Lecture Notes in Artificial Intellig

Subseries of Lecture Notes in Computer Science
Edited by J. G. Carbonell and J. Siekmann

Lecture Notes in Computer Science
Edited by G. Goos, J. Hartmanis and J. van Leeuwen

Springer

Berlin
Heidelberg
New York
Barcelona
Budapest
Hong Kong
London
Milan
Paris
Tokyo

Christine Froidevaux Jürg Kohlas (Eds.)

Symbolic and Quantitative Approaches to Reasoning and Uncertainty

European Conference, ECSQARU '95
Fribourg, Switzerland, July 3-5, 1995
Proceedings

Springer

Series Editors

Jaime G. Carbonell
School of Computer Science, Carnegie Mellon University
Pittsburgh, PA 15213-3891, USA

Jörg Siekmann
University of Saarland, German Research Center for AI (DFKI)
Stuhlsatzenhausweg 3, D-66123 Saarbrücken, Germany

Volume Editors

Christine Froidevaux
LRI, University of Paris-Sud
Bât. 490, F-91405 Orsay, France

Jürg Kohlas
Institute of Informatics, University of Fribourg
Site Regina Mundi, CH-1700 Fribourg, Switzerland

CIP data applied for

Die Deutsche Bibliothek - CIP-Einheitsaufnahme

Symbolic quantitative approaches to reasoning and uncertainty : European conference ; proceedings / ECSQARU '95, Fribourg, Switzerland, July 3 - 5, 1995. Christine Froidevaux ; Jürg Kohlas (ed.). - Berlin ; Heidelberg ; New York : Springer, 1995
(Lecture notes in computer science ; Vol. 946 : Lecture notes in artificial intelligence)
ISBN 3-540-60112-0
NE: Froidevaux, Christine [Hrsg.]; ECSQARU <1995, Fribourg>; GT

CR Subject Classification (1991): I.2.3, F.4.1

ISBN 3-540-60112-0 Springer-Verlag Berlin Heidelberg New York

Typesetting: Camera ready by author
SPIN 10486402 06/3142 – 5 4 3 2 1 0 Printed on acid-free paper

Preface

This volume contains the papers accepted for presentation at ECSQARU'95, the European Conference on Symbolic and Quantitative Approaches to Reasoning and Uncertainty, held at the University of Fribourg, Switzerland, July 3 to 5, 1995.

In recent years it has become apparent that an important part of the theory of Artificial Intelligence is concerned with reasoning on the basis of uncertain, vague, incomplete, or inconsistent information. Classical logic and probability theory are only partially adequate for this and a variety of other formalisms both symbolic and numerical have been developed, some of the most familiar being nomonotonic logics, modal logics, fuzzy sets, possibility theory, belief functions, evidence theory, and dynamic models of reasoning such as belief revision and Bayesian networks.

ECSQARU'95 is the third in a biennial series of conferences which provide a forum for the development, synthesis, and discussion of approaches to reasoning and uncertainty. The first was held in Marseille in 1991 (LNCS 548) and the second in Granada in 1993 (LNCS 747). Like its predecessors, ECSQARU'95 is sponsored and organized by the DRUMS consortium (Defeasible Reasoning and Uncertainty Management Systems, ESPRIT III Basic Research Action 6156), which involves twenty-one European partners, and by the European Society for Automated Practical Reasoning and Argumentation (ESAPRA).

The Executive Scientific Committee for the conference consisted of John Bell (QMW, University of London), Christine Froidevaux (LRI, University of Paris 11), Jürg Kohlas (University of Fribourg), Rudolf Kruse (University of Braunschweig), Ramon Lopez de Mantaras (CEAB, Blanes), Erik Sandewall (University of Linköping), Philippe Smets (IRIDIA, University of Brussels). We gratefully acknowledge the contribution of the many referees, who were involved in the reviewing process. Finally we would like to thank the University of Fribourg for the support it gave the organizers. Jürg Kohlas was responsible for the local organization in Fribourg.

April 1995

Christine Froidevaux, Jürg Kohlas
Co-chairs

Scientific Committee

J. Baldwin, J. Bell, F. Bergadano, Ph. Besnard, J. Bigham, B. Bouchon-Meunier, G. Brewka, M. Delgado, P. Doherty, D. Dubois, L. Farinas del Cerro, J. Fox, C. Froidevaux, D.M. Gabbay, P. Gärdenfors, E. Gregoire, P. Hájek, H. Herre, A. Hunter, J. Kohlas, P. Krause, R. Kruse, S. Lauritzen, R. Lopez de Mantaras, W. Lukasiewicz, E. Mamdani, J.J. Meyer, S. Moral, B. Nebel, H. Prade, M. Reinfrank, L. Saitta, E. Sandewall, T. Schaub, K. Schlechta, P. Siegel, P. Smets, K. Sundermeyer, Y.H. Tan, J. Treur, D. Vermeir, F. Voorbraak, N. Wilson, C. Witteveen, H.-J. Zimmermann.

Additional Referees

J.L. Arcos, S. Benferhat, A. Bonarini, A. Casales, L.M. de Campos, T. Drakengren, D. Driankov , G. Escalada-Imaz, F. Esteva, P. Fonck, P. Garcia, J. Gebhardt, L. Godo, D. Heerg, A. Herzig, W. van der Hoek, R. Kennes, U. Kjaerulff, F. Klawonn, F. Levy, T. Linke, J. Mengin, P.J.A. Monney, K.G. Olesen, U.G. Oppel, S. Parsons, E. Plaza, R.O. Rodriguez, A. Saffiotti, M. Sergot, C. Sierra, J. Valdes, J.L. Verdegay, W. Wobcke., H. Xu

Table of Contents

For all typical

Natasha Alechina

FWI, University of Amsterdam
Pl. Muidergracht 24, 1018 TV Amsterdam
The Netherlands
e-mail natasha@fwi.uva.nl

Abstract. In the paper a binary quantifier $\Pi x(\varphi, \psi)$ is studied. It can be read as 'typically, φ's are ψ's'. After investigating some formal properties of this quantifier, we compare the resulting logic with predicate conditional logic and discuss possible applications of binary quantifiers in formalizing defeasible reasoning.

1 Introduction

The present paper contains one more suggestion concerning a formal way to treat statements like 'φ's are (normally, typically) ψ's': common sense generalizations which can be used as premises in defeasible reasoning. The common feature of those statements is that they can be true while some exceptions (φ's which are not ψ's) are present. In the paper they are formalized with the use of a binary generalized quantifier Π, with $\Pi x(\varphi(x), \psi(x))$ informally meaning 'for all typical φ's ψ is true'. A related work in this respect is, first of all, Badaloni and Zanardo (1990), (1991). Another connection (which was already discussed by Badaloni and Zanardo) is the way such statements are formalized in the theory of circumscription: if $\varphi(x)$ and x *is not abnormal*, then $\psi(x)$. In section 4 possible applications of the logic with generalized quantifiers to defeasible reasoning are sketched. In section 3 we compare two possible readings of commonsense generalizations: 'normally, φ implies ψ' (cf. Morreau (1992)) and 'all typical φ's are ψ's'.

2 Language and models

Consider a first-order language $L_{\forall\Pi}$ with a binary generalized quantifier Π. A well-formed formula is defined as usual; if φ and ψ are well-formed formulas, so is $\Pi x(\varphi, \psi)$.

A model M for $L_{\forall\Pi}$ is a triple $< D, T, I >$, where D is a domain, I an interpretation function, and T is a function which takes a subset S of D and returns a set $S_T \subseteq D$ (the set of 'typical S's'). T obeys only one constraint, namely

$$S_T \subseteq S.$$

The truth definition for the generalized quantifier reads as follows:

$$M \models^{\alpha} \Pi x(\varphi, \psi) \Leftrightarrow \{d : M \models^{\alpha} \varphi[x/d]\}_T \subseteq \{d : M \models^{\alpha} \psi[x/d]\}$$

The notions of truth, validity and semantic consequence are standard. The following logical system corresponds to the described semantics.

Definition 1. The logic *Bin* is the least set of formulas closed under first-order derivability and

Reflexivity $\vdash \Pi x(\varphi, \varphi)$;
Distributivity $\vdash \Pi x(\varphi, \psi_1) \wedge \Pi x(\varphi, \psi_2) \rightarrow \Pi x(\varphi, \psi_1 \wedge \psi_2)$
Monotonicity $\vdash \forall x(\varphi(x) \rightarrow \psi(x)) \wedge \Pi x(\chi, \varphi) \rightarrow \Pi x(\chi, \psi)$;
Exchange $\vdash \forall y \Pi x(\varphi, \psi) \rightarrow \Pi x(\varphi, \forall y \psi)$, given that y is not free in φ;
Extensionality $\vdash \forall x(\varphi \leftrightarrow \psi) \rightarrow (\Pi x(\varphi, \chi) \leftrightarrow \Pi x(\psi, \chi))$;
Alphabetic variants $\vdash \Pi x(\varphi(x), \psi(x)) \rightarrow \Pi y(\varphi(y), \psi(y))$, given that y is free for x in $\Pi x(\varphi(x), \psi(x))$.

The notion of a proof is standard. Since in both logics the only inference rules are modus ponens and generalization, the deduction theorem has the same conditions (and proof) as in classical predicate logic.

It is easy to see that *Bin* is sound with respect to the semantics described above. A different question is whether the axioms are intuitively appealing given the intended interpretation of Π. Especially distributivity, exchange and extensionality can cause objections.

The first two axioms can be criticized as follows. There are reasonable interpretations of defaults under which even the closure for finite intersections in the consequent (distributivity) does not hold. For example, when $\Pi x(\varphi, \psi)$ is interpreted as 'in more than 50 per cent of cases φ's are ψ's'. Exchange axiom is even more questionable, since it presupposes the closure for arbitrary intersections. It fails under such strong interpretation of $\Pi x(\varphi, \psi)$ as $P(\{x : \psi(x)\}|\{x : \varphi(x)\}) = 1$. The following argument showing that the intersection property is counterintuitive, is given in Badaloni and Zanardo (1990). For every *specific* location y (for example, Rome), the generic 'Generally, birds live outside y' seems valid, that is, (after quantifying over locations)

$$\forall y \Pi x(Bird(x), Lives.outside(y, x))$$

can be accepted. But $\Pi x(Bird(x), \forall y Lives.outside(y, x))$ is obviously false.

However, there is an interpretation, namely the one underlying the semantics of *Bin*, which makes the axioms valid. If *there are* typical objects, then the intersection property must hold. The arguments above show that such 'absolute typicality' might be too strong an assumption. My suggestion would be to adopt the strategy used in the theory of circumscription and introduce 'typicality relative to an aspect'. Technically speaking, instead of one function T introduce a function for every aspect, $T_1, T_2, \ldots$, and corresponding quantifiers $\Pi^1, \Pi^2, \ldots$. The example above becomes $\Pi^1 x(Bird(x), Lives.outside(Rome, x))$, $\Pi^2 x(B(x), Lives.outside(Paris, x)), \ldots$, et cetera. The undesirable conclusion does not follow any more. To keep things simple, only one quantifier is considered in the sequel; but the analysis below will not change if the logic contained countably many quantifiers.

The extensionality property is also counterintuitive. If by chance the sets of A's and B's happen to contain precisely the same elements, it does not mean that typical A's are typical B's, and vice versa. To get rid of the extensionality, T can be defined syntactically, on formulas instead of sets; this is done in Alechina (1993) for a slightly different set up. But this also makes things too complicated, and for the present purposes we keep extensionality as well.

Theorem 2. *Bin is complete.*

Proof. The following principles, which are derivable in *Bin*, will be used in the proof:

Iteration $\vdash \Pi z(\varphi(z), \forall y_1 \ldots \forall y_n(\Pi x(\varphi(x), \psi(x)) \rightarrow \psi(z)))$, given that $y_1, \ldots, y_n$ are not free in φ (a derivation can be found in Alechina (1993)),

Monotonicity rule $\Sigma \vdash \varphi(x) \rightarrow \psi(x) \Rightarrow \Sigma \vdash \Pi x(\chi, \varphi) \rightarrow \Pi x(\chi, \psi)$, where x is not free in Σ.

We are going to show that every consistent in the sense of *Bin* set of formulas Δ has a model. Δ is extended to a maximally consistent set of formulas in a usual way, adding a witness for every existential quantifier. $\Sigma_0 = \Delta$, and the set of formulas which is obtained on the nth step will be denoted as Σ_n. If the $n+1$st formula is of the form $\neg\Pi x(\varphi, \psi)$ and it is consistent with Σ_n, add a new variable x' such that

(1) $\neg\psi[x/x']$;

(2) $\{\forall y_1 \ldots \forall y_k(\Pi x(\varphi(x), \chi(x)) \rightarrow \chi(x'))$:
for all formulas χ in the old alphabet, where $y_1, \ldots, y_k$ are the free variables of χ not occurring in $\varphi\}$

Assume that the above algorithm gives rise to inconsistencies. Then there is a finite subset of the formulas added on the nth step which is inconsistent with Σ_n, that is

$$\Sigma_n \vdash \bigwedge_i \forall y_{i1} \ldots \forall y_{ik}(\Pi x(\varphi(x), \chi_i(x)) \rightarrow \chi_i(x')) \rightarrow \psi(x')$$

and, by monotonicity,

$$\Sigma_n \vdash \Pi z(\varphi(z), \bigwedge_i \forall y_{i1} \ldots \forall y_{ik}(\Pi x(\varphi(x), \chi_i(x)) \rightarrow \chi_i(z))) \rightarrow \Pi z(\varphi(z), \psi(z))$$

and, by alphabetic variants,

$$\Sigma_n \vdash \Pi z(\varphi(z), \bigwedge_i \forall y_{i1} \ldots \forall y_{ik}(\Pi x(\varphi(x), \chi_i(x)) \rightarrow \chi_i(z))) \rightarrow \Pi x(\varphi(x), \psi(x)).$$

Since by iteration

$$\Sigma_n \vdash \Pi z(\varphi(z), \forall y_{i1} \ldots y_{ik}(\Pi x(\varphi(x), \chi_i(x)) \rightarrow \chi_i(z)))$$

for every χ_i, by Distributivity

$$\Sigma_n \vdash \Pi z(\varphi(z), \bigwedge_i \forall y_{i1} \ldots y_{ik}(\Pi x(\varphi(x), \chi_i(x)) \rightarrow \chi_i(z))),$$

therefore $\Sigma_n \vdash \Pi x(\varphi(x), \psi(x))$. A contradiction.

The model is based on the set $\Sigma = \cup_{n<\omega}\Sigma_n$. As usual, $, d_1, \ldots, d_n >\in I(P) \Leftrightarrow P(d_1, \ldots, d_n) \in \Sigma$. T is defined as follows:

$$u \in \{d : \varphi(x/d) \in \Sigma\}_T \;\Leftrightarrow\; \forall\chi(\Pi x(\varphi(x), \chi(x)) \in \Sigma \Rightarrow \chi(u) \in \Sigma).$$

The constraint on T: $\{d : \varphi(x/d) \in \Sigma\}_T \subseteq \{d : \varphi(x/d) \in \Sigma\}$ holds because of the Reflexivity axiom.

T is a function, i.e. if $\{d : \varphi(x/d) \in \Sigma\} = \{d : \psi(x/d) \in \Sigma\}$, then $\{d : \varphi(x/d) \in \Sigma\}_T = \{d : \psi(x/d) \in \Sigma\}_T$: this follows from Extensionality.

The construction of Σ guarantees that for every formula ψ, if $\Pi x(\varphi(x), \psi(x)) \notin \Sigma$, then there exists $u \in \{d : \varphi(x/d) \in \Sigma\}_T$ such that $\neg\psi(u) \in \Sigma$. Take u to be the witness x' for $\neg\Pi x(\varphi(x), \psi(x))$. Assume that x' is not in $\{d : \varphi(x/d) \in \Sigma\}_T$, that is, there is a formula χ containing some variables which were introduced after x', such that $\Pi x(\varphi(x), \chi(x)) \in \Sigma$ and $\neg\chi(x') \in \Sigma$. Then $\exists z_1 \ldots z_n(\Pi(\varphi(x), \chi(x)) \wedge \neg\chi(x')) \in \Sigma$, a contradiction. Now it is easy to prove that for any formula θ, $\theta \in \Sigma \Leftrightarrow \Sigma \models \theta$. □

3 Binary quantifiers and conditionals

In this section we will study the connections between the representation of defaults considered above and their representation in predicate conditional logic (cf. Delgrande (1991), Morreau (1992)).

Let $L_{\forall>}$ denote the language of first-order conditional logic (the language of the first-order predicate logic plus binary modal operator $>$). M is *a model* for $L_{\forall>}$ if $M =< D, W, S, I >$, where D is a non-empty universe (the same for all possible worlds), W is a non-empty set of possible worlds, $S : W \times \mathcal{P}(W) \rightarrow \mathcal{P}(W)$ is a selection function (given a world and a proposition, S provides a set of worlds which are *normal* with respect to this proposition from the point of view of this world), and I is an interpretation function. The truth definition for conditionals is as follows:

$$M, w \models^{\alpha} \varphi > \psi \Leftrightarrow S(w, [\varphi]_{M,\alpha}) \subseteq [\psi]_{M,\alpha},$$

where $[\varphi]_{M,\alpha} = \{w' : M, w' \models^{\alpha} \varphi\}$. The selection function satisfies the following constraint:

ID $S(w, [\varphi]_{M,\alpha}) \subseteq [\varphi]_{M,\alpha}$

Definition 3. *Cond* is the least set of formulas closed under first-order derivability and the axioms and rules below:

CI $\varphi > \varphi$;

CC $(\varphi > \psi_1) \wedge (\varphi > \psi_2) \rightarrow (\varphi > \psi_1 \wedge \psi_2)$;
E $\forall x(\varphi > \psi) \rightarrow (\varphi > \forall x\psi)$, if x is not free in φ;
RCEA

$$\frac{\vdash \varphi \leftrightarrow \psi}{\vdash (\varphi > \chi) \leftrightarrow (\psi > \chi)}$$

RCM

$$\frac{\vdash \varphi \rightarrow \psi}{\vdash (\chi > \varphi) \rightarrow (\chi > \psi)}$$

Cond is complete (see Morreau (1992)).

The resemblance between *Bin* and *Cond* is rather remarkable, and one can ask oneself if the two representations of defaults are not identical.

In Morreau (1992) generics are indeed informally understood as quantifying over normal (typical) individuals [1]. However, representing the sentence 'Normally, φ's are ψ's' by $\forall x(\varphi(x) > \psi(x))$ involves quantifying both over individuals and worlds and it is not obvious that this can be reduced to quantifying only over individuals.

A natural idea is to establish the connection between normal worlds and typical individuals as follows: call a world φ-normal, if it contains only φ-typical individuals (analogously, call an object a typical φ if it has the property φ in all φ-normal worlds). This works only if conditionals (quantifiers) are not iterated:

Theorem 4. *If φ and ψ are first-order formulas, then*

$$Bin \vdash \Pi x(\varphi, \psi) \;\Leftrightarrow\; Cond \vdash \forall x(\varphi > \psi).$$

Proof. The theorem easily follows from the two facts:
Fact 1. If φ, ψ are first-order formulas, $Cond \vdash \forall x(\varphi > \psi) \;\Leftrightarrow\; FOL \vdash \forall x(\varphi \rightarrow \psi)$;
Fact 2. If φ, ψ are first-order formulas, $Bin \vdash \Pi x(\varphi, \psi) \;\Leftrightarrow\; FOL \vdash \forall x(\varphi \rightarrow \psi)$.
In both cases, the direction from right to left is obvious. Assume that $FOL \nvdash \forall x(\varphi \rightarrow \psi)$. Then there is a first-order model M and an object d such that $M \models \varphi[d]$ and $M \not\models \psi[d]$. Let M' be a model for *Cond* consisting of just one world w, corresponding to M, and $S(w, [\varphi[d]]) = \{w\}$. Then $M', w \not\models \forall x(\varphi(x) > \psi(x))$. Therefore $Cond \nvdash \forall x(\varphi(x) > \psi(x))$. Analogously, let M" be a model for *Bin* with the same domain and interpretation function as that of M, and $\{a : M" \models \varphi(x/a)\}_T = \{a : M" \models \varphi(x/a)\}$. Then $M" \not\models \Pi x(\varphi, \psi)$ and $Bin \nvdash \Pi x(\varphi, \psi)$. □

[1] We assume for the present purposes that 'normal' and 'typical' have more or less the same meaning: a normal (typical) φ is an object which has all the properties one would expect from a φ-object without having any specific information about this very object. In particular, we are not going to make a distinction between 'normal' as 'average' and 'typical' as 'having all the features of its kind in the most condensed form'.

If φ or ψ contain conditionals / generalized quantifiers the statement does not hold: for example,

$$Bin \vdash \Pi x(\varphi(x), \Pi y(\psi(y), \varphi(x))),$$

but

$$Cond \nvdash \forall x(\varphi(x) > \forall y(\psi(y) > \varphi(x))).$$

It is however possible to find a translation from *Cond* into a two-sorted binary quantifier language, where conditionals of the form $\varphi(x) > \psi(x)$ are translated modulo some tricks as $\Pi w(\varphi(x,w), \psi(x,w))$. To make the embedding faithful, the extensionality axiom of *Bin* has to be restricted to the formulas with the same world variables. The proof can be found in Alechina (1993).

4 Applications to defeasible reasoning

The problem of defining defeasible inference (from the knowledge of defeasible generalizations to the knowledge of fact) in the language of binary quantifiers reminds of the so-called direct inference problem in probabilistic logic (from the knowledge of objective probabilities to subjective degrees of belief in individual events).

In Bacchus (1990) the latter problem was solved as follows. Let Γ be a finite knowledge base, and $\varphi(a)$ a statement concerning an object a [2]. The subjective degree of belief in $\varphi(a)$ given Γ, $prob(\varphi(a)|\Gamma)$, is computed from the objective probability $P(\{x : \varphi(x/a)\}|\{x : \Gamma(x/a)\})$. Our definition of defeasible inference is analogous.

Definition 5. Let Γ be a finite set of formulas, and $\varphi(x)$ a formula with one free variable x. Then $\varphi(a)$ defeasibly follows from Γ in *Bin* (in symbols $\Gamma \rhd \varphi(a)$), if $\Gamma \vdash_{Bin} \Pi x(\Gamma(x/a), \varphi(x/a))$.

The following principles of defeasible reasoning are widely accepted as the desirable ones:

Defeasible modus ponens (the names come from Morreau (1992)):
Normally, A's are B's; a is A $\rhd$ (It is plausible that) *a is B.*

Specificity *Normally, A's are B's; Normally, C's are not B's; All C's are A's; a is A; a is C* $\rhd$ (It is plausible that) *a is not B.*

Irrelevance *Normally, A's are B's; a is A; a is C* $\rhd$ (It is plausible that) *a is B* (if C is irrelevant or positive with respect to B).
Of course, if C is not irrelevant (for example, $C = \neg B$), the inference should not go through.

[2] We assume here that φ is a monadic property. For dealing with polyadic properties one can introduce a polyadic quantifier in an obvious way: quantifying over typical tuples of objects.

Those principles can be used as criteria of adequacy for the systems of defeasible reasoning.

One can easily see that our definition of defeasible inference for *Bin* makes the first two principles valid.

Theorem 6. *In Bin, defeasible modus ponens and specificity are valid, i.e.*

$$\Pi x(B(x), F(x)), B(a) \rhd F(a);$$
$$\Pi x(B(x), F(x)), \Pi x(P(x), \neg F(x)), \forall x(P(x) \to B(x)), B(a), P(a) \rhd \neg F(a).$$

Proof. The first statement is trivial. As for specificity, we need to show that

$$\Gamma \vdash \Pi x(\Gamma(x/a), \neg F(x/a)),$$

where $\Gamma(x/a)$ is

$$\Pi x(B(x), F(x)) \wedge \Pi x(P(x), \neg F(x)) \wedge \forall x(P(x) \to F(x)) \wedge B(x) \wedge P(x).$$

Clearly,

$$\Gamma \vdash \forall x(\Pi x(B(x), F(x)) \wedge \Pi x(P(x), \neg F(x)) \wedge \forall x(P(x) \to F(x)) \wedge B(x) \wedge P(x) \leftrightarrow$$
$$\leftrightarrow P(x)).$$

By extensionality and

$$\Gamma \vdash \Pi x(P(x), \neg F(x)),$$

we have

$$\Gamma \vdash \Pi x(\Gamma(x/a), \neg F(x/a)).$$

□

Note that above we essentially made use of the fact that

$$\forall x(P(x) \to B(x)) \vdash \forall x(B(x) \wedge P(x) \leftrightarrow P(x)).$$

Adding to Γ one more formula containing a, for example $Y(a)$, would block the inference, since

$$\Gamma \wedge Y(a) \nvdash \forall x(\Gamma(x/a) \wedge Y(x) \leftrightarrow P(x)).$$

Therefore, irrelevance in general is not a valid principle: we cannot justify the inference from 'Generally, birds fly', 'Tweety is a bird' *and* 'Tweety is yellow' to 'Tweety flies'.

However, there is one important special case of irrelevance which presents a difficulty for the minimal models approach but for this logic. Namely, if $\Gamma \rhd \varphi(a)$ and we add to Γ some irrelevant information Δ which does not contain a free, $\Gamma \cup \Delta \rhd \varphi(a)$, since

$$\Gamma, \Delta \vdash \forall x(\Gamma(x/a) \wedge \Delta(x/a) \leftrightarrow \Gamma(x/a)).$$

Therefore if irrelevant information is of the form 'There is a non-flying penguin' ($\exists x \neg F(x)$) or of the form 'Sam does not fly' ($\neg F(b)$), the reasoning goes thorough: we still are able to derive that Tweety flies.

5 Conclusion

We have seen that a very simple logic is suitable for representing commonsense generalizations if those are understood as talking about typical objects. Inside this logic one can perform some defeasible reasoning (defeasible modus ponens and specificity are valid), but it is in general sensitive to adding irrelevant information. Probably the only way to solve the latter problem is to use meta-theoretic arguments as it is done in other non-monotonic logics.

Comparing the properties of $\rhd$ above with the postulates of Kraus, Lehmann and Magidor (1990) shows that $\rhd$ is a very weak consequence relation. Namely, $\rhd$ satisfies Left Logical Equivalence, Right Weakening, Reflexivity, but does not satisfy Cumulativity postulates:

Cut $A \wedge B \rhd C, A \rhd B \Longrightarrow A \rhd C$
Cautious Monotony $A \rhd B, A \rhd C \Longrightarrow A \wedge B \rhd C$.

These postulates require an additional constraint on T: if all typical A's are B's ($A_T \subseteq B$), then typical A's are the same as typical $A \wedge B$'s ($A_T = (A \wedge B)_T$).

References

Alechina, N.: Binary quantifiers and relational semantics. ILLC Report LP-93-13 (1993), ILLC, Univ. of Amsterdam.

Bacchus, F.: Representing and reasoning with probabilistic knowledge. A logical approach to probabilities. Cambridge (Mass.) - London, The MIT Press (1990).

Badaloni, S., Zanardo, A.: A high plausibility logic for reasoning with incomplete time-sensitive knowledge. LADSEB-CNR (Italian National Research Council, Institute for Investigations in System Dynamics and Bioengineering), Int.Report 02/90 (1990).

Badaloni, S., Zanardo, A.: Typicality for plausible reasoning. In: Trends in Artificial Intelligence. Lecture Notes in Computer Science, Springer Verlag, (1991) 470–474.

Delgrande, J. P.: An approach to default reasoning based on a first-order conditional logic: Revised report. Artificial Intelligence **36**, (1991) 63–90.

Kraus, S., Lehmann, D., Magidor, M.: Nonmonotonic reasoning, preferential models, and cumulative logics. Artificial Intelligence **44** (1990) 167 - 207.

Morreau, M. Conditionals in Philosophy and Artificial Intelligence. PhD Thesis, Univ. of Amsterdam, Amsterdam (1992).

A Posteriori Knowledge: from Ambiguous Knowledge and Undefined Information to Knowledge

Matías Alvarado

LSI, Technical University of Catalonia
Pau Gargallo 5, 08028 Barcelona, Spain
e-mail: matias@lsi.upc.es

Abstract. Adequate treatment of incomplete and ambiguous information encourage research in theories about reasoning and action (*e. g.* [7]). In [10] is proposed to deal with this topic using Belnap's four-valued logic. In this paper, Driankov's semantic is used in a formalisation that captures the dynamic character of knowledge and belief. *Ambiguous* knowledge is present in several kind of situations that formally corresponds with knowing that a disjunction is true, but it is not known which element of the disjunction makes it true. We define an *a posteriori* knowledge operator that allows to extend knowledge from ambiguous knowledge or undefined information, being in the meanwhile, *potential* knowledge. In addition, belief is consider local knowledge.

1 Introduction

For knowledge and belief, the semantics of possible worlds [16] has been attractive for the intuitive way in which description of actual and possible worlds can be established. Kripke's possible worlds are sets of interpreted formulas according with classical two-valued semantic. Worlds are related through a relation called of *possibility*. World w is possible for the actual one w_0, whenever w_0 and w satisfy the relation. Logics of knowledge and belief using that semantics *e. g.* [12] [13], consider knowledge in w_0 as the true formulas in all the w_0-possible-worlds. Thus, if φ is knowledge and ψ is a logical consequence of φ, then ψ is true in all the worlds in which φ is and is knowledge as well. This *logical omniscience* is unintuitive to model *real* agents of knowledge and belief [19]
Based on classical Kleene's work [14], a formal tool that seems more flexible to model knowledge and belief is Partial Logic [5]. A partial interpretation of a set of formulas is such that some ones are *true* or *false* while the rest have no truth-value. The process to assign *true* or *false* to undefined formulas is a *refinement*. A possible world in partial logic thus corresponds to a partial interpretation. In this case, world w is possible for actual world w_0 if w is a refinement of w_0. Using partial interpretations, knowledge and belief can be defined more in accordance with real circumstances of incomplete information and limited resources [1], [9]. However, even in partial logics a disjunction is *true* whenever one literal is *true* [3], [14]. But there are several situations in which the known information is

a collection of alternatives only, and such that the especific true alternative is unknown. A so simple example is when a *coin* is flipped. The information provided by that action is ambiguous and the formal expression is given by a *true* disjunction with all its literal truth-values undefined. In [10] a four-valued logic that leads with *true* disjunction having no *true* literal is proposed.
The proposed logic in this paper is close to Driankov's logic. We define an *epistemic state* as a set of partial interpretation or *states* satisfing an informative partial order. In the epistemic state, given a *current state*, every possible one provides equal or more information. The intuitive meaning of this partial order is that there are alternative strands to be analized when extending knowledge from actual knowledge. The suitable use of informative order in modal logic has been mainly developed by N. Belnap [3] and J. Van Benthem [4].
Observe that possible states are refinaments of actual state and refinaments of possible state correspond to possible worlds, and so on. This gradual process of refinement provides to model the dynamic generation of *a posteriori* knowledge from ambiguous knowledge (or from undefined information) of the actual state. *Potential knowledge* can be defined as the *true* or *undefined* statements in possible worlds whenever the negated statement does not appear at any possible state. In this manner, potential knowledge can be considered the *meanwhile* step of *a posteriori* knowledge.
This paper is organized as follows: in section 2 an adapatation of Driankov's logic is developed. In section 3 modal operators to deal with knowledge and belief are defined. In additon, there we will comment our epistemic proposal with respect to other ones in the literature.

2

In this section is introduced a finite partial logic being a restriction of four-valued logic [10] to *true, false* and *undefined* truth-values. It is enough for the paper porpouse because *expansions* of actual state are defined in a cumulative a logic. While Driankov's logic is defined for single formulas we established definitions for finite sets by using partial interpretations.

Logical and Informative Lattices. Consider a propositional language L defined from a finite vocabulary of a set of propositional variables, Atm(L) $= \{p_1, ..., p_n\}$, and the logical connectives $\vee$, $\wedge$, and $\neg$. Let ψ be a finite set of sentences and $Atm(\psi)$ the propositional variables from Atm(L) which are used in the construction of formulas in ψ only. Then L(ψ) is the closed language from $Atm(\psi)$ under $\wedge, \vee$ and $\neg$.
On the semantic side, we consider the partial order $[L3; \leq]$ where $L3$ is the set of truth-values $\{u, t, f\}$ and $\leq$ is defined as follows: $f < u$, $f < t$, and $u < t$. The operations $a \vee b = max(a, b)$, and $a \wedge b = min(a, b)$, with a, $b \in L3$, turn this partial order into a *logical lattice*. The complement $\neg$, is defined as: $\neg(t) = f$ $\neg(f) = t$ and $\neg(u) = u$. These lattice operations are used to define, respectively, the the logical connectives *and*, *or*, and *negation*. On the information side, is

$\neg(f) = t$ and $\neg(u) = u$. These lattice operations are used to define, respectively, the the logical connectives *and*, *or*, and *negation*. On the information side, is considered the partial order $[I3; \sqsubseteq]$ where $I3$ is the set of truth-values $\{u, t, f\}$ and $\sqsubseteq$ is defined as follows: $u \sqsubset f$ and $u \sqsubset t$. The operations $\sqcap$ and $\sqcup$, defined as: $a \sqcap b = min(a, b)$, and $a \sqcup b = max(a, b)$, with a, $b \in I3$, turn this partial order into a *information lattice*. (Algebraical properties of these lattices are given in [10].)

Partial states. In this subsection logical and informative operations are extended over partial interpretations and its refinements. Let Q= $2^{Lit(\psi)}$ and P $\in$ Q. The symbol + denotes the expansion operation of AGM paradigm [9]. Any expansion E from ψ uses as expansion set an element from Q:

$$E = \psi^{+}_{\mathrm{P}}, \qquad \mathrm{P} \in \mathrm{Q}.$$

E = $\{E_0 = \psi, E_1, \ldots E_n\}$ is the set of expansions from ψ, that is finite whenever ψ is finite. Let F be the set of L(ψ)-formulas. Let t, f be the truth-values *true* and *false*, respectively.

Definition 1. A partial interpretation is a mapping I from a subset of $Atm(\psi)$ to $\{t, f\}$. Let $Atm^{+}(\psi) = \{P | I(P) = true\}$ and $Atm^{-}(\psi)\{P | I(P) = false\}$. The complement of $Atm^{-}(\psi) \cup Atm^{-}(\psi)$ are the undefined atoms. The truth-value of a formula $\alpha \in$ F in I, is defined in the usual inductive manner using the above introduced connectives and is denoted $I_E[\alpha]$.

(An equivalent formulation can be done by using three-valued interpretation with *true, false* and *undefined* truth-values (see [7]).

According to this definition it can be shown that there is a unique model for any conjunction in ψ and at least one model for any disjunction.

Let I be the set of all partial interpretations for all elements in E, I = $\{I_{E_i} : E_i \in \mathrm{E}\}$. The relation $\sqsubseteq$, can be introduced over the elements of I:

- $\forall E_1, E_2 \in \mathrm{E}$, $I_{E_1} \sqsubseteq I_{E_2}$ iff $\forall \alpha \in E_1 \cap E_2$, $I_{E_1}[\alpha] \sqsubseteq I_{E_2}[\alpha]$.

Easily can be shown that [I;$\sqsubseteq$] is a partial order and that operations $\sqcap$ and $\sqcup$, defined over partial interpretations, make it a lattice:

- $\forall \alpha \in E_1 \cap E_2$, $(I_{E_1} \sqcap I_{E_2})[\alpha] = I_{E_1}[\alpha] \sqcap I_{E_2}[\alpha]$, and $\forall \alpha \notin E_1 \cap E_2$, $(I_{E_1} \sqcap I_{E_2})[\alpha] = I_{E_1}[\alpha]$ if $\alpha \in E_1$, or $(I_{E_1} \sqcap I_{E_2})[\alpha] = I_{E_2}[\alpha]$ if $\alpha \in E_2$.
- $\forall \alpha \in E_1 \cap E_2$, $(I_{E_1} \sqcup I_{E_2})[\alpha] = I_{E_1}[\alpha] \sqcup I_{E_2}[\alpha]$, and $\forall \alpha \notin E_1 \cap E_2$ $(I_{E_1} \sqcup I_{E_2})[\alpha] = I_{E_1}[\alpha]$ if $\alpha \in E_1$, or $(I_{E_1} \sqcup I_{E_2})[\alpha] = I_{E_2}[\alpha]$ if $\alpha \in E_2$.

Now, IM_{E_1} can be defined as the informationally minimal model of E_1 such that there does not exist another model $M^{*}_{E_1}$, such that $M^{*}_{E_1} \sqsubseteq IM_{E_1}$. Again, if the set of formulas contains only conjunctions it has a unique IM_{E_1}. But when the set of formulas contains disjunctions, there is a number of informationally minimal models which can not be ordered amongst themselves with respect to $\sqsubseteq$ on I.

2.1 Epistemic States

Following Driankov, herein we define an epistemic state ES_ψ for a set ψ of formulas, as a set of partial interpretations of ψ, $ES_\psi = \{I_1, ..., I_n\}$, such that the truth-value of α in ES_ψ, denoted as $ES_\psi[\alpha]$, is given by $I_1[\alpha] \sqcap ... \sqcap I_n[\alpha]$. A *model epistemic state* of ψ, denoted as MES_ψ, is the epistemic state in which the truth value of the formulas in ψ is t. Let ES be the set of all epistemic states. The partial order $\sqsubseteq$ on I can be introduced over ES as follows:

- $\forall\, E_1,\ E_2 \in$ E, $ES_{E_1} \sqsubseteq ES_{E_2}$ iff $E_1 \cap E_2 \neq \emptyset$, and $\forall I_{E_2} \in ES_{E_2}$, $\exists\ I_{E_1} \in ES_{E_1}$, such that $I_{E_1} \sqsubseteq I_{E_2}$.

It is still possible to extend the $\sqcap$ and $\sqcup$ operations to elements of ES generalazing the one over [I; $\sqcup$] (for details see [2]).
Now, an *informationally minimal model epistemic state*, denoted as $IMES_{E_1}$, is defined as this model epistemic state of E_1 such that there does not exist another model epistemic state, $MES^*_{E_1}$, such that $MES^*_{E_1} \sqsubseteq IMES_{E_1}$. Again, for a set E containing only conjunctions, $IMES_E$ corresponds with its unique model. In the case of a set containing only a disjunctions α of n literals in E_1, it can be shown that $IMES_{E_1}$ can only be constructed as follows:

- Let $Lit(\alpha) = \{l_1, ..., l_n\}$ be the literals of α.
  $IMES_{E_1} = \{IMS^1_{E_1}, ..., IMS^n_{E_1}\}$, where
  $IMS^i[l_i] = t$ if $l_i \in Lit^+(\alpha)$, or
  $IMS^i[l_i] = f$ if $l_i \in Lit^-(\alpha)$, and
  $\forall p \neq l_i, IMS^i[p] = u$.

$Lit^+(\alpha)$ is the set of positive literals of α and $Lit^-(\alpha)$ the set of negative literals of α. The remarking thing about $IMES_{E_1}$ is the following property:

$$IMES_{E_1}[p] = u,\ \forall p \in Lit(\psi),\ \text{while } IMES_{E_1}[\alpha] = t$$

Observe that there are as many members in $IMES_{E_1}$ as literals in α. This property is very desirable to deal with ambiguous knowledge in a economic way. The construction for one disjunction is generalized for sets with any number of disjunctions taking the union of informationally minimal model epistemic state of each disjunction:

$$\bigcup_{\alpha \in E_1} IMES_\alpha.$$

Example 1. For $\psi = \{\alpha = a \vee b\}$, $IMES_\psi = \{(t, u), (u, t)\}$; $IMES_\psi[a] = u$, $IMES_\psi[b] = u$, but $IMES_\psi[\alpha] = t$.

The following structure defined by Doherty [9] is an epistemic state. To deal with the following epistemic definition we will do with respect to it.

Definition 2. A *model frame* is an ordered tupla M = $\langle$ I, $I_\psi, \sqsubseteq\rangle$, where I_ψ is the set of partial interpretation that satisfies ψ and I is the set of I_{E_i}, for $i = 0, \ldots, n$. For any $I' \in$ I we assume that $I \sqsubseteq I'$, for every $I \in I_\psi$.

Definition 3. An interpretation $I \in \mathrm{I}$ in the model frame M *satisfies* a sentence $\varphi \in \mathrm{L}$, $I \models_{\mathrm{M}} \varphi$, if and only if $I(\varphi) = t$. Is said that the frame satisfies φ, $\mathrm{M} \models \varphi$, if every $I \in \mathrm{I}$ satisfies φ. For a set Γ such that any sentencence of Γ is satisfied by M, is said that the frame M satisfies Γ, $\mathrm{M} \models \Gamma$

3 Knowledge and Belief

Propositional language L is extended by adding modal operators of **Knowledge** K, **Belief** B, **Potential Knowledge** K_p, and **Aposteriori Knowledge** K_{aps}. The language extended with these modal operators is called EL by epistemic language. Arguments of EL are any kind of object or epistemic formulas. In the satisfaction relation $I \models_{\mathrm{M}} \varphi$, whenever the model frame M is clear the subindex is ommited. (Easy reading of the following definitions could be done with example 2)

Definition 4. A formula φ is *knowledge* in the model frame M, $I \models_{\mathrm{M}} K(\varphi)$ if and only if,
1) $I \models_{\mathrm{M}} \varphi$ or
2) $I \models_{\mathrm{M}} K_{aps}(\varphi)$

Definition 5. An interpretation J *is maximal* for a set ψ in M, if and only if it assigns *true* or *false* truth-values to every subformula of any formula in ψ.

Definition 6. A formula φ is *a posteriori* knowledge in the model frame M, $I \models_{\mathrm{M}} K_{aps}(\varphi)$ if and only if,
1.) $I \models_{\mathrm{M}} \varphi^u$ and
2.) For all maximal J, such that $I \sqsubseteq J$, $J \models \varphi$

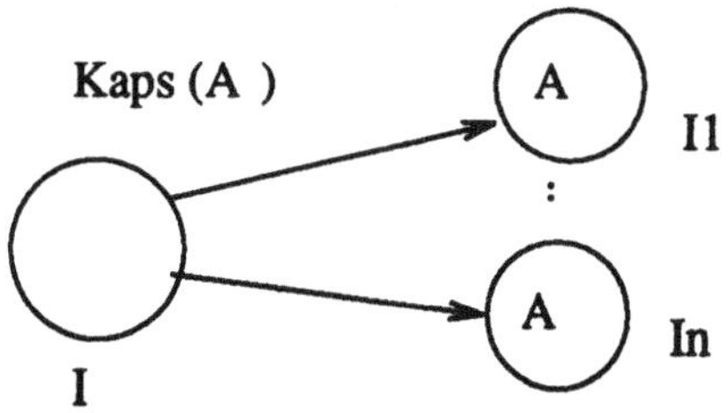

Fig. 1. Aposteriori Knowledge

Proposition 7. $I \models K_{aps}(\varphi \vee \beta)$ *if and only if* $(\forall J,\ J \models \varphi)$ *or* $(\forall J,\ J \models \beta)$ *with maximal* J.

Intuitively, ***a posteriori*** knowledge allows to know certain facts about ambiguous ***a priori*** knowledge: it is possible to know the possible alternatives about one fact altough not know which of them is really ***true***. For example, one can know that today will rain or not, but not know what effectively will occur. This is the case of tautological sentences; but not only that: I can know that my friend from Grenoble comes to Barcelone by plane, train or bus, altough I do not know which one of these transportations efectively he will use (see example 1).

Definition 8. A sentence φ *is believed* in the model frame M, $I \models B(\varphi)$ if and only if $I \not\models \varphi$, and $\exists\, I'$, with $I \sqsubseteq I'$ such that $I' \models \varphi$ (Fig. 2).

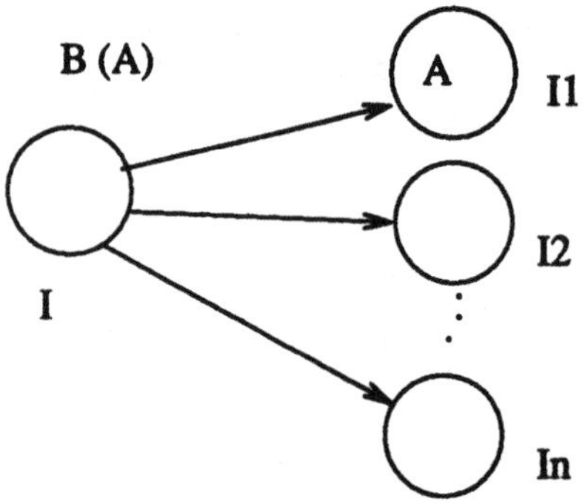

Fig. 2. Belief

Some useful *semantical observations* of defined operators are mentioned.

1. $I \models \neg B(\varphi)$ if and only if $I \not\models B(\varphi)$ if and only if $\forall I' > I,\ I' \not\models \neg\varphi$
2. $I \models \neg K_{apr}(\varphi)$ if and only if $I \not\models K_{apr}(\varphi)$ if and only if $I \not\models \varphi$
3. $I \models \neg K_{aps}(\varphi)$ if and only if $I \not\models K_{aps}(\varphi)\ ifandonlyif\ \exists I' > I,\ I' \not\models \varphi$

Definition 9. A formula φ is *potential knowledge* in the model frame M, $I \models_{\mathrm{M}} K_p(\varphi)$ if and only if,
1) $I \not\models \varphi$ and
2) $\forall\, I'$, such that $I \sqsubseteq I'$, $I' \not\models \neg\varphi$.

Observe that $I \models K_p(\varphi)$ if and only if $I \models \neg B(\neg\varphi)$. A particular case is when $I \models B(\varphi) \wedge \neg B(\neg\varphi) \rightarrow K_p(\varphi)$. Thus, potential knowledge is belief, but not necesarily the converse: a ***true*** formula in a state and ***false*** in another is belief but not potential knowledge.

Rationality of one agent concerns with consistency inside its set of beliefs. In this paper we consider that given a frame, a statement φ is consistent with beliefs of an agent whenever the agent does not believe in the frame the negation of

the statement. In that case the affirmative statement can become to be knowledge and can be considered potential knowledge for the agent. The converse is also intuitive: a default no contradictory conclusion can be considered potential knowledge.
In the other hand, in the case of an agent that is compelled to believe a statement affirmed and negated, except in the case to be trivial and uninteresting, the agent must deal with each one in local and different subframes. Our formalism provides this possibility. Consistency condition prevents to include contradictory statements in the same possible state. But any statement can be consider *true* in a subframe of full frame M, having a suitable meaning as *local knowledge*. The point is that in this case, any of the statements cannot be considereded potential knowledge, and thus cannot become to be knowledge (see example 3).

Example 2

ψ	E_1	E_2	Epistemic status in MES_ψ
$\{\alpha = a \vee b\}$	α, a	α, b	$K(\alpha)$, $B(a)$, $B(b)$, $K_p(a)$, $K_p(b)$
	α, a	$\alpha, \neg a$	$K(\alpha)$, $B(a)$, $B(\neg a)$, $\neg K_p(a)$, $K_p(b)$
	α, a	α, a, b	$K(\alpha)$, $K_{aps}(a)$, $B(b)$, $K_p(b)$

Each row represents possible expansion states from ψ. Epistemic sentences deppends of actual expansions. In model epistemic state of thirth row $E_1 \sqsubseteq E_2$ is satisfied.

Example 3. It is showed the application of epistemic definitions by modeling the well known Nixon Diamond problem. Let r be taken for republican, q for quacker and p for pacifist. It is guessed that republicans are not pacifist, quackers are pacifists and that Nixon is republican and quacker. In our approach this can be write as follows:

$$\{r \wedge \neg K_p(p) \rightarrow B(\neg p), \quad q \wedge \neg K_p(\neg p) \rightarrow B(p), \quad r \wedge q\}$$

The example shows that there is no problem to deal with contradictory information. Contradictory statements are treated in diferent expansion sets belonging to diferent *branches* of model frame M. So, divided opinion about Nixon pacificity, due to belong to both identified groups, can not be established as knowledge, but is possible to deal with it adequatetly (Cumulative Default Logic of Meyer and Hoeck [18] provides a close treatment of such kind of topics).

Recursivity and Epistemical Acceptance. Definitions of knowledge, potential knowledge and belief are recursive: they appeal the satisfaction of operators arguments in possibles states to decide if it is knowledge, potential knowledge or belief. Each succesor repeats the process. Whenever the conditions are satisfied the process stops and sentence epistemic status is established. This is

the process stops and sentence epistemic status is established. This is a constructive process because status of any sentence is determined whenever conditions are fulfilled.
Now we mentione some obvious epistemic observations satisfied by the epistemic operators: 1) $I \models K_{apr}(\wedge_1^n \alpha_i)$ then $I \models K_{apr}(\alpha_i)$ for $i = 1, \ldots, n$ and 2) $I \models B(\wedge_1^n \alpha_i)$ then $I \models B(\alpha_i)$ for $i = 1, \ldots, n$.

Metarules. The following rules introduce condition according with our epistemic intend in a model frame.
1.) $I \models K_{apr}(\vee_1^n \varphi_i) \wedge (\forall i \; \neg K_{apr}(\varphi_i)) \Longrightarrow K_{aps}\varphi_i$ for some $i \in \{1, \ldots, n\}$
2.) $I \models K_{apr}(\vee_1^n \varphi_i) \wedge (\exists i \; \neg B(\neg \varphi_i)) \Longrightarrow K_p \varphi_i$ for some i

1.) says that at least a part of an ambiguous knowledge sentence must be unambiguous in the future. Metarule 2.) established the plausibility of a substatement in a disjunctive knowledge sentence.

Proposition 10. *If $I \models K_{apr}((\wedge_1^n \varphi_i) \to \beta)$ and exists expansions $E_1, \ldots E_m$ of ψ such that respectively $\varphi_i \to \beta, \varphi_i \in E_i$, then $I \models K_{aps}(\beta)$.*

3.1 Related works

Awareness, Implicit and Explicit Beliefs. In the attempt to avoid logical omniscience and ideal reasoning Levesque introduced distinction between explicit and implicit beliefs [16]. Every explicit belief is implicit, but the last ones could be entailed from the explicits. However is not so clear how an implicit (undefined) belief can become to be explicit (*a posteriori*) one. In our model-based approach we can treat explicit belief as *a priori* knowledge and implicit belief as undefined or ambiguous ones. Deppendig of actual cappabilities of the agent is possible to extend explicit beliefs. The logic of awareness [12] defined over Kripke's possible worlds has intuitions close to our approach.

Defaults Theories. In our approach, we avoid to take a definitive position about any statement if there is not enough information to do it. In this sense, it is similar with default epistemic logics [6], [9], and essentially different with theories that use closed world assumption *e. g.* [17], in which the negation of information not explicitely deduced is taken. Our approach leads with non-monotone conclusions in the line of preferred default theories [20]. Belief and potential knowledge are satisfied by some preferred models. This graduality is as preferential entailment leads with non-monotonicity [21].

Concluding Remarks. A epistemic logic that captures —we hope in a suitable way— dynamical process to extend knowledge from ambiguous and undefined information is proposed. Modal operators of *a posteriori* knowledge, knowledge and belief have been defined. *A posteriori* knowledge is obtained from undefined information or from ambiguous knowledge, in such a way that intermediate step correspond with potential knowledge. Belief is consider local knowledge; thus an statement and its negation can be believed in an epistemic state without allowing global contradiction.

Aknowledgements. This work has been benefited with worth comments from Ll. Godó and R. Rodriguez (CSIC, Spain), G. Núñez (TII, Mexico), J. Larrosa (UPC, Spain) and the anonymous referees. The author is supported by a PhD scholarship of Universidad Nacional Autonoma de México.

References

1. Alvarado, M.: *Relatives Knowledge and Belief in SKL^{**} Preferred Model Frames* In Proc. of AIMSA94 (Sofia, Bulgaria, 1994)
2. Alvarado, M.: *A posteriori Knowledge: from Ambiguous Knowledge and Undefined Information to Knowledge.* Report de Recerca LSI-94-. (UPC, Spain 1994)
3. Belnap, N.: *A Useful Four-Valued Logic.* In Modern Use of Logic. (Reidel Publishing Co., 1976)
4. Van Benthem, J.: *A Manual of Intensional Logic* CSLI **1** (Stanford, 1988)
5. Blamey, S.: *Partial Logic* In *Handbook of Philosophical Logic*, **III**. D. Gabbay, F. Guenthner, (Eds.) (Reidel Publishing Co, 1986).
6. Brewka, G.: *Preferred Subtheories: an Extended Logical Framework for Default Reasoning.* In Proc. IJCAI89. (Detroit, USA, 1989).
7. Brewka, G., Hertzberg, J.: *How to do things with worlds: On formalizing revision and reasoning about action.* In Journal of Logic and Computation. (1993)
8. Del Val, A., Shoham, Y.: *Deriving Properties of Belief Update from Theories of Action (II).* In Proc. IJCAI'93
9. Doherty, P.: *NMR-3 A Three-Valued Approach to Non-Monotonic Reasoning.* PhD Theses (Linköping, 1992).
10. Driankov, D.: *Computing Effects of Ambiguous Actions in Incomplete Worlds: The Epistemic State Approach.* Linköping University (Sweden, 1994)
11. Gärdenfors, P.: *Knowledge in Flux* The MIT Press (1988).
12. J. Halpern, Moses, Y.: *A Guide to Completeness and Complexity for Modal Logics of Knowledge and Belief.* Artificial Intelligence **54** (1992) pp. 319 - 379.
13. Hintikka, J.: *Knowledge and Belief* (Cornell University Press 1962).
14. Kleene, S.: *Introduction to Metamathematical* (North Holland, Amsterdam, 1952).
15. Kripke, S.: *A completness theorem in modal logic.* The Journal of Symbolic Logic. **24 - 1** (1959) pp. 1-14.
16. Levesque, H.: *A Logic of Implicit and Explicit Belief.* Proceedings of the AAAI (1984).
17. McCArthy, J.: *Circumscription - A Form of Nonmonotonic Reasoning.* Artificial Intelligence (1986).
18. Meyer, J., Van der Hoek, W.: *A Cumulative Default Logic Based on Epistemic States.* Rapportnr. IR-288. August 1992. Vrije Universitet, Amsterdam
19. Núñez, G., Alvarado, M.: *Hacia una semántica realista de mundos posibles en lógica de creencias.* Reporte de Investigación LANIA (México, 1993).
20. Sandewall, E.: *The Semantics of Non-Monotonic Entailment Defined Using Partial Interpretations.* LiTH-IDA-R-88-31, Linköping University (Sweden, 1988)
21. Shoham, Y.: *Reasoning About Change* (The MIT Press, 1988).

Modeling Uncertain Relational Knowledge: the AV-Quantified Production Rules Approach

Pietro Baroni*, Giovanni Guida*, Silvano Mussi°
* Dipartimento di Elettronica per l'Automazione, Università di Brescia, Italy
° CILEA, Milano, Italy

Abstract

Relational knowledge is a very common form of knowledge, which allows direct inferences to be drawn from a premise to a conclusion. This paper focuses on the problem of representing and using relational knowledge affected by uncertainty. We first discuss the intuitive meaning of the uncertainty that may affect relational knowledge and we distinguish between A-uncertainty, concerning the applicability of a relation, and V-uncertainty, concerning the validity of a relation. Then we show how the difference between A-uncertainty and V-uncertainty has received so far only limited attention in various literature proposals. Finally, we introduce an original approach to deal with uncertain relational knowledge based on AV-quantified production rules, and we discuss its main features.

1 Introduction

One of the main features of intelligent behaviour is the ability to derive properties (called *conclusions*) about certain aspects of the world, inferring them from the available information relevant to different, but related, aspects (called *premises*). The simplest form of knowledge that can be used to this purpose consists in direct associations (*relations*) between the truth values attributed to a pair of propositions, one representing the premise and the other the conclusion of the inference process. For the sake of simplicity, we assume that propositions can assume just two truth values, i.e. true and false.

In many cases, the task of drawing an inference from a premise to a conclusion has to be accomplished in presence of uncertainty affecting both the truth value of the premise and the relation between the premise and the conclusion.

This paper focuses on the problem of representing and using uncertainty about the relation between the premise and the conclusion.

2 The Meaning of Uncertainty Affecting a Relation between Propositions

Given a proposition (expressing a fact about the world) and its possible truth values (supposed to be mutually exclusive), to be in a state of uncertainty about that proposition simply means to ignore which truth value has to be assigned to the proposition (given the hypothesis that the proposition has a truth value in the real world). The meaning of the term uncertainty is not so univocal and clear when dealing with uncertainty affecting (binary) relations between propositions. In fact, as we show below, uncertainty about a relation can carry two different meanings, depending on whether it affects the applicability or the validity of the relation.

Uncertainty about the applicability of a relation

This case is well exemplified by default rules [Reiter 80]. Here uncertainty arises from the fact that there are exceptions to these rules and that it is practically impossible to

enumerate and explicitly represent all the exceptions. For instance, given the default rule "birds fly", exceptions are represented by all the birds that do not fly, such as penguins, ostriches, emus ... (and broiled birds, according to [Pearl 91]).
Default rules may be viewed as rules with a weak, incomplete premise, that fails to capture all the conditions under which the rule is applicable. The meaning of the default rule "birds fly" is therefore not exactly

if is-a(X, bird) then fly(X)

but, more appropriately:

if is-a(X, bird) and "conditions"(X) then fly(X).

Often, we are unable (or unwilling) to specify all the "conditions" that make the rule applicable, since we have only incomplete knowledge about the relation existing between birds and the property of flying. However, we are intuitively certain about the validity of the rule, since in general, apart some exceptions, birds fly. "Birds fly" is in a sense an incomplete (or imprecise) rule, but it is definitely certain in nature. As it is evident, for any bird you meet - say Tweety - if you were able to correctly decide whether it meets "conditions" or not, you would able to deduce as well, without doubt, whether Tweety can fly or not. However, if you can not decide whether "conditions" are met or not - what is actually the case being "conditions" unknown - on the basis of the common experience that most birds fly, you may in any case assume that Tweety flies, until specific evidence against this assumption becomes available.
Uncertainty only affects the applicability of the rule, not its validity. This kind of uncertainty does not arise from a lack of evidence supporting the validity of the rule, but from the inherent incompleteness of its premise. We are simply unable to articulate all the conditions (that indeed exist) that make the rule applicable, either because they are too many and too intricate or because they are (partially) unknown.
We call this type of uncertainty that affects the applicability of a relation, but not its validity, *A-uncertainty*.

Uncertainty about the validity of a relation
In order to examine this case, let us consider the following two examples:

- "inveterate smokers catch lung cancer": it is definitely proved that smoke is a cause of lung cancer, but of course not all inveterate smokers necessarily catch lung cancer - statistically, an inveterate smoker has only 85% probabilities of contracting lung cancer;
- "inveterate smokers catch atherosclerosis": the causes of atherosclerosis are not exactly known, the majority of scholars (60%) indicates smoke as a probable cause of atherosclerosis, whereas others (40%) exclude this hypothesis.

The first rule represents a chunk of knowledge which is not really affected by uncertainty: there is no doubt that a (causal) relation exists between smoke and lung cancer. However, if your friend Tom is an inveterate smoker and you apply this knowledge to Tom, you can not be sure that Tom is among the 85% of smokers who will suffer from cancer. To put it another way, it is possible to consider the presence of inhibitors which prevent smoke from causing cancer and have a 15% statistical probability of being active; however, they are unknown. The nature of uncertainty in this case is not really different from that presented in the previous case of "birds fly". The first rule is clearly yet another example of A-uncertainty.

The second rule has a totally different meaning. It represents a case of uncertainty affecting the validity of relational knowledge: it is not certain that a (causal) relation exists between smoke and the disease atherosclerosis. Also in this case, you are not sure that your friend Tom will suffer from atherosclerosis, but the reason of uncertainty is quite different. While in the former case you were not sure about the applicability of the rule, assumed to be generally valid, to Tom, in this case you are not sure whether the rule is valid in general, i.e. if a relation exists between smoke and atherosclerosis or if they are totally unrelated, independently of the specific case of Tom. Note that this kind of uncertainty may be present even if a statistical correlation has been evidenced between smoke and atherosclerosis, since statistical correlation is a necessary, but not sufficient, condition to decide that a physical correlation exists between two phenomena. However, the discussion about this subtle point is beyond the scope of the present paper and, if the reader does not agree with this claim, s/he can assume that this type of uncertainty is simply due to a lack of information.

We call this type of uncertainty that affects the validity of a relation, but not its applicability, *V-uncertainty*.

This type of uncertainty - and especially the difference between A- and V-uncertainty - has escaped in the past the attention of most researchers. Also in the very rich and complete survey of Léa Sombé [Léa Sombé 90], uncertainty about a relation between propositions refers to the presence of exceptions only. Nevertheless, the distinction between A- and V-uncertainty has a huge practical relevance. In fact, they are clearly distinct in nature and should be treated differently. Therefore, when uncertain knowledge is acquired from an expert for some practical purpose, it is very important that this distinction is carefully taken into account, in order to avoid improper uses of knowledge or wrong deductions. In the next section, we investigate the ability of some of the known approaches to represent uncertainty to correctly capture and represent the difference between A- and V-uncertainty.

3 Representing Uncertain Relational Knowledge: a Focused Survey

Bayesian belief networks

In Bayesian belief networks [Pearl 91] the existence of a relation between two propositions associated to the nodes A and B of a network is represented through the value of P(B|A). Within this formalism (and also other Bayesian formalisms) it is not possible to have distinct representations for A- and V-uncertainty. Bayesian belief networks are appropriate to represent A-uncertainty: in fact, the example "inveterate smokers catch lung cancer" can be modeled as P(CANCER(x)|SMOKE(x)) = 0.85, which correctly implies that P(NOT CANCER(x)|SMOKE(x)) = 0.15, i.e. that 15% of smokers will not contract cancer. This kind of probabilistic representation fails, however, to capture the correct meaning of V-uncertainty.

In this case, considering the example "inveterate smokers catch atherosclerosis", we can model this situation as P(ATHEROSCLEROSIS(x)|SMOKE(x)) = 0.6. But, within a Bayesian formalism, we are forced by the probability axioms to derive that P(NOT ATHEROSCLEROSIS(x)|SMOKE(x)) = 0.4, which is a wrong a conclusion with respect to the knowledge we are intended to represent. In fact, in this case we may accept the statement that there is 60% probability that smoke causes atherosclerosis, and, therefore, that a smoker catches atherosclerosis; but we can not accept that 40% of smokers will not catch atherosclerosis, which is absolutely different from the original intended meaning that there is 40% probability that smoke is not a cause of atherosclerosis.

Probabilistic logic

Probabilistic logic [Nilsson 86] is a generalisation of ordinary first-order logic in which the truth values of sentences can range in the real interval [0, 1]. A relation between two sentences in logic is represented by the implication relation $\forall$ x, A(x) $\supset$ B(x), which is a shortcut for $\forall$ x, $\neg$A(x) $\vee$ B(x). Consider now the problem of representing the negation of the implication relation. One could represent the negation as $\neg$($\forall$ x, A(x) $\supset$ B(x)), which is equivalent to $\exists$ x, (A(x) $\wedge$ $\neg$B(x)). However this is equivalent to state the presence of exceptions, which are related to A-uncertainty. On the contrary, when dealing with V-uncertainty, we are in doubt if, in all cases, the relation is valid. This can be represented by $\forall$ x, $\neg$(A(x) $\supset$ B(x)), which is equivalent to $\forall$ x, A(x) $\wedge$ $\neg$B(x). This means that when trying to negate the validity of the implication, we introduce a stronger constraint between the truth values of A and B than the implication itself . In fact there are three possible worlds in which (A(x) $\supset$ B(x)) is true (namely: (A(x)=T, B(x)=T), (A(x)=F, B(x)=F), (A(x)=F, B(x)=T)), while there is just one possible world in which $\neg$(A(x) $\supset$ B(x)) is true (namely: (A(x)=T, B(x)=F)).

If, in order to represent V-uncertainty, a probability value p is ascribed to $\forall$ x,(A(x) $\supset$ B(x)), the probability value 1-p should be ascribed to $\forall$ x, $\neg$(A(x) $\supset$ B(x)). Therefore, it is clear that the negation of the implication in probabilistic logic, and in any extension of the ordinary logic, has nothing to do with what we have in mind when we say, for example, "smoke is not the cause of atherosclerosis". In fact, given this proposition, we consider as equally possible all the combinations of the values for smoke and the presence of atherosclerosis, because the proposition is intended to deny the existence of a relation between them. On the contrary when stating, in logic, that $\neg$(SMOKE(x) $\supset$ ATHEROSCLEROSIS(x)) only one possible combination of truth values for smoke and atherosclerosis is allowed.

It is well-known that logic has nothing to do with causality and that the concept of causality itself is simply rejected by a logic approach. However, this is not our point: we do not want to force probabilistic logic to capture the notion of causality, but we stress that it fails also to capture the notion of independence (causal or not causal). In fact, in ordinary logic, the independence between the truth values of two sentences A and B is implicit if nothing is said about them. However, as shown above, it is impossible to correctly express, in probabilistic logic, a state of uncertainty about the fact that there is a relation (or a dependency) between A and B or not.

Possibilistic logic

Possibilistic logic [Dubois et al. 94a] [Dubois et al. 94b] deals with propositional or first-order logic sentences to which a real number in the interval [0, 1] is associated, which quantifies the possibility or the necessity of the corresponding sentence. Namely Π(p) denotes the possibility degree of the sentence p and N(p) its necessity.

A relation between two sentences A (premise) and B (conclusion) is usually represented by the logical implication $\neg A \vee B$. Such an implication can be associated with a necessity degree or a possibility degree, to state that there is some uncertainty about it. This is definitely a promising step: we could interpret a necessity valued rule as representing A-uncertainty (the rule is considered fully possible but is not always applicable) and a possibility valued rule as representing V-uncertainty (doubts about the validity of the rule are expressed by the fact that it is not considered fully possible). However, at the best of our knowledge about possibilistic logic, no indication is given on the different kind of cognitive attitude underlying the fact that a rule has a necessity value less than 1 or a possibility value less than 1. In fact, even though, at a logical level, necessity and possibility have well distinct meanings, it is unclear which are the criteria to decide how to model uncertainty expressed in linguistic terms by a domain expert, either as a degree of necessity or as a degree of possibility.

Consider the example presented in [Dubois et al. 94a]: the rule "If John comes tomorrow, it is rather likely that Albert will come" is represented by ($\neg$comes(John,m) $\vee$ comes(Albert,m))(N 0.6), whereas the rule "someone will come to the meeting whose presence may (highly possibly, but not certainly at all) make the meeting not quiet" is represented by ($\neg$comes(a,m) $\vee$ $\neg$quiet(m))(Π 0.8). In these cases the distinction seems to be rather a matter of subtlety in the use of words than of different cognitive concepts, and it is easy to imagine that, asking different persons, they will express almost the same knowledge using different words such as: "If John comes tomorrow, it is possible, but not certain at all that Albert will come" or "Someone will come to the meeting whose presence is highly likely to make the meeting not quiet".

If knowledge analysis criteria are not specified, there is the risk of a totally imprecise, and perhaps meaningless, use of the formalism.

Moreover, since the relation $N(p) = 1 - \Pi(\neg p)$ holds, we have that when stating $(\neg A \vee B)(\Pi\ 0.8)$, $\neg(\neg A \vee B)(N\ 0.2)$, i.e. $(A \wedge \neg B)(N\ 0.2)$, is also implied. That is to say that also possibilistic logic suffers from the limitation previously showed for probabilistic logic: when we try to express our uncertainty about the validity of a relation between the truth values of two sentences, we necessarily introduce also some certainty for another stronger and, possibly, undesired relation between them.

Dempster-Shafer theory

The Dempster-Shafer (D-S) theory of evidence [Shafer 76], offers an alternative way to deal with uncertainty. In D-S theory, probability are not assigned to single events but to subsets of the frame of discernment (say Q), so that it is possible to express some degree of ignorance by assigning a non-null probability to the whole frame of discernment Q.

Given a probability assignment, it is possible, for each subset A of Q, to compute the value of a belief function Bel(A), which measures the total amount of belief in A: $Bel(A)=\Sigma_{B \subset A} m(B)$. The quantity $Pl(A)= 1 - Bel(\neg A)$ is called the plausibility of A and expresses the maximum amount of belief that can be assigned to A.

Since D-S theory allows an explicit representation of ignorance, it seems to be appropriate to capture the uncertainty present, for example, in "inveterate smokers catch atherosclerosis". In fact given the simple frame of discernment:

Q = {ATHEROSCLEROSIS, $\neg$ATHEROSCLEROSIS},

given the evidence SMOKE, and given the rule "inveterate smokers catch atherosclerosis", it is possible to derive the following probability assignment:

m({ATHEROSCLEROSIS}) = 0.6

m(Q) = 0.4,

which correctly captures our attitude to doubt the relation between SMOKE and ATHEROSCLEROSIS, and, therefore, ascribes some probability to Q, i.e. indifferently to ATHEROSCLEROSIS and ¬ATHEROSCLEROSIS, in presence of SMOKE. The attitude of D-S theory to capture "an interpretation of uncertainty (or, more precisely, epistemic uncertainty) as meta-knowledge about the validity of our knowledge" has been reported also by Saffiotti [Saffiotti 91] which considers the difference between the propositions "I am 80% sure that [all] birds fly" and "[I am sure that] 80% of birds fly". A thorough discussion about merits and flaws of D-S theory, which is a very active research field, is beyond the scope of this paper. However, let us only mention that, in many domains, it may be very difficult (and somewhat unnatural) to define the set of exhaustive and mutually exclusive hypotheses that constitute the frame of discernment.

4 Representing uncertain relational knowledge

Basic concepts: representing uncertainty of propositions

First of all, let us introduce the concept of belief: a *belief* is an evidential judgement about the credibility of the truth values ({true, false} in the case of ordinary two-valued logic) assigned to a proposition. Beliefs may assume values in an ordered set (even infinite) of *belief degrees*. For the sake of simplicity, we assume here the real interval [0, 1] as the set of possible belief degrees.

It is important to underline that, in our proposal, the concept of belief degree is related to the intuitive concept of "amount of evidence" supporting the credibility that a certain proposition should have a certain truth value. So, bel_E(A, V)=0 means that there is null (or negligible) evidence supporting the credibility that proposition A has the truth value V, and this is totally different from excluding that V is a possible truth value for A. Similarly, bel_E(A, V)=1 means that available evidence fully supports the credibility that proposition A has the truth value V, and this is again totally different from being absolutely certain that V is the correct truth value of A.

If we now consider a proposition and compute the belief degrees for all its possible truth values, we obtain a global representation of the uncertainty about which truth value should be assigned to the proposition, on the basis of the available evidence. Therefore, given a proposition A and a body of evidence E, the *belief state* of A under E, denoted by bels_E(A), is the pair (bel_E(A, true), bel_E(A, false)), (say (bt_A, bf_A) for short). The belief state represents how much one is authorized to believe in the association between a given proposition and its possible truth values, on the basis of the available evidence. A proposition accompanied by the relevant belief state is called a quantified proposition. Formally: for any proposition A, the pair (A, bels_E(A)) is called a *quantified proposition*. Intuitively, if we are fully convinced, on the basis of available evidence, that a proposition is true, this will be represented by the belief state (1, 0), whereas the opposite conviction will be represented by (0, 1). Moreover we can represent a state of total ignorance about a proposition (due to a lack of evidence) with the belief state (0, 0), which indicates the absence of evidence both supporting the value true and the value false. On the contrary, if we have, for any reason, strong evidences for both the values true and false, we can represent this contradictory situation by the belief state (1, 1). Of course, all the intermediate situations are possible, since the two components of a belief state are independent.

Uncertainty of relations between propositions

Let us now address the issue of representing uncertainty about relational knowledge. For the sake of simplicity, we will focus on the most common form of representation of relational knowledge, i.e. production rules. Production rules are considered here just as a simple example, useful to illustrate some basic initial ideas about the representation of uncertainty affecting relational knowledge. It is by no means our intention to propose the AV-quantified production rules approach, described in the following, as a generally valid formalism to deal with uncertainty.

A *production rule* is a relation between two propositions A and B, denoted by if A then B, whose intuitive meaning is "If proposition A is true, and the rule if A then B holds, then also proposition B is true". Proposition A is called the *if-part* and proposition B the *then-part* of the rule. To extend the formalism of production rules to deal with uncertainty, the first - most obvious - idea, derived from the representation of uncertainty in propositions, might be to quantify a production rule with a pair of belief states, one representing the applicability of the rule and the other the validity. However, two important points have to be considered.

- First of all, we note that, from a very general perspective, knowledge may be considered as partitioned in two classes, namely:
  - *Fresh knowledge* concerning the current state of the world, its current properties, and the currently occurring events. Fresh knowledge refers to the present time: it is acquired through observation.
  - *Consolidated knowledge* (also commonly called domain knowledge), concerning the steady properties of the world. Consolidated knowledge has been accumulated through observation and experimentation in the past.
- Second, fresh and consolidated knowledge greatly differ from the point of view of supporting evidence:
  - for fresh knowledge, acquired in the present time, detailed evidence can generally be collected in favor or against it;
  - for consolidated knowledge - acquired in the past, often through a long and complex process of successive refinements - the original evidence, in favour or against it, is generally not available anymore in analytical terms, being replaced by a more synthetic justification.

On the basis of the above remarks, the idea to quantify a production rule with two belief states seems impractical. Therefore, one has often to be satisfied with a more synthetic representation: instead of a belief state, only a belief degree is provided for representing A-uncertainty and V-uncertainty.

According to the above remark, we can extend the concept of belief state to production rules as follows. Given a production rule R and a body of evidence E, the *AV-belief state* of R under E, also denoted by $\underline{\text{AV-bels}}_E$(R), is the pair ($\underline{\text{bell}}_E$(R, true), $\underline{\text{bell}}_E$(R, false)), (say ($bt_R$, bf_R) for short) with:

- $\underline{\text{bell}}_E$(R, true) = $\underline{\text{bel}}_E$(applicable(R), true),
- $\underline{\text{bell}}_E$(R, false) = 1 - $\underline{\text{bel}}_E$(valid(R), true).

In intuitive terms, the AV-belief state of a production rule R has the following semantics:

- $\underline{\text{bell}}_E$(R, true) provides a measure of how much one is authorized to believe that the rule is universally applicable or - in other words - that there exist no exceptions to the applicability of the rule, i.e. the more one has reasons to believe that the rule is universally applicable the greater is $\underline{\text{bell}}_E$(R, true);
- $\underline{\text{bell}}_E$(R, false) provides a measure of how much one is authorized to believe that the rule is not fully valid, i.e. the more one has reasons for believing that the rule is fully valid the lesser is $\underline{\text{bell}}_E$(R, false).

For example, the rule "inveterate smokers catch lung cancer", affected by A-uncertainty only, can be AV-quantified by the AV-belief state (0.85, 0). The rule "inveterate smokers catch atherosclerosis", affected by V-uncertainty only, can be quantified by the AV-belief state (1, 0.4). If we consider a rule affected by both A- and V-uncertainty, for example "inveterate smokers get vesica cancer" we can quantify it by the AV-belief state (0.6, 0.3).
A production rule accompanied by the relevant AV-belief state is called an *AV-quantified production rule*. Formally: for any production rule R, the pair (R, $\underline{\text{AV-bels}}_E$(R)) is called an *AV-quantified production rule*.

At this stage of our work, we have not developed yet a complete theoretical framework for uncertain reasoning with AV-quantified production rules. Therefore, in the following, we will give only some preliminary indications about the problem of propagation of belief states. In fact, the behavior of the belief states during propagation formally defines the semantics of our representation of A- and V-uncertainty. This entails two aspects, namely (i) the identification of the role the four factors bt_A, bf_A, bt_R, bf_R are expected to play in determining bt_B, bf_B, and (ii) the formulas to be used in the computation of bt_B, bf_B. These issues are dealt with below.

The role of bt_A, bf_A, bt_R, bf_R in determining bt_B, bf_B
The role of bt_A, bf_A, bt_R, bf_R in determining bt_B, bf_B does not follow necessarily from the theory developed so far. In order to define it precisely, some assumptions have to be made. Consider, the following examples:

- "inveterate smokers catch lung cancer" quantified with (0.85, 0).
  Here we are faced with A-uncertainty. We are allowed to believe that the rule "inveterate smokers catch lung cancer" applies with a degree 0.85, but what happens in the cases where it does not apply ? Two answers are possible:
  - we know nothing about what might happen to inveterate smokers, as far as lung cancer is concerned,
  - inveterate smokers do not catch lung cancer.

  The former interpretation is more cautious and, possibly, safer, even if less telling; it corresponds to a *conservative* attitude. The latter is more flexible and, possibly, more riskier, even if more telling; it corresponds to an *evolutive* attitude. The evolutive perspective seems to capture more closely the semantics of A-uncertainty, which is strictly bound to the concept of default rules, or rules with exceptions. The intended meaning of "inveterate smokers catch lung cancer" quantified with (0.85, 0) is that the rule is not universally applicable: the majority of inveterate smokers catch lung cancer, but some inveterate smokers do not catch it. There is an implicit expectation - not just a lack of knowledge - about what should happen to the exceptions of a default rule: exceptional inveterate smokers not catching lung cancer.

- "inveterate smokers catch atherosclerosis", quantified with (1, 0.4).
  Here we are faced with V-uncertainty. We are allowed to believe that the rule "inveterate smokers catch atherosclerosis" is valid with a degree 0.6, but what happens in the cases where it is not valid ? Again, two answers are possible:
  - we know nothing about what might happen to inveterate smokers, as far as atherosclerosis is concerned,
  - inveterate smokers do not catch atherosclerosis.

  Similarly to the case of A-uncertainty, the former interpretation corresponds to a *conservative* attitude and the latter to an *evolutive* attitude. However, in this case, the conservative perspective seems to capture more closely the semantics of V-uncertainty. The intended meaning of "inveterate smokers catch atherosclerosis" quantified with (1, 0.4) is that the rule is not fully valid: there are intrinsic doubts about the fact that inveterate smokers catch atherosclerosis, and, consequently, we do not know what happens if the rule is not valid. There is no implicit expectation, but just a lack of knowledge.

Of course, the above reasoning does not pretend to offer an objective and definitely correct perspective on the semantics of A- and V-uncertainty. Rather, it is based on a subjective appreciation of what the semantics of A- and V-uncertainty should be in order to meet common sense and to be cognitively plausible. The proposed approach is not the only possible one; however, it is justified (it is based on plausible assumptions) and coherent (it brings to plausible deductions).
On the basis of the above discussion, we can now identify the specific role of bt_A, bf_A, bt_R, bf_R in determining bt_B, bf_B :

- The more one has reasons for believing in the truth of A (i.e., the higher is bt_A), the more he should believe in what can be inferred from A. Therefore, the higher is bt_A, the higher should be either bt_B or bf_B. Neither bt_B nor bf_B should however be greater than bt_A.
- The more one has reasons for believing in the falsity of A (i.e., the higher is bf_A), the more he should be ignorant about what can be inferred from A. Therefore, the higher is bf_A, the lower should be both bt_B and bf_B.
- The more one has reasons for believing in the applicability of the rule (i.e., the higher is bt_R), the more he should believe in the truth of the conclusion, and the less he should believe in its falsity. If the rule is universally applicable (i.e., bt_R=1), then one should completely transfer the belief in the truth of the premise to the belief in the truth of the conclusion; otherwise the belief in the premise should be distributed between the beliefs in the truth and in the falsity of the conclusion (according to the evolutive assumption about A-uncertainty).
- The more one has reasons for disbelieving in the validity of the rule (i.e., the higher is bf_R), the more he should be ignorant about what can be inferred from the rule. Therefore, the higher is bf_R, the lower should be both bt_B and bf_B (according to the conservative assumption about V-uncertainty).

The propagation formulas

Given bt_A, bf_A, bt_R, bf_R, several formulas may be proposed for computing (bt_B, bf_B) that meet the intuitive requirements stated above. For example, one might assume the following formulas:

$$bt_B = bt_A \cdot bt_R \cdot (1 - bf_A) \cdot (1 - bf_R)$$
$$bf_B = bt_A \cdot (1 - bt_R) \cdot (1 - bf_A) \cdot (1 - bf_R),$$

5 Conclusions and future work

In this paper we have discussed the distinction between two types of uncertainty affecting relational knowledge, namely A- and V-uncertainty, and we have introduced, as a preliminary proposal, an approach to represent and treat A- and V-uncertainty in the simple case of production rules. Many aspects of the research reported in the paper deserve further attention and will be the subject of a future work. Among others:

- the extension of the treatment to the case of fuzzy, instead of crisp, properties;
- the consideration of the case where a complete belief state is available about the applicability and the validity of a relation;
- the extension of the proposed approach to forms of relational knowledge more complex than production rules, such as, for example, causal-evidential networks.

Acknowledgments. This work has been supported by the Consiglio Nazionale delle Ricerche, Progetto Finalizzato Robotica, Obiettivo PANDE. The authors are indebted to the anonymous referees for incomparably insightful comments. Due to space limits, we could not deal with all their comments in this version of the paper, but we will take them into account in the development of our work.

References

[Dubois et al. 94a] Dubois D., Lang J., and Prade H. Automated reasoning using possibilistic logic: Semantics, belief revision, and variable certainty weights, *IEEE Trans. on Knowledge and Data Engineering* KDE-6(1), 64-71

[Dubois et al. 94b] Dubois D., Lang J., and Prade H. Possibilistic logic, in D.M. Gabbay, C.J.Hogger, and J.A. Robinson (Eds), *Handbook of Logic in Artificial Intelligence and Logic Programming*, Clarendon Press, Oxford, UK, 1994, 439-513.

[Léa Sombé 90] Léa Sombé Group. Reasoning under incomplete information in artificial intelligence: A comparison of formalisms using a single example, *International Journal of Intelligent Systems* 5(4), 1990, 323-472.

[Nilsson 86] Nilsson N.J. Probabilistic logic, *Artificial Intelligence* 28, 1986, 71-87

[Pearl 90] Pearl J. Bayesian and belief-functions formalisms for evidential reasoning: A conceptual analysis, in G. Shafer and J. Pearl (Eds.) *Readings in Uncertain Reasoning*, Morgan Kaufmann, San Mateo, CA, 1990, 540-574.

[Pearl 91] Pearl J. *Probabilistic Reasoning in Intelligent Systems: Networks of Plausible Inference*, Morgan Kaufmann, San Mateo, CA, 1991.

[Reiter 80] Reiter R. A logic for default reasoning, *Artificial Intelligence* 13, 81-132.

[Saffiotti 91] Saffiotti A. Using Dempster-Shafer theory in knowledge representation, in P.P. Bonissone, M. Henrion, L.N. Kanal, and J.F: Lemmer (Eds.) *Uncertainty in Artificial Intelligence 6*, Elsevier, New York, N.Y, 1991, 417-431

[Shafer 76] Shafer G. *A Mathematical Theory of Evidence*, Princeton University Press, Princeton, NJ, 1976.

Multiple Database Logic

Mario R. F. Benevides *

COPPE/Sistemas - UFRJ
Caixa Postal 68511
Rio de Janeiro - Brasil 21945-970
Email: mario@cos.ufrj.br - Fax: 55-21-2906626

Abstract. This work was inspired in Gabbay's ideas of multiple database logic [Gab91, Gab94]. Here, we study the viability of constructing a multiple database logic. The construction is based on the definition of local and global logics that guides each database of the system and their interactions.The local logic characterizes how each database works, and the global logic characterizes how they interact.
There is a variety of ways in which the databases can be interconnected to form a network. Each database in the network can even reason with different logic. In this work, we considered some possible architectures.

1 Introduction

This work is based in Gabbay's works on Labelled Deductive Systems - LDS. We claim that LDS is a natural framework to model a network of deductive databases (figure 1).

Our concerns are not in the epistemic aspects of each database. We are mainly interested in modeling the connections between databases.

In general, each deductive database t can be seen as a pair $(\Delta_t, \vdash_t)$. Where (Δ_t contains all the information of the database t expressed in some logical language and each database has its own answering logical system $\vdash_t$). The network of deductive databases is a set of databases $(\Delta_t, \vdash_t)|t \in T$ and some connections between the databases. According to Gabbay we have at least two options to describe the relationship between databases ([Gab94]):

- External (metalevel): to use a meta level language that allows explicit reference to each database and provides means to describe the relationship between the DB's.
- Internal: To enrich the language of each database with new connectives allowing it to relate to its neighbours. Example: $\Box A \in \Delta_i$ means all (some, most) neighbours databases answer yes to query ?A.

We use the second option, i.e., we use a modal language in each database to express properties that hold in the neighbours databases. The fact that we

* Partially supported by the Brazilian National Research Council - CNPq

use LDS alow us to express naturally, in the object level, properties of the interconnection between the databases. The network is modelled in LDS as a direct graph of databases.

We study the viability of constructing a multiple database logic. The need of having two logic components, one local and other global, on the description of a set of databases, is discussed by Gabbay in [Gab91, Gab94]. The local logic characterizes how each database works, and the global logic characterizes how they interact.

There is a variety of ways in which the databases can be interconnected to form a network. Moreover, each database in the network can even reason with different logic. In this work, we considered some possible architectures. Modal logic is used as global logic or network logic. Some important points about the interconnection of the database logics are analyzed. And finally, we discuss some issues about the use of local logics. All the interactions between the databases are handled in natural deduction style. In addition, we allow two kind of reasonings: hypothetical reasoning (reasoning about hypothetical databases) and non-hypothetical reasoning (reasoning about specific databases).

2 Labelled Deductive System

This section presents a very brief introduction to Labelled Deductive System. For more on LDS see [Gab94].

In a logical system presented in LDS formulas are labelled:

$t : A$

where A is a formula and t is label. There are many possible interpretations for the label t in $t : A$ ([Gab94]):

- A was obtained or assumed using the assumptions named in t
- Fuzzy reliability value, $0 \leq t \leq 1$
- Priority of A
- Time when A holds
- Possible world where A holds
- t indicates a proof of A
- t can be the situation where the property A holds

Definition 1. (Gabbay 94, [Gab94]): Let **A** be a first order language of the form **A**$=(A, R_1, ..., R_k, f_1, ..., f_m)$, where A is the set of terms of the algebra (individuals variables and constants) and R_i are predicates (on A, possibly binary but not necessarily so) and $f_1, ..., f_m$ are function symbols (on A) of various arity.

A diagram of labels is a set D containing elements generated from A by the function symbols together with predicates of the form $\pm R(t_1, ..., t_k)$ where $t_i \in D$ and R is a predicate symbol of the algebra.

Let **L** be a predicate language with connectives $\#_1, ..., \#_n$ of various arities, with quantifiers and with the same set of atomic terms A as the algebra.

We define the notion of declarative unit, database and label as follows:

1. An **atomic label** is any $t \in A$. A **label** is any term generated from the atomic labels by the functions f1,...,fm.
2. A **formula** is any formula of **L**.
3. A **declarative** unit is a pair $t : A$, where t is a label and A is a formula.
4. A **database** is either a declarative unit or has the form (D, f, d) where D is a finite diagram of labels, $d \in D$ is a distinguished label, and f is a function associating with each label t in D either a database or a finite set of formulas.

3 Modal Logic in LDS

In this section we present modal logics in LDS in natural deduction style. It is based on [BM92].

A labelled formula $t : A$ in LDS can be interpreted as "A holds at possible world t". In this sense labells are used to name possible worlds.

We use a propositional modal language, with the standard connectives: $\wedge, \vee, \rightarrow, \neg, \bot, \Box$ and $\Diamond$. In order to present modal logics in LDS, we need to define the labelling algebra:

Definition 2. A **Modal Labelling Algebra** is a triple $\mathbf{A} =< \{0\}, f^1_\Box, f^2_\Diamond >$. Where 0 is an individual constant and $f_\Box$ and $f_\Diamond$ are functions symbols of arity one and two respectively. We also say that 0 is an **atomic label** and a **label** is any term generated from the atomic labels by the functions symbols $f_\Box$ and $f_\Diamond$.

Definition 3. A *modal system* is a tuple : $< \Sigma_0, \Sigma, R_1, R_2 >$ where:
Σ_0 - the initial set of formulas labelled with 0;
Σ - the set of all sets generated from Σ_0 using inference rules of $R_i, i = 1, 2$;
R_1 - the set of inference rules which presents how the logical connectives work in each set of formulas;
R_2 - the set of inference rules which presents how $\Box$ and $\Diamond$ work;

The Set R_1 of Inference Rules

∧-I

$$\frac{s : A \quad s : B}{s : A \wedge B}$$

∧-E

$$\frac{s : A \wedge B}{s : A} \qquad \frac{s : A \wedge B}{s : B}$$

∨-I

$$\frac{s : A}{s : A \vee B} \qquad \frac{s : B}{s : A \vee B}$$

∨-E

$$\frac{s : A \vee B \quad \begin{array}{c}[s : A]\\ s : C\end{array} \quad \begin{array}{c}[s : B]\\ s : C\end{array}}{s : C}$$

→-I

$$\frac{\begin{array}{c}[s : A]\\ s : B\end{array}}{s : A \rightarrow B}$$

→-E

$$\frac{s : A \quad s : A \rightarrow B}{s : B}$$

¬-RAA

$$\frac{\begin{matrix}[s : \neg A] \\ s : \bot\end{matrix}}{s : A}$$

¬-Intuitionist

$$\frac{s : \bot}{s : A}$$

The Set R_2 of Inference Rules

□ - Rules

□-I

$$\frac{f_\Box(s) : A}{s : \Box A}$$

□-E

$$\frac{s : \Box A}{f_\Box(s) : A} \qquad \frac{s : \Box A \quad f_\Diamond(s,\alpha) : \alpha}{f_\Diamond(s,\alpha) : A}$$

◇ - Rules

◇-I

$$\frac{f_\Diamond(s,\alpha) : A}{s : \Diamond A}$$

◇-E

$$\frac{s : \Diamond A}{f_\Diamond(s,A) : A}$$

The function $f_\Box(s)$ opens a generic possible world accessible from s, and the $f_\Diamond(s, A)$ opens a particular possible world accesible from s where A holds.

As we want to have classical propositional modal logic the following rewrite rules must hold in order to cope with negated modalities:

$$\neg\Diamond A \Longrightarrow \Box\neg A \qquad \neg\Box A \Longrightarrow \Diamond\neg A$$

The modal logic obtained in this way is the classical propositional modal logic **K**. Other modal logics can be presented in a similar manner in LDS:

Modal Logic **T**

$$\frac{s : \Box A}{s : A}$$

Modal Logic **4**

$$\frac{f_\Box(s) : A}{f_\Box(s) : \Box A} \quad \text{or} \quad \frac{s : \Box A}{s : \Box\Box A}$$

Modal Logic **D** (Deontic)
Simplifying the □-E rule:

□-E

$$\frac{s : \Box A}{f_\Box(s) : A} \qquad \frac{s : \Box A}{f_\Diamond(s,\alpha) : A}$$

Modal Logic **S5**

$$\frac{f_\Diamond(s,\alpha) : A}{f_\Box(s) : \Diamond A}$$

Some remarks can be made about modal logics based in our presentation of modal logics in LDS:

- We have one actual (local) world, i.e., Σ_0;
- Deductions start and end in the set Σ_0 ;
- In Modal Logic not presented in LDS, it does not allow for naming possible world. We can only reasoning about Hypothetical Possible worlds;
- In Modal Logic presented in LDS we can extend the Labelling Algebra and allow for having more then one actual world and reasoning about particular (local) possible worlds.

4 Multiple Databases Logic

Our aim in this section is to model a network of deductive Each database has its own set of formulas (data), and has mechanisms to reasoning about its data. Each database can be interconnected with some neighbours.

In order to model a network of databases, as in figure 1, we must be able to name each database. That means that we must allow for several actual (local) worlds. And each database must be able to reasoning locally.

The network of databases forms a directed graph where the vertices are databases and the edges shows the interconnection between them.

Now we are ready to present the Multiple Databases Logic in LDS in natural deduction style.

A labelled formula $t : A$ in LDS now is interpreted as "A holds at database t". Labels are used to name databases.

We use a propositional modal language, with the standard connectives: $\wedge, \vee, \rightarrow, \neg, \perp, \Box$ and $\Diamond$. In order to present multiple database logic in LDS, we need to define the labelling algebra:

Definition 4. Definition 4.1: A **Multiple Databases Labelling Algebra** is a triple

$\mathbf{A} =< \{t_1, t_2, ..., t_n\}, f^1_\Box, f^2_\Diamond, C >$. Where $t_1, t_2, ..., t_n$ are individual constants, $f_\Box$ and $f_\Diamond$ are functions symbols of arity one and two, respectively and C is a binary predicate symbol. We also say that $t_1, t_2, ..., t_n$ are **atomic labels** and a **label** is any term generated from the atomic labels by the symbols $f_\Box$ and $f_\Diamond$.

Definition 5. A **Multiple Databases Logic** has the form $< D, f, \Sigma, R_1, R_2 >$, where

D - is a (finite) diagram (graph). A finite diagram is a (finite) set of terms of the labelling

algebra **A** and a binary relation C on individual terms of the algebra.

f - is a function associating with each $t \in D$ a formula A.

R_1- the set of inference rules which presents how the classical connectives work in each database.

R_2- the set of inference rules which presents how $\Box$ and $\Diamond$ work.

The set R_1 of Inference Rules

These rules presents the local logic, i.e., the logic of each database. In our case this is classical propositional logic. Each database reasons using the same logic.

The set R_1 for the Multiple Databases Logic is the same for the Modal Logic presented in section 3.

The set R_2 of Inference Rules

These rules model the interaction between the databases. They show how the $\Box$ and $\Diamond$ work in each database. There are two types of rules in this set: Hypothetical and Non-hypothetical rules. They model two forms of reasoning that each database can have.

Hypothetical (modal) rules allows each database to reasoning about its neighbours hypothetically. These are the modal rules. For instance, suppose database t_1 is connected with other databases in the network and we have $\{t_1 : \Box A; t_1 : \Diamond B\}$. we must be able to infer $t_1 : \Diamond(A \wedge B)$ without making any kind of interaction between t_1 and its neighbours. This inference can be done only using hypothetical reasoning about its neighbours.

The Hypothetical rules are the modal rules presented in section 3.

The Non-hypothetical rules allow each database to reason about its individuals neighbours. Let s and t be meta variables on terms of the algebra.

Non-hypothetical rules[2]

$\Box$ - Rules

$\Box$-E

$$\frac{t : \Box A \quad tCs}{s : A}$$

$\Box$-I

$$\frac{t : A \quad \text{for all t sCt}}{s : \Box A}$$

$\Diamond$ - Rules

$\Diamond$-E

$$\frac{t : \Diamond A \quad \begin{matrix}[s : A] \\ t : B\end{matrix} \quad \text{for all s tCs}}{t : B}$$

$\Diamond$-I

$$\frac{t : A \quad sCt}{s : \Diamond A}$$

Semantics

The semantics presented below to the Multiple Databases Logic is a particular case of the general framework proposed in [Gab94].

Definition 6. **A structure** of the semantics has the form $< W, R, v, g >$, where:

- W is the set of possible worlds.
- R is a binary relation on W, $R \subseteq W^2$.
- v is a function that associates each propositional symbol and a possible world $w \in W$ a value true or false. Let P be the set of all propositional symbols then $v : W \times \mathbf{P} \rightarrow \{T, F\}$.
- g is an one-to-one total function mapping the individual terms of the algebra into W, such that:

if $t, s \in D$ and tCs, then $g(t)Rg(s)$.

The notion of satisfaction $\models$ can be defined as follows:

1. $w \models P$ iff $v(w, P) = T$;
2. $w \models \neg A$ iff not $w \models A$
3. $w \models A \wedge B$ iff $w \models A$ and $w \models B$
4. $w \models A \vee B$ iff $w \models A$ or $w \models B$

---

[2] The Non-hypothetical rules can have the following readings:

$\Box - E$ - if in t we have $\Box A$ and t is connected with s, then in s we have A;

$\Box - I$ - if for all databases t accessible from s we have A, then in s we have $\Box A$;

$\Diamond - I$ - if in t we have A and s is connected with t, then in s we have $\Diamond A$

$\Diamond - I$ - if in the database t we have $\Diamond A$ and for all databases s accessible from t if we suppose A in s and deduce that in t we have B, then in t we can infer B.

5. $w \models A \rightarrow B$ iff not $w \models A$ or $w \models B$
6. $w \models \Box A$ iff for all $w' \in W$ s.t. wRw', $w' \models A$
7. $w \models \Diamond A$ iff there exists $w' \in W$ s.t. wRw', $w' \models A$

Example 1. Suppose we have just one database $t1$ and C is empty.

We cannot apply the non-hypothetical rules, therefore we have only propositional modal logic **K**. If the relation C has the pair $t1Ct1$ then we get the trivial modal logic. It is due to the fact that if we have A, then we have $\Box A$ and $\Box\Box A$ and so on.

Example 2. Suppose we have five databases $\{t1, t2, t3, t4\}$ and C is transitive.

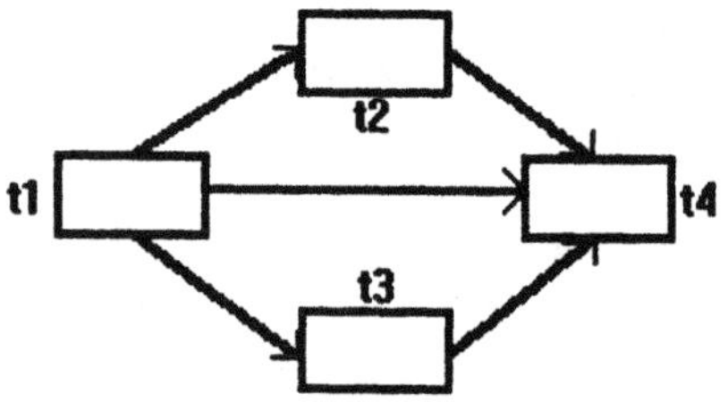

Fig. 1. Transitive Connection

Does we have **K4** in $t1$? The answer is no. We cannot prove $t1 : \Box A \rightarrow \Box\Box A$[3]. But, in $t1$, $t2$, and $t3$ we have **D**: $\Box A \rightarrow \Diamond A$ and in $t4$ we have **K**.

Example 3. Suppose we have four databases $\{t1, t2, t3, t4\}$ and in $t4$ we have intuitionistic logic.

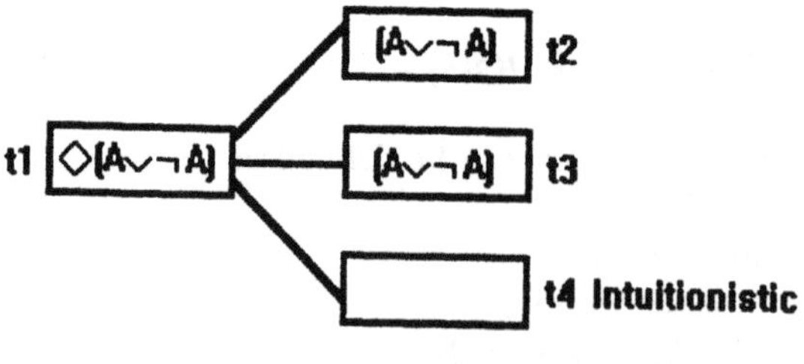

Fig. 2. Reasoning with different local logics

[3] In order to prove $t1 : \Box A \rightarrow \Box\Box A$ we suppose $t1 : \Box A$, then we have $t2 : A$, $t3 : A$ and $t4 : A$. As $t2Ct4$ and $t3Ct4$, then $t2 : \Box A$ and $t3 : \Box A$, but we do not have $t4 : \Box A$ (there is no database connected from $t4$). Therefore, we cannot infer $t1 : \Box\Box A$ and $t1 : \Box A \rightarrow \Box\Box A$.

The Multiple Databases Logic presented here can be easily modified to model this situation. But which modal logic do we get in $t1$? It is neither classical modal logic nor intuitionistic modal logic because we can not prove $\Box(A \vee \neg A)$ and we do prove $\Diamond(A \vee \neg A)$.

5 Conclusion

In this work we present Modal Logic in LDS, in natural deduction style, as a network of databases. As LDS allows for naming databases, we extend this presentation and propose a Multiple Databases Logic. We provide a proof theory and semantics for this logic.

We claim that LDS is a natural framework to model a network of deductive databases. It provides a variety of ways in which the databases can be interconnected to form a network. Moreover, each database in the network can even reason with different logic. Modal logic is used as global logic or network logic. Some important points about the interconnection of the database logics are analyzed. And finally, we discuss some issues about the use of local logics. All the interactions between the databases are handled in natural deduction style. In addition, we allow two kind of reasonings: hypothetical reasoning (reasoning about hypothetical databases) and non-hypothetical reasoning (reasoning about specific databases).

This work opens up some new possibilities of future works: the study of more general architectures; specification of distributed systems; detailed study of the use of different logics as local/global logics; the use of these ideas in specification of object oriented software; a semantical framework for multiple database logics and finally to establish a relation between this work and logics of knowledge and belief.

References

[BM92] M. R. F. Benevides and T. S. E. Maibaum. A constructive presentation for the modal connective of necessity. *Journal of Logic and Computation*, 2(No.1), 1992.

[BS93] M. R. F. Benevides and J. Silva. Um estudo em lógica de multiplos bancos de dados. In *Anais da XIX Conferência Latinoamericana de Informática y 22_a Jornadas Argentinas de Informática e Insetigación Operativa*, Buenos Aires, Argentina, 1993.

[Gab91] D. M. Gabbay. Theoretical foundations for non-monotonic reasoning part 2: structured non-monotonic theories. In *Proceedings of the 3rd Scandinavian AI Conference*, pages 19–40, 1991.

[Gab92] D. Gabbay. How to construct a logic for your application. 1992. Draft, October.

[Gab93] D. Gabbay. What is a logical system? 1993. Draft, July.

[Gab94] D. M. Gabbay. *LDS – Labelled Deductive Systems*. Volume 1, Max-Planck-Institut fur Informatik, Saarbrucken, Germany, May 1994.

A local approach to reasoning under inconsistency in stratified knowledge bases

Salem Benferhat, Didier Dubois and Henri Prade

I.R.I.T. – C.N.R.S. - Univ. Paul Sabatier - 31062 Toulouse Cedex, France
e-mail: {benferha, dubois, prade}@irit.irit.fr

Abstract. This paper investigates an approach for reasoning under inconsistency in a "local" way, in prioritized knowledge bases. In such bases, the higher the layer, the more certain, the more reliable are the formulas stored in this layer. The proposed approach is based on the notion of (consistent) *argument* whose strength depends on the layer of the least certain formulas involved in the argument. Each formula in the base is also associated with a "level of paraconsistency" which reflect to what extent there exists arguments that support both a formula and its negation. Three consequence relations are presented and compared. Two of them aim at maximizing the certainty degree and/or at minimizing the level of para-consistency of the conclusion. The third one produces consequences that are safely supported in the sense that there exists an undefeated argument for them (whose certainty is greater than its paraconsistency).

1. Introduction

Inconsistency may appear when a plausible consequence, obtained under incomplete information, has to be revised because further information is available. This issue has been extensively investigated in the nonmonotonic reasoning literature. In this paper we rather view inconsistency as being caused by the use (and the fusion) of multiple sources of information. Even if each source i of information provides a consistent knowledge base K_i, it may often happen in practice that the result of concatenating the K_i will be inconsistent. In such a situation, we further assume that the knowledge bases K_i store "regular" pieces of information rather than default rules liable to have explicit exceptions. In this paper, we will only deal with one inconsistent and prioritized (or if we prefer, stratified) knowledge base, denoted by Σ, which can be seen as the result of putting together several consistent knowledge bases. In this context, the introduction of priorities between pieces of information in Σ can be explained by the two following scenarios:

- Each consistent knowledge base K_i, issued from a source of information, is "flat" (i.e., without any priority between their elements). But there is a total pre-ordering between the sources of information according to their reliability. In this case merging different sources of information leads to a prioritized knowledge base Σ, where the certainty level of each formula reflects the reliability of the (best) source which provides it. A particular case is when each piece of information in Σ is supported by a different source.

- All sources of information are equally reliable (and thus have the same level of reliability), but inside each consistent knowledge base K_i there exists a preference relation between pieces of information given by an expert, which rank-orders them according to their level of certainty. Here again, the combination of the different sources of information gives an uncertain knowledge base, provided that the scales of uncertainty used in each knowledge base K_i are commensurate.

In this paper, we only consider a finite propositional language denoted by $\mathcal{L}$. The symbol $\vdash$ represents the classical consequence relation, Greek letters $\alpha,\beta,\delta,\ldots,\phi$,

$\psi, \chi, \ldots$ represent formulas. Let Σ be a set of propositional formulas, possibly inconsistent but not deductively closed. This paper deals with layered knowledge bases of the form $\Sigma = S_1 \cup \ldots \cup S_n$.

Possibilistic logic (e.g., [6]) offers a way of deriving non-trivial conclusions from an inconsistent knowledge base by taking advantage of the stratification of the base $\Sigma = S_1 \cup \ldots \cup S_n$ where formulas in S_i are considered as strictly more certain than the ones in S_j if $j>i$. This stratification is modelled in possibilistic logic [6] by attaching a weight $a \in [0,1]$ to each formula with the convention that $(\phi\ a_i) \in S_i$, $\forall i$ and $a_1 = 1 > a_2 > \ldots > a_n > 0$; for instance take $a_j = 1/j$. From now on, we will use a possibilistic representation of prioritized knowledge bases. A level of (partial) inconsistency for the base is computed as the level a_{j+1} such that $S_1 \cup \ldots \cup S_j$ is consistent but $S_1 \cup \ldots \cup S_{j+1}$ is not (consistency of Σ corresponds to inconsistency of level 0). The conclusions derived from $S_1 \cup \ldots \cup S_i$ with a_i strictly greater than the level of inconsistency are considered as well-grounded, since they are above the inconsistency level of Σ where inconsistency occurs, and more precisely since they can be logically deduced (in a non trivial way) using the most reliable part of Σ only. Although possibilistic reasoning can be successfully used for handling default information [1], it has two limitations for reasoning under inconsistency. Namely, formulas which do not take part to the inconsistency of the base but which have a level of certainty smaller or equal to the level of inconsistency of the base are not used in the inference process. Moreover, the user receives no information on the levels of certainty (smaller or equal to the level of inconsistency) of the formulas (if any) which contradict some of the formulas used for deriving the conclusion under consideration. The approach presented in this paper remedies these limitations. More precisely, the paper investigates three consequence relations capable of inferring non-trivial conclusions from an inconsistent knowledge base. In each case a level of paraconsistency is computed for each conclusion, which assesses to what extent there exists formulas which are somewhat certain in the base and which contradict some of the formulas used in the proof of the conclusion. These consequence relations treat inconsistency in a local way, by contrast with most of the approaches developed in the literature which work in a global way. See, e.g., Rescher & Manor[7]; Brewka[4]; Benferhat et al.[2].

The paper is organized as follows. Section 2 gives the background needed for the reading of this paper. Section 3 introduces the three proposed inconsistency-tolerant consequence relations which treat inconsistency in a local way. A comparative study between these consequence relations is given in Section 4.

2. Background

Throughout this paper, we denote sub-bases by capital letters A,B,C... and they are also represented in a stratified way. For the sake of simplicity, we will use the notation $A \vdash \psi$ to denote that ψ is a logical consequence of the formulas of A when we forget their weights. A sub-base A of Σ is said to be consistent if it is not possible to deduce a contradiction from A, i.e., $A \nvdash \bot$.

Def. 1: A sub-base A of Σ is said to be *minimal inconsistent* if and only if it satisfies the two following requirements: i) $A \vdash \bot$, and ii) $\forall (\phi\ a) \in A$, $A - \{(\phi\ a)\} \nvdash \bot$.

From now on, we denote by $Inc(\Sigma)$ the set of formulas belonging to at least one minimal inconsistent sub-base of Σ, namely:

$$Inc(\Sigma) = \{(\phi\ a), \exists A \subseteq \Sigma, \text{ such that } (\phi\ a) \in A \text{ and } A \text{ is minimal inconsistent}\}.$$

When we remove from Σ all elements of $Inc(\Sigma)$, the resulting base is called the free base of Σ, denoted by Free(Σ) [1]. In other words, the set Free(Σ) contains all the formulae, called *free formulas*, which are not involved in any inconsistency of the knowledge base Σ. Clearly Free(Σ) may be empty; Inc(Σ)=Ø when Σ is consistent. We now give the notion of free-consequence:

Def. 2: A formula ϕ is said to be a *free consequence* of Σ, denoted by $\Sigma \vdash_{Free} \phi$, if and only if ϕ is logically entailed from Free(Σ), namely: $\Sigma \vdash_{Free} \phi$ iff Free(Σ) $\vdash \phi$.

It is not hard to see that the Free-inference relation is very conservative, since it corresponds to a maximal revision of Σ, deleting all formulas involved in a conflict. We finish this section by defining the notion of argument:

Def. 3: A consistent sub-base A of Σ is said to be an ***argument*** to a degree a for a formula ϕ if it satisfies the following conditions: (i) $A \vdash \phi$, (ii) $\forall (\psi\ b) \in A$, $A - \{(\psi\ b)\} \nvdash \phi$, and (iii) $a = \min \{a_i \,/\, (\phi_i\ a_i) \in A\}$.

An argument for ϕ is then a minimal consistent sub-base of Σ which entails logically ϕ (in the sense of possibilistic logic, which requires condition (iii)). Note that this notion of argument is an extension of the one proposed by Simari and Loui [8]. These authors apply the notion of arguments to default reasoning (arguments are used to determine the relation of specificity between pieces of default information).

3. Local inconsistency-tolerant consequence relations

This section presents an approach to deal with inconsistent prioritized knowledge bases in a "local" way and studies three consequence relations in this framework. As in possibilistic logic, levels of priority or of certainty attached to formulas are used to distinguish between strong and less strong arguments in favour of a proposition or of its contrary. However it is possible to go one step further in the use of the certainty or priority levels by i) attaching to each proposition ϕ in the knowledge base not only its certainty weight a (obtained by computing the strongest argument in favour of ϕ in the sense of possibilistic logic), but also the weight b attached to the strongest argument in favour of $\neg\phi$ if any, and by ii) inferring from weighted premises such as (ϕ a b) by propagating the weights a and b. It will enable us to distinguish between consequences obtained only from "free" propositions in the knowledge base Σ for which b=0 (i.e., propositions for which there is no argument in Σ in favour of their negation), and consequences obtained using also propositions which are not free (for which there exists also a weighted argument in favour of their negation even if the latter has a smaller weight)[1].

More formally, the idea is first to attach to any formula in the stratified knowledge base Σ two numbers a and b reflecting respectively the extent to which we have some certainty that the formula is true and the extent to which we have some certainty that the formula is false. When b=0 then ϕ is *free* since ϕ is not involved in the inconsistency of Σ (otherwise there would exist an argument in favour of $\neg\phi$). When a≠0 and b≠0, ϕ is said to be *paraconsistent.* In the general case, we shall say that the pair (ϕ $\neg\phi$) has a level of "paraconsistency" equal to min(a,b). Classically and roughly speaking, the idea of paraconsistency is to say that ϕ is paraconsistent if there is a reason for stating both ϕ and $\neg\phi$. It corresponds to the situation where we have conflicting information about ϕ. This is why we speak here of paraconsistent information when min(a,b)>0, although the approaches presented in the following

---

[1] [5] already includes a brief suggestion of this approach by proposing an extension of the possibilistic resolution principle, handling paraconsistency degrees.

depart from classical paraconsistent logics (see [3] for their extension of these logics to the possibilistic framework). From now on, we denote by Σ' the set of triples $(\phi\ a\ b)$ such that $(\phi\ a_i)$ belongs to Σ, a is the weight attached to the strongest[2] argument in favour of ϕ and b is the weight attached to the strongest[2] argument in favour of its contrary $\neg\phi$. When $b \geq a$ then ϕ is said to be *defeated* by some argument. In the other case $(a>b)$ ϕ is said to be an *argumentative consequence* of Σ [2].

To see if a formula ψ is a plausible consequence of Σ, we first check if there is an argument in favour of ψ in Σ. It is clear that if there is no argument in favour of ψ in Σ then ψ cannot be a plausible consequence of Σ, since we have no reason to believe ψ in Σ. Assume that we have an argument A in favour of ψ where all elements of A are free formulas, then ψ can be considered as a plausible consequence of Σ (i.e., ψ is a free consequence of Σ). The situation differs if some elements of A are not free, and here we must be more careful in our inference. Indeed, let ϕ be a formula in A (the argument for ψ) such that there exists an argument in Σ which supports $\neg\phi$ with a certainty degree b higher than the one, a, of ϕ (namely ϕ is defeated), then the conclusion ψ must not be longer considered as a plausible consequence of Σ, as soon as, due to $a<b$, we do not consider ϕ as a plausible consequence of Σ (although $(\phi\ a\ b)$ is in Σ').

Once Σ' is constructed, we are going to associate two degrees to a conclusion ψ derived from an argument A in Σ: Cert(A), called the *certainty degree* of ψ using A, which just evaluates to what extent ψ is supported by an argument A, and Para(A), called the *paraconsistency degree* of ψ using A, which evaluates our degree of doubt to conclude ψ using A. These two measures are computed in the following way:

$$\mathrm{Cert}(A)=\min\{a_i \mid (\phi_i\ a_i\ b_i)\in\Sigma' \text{ and } (\phi_i\ a)\in A\},$$

$$\mathrm{Para}(A)=\max\{b_i \mid (\phi_i\ a_i\ b_i)\in\Sigma' \text{ and } (\phi_i\ a)\in A\}.$$

Cert(A) estimates the strength of argument A, and Para(A) its brittleness. In general, we can have several arguments which support ψ and we denote the set of all pairs thus obtained for ψ by:

$$\mathrm{Label}(\psi) = \{(\mathrm{Cert}(A_i), \mathrm{Para}(A_i)) \mid A_i \text{ is an argument for } \psi\}$$

From Label(ψ), we may think of two criteria to select the best argument for ψ: the certainty degree and the paraconsistency degree induced by the argument. It is clear that the best argument for ψ is the one which allows to deduce ψ with the highest certainty degree and the lowest paraconsistency degree. But in general, such argument does not always exist. Namely, we can have an argument for ψ with a high certainty degree, but also with a high paraconsistency degree, and another for ψ with low certainty and low paraconsistency. Then it is less obvious how to choose the best argument. We may: first either minimize the paraconsistency degree of a conclusion, or first maximize the certainty degree. These two possibilities lead to two definitions of inconsistency-tolerant consequence relations that we examine now.

Minimizing paraconsistency: One way to select the best argument among those which support ψ is to give a preference to arguments which minimize the paraconsistency degree of ψ. The knowledge base Σ can be viewed as decomposed into two sub-parts: the consistent (or free) sub-part, represented by Free(Σ), and the paraconsistent sub-part, represented by Inc(Σ). In this approach, the best argument for ψ is the one (if it exists) obtained from Free(Σ) even if the certainty degree of ψ induced by this argument is very low. If such argument does not exist in Free(Σ), then the best argument for ψ is obtained by i) using formulas from Free(Σ) as much as

---

[2] If there is an argument in favour of ϕ (resp. $\neg\phi$) to a degree c (resp. d) then $a \geq c$ (resp. $b \geq d$).

possible, ii) when necessary, using formulas from Inc(Σ) with the lowest paraconsistency degrees. More formally:

Def. 4: Let Label$_{Para}$(ψ) be the subset of Label(ψ) obtained by choosing the pairs with the lowest paraconsistency value. Let (Cert(A), Para(A)) be a pair of Label$_{Para}$(ψ) such that Cert(A) has the highest certainty value. Then ψ is said to be *PC-consequence* of Σ (PC: short for "first paraconsistency then certainty"), denoted by $\Sigma \vdash_{PC} \psi$, iff Cert(A) > Para(A).

Maximizing certainty: There is another view to selecting the best argument for ψ, where we prefer the argument which maximizes the certainty of ψ. This approach agrees with the principle that the lower is the certainty degree of formulas in a given argument, the lower is our degree of acceptation of the conclusion given by this argument.

Def. 5: Let Label$_{Cert}$(ψ) be the subset of Label(ψ) obtained by choosing pairs with the highest certainty value. Let (Cert(A), Para(A)) be a pair in Label$_{Cert}$(ψ) such that Para(A) has the lowest paraconsistency degree. Then ψ is said to be a *CP-consequence* of Σ (CP: short for "first certainty then paraconsistency"), denoted by $\Sigma \vdash_{CP} \psi$, iff Cert(A)>Para(A).

Definition 5 can be explained in a simpler way: to check if a conclusion ψ is a CP-consequence of Σ, first compute the greatest weight attached to the strongest argument, say A, for ψ. Next, compute the paraconsistency degree b of ψ with respect to A. Finally, if a>b then conclude that ψ is a CP-consequence of Σ. If the strongest argument A is not unique, take the one with the smallest paraconsistency degree.

Proceeding level by level: In this sub-section, we present a third local inference relation. We suggest that a formula ψ is a plausible consequence of Σ, if there exists a degree *a* such that ψ is a free-consequence of a sub-base of Σ composed of all formulas of Σ having a certainty degree higher or equal to *a*. It means that all formulas which are involved in the entailment of ψ must be either free formulas or have a level of paraconsistency less than *a* and thus less than the degree of certainty of ψ. More formally, let $\Sigma_a=\{(\phi\ b) \mid (\phi\ b)\in\Sigma \text{ and } b\geq a\}$ be the set of formulas of Σ having a certainty degree higher or equal to *a*, and Free(Σ_a) denotes the set of free formulas in Σ_a. It is clear that Free(Σ_a) is different from (Free(Σ))$_a$, and more precisely we have the following relation: (Free(Σ))$_a \subseteq$ Free(Σ_a). Note also that there is no inclusion relation between Free(Σ_a) and Free(Σ_b) where a>b. Indeed, since $\Sigma_a \subset \Sigma_b$, Σ_b may include new free formulas but also some which contradict formulas which were free in Σ_a. We define the inference relation that generates plausible results of Σ:

Def. 6: A formula ψ is said to be a ***safely supported consequence*** of Σ, denoted by $\Sigma \vdash_{SS} \psi$, if and only if there exists a positive number ***a*** such that $\Sigma_a \vdash_{Free} \psi$.

The degree of certainty of ψ is the greatest number *a* such that Free(Σ_a)$\vdash\psi$, namely

$$\text{Cert}(\psi)=\max\{a, \Sigma_a \vdash_{Free} \psi\}.$$

Thus, $\forall$b>Cert(ψ), $\Sigma_b \nvdash_{Free} \psi$. The paraconsistency degree of ψ is the lowest paraconsistency degree induced by arguments supporting ψ in $\Sigma_{Cert(\psi)}$, namely:

$$\text{Para}(\psi) = \min\{\text{Para}(A)/ A\subseteq\Sigma_{Cert(\psi)} \text{ and A is an argument for } \psi\}.$$

Notice that if for a given degree c<Cert(ψ) we have $\Sigma_c \nvdash_{Free} \psi$, then there is no longer a proof of ψ in Σ_c made only of free formulas and that at least one of the formulas, say ϕ, used in the free proof of ψ from Σ_a is paraconsistent. However, this

does not mean that we have an argument for $\neg\psi$ in Σ_c, although there is an argument for ψ in Σ_c obviously. Indeed, consider the following counter-example: $\Sigma=\{(\phi\ a),(\neg\phi\ a),(\neg\phi\vee\psi\ a)\}$. It is clear that we have an argument for ψ in the knowledge base Σ, and ψ is not a free-consequence of Σ, but we have no argument which supports $\neg\psi$.

The safely supported consequences can be described in terms of degrees Cert(A) and Para(A) for arguments A:

Proposition 1: $\Sigma \vdash_{SS} \psi$ iff there exists an argument A for ψ s.t. Cert(A)>Para(A).

Proof

Assume $\Sigma \vdash_{SS} \psi$, then let a=Cert(ψ) such that $\Sigma_a \vdash_{Free} \psi$. There is an argument A for ψ in Free(Σ_a), and Cert(A)=a. Assume Para(A)>Cert(A). Then it means that $\exists(\phi,a',b')\in\Sigma'$, $(\phi,a')\in A$, and b'>a. This means that there is in Σ an argument B of certainty b'>a that refutes ϕ. But this fact contradicts the assumption that $A\subset$Free(Σ_a). Conversely suppose A is an argument for ψ and Cert(A)>Para(A). It means that a=Cert(A)>max$\{b_i,(\phi,a_i)\in A, (\phi,a_i,b_i)\in\Sigma'\}$. Hence if B is an argument for $\neg\phi$, B is not a subset of Σ_a, and ϕ is free in Σ_a. Hence $A\subseteq$Free(Σ_a), and $\Sigma_a \vdash_{Free} \psi$. ■

Moreover the set of safely supported consequences of Σ is consistent:

Proposition 2: Let $K=\{\psi | \Sigma \vdash_{SS} \psi\}$. Then the set of formulas K is consistent.

Lemma: The set of formulas $\bigcup_{i=1,n}$ Free(Σ_{a_i}) is consistent.

Proof

Free(Σ_{a_n})=Free(Σ) is consistent. Then Free($\Sigma_{a_{n-1}}$) $\cup$ Free(Σ_{a_n}) is also consistent. Indeed assume it is not the case, it means that $\exists A\subseteq$Free($\Sigma_{a_{n-1}}$), $A\cup$Free(Σ_{a_n})$\vdash\bot$ where both A and Free(Σ_{a_n}) are consistent. This contradicts the fact that Free(Σ_{a_n}) only contains free formulas in Σ_{a_n} (since $A\subset\Sigma_{a_n}$). More generally, assume Free(Σ_{a_i})$\cup\ldots\cup$Free(Σ_{a_n})=F is consistent; let $A\subseteq$Free($\Sigma_{a_{i-1}}$), and assume $A\cup F\vdash\bot$. Let j be the smallest rank such that $A\cup$Free(Σ_{a_i})$\cup\ldots\cup$ Free(Σ_{a_j}) is inconsistent. This contradicts the fact that Free(Σ_{a_j}) only contains free formulas in Σ_{a_j} (since $A\subseteq\Sigma_{a_j}$ as well as Free(Σ_{a_i})$\subseteq\Sigma_{a_j}$ for $i\leq j$). ■

Proof of Proposition 2

We use the previous lemma. Clearly for each ϕ in K, there exists an argument say A(ϕ), in $\bigcup_{i=1,n}$ Free(Σ_{a_i}). Therefore $\bigcup_{\phi\in K}$ A(ϕ)$\subseteq\bigcup_{i=1,n}$ Free(Σ_{a_n}) and hence $\bigcup_{\phi\in K}$ A(ϕ) is consistent as well as its deductive closure. ■

Notice that when the knowledge base is flat (i.e., without any priority between their elements) the safely supported consequence relation as well as CP-consequence and PC-consequence relations are equivalent to the free-consequence relation defined in Section 2. Moreover, we can show that even if β and δ are safely supported consequences of Σ, their conjunction is not necessarily a safely supported consequence of Σ. Indeed, let us consider the following counter-example where our knowledge base is $\Sigma=\{(\alpha\ 1), (\neg\alpha\vee\beta\ .9), (\neg\rho\vee\delta\ .8), (\rho\ .7), (\neg\alpha\ .7)\}$. It is clear that β and δ are both safely supported consequences of Σ (since $\Sigma_{.9}\vdash_{Free}\beta$ and $\Sigma_{.7}\vdash_{Free}\delta$), while $\beta\wedge\delta$ is not since there is no *a*>0 such that $\Sigma_a\vdash_{Free}\beta\wedge\delta$. Indeed, a part of the argument $\{(\neg\rho\vee\delta\ .8), (\rho\ .7)\}$ for δ (namely ρ) has a certainty not greater than the level of paraconsistency of a part of the argument for β (namely α). This remark also holds for PC-consequence and CP-consequence (we can use the same counter-example). The failure of the "AND" property should not be a surprise when dealing with multi-source inconsistent information.

4. Comparative study and discussion

We first start this section by comparing the three above-mentioned inconsistency-tolerant consequence relations. To this aim we use the following example where the knowledge base is: $\Sigma = \{(\phi\ a), (\neg\phi\ b), (\neg\phi\vee\psi\ c), (\chi\ d), (\neg\chi\vee\psi\ e), (\neg\chi\ f)\}$.

Then: $\Sigma'=\{(\phi\ a\ b),(\neg\phi\ b\ a),(\neg\phi\vee\psi\ \max(b,c)\ 0),(\chi\ d\ f),(\neg\chi\vee\psi\ \max(e,f)\ 0),(\neg\chi\ f\ d)\}$.

Notice that only the formulas $\neg\phi\vee\psi$ and $\neg\chi\vee\psi$ are free in Σ, all the others are paraconsistent. We are interested in knowing if ψ can be deduced from Σ. We have:

$$\text{Label}(\psi) = \{(\min(a,c)\ b), (\min(d,e)\ f))\}$$

obtained using the following arguments respectively: $A=\{(\phi\ a), (\neg\phi\vee\psi\ c)\}$, and $B=\{(\chi\ d), (\neg\chi\vee\psi\ e)\}$. Then:

- Assume that a>c>b>f>d>e. Then minimizing the paraconsistency degree of the conclusion ψ will lead to select B as the best argument for ψ, and since min(d,e)<f then ψ will not be PC-inferred. This result is somewhat debatable since in the argument A, ψ is inferred from the two most certain formulas in Σ. In contrast, A is the strongest argument for ψ and hence ψ is a CP-consequence of Σ (since min(a,max(b,c))>b). More generally, if we have a pair (x y) with y>x and y is the lowest paraconsistency degree in Label(ψ) then ψ is completely inhibited by PC-consequence even if we have (1 z) in Label(ψ) with z slightly greater than y. Notice from the example, that the PC-consequence relation does not recover all the possibilistic consequences of the knowledge base (e.g., here ψ is a possibilistic consequence of the knowledge base). In contrast, CP-consequences do recover all the possibilistic consequences of the knowledge base.
- Assume that a>b>c>d>e>f then we obtain ψ as a plausible consequence of Σ if we first minimize the paraconsistency degree of ψ. In contrast, if we first maximize the certainty degree, A is selected since A is the best argument of ψ in this case, but ψ is no longer inferred since b>min(a,max(c,b)). This result is somewhat debatable especially if the certainty degree of $\neg\chi$ is very low. And more generally, if we have a pair (x y) with y>x and x is the highest certainty degree in Label(ψ) then ψ is completely inhibited by CP-consequence even if we have (z 0) in Label(ψ) (namely a free proof for ψ with z<x).
- Notice that in the two above cases, ψ is a safely supported consequence of Σ when we apply the third approach. Indeed, $\Sigma_c=\{(\phi\ a), (\neg\phi\vee\psi\ c)\}\vdash_{Free}\psi$ in the first case, and $\Sigma_e=\{(\phi\ a), (\neg\phi\ b), (\neg\phi\vee\psi\ c), (\chi\ d), (\neg\chi\vee\psi\ e)\}\vdash_{Free}\psi$ in the second case. Indeed Cert(A)>Para(A) in the first case and Cert(B)>Para(B) in the second case. The following proposition generalizes this remark and shows that $\vdash_{SS}$ produces more results than $\vdash_{PC}$ and $\vdash_{CP}$.

Proposition 3: If $\Sigma \vdash_{PC}\psi$ (resp. $\Sigma \vdash_{CP}\psi$) then $\Sigma \vdash_{SS} \psi$.

Proof

Indeed, if ψ is a PC-consequence (or a CP-consequence) of Σ then there exists an argument A for ψ in Σ such that a=Cert(A)>Para(A). Then use Proposition 1. ■

Furthermore, in [2] we have shown that $\vdash_{SS}$ recovers all the possibilistic consequences of Σ. Using Proposition 1 we can show that if there is in Label(ψ) a pair (a b) with a>b then $\Sigma \vdash_{SS} \psi$. This means that it cannot be that both ψ and $\neg\psi$

are PC-consequence or CP-consequence of Σ. Indeed, assume that both ψ and $\neg\psi$ are PC-consequences of Σ, namely there is a pair (a b)$\in$Label(ψ) with a>b, and a pair (c d)$\in$Label($\neg\psi$) with c>d, therefore using the remark above both ψ and $\neg\psi$ are paraconsistent consequences of Σ, and this is not possible using Proposition 2. Moreover, as suggested by the previous examples, we may have (a b)$\in$Label(ψ) with a>b (in this case ψ is a safely supported consequence), while ψ is neither a CP-consequence nor a PC-consequence of the knowledge base. Indeed, it is sufficient to imagine a situation where Label(ψ)=$\{(a+\varepsilon,1),(a,b),(\varepsilon',b-\varepsilon'')\}$ with $1>a>b>b-\varepsilon''\geq\varepsilon'$.

5. Conclusion

This paper has investigated a local approach to deal with inconsistency. Three consequence relations have been proposed and all are safe, namely we cannot have inconsistent sets of consequences of the knowledge base. Moreover, we have shown that only two of the consequence relations (CP-consequence and safely supported consequence relations) recover all the possibilistic results. On the other hand, the safely supported consequence relation generates more results than the CP-consequence, and hence $\vdash_{SS}$ seems to be a better approach to deal with inconsistency in a local way. Besides, in [2] we have shown that the so-called preferred sub-theories approach [4] generates more results than the safely supported consequence relation. However, some results given by preferred sub-theories may be debatable in a multi-source inconsistency reasoning perspective, as we can see in the following example: $\Sigma=\{(\phi\ 1.), (\neg\phi\ .9), (\neg\phi\vee\psi\ .8)\}$. Here ψ is a plausible consequence of Σ using the preferred sub-theories approach (since we remove simply $\neg\phi$ from the knowledge base) although the paraconsistency degree of ψ is greater than its certainty. The consequence relation $\vdash_{SS}$ which is based on undefeated arguments (since the inference requires the existence of a "free" argument) seems to be more satisfactory for reasoning with (possibly inconsistent) information coming from different sources. Lastly in [2] it is established that if the set of safely supported consequences of Σ is completed by deductive closure, then the obtained closed set is the set of possibilistic consequences of the intersection of all preferred sub-bases in the sense of Brewka [4].

References

1. S.Benferhat, D.Dubois, H.Prade. Representing default rules in possibilistic logic. Proc. KR'92, Cambridge, MA, Oct 26-29, 1992, pp. 673-684.
2. S.Benferhat, D.Dubois, H.Prade. Some syntactic approaches to the handling of inconsistent knowledge bases. Tech. Report IRIT/94-55-R, Univ. P.Sabatier, Toulouse.
3. P.Besnard, J.Lang. Possibility and necessity functions over non-classical logics. Proc. UAI'94, Morgan Kaufmann, pp. 69-76.
4. G.Brewka. Preferred subtheories: an extended logical framework for default reasoning. Proc. IJCAI'89, Detroit, MI, August, 1989, pp. 1043-1048.
5. D.Dubois, J.Lang, H.Prade. Handling uncertainty, context, vague predicates, and partial inconsistency in possibilistic logic. In: Fuzzy Logic and Fuzzy Control (Proc. IJCAI'91 Workshops) (D.Driankov et al., eds), Springer Verlag, LNAI N°833, pp. 45-55, 1994.
6. D.Dubois, J.Lang, H.Prade. Possibilistic logic. In: Handbook of Logic in Artificial Intelligence and Logic Programming, Vol. 3 (D.M.Gabbay et al., eds.), Oxford University Press, pp. 439-513, 1994.
7. N.Rescher, R. Manor. On inference from inconsistent premises. Theory and Decision, 1, 179-219, 1970.
8. G.R.Simari, R.P.Loui. A mathematical treatment of defeasible reasoning and its implementation. Artificial Intelligence, 53, 125-157, 1992.

Quasi-classical Logic: Non-trivializable classical reasoning from inconsistent information

Philippe Besnard[1] and Anthony Hunter[2]

[1] IRISA,Campus de Beaulieu, 35042 Rennes Cedex, France
[2] Department of Computing, Imperial College, London SW7 2BZ, UK

Abstract. Here we present a new paraconsistent logic, called quasi-classical logic (or QC logic) that allows the derivation of non-trivializable classical inferences. For this it is necessary that queries are in conjunctive normal form and the reasoning process is essentially that of clause finding. We present a proof-theoretic definition, and semantics, and show that the consequence relation observes reflexivity, monotonicity and transitivity, but fails cut and supraclassicality. Finally we discuss some of the advantages of this logic, over other paraconsistent logics, for applications in information systems.

1 Introduction

In practical reasoning, it is common to have 'too much' information about some situation. In other words, it is common to have to reason with classically inconsistent information. The diversity of logics proposed for aspects of practical reasoning indicates the complexity of this form of reasoning. However, central to practical reasoning seems to be the need to reason with inconsistent information without the logic being trivialized (Gabbay 1991, Finkelstein 1994). This is the need to derive reasonable inferences without deriving the trivial inferences that follow from ex falso quodlibet (EFQ):

$$\frac{\bot}{\alpha}$$

So for example, from the data $\{\alpha, \neg\alpha, \alpha \rightarrow \beta, \delta\}$, reasonable inferences include α, $\neg\alpha$, $\alpha \rightarrow \beta$, and δ by reflexivity, β by modus ponens, $\alpha \wedge \beta$ by introduction of conjunction, and $\neg\beta \rightarrow \neg\alpha$ by contraposition. In contrast, trivial inferences include γ, $\gamma \wedge \neg\delta$, etc, by ex falso quodlibet.

For classical logic, EFQ means that any conclusion can be drawn from inconsistent information. This renders the information useless, and therefore classical logic is obviously unsatisfactory for handling it. A possible solution is to weaken classical logic by dropping reductio ad absurdum. This gives a class of logics called paraconsistent logics such as C_ω (da Costa 1974). However, the weakening of the proof rules means that the connectives in the language do not behave in a classical fashion (Besnard 1991). For example, disjunctive syllogism does not hold, $((\alpha \vee \beta) \wedge \neg\beta) \rightarrow \alpha$ whereas modus ponens does hold. So, for example, α does not follow from $\{(\alpha \vee \beta), \neg\beta\}$, whereas α does follow from $\{(\neg\beta \rightarrow \alpha), \neg\beta\}$.

There are many similar examples that could be confusing and counter-intuitive for users of such a practical reasoning system.

An alternative, giving quasi-classical logic (or QC logic), which we explore in this paper, is to restrict the queries to being in conjunctive normal form, and restrict the proof theory to that of finding clauses that follow from the data. In the following we present a proof theory, and semantics for QC, and show how it provides a useful form of reasoning from inconsistent information.

2 Language for QC

In the following we present the usual classical definition for the language. In addition, we define the notion of a clause being trivial with respect to a set of formulae.

Definition 2.1 *Let $\mathcal{L}$ be the set of classical propositional formulae formed from a set of atoms and the $\wedge, \vee$ and $\neg$ connectives.*

Definition 2.2 *For each atom $\alpha \in \mathcal{L}$, α is a literal and $\neg\alpha$ is a literal. For $\alpha_1 \vee .. \vee \alpha_n \in \mathcal{L}$, $\alpha_1 \vee .. \vee \alpha_n$ is a clause iff each of $\alpha_1, .., \alpha_n$ is a literal. For $\alpha_1 \wedge .. \wedge \alpha_n \in \mathcal{L}$, $\alpha_1 \wedge .. \wedge \alpha_n$ is in a conjunctive normal form (CNF) iff each of $\alpha_1, .., \alpha_n$ is a clause.*

Definition 2.3 *For $\alpha_1 \wedge .. \wedge \alpha_n \in \mathcal{L}$, and $\beta \in \mathcal{L}$, $\alpha_1 \wedge .. \wedge \alpha_n$ is in a conjunctive normal form (CNF) of β iff $\alpha_1, .., \alpha_n$ is classically equivalent to β, and $\alpha_1, .., \alpha_n$ is in a CNF.*

For any $\alpha \in \mathcal{L}$, a CNF of α can be produced by the application of distributivity, double negation elimination, and de Morgan laws. We require the following function *Atoms*(Δ) which gives the set of atoms used in the set of formulae in Δ.

Definition 2.4 *Let $\Delta \in \wp(\mathcal{L})$, and α, β, $\gamma_1 \wedge .. \wedge \gamma_n$, $\delta_1 \vee .. \vee \delta_n \in \mathcal{L}$,*

$$Atoms(\Delta \cup \{\beta\}) = Atoms(\{\beta\}) \cup Atoms(\Delta)$$

$$Atoms(\emptyset) = \emptyset$$

$$Atoms(\{\beta\}) = Atoms(\{\gamma\}) \text{ where } \gamma \text{ is the CNF of } \beta$$

$$Atoms(\{\gamma_1 \wedge .. \wedge \gamma_n\}) = Atoms(\{\gamma_1\}) \cup .. \cup Atoms(\{\gamma_n\})$$

$$Atoms(\{\delta_1 \vee .. \vee \delta_n\}) = Atoms(\{\delta_1\}) \cup .. \cup Atoms(\{\delta_n\})$$

$$Atoms(\{\neg\alpha\}) = Atoms(\{\alpha\})$$

$$Atoms(\{\alpha\}) = \{\alpha\} \text{ if } \alpha \text{ is an atom}$$

Definition 2.5 *A clause $\alpha \in \mathcal{L}$ is trivial with respect to Δ iff $Atoms(\Delta) \cap Atoms(\{\alpha\}) = \emptyset$.*

3 Proof theory for QC

In the following, we present the QC proof rules, which are a subset of the classical proof rules, and we define the notion of a QC proof, which is a restricted version of a classical proof.

3.1 The QC proof rules

Definition 3.1 *Assume that $\wedge$ is a commutative and associative operator, and $\vee$ is a commutative and associative operator.*

$$\frac{\alpha \wedge \beta}{\alpha} \text{ [Conjunct elimination] } \quad \frac{\alpha \vee \alpha \vee \beta}{\alpha \vee \beta} \text{ [Disjunct contraction]}$$

$$\frac{\alpha}{\neg\neg\alpha} \text{ [Negation introduction] } \quad \frac{\neg\neg\alpha}{\alpha} \text{ [Negation elimination]}$$

$$\frac{\alpha \vee \beta \qquad \neg\alpha \vee \gamma}{\beta \vee \gamma} \text{ [Resolution]}$$

$$\frac{\alpha \vee (\beta \wedge \gamma)}{(\alpha \vee \beta) \wedge (\alpha \vee \gamma)} \quad \frac{(\alpha \vee \beta) \wedge (\alpha \vee \gamma)}{\alpha \vee (\beta \wedge \gamma)} \text{ [Disjunct distribution]}$$

$$\frac{\alpha \wedge (\beta \vee \gamma)}{(\alpha \wedge \beta) \vee (\alpha \wedge \gamma)} \quad \frac{(\alpha \wedge \beta) \vee (\alpha \wedge \gamma)}{\alpha \wedge (\beta \vee \gamma)} \text{ [Conjunct distribution]}$$

$$\frac{\neg(\alpha \wedge \beta)}{\neg\alpha \vee \neg\beta} \quad \frac{\neg\alpha \vee \neg\beta}{\neg(\alpha \wedge \beta)} \quad \text{[de Morgan laws]}$$

$$\frac{\neg\alpha \wedge \neg\beta}{\neg(\alpha \vee \beta)} \quad \frac{\neg(\alpha \vee \beta)}{\neg\alpha \wedge \neg\beta}$$

$$\frac{\alpha}{\alpha \vee \beta} \text{ [Disjunct introduction]}$$

3.2 Proofs in QC

Definition 3.2 *T is a proof-tree iff T is a tree where (1) each node is an element of $\mathcal{L}$; (2) for the trees with more than one node, the root is derived by application of any QC proof rule, where the premises for the proof rule are the parents of the root; (3) the leaves are the assumptions for the root; and (4) any node, that is not a leaf or root, is derived by the application of any QC proof rule - except the disjunct introduction rule - and the premises for the proof rule are the parents of the node.*

Definition 3.3 *Let $\Delta \in \wp(\mathcal{L})$. For a clause β, there is a QC proof of β from Δ iff there is a QC proof tree, where each leaf is an element of Δ, and the root is β.*

Definition 3.4 *Let $\Delta \in \wp(\mathcal{L})$, and $\alpha \in \mathcal{L}$. We define the QC consequence relation, denoted $\vdash_Q$, as follows:*

$\Delta \vdash_Q \alpha$ *iff for each β_i ($1 \leq i \leq n$) there is a QC proof of β_i from Δ*

where $\beta_1 \wedge .. \wedge \beta_n$ is a CNF of α.

Examples 3.1 *For $\Delta = \{\alpha \vee \beta, \alpha \vee \neg\beta, \neg\alpha \wedge \delta\}$, consequences of Δ include $\alpha \vee \beta$, $\alpha \vee \neg\beta$, α, $\neg\alpha$, and δ, but do not include $\neg\delta$, γ, $\gamma \vee \phi$, or $\neg\psi \wedge \neg\phi$. For $\Delta = \{\alpha \vee (\beta \wedge \gamma), \neg\beta\}$, consequences of Δ include $\alpha \vee \beta$, $\alpha \vee \gamma$, α, and $\neg\beta$.*

3.3 Properties of the QC consequence relation

Proposition 3.1 *Let $\Delta \in \wp(\mathcal{L})$, and $\alpha \in \mathcal{L}$. If $\Delta \vdash_Q \alpha$, then α is not trivial with respect to Δ. In other words, $Atoms(\Delta) \cap Atoms(\{\alpha\}) \neq \emptyset$.*

Proposition 3.2 *Cut, defined as follows, fails for the QC consequence relation.*

$$\frac{\Delta \cup \{\alpha\} \vdash_Q \beta \qquad \Gamma \vdash_Q \alpha}{\Delta \cup \Gamma \vdash_Q \beta}$$

Proof Consider that $\{\neg\beta \vee \delta, \alpha\} \cup \{\neg\alpha \vee \beta\} \vdash_Q \delta$ and $\{\neg\alpha\} \vdash_Q \neg\alpha \vee \beta$, but that $\{\neg\beta \vee \delta, \alpha\} \cup \{\neg\alpha\} \not\vdash_Q \delta$

Proposition 3.3 *Unit cumulativity, defined as follows, fails for the QC consequence relation.*

$$\frac{\Delta \vdash_Q \beta \qquad \Delta \cup \{\beta\} \vdash_Q \gamma}{\Delta \vdash_Q \gamma}$$

Proof Consider that $\{\neg\alpha, \alpha\} \vdash_Q \alpha \vee \beta$ and $\{\neg\alpha, \alpha\} \cup \{\alpha \vee \beta\} \vdash_Q \beta$, but $\{\neg\alpha, \alpha\} \not\vdash_Q \beta$

Proposition 3.4 *Reflexivity, defined as follows, succeeds for the QC consequence relation.*

$$\Delta \cup \{\alpha\} \vdash_Q \alpha$$

Proposition 3.5 *Monotonicity, defined as follows, succeeds for the QC consequence relation.*

$$\frac{\Delta \vdash_Q \alpha}{\Delta \cup \{\beta\} \vdash_Q \alpha}$$

Proposition 3.6 *Supraclassicality, defined as follows, fails for the QC consequence relation.*

$$\Delta \vdash \alpha \textit{ implies } \Delta \vdash_Q \alpha$$

Proposition 3.7 *For $\Delta = \emptyset$, there are no $\alpha \in \mathcal{L}$ such that $\Delta \vdash_Q \alpha$*

4 Semantics for QC

Definition 4.1 *Let S be some set. Let O be a set of objects defined as follows, where $+\alpha$ is a positive object, and $-\alpha$ is a negative object.*

$$O = \{+\alpha \mid \alpha \in S\} \cup \{-\alpha \mid \alpha \in S\}$$

We call any $X \in \wp(O)$ a model.

We can consider the following meaning for positive and negative objects being in or out of some model X,

- $+\alpha \in X$ means α is "satisfiable" in the model
- $-\alpha \in X$ means $\neg\alpha$ is "satisfiable" in the model
- $+\alpha \notin X$ means α is not "satisfiable" in the model
- $-\alpha \notin X$ means $\neg\alpha$ is not "satisfiable" in the model

This semantics can also be regarded as giving four truth values - called "Both", "True", "False", "Neither". For a literal α, and its complement α^*,

- α is "Both" if α is satisfiable and α^* is satisfiable
- α is "True" if α is satisfiable and α^* is not satisfiable
- α is "False" if α is not satisfiable and α^* is satisfiable
- α is "Neither" if α is not satisfiable and α^* is not satisfiable

This intuition coincides with that of four-valued logics (Belnap 1977). However, we will not follow the four-valued lattice-theoretic interpretation of the connectives, and instead provide a significantly different semantics.

Definition 4.2 *Let $\models_s$ be a satisfiability relation such that $\models_s \subseteq \wp(O) \times \mathcal{L}$. For $X \in \wp(O), \alpha \in \mathcal{L}$, we define $\models_s$ as follows,*

$$X \models_s \alpha \text{ if } +\alpha \in X$$

$$X \models_s \neg\alpha \text{ if } -\alpha \in X$$

$$X \models_s \alpha \wedge \beta \text{ iff } X \models_s \alpha \text{ and } X \models_s \beta$$

$$X \models_s \neg\neg\alpha \text{ iff } X \models_s \alpha$$

$$X \models_s \neg(\alpha \wedge \beta) \text{ iff } X \models_s \neg\alpha \vee \neg\beta$$

$$X \models_s \neg(\alpha \vee \beta) \text{ iff } X \models_s \neg\alpha \wedge \neg\beta$$

$$X \models_s \alpha \vee (\beta \wedge \gamma) \text{ iff } X \models_s (\alpha \vee \beta) \wedge (\alpha \vee \gamma)$$

$$X \models_s \alpha \wedge (\beta \vee \gamma) \text{ iff } X \models_s (\alpha \wedge \beta) \vee (\alpha \wedge \gamma)$$

$$\begin{aligned} X \models_s \alpha \vee \beta \text{ iff } & [X \not\models_s \neg\alpha \text{ or } X \models_s \beta] \\ & \text{and } [X \not\models_s \neg\beta \text{ or } X \models_s \alpha] \\ & \text{and } [X \models_s \alpha \text{ or } X \models_s \beta] \end{aligned}$$

Definition 4.3 *We extend the notion of satisfaction to that of weak satisfaction, denoted as $\models_w$, as follows, where $\models_w \subseteq \wp(O) \times \mathcal{L}$:*

$$X \models_w \alpha \text{ if } X \models_s \alpha$$

$$X \models_w \alpha \vee \beta \text{ if } X \models_s \alpha$$

Definition 4.4 *Let $\models_Q$ be an entailment relation such that $\models_Q \subseteq \wp(\mathcal{L}) \times \mathcal{L}$, and defined as follows,*

$$\{\alpha_1, .., \alpha_n\} \models_Q \beta$$
$$\text{iff for all models } X \text{ if } X \models_s \alpha_1 \text{ and } \ldots \text{ and } X \models_s \alpha_n \text{ then } X \models_w \beta$$

Examples 4.1 *Let $\Delta = \{\alpha\}$, and let $X1 = \{+\alpha\}$ and $X2 = \{+\alpha, -\alpha\}$. Now $X1 \models_s \alpha$, and $X2 \models_s \alpha$, whereas $X1 \models_s \alpha \vee \beta$, and $X2 \not\models_s \alpha \vee \beta$. However, $X1 \models_w \alpha \vee \beta$, and $X2 \models_w \alpha \vee \beta$, and indeed $\Delta \models_Q \alpha \vee \beta$. As another example, let $\Delta = \{\alpha \vee \beta, \neg\alpha\}$. For all models X, if $X \models_s \alpha \vee \beta$, and $X \models_s \neg\alpha$, then $X \models_s \beta$. Hence, $\Delta \models_Q \alpha \vee \beta$, $\Delta \models_Q \neg\alpha$, and $\Delta \models_Q \beta$.*

Proposition 4.1 *For all $\alpha \in \mathcal{L}$, $\{\} \not\models_Q \alpha$.*

Examples 4.2 *Consider $\alpha \vee \neg\alpha$. Here models that satisfy $\{\}$ include those, for example X, where $+\alpha \notin X$ and $-\alpha \notin X$, and so $X \not\models_Q \alpha$ and $X \not\models_Q \neg\alpha$ hold. Hence, it is not the case that for all models X that satisfies the empty set, X also satisfies $\alpha \vee \neg\alpha$.*

Proposition 4.2 *The $\vdash_Q$ relation is sound with respect to the $\models_Q$ relation.*
Proof See Besnard (1995).

Proposition 4.3 *The $\vdash_Q$ relation is complete with respect to the $\models_Q$ relation, where the formula on the right-hand side of both relations is in CNF.*

Proof See Besnard (1995).

5 Discussion

Developing a non-trivializable, or paraconsistent logic, necessitates some compromise, or weakening, of classical logic. The compromises imposed to give QC logic seem to be more appropriate than other paraconsistent logics for applications in computing. QC logic provides a means to obtain all the non-trivial resolvants from a set of formulae, without the problem of trivial clauses also following. Though the constraints on QC logic result in tautologies also being non-derivable, this is not usually a problem for applications.

QC logic exhibits the nice feature that no attention need to be paid to a special form that premises should have. This is in contrast with other paraconsistent logics where two formulae identical by definition of a connective in classical logic may not yield the same set of conclusions. An example given earlier in this paper is $\{(\neg\alpha \rightarrow \beta), \neg\alpha\}$ yielding the conclusion β as opposed to $\{\alpha \vee \beta, \neg\alpha\}$. QC logic is much better behaved in this respect, as illustrated by the the fact that more non-trivial classical conclusions are captured by QC-logic.

QC logic is more flexible than resolution (for the clause finding version, consult (Lee 1967)) which only deals with formulas in clausal form. In fact, QC logic could even be extended easily to handle arbitrary formulas, including implicative formulas. It only takes the following two inference rules to accommodate such formulae,

$$\frac{\alpha \rightarrow \beta}{\neg\alpha \vee \beta}$$

and

$$\frac{\neg(\alpha \rightarrow \beta)}{\alpha \wedge \neg\beta}$$

QC logic is also more appropriate than various approaches to reasoning from consistent subsets of inconsistent sets of formulae (for a review, see Benferhat 1993). In particular, QC logic does not suffer from the limitation due to "breaking off" formulae into compatible pieces: QC logic can make use of the contents of the formulas without being constrained by a consistency check. Moreover, it is obviously an advantage of QC logic to dispense with the costly consistency checks that are needed in all approaches to reasoning from consistent subsets. Finally, QC logic lends itself to a thorough analysis in terms of inference as proved in section 3.3 of this paper. In this way, we actually know what QC logic is, what it can do, what its limitations are, and, for these reasons, how it should be used.

In relation to other work, the proof theory we give for QC is quite close to Schutte's K1 axiomatization of classical logic (Schutte 1950). Also, QC logic extends the natural idea of tautological entailment without losing the demand that any conclusion is somehow contained in each disjunct of a conjunct when the premise is in a conjunctive normal form. In fact, our model theory for QC can be viewed as a natural simplification of Dunn's semantics for tautological entailement (Anderson 1975).

6 Acknowledgements

This work was funded by the ESPRIT DRUMS2 project, and by the UK Engineering and Physical Science Research Council project number GR/J 15483.

7 References

Anderson A R and Belnap N D Jr. (1975) Entailment: The logic of relevance and necessity, Princeton University Press

Belnap N (1977) A useful four-valued logic, in Dunn J and Epstein G, Modern Uses of Multiple-Valued Logic, 5-37, Reidel

Benferhat S, Dubois D, Prade H (1993) Argumentative inference in uncertain and inconsistent knowledge bases, Proceedings of the 9th Conference on Uncertainty in Artificial Intelligence, 411-419, Morgan Kaufmann

Besnard Ph (1991) Paraconsistent logic approach to knowledge representation, in de Glas M, and Gabbay D, Proceedings of the First World Conference on Fundamentals of Artificial Intelligence, Angkor

Besnard Ph and Hunter A (1995) Properties of quasi-classical logic, Technical Report, Department of Computing, Imperial College, London

da Costa N C (1974) On the theory of inconsistent formal systems, Notre Dame Journal of Formal Logic, 15, 497-510

Finkelstein A, Gabbay D, Hunter A, Kramer J, and Nuseibeh B (1993) Inconsistency handling in multi-perspective specifications, in IEEE Transactions on Software Engineering, 20(8), 569-578

Gabbay D and Hunter A (1991) Making inconsistency respectable, Part 1, in Jorrand Ph. and Keleman J, Fundamentals of Artificial Intelligence Research, Lecture Notes in Artificial Intelligence, 535, 19-32, Springer

Lee R C T (1967) A completeness theorem and a computer program for finding theorems derivable from given axioms. PhD dissertation, University of California, Berkeley

Schutte K (1950) Schlussweisen-Kalkuele der Praedikatenlogik, Mathematische Annalen, 122, 47-65

A Cost Bounded Possibilistic ATMS

John Bigham, Zhiyuan Luo, Debashis Banerjee

Department of Electronic Engineering,
Queen Mary & Westfield College, London University,
Mile End Road, London E1 4NS

Abstract. An incremental approach for generating multiple fault explanations when the system behaviour model is incomplete has been developed using a cost bounded ATMS as an underlying implementation mechanism. This paper describes an extension of the basic cost bounded ATMS suitable for cases when the incompleteness is modelled using possibilistic logic. The possibilistic cost bounded ATMS is integrated into a diagnostic system where uncertain and temporal information are used to discriminate hypotheses.

1 Overview

A cost bounded ATMS (CBATMS) which can be used as a computational mechanism to support diagnosis when there can be uncertainty and temporal dependencies in the model is described. An advantage in using a CBATMS is that explanations, which can include multiple fault explanations, can be generated incrementally. Initially only explanations below a chosen cost bound are generated and further explanations are generated, if required, by increasing the cost bound. In many diagnostic applications the structure of the model or the cost function can be such that the cost of explanations for the symptoms increase monotonically as explanations are generated in the (CB)ATMS network. Even if the condition for monotonicity is not true, in can be possible to restructure the model to ensure that it is. The CBATMS uses monotonic increase in costs to control the blocking and unblocking of propagation.

The approach to modelling uncertainty builds on using "causation events" to encode uncertain happenings, typically the generation of symptoms from causes. Temporal propositions are generated by backward reasoning from symptoms. The modified ATMS algorithm is used to generate explanations for the symptoms. The CBATMS is imbedded within a working diagnostic tool. This report concentrates on the basic CBATMS and its extension to allow possibilistic numerical uncertainty propagation.

2 The Unit-Port Representation Language

Applications are modelled in a knowledge representation language that has its roots in the diagnosis and maintenance of telecommunications systems. The essential elements of this language are given, to allow a description of the context of the CBATMS.

2.1 Functional Modelling

The functional model is built out of functional entities (FEs) which correspond to specific functionalities of the modelled system. A functional entity is for example a multiplexing functionality or the functionality of transmitting data from one FE to another FE, or the behaviour of a test and the corresponding test results. There is a mapping between the FEs of the functional model and the elements of the physical model. This mapping is not necessarily a one-to-one mapping. It can also be a many-to-one or one-to-many mapping. This separation into a functional and a physical model allows the functional model to be separate from the physical configuration of the system.

A functional entity consists of internal attributes called *states, input ports* and *output ports*. The ports are connected to the ports of other functional entities, e.g. the power-out port of a modelled converter is connected with the power-in port of a modelled multiplexer-group. The functional entities together with these port-to-port connections are the functional model.

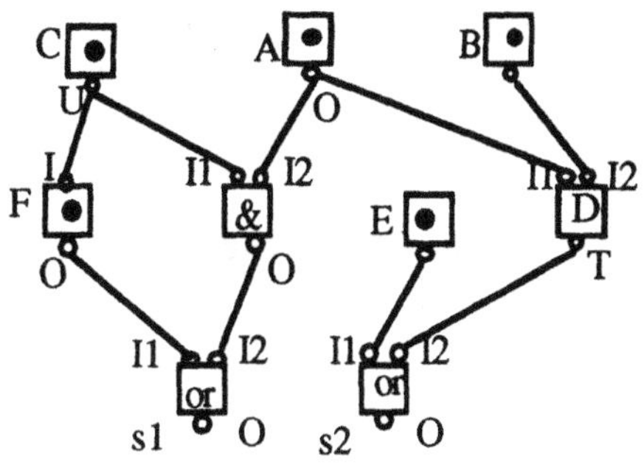

Fig. 1 A simple unit-port model

A simple example is given to clarify the approach. Because of space this example does not include temporal dependencies. In the example shown in figure 1, units A, B, C, D, E and F have eponymous state variables with domain {working, not-working} and all the ports in the model have domain {anomalous, not-anomalous}. State variables and ports have a user defined set of mutually exclusive values. The port T is observable. The units A, B, C, and E have rules which state that if the unit is not working their output port is anomalous, otherwise the port is not-anomalous, i.e.

A= not-working → O=anomalous

A=working → O=not-anomalous

where O is the output port of A. The "&" unit has input ports I1 and I2 and output port Output with logic

I1=anomalous & I2=anomalous → Output= anomalous

I1= not-anomalous or I2=not-anomalous → Output= not-anomalous

i.e. both inputs have to be abnormal before the output is. (A form of built in redundancy often found in electrical systems.) The "or" unit has input ports I1 and I2 and output port Output with logic

I1= anomalous or I2=not-anomalous → Output= anomalous

I1=not-anomalous & I2=not-anomalous → Output= not-anomalous

i.e. if any input is anomalous then the output will be.
F and D have an incomplete models, specified by causation events and described below. The rules in italics correspond to the nominal behaviour of the units.

An output port can be connected to any number of input ports, but an input port may only be connected to one output port. This is to ensure that there is no logic implied by the connections between the ports. A link between two ports only signifies that the ports correspond. A more detailed description of the unit-port language and how it has been used can be found in Bigham 93 & 95. Rule antecedents that model the inputs to a particular port value are not required to be mutually exclusive. This differs from the modelling used by Poole (Poole 93) where all the antecedents are mutually exclusive. The generated explanations can be made mutually exclusive afterwards if necessary.

2.2 Possibilistic Logic

Logical rules can also be used to model different uncertainty calculi. An example is Possibilistic Logic (Dubois, Lang & Prade). Here belief in a proposition requires two numbers to represent its value. These are called the Necessity N and Possibility Π. The number pairs (N, Π) are however constrained to lie on the thick line shown on figure 2. Only when a proposition is completely possible, can we talk about how necessarily true it is. Positive evidence for a proposition increases the necessity. Evidence against (i.e.. evidence for the negation of the proposition) decreases the possibility.

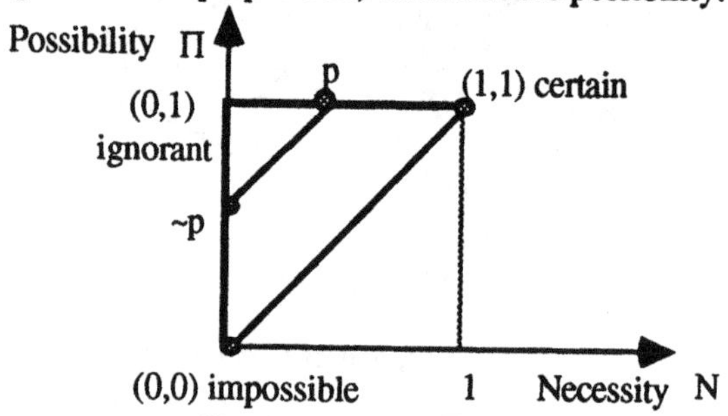

Fig. 2 $N(p) = 1 - \Pi(\sim p)$

Complementary propositions have (N, Π) pairs which lie on points equidistant from the point corresponding to ignorance. When using Possibilistic Logic port values and the causation events each have a belief specified by a (N, Π) pair. The possibility figure is always an upper bound. The necessity figure is always a lower bound. The inequalities arise because whilst $N(p \wedge q) = \min \{ N(p), N(q) \}$, we only have $N(p \vee q) \geq \max \{ N(p), N(q) \}$; and whilst $\Pi(p \vee q) = \max \{ \Pi(p), \Pi(q) \}$ we only have $\Pi(p \wedge q) \leq \min \{ \Pi(p), \Pi(q) \}$.

2.3 Representing Uncertainty Using Rules and Possibilistic Logic

The approach to modelling uncertainty builds on using "causation events" to represent uncertain happenings (Peng & Reggia 1987), and model the generation of symptoms from causes. If the causation event is required to appear as part of an explanation for the symptoms then it is included explicitly by introducing a state variable to represent each such causation event. Otherwise only a numerical value is used. Here we illustrate the use of Possibilistic logic. A common kind of unit found in applications arises when modelling a situation where failure in the unit can cause anomalous output, or anomalous input can cause anomalous output. Suppose F has an incomplete model, specified by the causation events α, β, γ and δ. α reads for example as "the state α holds". α, β, γ and δ may have physical significance.

F= not-working & $\alpha \rightarrow$ F.O=anomalous
F.I= anomalous & $\gamma \rightarrow$ F.O=anomalous
F= working & $\sim\beta \rightarrow$ F.O=anomalous
F.I= not-anomalous & $\sim\delta \rightarrow$ F.O=anomalous

Suppose α, β, γ and δ have necessities $\alpha*$, $\beta*$, $\gamma*$ and $\delta*$. Since we are illustrating the case where we do not want the causation events to appear in the explanations then, for example, the third of the above rules would be expressed as:

F= working $\rightarrow$ F.O=anomalous with $(N,\Pi) = (0, 1-\beta*)$

This is a form of noisy "or", the problem being that the antecedents are not mutually exclusive. If the modeller says that the above are the only ways in which we can have anomalous output (i.e. the above rules are covering) then the complementary rules can be derived as:

F= working & F.I= not-anomalous & $\beta\delta \rightarrow$ *F.O=not- anomalous*
F= working & F.I= anomalous & $\beta\text{~}\gamma \rightarrow$ *F.O=not- anomalous*
F= not-working & F.I= not-anomalous & $\text{~}\alpha\delta \rightarrow$ *F.O=not- anomalous*
F= not-working & F.I= anomalous & $\text{~}\alpha\text{~}\gamma \rightarrow$ *F.O=not- anomalous*

and the possibilistic form of the ruleset can be expressed as:

F= working & F.I=not-anomalous $\rightarrow$ F.O=not- anomalous with $(N, \Pi) = (\min\{\beta*, \delta*\}, 1)$
F= working & F.I=anomalous $\rightarrow$ F.O=not- anomalous with $(N, \Pi) = (0, 1-\gamma*)$
F= not-working & F.I=not-anomalous $\rightarrow$ F.O=not- anomalous with $(N, \Pi) = (0, 1-\alpha*)$
F= not-working & F.I=anomalous $\rightarrow$ F.O=not- anomalous with $(N, \Pi) = (0, \min\{1-\alpha*, 1-\gamma*\})$

D has an incomplete model, specified by the causation events τ, η, and φ.

D.I1= anomalous & D.I2= anomalous & $\varphi \rightarrow$ D.O=anomalous
D.I1= anomalous & D.I2= not- anomalous & $\text{~}\tau \rightarrow$ D.O=anomalous
D.I1= not-anomalous & D.I2= anomalous & $\text{~}\eta \rightarrow$ D.O=anomalous

Here the antecedents are mutually exclusive and the complementary ruleset is obvious.

3 The Cost Bounded ATMS

3.1 Context of application

The network used by the cost bounded ATMS is created by a reasoning scheme. The three main components of the diagnostic reasoning system are an *Explanations Generator* , a *Reasoning Controller* and an *Expected Symptoms Generator.* Together they allow forward and backward reasoning and construct the ATMS network which is used to store the necessary relationships required to compute explanations. A network segment is created from each symptom and other segments created to combine the explanations from individual symptoms to find consistent explanations for all the symptoms. Assumptions in the ATMS correspond to possible values of state variables, which include causation event assumptions if they are modelled explicitly. Environments in the network constructed correspond to partial explanations of the symptoms. Details of how the network is constructed can be found in Bigham 95

3.2 The Cost Bounded Algorithm

Following Ngair & Provan 93 each environment has a cost computed using a cost function which preserves the partial ordering on sets of assumptions induced by set inclusion, i.e. the cost function has to satisfy $\rho(e_1) \leq \rho(e_2)$ iff $e_1 \subseteq e_2$. Ngair & Provan's algorithm is as follows:

Set the cost bound to be the lowest possible, i.e. the cost associated with the empty environment and introduce all assumptions with cost lower or equal to the current bound. Run the basic ATMS algorithm with the current cost bound
Here if l_1 and l_2 are labels, then rather than $l_1 \wedge l_2$ being computed as the smallest subsets in $\{ e_1 \cup e_2 \mid e_1 \in l_1, \text{and } e_2 \in l_2\}$, it is computed as:
the smallest subsets $\{e = e_1 \cup e_2 \mid e_1 \in l_1, \text{and } e_2 \in l_2, \text{and } \rho(e) \leq \text{current cost bound}\}$
As before if l_1 and l_2 are labels then $l_1 \vee l_2$ is computed as the smallest subsets in $\{l_1 \cup l_2\}$. Note that this assumes that hyper-resolution is not required.

The CBATMS has a special node in which the environments are considered as solutions. In our application, this node correspond to the "Explanations Node". If an environment appears in the label of Explanations, stop and report the result, otherwise increase the cost bound to the next higher cost and introduce more assumptions. The CBATMS ensures that the cost of explanations increase monotonically as assumptions are added. A computational approach which allows incremental updating of the labels has been implemented.The following section describes how this has been augmented to allow for uncertainty in the justifications.

3.3 Environments and Updating Rules - Possibilistic Case

Following the approach Dubois, Lang and Prade used in their Possibilistic ATMS we will extend the definition of an environment to include additional belief information derived from the implicit assumptions. There may also be beliefs associated with the explicit assumptions.

The pair (N_1, Π_1) is defined to be $\geq (N_2, \Pi_2)$ iff $N_1 \geq N_2$ or if $N_1 = N_2$ then $\Pi_1 \geq \Pi_2$. An environment for a proposition is defined as the pair $e = [E\ (\nu, \pi)]$ if when we believe the assumptions in E - the explicit assumptions, then the (N,Π) for the implicit assumptions is $\geq (\nu, \pi)$.

If $[E1\ (N_1, \Pi_1)]$ and $[E2\ (N_2, \Pi_2)]$ are environments and $E1 \subseteq E2$ and $(N_1, \Pi_1) \geq (N_2, \Pi_2)$ then we can remove $[E2\ (N_2, \Pi_2)]$.

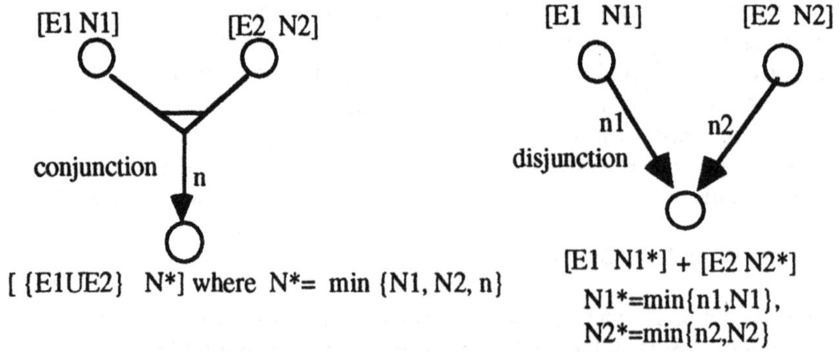

Fig. 3 Combination rules for necessities

The overall cost of $[E1\ (N_1, \Pi_1)]$, for example, is computed from the belief in the conjunction of independent assumptions in E1 and the propagation necessity

/possibility. The propagation rules in figure 3 are described in terms of necessities. The rules for possibilities are similar. Each of these combination rules satisfy the conditions of the CBATMS.so can be integrated into the incremental algorithm. For nodes with no inputs the initial value given to (N,Π) is $(1, 1)$. This does not correspond to any prior beliefs in the assumptions. These beliefs are used when computing the belief in E.

Several cost functions are possible. In the current application prototype the cost function is defined as pair $\rho^*(e)$:

$$\rho^*(e) = < (\nu, \pi), \varpi(E) > \text{ where } e = [E\ (\nu, \pi)]$$

where ϖ = number of not-working assumptions. $< (N_1\ \Pi_1), \varpi_1 > \geq\ < (N, \Pi), \varpi_2 >$ iff $(N_1, \Pi_1) \geq (N_2, \Pi_2)$ or if $(N_1, \Pi_1) = (N_2, \Pi_2)$ then $\varpi_1 \geq \varpi_2$. Here we start looking for solutions with $(N, \Pi) = (1, 1)$ and gradually reduce the threshold till solutions are found. An advantage of this cost function is that hyper-resolution is not necessary for the algorithm, as given above, to find the globally least cost solution incrementally. In general the requirement for hyper-resolution depends on the cost function and the structure of the network.

4 Temporal Delays

The temporal model corresponds closely to a form of extended Petri net. In fact a behaviour rule in the UP language corresponds to a transition in a modified stochastic Petri net. Because a Petri net gives a better intuitive description than the textually based language, the modelling will, in this section, be described in the context of Petri nets.

Petri nets are often used to model systems where there may be asynchronous or concurrent behaviour, and there are constraints on the precedence or frequency of the concurrence. In its simplest variant a net consists of two kinds of nodes. These are called *places* and *transitions* . Places are drawn as circles and transitions are drawn as bars. The nodes are connected by directed arcs. *Tokens* are associated with places. A transition is *enabled* when all its input places have a token in them, and when a transition *fires* the enabling tokens are removed from the input places and a token is added to all of the output places. A formal definition of a Petri Net can be found in Murata.

Figure 4 shows a transition which is enabled but not fired, and the state of the network after firing. In diagnosis a concern is to model the propagation of faults where there may be temporal delays. In a *deterministic timed* Petri net deterministic delays between enablement and firing are associated with the transitions. In a *stochastic net* the imprecision of the delay is specified, e.g. by a probability distribution. In our implementation the delay is specified by an interval.

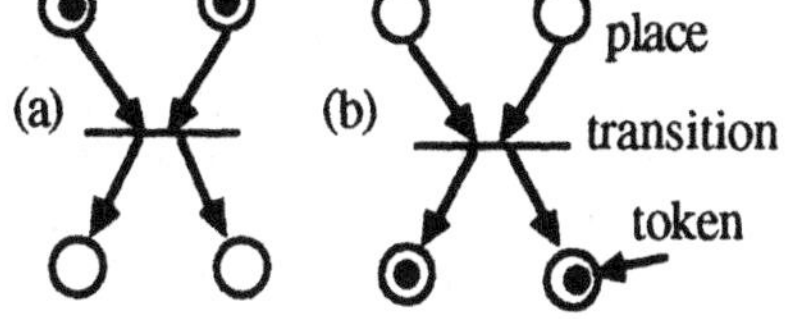

Fig. 4 (a) An enabled transition (b) the network after firing

We modify the stochastic Petri net to additionally allow a belief to be associated with the presence of a token in a set of mutually exclusive places. The tokens are allocated to those places used to control the uncertain triggering before the network is used to model event propagation. Once the transtion is selected the firing is sure to happen at some time as specified by distribution specifying the imprecision.

5 Complexity And Performance

An analysis of the complexity of the algorithm has been undertaken using the number of assumptions as the cost function. The basic ATMS algorithm (de Kleer 86) is NP-complete. A polynomial time behaviour can be achieved using a cost function and assuming the ATMS network contains no cycles and the network is considered sparse, i.e. it has O(q) connections for q network nodes . (It is still polynomial for a dense network of $O(q^2)$ connections.) The order of the polynomial increases with the number of assumptions in the cost threshold.

The system is still being improved but currently, for example, in a randomly generated test network with 150 nodes, over 100 assumptions and a cost function corresponding to the number of assumptions in an environment, the 1000 (approx.) possible explanations are created (incrementally) in 30 seconds on a Macintosh with all the cheapest solutions found in less than 1 second. This is shown in figure 5.

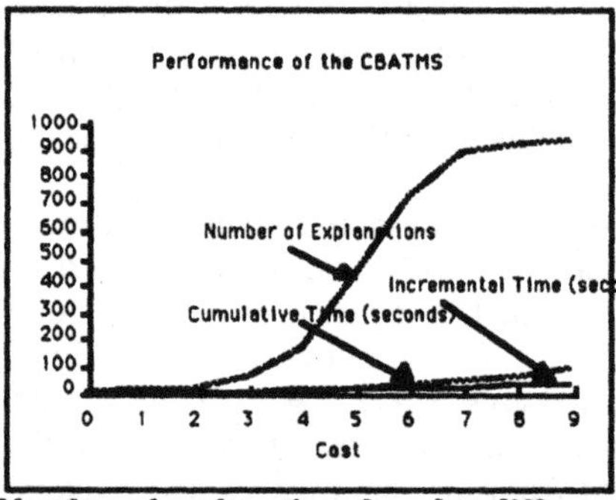

Fig. 5 Number of explanations found at different cost bounds

When there are complementary assumptions (as is usually the case when modelling uncertainty) then for certain cost functions the global least cost solution cannot be found without hyper-resolution. An example of such a cost function is $<\varpi(E), \omega(E).>$ where ω is the number of assumptions in E. If hyper-resolution is required the solution found using the CBATMS may not be the cheapest as it violates the assumption of the cost bounded ATMS that $l_1 \vee l_2$ is computed as the smallest subsets in $\{l_1 \cup l_2\}$, and so the cost of the explanations do not increase monotonically as assumptions are added. This condition was to ensure that the CBATMS creates all explanations below the cost bound. It is worthwhile noting that even if the cost function chosen should in general require hyper resolution it can be established for the network in question whether it is actually necessary. This could be done by running the ATMS for individual symptom possibilities prior to run time. Additionally hyper-resolution is *only* a possibility when there is disjunctive input to an ATMS node. When we combine explanations for individual symptoms, this is done by creating conjunctions of the explanation nodes for the individual symptoms. So hyper-resolution is *only* possible in that part of the network which can reasonably be examined before run time. The solution is to establish before run time if hyper-resolution is required, and if so ensure that the rulesets are (re-)written so that it is. This is not as difficult as it may at first sound as it can be done for each potential symptom individually, and does *not need to be done for symptom combinations.* Given that in a real time situation the network for each possible symptom may well be precompiled anyway, the ATMS algorithm itself could also be used as a basis for checking if the structure of the network was satisfactory. Additionally networks of the wrong structure are unlikely to be created by the modeller anyway, as the potential for simplification usually indicates redundant conditions in the rulesets.

A strength of the approach is the apparent ability to scale up, and the feasibility of integration within the same computational framework both uncertainty and a form of temporal reasoning. This will be described in future reports of the UNITE and DRUMS projects.

Acknowledgements

This work was funded in part by the DRUMS II and Esprit UNITE projects.

References

Bigham, J., Pang, P., (1993) "A model based reasoning system for the maintenance of telecommunications networks", International Journal of Engineering Intelligent Systems for Electrical Engineering and Communications", No 1, Vol. 1

Bigham, J., Luo, Z., (1995) "An integrated tool for uncertain and temporal reasoning in diagnostic problems", Internal Report, Department of Electronic Engineering, Queen Mary & Westfield College (London University), Mile End Road, London E1 4NS.

de Kleer, J. (1986) "Extending the ATMS", Artificial Intelligence **28** pp163-196, Elsevier Science

Dubois, D., Lang, J., Prade H., (1989) "A Possibilistic Assumption-based Truth Maintenance System with uncertain justifications and its application to belief revision", Truth Maintenance Systems, Springer Verlag, pp 87-106.

Murato, T., (1989) "Petri Nets:Properties, Analysis and Applications", Proc. IEEE, Vol 77, No 4, April 1989

Peng, Y., Reggia, J.A., (1987)"A probabilistic causal model for diagnostic problem solving - Parts I and II", IEEE Transactions on Systems, Man and Cybernetics, Vol SMC-17

Poole, D., (1993) "Probabilistic Horn Clause Abduction and Bayesian Networks", Artificial Intelligence, 64, (1993) pp81-129, Elsevier Science Publishers

Ngair, T. H. and Provan G. (1993) "A Lattice-Theoretic Analysis of Assumption-based Problem Solving", Institute of System Science, National University of Singapore, Kent Ridge, S(0511), Republic of Singapore

A Substructural Connective for Possibilistic Logic *

Luca Boldrin

Dept. of Pure and Applied Mathematics, University of Padova
Via Belzoni 7, 35131 Padova, Italy

Abstract. We investigate the use of substructural logics for dealing with uncertainty. In this paper possibilistic logic is enriched with a new connective for combining information; the language allows then for two combinators: the usual "and" for performing expansion and the new "and" for combining information from distinct independent sources, as argued in [Dubois and Prade 85]. A negation is introduced which corresponds to fuzzy set complementation. The resulting logic is given the expected semantics and a proof system in sequent calculus, which is proved sound and complete.

1 Introduction

The modeling of uncertain and incomplete knowledge has been widely studied in the literature, giving rise to various tools like belief functions, probability functions, possibility functions; various ways have also emerged for the combination of evidence in these frameworks (see. [Dubois and Prade 94] for a wide survey).

From a logical point of view, some languages and inference mechanisms have been developed whose semantics rest on belief, probability or possibility functions (see [Dubois, Lang and Prade 94], [Fagin and Halpern 94], [Saffiotti 92]), and links to classical epistemic logics have been provided by [Alechina and Smets 94], [Hajek et. al 94], [Murai et al. 93] and [Voorbraak 93]. However, most of these languages are static, in the sense that they deal with a unique information state; no logical counterpart has been established to the combination of evidence which, semantically, is a change of information state.

To explain better this concept, assume we are given some uncertain information in the form of a set of labeled formulae $\Gamma = \{(A_i, \alpha_i) : i \in I\}$, where the labels express some degree of belief (certainty, probability,...) on the formulae. This set may be thought of as representing an information state. We may content ourselves with determining what else is true in this information state, by using some inference mechanism $\vdash$; soundness guarantees that if $\Gamma \vdash (B, \beta)$, then the formula B is supported to the degree β by the information state. This is what we call static inference. We may also want some automatic means for changing the information state after the acquisition of more information; if we are given the new token of information (A, α), we can proceed in two ways:

* This work has been conceived during a visit at IRIDIA (ULB – Bruxelles, Belgium); it has then been carried on at the institute LADSEB (CNR – Padova, Italy)

- Look for an extra-logical operator * such that $\Gamma * (A, \alpha)$ yields a new set Γ' such that Γ' exactly represents the information state that we should reach (this is the approach of belief revision).
- Interpret the set Γ as the logical formula $\gamma = \bigwedge_{i \in I}(A_i, \alpha_i)$, and add a new connective $\otimes$ to the language. We require that $\gamma \otimes (A, \alpha) \vdash (B, \beta)$ if B is held to the degree β in the new information state (this approach resembles that of non-monotonic reasoning).

This second statement is the one we are going to explore.

A parallel can be drawn with the representation of certain knowledge; in that case, since there is no way of weighing evidence from different sources, the only meaningful operators correspond to expansion, revision or update. An interesting work in the direction of representing these dynamic operators as logical connectives is [de Rijke 94], which captures the non-determinism of revision. The uncertain setting has to cope with a much wider set of operators, some of which we try to represent *inside* the language. The introduction of several connectives into a language for modeling different combinations of truth values is not a new thing, since it is already present in works on fuzzy logic like [Pavelka 79]; however, differently from Pavelka, we do not cope with fuzzy truth values since we do not aim at representing *fuzziness*, but *uncertainty*; consequently, formulae of our language represent *crisp* tokens of evidence which are mapped into a lattice of possibility distributions, and the connectives correspond to operators for combining these distributions.

This paper is focussed on possibilistic logic; while it is not our intent to discuss the semantic framework, which we take for granted, our contribution is limited to the syntactic treatment of uncertainty in a possibilistic framework; we show how different connectives, which correspond to some kind of combination of evidence, can be added to possibilistic logic in a substructural framework. However, a similar extension of the language is also arguable in other settings: for instance, we can think of a Dempster-Shafer combination operator for belief function-based logic (a syntactic characterization of Dempster conditionalization has been proposed in [Alechina and Smets 94]), or to a Jeffrey conditionalization operator for probabilistic logic.

Let us assume that a piece of evidence is modeled by a possibility distribution on a set of possible worlds; as reported in [Dubois and Prade 85], there are several ways of aggregating information, depending on the relation among the sources of information, and on assumptions on their reliability. In this paper we focus on two operators for combining possibility distributions: $\wedge$ defined by $(\pi_1 \wedge \pi_2)(w) = \pi_1(w) \wedge \pi_2(w)$ and the Łukasiewicz operator $\times$, defined by $(\pi_1 \times \pi_2)(w) = (\pi_1(w) + \pi_2(w) - 1) \vee 0$; both of these operators are T-norms. The first one, up to when the result remains consistent, can be used to model expansion, i.e. the combination of coherent information (think for instance of tokens of information coming from the same source): we represent it syntactically with "&"; it corresponds to the set union of possibilistic formulae in the logic of [Dubois, Lang and Prade 94], or to the $\wedge$ between modal formulae in modal approaches. The second operator models the combination of evidence coming from distinct sources: if the two evidences agree, combination yields an evidence stronger than both. We introduce it in the language as "$\otimes$", which has no explicit representation in standard possibilistic logic. Moreover, it comes very natural to add to the language a negation, which corresponds to the operation of fuzzy set complementation with respect to $\times$ (it has nothing to do with the negation of modal logics, as we are going to discuss later).

This approach, while owing much to modal approaches, as it can be evinced from the semantics, differs from them in that it distinguishes between an object level language and a language at a meta level. The first is the language which speaks of the world as it is, and for this reason we found it convenient to use a classical propositional language. The meta-language is a resource-oriented language which speaks of the beliefs that the agent maintains on the world (i.e. on object level formulae). It makes use of the different connectives we were speaking about and is essentially independent of the object language. In this sense, the work can be related to the field of "combination of logics" [Gabbay 92]. The result is a sound and complete sequent calculus for the overall logic; we named it Substructural Possibilistic Logic (SLP), since the connective $\otimes$ happens to miss a structural rule of classical logic (namely *contraction*).

In our opinion the system we present could be relevant to the modeling of autonomous agents in AI. Think of an agent moving in an unknown environment, from which he receives (uncertain and incomplete) information. We assume that evidence from the external world comes in tokens of the form $N_\alpha A$, i.e. lower bounds on the necessity of some formula. The agent can connect these tokens in two different ways: by & if the tokens come from the same source, or by $\otimes$ if the tokens come from different sources[2]. At any time the agent can use the evidence he has accumulated up to then, which is represented by the formula he has built piece to piece, to infer new facts which are granted to by true in the final information state.

In the following paragraphs we present the language, the semantics, the proof system and state soundness and completeness theorems. Proofs, which are omitted for the sake of space, can be found in [Boldrin 94].

2 The Language

We assume the following language, which is made of a classical propositional language (the *object language*) and, on top of it, a simple language with two conjunctions and a negation; the basic formulae of this level are built from object formulae with the constructor N_α, where α is a real number in $[0, 1]$. The set $\mathcal{L}_0$ of atomic propositions is assumed to be finite.

obj-formula ::= atomic_proposition | obj-formula $\wedge$ obj-formula | $\neg$ obj-formula
π-formula ::= $\mathbf{1}$ | N_α obj-formula | $\neg$ π-formula | π-formula & π-formula | π-formula $\otimes$ π-formula

[2] A further improvement would consist in allowing for more connectives, to allow the combination of tokens of information with a different relative weight

We take $\mathcal{L}$ to be the set of π-formulae, and $\mathcal{L}_1$ that of object-formulae; connectives $\vee$ and $\rightarrow$ and the constant $\top$ at the object level are defined as usual. We use upper case latin letters (A, B, C,...) for obj-formulae, lower case greek letters (ϕ, ψ, ...) for π-formulae and upper case greek letters (Γ, Δ, ...) for sets of π-formulae; the greek letters α and β represent real numbers in $[0,1]$. $\otimes$ is intended to represent combination of the evidence coming from different sources, while & combines tokens of information from the same source. It is then natural to require that $N_\alpha A \otimes N_\alpha A$ be a stronger evidence than $N_\alpha A$, so we reject idempotence for the operator $\otimes$. This is not true for the & operator, since we want to have the equivalence between $N_\alpha A \,\&\, N_\alpha A$ and $N_\alpha A$. The connectives $\neg$, & and $\otimes$ are the ones we are particularly interested in; in fact we can also introduce new symbols (typical of substructural logics) via the definitions:

$$\mathbf{0} =_{\text{def}} \neg\mathbf{1}; \quad \phi \rightarrow \psi =_{\text{def}} \neg(\phi \otimes \neg\psi); \quad \phi \oplus \psi =_{\text{def}} \neg(\neg\phi \& \neg\psi)$$

3 The Semantics

Let $\mathcal{P}$ denote the set of functions (which we call possibility distributions) from a non-empty set W to the real interval $[0,1]$, with the order $\leq$ ($\pi_1 \leq \pi_2$ iff for any w it holds that $\pi_1(w) \leq \pi_2(w)$); the lattice operations $\vee$ and $\wedge$ on possibility functions are defined with respect to the order $\leq$; $\langle P, \vee, \wedge \rangle$ is a complete lattice. The operation $\times$ is defined by $\pi = \pi_1 \times \pi_2$ iff for any w $\pi(w) = 0 \vee (\pi_1(w) + \pi_2(w) - 1))$. To define the semantics of negation, we make use of fuzzy set complementation with respect to $\times$, which makes our negation coincide with Girard's, where the inconsistent set contains only the function identically zero.

We need the following definitions:

Definition 1. 1. For any $\pi \in \mathcal{P}$, $\downarrow \pi = \{\sigma \in \mathcal{P} : \sigma \leq \pi\}$.
2. For any $\alpha \in [0,1]$, $\boldsymbol{\alpha}$ is the function identically equal to α (in particular $\mathbf{1}(w) = 1$ and $\mathbf{0}(w) = 0$ for any w).
3. For any $G \subseteq \mathcal{P}$ and $H \subseteq \mathcal{P}$, $G \Rightarrow H = \{\sigma \in \mathcal{P} :$ for any $\pi \in G, \pi \times \sigma \in H)\}$.
4. For any $G \subseteq \mathcal{P}$, $G^\perp = G \Rightarrow \{\mathbf{0}\}$.

It can be easily verified that $^{\perp\perp}$ is a closure operator on $2^{\mathcal{P}}$ (see [Girard 87]).

Theorem 2. *For any $G \subseteq \mathcal{P}$, let $\pi_G = \bigvee_{\pi \in G} \pi$; then:*

1. $G^\perp = \{\pi \in \mathcal{P} : \pi \times \pi_G = \mathbf{0}\}$
2. $G^{\perp\perp} = \downarrow \pi_G$

The structure $\langle \mathcal{P}, \times, \mathbf{1} \rangle$ is a commutative monoid with unit, and $\perp = \{\mathbf{0}\} \subseteq \mathcal{P}$. Hence the structure $\langle \mathcal{P}, \times, \mathbf{1}, \perp \rangle$ is a phase space in Girard's sense. The closure operator is exactly the one of Girard, so the set $\mathcal{Q} = \{G \subseteq \mathcal{P} : G = G^{\perp\perp}\}$ is the set of *facts*, and belongs to the class of *Girard quantales*[3] as defined in [Rosenthal 90].

[3] Almost the same as *residuated lattices* in [Pavelka 79]

A frame for our language is a couple $F = \langle W, V_0 \rangle$, where W is a nonempty set of worlds, $V_0 : \mathcal{L}_0 \to 2^W$ is a propositional assignment over the worlds which is extended to $V : \mathcal{L}_1 \to 2^W$, as usual.

Definition 3. Given the frame F, let us define the function $\|\cdot\|_F : \mathcal{L} \to \mathcal{Q}$:

$$\begin{aligned}
\|\mathbf{1}\|_F &= \mathcal{P} \\
\|N_\alpha A\|_F &= \{\pi : Nec_\pi(V(A)) \geq \alpha\} \\
\|\neg\phi\|_F &= \|\phi\|_F^\perp \\
\|\phi \mathbin{\&} \psi\|_F &= \|\phi\|_F \cap \|\psi\|_F \\
\|\phi \otimes \psi\|_F &= \|\phi\|_F \times \|\psi\|_F
\end{aligned}$$

where $Nec_\pi : 2^w \to [0,1]$ is the necessity function associated to the possibility distribution π: $Nec_\pi(X) = 1 - \bigvee_{w \notin X} \pi(w)$. The $\times$ product between sets is the point-to-point product. It can be verified that :

$$\|\phi \mathbin{\&} \psi\|_F = \|\phi\|_F \wedge \|\psi\|_F \text{ (the point-to-point } \wedge); \quad \|\mathbf{0}\|_F = \{\mathbf{0}\};$$

$$\|\phi \to \psi\|_F = \|\phi\|_F \Rightarrow \|\psi\|_F; \quad \|\phi \oplus \psi\|_F = \|\phi\|_F \vee \|\psi\|_F$$

It follows from theorem 2 that $\|A\|_F$ as above defined is a fact (i.e. belongs to $\mathcal{Q}$) for any $A \in \mathcal{L}$.

Definition 4. A model is a couple $K = \langle F, \pi \rangle$ we say that $K \models \phi$ iff $\pi \in \|\phi\|_F$. A formula ϕ is valid in F iff for any model K in the frame F, $K \models \phi$ (this can be shown to be equivalent to $\mathbf{1} \in \|\phi\|_F$).

In a fixed frame a formula $N_\alpha A$ is true in the models whose possibility distribution gives A at least α support; a formula $\neg\phi$ is true in the models which are inconsistent with the models for ϕ; a formula $\phi \mathbin{\&} \psi$ is true in those models which fit both ϕ and ψ; and, eventually, a formula $\phi \otimes \psi$ is true in any model whose possibility distribution is the product of one of a ϕ-model and one of a ψ-model. Since the lattice $\mathcal{P}$ is complete, we can establish a correspondence between formulae of the language and their least informative model in a frame (keep in mind that least informative means higher in the order $\leq$): $\pi_\phi^F =_{\text{def}} \bigvee_{\pi \in \|\phi\|_F} \pi$

Theorem 5. *Given a frame F, $\|\phi\|_F = \|\phi\|_F^{\perp\perp} = \downarrow \pi_\phi^F$. Moreover, the following statements hold (we omit all the superscripts F):*

1. $\pi_{\mathbf{1}} = \mathbf{1}$; $\pi_{\mathbf{0}} = \mathbf{0}$
2. $\pi_{N_\alpha A} = \lambda w. \begin{cases} 1 & \text{if } w \in V(A) \\ 1 - \alpha & \text{otherwise} \end{cases}$
3. $\pi_{\neg\phi} = \sim \pi_\phi =_{\text{def}} \mathbf{1} - \pi_\phi$
4. $\pi_{\phi \& \psi} = \pi_\phi \wedge \pi_\psi$
5. $\pi_{\phi \otimes \psi} = \pi_\phi \times \pi_\psi$
6. $\pi_{\phi \oplus \psi} = \pi_\phi \vee \pi_\psi$
7. $\pi_{\phi \to \psi} = (\mathbf{1} - \pi_\phi + \pi_\psi) \wedge \mathbf{1}$

To define the semantic entailment relation, we first consider the entailment between formulae: $\phi \models \psi$ iff for any frame F, $\pi_\phi^F \leq \pi_\psi^F$. We can now state the following

Theorem 6. *Let the frame $C = \langle W_c, V_0^c \rangle$ be defined as follows: W_c is the set of classical propositional valuations for $\mathcal{L}_0$ (i.e. the set of functions from $\mathcal{L}_0$ to $\{True, False\}$) and $V_0^c(p) = \{w \in W_c : w \models p \text{ (classically)}\}$. Then $\pi_\psi^C \leq \pi_\phi^C$ implies $\pi_\psi^F \leq \pi_\phi^F$ for any frame F.*

An important consequence of the theorem above is that we can restrict our attention to a unique quantal, which is the one made from the set of possibility distributions over the set W_c, via the closure operation. In fact, we can define the semantic entailment relation as follows (here and in the following we write π_ϕ for π_ϕ^C): $\phi \models \psi$ iff $\pi_\phi \leq \pi_\psi$. Eventually, since the intended meaning of the sequent $\Gamma \vdash \phi$ is $\bigotimes_{\psi \in \Gamma} \psi \rightarrow \phi$, we say that the sequent $\Gamma \vdash \phi$ is valid iff $\bigotimes_{\psi \in \Gamma} \psi \models \phi$.

We know that the proof system of linear logic is sound (and complete) with respect to interpretations in any quantales. By theorem 2, π_x is such a valuation, so linear logic rules must be sound with respect to our semantics. Moreover, since we allow weakening (which corresponds to monotonicity of $\times$) and double negation, it results that our logic is a specialization of *direct logic* [Ketonen and Weyhrauch 84].

Let us briefly comment on negation. Possibilistic models on the same frame represent a state of information about the possible worlds of the frame; they are informationally ordered: $\pi_1 \leq \pi_2$ means that π_1 is more informative then π_2, since it better constrains the set of possible worlds. Since a formula ϕ is interpreted in the least informative information state which satisfies it (π_ϕ), we have two possible readings for negation:

- The *modal* one, which refers to absent information. In this case the statement $K \models \neg N_\alpha A$ must be read as: "in the given state of information it is not possible to prove that A is necessary at least α (while it may become possible in a refinement of the information state)".
- The *internal* one (which we use in our language), where the statement $K \models \neg N_\alpha A$ is read as: "in the given state of information we definitely refuse to accept the token $N_\alpha A$ (and no refinement will allow to prove the opposite)". The formula $\neg N_\alpha A$ then expresses a positive token of information, and does not deal with absence of information. Note that, in this second reading, $\neg N_1 A$ is equivalent to $N_1 \neg A$, but the same is not true for the general N_α.

Moreover, the reader can verify that there are models with non-zero possibility functions which satisfy both ϕ and $\neg\phi$; all of these functions are, however, smaller than **0.5**. So we tolerate that a partially consistent information state support both a token of information and its negation.

4 The Proof System SPL

The proof system will be given in a Gentzen-style calculus, since it is the most comfortable way to deal with multisets (remember that, because of the absence of contraction [4], it does matter how many times a formula is given). The calculus

[4] Contraction is the rule: contraction) $\dfrac{\Delta, \phi, \phi, \Gamma \vdash \chi}{\Delta, \phi, \Gamma \vdash \chi}$

SPL will be made of four parts: structural rules, logical rules (adjusted from [Sambin 95].), the calculus for standard possibilistic logic (apart of N_0, exactly the propositional fragment of the system in [Dubois, Lang and Prade 94]), and some further axioms which characterize our logic.

1. *Structural rules:*

$$\text{id)}\quad \phi \vdash \phi \qquad\qquad \text{cut)}\ \frac{\Gamma \vdash \psi \quad \Delta, \psi \vdash \phi}{\Delta, \Gamma \vdash \phi}$$

$$\text{exchange)}\ \frac{\Delta, \psi, \phi, \Gamma \vdash \chi}{\Delta, \phi, \psi, \Gamma \vdash \chi} \qquad \text{weakening)}\ \frac{\Delta \vdash \psi}{\Delta, A \vdash \psi}$$

2. *Logical rules:*

$$\&\ \text{L)}\ \frac{\Delta, \phi \vdash \chi}{\Delta, \phi \,\&\, \psi \vdash \chi} \quad \frac{\Delta, \psi \vdash \chi}{\Delta, \phi \,\&\, \psi \vdash \chi} \qquad \&\ \text{R)}\ \frac{\Delta \vdash \phi \quad \Delta \vdash \psi}{\Delta \vdash \phi \,\&\, \psi}$$

$$\otimes\ \text{L)}\ \frac{\Delta, \psi, \phi \vdash \chi}{\Delta, \psi \otimes \phi \vdash \chi} \qquad \otimes\ \text{R)}\ \frac{\Delta \vdash \phi \quad \Gamma \vdash \psi}{\Delta, \Gamma \vdash \phi \otimes \psi}$$

$$\oplus\ \text{L)}\ \frac{\Delta, \phi \vdash \chi \quad \Delta, \psi \vdash \chi}{\Delta, \psi \oplus \phi \vdash \chi} \qquad \oplus\ \text{R)}\ \frac{\Delta \vdash \phi}{\Delta, \vdash \phi \oplus \psi} \quad \frac{\Delta \vdash \psi}{\Delta, \vdash \phi \oplus \psi}$$

$$\neg\ \text{L)}\ \frac{\Delta \vdash \phi}{\Delta, \neg\phi \vdash \mathbf{0}} \qquad \neg\ \text{R)}\ \frac{\Delta, \phi \vdash \mathbf{0}}{\Delta \vdash \neg\phi}$$

$$\neg\neg)\quad \neg\neg\phi \vdash \phi \qquad \mathbf{0})\quad \Gamma, \mathbf{0} \vdash \phi$$

$$\mathbf{1}\ \text{L)}\ \frac{\Delta \vdash \chi}{\Delta, \mathbf{1} \vdash \chi} \qquad \mathbf{1}\ \text{R)}\quad \Gamma \vdash \mathbf{1}$$

3. *Possibilistic rules:*

A1) $\vdash N_1(A \to (B \to A))$
A2) $\vdash N_1((A \to (B \to C)) \to ((A \to B) \to (A \to C)))$
A3) $\vdash N_1((\neg A \to \neg B) \to ((\neg A \to B) \to A))$
GMP) $N_\alpha A \,\&\, N_\beta(A \to B) \vdash N_{\alpha\wedge\beta}B$
S) $N_\alpha A \vdash N_\beta A$ for any $\beta \leq \alpha$
N_0) $\vdash N_0 A$

4. *Reduction rules:*

$\otimes$-& distr) $(\phi \,\&\, \psi) \otimes \chi \dashv\vdash (\phi \otimes \chi) \,\&\, (\psi \otimes \chi)$
$\otimes$ red) $N_\alpha A \otimes N_\beta B \dashv\vdash N_\beta(A \to B) \,\&\, N_\alpha(B \to A) \,\&\, N_{(\alpha+\beta)\wedge 1}(A \vee B)$
$\neg$ red) $\neg N_\alpha A \dashv\vdash N_{1-\alpha} A \,\&\, N_1 \neg A$

We remind the reader that distributivity of $\otimes$ with respect to $\oplus$, i.e. the sequent $(\phi \oplus \psi) \otimes \chi \dashv\vdash (\phi \otimes \chi) \oplus (\psi \otimes \chi)$ holds by the logical rules; we shall refer to it as $\otimes$-$\oplus$ distr). In fact, also the left-to-right direction of $\otimes$-& distr) can be obtained from the logical rules. Reduction rules represent the central part of this axiomatization, since they allow to perform calculations on composite π-formulae, i.e., on states of information. Rule $\otimes$ red), which is the most complex, has the following intuitive reading: the information we get from the two tokens "A with degree α" and "B with degree β" coming from two distinct sources, is equivalent to the information we would obtain by receiving the three tokens "$\neg A \vee B$ with degree β", "$\neg B \vee A$ with degree α" and "$A \vee B$ with degree $(\alpha + \beta) \wedge 1$" from a unique source.

5 Soundness and Completeness

Soundness can be easily proved by induction on the proof length. To prove completeness, we first state the following:

Theorem 7. *Any π-formula χ is provably equivalent in the calculus SPL to an &-formula ξ, i.e. a π-formula with no occurrences of the $\neg$ and $\otimes$ operators.*

This fact shows that the $\otimes$ and $\neg$ connectives are in fact (recursively) definable inside standard possibilistic logic [Dubois, Lang and Prade 94], where they would however become meta-connectives between sets of formulae. We found several reasons for producing a new calculus in sequent form:

- we obtain a logic with two distinct conjunctions, where the second one misses the contraction property; this would be somehow hidden in possibilistic logic, where conjunction is represented by means of set union.
- the logic can be extended to new connectives, corresponding to some operation on the lattice of possibility distributions, and the connectives are not forced to obey to structural rules;
- last, and most important, the reduction of the $\otimes$ and $\neg$ operators seems to be a very fortunate case due to the nature of possibility distributions and to the simplicity of the operators we have chosen; the reduction may be not possible in other settings such as, for instance, that one of belief functions.

By the above theorem, completeness of our system is an immediate consequence of completeness of the calculus for standard possibilistic logic, since we identify the formula $\&_{i \in I} N_{\alpha_i} A_i$ with the set $\{(A_i, \alpha_i) : i \in I\}$. At this point we state the main theorem:

Theorem 8. *The calculus SPL is sound and complete with respect to the above semantics, i.e. the calculus proves $\Gamma \vdash \phi$ iff the sequent $\Gamma \vdash \phi$ is valid.*

6 Open Issues

This paper presents a syntactic treatment of two easy combinators in a representation of uncertainty based on possibility functions. It is natural to look forward in two directions:

- The representation of some more connectives of practical use; we think for instance of different combinators of evidence, as well as revision (conditioning) and update (imaging) operators, as described in [Dubois and Prade 94].
- The shift to more sophisticated frameworks like that of belief functions; things are much more complex because the information state space is not even a lattice.

Moreover we believe that the proximity to widely studied substructural logics could help in the development of automated deduction systems for this and similar calculi.

Acknowledgments

This work was born from several discussions with Alessandro Saffiotti and Claudio Sossai, who gave me constant help. I am also indebted to Natasha Alechina and Philippe Smets for introducing me to the modal treatment of uncertainty, to Marcello d'Agostino for some precious lectures on linear logic, to Silvio Valentini for his careful supervision, and to some anonymous referees for helpful and encouraging comments.

References

[Alechina and Smets 94] N. Alechina and P. Smets. A note on modal logics for partial beliefs (manuscript), 1994.

[Boldrin 94] Substructural connectives for merging information in possibilistic logic. LADSEB-CNR Int. Rep. 09, 1994.

[Dubois and Prade 85] D. Dubois and H. Prade. A review of fuzzy set aggregation connectives. Information Sciences 36, 1985, pp. 85-121.

[Dubois and Prade 94] D. Dubois and H. Prade. A survey of belief revision and updating rules in various uncertainty models. Int. J. of Intelligent Systems 9, 1994, pp. 61-100.

[Dubois, Lang and Prade 94] D. Dubois, J. Lang and H. Prade. Possibilistic logic In: D. Gabbay, C. Hogger and J. Robinson (eds.) Handbook of Logic in Artificial Intelligence and Logic Programming, vol. 3. Clarendon Press 1994.

[Fagin and Halpern 94] R. Fagin and J. Y. Halpern. Reasoning about knowledge and probability. J. of the ACM, 41, 1994, pp. 340-367.

[Gabbay 92] D. Gabbay. Fibred semantics and the weaving of logics. Draft, Imperial College, 1992.

[Girard 87] J. Y. Girard. Linear logic. Theoretical computer science, 50, 1987, pp. 1-101.

[Hajek et. al 94] P. Hajek, D. Harmancova and R. Verbrugge. A qualitative fuzzy possibilistic logic. Int. J. of Approximate Reasoning 7, 1994.

[Ketonen and Weyhrauch 84] J. Ketonen and R. Weyhrauch. A decidable fragment of predicate calculus. Theoretical computer science 32, 1984, pp. 297-307.

[Murai et al. 93] T. Murai, M. Miyakoshi and M. Shimbo. Measure-based semantics for modal logic. In: R. Lowen and M. Roubens (eds.). Fuzzy logic. Kluwer Academic Publishers, 1993, pp. 395-405.

[Pavelka 79] J. Pavelka. On fuzzy logic II. Zeitschr. f. math. Logik und Grundlagen d. Math 25, 1979, pp. 119-131.

[de Rijke 94] Meeting some neighbours. A dynamic logic meets theories of change and knowledge representation. In J. van Eijck and A. Visser: Logic and information flow. The MIT Press, 1994.

[Rosenthal 90] K. I. Rosenthal. Quantales and their applications. Longman 1990.

[Saffiotti 92] A. Saffiotti. A belief function logic. Proceedings of AAAI 1992, pp. 642-647.

[Sambin 95] G. Sambin. Pretopologies and the completeness proof. To appear in The J. of Symbolic Logic.

[Voorbraak 93] F. Voorbraak. As far as I know. Epistemic logic and uncertainty. Phd dissertation, Dept. of Philosophy - Utrecht University, 1993.

Chain graphs: semantics and expressiveness*

Remco R. Bouckaert[1] and Milan Studený[2]

[1] Utrecht University, Department of Computer Science, P.O.Box 80.089, 3508 TB Utrecht, The Netherlands, remco@cs.ruu.nl
[2] Inst. of Inform. Theory & Autom., Czech Academy of Sciences, Pod vodárenskou věží 4, 182 08 Prague, Czech Republic, studeny@utia.cas.cz

Abstract. A *chain graph* (CG) is a graph admitting both directed and undirected edges with forbidden directed cycles. It generalizes both the concept of undirected graph (UG) and the concept of directed acyclic graph (DAG). CGs can be used efficiently to store *graphoids*, that is, independency knowledge of the form "X is independent of Y given Z" obeying a set of five properties (axioms).
Two equivalent criteria for reading independencies from a CG are formulated, namely the *moralization criterion* and the *separation criterion*. These criteria give exactly the graphoid closure of the input list for the CG. Moreover, a construction of a CG from a graphoid (through an input list), which produces a minimal I-map of that graphoid, is given.

1 Introduction

Using graphs to describe independency structure arising among variables has a long and rich tradition. One can distinguish two classic approaches (for details see the book [11]): using *undirected graphs* (UGs), called also Markov networks, or using *directed acyclic graphs* (DAGs), named also Bayesian networks, recursive models or influence diagrams. The aim is to describe efficiently independency models in the form of lists of statements "X is independent of Y given Z", where X, Y, Z are disjoint sets of variables. Such structures can arise in several calculi for dealing with uncertainty in artificial intelligence: in probabilistic reasoning, in theory of natural conditional functions known also as kappa-calculus, in possibility theory or Dempster-Shafer theory of evidence (for overview see [12]) but also in the theory of relational databases. Of course, different calculi produce different independency models, but in case of non-extreme knowledge representation they share five properties which define the class of *graphoids*.

Graphoids can be sometimes described graphically. Thus, every UG defines by means of *separation criterion* an independency model which is a graphoid. The use of UGs in probabilistic reasoning justified by the result from [5], where every such UG-model is shown to be a probabilistic independency model. Nevertheless, a lot of graphoids (even probabilistic models) have no UG representation (that is, are not UG-models). Therefore Pearl [11] proposed to approximate graphoids

* This work was partially supported by the grants: GA AVČR no. 275105 and CEC no. CIPA3511CT930053.

by their contained UG-models (I-maps) and showed that for every graphoid M there exist a unique maximal UG-model contained in M, called *minimal I-map of M*.

Evolution of DAG-models was more complicated. Originally, DAGs were used to describe recursive factorizations of probability distributions. But such a factorization is equivalent to the requirement that the considered distribution complies with a set of independencies called often *causal input list*. Nevertheless, the distribution usually complies with many other independencies outside the input list. A lot of effort was exerted to achieve a graphical criterion which makes it possible to read from the DAG all independencies in the factorizable distribution.

In fact, two equivalent criteria were found. Lauritzen *et. al.* [10] generalized an incomplete criterion from [6] and formulated a *moralization criterion* where testing consist of 3 steps: restriction of the DAG to certain set of nodes, transforming it properly to an UG (called *moral graph*), and using the separation criterion for UGs with respect to the moral graph. The group around Pearl developed a direct *separation criterion* [3], for this purpose they introduced the concept of *d-separation* (*d-* stands for directional) for paths in DAGs. It was shown that the criteria are equivalent [10] and that they give exactly the graphoid closure of the input list [13]. Finally, the criteria were shown to be complete for probabilistic reasoning by showing that every independency model defined by the separation criterion is a probabilistic model [4]. Thus, DAG-models were established and their use in probabilistic reasoning was justified. Like in case of UGs Pearl [11] considered the problem of inner approximation of graphoids by DAG-models. In contrast to the case of UGs several maximal DAG-models contained in a graphoid (*minimal I-maps*) may exist. In fact, any ordering of variables can generate such a minimal I-map, the corresponding construction is given in [13].

This paper deals with *chain graphs* (CGs) which allow both directed and undirected edges. This class of graphs, introduced by Lauritzen and Wermuth [7], generalizes both UGs and DAGs. To establish semantics of CGs one should associate an independency model to every CG. Some steps were already made. Lauritzen and Wermuth [8] intended to use CGs to describe independency models for positive distributions and introduced the concept of *chain Markov property* which is an analogy of the concept of causal input list for DAGs. Frydenberg [2] generalized the concept of moral graph and introduced a *moralization criterion* for reading independencies from a CG.

In this paper some of above mentioned results concerning UGs and DAGs are extended to the case of CGs. We introduce the concept of *c-separation* (chain separation) for trails in CGs, which generalizes both separation in UGs and d-separation in DAGs. This gives a direct *separation criterion* for reading independencies from a CG. The main result of the contribution says that an independency statement belongs to the graphoid closure of the *input list* for a CG iff it is derived by the moralization criterion, which is equivalent to the separation criterion. Moreover, the construction of a minimal I-map from [13] is generalized to the case of CGs.

2 Independency models

Throughout the paper, in apposite situations, we will use a reduced notation: juxtaposition XY instead of $X \cup Y$, u instead of $\{u\}$ and $X - Y - u$ instead of $X \setminus (Y \cup \{u\})$.

Supposing N is a nonempty finite set the symbol $T(N)$ will denote the class of all triplets $\langle X, Y|Z\rangle$ of disjoint subsets of N whose first two components X and Y are nonempty. An *independency model* over N is a subset of $T(N)$. It is called *graphoid* iff it satisfies the following properties:

$\langle X,Y|Z\rangle \rightarrow \langle Y,X|Z\rangle$ symmetry

$\langle X,YW|Z\rangle \rightarrow \langle X,W|Z\rangle$ decomposition

$\langle X,YW|Z\rangle \rightarrow \langle X,Y|WZ\rangle$ weak union

$[\langle X,Y|WZ\rangle \;\&\; \langle X,W|Z\rangle] \rightarrow \langle X,YW|Z\rangle$ contraction

$[\langle X,Y|WZ\rangle \;\&\; \langle X,W|YZ\rangle] \rightarrow \langle X,YW|Z\rangle$ intersection

Having a set $L \subset T(N)$ its *graphoid closure*, denoted by $gr(L)$ consists of all triplets in $T(N)$ derivable from L by means of consecutive application of graphoid properties.

3 Graphs

A graph is a couple (N, E) where N is a nonempty finite set of *nodes* and E is a set of *edges*, that is, two-element subsets of N. In this paper we consider several types of edges (every edge belongs exclusively to one of possible types) and this gives several types of graphs. An *undirected graph* (UG) admits only undirected edges, called *links*. We will write $u - v$ to denote that there exists a link between a node u and a node v. A *directed acyclic graph* (DAG) is a graph having only directed edges called *arcs* (we will write $u \rightarrow v$ to denote that there exists an *arc* from a node u to a node v) such that there exists no directed cycle in the graph (that is, sequence of distinct nodes $v_1, \ldots, v_k$, $k \geq 2$ with $v_i \rightarrow v_{i+1}$, $i = 1, \ldots, k-1$ and $v_k \rightarrow v_1$).

A *chain graph* (CG) admits both links and arcs. It is required that the set of nodes can be partitioned into ordered disjoint (nonempty) subsets $B_1, \ldots, B_n$, $n \geq 1$ called *blocks* in such a way that the types of edges are determined as follows:

(i) if $\{u, v\}$ is an edge with $u, v \in B_i$ then $u - v$,

(ii) if $\{u, v\}$ is an edge with $u \in B_i, v \in B_j, i < j$ then $u \rightarrow v$.

Note that CGs were characterized in [2] as graphs not having any directed cycles, but the definition above is more suitable for our purposes. It is evident that CGs involve both UGs and DAGs. Every ordered partitioning satisfying (i)-(ii) will be called a *chain* for the CG. Of course, a CG admits several chains.

A *subgraph* of a graph $G = (N, E)$ is a graph $H = (V, F)$ with $V \subset N$ and $F \subset E$; its *restriction* to a nonempty set $T \subset N$ is the subgraph $G_T = (T, E_T)$, where $E_T = \{\, \{u, v\} \in E\,;\, u, v \in T\,\}$. Of course, the types respectively orientations of edges remain unchanged. Let us mention that a restriction of a CG is again a CG.

A *path* in a CG is a sequence of its distinct nodes $v_1, \ldots, v_k$, $k \geq 1$ such that $\forall i = 1, \ldots, k-1$ $\{v_i, v_{i+1}\}$ is an edge. We will say that it is a path *from* a node u *to* a node w iff $v_1 = u$ and $v_k = w$. We will say that a path $v_1, \ldots, v_k$, $k \geq 1$ *meets* a set of nodes Z iff $\{v_1, \ldots v_k\} \cap Z \neq \emptyset$. The path is *undirected* iff $\forall i = 1, \ldots, k-1$ $v_i - v_{i+1}$. The path is *descending* iff $\forall i = 1, \ldots, k-1$ either $v_i \rightarrow v_{i+1}$ or $v_i - v_{i+1}$. If there exists a descending path from a node u to a node v, then v is a *descendant* of u, or dually u is an *ancestor* of v. The symbol $ds_G(u)$ will denote the set of descendants of u; $ds_G(X)$ is the union of $ds_G(u)$'s for $u \in X$ (X is a set of nodes). It is worthwhile to realize the following simple fact.

FACT 1 If there exists an undirected path from u to v, then $ds_G(u) = ds_G(v)$.

Similarly, $an_G(X)$ denotes the set of ancestors of nodes from X. We will omit the symbol of the graph G if it will be clear from the context. A set of nodes X is *ancestral* (in G) iff it contains ancestors of its nodes, that is, $an_G(X) \subset X$.

4 Moralization criterion

The moralization criterion for CGs is based on the classic separation criterion for UGs. Thus, we recall that a triplet $\langle X, Y|Z\rangle \in T(N)$ is *represented* in an UG $H = (N, E)$, denoted by $\langle X, Y|Z\rangle_H$, iff every path in H from a node of X to a node of Y in G meets Z.

Given a CG $G = (N, E)$ its *moral graph*, denoted by G^{mor}, is an UG having the same set of nodes as G, but the set of links established as follows: $u - v$ in G^{mor} iff $u - v$ in G or $u \rightarrow v$ in G or $u \leftarrow v$ in G or there exists a path $v_1, \ldots, v_k$, $k \geq 3$ from u to v in G such that $v_1 \rightarrow v_2, \forall i = 2, \ldots, k-2$ $v_i - v_{i+1}$, $v_{k-1} \leftarrow v_k$.

Let $G = (N, E)$ be a CG, $\langle X, Y|Z\rangle \in T(N)$ and H be the moral graph of $G_{an(XYZ)}$. We will say that $\langle X, Y|Z\rangle$ is *represented* in G according to the *moralization criterion* and write $\langle X, Y|Z\rangle_G^{mor}$ iff $\langle X, Y|Z\rangle_H$. Let us mention that the moral graph H depends on $\langle X, Y|Z\rangle$. The reader can verify that this moralization criterion specified to DAGs gives exactly the criterion from [10].

5 Separation criterion

To formulate the separation criterion for CGs we have to introduce some special graphical concepts. Given a CG, a *slide* from a node u to a node w is a path $v_1, \ldots, v_k$, $k \geq 2$ such that $u = v_1 \rightarrow v_2$, $\forall i = 2, \ldots, k-1$ $v_i - v_{i+1}$ and $v_k = w$.
A *trail* in a CG is a sequence of its nodes $v_1, \ldots, v_k$, $k \geq 1$ such that
(i) $\forall i = 1, \ldots, k-1$ $\{v_i, v_{i+1}\}$ is an edge of G,
(ii) $\forall i = 2, \ldots, k-1$ the nodes v_{i-1}, v_i, v_{i+1} are distinct,
(iii) every its undirected subsequence $v_j - v_{j+1} - \ldots - v_{j+t}$, $1 \leq j \leq k$, $0 \leq t \leq k-j$ consists of distinct nodes.
The concept of trail is more general than the concept of path since a node can occur several times in a trail.

In contrast to d-separation in DAGs we will not define blocking for nodes of a trail, but for its *sections*, that is, maximal undirected subpaths. Evidently, every trail can be decomposed uniquely into sections. Moreover, sections of a trail can be classified according to types (or existence) of edges of the trail entering the section. Namely, just one of the following three possibilities can occur for the first terminal node v_j of a section $S : v_j, \ldots, v_{j+t}$, $1 \leq j \leq k$, $0 \leq t \leq k - j$. If $j > 1$ & $v_{j-1} \rightarrow v_j$, then v_j is a *head-terminal* node of S; if $j > 1$ & $v_{j-1} \leftarrow v_j$, then v_j is a *tail-terminal* node of S; if $j = 1$, then v_j is an *end-terminal* node of S. An analogous classification holds for the second terminal node v_{j+t}. Thus, according to the type of terminal nodes[3] one can classify sections of a trail into the following 6 classes. A section of a trail is called a *head-to-head* section iff it has two head-terminal nodes, or a *head-to-tail* section iff it has one head-terminal node and one tail-terminal node. Analogously are defined *head-to-end*, *tail-to-tail*, *tail-to-end* and *end-to-end* sections.

Let $G = (N, E)$ be a CG, $Z \subset N$ and S be a section of a trail in G. The definition of *blocking* of S by Z depends on the type of the section S:
• if S is a head-to-head section, then S is blocked by Z iff $ds(S) \cap Z = \emptyset$[4],
• if S is a head-to-tail (respectively head-to-end) section, then S is blocked by Z iff $S \cap Z \neq \emptyset$ & every slide to the tail-terminal (respectively end-terminal) node of S meets Z,
• if S is a tail-to-tail or tail-to-end or end-to-end section, then S is blocked by Z iff $S \cap Z \neq \emptyset$ & every slide to any of the terminal nodes of S meets Z.
A trail in a CG is *c-separated* (chain separated) by Z iff there exists a section of the trail which is blocked by Z.

Let $G = (N, E)$ be a CG and $\langle X, Y|Z\rangle \in T(N)$. We will say that $\langle X, Y|Z\rangle$ is *represented* in G according to the *separation criterion* and write $\langle X, Y|Z\rangle_G^{sep}$ iff every trail from X to Y in G is c-separated by Z. We left to the reader to verify that c-separation specified to the case of DAGs gives exactly d-separation from [11]. Note that in case of c-separation we have to consider trails, the requirement of blocking paths only is indeed weaker.

Lemma 1. *Let $G = (N, E)$ be a CG, $\langle X, Y|Z\rangle \in T(N)$. Then $\langle X, Y|Z\rangle_G^{sep}$ iff $\langle X, Y|Z\rangle_G^{mor}$.*

The proof of this lemma is beyond the scope of a conference contribution and can be found in [1]. To prove the lemma the concept of moral graph is formally modified: edges of the original graph keep their type (that is, links or arcs) and the added edges are consider of a third type, say, virtual edges called *virts*. We can extend the concept of blocking for head-to-virt, tail-to-virt, virt-to-virt and end-to-virt sections. Then we show that for every $\langle X, Y|Z\rangle \in T(N)$, there exists a path from X to Y outside Z in the moral graph of $G_{an(XYZ)}$ iff there exists a trail from X to Y in G which is not blocked by Z. Both implications can be

[3] If $t = 0$, then the terminal nodes v_j and v_{j+t} coincide. In this case the node $v_j = v_{j+t}$ is considered as a double terminal node, that is, it can be for example both head- and tail-terminal, or for example twice head-terminal node and so on.

[4] It follows from Fact 1 that $ds(S) = ds(u)$ for any $u \in S$.

verified by consecutive transformation of the considered trail (respectively path) – by replacing sections meeting Z (respectively virts) by a 'detour'.

6 Input list

Let $G = (N, E)$ be a CG and $\mathcal{B} : B_1, \ldots, B_n$ a chain for G. The *domain* of a node u, written $dom^{\mathcal{B}}(u)$, is the union of blocks $B_1, \ldots, B_k$, where B_k is the block containing u. The set *adjacents* of u, written by $ad_G(u)$, is $\{v \in N;\ v - u \text{ in } G\}$, the *neighborhood* of u, written $nb_G(u)$ is $\{v \in N;\ v \to u \text{ or } v - u \text{ in } G\}$. Note that for every chain $\mathcal{B}$ for G and $u \in N$ it holds $nb_G(u) \subset dom^{\mathcal{B}}(u)$.

The *input list* associated with G and a chain $\mathcal{B}$ for G is the set of triplets:

$$L_G^{\mathcal{B}} = \{\langle u, dom^{\mathcal{B}}(u) - nb_G(u) - u | nb_G(u) \rangle;\ u \in N\}.$$

Note, that it generalizes the concept of causal input list for a DAG. Input lists have the following properties.

Lemma 2. *Every triplet from the input list is represented in G according to the moralization criterion.*

Proof. Consider the triplet corresponding to $u \in N$. The corresponding ancestral set is $dom(u)$, and moreover $ad_H(u) = nb_G(u)$, where H is the corresponding moral graph. Hence, $nb_G(u)$ separates u from the rest of $dom(u)$ in H.

Lemma 3. *The independency model given by the moralization criterion is a graphoid.*

A proof can be found in [1]. The lemma can be shown by checking for each graphoid axiom that if the moralization criterion holds for the triplets on the left-hand side of the axiom, then it implies that the moralization criterion holds for the triplet on the right-hand side.

Lemma 4. *Let* $G = (N, E)$ *be a CG,* $\mathcal{B}$ *a chain for G,* $\langle X, Y | Z \rangle \in T(N)$. *Then* $\langle X, Y | Z \rangle_G^{mor}$ *implies* $\langle X, Y | Z \rangle \in gr(L_G^{\mathcal{B}})$.

A proof can be found in [1]. The lemma states that every triplet for which the moralization criterion holds in a CG is in the graphoid closure of the input list of the CG.

We can summarize Lemmas 1, 2, 3 and 4 as follows:

Theorem 5. *Supposing* $G = (N, E)$ *be a CG and* $\mathcal{B}$ *be a chain for G, the following conditions are equivalent for a triplet t from* $T(N)$:
(i) t is represented in G according to the moralization criterion,
(ii) t is represented in G according to the separation criterion,
(iii) t belongs to the graphoid closure of the input list associated with G and $\mathcal{B}$.

It follows from the theorem that the graphoid closure of the input list does not depend on the choice of the chain.

7 Minimal I-map

In this section we generalize the construction of a minimal I-map (see [11]) to the case of CGs. Let $M \subset T(N)$ be a graphoid and $\mathcal{B} : B_1, \ldots, B_n$, $n \geq 1$ an ordered partition of N (into nonempty sets). Then for every $u \in N$ there exists the least set $X \subset dom^{\mathcal{B}}(u) - u$ for which $\langle u, dom^{\mathcal{B}}(u) - X - u | X \rangle \in M$.[5] Its existence and uniqueness follows from the assumption that M is a graphoid. Let us denote it by X_u. Our aim is to establish a CG with such a prescribed input list.

Lemma 6. *There exists a CG G having the given ordered partition $\mathcal{B}$ as its chain and the list $\{ \langle u, dom^{\mathcal{B}}(u) - X_u - u | X_u \rangle \, ; \, u \in N \}$ as its input list $L_G^{\mathcal{B}}$. This CG is moreover a minimal I-map of M.*

A proof can be found in [1].

8 Conclusions

In this paper we have introduced a causal input list for chain graphs whose graphoid closure is shown in [1] to be exactly the set of triplets for which the moralization criterion holds. This implies that chain graphs are indeed a generalization of both DAGs and UGs as formalisms for representing independency relations. So, the concept of *chain graph* (CG) makes it possible to describe a wider class of independency models involving both UG-models and DAG-models. This raises expressiveness of graphical models. The presented results give certain unifying point of view on graphical models and establishes semantics for CGs.

Further, we have presented a separation criterion which is shown in [1] to be equivalent with the moralization criterion. The new separation criterion, based on the concept *c-separation* has its own significance. For example, it easily implies that every CG-model satisfies *composition* property [11][6] which may be complicated to verify using the moralization criterion. Nevertheless, its main profit is expected in future. In [4] it is shown that for every DAG there exists a probability distribution in which exactly those conditional independency statements hold that are represented in the graph. We hope that analogously to this result the concept of c-separation will help to prove a similar result for CGs. In fact, in [9] this is claimed to be an open question, and in [2] even a wish to have a proper separation criterion for this purpose is expressed. Such a result would justify completely the use of CG in probabilistic reasoning. We expect analogous results also in other calculi for dealing with uncertainty in artificial intelligence.

---

[5] We keep the notation $dom^{\mathcal{B}}(u)$ from the preceding section, by convention $\langle u, \emptyset | dom^{\mathcal{B}}(u) - u \rangle \in M$.

[6] The composition property: $[\langle X, Y | Z \rangle \;\&\; \langle X, W | Z \rangle] \;\rightarrow\; \langle X, YW | Z \rangle$.

References

1. R. Bouckaert and M. Studený: Chain graphs: semantics and expressiveness - extended version. Res. rep. Institute of Information Theory and Automation, Prague 1995 (in preparation).
2. M. Frydenberg: The chain graph Markov property. Scand. J. Statist. 17 (1990), 333-353.
3. D. Geiger, T. Verma, J. Pearl: Identifying independence in Bayesian networks. Networks 20 (1990), 507-534.
4. D. Geiger, J. Pearl: On the logic of causal models. In Uncertainty in Artificial Intelligence 4 (R. D. Shachter, T. S. Lewitt, L. N. Kanal, J. F. Lemmer eds.), North-Holland 1990, 3-14.
5. D. Geiger, J. Pearl: Logical and algorithmic properties of conditional independence and graphical models. Ann. Statist. 21 (1993), 2001-2021.
6. H. Kiiveri, T. P. Speed, J. B. Carlin: Recursive causal models. J. Aust. Math. Soc. A 36 (1984), 30-52.
7. S. L. Lauritzen, N. Wermuth: Mixed interaction models. Res. rep. R-84-8, Inst. Elec. Sys., University of Aalborg 1984 (the report was later changed and published as an journal paper here referenced as [8]).
8. S. L. Lauritzen, N. Wermuth: Graphical models for associations between variables, some of which are qualitative and some quantitative. Ann. Statist. 17 (1989), 31-57.
9. S. L. Lauritzen: Mixed graphical association models. Scand. J. Statist. 16 (1989), 273-306.
10. S. L. Lauritzen, A. P. Dawid, B. N. Larsen, H.-G. Leimer: Independence properties of directed Markov fields. Networks 20 (1990), 491-505.
11. J. Pearl: Probabilistic Reasoning in Intelligent Systems: Networks of Plausible Inference. Morgan Kaufmann, San Mateo, CA 1988.
12. M. Studený: Formal properties of conditional independence in different calculi if AI. In Symbolic and Quantitative Approaches to Reasoning and Uncetainty (M. Clarke, R. Kruse, S. Moral eds.), Springer-Verlag, Berlin Heidelberg 1993, 341-348.
13. T. Verma, J. Pearl: Causal netwoks: semantics and expressiveness. In Uncertainty in Artificial Intelligence 4 (R. D. Shachter, T. S. Lewitt, L. N. Kanal, J. F. Lemmer eds.), North-Holland 1990, 69-76.

Axiomatic Treatment of Possibilistic Independence *

Luis M. de Campos[1], Jörg Gebhardt[2], and Rudolf Kruse[2]

[1] Dept. of Computer Science and Artificial Intelligence, University of Granada 18071 Granada, Spain
[2] Dept. of Mathematics and Computer Science, University of Braunschweig 38106 Braunschweig, Germany

Abstract. The clarification of the concepts of independence, marginalization, and combination of modularized information is one of the major topics concerning the efficient treatment of imperfect data in complex domains of knowledge. Confining to the uncertainty calculus of possibility theory, we consider a syntactic (based on a set of axioms) as well as a semantic approach (in a random set framework) to appropriate definitions of possibilistic independence. It turns out that well-known, but also new proposals for the concept of possibilistic independence can be justified.

1 Introduction

The concept of irrelevance or independence among events or variables has been identified as one of the most important to perform efficiently reasoning tasks in extensive and/or complex domains of knowledge. Independence allows us to modularize the knowledge in such a way that we only need to consult the information that is relevant to the particular question which we are interested in, instead of having to explore a complete knowledge base. In this way, the reasoning systems that consider independence relationships gain in efficiency. This is the case, for example, in belief networks [20], which codify the independence relations by means of graphs.

In the framework of systems which handle uncertain knowledge, the concept of independence and conditional independence has been studied in-depth only for probability measures (see, for example, [6, 19]), although there are also some results for other theories of uncertain information [3, 4, 22], as well as works that consider the problem from an abstract point of view [20, 28].

The aim of this paper is to investigate several ways to define independence relationships in the framework of possibility theory [30, 8], as well as to study some semantic aspects of possibilistic independence. Some other investigations about the same topic have recently appeared [1, 2, 5, 7, 11, 12, 25].

The paper is divided in five sections: In section 2 we introduce the properties that are usually required to an independence relation. They lead to a graphical

* This work has been supported by the European Economic Community under Project ESPRIT III BRA 6156 (DRUMS II), and by the DGICYT under Project PB92-0939

representation. In section 3, after introducing the concepts of marginalization and conditioning for possibility measures, we study different (syntactic) definitions of possibilistic independence. A discussion about two different semantic views of possibilistic independence, based on either imprecision or uncertainty, is topic of section 4. Section 5 summarizes our considerations and gives some concluding remarks.

2 Axioms for Independence Relations

The study of the concept of conditional independence in probability theory (also in relational database theory and graph theory) has resulted in the identification of several properties that could be reasonable to demand to a relation which tries to capture the intuitive notion of independence [20, 28]. If we denote by $I(X,Y|Z)$ the sentence 'X is independent of Y given Z', where X,Y, and Z are (disjoint) sets of variables in a given domain, such properties are the following:

- A1 Trivial Independence: $I(X,\emptyset|Z)$
- A2 Symmetry: $I(X,Y|Z) \Rightarrow I(Y,X|Z)$
- A3 Decomposition: $I(X,Y\cup W|Z) \Rightarrow I(X,Y|Z)$
- A4 Weak Union: $I(X,Y\cup W|Z) \Rightarrow I(X,W|Z\cup Y)$
- A5 Contraction: $I(X,Y|Z)$ and $I(X,W|Z\cup Y) \Rightarrow I(X,Y\cup W|Z)$
- A6 Intersection: $I(X,Y|Z\cup W)$ and $I(X,W|Z\cup Y) \Rightarrow I(X,Y\cup W|Z)$

For example, in probability theory, using the concepts of marginalization and conditioning, $I(X,Y|Z)$ is true if and only if the distribution of X conditioned to Y and Z equals the distribution of X conditioned to Z, that is

$$I(X,Y|Z) \Leftrightarrow P(x|yz) = P(x|z), \quad \forall x,\ \forall y,\ \forall z \text{ s.t. } P(yz) > 0\ . \tag{1}$$

This relation of probabilistic independence satisfies all the axioms A1–A5, and it also satisfies A6 for probability distributions which are strictly positive.

Having an independence model M, that is, a set of conditional independence statements about the variables of a given domain, the aim is to find a graphical representation for it, or in other words, a correspondence between the variables in the model and the nodes in a graph G such that the topology of G reflects some properties of M. The kind of topological property of G which corresponds to the independence relations in M is separation if we choose a representation based on undirected graphs, and d-separation for directed acyclic graphs [20]. Due to what properties are verified in each particular situation for a given independence model, it is possible to construct, using different methods, different types of graphs which display (through the separation or d-separation criteria) some or all the independencies represented in the model [24, 20].

After this brief review of the abstract aspects of independence and its relation to graphical structures, we are in the position to study some specific formalisms. We are going to focus on possibility theory, although some of the ideas presented here could also be applied to other uncertainty calculi.

3 Syntactic Aspects of Possibilistic Independence

Consider a variable X_1 taking its values in a finite domain Ω_1. From a purely syntactic point of view, a possibility measure defined on X_1 is simply a set function

$$\Pi : \mathcal{P}(\Omega_1) \rightarrow [0,1],$$

such that

1. $\Pi(\Omega_1) = 1$,
2. $\Pi(A \cup B) = \max(\Pi(A), \Pi(B)),\ \forall A, B \subseteq \Omega_1$.

Associated with the possibility measure Π, the possibility distribution

$$\pi : \Omega_1 \rightarrow [0,1]$$

is defined by means of

$$\pi(x_1) = \Pi(\{x_1\}),\ \forall x_1 \in \Omega_1.$$

The information contained in the possibility distribution is sufficient to recover the possibility measure, since $\forall A \subseteq \Omega_1,\ \Pi(A) = \max_{x_1 \in A} \pi(x_1)$. So, we can restrict our study to deal only with possibility distributions.

3.1 Marginalization and Conditioning

Given a joint possibility distribution π defined on two variables X_1 and X_2, whose common universe of discourse is the cartesian product $\Omega = \Omega_1 \mathrm{x} \Omega_2$, the marginal possibility distribution of X_2, π_{X_2}, is defined by means of

$$\pi_{X_2}(x_2) = \max_{x_1 \in \Omega_1} \pi(x_1, x_2),\ \forall x_2 \in \Omega_2. \tag{2}$$

However, the concept of a conditional possibility distribution is not so universal, there exist different alternatives to define it. We will mainly consider the following definition:
The possibility distribution on X_1 conditioned to the event $[X_2 = x_2]$, $\pi(.|x_2)$, is defined as

$$\pi(x_1|x_2) = \begin{cases} \pi(x_1, x_2) & \text{if } \pi(x_1, x_2) < \pi_{X_2}(x_2) \\ 1 & \text{if } \pi(x_1, x_2) = \pi_{X_2}(x_2) \end{cases} \quad \forall x_1 \in \Omega_1 \tag{3}$$

A slightly different version of this definition was considered in [17], as the solution of the equation $\pi(x_1, x_2) = \min\left(\pi(x_1|x_2), \pi_{X_2}(x_2)\right),\ \forall x_1$. The definition above is the least specific solution of this equation [10].

A completely different definition of conditioning that will not be considered here (see [2]) is the following: The possibility distribution of X_1 conditioned to the event $[X_2 = x_2]$, $\pi_d(.|x_2)$, is defined as

$$\pi_d(x_1|x_2) = \frac{\pi(x_1, x_2)}{\pi_{X_2}(x_2)}\quad \forall x_1 \in \Omega_1. \tag{4}$$

This is Dempster's rule of conditioning, specialized to possibility measures [21].

Observe that the difference between these two definitions of conditioning is the kind of normalization used. In both cases we first focus on the values compatible with the available information $[X_2 = x_2]$, that is $\{(x_1, x_2') \mid x_1 \in X_1, x_2' = x_2\}$, and next we must normalize the values $\pi(x_1, x_2)$ to get a possibility distribution. In the second case the normalization is carried out by dividing by the greatest value, $\pi_{X_2}(x_2)$ ($= \max_{x_1' \in \Omega_1} \pi(x_1', x_2)$), whereas in the first case the normalization is achieved by increasing only the greatest values of $\pi(x_1', x_2)$ up to 1.

Obviously these definitions of marginal and conditional possibility distributions can be immediately extended to the n-dimensional case. From now on, to simplify the notation of a marginal possibility distribution, we will drop the subindex, thus writing $\pi(x_2)$ instead of $\pi_{X_2}(x_2)$.

3.2 New Approaches to Possibilistic Independence

Consider a finite set of variables $V = \{X_1, X_2, \ldots, X_n\}$, and a n-dimensional possibility distribution π defined on V. Given three disjoint subsets of variables in V, X,Y and Z, we will represent by means of $I(X, Y|Z)$ the sentence X is conditionally independent of Y given Z, for the model associated to the distribution π. We will denote by x, y, z the values that the respective variables can take on, which can vary in the domains Ω^X, Ω^Y and Ω^Z, respectively. The values of, for example, $Y \cup Z$, will be denoted simply by yz, and they can vary in the set $\Omega^{Y \cup Z} = \Omega^Y \times \Omega^Z$

The most obvious way to define the conditional independence is to proceed in a way similar to the probabilistic case, eq.(1), that is:

$$I(X, Y|Z) \Leftrightarrow \pi(x|yz) = \pi(x|z)\ \forall x, y, z \tag{5}$$

This means that the knowledge about the value of the variable Y does not modify our belief about the values of X, when the value of the variable Z is known. This definition of independence satisfies all the axioms except A2. By defining a new relation $I'(.,.|.)$ by means of $I'(X, Y|Z) \Leftrightarrow I(X, Y|Z)$ and $I(Y, X|Z)$, we get a definition of independence that verifies all the axioms A1–A6 [12].

One problem with the previous definition could be, in our opinion, that it is too strict, because it requires the equality of the distributions, and these distributions represent imprecise knowledge. The problem becomes worse when the distributions must be estimated from data or human judgements.

The definition in eq.(5) represents that our information about X remains unchanged after conditioning to Y. A different idea could be to assert the independence when we do not gain additional information about the values of X after conditioning to Y (but we could lose some information) [3, 4]. The idea of a possibility distribution being more or less informative than another one is adequately captured by the well-known definition of inclusion for possibility distributions:

Given two possibility distributions π and π', π' is said to be included in (or gives less information than) π if and only if $\pi(x) \leq \pi'(x)\ \forall x$.

Using the relation of inclusion between possibility distributions, the previous idea can be expressed more formally by means of

$$I(X,Y|Z) \Leftrightarrow \pi(x|yz) \geq \pi(x|z)\ \forall x,y,z \tag{6}$$

It can be proved that this definition satisfies the properties A1–A5 and does not verify A6 in general. Moreover, this definition turns out to be equivalent to the following:

$$I(X,Y|Z) \Leftrightarrow \pi(xyz) = \min\left(\pi(xz), \pi(yz)\right)\ \forall x,y,z \tag{7}$$

If we consider the case of marginal independence ($Z = \emptyset$), from eq.(7) we obtain

$$I(X,Y|\emptyset) \Leftrightarrow \pi(x,y) = \min\left(\pi(x), \pi(y)\right)\ \forall x,y\ , \tag{8}$$

and thus the well-known concept of non-interactivity for possibility measures[8]. The definition of independence in eq.(6) could therefore be called *conditional non-interactivity*.

Observe that for the kind of conditioning we are using, the only necessary operation is comparison, that is to say, we only need to have an order relation. So, we could easily consider possibility distributions taking values in sets having less properties than the [0, 1] interval (for example, a set of linguistic labels). We could speak about these generalized possibility measures as qualitative possibility measures. In these conditions we could define the conditioning and the independence in exactly the same way as before (eqs.(3) and (6)), obtaining the same properties.

A different approach to possibilistic independence considers that the idea of independence as a non-gain of information after conditioning, eq.(6), has not been carried out until the end of the reasoning process: If after conditioning we lose information, it seems more convenient to keep the initial information. This is debatable, but it represents a sort of default rule: If in a very specific context we do not have much information, then we use the information available in a less specific context. In practical terms, this idea implies a change in the definition of conditioning:

$$\pi_c(x|y) = \begin{cases} \pi(x) & \text{if } \pi(x|y) \geq \pi(x)\ \forall x \\ \pi(x|y) & \text{if } \exists x' \text{ such that } \pi(x'|y) < \pi(x') \end{cases} \tag{9}$$

If $\pi(x|y)$ is always greater than or equal to $\pi(x)$, that is, it gives not more information than $\pi(x)$, then maintain $\pi(x)$; otherwise use the previous conditioning.

Applying this conditioning, the new definition of independence is

$$I(X,Y|Z) \Leftrightarrow \pi_c(x|yz) = \pi_c(x|z)\ \forall x,y,z. \tag{10}$$

In this case, all the axioms A1–A6 are satisfied, except A2. Once again, we could obtain symmetry by defining a new relation $I'(.,.|.)$ by means of $I'(X,Y|Z) \Leftrightarrow I(X,Y|Z)$ and $I(Y,X|Z)$, but in this case is not clear so far that all the other axioms A1 and A3–A6 will still be satisfied.

It can be seen that this relation is more restrictive than the conditional non-interactivity, eq.(6): Every independence statement which is true using eq.(10) is also true if we use eq. (6), but the converse does not hold.

4 Semantic Aspects of Possibilistic Independence

Similar to the many semantic approaches to probability theory, recent years of research provided a variety of proposals for the concept of a possibility distribution and the meaning of a degree of possibility. Although these proposals differ from one another concerning the semantic background and the chosen formal framework, they all introduce possibility theory as an appropriate calculus for an information–compressed modelling of uncertain and imprecise (set–valued) information. For illustration, we mention possibility distributions as one–point coverages of random sets [16], contour functions of belief functions [21], and falling shadows in set–valued statistics [27].

In comparison to probability theory, from the viewpoint of representing imperfect data, this is more general, since using a single probability space covers only uncertainty modelling of precise data. In a corresponding way, relational database theory applies relations in order to represent imprecise (set–valued), but certain information about dependencies among variables. Due to their restrictions to different kinds of imperfect data, the two frameworks supply different concepts of independence, which are probabilistic independence and lossless–join decomposability [26], respectively. Probabilistic independence may be viewed as an *uncertainty–driven* type of independence, whereas lossless–join decomposability reflects an *imprecision–driven* type of independence. Since possibility theory addresses both kinds of imperfect knowledge, concepts of possibilistic independence can be uncertainty–driven or imprecision–driven, so that there are at least two ways of introducing and justifying them.

In our following investigations we clarify that imprecision–driven possibilistic independence coincides with non–interactivity [9] of possibility distributions, while uncertainty–driven possibilistic independence strongly refers to applying Dempster's rule of conditioning [21], specialized to possibility measures.

4.1 Imprecision–driven Possibilistic Independence

Considering possibility theory as a calculus for an information–compressed modelling of uncertainty and imprecision (both to be separated from one another), we first start with a concept of relational independence and then generalize it to the possibilistic setting.

Relational Independence
Let $V = \{X_1, X_2, \ldots, X_n\}$ be a set of variables (attributes), $\Omega_i = \mathrm{Dom}(X_i)$, $i = 1, \ldots, n$, their domains, and $\Omega = \Omega_1 \times \cdots \times \Omega_n$ their common domain (Universe of discourse) for specifying the possible states of objects that are characterized by $X_1, \ldots, X_n$.

Based on certain, but in general imprecise knowledge about an actual object state $\omega_0 \in \Omega$ of interest, any non–empty relation $R \subseteq \Omega$ among attribute values is appropriate for representing the most specific correct set–valued specification of ω_0. In this context, R is called *correct* w.r.t. ω_0, iff $\omega_0 \in R$. For any $R' \subseteq \Omega$, we call R' *at least as specific as* R, iff $R' \subseteq R$.

A correct relation R is therefore most specific w.r.t. ω_0, iff for all proper subsets R' of R, considering our actual knowledge about ω_0, it is not guaranteed that R' is correct w.r.t. ω_0.

Referred to these definitions, the concept of *relational independence* can be introduced as follows:

Let X, Y, and Z denote disjunct subsets of V, and let $X \neq \emptyset, \emptyset \neq R \subseteq \Omega$. X *is independent of* Y *given* Z *w.r.t.* R, iff any additional certain knowledge about Y (i.e.: knowledge beyond R) does not further specify our knowledge about X.

Formally spoken, for any $W \subseteq U \subseteq V$, let Ω^W denote the product of the domains of the variables in W, Π_W^U the projection from Ω^U onto Ω^W, and $\hat{\Pi}_W^U$ the cylindrical extension from Ω^W to Ω^U.

X *is independent of* Y *given* Z *w.r.t.* R (in symbols: $I_R(X, Y|Z)$), iff for any instantiations $Y = y$ and $Z = z$ (i.e. $y \in \Omega^Y, z \in \Omega^Z$),

$$R(X|z) = R(X|yz), \tag{11}$$

where

$$\begin{aligned} R(X|z) &\stackrel{\text{Df}}{=} \Pi_X^V(R \cap \hat{\Pi}_Z^V(z)), \\ R(X|yz) &\stackrel{\text{Df}}{=} \Pi_X^V(R \cap \hat{\Pi}_Y^V(y) \cap \hat{\Pi}_Z^V(z)). \end{aligned}$$

Note that $R(X|yz)$ is the most specific set-valued specification of $\Pi_X^V(\omega_0)$, given the correctness of R w.r.t. ω_0 and the information that $\Pi_Y^V(\omega_0) = y$ and $\Pi_Z^V(\omega_0) = z$.

It is easy to prove that

$$I_R(X, Y|Z) \Leftrightarrow R(X \cup Y|z) = R(X|z) * R(Y|z) \, \forall z \tag{12}$$

with

$$R(X|z) * R(Y|z) = \hat{\Pi}_X^{X \cup Y}(R(X|z)) \cap \hat{\Pi}_Y^{X \cup Y}(R(Y|z)),$$

which means that $R(X \cup Y|z)$ has a lossless-join decomposition w.r.t. the variables in X and Y.

The eq. (11) is the basic definition of independence in the relational setting. Stating this definition, it follows that $I_R(X, Y|Z)$ satisfies the axioms A1–A5. On the other hand, the intersection axiom A6 does not hold in general, because it is more oriented at uncertainty-driven independence (for example, probabilistic independence) than referred to imprecision-driven independence.

Generalization to Possibilistic Independence

In this subsection we confine to the view of possibility distributions as one-point coverages of random sets. Let $(C, 2^C, P), C = \{c_1, c_2, \dots, c_m\}$, denote a finite probability space, and $\gamma : C \rightarrow 2^{\Omega}$ a set-valued mapping. C is interpreted as a set of contexts that are distiguished for set-valued specifications of ω_0.

The relation $\gamma(c_j)$ is assumed to be the most specific set-valued specification of ω_0, implied by the frame conditions that describe c_j. The quantity $P(\{c_j\})$ is the (subjective) probability of applying c_j for the specification of ω_0. The resulting *random set* $\Gamma = (\gamma, P)$ is an imperfect (set-valued and uncertain) specification of ω_0. Let π_Γ denote the *one-point coverage of* Γ (the *possibility distribution induced by* Γ), defined as

$$\pi_\Gamma : \Omega \rightarrow [0,1],$$
$$\pi_\Gamma(\omega) \stackrel{\text{Df}}{=} P(\{c \in C \mid \omega \in \gamma(c)\}).$$

In a complete modelling, the contexts in C must be specified in detail, so that the relationships among all contexts c_j and their context-dependent specifications $\gamma(c_j)$ of ω_0 are clarified. On the other hand, if the contexts are unknown or ignored, then $\pi_\Gamma(\omega)$ is the total mass of all contexts c that provide a correct specification $\gamma(c)$ of ω_0, and this quantifies the *possibility of truth* of "$\omega = \omega_0$". More details on this context approach to possibility theory can be found in [13, 14, 15].

Our (information-compressed) imperfect knowledge about ω_0, represented by π_Γ, can be specialized in the way that uncertainty is excluded by stating *α-correctness of Γ w.r.t.* ω_0, which means that there exists a subset $C' \subseteq C$ of contexts such that $P(C') \geq \alpha$ and $\forall c' \in C' : \omega_0 \in \gamma(c')$. In this case, the *$\alpha$-cut* $[\pi_\Gamma]_\alpha \stackrel{\text{Df}}{=} \{\omega \mid \pi_\Gamma(\omega) \geq \alpha\}$ of the possibility distribution π_Γ turns out to be the most specific correct set-valued specification of ω_0, given the representation Γ of our background knowledge about ω_0, and the α-correctness assumption w.r.t. ω_0.

Operating on α-cuts reduces the possibilistic setting to the relational setting. By this we obtain a straight-forward generalization of the concept of relational independence to possibilistic independence:

X is independent of Y given Z w.r.t. π_Γ, iff any additional certain knowledge about Y ($\Pi_Y^V(\omega_0) = y$), given any certain knowledge about Z ($\Pi_Z^V(\omega_0) = z$), does not further specify our knowledge about X, assuming any degree of α-correctness of Γ w.r.t. ω_0.

Formally spoken, defining $\pi \stackrel{\text{Df}}{=} \pi_\Gamma$,

X is independent of Y given Z w.r.t. π (in symbols: $I_\pi(X, Y \mid Z)$), iff for any instantiations y of Y and z of Z, and any $\alpha \in [0,1]$,

$$[\pi(X \mid z)]_\alpha = [\pi(X \mid yz)]_\alpha, \tag{13}$$

where the possibility distributions $\pi(X \mid z)$ and $\pi(X \mid yz)$ denote the canonical generalization of $R(X \mid z)$ and $R(X \mid yz)$ to the possibilistic setting, which result from applying the extension principle [29] to the needed set-theoretical operations of intersection, projection, and cylindrical extension.

Note that $[\pi(X|z)]_\alpha$ is the most specific set-valued specification of $\Pi_X^V(\omega_0)$, given the α-correctness of π w.r.t. ω_0 and the additional certain information $\Pi_Y^V(\omega_0) = y$ and $\Pi_Z^V(\omega_0) = z$.

It is easy to prove that

$$I_\pi(X,Y|Z) \Longleftrightarrow \pi(X \cup Y|z) \equiv \min\left(\pi(X|z), \pi(Y|z)\right) \forall z\,, \tag{14}$$

which is non-interactivity of possibility distributions as a generalization of the lossless-join-decomposition property from the relational setting to the possibilistic setting.

Conform to the properties of a generalization, it is clear that $I_\pi(X,Y|Z)$ in general does not satisfy the intersection axiom A6, but, starting with equality (13) as the basic definition of possibilistic independence, it can be shown that A1–A5 still hold.

4.2 Uncertainty–driven Possibilistic Independence

Concerning the treatment of imperfect information, one should consider two different levels of reasoning, namely the *credal level*, where all operations on our pieces of knowledge take place, and the *pignistic level*, where the final step of decision making follows [23]. Imprecision–driven possibilistic independence is strongly oriented at the credal level, applying the extension principle as the basic concept of operating on possibility distributions, and avoiding normalization, which would change their meaning from quantifying absolute to relative degrees of possibility.

In opposite to this, an uncertainty–driven approach to possibilistic independence should be referred to the pignistic level, taking decision making aspects into account and thus quantifying the relative degrees of possibility of events. On this level, the need of normalization is obvious.

In order to define possibilistic independence, we therefore use the normalizations of the possibility distributions $\pi(X|z)$ and $\pi(X|yz)$, respectively.

Normalization yields

$$\pi^*(X|z) \overset{\text{Df}}{=} \frac{\pi(X|z)}{\pi(V|z)} \quad \text{and} \tag{15}$$

$$\pi^*(X|yz) \overset{\text{Df}}{=} \frac{\pi(X|yz)}{\pi(V|yz)}\,,$$

where $\pi(V|yz) > 0$ is required to be satisfied.

From this we obtain the following notion of possibilistic independence on the pignistic level:

X is independent of Y given Z w.r.t. π, iff any additional certain knowledge about Y ($\Pi_Y^V(\omega_0) = y$), given any certain knowledge about Z ($\Pi_Z^V(\omega_0) = z$), does not change the possibility degree of X.

Formally spoken,

X is independent of Y given Z w.r.t. π (in symbols: $I^*_\pi(X,Y|Z)$), iff for any instantiations $Y = y$ and $Z = z$,

$$\pi^*(X|z) \equiv \pi^*(X|yz) \tag{16}$$

holds for all $y \in \Omega^Y$ and $z \in \Omega^Z$ sucht that $\pi(V|yz) > 0$.

It is straight–forward to prove that

$$I^*_\pi(X,Y|Z) \Longleftrightarrow \pi_d(X|z) \equiv \pi_d(X|yz) \tag{17}$$

for all y and z that fulfil the above specified restrictions, with π_d denoting Dempster's conditioning of π, specialized to possibility measures (see (4)).

Note that $I^*_\pi(X,Y|Z)$ satisfies axioms A1–A5, and also A6, if π is strictly positive. This is analogous to the probabilistic setting, when π is a probability distribution.

Hence, it is

$$I^*_\pi(X,Y|Z) \Longleftrightarrow \pi_d(X \cup Y|z) \equiv \pi_d(X|z) \cdot \pi_d(Y|z) \tag{18}$$

for all $z \in \Omega^Z$ such that $\pi(V|z) > 0$. This reflects another kind of decomposition, characterized by multiplying the (relative) degrees of possibility with respect to marginal possibility distributions.

5 Concluding Remarks

In this paper, several definitions of possibilistic independence have been proposed. Starting from a pure syntactic point of view, we studied their properties with respect to a well-known set of axioms that tries to capture the intuitive idea of independence. Related to various kinds of possibilistic conditioning, we obtained new proposals for possibilistic independence, which are appropriate for constructing independence graphs and propagating possibilistic information in these structures.

Focussing our interest on a pure semantic approach to possibility theory in a random set framework, we pointed out that one should distinguish between imprecision- and uncertainty-driven possibilistic independence. In this connection, we justified non-interactivity as well as independence with respect to Dempster's rule of conditioning.

Based on this background, our future work will consider how to extract possibility distributions from raw data, and how to merge this information with subjective judgments from experts. A first result concerning the problem of inducing possibilistic networks from databases of sample cases, using non-interactivity as a concept of possibilistic independence, is given in [15].

References

1. Benferhat, S., Dubois, D., and Prade, H.: Expressing independence in a possibilistic framework and its application to default reasoning, in: Proceedings of the Eleventh ECAI Conference, 150–154 (1994).
2. Campos, L.M. de: Independence relationships in possibility theory and their application to learning belief networks, to appear in Proceedings of the ISSEK Workshop 'Mathematical and Statistical Methods in Artificial Intelligence' at Udine, Italy (1995).
3. Campos, L.M. de and Huete, J.F.: Independence concepts in upper and lower probabilities, in: Uncertainty in Intelligent Systems (Eds. B. Bouchon-Meunier, L. Valverde, R.R. Yager), North-Holland, 49–59 (1993).
4. Campos, L.M. de and Huete, J.F.: Learning non probabilistic belief networks, in: Symbolic and Quantitative Approaches to Reasoning and Uncertainty, Lecture Notes in Computer Science 747 (Eds. M. Clarke, R. Kruse, S. Moral), Springer Verlag, 57–64 (1993).
5. Cooman, G. de and Kerre, E.E.: A new approach to possibilistic independence, in: Proceedings of the Third IEEE International Conference on Fuzzy Systems, 1446–1451 (1994).
6. Dawid, A.P.: Conditional independence in statistical theory, J.R. Statist. Soc. Ser. B 41, 1–31 (1979).
7. Dubois, D., Farinas del Cerro, L., Herzig, A. and Prade, H.: An ordinal view of independence with applications to plausible reasoning, in: Uncertainty in Artificial Intelligence: Proceedings of the Tenth Conference (Eds. R. López de Mántaras, D. Poole), Morgan Kaufmann, 195–203 (1994).
8. Dubois, D. and Prade, H.: Possibility Theory: An approach to computerized processing of uncertainty, Plenum Press (1988).
9. Dubois, D. and Prade, H.: Fuzzy sets in approximate reasoning, Part 1: Inference with possibility distributions, Fuzzy Sets and Systems 40, 143–202 (1991).
10. Dubois, D. and Prade, H.: Belief revision and updates in numerical formalisms — An overview, with new results for the possibilistic framework, in: Proceedings of the 13th IJCAI Conference, Morgan and Kaufmann, 620–625 (1993).
11. Farinas del Cerro, L. and Herzig, A.: Possibility theory and independence, in: Proceedings of the Fifth IPMU Conference, 820–825 (1994).
12. Fonck, P.: Conditional independence in possibility theory, in: Uncertainty in Artificial Intelligence, Proceedings of the Tenth Conference (Eds. R. López de Mántaras, D. Poole) Morgan and Kaufmann, 221–226 (1994).
13. Gebhardt, J. and Kruse, R.: A new approach to semantic aspects of possibilistic reasoning, in: Symbolic and Quantitative Approaches to Reasoning and Uncertainty, Lecture Notes in Computer Science 747 (Eds. M. Clarke, R. Kruse, S. Moral), Springer Verlag, 151–160 (1993).
14. Gebhardt, J. and Kruse, R.: On an information compression view of possibility theory, in; Proc. of the Third IEEE Int. Conf. on Fuzzy Systems, Orlando, 1285–1288 (1994).
15. Gebhardt, J. and Kruse, R.: Learning possibilistic networks from data, in: Proc. of the Fifth Int. Workshop on Artificial Intelligence and Statistics, Fort Lauderdale, Florida, 233–244 (1995).
16. Hestir, K., Nguyen, H.T., and Rogers, G.S.: A random set formalism for evidential reasoning, in: Conditional Logic in Expert Systems, (Eds. I.R. Goodman,

M.M. Gupta, H.T. Nguyen, and G.S. Rogers), North Holland, New York, 209–344 (1991).
17. Hisdal, E.: Conditional possibilities, independence and noninteraction, Fuzzy Sets and Systems 1, 283–297 (1978).
18. Kruse, R., Gebhardt, J., and Klawonn, F.: Foundations of Fuzzy Systems, Wiley, Chichester (1994).
19. Lauritzen, S.L., Dawid, A.P., Larsen, B.N., and Leimer, H.G.: Independence properties of directed Markov fields, Networks 20, 491–505 (1990).
20. Pearl, J.: Probabilistic reasoning in intelligent systems: Networks of plausible inference, Morgan and Kaufmann (1988).
21. Shafer, G.: Mathematical theory of evidence, Princeton University Press, Princeton (1976).
22. Shenoy, P.P.: Conditional independence in uncertainty theories, in: Uncertainty in Artificial Intelligence, Proceedings of the Eighth Conference (Eds. D. Dubois, M.P. Wellman, B. D'Ambrosio, P. Smets), Morgan and Kaufmann, 284–291 (1992).
23. Smets, P. and Kennes, R.: The transferable belief model, Artificial Intelligence 66, 191–234 (1994).
24. Spirtes, P., Glymour, C., and Scheines, R.: Causation, Prediction and Search, Lecture Notes in Statistics 81, Springer-Verlag (1993).
25. Studený, M.: Formal properties of conditional independence in different calculi of AI, in: Symbolic and Quantitative Approaches to Reasoning and Uncertainty, Lecture Notes in Computer Science 747, (Eds. M. Clarke, R. Kruse, S. Moral Springer Verlag, 341-348 (1993).
26. Ullman, J.D.: Principles of Database and Knowledge-Base Systems, Vol. 1, Computer Science Press Inc., Rockville, Maryland (1988).
27. Wang, P.Z.: From the fuzzy statistics to the falling random subsets, in: Advances in Fuzzy Sets, Possibility and Applications, (Eds. P.P. Wang), Plenum Press, New York, 81–96 (1983).
28. Wilson, N.: Generating graphoids from generalized conditional probability, in: Uncertainty in Artificial Intelligence, Proceedings of the Tenth Conference, (Eds. R. López de Mántaras, D. Poole) Morgan and Kaufmann, 221–226 (1994).
29. Zadeh, L.A.: The concept of a linguistic variable and its application to approximate reasoning, Inform. Sci. 8, 199–249, 301–37, Inform. Sci. 9, 43–80 (1975)
30. Zadeh, L.A.: Fuzzy sets as a basis for a theory of possibility, Fuzzy Sets and Systems 1, 3–28 (1978).

Parametric Structure of Probabilities in Bayesian Networks

Enrique Castillo[1], José Manuel Gutiérrez[1] and Ali S. Hadi[2]

[1] Department of Applied Mathematics and Computational Science, University of Cantabria, SPAIN
[2] Department of Statistics, Cornell University, USA

Abstract. The paper presents a method for uncertainty propagation in Bayesian networks in symbolic, as opposed to numeric, form. The algebraic structure of probabilities is characterized. The prior probabilities of instantiations and the marginal probabilities are shown to be rational functions of the parameters, where the polynomials appearing in the numerator and the denominator are at the most first degree in each of the parameters. It is shown that numeric propagation algorithms can be adapted for symbolic computations by means of canonical components. Furthermore, the same algorithms can be used to build automatic code generators for symbolic propagation of evidence. An example of uncertainty propagation in a clique tree is used to illustrate all the steps and the corresponding code in *Mathematica* is given. Finally, it is shown that upper and lower bounds for the marginal probabilities of nodes are attained at one of the canonical components.

1 Introduction

Bayesian networks are powerful tools for handling uncertainty in expert systems. A key problem in Bayesian networks is evidence propagation. There are several well-known methods for exact and approximate propagation of evidence in a Bayesian network; see, for example, Pearl [1, 2], Lauritzen and Spiegelhalter [3], Castillo and Alvarez [4], and Castillo, Gutiérrez and Hadi [5, 6]. These methods, however, require that the joint probabilities of the nodes be given in a numeric form. In practice, exact numeric specification of these parameters may not be available. In such cases, there is a need for methods which are able to deal with the parameters symbolically. Symbolic propagation leads to probabilities which are expressed as functions of the parameters instead of real numbers. Thus, the answers to specific queries can then be obtained by plugging the values of the parameters in the solution, without need to redo the propagation. Furthermore, a real practical use of this approach is the possibility of performing a sensitivity analysis of the parameter values without the need of redoing the computations.

2 Notation and Basic Framework

Let $X = \{X_1, X_2, \ldots, X_n\}$ be a set of n discrete variables and let r_i be the cardinality (number of states) of variable X_i. A Bayesian network B over X is a

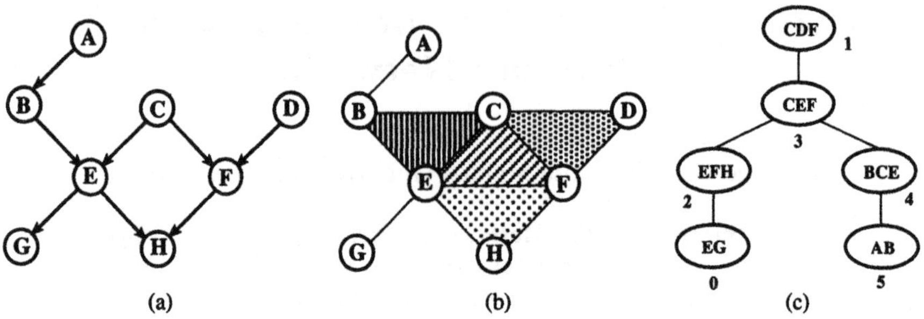

Fig. 1. Example of a Bayesian Network with its cliques and associated clique tree.

pair (B_S, B_P), where the network structure B_S is a directed acyclic graph with one node for each variable in X. We refer to the parents of a node X_i in the network structure as Π_i and to the set of instances of Π_i (specific combination of values in the parent set) as π_i (in lower case). B_P is a set of n conditional probabilities $P_i(X_i|\Pi_i)$, one for each variable, which gives the probabilities of X_i, given the values of the variables in its parent set Π_i. Using the chain rule, the joint probability density of X can be written as

$$P(X_1, X_2, \ldots, X_n) = \prod_{i=1}^{n} P_i(X_i|\Pi_i). \tag{1}$$

An advantage of this decomposition of the joint probability density is that each conditional probability $P_i(X_i|\Pi_i)$ can be given independently of the other probabilities. We can consider $P_i(X_i|\Pi_i)$ as a parametric family. A natural choice of parameters is given by

$$\theta_{ijk} = P_i(k|j),\ k \in \{1, \ldots, r_i - 1\},\ 0 \leq j \leq q_i;\ \sum_{k=1}^{r_i-1} \theta_{ijk} \leq 1,\ i \in \{1, \ldots, n\}, \tag{2}$$

where $q_i = \prod_{i \in I_{\Pi_i}} r_i$ is the cardinal of Π_i, I_{Π_i} is the set of indices of Π_i, and

$$\theta_{ijr_i} = 1 - \sum_{k=1}^{r_i-1} \theta_{ijk}. \tag{3}$$

For illustrative purpose, we shall use the following example:

Example 1. Assume a Bayesian network (B_S, B_P) where B_S is the directed graph in Fig. 1(a) with the corresponding cliques in Fig. 1(b) and associated clique tree in Fig. 1(c), which imply a joint probability of the set of nodes X of the form:

$$P(X) = P(A)P(B|A)P(C)P(D)P(E|BC)P(F|CD)P(G|E)P(H|EF). \tag{4}$$

Assume that all nodes represent binary variables with values in the set $\{0, 1\}$ and that the conditional probabilities, numeric and symbolic, are given in Table 1.

$P(A=0)=p_0$ $P(C=0)=0.4$	$P(B=0\|A=0)=0.3$ $P(B=0\|A=1)=0.5$
$P(E=0\|B=0,C=0)=0.2$ $P(E=0\|B=0,C=1)=0.3$ $P(E=0\|B=1,C=0)=0.4$ $P(E=0\|B=1,C=1)=0.5$	$P(F=0\|C=0,D=0)=0.1$ $P(F=0\|C=0,D=1)=0.4$ $P(F=0\|C=1,D=0)=0.3$ $P(F=0\|C=1,D=1)=0.2$
$P(D=0)=p_1$ $P(G=0\|E=0)=0.3$ $P(G=0\|E=1)=0.6$	$P(H=0\|E=0,F=0)=0.2$ $P(H=0\|E=0,F=1)=0.4$ $P(H=0\|E=1,F=0)=0.6$ $P(H=0\|E=1,F=1)=0.3$

Table 1. Conditional probability tables showing two symbolic parameters: p_0 and p_1.

3 Exact Propagation in Bayesian Networks

In this section we consider an exact method for the propagation of uncertainties (see, for example, Shachter, Andersen, and Szolovits [7]). This method will serve as the basis for the symbolic methods in the following sections. Initially, each conditional probability distribution $P(X_i|\Pi_i)$ is assigned to exactly one clique containing the X_i's family, (X_i, Π_i). The product of the conditional probability distributions assigned to clique S_i is called the *potential function*, $\Psi_i(S_i)$, for clique S_i. With this, once the evidence $\mathcal{E}$ is known, the joint distribution for all the variables can be written as

$$P(X) = \prod_{X_i \in X - \mathcal{E}} P(X_i|\Pi_i) \prod_{e_k \in \mathcal{E}} P(e_k|\Pi_k) = \prod_{k=1}^{N_c} \Psi_k(S_k), \tag{5}$$

where N_c is the number of cliques and e_k is the evidence. Shachter, Andersen, and Szolovits [7] show that the joint probability for clique S_i is

$$P_i(S_i) = \Psi_i(S_i) \prod_{k \in A_i} M_{ki}, \tag{6}$$

where A_i is the set of all cliques adjacent to S_i and M_{ki} is the message sent by clique S_k to S_i, which is given by:

$$M_{ij} = \left(\sum_{(S_i - S_j)} \Psi_i(S_i) \prod_{k \in A_i - j} M_{ki} \right). \tag{7}$$

Once $P_i(S_i)$ is known, the node marginals can be easily calculated by marginalizing in the cliques. These expressions lead to well-known numerical propagation algorithms.

4 Symbolic Computations

Dealing with symbolic computations is the same as dealing with numeric values with the only difference being that all the required operations must be performed by a program with symbolic manipulation capabilities. Symbolic computations, however, are intrinsically slow and require more memory. A code generator can be easily written based on any standard propagation algorithm if, instead of building the potential functions $\Psi_i(S_i)$, and calculating the M_{ij} messages, the probability function of the cliques, and the node marginals, we write the corresponding code in the order indicated by the algorithm. We have written such a program in C++ language. In fact the code in Fig. 2 has been generated by this computer program given the network in Example 1. Table 2 shows that the initial marginal probabilities of the nodes are polynomials in the parameters.

Node	P(Node=0)	Node	P(Node=0)
A	p_0	B	$0.5 - 0.2p_0$
C	0.4	D	p_1
E	$0.04(9 + p_0)$	F	$0.02(14 - 3p_1)$
G	$0.012(41 - p_0)$	H	$0.0004(930 - 4p_0 - 30p_1 + 3p_0p_1)$

Table 2. Initial probabilities of nodes.

The previous results have been obtained without any instantiation of evidence. Suppose now we have the following evidence: $\{D = 0, E = 0\}$. To this aim, we make the ranges of variables D and E equal to $(0, 0)$, that is, $ul[3] = ul[4] = 0$ and repeat the calculations. Table 3 gives the new probabilities of the nodes given this evidence. We get rational functions, i.e., quotients of polynomial functions in the parameters with unit exponents. The fact that the probability of any instantiation is a polynomial in the parameters is proven in Sect. 5.

Node	P(Node=0)	Node	P(Node=0)
A	$(10p_0)/(9 + p_0)$	B	$0.65(5 - 2p_0)/(9 + p_0)$
C	$0.2(15 + 2p_0)/(9 + p_0)$	D	1
E	1	F	$0.02(105 + 11p_0)/(9 + p_0)$
G	0.3	H	$0.004(795 + 89p_0)/(9 + p_0)$

Table 3. Conditional probabilities of the nodes, given $\{D = 0, E = 0\}$, showing the common denominator

```
(* Probability Tables and Initialize ranges*)
T={p0,1-p0};n=1; Do[PA[i1]=T[[n]];n++,{i1,0,1}];
T={0.3,0.5,0.7,0.5};n=1; Do[PB[i1,i2]=T[[n]];n++,{i1,0,1},{i2,0,1}];
T={0.4,0.6};n=1; Do[PC[i1]=T[[n]];n++,{i1,0,1}];
T={p1,1-p1};n=1; Do[PD[i1]=T[[n]];n++,{i1,0,1}];
T={0.2,0.3,0.4,0.5,0.8,0.7,0.6,0.5};
n=1; Do[PE[i1,i2,i3]=T[[n]];n++,{i1,0,1},{i2,0,1},{i3,0,1}];
T={0.1,0.4,0.3,0.2,0.9,0.6,0.7,0.8};
n=1;Do[PF[i1,i2,i3]=T[[n]];n++,{i1,0,1},{i2,0,1},{i3,0,1}];
T={0.3,0.6,0.7,0.4}; n=1; Do[PG[i1,i2]=T[[n]];n++,{i1,0,1},{i2,0,1}];
T={0.2,0.4,0.6,0.3,0.8,0.6,0.4,0.7};
n=1; Do[PH[i1,i2,i3]=T[[n]];n++,{i1,0,1},{i2,0,1},{i3,0,1}];
Do[u0[i]=0; u1[i]=1, {i,0,7}];

(* Potential Functions *)
F0[G_,E_]:=PG[G,E];F1[D_,C_,F_]:=PC[C]*PD[D]*PF[F,C,D];
F2[H_,E_,F_]:=PH[H,E,F];F3[F_,E_,C_]:=1;
F4[C_,B_,E_]:=PE[E,B,C];F5[B_,A_]:=PA[A]*PB[B,A];

(* Messages *)
L02[E_]:=Sum[F0[G,E],{G,u0[6],u1[6]}];
L13[C_,F_]:=Sum[F1[D,C,F],{D,u0[3],u1[3]}];
L23[E_,F_]:=Sum[F2[H,E,F]*L02[E],{H,u0[7],u1[7]}];
L34[E_,C_]:=Sum[F3[F,E,C]*L13[C,F]*L23[E,F],{F,u0[5],u1[5]}];
L45[B_]:=Sum[F4[C,B,E]*L34[E,C],{C,u0[2],u1[2]},{E,u0[4],u1[4]}];
L54[B_]:=Sum[F5[B,A],{A,u0[0],u1[0]}];
L43[E_,C_]:=Sum[F4[C,B,E]*L54[B],{B,u0[1],u1[1]}];
L31[C_,F_]:=Sum[F3[F,E,C]*L23[E,F]*L43[E,C],{E,u0[4],u1[4]}];
L32[E_,F_]:=Sum[F3[F,E,C]*L13[C,F]*L43[E,C],{C,u0[2],u1[2]}];
L20[E_]:=Sum[F2[H,E,F]*L32[E,F],{H,u0[7],u1[7]},{F,u0[5],u1[5]}];

(* Cluster and Node Marginals *)
Q0[G_,E_]:=F0[G,E]*L20[E];Q1[D_,C_,F_]:=F1[D,C,F]*L31[C,F];
Q2[H_,E_,F_]:=F2[H,E,F]*L02[E]*L32[E,F];
Q3[F_,E_,C_]:=F3[F,E,C]*L13[C,F]*L23[E,F]*L43[E,C];
Q4[C_,B_,E_]:=F4[C,B,E]*L34[E,C]*L54[B];Q5[B_,A_]:=F5[B,A]*L45[B];
M[0,A_]:=Sum[Q5[B,A],{B,u0[1],u1[1]}];M[1,B_]:=Sum[Q5[B,A],{A,u0[0],u1[0]}];
M[2,C_]:=Sum[Q4[C,B,E],{B,u0[1],u1[1]},{E,u0[4],u1[4]}];
M[3,D_]:=Sum[Q1[D,C,F],{C,u0[2],u1[2]},{F,u0[5],u1[5]}];
M[4,E_]:=Sum[Q0[G,E],{G,u0[6],u1[6]}];M[6,G_]:=Sum[Q0[G,E],{E,u0[4],u1[4]}];
M[5,F_]:=Sum[Q3[F,E,C],{E,u0[4],u1[4]},{C,u0[2],u1[2]}];
M[7,H_]:=Sum[Q2[H,E,F],{E,u0[4],u1[4]},{F,u0[5],u1[5]}];

(* Normalizations *)
Do[sumConst=Chop[Simplify[Sum[M[i,t],{t,u0[i],u1[i]}]]];Do[R[i,t]:=
Simplify[Chop[M[i,t]]/sumConst];Print["P(Node",i,"=",t,")=",R[i,t]],
{t,u0[i],u1[i]}];Print[" "],{i,0,7}]
```

Fig. 2. Mathematica statements for symbolic propagation of evidence.

Tables 2 and 3 can then be used to answer all queries regarding initial or evidential marginal probabilities associated with the network in Example 1 simply by plugging in specific values for the parameters.

We note that the symbolic part of computations increases exponentially with the number of parameters but not with the number of nodes.

5 Algebraic Structure of Probabilities

In this section we discuss the algebraic structure of probabilities of single nodes. We start with the prior and later we analyze the case of posterior probabilities.

Theorem 1. *The prior probability of any instantiation is a polynomial in the parameters of degree less than or equal to the minimum of the number of parameters or nodes. However, it is a first degree polynomial in each parameter.*

Proof. According to (1) the probability of an instantiation $(x_1, \ldots, x_n)$ is

$$\prod_{i=1}^{n} P(x_i|\pi_i),$$

that is, a product of n factors. Each factor is either θ_{ijk}, if $x_i < r_i$ or

$$1 - \sum_{k=1}^{r_i-1} \theta_{ijk},$$

if $x_i = r_i$ (see (3)), that is, a parameter or a first degree polynomial in some parameters.

In addition, each parameter appears at most in one factor and dependent parameters, such as θ_{ijk_1} and θ_{ijk_2}, do not appear in the same factor. Thus, we get a polynomial of degree less than or equal to the minimum of the number of parameters or nodes, which is first degree in each parameter. □

Corollary 2. *The prior node marginals are polynomials in the parameters of the same form.*

Proof. The prior marginals of any node are the sum of the probabilities of a subset of instantiations. □

It is well-known from probability theory, that after some evidence is available, the joint probability of the remaining nodes is proportional to (1) with the evidential nodes instantiated to their evidence values. Thus, while Equation (1) gives the true (normalized) joint probability of nodes, instantiation of the evidential variables in (1) leads to the unnormalized joint probability of the remaining nodes. Thus, the same methods can be used for prior and posterior probabilities, the only difference being that in the later case the normalization constant must be determined. However, this constant is common to the joint and to any of the possible marginal probabilities. Thus, we have the following corollary.

Corollary 3. *The posterior node marginals, i.e., the node marginals given some evidence $\mathcal{E}$, are rational functions of the parameters, that is, quotient of polynomials in the parameters of the same form. The denominator polynomial is the same for all nodes.*

Proof. When normalizing probabilities we divide by their sum, that is, by a polynomial of the same form; then, the rational functions arise. □

Because the denominator polynomial is the same for any of the possible marginals, for implementation purposes, it is more convenient to calculate and store all the numerator polynomials for each node and calculate and store the common denominator polynomial separately.

It is interesting to know the total number of monomials involved. This is given by the following theorem.

Theorem 4. *The total number of monomials is given by*

$$\prod_{i=1}^{n}(1+s_i), \tag{8}$$

where s_i is the number of parameters θ_{ijk}, i.e., those related to node i.

Proof. Each monomial is generated from n factors, each associated with a given node. Each factor can be a constant value or one of the parameters. □

Corollary 5. *The maximum number of monomials is given by*

$$\prod_{i=1}^{n}[1+q_i(r_i-1)]. \tag{9}$$

Proof. The maximum number of parameters related to node i is $q_i(r_i-1)$ and using (8), (9) holds. □

Once we know the structure of the marginal probabilities we can exploit it to obtain symbolic results using numerical procedures, as follows.

6 Symbolic Propagation and Numeric Methods

In this section we show how symbolic propagation can be performed using numeric methods. This has special importance for large networks. Consider the network in Example 1 and assume that we want to know the influence of the parameters p_0 and p_1 on the conditional probabilities of the remaining nodes given the evidence $\{D=0, E=0\}$. Then, for any node i we know that the unnormalized marginal probability $p^*_{ik}(p_0,p_1)$ is a polynomial of the form

$$P(X_i=k|D=0,E=0)=a_{ik}+b_{ik}p_0+c_{ik}p_1+d_{ik}p_0p_1=p^*_{ik}(p_0,p_1). \tag{10}$$

Choosing $C = \{(0,0),(0,1),(1,0),(1,1)\}$, which is the so-called *canonical component* set, we get the system of equations

$$\begin{pmatrix} 1\,0\,0\,0 \\ 1\,1\,0\,0 \\ 1\,0\,1\,0 \\ 1\,1\,1\,1 \end{pmatrix} \begin{pmatrix} a_{ik} \\ c_{ik} \\ b_{ik} \\ d_{ik} \end{pmatrix} = \begin{pmatrix} p^*_{ik}(0,0) \\ p^*_{ik}(0,1) \\ p^*_{ik}(1,0) \\ p^*_{ik}(1,1) \end{pmatrix}, \tag{11}$$

from which the polynomial coefficients can be calculated.

In fact, we can use any set of (p_0, p_1), normalized or unnormalized, values such that the leading matrix in (11) becomes non-singular. We use the fact that our probability can be written as a linear convex combination of a given generating set of probabilities (the canonical probabilities), i.e., it belongs to the convex hull generated by them.

Adding the unnormalized probabilities of any node we get the normalization polynomial (common denominator). Note that with this method we can deal with symbolic propagation using numeric programs. Note also that exact and approximate numeric algorithms can be used.

6.1 Computing Canonical Components

When propagating uncertainty in the canonical cases we can save many calculations because some messages are common to all of them. Fig. 3 shows all the clique messages indicated by arrows. We can distinguish three types of messages:

1. Messages with no index. These are common messages that need to be calculated only once.
2. Messages with only one index D or E. These messages depend on the parameters associated with the index node and then we must calculate as many different messages as the number of monomials associated with it.
3. Messages with two indices D and E. These messages depend on the parameters associated with nodes D and E and then we must calculate as many different messages as the number of monomials associated with them.

We can build the rational function associated with the node marginals based only on numeric calculations. Thus, we have a numeric method that efficiently solves the symbolic problem.

7 Symbolic Treatment of Random Evidence

Until now we have dealt with deterministic evidence. In this section we deal with random evidence. Let $Q_{e_1,\ldots,e_k}(x_i)$ denote the marginal of node X_i when the evidence nodes take values $e_1,\ldots,e_k$, where k is the cardinality of $\mathcal{E}$. If we assume a lottery $q(e_1,\ldots,e_k)$, that is, a probability over $\mathcal{E}$, then the marginal of node X_i becomes

$$P_q(x_i) = \sum_{e_1,\ldots,e_k} q(e_1,\ldots,e_k) Q_{e_1,\ldots,e_k}(x_i); \quad \sum_{e_1,\ldots,e_k} q(e_1,\ldots,e_k) = 1. \tag{12}$$

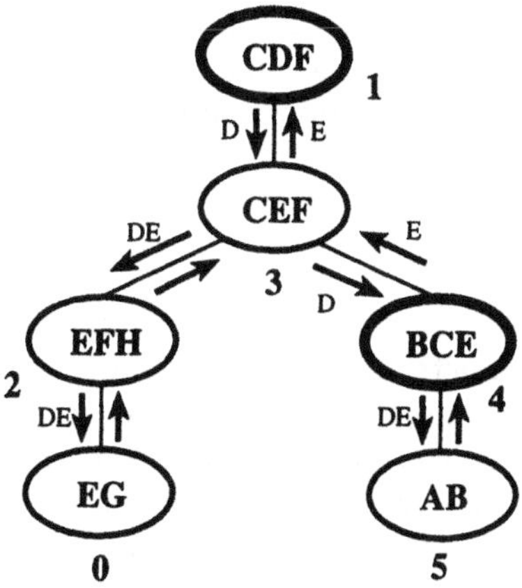

Fig. 3. Clique tree and messages affected by the parameters in nodes D and E. Cliques involving potential functions depending on parameters p_0 and p_1 are outlined.

It is important to note that $P_q(x_i)$ is also a rational function because it is a linear convex combination of the rational functions $Q_{e_1,\ldots,e_k}(x_i)$. However, in this case the conditional probability table parameters can appear with exponents larger than one, which implies polynomial of order larger than one in each of the parameters. The following theorem states this result.

Theorem 6. *The probabilities of the nodes given a random evidence are rational functions where the degree in each parameter of the polynomials involved is at most the sum of the cardinalities of the evidential nodes.*

Proof. The polynomial denominators of the rational functions $Q_{e_1,\ldots,e_k}(x_i)$ are in general different for different combinations of the evidence set $(e_1,\ldots,e_k)$. Thus, reduction to common denominator to get the rational function (12) implies their product and then the result. □

As an example, the probabilities of node $C = 0$ for the random evidence $P(F = 0) = a$ is given by

$$a\ P(C=0|F=0)+(1-a)\ P(C=0|F=1) = \frac{2(3p_1^2+40ap_1-8p_1-20a-28)}{3p_1^2+22p_1-168}.$$

8 Upper and Lower Bounds for Probabilities

Symbolic expressions, such as those in Tables 2 and 3, can also be used to obtain upper and lower bounds for the marginal probabilities which is a valuable information. This can be easily done by considering non-informative $\{0, 1\}$ bounds or other bounds given by experts. Using a theorem given by Bela-Martos (see [8]) it is immediate to see that upper and lower bounds are attained at one of the canonical components (vertices of the feasible convex parameter set). As an example, from Table 2 the maximum and minimum values for the initial probabilities of node $H = 0$ are attained in the set $\{0.372, 0.36, 0.3704, 0.3596\}$.

9 Conclusions

The symbolic structure of prior and posterior marginal probabilities of Bayesian networks have been characterized as polynomials or rational functions of the parameters, respectively, and the degrees of the polynomials have been shown to be dependent on the deterministic or random character of evidence. This characterization allows the symbolic propagation of evidence to be converted to a numeric problem using the canonical components, leading to an important saving in computation. An extra saving is obtained by identifying those messages which are common for all or some canonical components. These components are also shown to attain upper and lower bounds for the probabilities.

Acknowledgements

We thank the University of Cantabria and Dirección General de Investigación Científica y Técnica (DGICYT) (project PB92-0504), for support of this work.

References

1. Pearl, J.: Fusion, Propagation and Structuring in Belief Networks. Artificial Intelligence, **29** (1986) 241–288
2. Pearl, J.: Evidential Reasoning Using Stochastic Simulation of Causal Models. Artificial Intelligence, **32** (9186) 245– 287
3. Lauritzen, S. L., Spiegelhalter, D. J.: Local Computations with Probabilities on Graphical Structures and Their Application to Expert Systems. Journal of the Royal Statistical Society (B), **50** (1988) 157–224
4. Castillo, E., Alvarez, E.: Experts Systems: Uncertainty and Learning. Computational Mechanics Publications and Elsevier Science. London (1991)
5. Castillo, E., Gutiérrez, J. M., Hadi, A. S.: Modelling Probabilistic Networks Based on Conditional Probabilities. Technical report No. 93-2, (1993) University of Cantabria.
6. Castillo, E., Gutiérrez, J. M., Hadi, A. S.: Expert Systems and Bayesian Networks, to appear.
7. Shachter, R. D., Andersen, S. K., Szolovits, P.: Global Conditioning for Probabilistic Inference in Belief Networks. Proceedings UAI, Morgan Kaufmann Publishers (1994) 514–522.
8. Martos, B.: Hyperbolic programming. Naval Research Logistic Quarterly, **11** (1964) 135–156

From Non-Monotonic Syntax-Based Entailment to Preference-Based Argumentation

Claudette CAYROL

Institut de Recherche en Informatique de Toulouse (I. R. I. T.)
Université Paul Sabatier, 118 route de Narbonne, 31062 Toulouse Cedex (FRANCE)
E-mail: testemal@irit.fr

Abstract. We briefly discuss and compare two frameworks for reasoning with inconsistent belief bases: argumentation systems, based on the construction and selection of acceptable arguments in favor of a conclusion, and syntax-based approaches to non-monotonic entailment, based on the selection of preferred consistent subbases. In the case of a flat belief base (i.e. without any priority between its elements), we show that most of the argument-based inference relations can be exactly restated in the framework of syntax-based entailment. Then, taking advantage of the modelling of prioritized syntax-based entailment, we propose a methodological approach to the integration of preference orderings in argumentation frameworks.

1 Introduction

Reasoning with inconsistent beliefs is a significant problem in Artificial Intelligence. Among the wide variety of formalisms, two promising approaches have recently emerged: argumentation-based reasoning [14,18,17,9,10,11,13] and non-monotonic syntax-based entailment [4,15,16,1,6,7]. On one hand, argumentation is a general principle based on the construction and use of arguments. Due to the inconsistency of the available knowledge, arguments may be constructed in favor of a statement and other arguments may be constructed in favor of the opposite statement. The basic idea is to view reasoning as a process of first constructing arguments in favor of a conclusion, and then selecting the most acceptable of them. The notion of acceptability has been most often defined purely on the basis of other constructible arguments. Other criteria such as specificity [12,17], or explicit priority on the beliefs [2,8,11] may be taken into account for comparing arguments. However, few works have been devoted to preference-based argumentation. On the other hand, non-monotonic syntax-based entailment from an inconsistent belief base can be defined as the combination of a mechanism for generating "preferred" consistent belief subbases, a principle for selecting some of these subbases and the classical inference. Various kinds of "preference" have been considered, from maximality for set-inclusion to preference orderings induced by an underlying stratification of the belief base [1,8,12]. As a selection principle, we usually find the existential one, selecting one of the preferred subbases, or the universal one, selecting all the preferred subbases. An intermediary principle, called argumentative in [2], leads to the following consequence

relations "I conclude ϕ if at least one preferred subbase classically entails ϕ and no preferred subbase classically entails $\neg\phi$".
The topic of this paper is twofold. First, we establish tight relationships between the two methodologies described above. We show that most of the argument-based inference relations can be exactly restated in the framework of syntax-based entailment with appropriate selection principles on maximal consistent subbases. Then, taking advantage of the modelling of prioritized syntax-based entailment, we propose a methodological approach to the integration of preference orderings in argumentation frameworks. Our aim is not to provide one more formalism to reason from inconsistency, but rather to show that a priori independent proposals can be restated in a common framework. The structure of the paper follows the above discussion. We start by successively presenting argument-based inference within argumentation systems and a taxonomy of syntax-based non-monotonic consequence relations.

2 Argument-Based Inference

2.1 Argumentation Systems

Throughout this paper L is a propositional language. $\vdash$ denotes classical entailment. K and E denote sets of formulas of L. K, which may be empty, represents a core of knowledge and is assumed consistent. Contrastedly, formulas of E represent defeasible pieces of knowledge, or beliefs. So K $\cup$ E may be inconsistent. E will be referred to as the *beliefbase*. We introduce the notion of argument in the framework (K, E). A similar definition appears for instance in [17].

Definition1. An *argument* of E is a pair (H, h), where h is a formula of L and H is a subbase of E satisfying: (i) K $\cup$ H is consistent, (ii) K $\cup$ H $\vdash$ h, (iii) H is minimal (no strict subset of H satisfies ii). H is called the *support* and h the *conclusion* of the argument. AR(E) denotes the set of all the arguments of E.

According to [9], an argumentation system is defined given any set of arguments equipped with a binary relation R. The intended meaning of "R(A1, A2)" is "the argument A1 defeats the argument A2". In this paper, we focus on two definitions of "defeat", within the above context where arguments are built from a belief base.

Definition2. (see [10]) (H1, h1) *rebuts* (H2, h2) iff h1 $\equiv$ $\neg$h2. (H1, h1) *undercuts* (H2, h2) iff for some h $\in$ H2, h $\equiv$ $\neg$h1. ($\equiv$ means logical equivalence).

The main approaches which have been developed for reasoning within an argumentation system rely on the idea of differentiating arguments with a notion of acceptability. In the proposal by [10,11] acceptability levels are assigned to arguments on the basis of other constructible arguments. Then, from a taxonomy of acceptability classes, consequence relations are defined. Quite independently, Dung [9] formalized a kind of global acceptability. The set of all the arguments that a rational agent may accept must defend itself against all attacks on it. This leads to the definition of extensions of an argumentation system.

In this section, we apply both methodologies on the same argumentation system.

2.2 Hierarchy of Acceptability Classes

Definition3. (see [10]) AR*(E) denotes the set of arguments of E with an empty support. $AR^+(E)$ denotes the set of arguments of E which are not rebutted by some argument of E. $AR^{++}(E)$ denotes the set of arguments of $AR^+(E)$ (or equivalently of E, as proved in [10]) which are not undercut by some argument of E.

The following inclusions hold between the so-called acceptability classes:

$C4 = AR^*(E) \subseteq C3 = AR^{++}(E) \subseteq C2 = AR^+(E) \subseteq C1 = AR(E)$. (H1, h1) is said more acceptable than (H2, h2) iff there exists a class Ci ($1 \leq i \leq 4$) containing (H1, h1) but not containing (H2, h2). Consequence relations are defined by:

Definition4. (see [10]) ϕ is a *certain* consequence of E ($E \mid\sim_{ce} \phi$) iff AR*(E) contains an argument concluding ϕ. ϕ is a *confirmed* consequence of E ($E \mid\sim_{co} \phi$) iff there exists $H \subseteq E$ with $(H, \phi) \in AR^{++}(E)$. ϕ is a *probable* consequence of E ($E \mid\sim_{pr} \phi$) iff there exists $H \subseteq E$ with $(H, \phi) \in AR^+(E)$. ϕ is a *plausible* consequence of E ($E \mid\sim_{pl} \phi$) iff there exists $H \subseteq E$ with $(H, \phi) \in AR(E)$.

2.3 Stable Extensions

Let (AR, "defeats") denote an argumentation system.

Definitions5. (see [9]) A subset S of AR is *conflict-free* iff there are no two arguments A1, A2 in S such that A1 "defeats" A2. A subset S of AR is a *stable extension* iff S is conflict-free and for each argument A not belonging to S, there exists an argument B in S such that B "defeats" A. In other words, S "defeats" each argument which does not belong to S.

For instance, $AR^+(E)$ is conflict-free in the system (AR(E), "rebuts") and $AR^{++}(E)$ is conflict-free in the system (AR(E), "undercuts"). Intuitively, a stable extension corresponds to a maximal set of "acceptable" arguments for a rational agent.

Now, we consider the argumentation system (AR(E), "undercuts"). Let For(S) denote the set of conclusions of arguments of S and Supp(S) denote the union of the supports of arguments of S. T being a subbase of E, let Arg(T) denote $\{(H, h) \in AR(E) / H \subseteq T\}$. We obtain the following characterization of stable extensions:

Proposition1. In the argumentation system (AR(E), "undercuts"), the stable extensions are exactly the Arg(T), where T is a maximal (for set-inclusion) K-consistent subbase of E. (proof in [5])

3 Syntax-Based Non-Monotonic Entailment

We briefly present another promising framework for reasoning from inconsistency. Then we show that it enables to recover argument-based inference schemas.

3.1 Syntax-Based Non-Monotonic Consequence Relations

First, we emphasize the syntactic status of the belief base: each belief is a distinct piece of information and only beliefs which are explicitely present in the base are taken into account. It departs from the logical point of view where a base is identified with the set of its models. Following [16], it is convenient to see non-monotonic syntax-based entailment as a two-step procedure which first generates and selects preferredconsistent subbases (the "generation mechanism") and then manages these multiple subbases in order to conclude (the "conflict resolution principle"). As preferred subbases, maximal (for set-inclusion) K-consistent subbases, or K-consistent subbases of maximal cardinality may be considered. But, the presence of an ordering on E enables to refine the preference. From now on, we assume that the belief base E is equipped with a complete pre-ordering structure (a priority relation) which is not related to the semantical entailment ordering. Then, the selection of preferred subbases relies upon the definition of aggregation modes which extend the priority ordering (defined on the initial belief base) into a preference relation between subbases. This problem has been already considered in [1], and [8] from a more general point of view on preference-based reasoning.

In this section, Pref will denote a preference relation (partial pre-ordering) on the set of K-consistent subsets of E, as well as the mechanism which produces the associated preferred subbases. As a particular case, T will denote the mechanism which produces the maximal (for set-inclusion) K-consistent subbases of E.

Syntax-based non-monotonic consequence relations are defined by:

Definition6. E $\mid\!\sim^{p,\mathrm{Pref}} \phi$ iff ϕ is inferred from the set of preferred (w.r.t. Pref) subbases of E according to the principle p.

The most commonly encountered conflict resolution principles are:

Cautious, denoted by CAU: ϕ is classically entailed by (the union[1] of K and) the intersection of the preferred subbases. Universal (or skeptical), denoted by UNI: ϕ is classically entailed from *each* preferred subbase. Existential (or credulous), denoted by EXI: ϕ is classically entailed from *at least one* preferred subbase.

Since the EXI principle leads to unsafe consequence relations (i.e. pairwise contradictory conclusions may be produced), the so-called Argumentative (denoted by ARG) principle has been considered: ϕ is classically entailed from *at least one* preferred subbase *and* no preferred subbase classically entails $\neg\phi$.

Two other principles were introduced in [16]. AP principle: ϕ is classically entailed from *at least one* consistent subbase S *and* no subbase strictly preferred to S (w.r.t. Pref) classically entails $\neg\phi$. SAP principle (safe counterpart of AP): ϕ is classically entailed from *at least one* consistent subbase S *and* S is strictly preferred (w.r.t. Pref) to any consistent subbase which classically entails $\neg\phi$.

A taxonomy of these principles (except CAU) according to cautiousness[2] has been proposed in [16] (see Figure1). Other works considered consequence relations of the form E $\mid\!\sim^{p,\mathrm{Pref}} \phi$. Logical properties of $\mid\!\sim^{\mathrm{CAU,T}}$, $\mid\!\sim^{\mathrm{UNI,T}}$, $\mid\!\sim^{\mathrm{EXI,T}}$ have been studied in [3]. Besides, note that $\mid\!\sim^{\mathrm{CAU,T}}$ exactly corresponds to the Free consequence of [2]. A thorough discussion of $\mid\!\sim^{\mathrm{UNI,Pref}}$ can be found in [1], with different preference relations. A comparative study of $\mid\!\sim^{p,\mathrm{Pref}}$ consequence relations has been recently proposed in [6,7], according to three points of view: The computational

---

[1] From now on, K is assumed empty. However, all the results hold in the general case.

[2] Given two consequence relations R1 and R2, R1 is said more cautious than R2 iff every conclusion obtained by R1 is also obtained by R2.

complexity, the cautiousness and the validity of deduction rules. The comparison concerns the EXI, UNI, ARG principles and four preference relations.

3.2 Argument-Based Inference as Syntax-Based Entailment

Here, we do not take into account the pre-ordering structure on E (if any). Tight relationships can be established between the argument-based inference schemas presented in section2 (namely the consequence relations of Definition4) and the syntax-based consequence relations of the form $\vdash^{P,T}$. More precisely, we obtain the following characterizations, pictured on Figure1 (proofs in [5]):

Proposition2.

ϕ is a *plausible* consequence of E ($E \mid\!\sim_{pl} \phi$) iff $E \vdash^{EXI,T} \phi$ iff there exists at least one stable extension S of (AR(E), "undercuts") such that $\phi \in$ For(S).

ϕ is a *probable* consequence of E ($E \mid\!\sim_{pr} \phi$) iff $E \vdash^{ARG,T} \phi$ iff there exists at least one stable extension S of (AR(E), "undercuts") such that $\phi \in$ For(S) and no stable extension S' such that $\neg\phi \in$ For(S').

ϕ is a *confirmed* consequence of E ($E \mid\!\sim_{co} \phi$) iff $E \vdash^{CAU,T} \phi$ iff there exists an argument (H, ϕ) which belongs to *each* stable extension of (AR(E), "undercuts").

4 Preference-Based Argumentation

As mentioned in the introduction, our purpose is now to take advantage of the above results in order to propose a methodological approach to the integration of preference orderings in argumentation frameworks. Following the methodology used in section3, we distinguish two problems: the definition of preference relations in order to compare conflicting arguments and the specification of principles which take into account these preference relations in order to select acceptable arguments.

The first problem is not the topic of this paper. We just mention some references to preliminary work on the subject. The notion of specificity [12,17], which is syntactically extracted from the belief base, is a first way of comparing conflicting arguments. Taking into account certainty degrees on the beliefs leads to define certainty levels for arguments [2]. Other preference relations can be aggregated from an underlying priority ordering on the belief base [8,11].

Let *APref* denote a preference relation available for comparing arguments of AR(E). For instance, if *Pref* denotes a partial pre-ordering on consistent subsets of E, we may define "(H1, h1) is preferred to (H2, h2) w.r.t. *APref*" by "H1 is better than H2 w.r.t. *Pref*". Again, we assume that K is empty. Our discussion will be organized around an argumentative principle analogous to the principle called SAP in section3.

4.1 Argument-Based Inference Through SAP-Principle

Definition7. $E \mid\!\sim_{APref} \phi$ iff there exists (H, ϕ) in AR(E) which is strictly preferred (w.r.t. *APref*) to any argument concluding $\neg\phi$.

It is easy to show that $\mid\!\sim_{APref}$ is less cautious than $\vdash^{ARG,T}$ but remains safe and is more cautious than $\vdash^{EXI,T}$.

Proposition3. When the preference *APref* between arguments is defined from a preference *Pref* between the supports, and if the relation *Pref* respects minimality for set-inclusion, (i.e. a consistent subbase S of E is preferred to each consistent subbase which contains S), then E $|\sim_{APref}$ ϕ iff ϕ is inferred through the SAP principle of section3.

Now, we prove that the argumentative consequence proposed by [2] in the context of possibilistic logic can be viewed as an illustration of Proposition3. Indeed, in [2], the belief base is stratified $E = E1 \cup E2 \cup \ldots \cup En$, such that beliefs in Ei have the same level of certainty, and are more reliable than beliefs in Ej where j>i. The level of a non-empty consistent subbase S is defined as level(S) = min $\{j \mid Sj+1 \cup \ldots \cup Sn = \emptyset\}$, where Si denotes $S \cap Ei$. Then, the relation defined by "a subbase S is better than S' iff level(S) $\leq$ level(S')" is a total pre-ordering which respects minimality for set-inclusion. This total pre-ordering induces a preference between conflicting arguments such that: ϕ is an argumentative consequence of E iff there is an argument for ϕ which is strictly preferred to each argument for $\neg\phi$.

4.2 Argumentation Systems and Preference

Another way of combining preference and argumentation is to account for preference in the argumentation system itself, either in the definition of the acceptability classes, or even in the definition of the relation "defeats". We successively consider both approaches. Following definition3, we define two new acceptability classes:

Definition8. $AR^{+}_{Pref}(E)$ denotes the set of arguments of E which are strictly preferred (w.r.t. *APref*) to each rebutting argument. $AR^{++}_{Pref}(E)$ denotes the set of arguments of E which are strictly preferred to each undercutting argument.

A similar definition for $AR^{+}_{Pref}(E)$ appears in [11] with a preference relation induced by a pre-ordering on the supports which does not respect minimality for set-inclusion. The following inclusions hold: $AR^{+}(E) \subseteq AR^{+}_{Pref}(E) \subseteq AR(E)$ and $AR^{++}(E) \subseteq AR^{++}_{Pref}(E) \subseteq AR(E)$. However, in the general case, no inclusion holds between $AR^{++}_{Pref}(E)$ and $AR^{+}_{Pref}(E)$.

Proposition4. The consequence relation induced by the class AR+Pref(E) exactly corresponds to the relation $|\sim_{APref}$ of Definition7.

Indeed, there exists $H \subseteq E$ with $(H, \phi) \in AR^{+}_{Pref}(E)$ iff there exists (H, ϕ) in AR(E) which is strictly preferred (w.r.t. *APref*) to any argument concluding $\neg\phi$.

As a consequence, we obtain a characterization of the SAP principle in terms of classes of arguments, when the relation *APref* is defined from a preference on the supports which respects minimality for set-inclusion.

Preference orderings may be also used to provide new definitions of the relation "defeats", while keeping the same construction for acceptability classes. For instance, once again, the relation $|\sim_{APref}$ of Definition7 is recovered if we consider the relation "conflicts" of [13]. An argument A concluding $\neg\phi$ *conflicts with* an argument B concluding ϕ iff B is not strictly preferred to A. Then, E $|\sim_{APref}$ ϕ iff there exists (H, ϕ) in AR(E) such that no argument conflicts with (H, ϕ). In the framework of conditional entailment, Geffner [12] proposed to define "A *defeats* B" iff A contains a subargument preferred than B and rebutting B. However, the consequence relation associated with the class of arguments which are never defeated is less cautious than

$|\sim_{APref}$. Following [17], another definition may be given: (H1, h1) *defeats* (H2, h2) iff there exists a subargument of (H2, h2) which rebuts (H1, h1) and is not strictly preferred to (H1,h1). Then, let $A_{SL}(E)$ denote the set of arguments which are not defeated by some argument of E. The following inclusions hold (proof in [5]): $AR^{++}(E) \subseteq A_{SL}(E) \subseteq AR^{+}_{Pref}(E)$. Indeed, (H, h) belongs to $A_{SL}(E)$ iff each subargument of (H, h) belongs to $AR^{+}_{Pref}(E)$.
All the results of this section are summarized in the figure below:

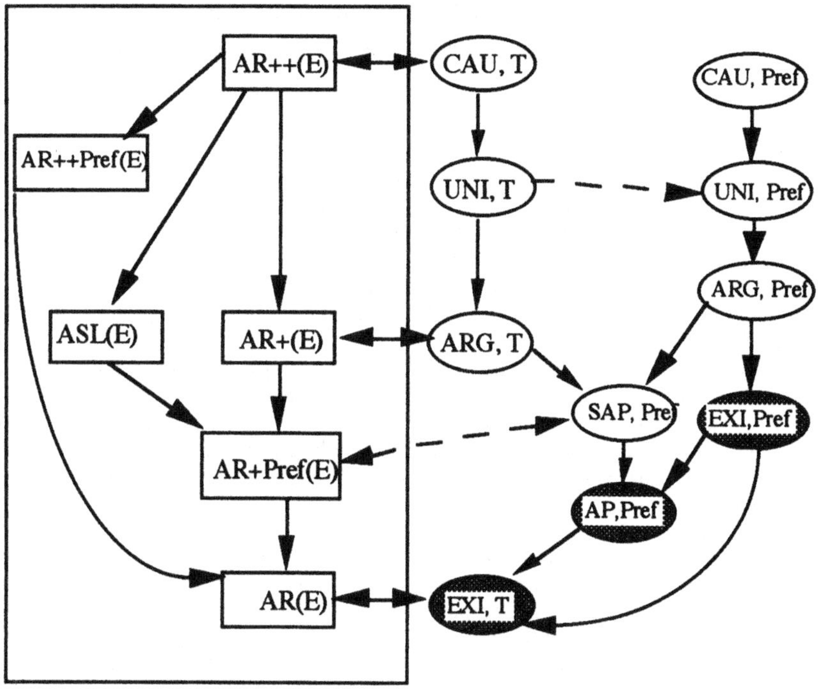

Fig. 1 A consequence relation is represented by the associated principle p and generation mechanism Pref and is simply denoted by the pair (p, Pref).
In the right part of the figure: The arrow means "more cautious than". Shaded relations are unsafe. The relation between UNI,T and UNI,Pref (dotted arrow) holds if the preference respects maximality for set-inclusion.
For each of the relations (CAU,T), (ARG,T), (EXI,T), (SAP,Pref), we find the corresponding acceptability class of arguments. The correspondence showed by the dotted arrow holds if the preference between arguments is induced by a relation Pref between subbases which respects minimality for set-inclusion. In the framed part of the figure, the vertical arrow means "is included in".

5 Conclusion

We think that the work reported here contributes to a better understanding of the fundamental mechanisms of defeasible reasoning. We have outlined the similarity of the paradigms of syntax-based entailment and argumentation: Each one may be viewed as a two-step process which first generates either consistent belief subbases or arguments and then selects preferred or most acceptable of them. An exact correspondence between inference operations has been established in the case of a flat belief base. Taking advantage of this result and of recent work on prioritized syntax-based entailment, we have proposed some principles for integrating preference orderings in the selection of arguments. However much work must be devoted to the definition of preference orderings for comparing arguments, and more particularly conflicting arguments. There is a need for aggregation modes for combining implicit priority such as specificity with explicit priority expressed on the beliefs. Once this problem has been investigated, it will be interesting to study the logical properties of the argument-based consequence relations, as it has been done for non-monotonic syntax-based inference relations.

6 References

1. S. Benferhat, C. Cayrol, D. Dubois, J. Lang, H. Prade. Inconsistency management and prioritized syntax-based entailment. IJCAI'93, 640-645.

2. S. Benferhat, D. Dubois, H. Prade. Argumentative Inference in Uncertain and Inconsistent Knowledge Bases. UAI'93, 411-419.

3. S. Brass. On the semantics of supernormal defaults. IJCAI'93, 578-583.

4. G. Brewka. Preferred subtheories: An extended logical framework for default reasoning. IJCAI'89, 1043-1048 .

5. C. Cayrol. Reasoning from inconsistent belief bases: On the relation between Argumentation and Coherence-Based Non-monotonic Entailment. Research Report IRIT, n° 95/09/R, April 1995.

6. C. Cayrol, M.C. Lagasquie-Schiex. On the complexity of non-monotonic entailment in syntax-based approaches. Proc. ECAI-94 Workshop on Algorithms, Complexity and Commonsense Reasoning.

7. C. Cayrol, M.C. Lagasquie-Schiex. Non-monotonic Syntax-Based Entailment: A Classification of Consequence Relations. ECSQARU'95, in this volume.

8. C. Cayrol, V. Royer, C. Saurel. Management of preferences in Assumption-Based Reasoning. In: Lecture Notes in Computer Science (B. Bouchon-Meunier, L. Valverde, R.Y. Yager Eds.), Springer Verlag, Vol. 682, 13-22, 1993.

9. P.M. Dung. On the acceptability of arguments and its fundamental role in non-monotonic reasoning and logic programming. IJCAI'93, 852-857.

10. M. Elvang-Goransson, J. Fox, P. Krause. Acceptability of arguments as "logical uncertainty". Proc. ECSQARU'93, Lecture Notes in Computer Science (Springer Verlag ed.), Vol. 747, 85-90, 1993.

11. M. Elvang-Goransson, J. Fox, P. Krause. Dialectic reasoning with inconsistent information. UAI'93, 114-121.

12. H. Geffner. Default Reasoning: Causal and Conditional Theories. MIT Press, 1992.

13. A. Hunter. Defeasible reasoning with structured information. KR'94, 281-292.

14. F. Lin, Y. Shoham. Argument Systems: An uniform basis for non-monotonic reasoning. KR'89, 245-255.

15. B. Nebel. Belief revision and Default Reasoning: Syntax-based approaches. KR'91, 417-428.

16. G. Pinkas, R.P. Loui. Reasoning from inconsistency: a taxonomy of principles for resolving conflicts. KR'92, 709-719.

17. G.R. Simari, R.P. Loui. A mathematical treatment of defeasible reasoning and its implementation. Artificial Intelligence, 53, 125-157, 1992.

18. G. Vreeswijk. The feasibility of Defeat in Defeasible Reasoning. KR'91, 526-534.

Non-monotonic Syntax-Based Entailment: A Classification of Consequence Relations

Claudette Cayrol and Marie-Christine Lagasquie-Schiex

Institut de Recherche en Informatique de Toulouse
118 route de Narbonne 31062 Toulouse Cedex
France
e-mail: {testemal, lagasq}@irit.fr

Abstract. The purpose of this paper is to provide a comparative study of non-monotonic syntax-based consequence relations, from different points of view. Starting from a (not necessarily consistent) belief base E and a pre-ordering on E, we first remind different mechanisms for selecting preferred consistent subbases in syntax-based approaches. Then, we present three entailment principles in order to cope with these multiple subbases. The crossing point of each generation mechanism and each principle defines a syntax-based consequence relation. Pursuing previous work of the authors concerning the computational complexity point of view, we first provide a comparison from the cautiousness point of view. Our proposal restates previous results [18] in a single framework and provides new results. In the last part of this paper, we study the validity of deduction rules (such as those introduced by [15, 12]). Results are discussed in the conclusion.

1 Introduction

In this paper, we focus on syntactic approaches to non-monotonic inference. We assume that a set of formulae E (the belief base) is equipped with a complete pre-ordering structure (a priority relation) which, contrarily to [12], is not related to the semantical entailment ordering. Following [18], it is convenient to see non-monotonic syntax-based entailment as a two-step procedure which first generates and selects preferred consistent subbases (the "generation mechanism") and then manages these multiple subbases in order to conclude (the "conflict resolution principle"). For instance, the kind of inference "E infers Φ iff Φ is classically inferred in all the preferred consistent subbases of E" has been extensively considered in [2], with several meanings given to the term "preferred". A taxonomy of conflict resolution principles, according to cautiousness, can be found in [18]. The selection of preferred subbases relies upon the definition of aggregation modes which enable to extend the priority ordering (defined on the initial belief base) into a preference relation (between subbases). This problem has been already considered in [2, 9] from a more general point of view on preference-based reasoning.

In the framework described above, our purpose is to propose a comparative study of various syntax-based consequence relations, from different points of view. We have extensively studied the computational complexity of these relations (see [8]). Here, we first recall the three mechanisms for selecting preferred consistent subbases and the three conflict resolution principles, which were used to define the considered syntax-based consequence relations. Then, we provide a comparison from the cautiousness point of view. Our proposal restates previous results [18] in a single framework and provides new results. In the third part of this paper, we study the validity of deduction rules (such as those introduced by [15, 12]). Results are discussed in the conclusion.

2 Syntax-Based Consequence Relations

Throughout the paper, E denotes a non-empty finite set of propositional formulae and is referred to as the *belief base*. The belief base is considered syntactically, as in [17]: each belief is a distinct piece of information and only beliefs which are explicitely present in the base are taken into account. It departs from the logical point of view where a base is identified with the set of its models. Due to the belief status of its elements, E is not assumed to be consistent. Moreover, we assume that E is equipped with a complete pre-ordering $\leq$ (a priority relation), which modelizes an epistemic relevance ordering. It is equivalent to consider that E is stratified in a collection $(E_1, \ldots, E_n)$ of belief bases, where E_1 contains the formulae of highest priority (or relevance) and E_n those of lowest priority. The pair $(E, \leq)$ is called a *prioritized* (or *stratified*) belief base[1]. Each E_i is called a *stratum* of E. In the literature on non-monotonic inference, the most usual proposal for handling inconsistency is to work with maximal (w.r.t. set-inclusion) consistent subbases of E. Different approaches have been proposed to use the priority relation in order to select "preferred" consistent subbases (see [8] for a survey). For the purpose of our comparative study, we focus on three preference relations: the best-out preference which has been related to possibilistic inference, the inclusion-based preference which combines priorities and maximal consistent subbases and the lexicographic preference which combines priorities and subbases of maximal cardinality.

Definition 1 *Let $X = (X_1 \cup \ldots \cup X_n)$ and $Y = (Y_1 \cup \ldots \cup Y_n)$ be two consistent subbases of E (where $X_i = (X \cap E_i)$ and $Y_i = (Y \cap E_i)$), we define:*

- *best-out preference (see [2]): let X be a consistent subbase of E and $a(X) = \min \{i \mid \exists \Phi \in E_i \setminus X\}$. The best-out preference is the complete pre-ordering defined by $X \ll^{bo} Y$ iff $a(X) \leq a(Y)$[2] ; we say that Y is bo-preferred than X.*
- *inclusion-based preference (see [9] and [13] for equivalent definitions): this is the strict partial ordering defined by $X \ll^{incl} Y$ iff $\exists i \mid X_i \subset Y_i$ and $\forall j \mid 1 \leq j < i$, $X_j = Y_j$; we say that Y is incl-preferred than X.*
- *lexicographic preference (see [16, 2]): this is the strict ordering defined by $X \ll^{lex} Y$ iff $\exists i \mid |X_i| < |Y_i|$ and $\forall j \mid 1 \leq j < i$, $|X_j| = |Y_j|$ ($|Y|$ denotes the cardinality of Y) ; we say that Y is lex-preferred than X[3].*

---

[1] In the following, the underlying pre-ordering will be omitted and a prioritized belief base will be denoted by E. The case of a flat belief base (*i.e.*, all the formulae are equally important) is a particular case.

[2] This ordering depends only on the most prioritary stratum where at least one formula has been removed in order to restore consistency.

[3] The lexicographic pre-ordering is complete. For any subbases X and Y of E, either $X \equiv^{lex} Y$ (*i.e.*, $|X_i| = |Y_i|$ for $i = 1 \ldots n$) or one of them is lex-preferred to the other one ($X \ll^{lex} Y$ or $Y \ll^{lex} X$).

The best-out preference is not very selective since some of the preferred subbases are not maximal for set-inclusion. Indeed, let $amax(E) = \max\ \{i \mid E_1 \cup \ldots \cup E_i$ is consistent$\}$. If $amax(E) = k$, then the best-out preferred consistent subbases of E are exactly the consistent subbases of E which contain $(E_1 \cup \ldots \cup E_k)$. The inclusion-based preference refines the set-inclusion in the sense that inclusion-based preferred consistent subbases are maximal consistent subbases. These incl-preferred subbases are of the form $(X_1 \cup \ldots \cup X_n)$ such that $(X_1 \cup \ldots \cup X_i)$ is a maximal-consistent subbase of $(E_1 \cup \ldots \cup E_i)$ for $i = 1 \ldots n$. It follows that incl-preferred subbases are also bo-preferred subbases. Note that incl-preferred consistent subbases are also called preferred sub-theories in [5], and exactly correspond to strongly maximal-consistent subbases in [10]. The lexicographic preference refines the inclusion-based preference. Any lex-preferred consistent subbase of E is an incl-preferred consistent subbase, but the converse is false.

As mentioned in the introduction of this paper, non-monotonic entailment from a given belief base can be viewed as a two-step procedure which first generates "preferred" belief states, and then manages these different belief states according to cautiousness principles. In the following, we call T (resp. INCL, LEX, BO) the mechanism which produces the set of maximal (resp. incl-preferred, lex-preferred, bo-preferred) consistent subbases of E. The two main entailment principles activated in presence of multiple conflicting belief states are the skeptical and credulous principles. A taxonomy of numerous entailment principles has been established by Pinkas and Loui [18] according to their cautiousness. Here, we focus on three of them.

Definition 2 *Let $m(E)$ denote a set of consistent subbases of E. For instance, $m(E)$ may be obtained with one of the mechanisms T, INCL, LEX or BO. Let Φ be a propositional formula. We define:*

- *UNI principle: Φ is inferred from $m(E)$ according to the skeptical (or universal) entailment principle iff Φ is classically inferred from each element of $m(E)$.*
- *EXI principle: Φ is inferred from $m(E)$ according to the credulous (or existential) entailment principle iff Φ is classically inferred from at least one element of $m(E)$*[4].
- *ARG principle: this intermediary principle consists in keeping only the credulous consequences whose negation cannot be inferred (see [3] for a discussion on the so-called argumentative inference). Φ is inferred from $m(E)$ according to the argumentative entailment principle iff Φ is classically inferred from at least one element of $m(E)$ and no element of $m(E)$ classically entails $\neg\Phi$.*

We are now ready to give a precise definition of syntax-based consequence relations generated by a prioritized belief base. Each one appears at the crossing point of a belief state generation mechanism m and an entailment principle p.

Definition 3 *Let E be a prioritized belief base and Φ a propositional formula. $E \mid\!\sim^{p,m} \Phi$ iff Φ is inferred from $m(E)$ according to the principle p ; $m(E)$ denotes the set of consistent subbases of E which are preferred for the mechanism m.*

---

[4] Obviously, each conclusion inferred from $m(E)$ by UNI principle is also obtained by EXI principle.

For our comparative study, m belongs to {T, INCL, LEX, BO} and p belongs to {UNI, EXI, ARG}. More generally, we will consider non-monotonic consequence relations of the form "Φ is inferred from Ψ with respect to E".

Following previous works on the relationship between non-monotonic inference and belief revision [17, 12], we define:

Definition 4 *$\Psi \mid\!\sim_E^{p,m} \Phi$ iff $\Psi \oplus E \mid\!\sim^{p,m} \Phi$, where $\Psi \oplus E$ denotes the prioritized belief base obtained from E by adding $\{\Psi\}$ as first stratum. More precisely, if E is stratified into $(E_1, \ldots, E_n)$, then $\Psi \oplus E = (E_0 = \{\Psi\}, E_1, \ldots, E_n)$ and if E is a flat belief base, then $\Psi \oplus E = (E_0 = \{\Psi\}, E)$.*

3 The Cautiousness Ordering

In this section, we compare syntax-based consequence relations generated by a belief base, from the point of view of cautiousness [18]. Given two consequence relations R_1 and R_2, R_1 is said more cautious than R_2 iff every conclusion obtained by R_1 is also obtained by R_2. Results have already been obtained for some of the relations considered in section 2. Our proposal restates these previous results in a single framework and provides new results (proofs are in [7]). We obtain the taxonomy depicted in Figure 1.

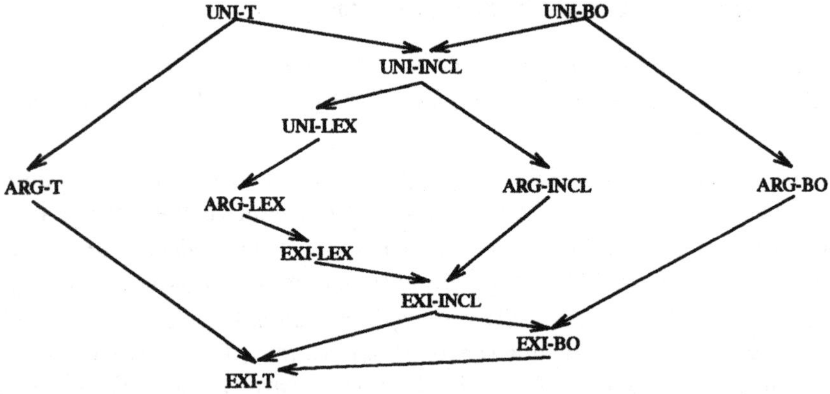

Fig. 1. Cautiousness ordering. A syntax-based consequence relation is represented by the associated selection principle p and generation mechanism m and is simply denoted by the pair p-m. The arrow means "more cautious than".

Remarks about previous works: The taxonomy proposed in [18] contains other selection principles (than EXI, ARG and UNI) but does not specify the generation mechanism. We propose a refinement since the relationships we establish concern four specified generation mechanisms. Brass [4] compared four selection principles (including EXI and UNI) on the particular case of the INCL mechanism and a belief base stratified in two levels, the first one being consistent. A comparison of $\mid\!\sim^{\text{UNI,T}}$, $\mid\!\sim^{\text{EXI,T}}$, $\mid\!\sim^{\text{ARG,T}}$ can be found in [3]. The relations $\mid\!\sim^{\text{UNI,BO}}$, $\mid\!\sim^{\text{UNI,INCL}}$, and $\mid\!\sim^{\text{UNI,LEX}}$ are thoroughly discussed in [2] but with a different definition. However, both presentations are equivalent due to the following property:

Proposition 1 *Let E be a prioritized belief base and Φ a propositional formula. For each m in $\{BO, INCL, LEX\}$: the m-preferred consistent subbases of $\Psi \oplus E$ are of the form $\{\Psi\} \cup S$, where S is a subbase of E which is m-preferred among the Ψ-consistent subbases of E.*

4 Classification According to Deduction Rules

Much work has been done concerning the characterization of classes of non-monotonic consequence relations by means of logical properties, or deduction rules. The best known classes are:

- the preferential relations defined by the rules of the System P (see [15]): Supraclassicality (SCL), Left Logical Equivalence (LLE), Right Weakening (RW), Cut, Cautious Monotony (CM), Or.
- the rational relations defined by the system P and the Rational Monotony (RM).
- the non-monotonic relations defined by the Basic Postulates (see [12]): Supraclassicality (SCL), Left Logical Equivalence (LLE), Right Weakening (RW), And, Weak Rational Monotony (WRM), Weak Conditionalization (WC), Consistency Preservation (CP).
- the comparative relations defined by the set of Extended Postulates (see [12]): Basic postulates with Cumulativity (CUM)[5], Rational Monotony (RM), Or.

Here, we study the validity of the above deduction rules for the relations considered in definition 4. The mechanism T will not be considered when studying relations of the form $\Psi \mid\!\sim_E^{p,m} \Phi$, since the base $\Psi \oplus E$ is stratified. Let us first recall the previous results on the subject. Brass [4] has proved characterization theorems for $\mid\!\sim^{\mathrm{UNI,INCL}}$ and $\mid\!\sim^{\mathrm{EXI,INCL}}$ in the particular case of a belief base stratified in two levels, the first one being consistent. For instance, $\mid\!\sim^{\mathrm{UNI,INCL}}$ is the more cautious "semantics" for the set of rules REF, RW, AND, OR, LLE, CWA[6]. Two important characterizations can be found in [2]: The set of $\mid\!\sim^{\mathrm{UNI,LEX}}$ relations is exactly the set of comparative inference relations (defined by the extended postulates). The set of $\mid\!\sim^{\mathrm{UNI,INCL}}$ relations strictly contains the set of comparative relations and is strictly included in the set of preferential relations. [1] discusses $\mid\!\sim^{\mathrm{UNI,BO}}$ and the relationship with possibilistic inference. Due to space limitations, we summarize our results in the Table 1. All the proofs are in [7].

5 Conclusions

First of all, we did not consider the semantical point of view but rather an operational point of view. However, the $\mid\!\sim^{\mathrm{UNI},m}$ relations can be given a preferential-models seman-

[5] CUM is a consequence of CUT, CM, LLE, SCL.

[6] A consequence relation R satisfies the rule CWA iff for each Ψ, if the union of all the INCL-preferred subbases of $\Psi \oplus E$ is consistent and entails Φ, then $(\Psi \oplus \mathrm{E})\, R\, \Phi$.

	UNI-BO	UNI-INCL	UNI-LEX	EXI-BO	EXI-INCL	EXI-LEX	ARG-BO	ARG-INCL	ARG-LEX
Kraus, Lehmann and Magidor's systems									
System P									
REF	♦	♦	♦	♦	♦	♦	♦	♦	♦
LLE	♦	♦	♦	♦	♦	♦	♦	♦	♦
RW	♦	♦	♦	♦	♦	♦	♦	♦	♦
CUT	♦	♦	♦	–	–	–	–	–	–
CM	♦	♦	♦	–	–	–	–	–	–
OR	♦	♦	♦	–	–	–	–	–	–
RM	♦	–	♦	♦	♦	♦	–	–	–
Gärdenfors and Makinson's postulates									
Extended Postulates									
Basis Postulates									
SCL	♦	♦	♦	♦	♦	♦	♦	♦	♦
LLE	♦	♦	♦	♦	♦	♦	♦	♦	♦
RW	♦	♦	♦	♦	♦	♦	♦	♦	♦
AND	♦	♦	♦	–	–	–	–	–	–
WRM	♦	–	♦	♦	♦	♦	–	–	–
WC	♦	♦	♦	♦	♦	♦	♦	♦	♦
CP	♦	♦	♦	♦	♦	♦	♦	♦	♦
CUM	♦	♦	♦	–	–	–	–	–	–
RM	♦	–	♦	♦	♦	♦	–	–	–
OR	♦	♦	♦	–	–	–	–	–	–

Table 1. Deduction rules – ♦ (resp. –) = means that the rule is (resp. is not) satisfied

tics (see [2, 15]). More generally, the preference relations defined on consistent subbases of E induce pre-ordering on models (see [2]).

Following [12, 15] approaches to non-monotonic inference leads to prefer the class of $\vdash\!\!\sim^{\mathrm{UNI},m}$ relations, which are the more cautious relations. Hence, it is not surprising that the $\vdash\!\!\sim^{\mathrm{EXI},m}$ and $\vdash\!\!\sim^{\mathrm{ARG},m}$ relations obtain bad results in the Table 1 (because these rules are basically defined for the $\vdash\!\!\sim^{\mathrm{UNI},m}$ relations). The Rational Monotony has been justified by the ability to cope with the problem of irrelevance: If Φ is a plausible consequence of Ψ_1 and if Ψ_2 has nothing to do with Ψ_1, then Φ should be also a plausible consequence of $(\Psi_1 \wedge \Psi_2)$. However, the relation $\vdash\!\!\sim^{\mathrm{UNI,BO}}$ (which satisfies the property of Rational Monotony) suffers from the so-called "drowning effect" [2]: the beliefs which appear below $amax(E)$ are completely ignored by the inference process. Contrastedly, the problem of "drowning effect" is solved with the relations $\vdash\!\!\sim^{\mathrm{UNI,LEX}}$ and $\vdash\!\!\sim^{\mathrm{UNI,INCL}}$ (which rely upon a selection of maximal consistent subbases). However, with $\vdash\!\!\sim^{\mathrm{UNI,INCL}}$ Rational Monotony is lost, while it is recovered with $\vdash\!\!\sim^{\mathrm{UNI,LEX}}$. Besides, the LEX-based approaches are very sensitive to redundance of information, since they rely upon cardinality. They should be probably reserved to specific applications (such as for instance consistency-based approaches to model-based diagnosis).

At the other extremity, the $\mid\!\sim^{\mathrm{EXI},m}$ relations are too permissive. In particular, they may lead to pairs of mutually exclusive conclusions. It seems reasonable to require the property of safety for a relation. A relation is safe if it does not produce pairwise contradictory conclusions. Requiring safety naturally leads to the third class of relations, the $\mid\!\sim^{\mathrm{ARG},m}$ relations.

The $\mid\!\sim^{\mathrm{ARG},m}$ relations are more productive than the $\mid\!\sim^{\mathrm{UNI},m}$ relations, while respecting safety[7]. They are well-suited to applications where the inconsistency of the belief base may be generated by the fusion of different belief bases. In that case, it seems that with the ARG principle, the inference process remains faithful to the contents of the base. That point is illustrated by the following example: $E = E_1 \cup E_2 \cup E_3$ with $E_1 = \{a, b, c, a \rightarrow \neg b\}$, $E_2 = \{a \rightarrow \neg c\}$ and $E_3 = \{a \rightarrow d\}$. The incl-preferred consistent subbases are: $S_1 = \{a, c, a \rightarrow \neg b, a \rightarrow d\}$, $S_2 = \{a, b, c, a \rightarrow d\}$, $S_3 = \{b, c, a \rightarrow \neg b, a \rightarrow \neg c, a \rightarrow d\}$. Only one subbase is lex-preferred: S_3. The conclusion d is inferred by $\mid\!\sim^{\mathrm{ARG,INCL}}$ (but not by $\mid\!\sim^{\mathrm{UNI,INCL}}$). Besides, note that d is not inferred by $\mid\!\sim^{\mathrm{ARG,LEX}}$. Indeed, due to cardinality considerations, the LEX mechanism hides the argument in favor of d. Another example shows that the ARG principle can solve the "drowning effect", even when the mechanism BO is chosen. $E = E_1 \cup E_2 \cup E_3 \cup E_4$ with $E_1 = \{a \rightarrow \neg b\}$, $E_2 = \{a\}$, $E_3 = \{b\}$ and $E_4 = \{c\}$. c is not inferred by $\mid\!\sim^{\mathrm{UNI,BO}}$ but is inferred by $\mid\!\sim^{\mathrm{ARG,BO}}$.

Some directions for further research may be drawn from the above discussion. First, we think that syntax-based inference based on the ARG principle deserves deeper investigation. Promising approaches to defeasible reasoning have been recently proposed in the framework of argumentation (for instance in [19, 11, 14]). Roughly speaking, a conclusion is inferred if the arguments supporting it can be successfully defended against the arguments supporting the opposite statement. In the case of a flat belief base, most of the argument-based inference relations have been restated in the framework of syntax-based entailment described in this paper (see [6] for a report on that topic). The comparison of both methodologies will be extended to stratified belief bases. Another interesting problem is the complete characterization of the so-called irrelevance principle (which is not achieved by the Rational Monotony). More generally, other logical properties should be outlined in order to characterize the $\mid\!\sim^{\mathrm{EXI},m}$ and $\mid\!\sim^{\mathrm{ARG},m}$ relations in counterbalancing the preference for the $\mid\!\sim^{\mathrm{UNI},m}$ relations due to the logical properties of [15, 12].

Our main contribution is a unifying framework which enables to provide:

- a comparative study according to different points of view: computational complexity (previous work), cautiousness, and validity of deduction rules,
- a better understanding of underlying mechanisms and a help for choosing one of the specified mechanisms/principles depending on the pragmatics of the application or on complexity considerations.

---

[7] The price paid for these advantages is an expensive computational complexity.

References

1. Salem Benferhat. *Raisonnement non-monotone et traitement de l'inconsistance en logique possibiliste*. PhD thesis, UPS-IRIT. France, February 1994.
2. Salem Benferhat, Claudette Cayrol, Didier Dubois, Jérôme Lang, and Henri Prade. Inconsistency management and prioritized syntax-based entailment. In *Proc. of the 13th IJCAI*, pages 640–645, Chambéry, France, 1993. Morgan-Kaufmann.
3. Salem Benferhat, Didier Dubois, and Henri Prade. Argumentative inference in uncertain and inconsistent knowledge bases. In *Proc. of the 9th UAI*, pages 411–419, Washington, DC, 1993. Morgan-Kaufmann.
4. Stefan Brass. On the semantics of supernormal defaults. In *Proc. of the 13th IJCAI*, pages 578–583, Chambéry, France, 1993. Morgan-Kaufmann.
5. Gerhard Brewka. Preferred subtheories : An extended logical framework for default reasoning. In *Proc. of the 11th IJCAI*, pages 1043–1048, Detroit, MI, 1989. Morgan-Kaufmann.
6. Claudette Cayrol. From non-monotonic syntax-based entailment to preference-based argumentation. In *Proc. of ECSQARU-95*, in this volume, Fribourg, Switzerland, 1995.
7. Claudette Cayrol and Marie-Christine Lagasquie-Schiex. Classification de relations d'inférence non-monotone : la prudence et les propriétés de déduction. Technical Report 94-49R, UPS-IRIT. France, November 1994.
8. Claudette Cayrol and Marie-Christine Lagasquie-Schiex. On the complexity of non-monotonic entailment in syntax-based approaches. In *Proc. of the 11th ECAI workshop on Algorithms, Complexity and Commonsense Reasoning*, Amsterdam, Nederland, 1994.
9. Claudette Cayrol, Véronique Royer, and Claire Saurel. Management of preferences in assumption-based reasoning. In *Advanced methods in AI. Lecture notes in computer science 682*, pages 13–22. Springer Verlag, 1992.
10. Didier Dubois, Jérôme Lang, and Henri Prade. Inconsistency in possibilistic knowledge bases - to live or not to live with it. In *Fuzzy logic for the Management of Uncertainty*, pages 335–351. Wiley and sons, 1991.
11. M. Elvang-Goransson, J. Fox, and P. Krause. Dialectic reasoning with inconsistent information. In *Proc. of the 9th UAI*, pages 114–121, Washington, DC, 1993. Morgan-Kaufmann.
12. Peter Gärdenfors and David Makinson. Nonmonotonic inference based on expectations. *Artificial Intelligence*, 65:197–245, 1994.
13. H. Geffner. *Default reasoning: Causal and Conditional Theories*. MIT Press, 1992.
14. A. Hunter. Defeasible reasoning with structured information. In *Proc. of the 4th KR*, pages 281–292, Bonn, Germany, 1994.
15. Sarit Kraus, Daniel Lehmann, and Menachem Magidor. Nonmonotonic reasoning, preferential models and cumulative logics. *Artificial Intelligence*, 44:167–207, 1990.
16. Daniel Lehmann. Another perspective on default reasoning. Technical Report 92-12, Leibniz Center for Research in Computer Science. Hebrew University of Jerusalem, Israel, July 1992.
17. Bernhard Nebel. Belief revision and default reasoning: Syntax-based approaches. In *Proc. of the 2nd KR*, pages 417–428, Cambridge, MA, 1991. Morgan-Kaufmann.
18. Gadi Pinkas and Ronald P. Loui. Reasoning from inconsistency : A taxonomy of principles for resolving conflict. In *Proc. of the 3rd KR*, pages 709–719, Cambridge, MA, 1992. Morgan-Kaufmann.
19. G.R. Simari and R.P. Loui. A mathematical treatment of defeasible reasoning and its implementation. *Artificial Intelligence*, 53:125–157, 1992.

Local Möbius Transforms of Monotone Capacities

Alain CHATEAUNEUF
CERMSEM, Université PARIS I

Jean-Yves JAFFRAY
LAFORIA, Université PARIS VI

Abstract

The concept of local Möbius transform of a capacity is introduced and shown to provide a handier characterization of K-monotonicity than the standard Möbius transformation. It is moreover used to give a new proof of the preservation of K-monotonicity by conditional lower probabilities.

1. Introduction

Möbius inversion (Rota [9], Shafer [10]) has proved to be an extremely useful tool in the study of belief functions, i.e., of infinite monotone capacities considered as measures of uncertainty (see, e.g., Shafer [10], Smets [11]).

However, situations are also met where the natural representation of uncertainty only consists in a convex, i.e., 2-monotone, capacity, or, more generally in a K-monotone capacity, in which case the usefulness of Möbius inversion is somewhat lessened by the fact that Möbius transforms of K-monotone capacities do not possess a very simple characterization.

In this paper, we introduce the concept of local Möbius transform of a capacity, which offers a handier characterization of K-monotonicity, and we show its usefulness by giving a new proof of the preservation of K-monotonicity by conditional lower probabilities (Sundberg and Wagner [12]).

2. Properties of Convex Capacities and Monotone Mappings

2.1. Monotone and weakly monotone mappings

Given a mapping $f : \mathcal{A} \to \mathbb{R}$, where $\mathcal{A} = 2^{\mathcal{X}}$ and $\mathcal{X}$ is a finite set (whe shall later interpret the elements of $\mathcal{X}$ and $\mathcal{A}$ as, respectively, *states of nature* and *events*). Choquet [2] derives from f *difference functions* $\Delta_K f$, $K \in \mathbb{N}$, defined on $\mathcal{A}^{K+1}$ by the recursive formula

$$\Delta_K f(A,B_1,\dots,B_k,\dots,B_K) = \Delta_{K-1} f(A,B_1,\dots,B_k,\dots,B_{K-1}) - \Delta_{K-1} f(A \cap B_K,B_1,\dots,B_k,\dots,B_{K-1}) \qquad (1)$$

for all $A,B_k \in \mathcal{A}$, $k \in I(K)$ [1] and $K \geq 1$, and the initial term $\Delta_0 f = f$.

It is easy to check that $\Delta_K f$ is given by

$$\Delta_K f(A,B_1,\dots,B_k,\dots,B_K) = \sum_{J \subseteq I(K)} (-1)^{|J|} f(A \cap [\bigcap_{j \in J} B_j]), \qquad (2)$$

which implies that neither a permutation of the B_k's nor the substitution of $B_k \cap A$ for B_k has an effect on the value of $\Delta_K f$. Let us also note that difference operators Δ_K are additive, i.e., $\Delta_K(f+g) = \Delta_K f + \Delta_K g$. By definition (Choquet [2]), f is *monotone of order* K, or K-*monotone*, for $K \geq 1$, when $\Delta_K f \geq 0$. (3)

Note that a K-monotone function is also K'-monotone for $1 \leq K' < K$ and that a 1-monotone function is monotone (increasing) in the usual sense.

We shall say that f *is weakly* K-*monotone*, for $K \geq 2$, when

$$f\Big(\bigcup_{k=1}^{K} B_k\Big) \geq \sum_{\emptyset \neq J \subseteq I(K)} (-1)^{|J|+1} f\Big(\bigcap_{j \in J} B_j\Big), \text{ for all } B_k \in \mathcal{Q},\ k \in I(K). \quad (4)$$

A weakly K-monotone function is also weakly K'-monotone for $2 \leq K' < K$.

The following Lemma clarifies the relation between monotonicity and weak monotonicity properties.

Lemma 1. *For* $f : \mathcal{Q} \to \mathbb{R}$ *and* $K \geq 2$, *the following statements are equivalent :*

(i) f is K-*monotone ; (ii) f is weakly* K-*monotone and* 1-*monotone.*

2.2. Convex capacities

Thus the difference between K-monotonicity and weak K-monotonicity vanishes for 1-monotone functions, and, in particular, for *(normalized) capacities* which are defined as mappings : $f : \mathcal{Q} \to \mathbb{R}$ satisfying 1-monotonicity and

$$f(\emptyset) = 0,\ f(\mathfrak{X}) = 1\ . \quad (5)$$

A *convex capacity* is a capacity which is weakly 2-monotone, i.e., a mapping $\mathcal{Q} \to \mathbb{R}$ which satisfies 1-monotonicity, (5) and

$$f(B_1 \cup B_2) \geq f(B_1) + f(B_2) - f(B_1 \cap B_2) \text{ for all } B_1, B_2 \in \mathcal{Q} \quad (6)$$

or, equivalently, (5) and 2-monotonicity property

$$[\Delta_2 f(A,B_1,B_2)=]\ f(A) - f(A \cap B_1) - f(A \cap B_2) + f(A \cap B_1 \cap B_2) \geq 0$$

for all $A, B_1, B_2 \in \mathcal{Q}$. (7)

As defined by Shafer [10], a *belief function* is a capacity which is weakly K-monotone for all $K \geq 2$, or, equivalently, a mapping $\mathcal{Q} \to \mathbb{R}$ which is K-monotone for all $K \geq 1$ and satisfies (5).

2.3. Möbius inversion

Any mapping $f : \mathcal{A} \to \mathbb{R}$ has a *Möbius transform* (Rota [9]) $\varphi : \mathcal{A} \to \mathbb{R}$ defined by

$$\varphi(A) = \sum_{B \subseteq A} (1)^{|A-B|} f(B) \quad \text{for all } A \in \mathcal{A}, \tag{8}$$

which characterizes f, since f is retrievable from φ by (Shafer [10])

$$f(A) = \sum_{B \subseteq A} \varphi(B) \text{ for all } A \in \mathcal{A}. \tag{9}$$

The support of φ, $\mathcal{B} = \{B \in \mathcal{A} : \varphi(B) \neq \emptyset\}$ is the *focal set* of f.

The Möbius transform of a mapping informs one of its monotonicity properties. In particular, as proven in Chateauneuf & Jaffray [1] :

Proposition 1. *Let* φ *be the Möbius transform of mapping* $f : \mathcal{A} \to \mathbb{R}$. *Then :*

(i) f *is 1-monotone if and only if*

$$\sum_{\{x\} \subseteq B \subseteq A} \varphi(B) \geq 0 \text{ for all } A \in \mathcal{A}, \text{ all } x \in A ; \tag{10}$$

(ii) f *is weakly* K*-monotone* (K ≥ 2) *if and only if*

$$\sum_{B \subseteq \cup A_k, \text{not } B \subseteq A_k} \varphi(B) \geq 0 \text{ for all } A_k \in \mathcal{A}, k \in I(K), \tag{11}$$

or, alternatively, if and only if

$$\sum_{C \subseteq B \subseteq A} \varphi(B) \geq 0 \textit{ for all } A \in \mathcal{A}, \textit{ all } C \in \mathcal{A} \textit{ such that } 2 \leq |C| \leq K. \tag{12}$$

Since conditions (5) are clearly equivalent to

$$\varphi(\emptyset) = 0 \;;\; \sum_{B} \varphi(B) = 1, \tag{13}$$

one gets the following characterizations :

Corollary 1. *Let* φ *be the Möbius transform of mapping* $\mathcal{A} \to \mathbb{R}$. *Then :*

(i) f *is a capacity if and only if* φ *satisfies* (10) *and* (13) ;

(ii) f *is a belief function if and only if* $\varphi \geq 0$ *and* (13) *holds true.*

The characterization of K-monotonicity provided by the conjunction of Lemma 1 and Proposition 1 is not simple. A handier characterization can however be found by using Möbius inversion "locally".

2.4. Local Möbius inversion

Let us prove

Proposition 2. (i) *Consider* $f : \mathcal{C} \to \mathbb{R}$ *.Given* $K \geq 1$ *and a sequence* $S = (A, B_1, \dots, B_k, \dots, B_K)$ *of elements of* $\mathcal{C}$, *there exists a unique mapping* $\mu_S : 2^{I(K)} \to \mathbb{R}$ *satisfying*

$$f(A \cap [\bigcap_{i \in I} B_i]) = \sum_{J \supseteq I} \mu_S(J) \text{ for all } I \subseteq I(K), \tag{14}$$

which is defined by

$$\mu_S(I) = \Delta_{K-|I|} f(A \cap [\bigcap_{i \in I} B_i], \{B_\ell, \ell \in \overline{I}\})$$

$$\text{for all } I \subseteq I(K), \overline{I} = I(K) - I\,; \tag{15}$$

(ii) f *is K-monotone if and only if*

$\mu_S(I) \geq 0$ for all S in $\mathcal{C}^{K+1}$, all $I \subset I(K)$;

(iii) f *is K-monotone and nonnegative if and only if*

$\mu_S(I) \geq 0$ *for all* S *in* $\mathcal{C}^{K+1}$, *all* $I \subseteq I(K)$.

Proof. (i) Mapping $\overline{f} : 2^{I(K)} \to \mathbb{R}$ defined by $\overline{f}(\overline{I}) = f(A \cap [\bigcap_{i \in I} B_i]), I = I(K) - \overline{I}$, for all $\overline{I} \subseteq I(K)$, has a unique Möbius transform $\overline{\mu}$, given by

$$\overline{\mu}(\overline{I}) = \sum_{J \subseteq \overline{I}} (-1)^{|\overline{I} - J|} \overline{f}(J), \text{ for all } \overline{I} \subseteq I(K), \text{ or}$$

$$\overline{\mu}(\overline{I}) = \sum_{J \subseteq \overline{I}} (-1)^{|J|} \overline{f}(\overline{I} - J) = \sum_{J \subseteq \overline{I}} (-1)^{|J|} f(A \cap [\bigcap_{i \in I} B_i] \cap [\bigcap_{j \in J} B_j])$$

$$= \Delta_{K-|I|} f(A \cap [\bigcap_{i \in I} B_i], \{B_\ell, \ell \in \overline{I}\}).$$

Thus $\mu_S : 2^{I(K)} \to \mathbb{R}$ defined by $\mu_S(I) = \overline{\mu}(\overline{I}), \overline{I} = I(K) - I$ for all $I \subseteq I(K)$, satisfies (15) ; moreover since $\overline{\mu}$ is the unique solution to $\overline{f}(\overline{I}) = \sum_{J \subseteq \overline{I}} \overline{\mu}(\overline{J})$, all $\overline{I} \subseteq I(K)$, and $\sum_{J \subseteq \overline{I}} \overline{\mu}(J) = \sum_{L \supseteq I} \mu_S(L)$, μ_S is the unique solution to (14).

(ii) and (iii). If f is K-monotone, it is also K'monotone for $1 \leq K' < K$, and thus (15) shows that $\mu_S(I) \geq 0$ for $K - |I| \geq 1$, which property extends to $|I| = K$ (i.e., to $I = I(K)$) when $\Delta_0 f = f \geq 0$. The converse statements follow from the fact that, by (15) again, $\Delta_K f(A, B_1, \dots, B_k, \dots, B_K) = \mu_S(\emptyset)$ for $K \geq 1$, and, for k = 1 and $S = (A, \mathfrak{X})$, $f(A) = f(A \cap \mathfrak{X}) = \Delta_0 f(A \cap \mathfrak{X}) = \mu_S(I(K))$. ∎

μ_S given by (15) is called the *local Möbius transform* [2] of f at S.

As an application of Proposition 2 let us show that

Proposition 3. *The product* $f = f_1 f_2$ *of two* K-*monotone mappings* $f_1, f_2 : \mathcal{C} \to \mathbb{R}_+$ *is itself* K-*monotone* (K *integer* $K \geq 1$).

Proof. Let $S = (A, B_1, \ldots, B_k, \ldots, B_K) \in \mathcal{C}^{K+1}$ and let μ_S, μ_S^1, μ_S^2 be defined by (15) applied to f, f_1 and f_2 respectively. Then, by (14),

$$f(A \cap [\bigcap_{i \in I} B_i]) = \sum_{L_1 \supseteq I} \mu_S^1(L_1) \sum_{L_2 \supseteq I} \mu_S^2(L_2)$$

$= \sum_{L \supseteq I} \sum_{L_1 \cap L_2 = L} \mu_S^1(L_1) \mu_S^2(L_2)$, for all $I \subseteq I(K)$, which implies, μ_S being the only solution to (14), that

$$\mu_S(I) = \sum_{I_1 \cap I_2 = I} \mu_S^1(I_1)\ \mu_S^2(I_2) \quad \text{for all } I \subseteq (K). \tag{16}$$

The conclusion easily follows from the validity of this relation for all $S \in \mathcal{C}^{K+1}$ and statement (iii) of Proposition 2. ■

2.5. Probabilities which are consistent with a mapping

Given a mapping $f : \mathcal{C} \to \mathbb{R}$, let us define the set of all probability measures which are *consistent* with f as

$$\mathcal{P}_f = \{P \in \mathcal{L} : P \geq f\}. \tag{17}$$

Note that $\mathcal{P}_f$ can also be described as

$$\mathcal{P}_f = \{P \in \mathcal{L} : f \leq P \leq F\}, \tag{18}$$

where $F : \mathcal{C} \to \mathbb{R}$ is the *dual* of f, defined by $F(A) = 1 - f(A^c)$, $A \in \mathcal{C}$. Clearly $\mathcal{P}_f$ may be empty (for instance, if $f(A) + f(A^c) > 1$ for some $A \in \mathcal{C}$). Moreover, when $\mathcal{P}_f$ is not empty, f is not necessarily *representable by* $\mathcal{P}_f$ in the sense that

$$f = \inf\{P : P \in \mathcal{P}_f\} \tag{19}$$

Huber [5], Ch.10, gives n.s. conditions for the validity of (19). For convex capacities however, (19) is a direct consequence of the following characteristic property :

Proposition 4. *For any mapping* $f : \mathcal{C} \to \mathbb{R}$*, with dual mapping* F, *the following statements are equivalent : (i) f is a convex capacity ; (ii) for any events* $A, B \in \mathcal{C}$ *such that* $A \cap B = \emptyset$ *there exists a probability measure* P *consistent with* f *and such that* $P(A) = f(A)$ *and* $P(B) = F(B)$.

3. Bayesian conditioning and convex lower probabilities

3.1. Convex lower probability representation of uncertainty

Consider a situation of uncertainty in which data concerning the events are completely summarized by the specification of $\mathcal{P}$, a non empty subset of $\mathcal{L}$. In other words, suppose that a probability measure is known to exist and to be located in $\mathcal{P}$, and that there is complete ignorance on its location in $\mathcal{P}$.

The *lower envelope* of $\mathcal{P}$, capacity $f = \inf \{P \in \mathcal{L} : P \in \mathcal{P}\}$, also called the *lower probability* defined by $\mathcal{P}$, can be used to characterize $\mathcal{P}$, provided it is retrievable from f, which requires that

(H1) $\qquad \mathcal{P} = \mathcal{P}_f, \text{ i.e., } \quad \mathcal{P} = \{P \in \mathcal{L} : P \geq f\},$

whereas in general $\mathcal{P}_f$ may strictly contain $\mathcal{P}$.

When (H1) holds, one says that uncertainty admits of a *lower probability representation.*

A lower probability is always a capacity but need not be K-monotone, even for $K = 2$. Thus, to ensure some desirable properties of $\mathcal{P}$ and f, we must introduce the additional assumption that

(H2) $\qquad$ *capacity* f *is convex.*

Fortunately, in many applications, (H2) turns out to be satisfied. As a matter of fact, f is even a belief function whenever $\mathcal{P}$ is generated by a random set (Nguyen [8]), and Jaffray [7] assumes f to be a belief function. However (H2) allows the model to encompass other natural situations such as the following ones :

Example 1. (Huber & Strassen [6])

$\mathcal{P} = \{P \in \mathcal{L} : |P(A) - P_0(A)| \leq \varepsilon \text{ for all } A \in \mathcal{A}\}$, where $P_0 \in \mathcal{L}$ and $\varepsilon > 0$.

Example 2. (De Robertis & Hartigan [3])

$\mathcal{P} = \{P \in \mathcal{L} : (1-\varepsilon)\, P_0(A) \leq P(A) \leq (1+\varepsilon)\, P_0(A) \text{ for all } A \in \mathcal{A}\}$, where $P_0 \in \mathcal{L}$, and $\varepsilon \in (0,1)$.

Example 3. Partial information concerning the content of an urn is that its balls can have (K+1) ($K \geq 2$, given) different colours and that the percentage of balls of any given colour is at most (1-1/K). Thus, if $\mathcal{X} = \{x_1, \ldots, x_k, \ldots, x_{K+1}\}$ is the set of colours, the probability that the colour of a randomly drawn ball is x_k is known to be at most (1-1/K) or, equivalently : $P(A) \geq 1/K$ for $A \in \mathcal{A}$ and $|A| = K$.

The lower envelope of $\mathcal{P}$ is easily seen to be the capacity f given by $f(A) = 0$ for $|A| \leq K - 1$; $f(A) = 1/K$ for $|A| = K$, (and of course, $f(A) = 1$ for $|A| = K+1$). The validity of (H1) is straightforward.

In order to show that f, which is 1-monotone, is in fact K-monotone, it is sufficient to show that it is weakly K-monotone, i.e., that for $k = K$,

$$\Delta_k f\left(\bigcup_{i=1}^{k} A_i, A_1, \ldots, A_i, \ldots, A_k\right) \geq 0 . \tag{20}$$

Alternatively, f could be shown to be weakly K-monotone but not weakly K+1 monotone by calculating the Möbius transform φ of f and checking the validity of inequalities (12) of Proposition 1 (which is easy since $\varphi(A) = 0$ for $|A| < K$, $\varphi(A) = 1/K$ for $|A| = K$, and $\varphi(\mathcal{X}) = -1/K$). ■

3.2. Bayesian conditioning

Given a situation of uncertainty characterized by a set of probability measures $\mathcal{P}$, suppose that one observes an event E of $\mathcal{A}$ such that $P(E) > 0$ for all $P \in \mathcal{P}$.

There exists then for every P in $\mathcal{P}$ a conditional probability measure P given E, denoted P^E, on the subalgebra of events $\mathcal{A}^E = \{A \in \mathcal{A} : A \subseteq E\}$, which is given by Bayes rule : $P^E(A) = P(A)/P(E)$ for all $A \in \mathcal{A}^E$.

Bayesian conditioning is defined as transformation

$$\mathcal{P} \rightarrow \mathcal{P}^E = \{P^E \in \mathcal{L}^E : P \in \mathcal{P}\} \tag{21}$$

where $\mathcal{L}^E$ is the set of all probability measures on $(E, \mathcal{A}^E)$.

When the initial situation corresponds to complete ignorance in $\mathcal{P}$, it is natural to admit that the new situation, after the observation of E, corresponds to complete ignorance in $\mathcal{P}^E$, and is therefore characterizable by this last set.

The question then arises whether $\mathcal{P}^E$ inherits, or not, the properties of $\mathcal{P}$. For (H1), the answer is known to be negative, since Jaffray [7] has shown that $\mathcal{P} = \mathcal{P}_f$ does not imply in general $\mathcal{P}^E = \mathcal{Q}^E$, where

$$\mathcal{Q}^E = \{Q \in \mathcal{L}^E : Q \geq f^E\}, \tag{22}$$

even when f is a belief function (in fact the validity of $\mathcal{P}^E = \mathcal{Q}^E$ for all E requires f to be "almost" additive).

The monotonicity properties of f, on the other hand, are always inherited by f^E. This was first shown for belief functions by Fagin & Halpern [4], for convex capacities by Walley [13], and later extended to other K-monotone capacities by Sundberg & Wagner [12]. Local Möbius inversion is a useful tool for proving these results. As a preliminary step, let us recall a well-known expression relating f^E to f.

Proposition 5. *Let* $f : \mathcal{A} \to \mathbb{R}$ *be a convex capacity,* F *its dual mapping, and* $\mathcal{P} = \mathcal{P}_f = \{P \in \mathcal{L} : P \geq f\}$. *Given event* $E \in \mathcal{A}$ *such that* $f(E) > 0$, *let* $f^E = \inf\{P^E : P \in \mathcal{P}\}$. *Then* f^E *is a capacity and, for all* $A \in \mathcal{A}^E$,

$$f^E(A) = f(A)/[f(A) + F(E-A)] = f(A)/[f(A)+1-f(A \cup E^c)]. \tag{23}$$

The proof (see e.g. Jaffray [7]) consists basically in remarking that

$$f^E(A) = \inf\{P(A)/[P(A)+P(E-A)] : P \in \mathcal{P}\} = 1/[1+\sup\{P(E-A)/P(A) : P \in \mathcal{P}\}]$$

and applying Proposition 4 to A and $B = E-A$. Note that by convexity, for $C \in \mathcal{A}^E$, $f(C) + 1 - f(C \cup E^c) \geq f(E) > 0$. Thus the denominator of expression (23) is positive. Moreover, since it involves the difference function $\Delta_1 f(A \cup E^c, E) = f(A \cup E^c) - f(A)$, the following properties will be useful :

Lemma 2. *Given* $f : \mathcal{A} \to \mathbb{R}$ *and* $E \in \mathcal{A}$, *let* $g : \mathcal{A}^E \to \mathbb{R}$ *be defined by*

$$g(A) = \Delta_1 f(A \cup E^c, E) = f(A \cup E^c) - f(A) \quad \text{for all } A \in \mathcal{A}^E, \tag{24}$$

and let $k \in \mathbb{N}^*$.

(i) The local Möbius transform of g *at* $S = (A, \{B_i, i \in I(K)\}) \in (\mathcal{A}^E)^{K+1}$ *is function* υ_S *given by*

$$\upsilon_S(I) = \Delta_{K-|I|+1} f([A \cap (\bigcap_{i \in I} B_i)] \cup E^c, \{B_\ell \cup E^c, \ell \in \bar{I}\}, E) \text{ for all}$$

$$I \subseteq I(K) \text{ and } \bar{I} = I - I(K). \tag{25}$$

(ii) If f *is* K*-monotone, then* $\upsilon_S(I) \geq 0$ *for all* $I \subseteq I(K)$ *with* $I \neq \emptyset$ (26)

and $\upsilon_S(\emptyset) = \mu_T(\emptyset) - \mu_S(\emptyset)$, (27)

where μ_S *and* μ_T *are the local Möbius transforms of* f *at* S *and* $T = (A \cup E^c, \{B_i \cup E^c, i \in I(K)\})$, *respectively, and thus* $\mu_S(\emptyset) \geq 0$ *and* $\mu_T(\emptyset) \geq 0$.

3.3. Preservation of K-monotonicity

Proposition 6. *Let* $f : \mathcal{A} \to \mathbb{R}$ *be a* K*-monotone capacity, with* $K \geq 2$, *and let event* $E \in \mathcal{A}$ *be such that* $f(E) > 0$. *Then* $f^E = \inf\{P^E : P \in \mathcal{P}_f\}$ *is a* K*-monotone capacity on* $\mathcal{A}^E$.

<u>Proof.</u> (i) According to (23), since $K \geq 2$, $f(A) = f^E(A)\,[1 - (f(A \cup E^c) - f\,A))]$ *for all* $A \in \mathcal{Q}^E$, or, equivalently $\overline{f} = f^E - f^E.g$ where $\overline{f}$ is the restriction of f to $\mathcal{Q}^E$ and g is defined by (24). For any $S \in (\mathcal{Q}^E)^{K+1}$, $\overline{f}$ has the same local Möbius transform at S, μ_S , as f (see (15)). Moreover, it results from the additivity of operator Δ_K and formula (16), that the local Möbius transform at S, λ_S, of f^E is related to that, υ_S, of g and to μ_S by

$$\mu_S(I) = \lambda_S(I) - \sum_{I_1 \cap I_2 = I} \lambda_S(I_1).\upsilon_S(I_2) \text{ for all } I \subseteq I(K). \tag{28}$$

We want to prove that capacity f^E is K-monotone, which, by Proposition 2, amounts to prove that $\lambda_S(I) \geq 0$ for all $S \in (\mathcal{Q}^E)^{K+1}$, all $I \subset I(K)$.

(ii) Let us first rewrite (28) successively as

$$\lambda_S(I) = \mu_S(I) + \lambda_S(I) \sum_{I_2 \supseteq I} \upsilon_S(I_2) + \sum_{I_1 \supset I} \lambda_S(I_1) \sum_{I \cup I_1^c \supseteq I_2 \supseteq I} \upsilon_S(I_2)$$

and, since $\sum_{I_2 \supseteq I} \upsilon_S(I_2) = g(C)$ with $C = A \cap [\bigcap_{i \in I} B_i]$, as

$$\lambda_S(I)\,[1 - g(C)] = \mu_S(I) + \sum_{I_1 \supset I} \lambda_S(I_1) \sum_{I \cup I_1^c \supseteq I_2 \supseteq I} \upsilon_S(I_2) \tag{29}$$

Since $1 - g(C) > 0$, $\mu_S(I) \geq 0$ for all $I \subseteq I(K)$, and $\upsilon_S(I_2) \geq 0$ for all $I \subseteq I(K)$ with $I \neq \emptyset$, the following implication is valid for $r \geq 1$:

$$[\lambda_S(I) \geq 0 \text{ for } K \geq |I| > r] \Rightarrow \lambda_S(I) \geq 0 \text{ for } |I| = r. \tag{30}$$

Moreover, for $|I| = K$, i.e., for $I = I(K)$, (29) reduces to $\lambda_S(I(K))\,[1 - g(C)] = \mu_S(I(K))$, which shows that $\lambda_S(I(K)) \geq 0$, and thus, by applying (30) recursively, that $\lambda_S(I) \geq 0$ for all $I \neq \emptyset$.

(iii) It remains to prove that $\lambda_S(\emptyset) \geq 0$. For $I = \emptyset$, (29) becomes

$$\lambda_S(\emptyset)\,[1\text{-}g(A)] = \mu_S(\emptyset) + \sum_{I_1 \neq \emptyset} \lambda_S(I_1) \sum_{\emptyset \neq I_2 \subseteq I_1^c} \upsilon_S(I_2)$$

$$+ [\sum_{I_1 \neq \emptyset} \lambda_S(I_1)]\, \upsilon_S(\emptyset) \tag{31}$$

and since $\sum_{I_1 \neq \emptyset} \lambda_S(I_1) = f^E(A) - \lambda_S(\emptyset)$ and $\upsilon_S(\emptyset) = \mu_T(\emptyset) - \mu_S(\emptyset)$, one gets

$$\lambda_S(\emptyset)\,[1\text{-}g(A)] + \upsilon_S(\emptyset)] = \mu_S(\emptyset)\,[1\text{-}f^E(A)] + \mu_T(\emptyset) f^E(A)$$

$$+ \sum_{I_1 \neq \emptyset} \lambda_S(I_1) \sum_{\emptyset \neq I_2 \subseteq I_1^c} \upsilon_S(I_2) \geq 0 \tag{32}$$

and thus $\lambda_S(\emptyset) \geq 0$ as soon as $[1-g(A)] + \upsilon_S(\emptyset)] > 0$.

If not, $f(A) + \upsilon_S(\emptyset)\, f^E(A) = [1-g(A)]\, f^E(A) + \upsilon_S(\emptyset)\, f^E(A) \leq 0$,

hence $f(A) \leq [\, \mu_S(\emptyset) - \mu_T(\emptyset)]\, f^E(A) \leq \mu_S(\emptyset)\, f^E(A) \leq \mu_S(\emptyset)$,

which implies, since $f(A) = \sum_I \mu_S(I)$ and $\mu_S(I) \geq 0$ for all I, that

$f(A) = \mu_S(\emptyset)$ and $\mu_S(I) = 0$ for $I \neq \emptyset$. This implies in turn, by (14) that $f(A \cap [\bigcap_{i \in I} B_i] = 0$ and thus $f^E(A \cap [\bigcap_{i \in I} B_i] = 0$ for all $I \neq \emptyset$, hence by (15) that $\lambda_S(I) = 0$ for all $I \neq \emptyset$, and by (14) again, that $\lambda_S(\emptyset) = f^E(A) \geq 0$. ∎

Remark. Although we have only considered here capacities on finite sets, the definition and properties of local Möbius inversion are still valid in an infinite setting so that many results such as the previous ones could be directly transposed from the finite case to the infinite one.

Notes

[1]By definition $I(K) = \{1,\ldots,k,\ldots K\}$. Note also the use of $\subseteq$ (resp. $\subset$) for large (resp. strict) inclusion, and the definition of K-monotonicity differ from those in [1].

[2]Note that the restriction of f to any subalgebra of $\mathcal{A}$ that contains all elements of S has the same local Möbius transform at S as f.

References

[1] A. Chateauneuf & J.Y. Jaffray, Some characterizations of lower probabilities... through the use of Möbius inversion, Math. Soc. Sc., 17 (1989), 263-283.

[2] G. Choquet, Théorie des capacités, Ann. Inst. Fourier (Grenoble) (1953)V.131-295.

[3] De Robertis & J.A. Hartigan, Bayesian inference using intervals of measures, Ann. Statist., 9 (1981) 235-244.

[4] R. Fagin & J.Y. Halpern, A new approach to updating beliefs, in Proc. 6th Conf. Uncertainty in A.I. (1990).

[5] P.J. Huber, The use of Choquet capacities in statistics, Bull. Int. Statist. Inst. XLV, Book 4 (1973).

[6] P.J. Huber & V. Strassen, Minimax tests and the Neyman-Pearson lemma for capacities, Ann. Stat.1 (1973) 251-263.

[7] J.Y. Jaffray, Bayesian updating and belief functions, I.E.E.E. trans. on Systems, Man and Cybern. 22, N°5 (1992) 1144-1152.

[8] H.T. Nguyen, On random sets and belief functions, J. of Math. Anal. and Appl. 65 (1978) 531-542.

[9] G.C. Rota, Theory of Möbius functions, Z. für Wahrscheinlichkeitstheorie und Verwandte Gebiete 2 (1964) 340-368.

[10] G. Shafer, A Mathematical Theory of Evidence, Princeton University Press, Princeton, New Jersey (1976).

[11] Ph. Smets, Belief functions in Smets & al. (Eds) "Non standard logics for automated reasoning", (Academic Press, London, 1988) 253-286.

[11] G. Sundberg and C. Wagner, Generalized finite differences and Bayesian conditioning of Choquet capacities, Adv. in Appl. Math., 13, (1992), 262-272.

[13] P. Walley, Coherent lower and upper probabilities, Research Report (1981), University of Warwick, Coventry.

Automated reasoning with merged contradictory information whose reliability depends on topics

Laurence Cholvy
ONERA-CERT
2 avenue Edouard Belin,31055 Toulouse, France
cholvy@tls-cs.cert.fr

Abstract

This paper presents a theorem prover for reasoning with information which is provided by several information sources and which may be contradictory.

This prover allows the user to assume that the different sources are more or less reliable, depending on the topics of the information.

Theorems which can be proved by this prover are of the form : if the sources were ordered in such a way for such a topic, then such a formula would be deducible.

1 Introduction

This paper addresses the problem of reasoning with merged information which is contradictory.

Such a problem is raised in case of multi-database systems [10] [13] [23] where one wants to access several distributed databases or when one wants to build a new database from several existing databases which have been independently developped. The problem of merging information is also generated when adding a new piece of information to an initial set of information. This problem has been studied in many ways : it has initially been studied in database area [1], [17], [25], [14], [24]... It has also been studied in the area of belief revision [15], [21], [16]... Finally, the problem of merging information is generated in multi-source environment [2], [3], [9], [6], [5]...

Roughly speaking, our solution to the problem of merging contradictory information consists in considering the relative reliability of the information i.e. considering the relative reliability of the sources which provide the information. In a first step, we had considered that this reliability only depends on the sources. But in fact, to be more realistic, we have considered that the reliability of an information source also depends on what the information is talking about i.e. its topics. So our present solution consists in considering as many orders between the sources, as topics of information. Each order associated to a topic, represents the relative reliability of the sources as regard to the information which belongs to this topic.

Let us take an example. Consider a police inspector who collects information provided by two witnesses of a crime who are a woman and a man. They both provide information about what they have seen. The woman says that she saw a girl, wearing a Chanel suit, jumping into a sport Volkswagen car. The man says that he saw a girl wearing a dress. He assumed that she jumped into a car that he did not see but he heard that it was a diesel. The two accounts are contradictory : Did the girl wear a dress or a suit ? Was the car a sport car or not ? For solving these contradictions, the inspector may use the fact that, when speaking about "clothes", women are generally more expert than men ; and when speaking about "mechanics", men are generally more expert than women. This leads the inspector to assume two orders, depending on the two topics "clothes" and "mechanics" : the woman is more reliable than the man as regard to "clothes" and the man is more reliable than the woman as regard to "mechanics". Using such orders, the inspector can adopt two attitudes we called "trustful" and "suspicious" [6]. Adopting a "trustful" attitude, the inspector could conclude that there was a girl, wearing a Chanel suit, jumping into a diesel car which was a Volkswagen make. Adopting a "suspicious" attitude, the inspector had derived that there was a girl, wearing a Chanel suit, jumping into a diesel car whose brand is unkown.

In section 2, we recall the semantics we have defined, in previous works, for reasoning with merged information using topics-dependent orders and according to "trustful" attitude.

In section 3, we define a theorem-prover for automatically reasoning according to this semantics. This prover, which takes into account the reliability of the sources depending on the topics, constitutes the main contribution of our paper.

2 A semantics for merging information sources with topic-dependent orders

2.1 Modelisation of topics for the problem of merging

The notion of topic has been investigated to characterize sets of sentences from the point of view of their meaning, independently of their truth values. For example, in the context of Cooperative Answering, topics can be used to extend an answer to other facts related to the same topic [8, 4] . In the context of Knowledge Representation [18] , topics are used to represent all an agent believes about a given topic. In other works [22, 12] the formal definition of the notion of "aboutness" is investigated in general. The purpose of this paper is not to define a logic for reasoning about the links between a sentence and a topic in general, but to define a logic that is based on source orders which depend on topics. We assume that the underlying propositional language is associated to a finite number of topics which are sets of literals such that : each literal of L belongs to a topic ; topics may intersect ; if a literal of L belongs to a topic, its negation belongs to this topic too.

Definition 1

Let $t_1 \ldots t_m$ be the topics of L. Let $O_1 \ldots O_m$ be total orders on the bases, associated with the topics $t_1 \ldots t_m$. $O_1 \ldots O_m$ are $(t_1 \ldots t_m)$-compatible iff
$\forall\, k = 1 \ldots m \,, \forall\, r = 1 \ldots m \quad t_k \cap t_r \neq \emptyset \implies O_k = O_r$.

Intuitively, this definition characterizes orders which, in some sense, "agree on" the structure of the topics.

2.2 Semantics of the logic

The databases we consider are finite sets of literals which are satisfiable but not necessarily complete. We will note them 1...n. Let us note L the underlying propositional language and let $t_1...t_m$ be the topics on L. We define a language L' by adding to language L, a finite number of modalities noted $[O_1...O_m]$, where the O_i's are orders on subsets of the databases, which are assumed to be total and to be $(t_1...t_m)$-compatible.

Let $O_1, ..., O_m$ be total and $(t_1...t_m)$-compatible orders on k databases, then the formula $[O_1...O_m]$ F will mean that F is deducible in the database obtained by merging the k databases when considering that their relative reliability are expressed by orders $O_1...O_m$.

Notice that the general form of these modalities allows us to represent the particular case when $k = 1$. In such a case, there is only one base to order, say i_0, thus $O_1 = ... = O_m = i_0$.

Definition 2
Let m be an interpretation of L and let t be a topic. We define the projection of m on t, noted $m \mid t$ by : $m \mid t \stackrel{def}{=} \{l : l \in m \text{ and } l \in t\}$

Definition 3
Let E be a set of interpretations of L and let t be a topic. We define :
$E \mid t \stackrel{def}{=} \{m \mid t : m \in E\}$

Definition 4
Let t be a topic and O the total order $(i_1 > \cdots > i_k)$ on k databases, relatively to topic t. We define :
$R_t(O) \stackrel{def}{=} f_{i_k,t}(\cdots(f_{i_2,t}(R(i_1) \mid t))\cdots)$, with : $f_{i_j,t}(E) = \bigcup_{m \in R(i_j)|t} Min(E, \leq_m)$

Definition 5
An interpretation of FUSION-T is a pair M = (W,r), where W is the set of all the interpretations of L, and r is a finite set of subsets of W such that every modality $[O_1...O_m]$ is associated to one of these subsets which is noted $R(O_1...O_m)$. Sets $R(O_1...O_m)$ are recursively defined by :

R(i...i) is a non empty subset of W

$$R(O_1...O_m) \stackrel{def}{=} \{w : w = w_1 \cup ... \cup w_m, \text{ where : } \forall t \in [1..m], w_t \in Rt(Ot) \text{ and } \forall l \in L, l \notin w \text{ or } \neg l \notin w\}$$

Definition 6 (Satisfaction of formulas)
Let F be a formula of L. Let F1 and F2 be two formulas of L'.
Let $O_1...O_m$ be $(t_1...t_m)$-compatible total orders on some databases.
Let (W,r) an interpretation of FUSION-T, let $w \in W$. The satisfaction of formulas is defined by :

FUSION-T,r,w $\models$ F iff w $\models$ F
FUSION-T,r,w $\models$ $[O_1...O_m]$ F iff $\forall$ w', if w' $\in$ $R(O_1...O_m)$ then w' $\models$ F
FUSION-T,r,w $\models$ $\neg$ F1 iff FUSION-T,r,w $\not\models$ F1)
FUSION-T,r,w $\models$ F1 $\wedge$ F2 iff (FUSION-T,r,w $\models$ F1) and (FUSION-T,r,w $\models$ F2)

Definition 7 (Valid formulas)
let F be a formula of L'. F is a valid formula in FUSION-T, iff $\forall$ M = (W,r), $\forall$ w $\in$ W, FUSION-T,r,w $\models$ F. (We note them FUSION-T $\models$ F)

Definition 8
We note ψ the conjunction, for any database, of all the literals it believes and the clauses it does not believe. $\psi = \bigwedge_{i=1}^{n}(\bigwedge_{l \in i}[i]l \wedge \bigwedge_{i \not\vdash c} \neg[i]c)$, where l is a literal, c is a clause and i's are the databases.

We are interested in finding valid formulas of the form : $(\psi \rightarrow [O_1...O_m]\ F)$, i.e finding formulas F which are deducible in the database obtained by merging several databases ordered by topic-dependent orders $O_1...O_m$.

Let M0 be the interpretation of L' in which each set R(i...i) is the set of all the models of the ith base. Let $O_1...O_m$ be topic-compatible orders. We have proved, in previous works, that the set $R(O_1...O_m)$, associated in M0 to the modality $[O_1...O_m]$ is not empty. This guarantees that, when the databases to be merged are satisfiable sets of literals and when the orders are topic-compatible, the semantics defines a database whose set of models, $R(O_1...O_m)$ is never empty. Thus, this database is satisfiable even if the merged databases are contradictory.

We have also proved that FUSION-T $\models$ $(\psi \rightarrow [O_1...O_m]F)$ if and only if $\forall$ w $\in$ $R(O_1...O_m)$, w $\models$ F. So, for proving that a formula F is deducible in the database obtained by merging several databases ordered by topic-compatible orders $O_1...O_m$, we just have to compute $R(O_1...O_m)$ by definition 5, assuming that sets R(i...i) are the sets of all the models of the ith base.

Let us add that a complete and sound axiomatics has been given for this semantics [7]

2.3 Example

Let us come back to the police inspector example and consider the two topics "clothes" and "mechanics". The orders, relatively to these topics were :
$O_{clothes}$ = (woman > man) and $O_{mechanics}$ = (man > woman)

Here are some deductions the inspector can make :

FUSION-T $\models$ $(\psi \rightarrow [O_{clothes}\ O_{mechanics}]$ (Chanel $\wedge$ tailleur $\wedge$ $\neg$ dress))

FUSION-T $\models$ $(\psi \rightarrow [O_{clothes}\ O_{mechanics}]$ (diesel $\wedge$ $\neg$ sport-car $\wedge$ Volkswagen))

FUSION-T $\models$ $(\psi \rightarrow \neg [O_{clothes}\ O_{mechanics}]$ ($\neg$ Volkswagen))

In other terms, when assuming that the woman is more reliable than the man on "clothes" and that the man is more reliable than the woman on "mechanics", the inspector can deduce that the girl was wearing a Chanel suit, and not a dress, and that she jumped into a diesel car, and not a sport-car, which was a Volkswagen make.

3 Automated deduction

In this section, we deal with the implementation aspects of the logic FUSION-T introduced in the previous section. We describe a theorem prover which allows us to answer questions of the form : is formula F deducible in the database obtained from trustfully merging several databases ordered by topic-dependent orders [O1...Om] ? This theorem-prover is an extension of the one described in [5] since instead of considering only one order on information sources, it considers several orders depending on topics. It is specified at the meta-level and implemented in a PROLOG-like language.

3.1 The meta-language

Let us consider a meta-language ML, based on language L, defined by :

Constants :
- Propositions of L are constants of ML
- There is a constant noted nil which will represent the empty order
- There are as many constants as databases 1...n

Functions :
- An unary function noted $\neg$. $\neg$ l will represents the negation of literal l.
- A function noted >. The term O > i represents the extension of the order O with i. For instance $(i_1 > i_2) > i_3$ is the order $(i_1 > i_2 > i_3)$. By definition, the order $(i_1 > .. > i_n > nil)$ will be the order $(i_1 > ... > i_n)$.
- A function noted $-$. By definition, the term $(O - i)$ represents the order obtained from O by deleting i. For instance $((i_1 > i_2 > i_3) - i_2)$ is the order $(i_1 > i_3)$.
- A m-ary function noted (). $(O_1 ... O_m)$ is a set of m orders.

Predicates :
- Predicate symbols of ML are : TFUSION, EMPTY, TOPIC.

The intuitive semantics of the predicates is the following :

- TFUSION($(O_1...O_m)$, l) means that it is the case that literal l is true in the database obtained by merging the databases according to the orders : $O_1 ... O_m$.

- EMPTY($O_1, ..., O_m$) is true if and only if all the orders O_i are empty.

- TOPIC(l,t) means that literal l belongs to the topic t.

3.1.1 The meta-program

Let us consider META, the following set of the ML formulas :

(0) TOPIC(l,k) for any literal l belonging to topic k
(1) TFUSION((i...i), l) for any literal l in database i
(2) TOPIC(l,k) $\wedge$
TFUSION($((O_1 - i)...(O_{k-1} - i)\ \ O_k\ \ (O_{k+1} - i)...(O_m - i))$, l) $\wedge$
$\neg$ EMPTY($(O_1 - i), ..., (O_{k-1} - i), O_k, (O_{k+1} - i), ..., (O_m - i)$) $\rightarrow$
TFUSION($(O_1...O_{k-1}\ \ O_k > i\ \ O_{k+1}...O_m)$, l)
(3) TOPIC(l,k) $\wedge$
TFUSION((i...i), l) $\wedge$
$\neg$ TFUSION($((O_1 - i)...(O_{k-1} - i)\ \ O_k\ \ (O_{k+1} - i)...(O_m - i))$, $\neg$ l) $\wedge$
$\neg$ EMPTY($(O_1 - i), ..., (O_{k-1} - i), O_k, (O_{k+1} - i), ..., (O_m - i)$) $\rightarrow$
TFUSION($(O_1...O_{k-1}\ \ O_k > i\ \ O_{k+1}...O_m)$, l)
(4) EMPTY(nil...nil)

Proposition (soundness and completeness)
Let l be a literal of L, let $O_1...O_m$ be m topic-compatible total orders on a subset of {1..n}. Using negation-as-failure on the meta-progran META, PROLOG succeeds in proving TFUSION($(O_1...O_m)$, l) iff FUSION-T $\models (\psi \rightarrow [O_1...O_m]l)$. it fails iff FUSION-T $\models (\psi \rightarrow \neg\ [O_1...O_m]\ l)$

Sketch of proof
We first introduce an intermediate meta-program where the negation of literals TFUSION and EMPTY are explicitely represented by new predicates nonTFUSION and nonEMPTY. PROLOG without negation-as-failure, can be used on this meta-program. And we can show that it proves TFUSION($(O_1...O_m)$, l) iff FUSION-T $\vdash (\psi \rightarrow [O_1...O_m]\ l)$. Its proves nonTFUSION($(O_1...O_m)$, l) iff FUSION-T $\vdash (\psi \rightarrow \neg\ [O_1...O_m]\ l)$.

In a second step,, we optimize this intermediate program by only using predicates TFUSION and EMPTY and applying PROLOG with negation-as-failure.

3.2 Extension to any propositional formula

We consider four new meta-axioms and a new function, noted $\cup$, for the management of conjunctions and disjunctions :

(5) CFUSION($(O_1...O_m)$,nil)
(6) DFUSION($(O_1...O_m)$,d) $\wedge$ CFUSION($(O_1...O_m)$,c) $\rightarrow$ CFUSION($(O_1...O_m)$,d $\cup$ c)
(7) TFUSION($(O_1...O_m)$,l) $\rightarrow$ DFUSION($(O_1...O_m)$,l $\cup$ d)
(8) DFUSION($(O_1...O_m)$,d) $\rightarrow$ DFUSION($(O_1...O_m)$, l $\cup$ d)

Proposition .
Let F be a formula under its conjunctive normal form in which no disjunction is a tautology . Let $(O_1 ... O_m)$ be m topic-compatible total orders on a subset of {1..n}. Using negation-as-failure on the meta-progran obtained by adding these four axioms to META, PROLOG proves the goal CFUSION($(O_1 ... O_m)$,F) iff FUSION-T $\models (\psi \rightarrow [(O_1 ... O_m)]F)$; it fails iff FUSION-T $\models (\psi \rightarrow \neg [(O_1 ... O_m)] F)$

Sketch of proof
This result is essentially due to the fact that these new axioms are definite Horn clauses with no function symbols in the left side, and to the fact that the databases we consider are sets of literals.

4 Discussion

Let us notice that the notion of reliability we have introduced in our work, expressed by an order between the databases, is a relative notion. Indeed, we only assume that a database is assumed to be more reliable than another one. We do not assume that even the most reliable database is providing information which is true in the real world. In other terms, none of the databases, even the most reliable, is assumed to be safe [20], [11] i.e to tell the truth. In our work, the database obtained by merging several information sources still remains of collection of beliefs.

Recently, in [19], A. Motro also attacked the problem of multiple information sources. Like us, he is interested in providing a way to answer queries addressed to a collection of information sources, and particularly, answers which are "inconsistent". However, his notion of inconsistency is not exactly the same as ours : indeed, he considers that two information sources are inconsistent as soon as they describe differently the same portion of the real world. This does't mean that they are necessarily contradictory : two information sources may be inconsistent according to Motro, if for instance, one is more precise the other. He assumes that the information is provided by the sources with a degree of "goodness" (or in the previous terminology, a degree of safety) which estimates its relationship to the true information of the real world. The main problem is then to integrate information in a set of the highest goodness. Again, the problem we attacked here is a bit different since we do not consider in our work the relation between the information (stored in the databases), and the information of the real world it is supposed to represent.

Finally, we think that the notion of topics we have used in our work to order the information sources topic-by-topic, could also be used to the particular problem of belief revision in the following way : instead of considering that the new belief is always more reliable that the initial set of beliefs (this is what one of the postulate of revision, named R1 in [16], expresses), we could consider that for some topics, the new belief is more reliable, but for some other topics, this is the initial set of beliefs which is more reliable.

References

[1] S. Abiteboul and G. Grahne. Update semantics for incomplete databases. In *Proceedings of VLDB*, pages 1–12, 1985.

[2] J. Minker C. Baral, S. Kraus and V.S. Subrahmanian. Combining multiple knowledge bases. *IEEE Trans. on Knowledge and Data Engineering*, 3(2), 1991.

[3] J. Minker C. Baral, S. Kraus and V.S. Subrahmanian. Combining knowledge bases consisting of first order theories. *Computational Intelligence*, 8(1), 1992.

[4] S. Cazalens and R. Demolombe. Intelligent access to data and knowledge bases via users' topics of interest. In *Proceedings of IFIP Conference*, pages 245–251, 1992.

[5] L. Cholvy. Proving theorems in a multi-sources environment. In *Proceedings of IJCAI*, pages 66–71, 1993.

[6] L. Cholvy. A logical approach to multi-sources reasoning. In *Lecture notes in Artificial Intelligence*, number 808, pages 183–196. Springer-Verlag, 1994.

[7] L. Cholvy and R. Demolombe. Reasoning with information sources ordered by topics. In *Proc of AIMSA*, 1994.

[8] F. Cuppens and R. Demolombe. Cooperative Answering: a methodology to provide intelligent access to Databases. In *Proc of Eexpert Database Systems*, 1988.

[9] J. Lang D. Dubois and H. Prade. Dealing with multi-source information in possibilistic logic. In *Proceedings of ECAI*, pages 38–42, 1992.

[10] L. G. Demichiel. Resolving database incompatibility : an approach to performing relational operations over mismatched domains. *IEEE Transactions on Knowledge and Data Engineering*, 1(4), 1989.

[11] R. Demolombe and A. Jones. Deriving answers to safety queries. In *Proc of International workshop on nonstandard queries and answers (Toulouse)*, 1991.

[12] R.L. Epstein. *The Semantic Foundations of Logic, Volume1: Propositional Logic*. Kluwer Academic, 1990.

[13] Y. Breitbart et al. Panel : interoperability in multidatabases : semantic and systems issues. In *Proc of VLDB*, pages 561–562, 1991.

[14] L. Farinas and A. Herzig. Reasoning about database updates. In *Workshop of Foundations of deductive databases and logic programming.*

[15] P. Gardenfors. *Knowledge in Flux : Modeling the Dynamics of Epistemic States.* The MIT Press, 1988.

[16] H. Katsuno and A. Mendelzon. Propositional knowledge base revision and minimal change. *Artificial Intelligence*, 52, 1991.

[17] G.M. Kupper, J.D. Ullman, and M. Vardi. On the equivalence of logical databases. In *Proc of ACM-PODS*, 1984.

[18] G. Lakemeyer. All they know about. In *Proc. of AAAI-93*, 1993.

[19] A. Motro. A formal framework for integrating inconsistent answers from multiple information sources. Technical Report ISSE-TR-93-106, George Mason University.

[20] A. Motro. Integrity = validity + completeness. In *ACM TODS*, volume 14(4).

[21] B. Nebel. A knowledge level analysis of belief revision. In *Proc of KR'89.*

[22] R. Demolombe S. Cazalens and A. Jones. A logic for reasoning about is about. Technical report, ESPRIT Project MEDLAR, 1992.

[23] M. Siegel and S. E. Madnick. A metadata approach to resolving semantic conflicts. In *Proceedings of VLDB*, pages 133–146, 1991.

[24] M. Winslett. *Updating Logical Databases.* Cambridge University Press, 1990.

[25] M. Winslett-Wilkins. A model theoretic approach to updating logical databases. In *Proceedings of International Conference on Database Theory*, Rome, 1986.

Linking transition-based update and base revision*

Marie-Odile Cordier[1] and Jérôme Lang[2]

[1] IRISA, Campus de Beaulieu, RENNES Cedex, France, cordier@irisa.fr
[2] IRIT, 118 route de Narbonne, 31062 TOULOUSE Cedex, France, lang@irit.fr

Abstract. This paper gives several different translations between the transition model proposed for belief update in [6] and base revision [14], which sheds some new light on the links between update and revision.

1 Introduction

Katsuno and Mendelzon [13] oppose belief revision (we introduce a new piece of information in a static world, i.e. we learn that the actual world satisfies α) to belief update (the new piece of information α is verified after an evolution of the world). Among the postulates that Katsuno and Mendelzon require for belief update operators, the following one : if $KB \models \alpha$ then $Update(KB, \alpha) \equiv KB$ $(U2)$ has been criticized by different authors; namely, this axiom enforces *inertia*, i.e. fluents tend to persist if nothing contradicts it. Some authors (see Section 5) propose extended or alternative frameworks for reasoning about world change where inertia $(U2)$ is not necessarily taken for granted.

A point which is left aside in the work of Katsuno and Mendelzon is that it is often practically unreasonable to assume that the transition structure (i.e. the collection of $\leq_M$) is explicitely specified by the user. This assumption is even more unreasonable when inertia is not required. In [6], Cordier and Siegel proposed to generate the transition structure from a set of syntactic *transition constraints* of the form "if α holds in a state then β is expected to hold in the next state, i.e. the state resulting from the update". (See Section 5 for alternative ways to generate this transition structure). In this paper, we argue that this transition-based approach is the counterpart for update of the so-called *syntax-based* approaches for belief revision, as proposed and studied by many authors, especially Nebel [14] [15]. We show first that, in the particular case where the knowledge base is complete, transition-based update can be viewed as base revision. Namely, we propose two different translations highlighting two different views on the relation existing between transition-based update and base revision. Then, in the general case where the initial knowledge base is not complete (i.e. does not determine a unique world), we show that after an adequate change of language, it is still possible to translate a transition-based update operator into a base revision operator.

---

* This work is partially supported by the French national project entitled "Gestion de l'évolutif et de l'incertain" (Handling of Uncertainty in a Dynamical World)

2 Preliminaries

2.1 Notations

In the rest of the paper, $\mathcal{L}$ is a propositional language generated by a finite number of propositional variables; α, β, φ, ψ, ..., are formulas of $\mathcal{L}$; $\top$ and $\bot$ denote respectively tautology and contradiction; M, M', ... denote interpretations (possible worlds) for $\mathcal{L}$; the set of all possible worlds is denoted by $\mathcal{M}$; $Mod(\alpha)$ denotes the set of models of α; if S is a set of formulas then $M[S] = \{\varphi \in S | M \models \varphi\}$; $\subset$ denotes strict inclusion. For each model M, $for(M)$ denotes the propositional formula whose only model is M (i.e. the conjunction of all literals satisfied by M).

2.2 Updates induced from transition constraints

In [6], Cordier and Siegel propose a syntactic *transition model* for update. We recall a simplified version of this approach (we introduce only what we need in the paper).

A *transition* is a pair $\langle \varphi, \psi \rangle$ of propositional formulas. Intuitively, it means that if φ is true at a given time point, then normally the world should evolve in such a way that ψ is verified at the next time point. The approach considers only two time points, namely the *initial* time point t, and the *final* one t' : t (resp. t') is the time point corresponding to the world *before* (resp. *after*) its evolution. A *transition model* is a ranked collection of transitions, where the ranks corresponds to priorities: $TR = TR_1 \cup ... \cup TR_n$, where each TR_i is a finite set of transitions. Level 1 corresponds to the most prioritary transitions and level n to the least prioritary ones.

A transition model TR induces a collection of preference relations on worlds $\leq_{TR,M}$ for each $M \in \mathcal{M}$, defined as follows: for each $i = 1...n$, let $Diff_i(M, M') = \{\langle \varphi, \psi \rangle \in TR_i$ such that $M \models \varphi$ and $M' \models \neg\psi\}$. Now, $M' <_{TR,M} M''$ iff $\exists i$ such that $Diff_i(M, M') \subset Diff_i(M, M'')$ and $\forall j < i, Diff_j(M, M') = Diff_j(M, M'')$. $<_{TR,M}$ is a strict ordering; the partial preordering $\leq_{TR,M}$ is now defined by $M' \leq_{TR,M} M''$ iff $M' <_{TR,M} M''$ or $\forall i, Diff_i(M, M') = Diff_i(M, M'')$. We do not consider here *sure transitions* as in the original framework (see [6]).

Now, let KB be a knowledge base, representing what we know about the initial world at time t, and α a formula that we know to hold in the world at time t'. We do not require any assumption about whether the meaning of the update by α is action-oriented (the agent makes the world satisfy α) or event-oriented (an event has occurred, which has made the world satisfy α). The *update* of world M by α w.r.t. the transition model TR is the set of worlds $Update\_model(M, TR, \alpha) = Min(<_{M,TR}, Mod(\alpha))$. Now, the new knowledge base resulting from the update of KB by α w.r.t. TR is defined by $\beta \in Update(KB, TR, \alpha)$ iff $\cup_{M \models KB} Update\_model(M, TR, \alpha) \subseteq Mod(\beta)$.

In the rest of the paper, we will often consider the simple case of a non-prioritised transition model: we will thus establish first the results in this simpler case - the generalisation to the prioritised case being most of the time easy.

2.3 Base revision as inconsistency handling

Inconsistency handling consists in restoring the consistency of an inconsistent set of formulas. More specifically, *syntax-based inconsistency handling* (see e.g. [1] for a discussion) consists in selecting preferred consistent subsets of a knowledge base K. A straightforward choice for a preference criterion are maximality w.r.t. set inclusion (i.e. select maximal consistent subsets) This criterion can be easily generalized to the prioritised case: if $K = K_1 \cup \ldots \cup K_n$ (where 1 is the highest priority level) then, if $K' = K'_1 \cup \ldots \cup K'_n$ and $K'' = K''_1 \cup \ldots \cup K''_n$ are two consistent subsets of K, then $K' <^{inc}_K K''$ iff $\exists i$ such that $K'_i \supset K''_i$ and $\forall j < i, K'_j = K''_j$. The $<^{inc}_K$-preferred subsets are those which are minimal w.r.t. $<^{inc}_K$. These $<^{inc}_K$-preferred subsets were called "preferred subtheories" by Brewka [3].[3]

Base revision [14] [15] [16] is a *syntax-based* approach to belief revision which consists roughly in restoring the consistency after adding a new formula α to a belief base KB (a consistent set of formulas). The terminology *syntax-based*, introduced by Nebel [14], means that the syntactic way the knowledge base K is written will influence the revision operator: each formula of K is considered a distinct piece of information which will be kept or rejected in a whole. For instance, $K = \{a, b\}$ will not be revised the same way as $K' = \{a \wedge b\}$ by the new formula $\neg a$: $b \in Revise(K, \neg a)$ while $b \notin Revise(K', \neg a)$. More formally, the prioritised base revision operator was defined first by Nebel [14] by $\beta \in Revise(K, \alpha)$ iff for any $<_{inc}$-preferred subset S of K among those consistent with α, then $S \cup \{\alpha\} \models \beta$. This specific base revision operator will be referred to in the rest of the paper as Nebel's base revision operator. Obviously, other base revision operators can be obtained by letting the preference criterion vary.

Thus, base revision is directly related to inconsistency handling. Both can be characterized by means of preferential models [1]: $M \leq_K M'$ (i.e. M is preferred to M' w.r.t. K) iff $\exists i$ such that $M[K_i] \supset M'[K_i]$ and $\forall j < i, M[K_i] = M'[K_i]$; then, $\beta \in Revise(K, \alpha) \Leftrightarrow Min(\leq_K, Mod(\alpha)) \subseteq Mod(\beta)$. We will show in the next section that up to a certain extent, transition-based update as defined by Cordier and Siegel in [6] is the syntax-based version of belief update in the sense of [13].

3 Transition-based update on a complete knowledge base = transition + inconsistency handling

In this section we consider a transition model TR and an initial knowledge base which is *complete*, i.e. it has only one model M. In practice, this means that we know which transitions are applicable at t. So, when all applicable transitions can be applied without generating any inconsistency at time t', the result of the update will be the conjunction of the results obtained by applying these constraints; more generally, when they generate an inconsistency, then the result of the update will be obtained by syntax-based inconsistency handling of the (inconsistent) set of formulas consisting in the results of applicable constraints. We are now investigating more formally this principle UPDATING = TRANSITION + INCONSISTENCY HANDLING. Let us first introduce several preliminary definitions.

[3] Of course, this preference selection criterion is not the only possible one. For instance, [1] propose to select subsets of maximal cardinality. However, when we refer in the rest of the paper to "syntax-based inconsistency handling", we refer by default to $<^{inc}_K$ (unless stated otherwise).

Definition 1 *The set of applicable transitions w.r.t. a transition model TR and a model M is defined by*

$$App(TR, M) = \{\langle\varphi, \psi\rangle \in TR \mid M \models \varphi\}$$

Definition 2 *The result of applying a transition model TR to a model M is the set of formulas obtained by projecting the set of applicable transitions on the effect part of the constraints:*

$$Result(TR, M) = \{\psi \mid \langle\varphi, \psi\rangle \in App(TR, M)\}$$

If TR is a prioritised transition model, then $App(TR, M)$ and $Result(TR, M)$ are prioritised too, the priorities being directly inherited from the priorities of the transitions.

Let us see now how, for complete knowledge bases, transition-based update can be viewed as base revision.

Proposition 1 *Let TR be a transition model, KB a complete knowledge base whose model is M, and let α, β two formulas. Then*

$$\beta \in Update(TR, M, \alpha) \text{ iff } \beta \in Revise(Result(TR, M), \alpha)$$

(where $Revise$ is Nebel's base revision operator).

Proof: For the sake of simplicity we give the proof in the non-prioritised case . Since KB is complete, $Update(KB, TR, \alpha) = Update - model(M, \alpha) = Min(<_{M,TR}, Mod(\alpha))$ and thus $\beta \in Update(KB, TR, \alpha)$ iff $Min(<_{M,TR}, Mod(\alpha)) \subseteq Mod(\beta)$. Now, $\beta \in Revise(Result(TR, M), \alpha)$ iff $Min(<_{Result(TR,M)}, Mod(\alpha)) \subseteq Mod(\beta)$, where $M' <_{Result(TR,M)} M''$ iff $Result(TR, M) \cap Mod(M') \supset Result(TR, M) \cap Mod(M'')$. Thus, what remains only to be showed is that $<_{Result(TR,M)}$ and $<_{M,TR}$ are identical. This last step is easy:

$M' <_{M,TR} M''$
$\Leftrightarrow Diff(M, M', TR) \subset Diff(M, M'', TR)$
$\Leftrightarrow \{\langle\varphi, \psi\rangle \in App(TR, M) | M' \models \neg\psi\} \subset \{\langle\varphi, \psi\rangle \in App(TR, M) | M'' \models \neg\psi\}$
$\Leftrightarrow \{\psi \in Result(TR, M) | M' \models \neg\psi\} \subset \{\psi \in Result(TR, M) | M'' \models \neg\psi\}$
$\Leftrightarrow \{\psi \in Result(TR, M) | M' \models \psi\} \supset \{\psi \in Result(TR, M) | M'' \models \psi\}$
$\Leftrightarrow M' <_{Result(TR,M)} M''$. QED.

Thus, using a transition model for updating a complete knowledge base KB can be viewed as the sequence of the two following steps: first, the applicable transitions are "fired" no matter if the resulting set of formulas representing knowledge at time t' is inconsistent; then, if it is inconsistent, this inconsistency is handled by the well-studied inclusion-based preference relation.

Thus, *any transition-based update operator applied to a complete knowledge base corresponds to a base revision operator.* The converse, which is straightforward, establishes that transition-based update of complete knowledge includes base revision as a particular case:

Proposition 2 *Any base revision operator corresponds to a transition-based update operator applied to a complete knowledge base.*

Proof: (in the non-prioritised case): let $K = \{\varphi_1, ..., \varphi_n\}$ be a belief base. Define $TM(K) = \{\langle\top, \varphi_1\rangle, ..., \langle\top, \varphi_n\rangle\}$. Obviously, $Result(TM(K), M) = K$, hence the result. QED.

Actually, with base revision we reason only about the knowledge base at time t', and the degenerate update is then completely independent from KB_t and therefore also from the premise parts of the transition constraints (indeed, base revision deals with a *static* world).

Translating KB to $Result(KB, TM)$ has to be done each time we will use a given transition model to a specific knowledge base KB. Doing so yields a loss of knowledge since the revision operator does not contain any longer anything corresponding to the transition constraints. We propose now another translation, which really encodes the transitions, and which gives a different view on how to see update as a revision operator in the case of complete knowledge. Thus, from a knowledge representation point of view, both translations are interesting. This second translation assumes a change of language. It is the same translation as that defined in [6] for establishing the link between transition-based change and prioritised circumscription. Each propositional variable a is "split" into two new ones a_t and $a_{t'}$. If φ is a complex formula then φ_t (resp. $\varphi_{t'}$) is the formula obtained by replacing each occurence of a propositional variable x by x_t (resp. $x_{t'}$). To the (complete) knowledge base KB we associate the formula KB_t. The transition model TR is then translated in $f(TR)$ as follows:

Definition 3 $f(\langle\varphi, \psi\rangle) = \varphi_t \rightarrow \psi_{t'}; f(TR) = \{f(\langle\varphi, \psi\rangle) | \langle\varphi, \psi\rangle \in TR\}$

Then we have:

Proposition 3

$$\beta \in Update(KB, TR, \alpha) \Leftrightarrow \beta_{t'} \in Revise(f(TR), \{KB_t, \alpha_{t'}\})$$

This translation sheds some new light on viewing update as revision. In Propositions 1 and 3, what we revise are *beliefs* while what we apply the update operator on are only *facts holding at* t, the truth of which cannot be questioned. Therefore,

- either (Proposition 1) we start from the facts known at t (the complete knowledge base KB whose model is M), and by the transition model we obtain beliefs about what should be true at t'. These beliefs ($Result(TR, M)$) are then revised by α.
- or (Proposition 3) we consider directly the transition model as beliefs on the way the world should change, and then we revise these beliefs by what is holding for sure at t (KB) and at t' (α).

4 The general case

In this section TR denotes a transition system and KB an initial knowledge base whose model set is $Mod(KB) = \{M_1, ...M_p\}$. From the results of Section 3 and the definition of transition-based updates we have

$\beta \in Update(KB, TR, \alpha)$
$\Leftrightarrow \beta \in \cap_{i=1}^{p} Revise(Result(M_i, TR), \alpha)$
$\Leftrightarrow \beta_{t'} \in \cap_{i=1}^{p} Revise(f(TR), \{(M_i)_t, \alpha_{t'}\})$

So, transition-based update does not straightforwardly correspond to a single base revision operator but to an *intersection* of base revision operators. To see that the translation of Proposition 3 does not work if KB is incomplete, consider this version of Sandewall's hiding turkey scenario (where h, l and d stand for "hidden", "loaded" and "deaf"). [18] [6]: $TR = \{\langle \neg d, l \rightarrow h \rangle, \langle \neg h, \neg h \rangle, \langle \neg d, \neg d \rangle, \langle d, d \rangle\}$, $KB = \neg h$ and $\alpha = l$. $f(TR) \wedge KB_t \wedge l_{t'}$ is consistent, so this is the only preferred subset, and $KB_t \wedge l_{t'} \wedge (\neg d_t \wedge l_{t'} \rightarrow h_{t'}) \wedge (h_t \rightarrow h_{t'}) \models d_t \wedge h_{t'}$, which is not the intended result.

Translating transition-based update into base revision:

In the case of a complete initial knowledge base we had shown that it was possible to find an equivalent base revision operator *using the same propositional language* (Proposition 1). This result cannot be generalized to the general case; however, it is still possible in the general case to find an equivalent base revision operator *modulo a change of the language* (as in Proposition 3 but with a more complex translation).

Proposition 4 *Let* $\Delta_{TR,KB} = \Delta_0 \cup \Delta_1 \cup \ldots \cup \Delta_n$ *be the prioritised knowledge base induced from* TR *and* KB *by:* $\Delta_0 = \{for(M)_t | M \models KB\}$ *and for any* $i = 1 \ldots n$, $\Delta_i = \{\varphi_t \rightarrow \psi_{t'} | \langle \varphi, \psi \rangle \in TR_i\} = f(TR_i)$. *Then* $\beta \in Update(KB, TR, \alpha) \Leftrightarrow \beta_{t'} \in Revise(\Delta_{TR,KB}, \alpha t')$

Proof sketch: unformally, the role of Δ_0 is that all $\leq_{\Delta_{TR,KB}}$-preferred models will satisfy a maximal subset of Δ_0, which means exactly one formula of Δ_0 (corresponding to one model of KB) since they are mutually inconsistent. Now, for a fixed model M_t of KB, the Δ_i's for $i \geq 1$ ensure that $M_t \cup M'_{t'} \in Min(\leq_{\Delta_{TR,KB}}) \Leftrightarrow M' \in Min(\leq_{TR,M}, Mod(\alpha))$.

Example : let us come back to the hiding turkey scenario considered at the beginning of the Section. Its translation is
$\Delta_0 = \{h_t \wedge \neg d_t, h_t \wedge d_t\}$,
$\Delta_1 = \{\neg d_t \rightarrow (l_{t'} \rightarrow h_{t'}), \neg h_t \rightarrow \neg h_{t'}, d_t \rightarrow d_{t'}, \neg d_t \rightarrow \neg d_{t'}\}$.

Thus, any transition-based update operator can be translated into a base revision operator in the sense of Nebel [14], up to a change of language. Note that if KB_t has only one model, the latter translation becomes equivalent to the one of Proposition 3.

As it was the case for complete knowledge, the transition model TM is considered as beliefs on the way the world should change; what is holding for sure at t (given by $\{for(M)_t | M \models KB\}$) is considered as prioritary beliefs by belonging to Δ_0. This prioritised set of beliefs $\Delta_{TR,KB}$ can then be revised by $\alpha_{t'}$. This translation between transition-based update and revision clearly does not mean that update is equivalent to revision, but that update can be seen as revision after an adequate change of representation.

5 Related work

As already mentioned in the introduction, some authors have proposed to induce update operators in a "more friendly" way than specifying explicitely the whole transition structure $\{\leq_M, M \in \mathcal{M}\}$. In the work of Winslett [19], the update operator is only induced by inertia (since it minimizes the set of propositional variables whose truth value changes). It can be checked easily that Winslett's update operator can be recovered by a transition model which contains exactly all transitions $\langle a, a \rangle$ and $\langle \neg a, \neg a \rangle$, for all propositional variables a.

Goldszmidt and Pearl [12] propose a machinery based on a causal network and Z^+ stratified rules (where the stratification is computed automatically and takes account of specificity) to encode persistence and causation. The update of KB by φ is encoded by $\{\varphi_t \rightarrow \varphi_{t'}, \neg\varphi_t \rightarrow \neg\varphi_{t'}, do(\varphi) \rightarrow \varphi_{t'}\}$, where $\varphi_t, \varphi_{t'}$ denote respectively φ before and after the update, and $do(\varphi)$ is a new propositional literal whose truth expresses that the update by φ is performed. The last rule $do(\varphi) \rightarrow \varphi_{t'}\}$ is more specific than the persistence rule $\neg\varphi_t \rightarrow \neg\varphi_{t'}$ and will thus override it when the update by φ is performed. The resulting update operator does not satisfy inertia. Note that this is a nice way to generate automatically (prioritised) transition constraints, which can then be used as discussed in [6] and in this paper. Recently, Dubois et al. [9] proposed an approach similar to Goldszmidt and Pearl's approach without requiring the existence of an acyclic causal network.

Del Val and Shoham [8] induce update operators from a theory of action based on the situation calculus and using persistence axioms (which, roughly, specify which fluents tend to persist in which state); their updates are more general than KM updates (they do not generally satisfy inertia) and they show under which conditions on the persistence axioms they do satisfy these postulates. This different approach (less syntactic) to generate updates is somewhat less intuitive than transition-based update, more so because (to our opinion) from the point of view of the user, persistence axioms are harder to specify to transition constraints.

Some other works induce updates from explicit action models (and thus are more concerned with planning). Brewka and Hertzberg [4] encode the effects of actions by a disjunctive collection of transitions $\langle precondition, postcondition \rangle$ and then they minimize the set of violated transitions (for a comparison of both approaches see [6]).

Boutilier [2] proposes an alternative, event-based view of update operators, based on an set of possible events E, where an event e maps each world M to a set of worlds $e(M)$ (representing the possible results of the event), and equipped with a plausibility ordering of events $\leq_M$ for each world M; then, updating KB by α means: if after the evolution of the world, we observe α, then we look for the most plausible explanations, i.e. the most plausible events which may have occurred, and we use these explanations to predict further consequences about the new state of the world. The update operator induced by an event model does not generally satisfy inertia [4]. This view of update is compatible with transition-based update, and the underlying ideas are very similar; we can view an applicable transition as a possible event, which suggests that the transition model can be

[4] It does if the following condition is assumed: whatever the initial state of the world, the most plausible event is always the null event, i.e. the event where nothing changes.

viewed as a syntactic counterpart of Boutilier's event model, which furthermore would avoid the explicit specification of all ordered sets of events for all worlds. However, a difference between both frameworks prevents us from translating simply any transition model into an event model by associating to each constraint $\langle\alpha, \beta\rangle$ an event e such that $\forall M \models \alpha, e(M) = Mod(\beta)$: whereas Boutilier allows at most one event to occur at once, the results of several transitions are simultaneously considered[5].

In [5], Cordier and Siegel proposed another transition model, different from the one detailed in Section 2 in several points, the most important being that in the case of an incomplete initial knowledge base, its models were not updated independently. See [6] for further comparisons between both approaches.

In many works, including [17] and [18], Sandewall proposes a classification of problems in the field of reasoning about action and change w.r.t the assumptions that are made how the world changes w.r.t. actions and what we know about the world and the occurrences of actions. Although transition-based updating does not deal with explicit time (but it could be done without difficulty), while Sandewall's classification does, it is worth looking for the class of problems adressed by transition constraints: it does not necessarily include inertia (I) unless specifying further assumptions (cf. Section 5), and includes the following ontological specialities: actions encoded by transition constraints may have alternative results (A), they may be concurrent (C), there may be surprises, i.e. changes which are not justified by any known occurrence of an action (S). As to the epistemological specialities, updating based on transition constraints assumes correct and accurate knowledge of the world ($\mathcal{K}$), but in general no complete knowledge about neither the initial nor the next states.

Fariñas and Herzig [11] induce update operators from an interference relation between formulas, following the principle: $\beta \in Update(KB, \alpha)$ iff α and β do not interfere - and then they give several possible definitions for practically generating an interference relation.

6 Conclusion and further work

In this paper we have established some connections between Cordier and Siegel's transition-based appoach to update [6] and the so-called syntax-based approaches to inconsistency handling and belief revision. For the sake of brevity we have considered all along this paper that the selection criterion fo inducing $<_{M,TR}$ was fixed. A immediate extension would be to generalize the connections when it varies. Some other criteria include using cardinality instead of set inclusion , taking account of an additional level of *sure* transitions [6] which can never be violated, or even switching to a more quantitative approach: for instance, we may think of associating to each transition the prior probability that it is not violated. Then it would be reasonable to integrate explicit time and then to consider also a probabilistic model of decreasing persistence such as Dean and Kanazawa's [7]: the probability of a transition $\langle\alpha, \alpha\rangle$ would then be a function $f(\alpha, t, t')$ which decreases when $t' - t$ increases.

[5] Now, in the other direction, it is possible to translate in a rather intuitive way any *complete* event model into an equivalent set of transitions constraints (i.e. generating the same update operator) which has the nice feature to be written more compactly.

Another point which is not considered in this paper is the particular case of inertia (U2). An example of transition model where the associate update operator satisfies inertia is Winslett's update operator [19] which can be obtained by the set of all transitions $\langle a, a \rangle$ and $\langle \neg a, \neg a \rangle$ for all propositional variables a. More generally, the conditions on the transition model under which the associated update operator satisfies inertia are of special interest. So is the connection with the work done by Dubois et al. [10] on updating without inertia. These are topics for further research.

References

1. Salem Benferhat, Claudette Cayrol, Didier Dubois, Jérôme Lang and Henri Prade, *Inconsistency management and prioritized syntax-based entailment*, Proc. of IJCAI'93, 640-645.
2. Craig Boutilier, *Abduction to plausible causes: an event-based model of belief update*, Tech. Report 94-9, Department of Computer Science, University of British Columbia, March 94.
3. Gerd Brewka, *Preferred subtheories: an extended logical framework for default reasoning*, Proceedings of IJCAI'89, 1043-1048.
4. Gerd Brewka and Joachim Hertzberg, *How to do things with worlds: on formalizing actions and plans*, J. of Logic and Computation, 3(5), 1993.
5. Marie-Odile Cordier and Pierre Siegel, *A temporal revision model for reasoning about world change*, Proc. of KR'92, 732-739.
6. Marie-Odile Cordier and Pierre Siegel, *Prioritised transitions for updates*, Tech. Report IRISA (Rennes - France), nb. 884, 1994. Short version somewhere in this volume.
7. Thomas Dean and Keiji Kanazawa, *A model for reasoning about persistence and causation*, Computational Intelligence 5 (1989), 142-150.
8. Alvaro del Val and Yoav Shoham, *Deriving properties of belief update from theories of action* Part 1 in Proc. of AAAI'92, 584-589. Part 2 in Proc. of IJCAI'93, 732-737.
9. Didier Dubois, Florence Dupin de Saint-Cyr and Henri Prade, *Updating, transition constraints and possibilistic Markov chains*, Proc. of IPMU'94, 826-831.
10. Didier Dubois, Florence Dupin de Saint-Cyr and Henri Prade, *Update postulates without inertia*, somewhere in this volume.
11. Luis Fariñas del Cerro and Andreas Herzig, *Revisions, updates and interference*, in Logic, Action and Information (A. Fuhrmann, H. Rott eds.), DeGruyter, 1993.
12. Moises Goldszmidt and Judea Pearl, *Rank-based systems: a simple approach to belief revision, belief update and reasoning about evidence and actions*, Proc. KR'92, 661-672.
13. Hirofumi Katsuno and Alberto O. Mendelzon, *On the difference between updating a knowledge base and revising it*, Proc. of KR'91, 387-394.
14. Bernhard Nebel, *Belief revision and default reasoning: syntax-based approaches*, Proceedings of KR'91, 417-428.
15. Bernhard Nebel, *Base revision operations and schemes: semantics, representation and complexity*, Proceedings of ECAI'94, 341-345.
16. Hans Rott, *Belief contraction in the context of the general theory of rational choice*, Journal of Symbolic Logic 58 (1993), 1426-1450.
17. Erik Sandewall, *The range of applicability of nonmonotonic logics for the inertia problem*, Proc. if IJCAI'93, 738-743.
18. Erik Sandewall, *Feature and Fluents*, Oxford University Press, 1995.
19. Marianne Winslett, *Reasoning about actions using a possible model approach*, Proc. of AAAI'88, 89-93.

Prioritized Transitions for Updates

Marie-Odile Cordier[1] and Pierre Siegel[2]

[1] IRISA, Campus de Beaulieu, 35042 RENNES Cedex, France, cordier@irisa.fr
[2] LIM, 3 place Victor Hugo, 13331 MARSEILLE Cedex 3, France, siegel@gyptis.univ-mrs.fr

Abstract. An update operation presupposes that one can predict how the world changes along time. In the absence of a predictive model of evolution, the common sense law of inertia is usually used and justifies the minimal change approach to the frame problem. Instead of relying on an implicit modeling of persistence, we propose to use an *explicit* modeling of the expected evolution. We first explain why our previous proposal was not quite satisfactory. We then propose a model-driven semantics of the update operation which can take into account an explicit transition model. The transition model provides a more powerful and flexible way to represent the persistence of information. It can moreover be stressed that non only persistence information but also default and transition rules can be expressed in this transition model. It can then be used to represent evolutive systems as required for example in a monitoring or diagnosis context.

1 Introduction

Update is an operation which turns a knowledge base KBt, describing the state of the world at time t, into a knowledge base KBt' describing the state of the world at time t'. This change is generally triggered by an event, supposed in the following to be the arrival of some new piece of information A known to be true at time t'. A then has to belong to KBt'. An update operation presupposes that one can predict how the world changes along time. It requires that the tendency for propositions describing the world to persist along time be known. In absence of a predictive modeling of evolution, the common sense law of inertia is usually used and justifies the minimal change approach to the frame problem [McCarthy and Hayes, 1969]: a proposition true at time t remains true at time t' unless it can be proved to be false in t'. KBt' describes the "closest" world to KBt accounting for the new piece of information A. This minimal change principle is the basis of the syntax-oriented approach (PWA) proposed by [Ginsberg and Smith, 1987] as well as the model-driven approach (PMA) proposed by [Winslett, 1988]. In the first case, the set of formulas describing KBt is changed as little as possible to account for the new piece of information. In the second case, each model of KBt is changed as little as possible to account for the new piece of information.

Instead of relying on an implicit notion of persistence as Winslett does, we propose to use an *explicit* and symbolic transition model [3]; a similar proposal has been done by [Dean and Kanazawa, 1989] who proposed to use an explicit probabilistic model

[3] The word "model" in transition model (as well as in model of persistence or model of transition) has no logical connotation. Transition model means here a formal representation of the evolution of a system.

of persistence and causation. This explicit modeling encodes the expected evolution and provides a more powerful and flexible way to represent how information tends to change along time. A proposal in that direction was made in [Cordier and Siégel, 1992]. Its major flaw is its inability to respect the model-driven principle which was shown to be crucial in an update context [Katsuno and Mendelzon, 1991]. According to this principle, each model of the theory has to be considered independently for update. It is not the case in this first proposal and its default-based semantics appears to be not adequate for update. Applying for example [Cordier and Siegel, 1992] to the *turkey scenario* leads to non-intuitive results, as we show in section 2.

In this paper, we propose a *model-driven* semantics for an update operation capable of taking into account an explicit transition model. It extends the model-driven semantics defined in [Winslett, 1989] for the Possible Model Approach by allowing an explicit expression of persistence. The transition model provides a more powerful and flexible way to represent how the world tends to change along time. It can moreover be stressed that non only persistence information but also default and transition rules can be expressed in this transition model. It can then be used to represent evolutive systems as required for example in a monitoring or diagnosis context.

The paper is structured as follows : we begin by showing on a motivating example the main issues of the update operation and we point out the flaws of our [Cordier and Siegel, 1992] proposal. The transition model is presented in section 3. The semantics of the update operation is defined in section 4 and illustrated by examples in section 5. In the last section, we conclude by comparing our approach to the related ones more precisely.

2 A Motivating Example

The following example [4] illustrates first that updating a knowledge base requires a model-driven approach, as demonstrated by [Winslett, 1988] and [Katsuno and Mendelzon, 1991]. In scenario 1, not considering independently each model leads clearly to non intuitive results. Scenario 2 illustrates that common-sense reasoning about change makes use of an a priori ordering on the expected transitions. This was first shown by [Winslett, 1988] who proposed to extend PMA with priorities.

At the end of this section, we rely on this example to point out the major flaws of [Cordier and Siegel, 1992] and to justify this new proposal.

Scenario 1. Let us suppose that we know that a turkey is sleeping at time t. We know as a constraint that "as soon as the alarm rings, the turkey is awake or it is deaf" [5].

$KBt = Th(Asleep, Alarm \Rightarrow (Deaf \vee \neg Asleep))$.

At time t', we learn that the alarm rings. This corresponds to the arrival of a new piece of information A with $A = Alarm$. We would like to know what happens to the turkey at time t', i.e. what is the next state KBt' where KBt' = Update(KBt, A). Remember that A has to belong to KBt'.

---

[4] This example is inspired by *the hiding turkey scenario* from [Sandewall, 1995].

[5] We do not take into account the short delay between the alarm and its effects.

Let us see how we would reason (using commonsense) on this scenario. We do not know if the turkey is deaf or not at time t. Two cases have then to be considered. In the first case, the turkey is deaf at time t; we can consider that it is an immutable information and that it will still be deaf at time t'; it will then remain asleep. In the second case, the turkey is not deaf at time t. What happens next depends on the relative persistence of $\neg Deaf$ and $Asleep$. Supposing $\neg Deaf$ to be more persistent than $Asleep$, (i.e. the change from being asleep to not being asleep is more expected than the change from being not-deaf to being deaf), the turkey remains not-deaf and not to be asleep at time t'. Considering these two cases, we get that the turkey is either deaf and asleep or not-deaf and not-asleep.

This first scenario demonstrates clearly that the possible worlds in t (or the models of KBt) and their expected changes have to be considered independently. Not doing so, we would obtain as KBt' $\{\{Asleep, Deaf, Alarm\}\}$ which is clearly not the expected result (an alarm does not make someone deaf!).

Scenario 2. In this second scenario, the only thing we know at time t is that the turkey is not deaf. $KBt = Th(\neg Deaf, Alarm \Rightarrow Deaf \vee \neg Asleep)$. We learn that the alarm rings at time t'. In this case, supposing as before that $\neg Deaf$ is more persistent than $Asleep$, we do not need to wonder whether or not the turkey was sleeping at time t. The turkey remains not-deaf and will be awaken : KBt' $\{\{\neg Asleep, \neg Deaf, Alarm\}\}$

This second scenario demonstrates that common-sense reasoning about change makes use of an a priori ordering on the expected transitions. Not doing so would result in the turkey being still not-deaf and awake *or* being asleep as long as it is now deaf! This latter case clearly disagrees with our common-sense expectations.

Using this example, we can now point out the major flaws of the [Cordier and Siegel, 1992]'s approach which cannot correctly dealt with these two scenarios. Let us recall briefly that, in [Cordier and Siegel, 1992], persistence is expressed by elementary transitions which can be seen as temporal defaults. An axiomatisation was proposed to combine the elementary transitions by three operators : σ(substitution), $\wedge$(and) and $\vee$(or). The $\vee$ operator was quite important in that it allowed to get the persistence of a disjunctive formula. It was adequate to solve the well-known examples of the update literature, as the door-and-window example. Knowing that a door or a window is open at time t, you do not want that the closure of the door at time t' makes you infer that the window is now (magically) closed. But it was not sufficient to provide a model-driven approach, assuring that each model is updated independently. Applied to scenario 1, it leads to the non intuitive result explained before : not knowing whether the turkey is Deaf or not, persistent formulas concerning Deaf cannot be applied; on the contrary, persistent formulas concerning Asleep can be applied and the turkey is considered as deaf. The key point in this scenario is not the question of the persistence for a disjunctive formula, but that of considering for updates the two cases, deaf and not-deaf, separately. The default-based semantics we used proved to be not adequate for that.

Concerning the scenario 2, only three classes of formulas can be expressed in our [Cordier and Siegel, 1992] transition model, constraints, immutable and persistant formulas [5] , which appears not to be sufficient. $\neg Deaf$ and $Asleep$ are both persistant formulas; no preference can be given to one on the other. As we see in section 3, we propose now a transition model where formulas can be ordered in a more powerful way by giving them priorities.

These scenarios have motivated the main points of this new proposal : to define a *model-driven* semantics for an update operation while taking into account an *explicit model of transition* where formulas can be ordered by *priorities*.

3 The Transition Model

Let us first define the transition model which allows us to explicitly express the way information tends to persist along time.

A state of the world is represented by a deductively closed set *KB* of first-order formulas. A formula belonging to *KBt* is a formula true at time *t*. [6]

The transition model *TM* is composed of a set of elementary transitions. An elementary transition is described as a pair $\langle X, Y\rangle$ where X and Y are formulas. There exist two kinds of elementary transitions : sure transitions ST and (more or less) expected transitions ET.

- A sure transition $ST : \langle X, Y\rangle$ expresses that : if X is true in a state *KBt*, then Y must be true in the successing state *KBt'*.
- An expected transition $ET : \langle X, Y\rangle$ expresses that : if X is true in a state *KBt*, then Y is expected to be true in the successing state *KBt'*. Expected transitions are partially ordered : $ET_i > ET_j$ means that ET_i is more expected than ET_j.

This model allows us to express constraints, time-dependent formulas such as immutable and persistent formulas, [7] and other typical kinds of change.

A *constraint* (or protected formula) K is a formula which is always true. It is expressed by a sure transition $ST : \langle True, K\rangle$. For example, $ST : \langle True, Male \vee Female\rangle$ means that $Male \vee Female$ has to be true in the world at any time.

An *immutable* formula F is a formula which as soon as it has become true remains true along time. It is expressed by a sure transition $ST : \langle F, F\rangle$. For example $ST : \langle Dead, Dead\rangle$ or $ST : \langle Deaf, Deaf\rangle$ means that if we know at time *t* that someone is dead (or deaf), we consider it to be true in all the subsequent states.

A *persistent* formula is a formula which, if true at time t, remains true as long as possible; it is then expected to be true at time t' unless it leads to a inconsistency. A persistent formula F is expressed by an expected transition $ET : \langle F, F\rangle$. For example, $ET : \langle Married, Married\rangle$ means that if we know that someone is married, we expect it to be true as long as there is no evidence to the contrary.

Other typical kinds of change can also be expressed in this formalism by $ST : \langle F, G\rangle$ or $ET : \langle F, G\rangle$: they correspond to sure or expected change from F to G. As for example:

$ST : \langle clock(i), clock(i+1)\rangle$ states that the clock is increased of one unit at each transition.

---

[6] We suppose a discrete representation of time.

[7] Notice that we changed our vocabulary to conform to common use : what we named persistent formulas in [Cordier and Siegel, 1992] are now named immutable formulas and remanent formulas are named persistent formulas.

$ET : \langle True, F \rangle$ expresses default formulas as $ET : \langle True, On(Switch) \rangle$ which expresses the default value of a switch.

$ET : \langle lighton, deadbattery \rangle$ expresses that if the lights have been on, we expect that the battery will be dead in the next state [8].

In the following we consider that the partial ordering between the expected transitions allows us to partition the set of expected transitions into strata, numbered from $S1$ to Sn. For $i > j$, the transitions of the ith stratum are more expected than the transitions of the jth stratum. We have $Sn > Sn - 1 > ... > S1$. Each element of $Si - 1$ are those directly less than the elements of Si. It can be noticed that an expected transition belonging to the maximal stratum (the nth stratum) does not have the same semantics as a sure transition. A sure transition cannot be overruled by any arriving piece of information. It has to be satisfied. An expected transition, even if it belongs to the maximal stratum, can be overruled by an arriving piece of information; however, it maintains in any case priority over other expected transitions belonging to inferior strata.

4 Semantics for Updates using a Transition Model

The update operation of a state *KBt* by some piece of information A using a transition model *TM* is denoted $\text{Update}_{TM}(KBt, A)$ or Update(KBt, A) for short. This update operation corresponds to considering each possible world at time t (or model of *KBt*) in turn; for each of these models, looking for the set of models which account for A and are the "closest" to what is expected to be true in t' for this model according to *TM*. As explained in section 3, we note $TM : \{ ST, ET \}$ where ST (resp. ET) represents here the set of sure (resp. expected) transitions, and $ET : \{ S1, S2, \ldots, Sn \}$ where Si represents the ith stratum.

We define an update operation on *KBt* by first defining update operations on the models M of *KBt*, noted Update-Model(M, A). We want to evaluate the distance between an interpretation M of *KBt* and an interpretation M' of *KBt'* with respect to the transition model. Let us first define $Diff_i(M, M')$ which evaluates the distance between two interpretations with respect to the ith stratum Si of ET. This distance is evaluated by looking at the expected transitions belonging to Si and which are not satisfied when M is changed to M': $Diff_i(M, M') = \{\langle X, Y \rangle \in Si$ where X is true in M and Y is false in $M'\}$.

It is then possible to map each interpretation M to a partial order [9] $\leq_M$. Let M' and M'' be two interpretations. We define $\leq_M$ by:

[8] The model of transition depends on an implicit period of time between two updates : after one day, when the lights of a car have been on, the battery is expected to be dead; after one second, it will not be the case. After one second, when the key has been turned, the car is expected to start; after on day, it makes no sense.

[9] Remark that, due to the transition model, this assignment is not a faithful relation as defined in [Katsuno and Mendelzon, 1991]. We don't have that $\forall M' M \leq_M M'$. Let us take *TM* to be $\{ET_1 : \langle A, \neg B \rangle, ET_2 : \langle B, \neg A \rangle\}$ (describing a flip-flop), M be $\{A, \neg B\}$ and M' be $\{\neg A, B\}$. We have $M \not\leq_M M'$.

$M' <_M M''$ iff:

- $\exists i$ such that $Diff_i(M, M') \subset Diff_i(M, M'')$
- $\forall j > i \; Diff_j(M, M') = Diff_j(M, M'')$.

$M' =_M M''$ iff $\forall i \; Diff_i(M, M') = Diff_i(M, M'')$
$M' \leq_M M''$ iff $M' <_M M''$ or $M' =_M M''$.

Update-Model(M, A) is defined as the set of models M' satisfying the sure transitions with M and being the "closest" to M by $\leq_M$ by :

1. A is true in M' (M' is a model for A)
2. $\forall \langle X, Y \rangle \in ST$, if X is true in M, then Y is true in M'
3. There is no other model M'' such that M'' satisfies 1-3 and $M'' <_M M'$

We have then $KBt' =$ Update(KBt, A) $= \bigcup_{M \in Models(KBt)}$Update-Model($M, A$).

Update(KBt, A) $\models F$ iff F is true in all the models preferred by the Update-Model operation. It can be noticed that this definition extends the definition given in [Winslett, 1989] by taking into account the transition model (see section 6 for a more detailed comparison).

5 Illustrative examples

Let us see now how the scenarios presented in 2 are solved by using the transition model as defined in section 3 and the semantics proposed for update in section 4.

The transition model allows us to express the constraint as well as the persistence of the formulas by :
$ST_1 : \langle True, Alarm \Rightarrow (Deaf \vee \neg Asleep) \rangle$
$ST_2 : \langle Deaf, Deaf \rangle$ "*Deaf is an immutable fact*"
$ET_1 : \langle \neg Deaf, \neg Deaf \rangle$ "*¬Deaf is a persistent fact*"
$ET_2 : \langle Asleep, Asleep \rangle$ "*Asleep is a persistent fact*"
with $ET_1 > ET_2$. "*¬Deaf is more persistent than Asleep*"

Scenario 1 continued. We have
$KBt = Th(Asleep, Alarm \Rightarrow (Deaf \vee \neg Asleep))$ and $A = Alarm$.
KBt has three models :
$M1 : \{Asleep, Deaf, Alarm\}$,
$M2 : \{Asleep, Deaf, \neg Alarm\}$,
$M3 : \{Asleep, \neg Deaf, \neg Alarm\}$.
By looking to the models of KBt and applying the definitions given in section 4, we get :
Update-Model($M1, A$) $= \{\{Asleep, Deaf, Alarm\}\}$
Update-Model($M2, A$) $= \{\{Asleep, Deaf, Alarm\}\}$
Update-Model($M3, A$) $= \{\{\neg Asleep, \neg Deaf, Alarm\}\}$.
$KBt' =$ Update(KBt, A) $= \bigcup_{M \in Models(KBt)}$Update-Model($M, A$)
We get then
$KBt' = Th(Alarm, Deaf \Leftrightarrow Asleep)$, which is the expected result.

Scenario 2 continued. We have

$KBt = Th(\neg Deaf, Alarm \Rightarrow (Deaf \vee \neg Asleep))$.

In the same way as before, by looking to the models of KBt and applying the definitions, it can be checked that we obtain

$KBt' = \text{Update}(KBt, A) = Th(Alarm, \neg Deaf, \neg Asleep)$, which is what is expected.

6 Related Works

As remarked before, this work extends the Possible Model Approach with priorities proposed by [Winslett, 1989]. Instead of relying on an implicit notion of persistence as she does, we propose to use an *explicit* model of transition and we give a model-based semantics for update taking into account this model. [Winslett, 1989] relies on an implicit transition model where protected formulas correspond to the constraints and *all* the predicates are considered as persistent (with priorities).

We propose to use an explicit transition model; we can then express constraints and persistent information; but also immutable information, certain and expected transitions, and all what is known about the way the world is going to change. If, for example, an update contradicts a fact known to be immutable (once it is known, it cannot change), it is rejected. It is possible to describe instantaneous (or contingent) pieces of information: i.e information which can be true in KBt, but will be true in KBt' only if it can be deduced from other facts known to be true in t'. For example, a noise can happen in KBt but we have no reason to think that it will be true in KBt'. These formulas have no proper persistence, and consequently, nothing has to be said about them in the transition model. Transition constraints, as used in databases, can be expressed by sure transitions, as for example that the age of a person (or the salary?) cannot decrease from one time to the successing one. Default rules and expected transitions can be quite useful to describe the behaviour of evolutive systems. All this cannot be taken into account by an implicit model as the one by [Winslett, 1989].

[Brewka and Hertzberg, 1993] propose to use some kind of stratified priorities in order to choose the minimal models of the new theory T'. Their approach is not far away from [Winslett, 1989]'s approach with priorities. These priorities are not given a priori but result from causal relations existing between formulas. This is an interesting point as it is clear that there exists a link between persistence and causal relations. If A causes B, then the persistence of ¬B depends on A: If A is true at time t', even if ¬B was true at time t, it cannot persist at time t'. Before deciding of the persistence of ¬B we have to look if A will be true or not at time t'. The degree of persistence of ¬B should then be less than the degree of persistence of A. This is exactly the case in the above example. There is a causal link between ¬Deaf and ¬Asleep (i.e. awaken); in the case of an alarm, ¬Deaf causes ¬Asleep. This is why before deciding if Asleep true at time t remains true at time t', we have first to look at ¬Deaf. But it seems also clear that causal relations are not the only source of the ordering concerning the persistence of information. Let us discuss the following example : we know as a constraint that "in the case of an alarm, if the turkey is not deaf *and if it is not tired*, then it will get up from bed". Suppose we know that, at time t, it is in its bed, it is not tired and that it is not deaf. We learn at time t' that the alarm rings and that the turkey does not get up. We are probably be more willing to suppose that it changes from not-tired to tired than from not-deaf to deaf. The persistence of not-deaf is greater than the persistence of not-tired. And there is clearly no causal link between these two pieces of information.

Finally, we can compare this work with [Dean and Kanazawa, 1989] who propose to use a probabilistic model of persistence. The truth value of a fact at time t depends on whether or not it was true at the preceding time t. This dependency is represented by conditional probabilities. They encode the change expectation of facts. It can then be seen as the probabilistic equivalent of our transition model. In such approaches, the persistence degree of a fact varies according to time. The time between two updates can be taken into account, which is not the case in our approach. The main problem is that you need to be aware of each possible cause-effect relation in order to get valid probabilistic information. In our approach, we only require a partial ordering between elementary transitions.

The relation between PMA and preferential models and circumscription has been highlighted by [Winslett, 1989]'s and [Satoh, 1988]'s. We show in [Cordier and Siegel, 1994] that it can be extended to take into account an explicit transition model. With an adequate change of representation, the semantics of the update operation can be expressed as the preferred models of a theory T, according to a preference relation given in [Cordier and Siegel, 1994]. The updated theory can then be obtained by using the corresponding circumscriptive schema. Preferred models and prioritized circumscription can then give a formal account to the semantics described in section 4.

7 Conclusion

In this paper, we argue that updating a knowledge base requires to have information on how the world change along time. We propose to use an explicit transition model and to order the transitions by priorities. We define a model-driven semantics of the update operation which extends [Winslett, 1989] by taking into account the transition model. The main approaches in update do not use an explicit model of evolution and rely on the simple but limited minimal change principle. Our formalism provides a more powerful and flexible way to represent the persistence. We focussed on persistence in this paper; however it can be stressed that non only persistence but also default and transition rules can be expressed as well. This point is quite interesting to represent evolutive systems, as required for example in a monitoring or diagnosis context. We are currently investigating the updating problem when multiple, successive or even concurrent transitions have to be considered.

Acknowledgments: This work has been partially supported by the French national project entitled "Gestion de l'évolutif et de l'incertain"(Handling of Unvertainty in a Dynamical World). The paper has benefited from discussions with G. Brewka, J. Hertzberg and S. Thiebaux. Many thanks also to T. Schaub for his helpful comments.

References

Gerhard Brewka and Joachim Hertzberg. How to do things with worlds: On formalizing actions and plans. *J. of Logic and Computation*, 3(5), 1993.

Marie Odile Cordier and Pierre Siegel. A temporal revision model for reasoning about world change. In Bernhard Nebel, Charles Rich, and William Swartout, editors, *Principles of Knowledge Representation and Reasoning (KR'92)*, pages 732–739. Morgan Kaufmamm, 1992.

Marie-Odile Cordier and Pierre Siegel. Prioritized transitions for updates. Technical Report 884, IRISA, Rennes, France, 1994.

Thomas Dean and Keiji Kanazawa. A model for reasoning about persistence and causation. *Computational Intelligence*, 5:142–150, 1989.

Matthew L. Ginsberg and D. E. Smith. *Readings in Non Monotonic Reasoning*. Morgan Kaufmann, 1987.

Hirofumi Katsuno and Alberto O. Mendelzon. On the difference between updating a knowledge base and revising it. In *Principles of Knowledge Representation and Reasoning (KR'91)*, pages 387–394, 1991.

John C. McCarthy and Patrick H. Hayes. Some philosophical problems from the standpoint of artificial intelligence. In B. Meltzer and D. Michie, editors, *Machine Intelligence*, volume 4, pages 463–502, New-York, 1969. American Elsevier.

Erik Sandewall. *Features and Fluents (volume I)*. Oxford University Press, 1995.

Ken Satoh. Nonmonotonic reasoning by minimal belief revision. In *Proceedings of the International Conference on Fifth Generation Computer Systems*. ICOT, 1988.

Marianne Winslett. Reasoning about actions using a possible model approach. In *Proceedings of the Seventh National AAAI Conference*, pages 89–93, 1988.

Marianne Winslett. Sometimes updates are circumscription. In *Proceedings of the IJCAI Conference*, pages 859–863, Detroit, 1989.

Probabilistic Satisfiability and Decomposition

Guy-Blaise Douanya Nguetsé[1] Pierre Hansen[2] Brigitte Jaumard[3]

1. École Polytechnique de Montréal, Canada
2. GERAD and École des Hautes Études Commerciales de Montréal, Canada
3. GERAD and École Polytechnique de Montréal, Canada

Abstract

Given a set of logical sentences together with probabilities that these sentences are true, the probabilistic satisfiability (PSAT) problem consists, in its decision version, in finding whether these probabilities are consistent, and in its optimization version in determining best possible lower and upper bounds on the probability that an additional sentence be true. Van der Gaag recently proposed a partially quantified belief network model which may be viewed as a decomposition-oriented version of PSAT. Both models give the same bounds, which implies that PSAT implicitly takes into account some independence relations. A column-generation algorithm is proposed for the decomposition form of PSAT and shown to have several advantages over a similar algorithm for the usual form, mainly in the exploitation of the sparsity of the matrix of coefficients.
Keywords: Probabilistic Satisfiability; Decomposition; Belief Network.

1 Introduction

After a period of relative disfavor, models based on probability theory are increasingly used for reasoning under uncertainty in knowledge-based systems. Such models differ in the independence assumptions which are made and in the amount of information required from the expert. At one extreme of the spectrum, belief networks [18], [21], [22] which represent graphically the variables of the domain under study and their probabilistic relationship, make strong conditional independence assumptions and require sufficient information for the joint probability distribution on the space of possible outcomes to be entirely specified. When those requirements are satisfied the probability of any event may be computed, often in moderate time. Moreover, evidence can be efficiently propagated through the network. However, the requirement of giving precise conditional probabilities for an often large number of configurations is very demanding and may be irrealistic. At the other extreme of the spectrum some models make no explicit independence assumptions and require only as little and as much probability information as is available. Moreover, this information may be given by intervals instead of single values. Among such models, probabilistic satisfiability (or PSAT, better known under the names of probabilistic logic or probabilistic entailment in artificial intelligence (Nilsson [19])) has attracted much attention. Given a set of logical sentences together with probabilities that these sentences are true, the decision version of PSAT consists in assessing whether these probabilities are consistent or not. The optimization version of PSAT consists in determining best possible lower and upper bounds on the probability of an additional sentence to be true. PSAT is defined mathematically in the next section; algorithms and extensions are also briefly reviewed. Recently, Van der Gaag [24], [25] has proposed a partially quantified belief network model, which may be viewed as a decomposition-oriented version of PSAT, together with an algorithm. This model is decribed and discussed in Section 3. It is noted that both versions of PSAT give the same bounds on the truth probability of the objective function sentence. As a consequence, the usual version of PSAT takes implicitly into account, in terms of objective function value, the conditional independence relations expressed in the decomposition-oriented version. The algorithm of Van der Gaag is summarized and discussed in Section 4. In particular, the impact of the feasibility domain assessment and projection step on the theoretical and pratical complexity is examined, and shown to be an obstacle to solution of large instances. A column generation algorithm for the decomposition-oriented version of PSAT is proposed in the same section. It is argued that it has several advantages, mainly in the exploitation of the sparsity of the matrix of coefficients, over a similar algorithm for the usual version.

2 PSAT

The probabilistic satisfiability problem may be defined mathematically as follows. Let $x_1, x_2, \ldots, x_n$ be n logical variables and $S_1, S_2, \ldots, S_m$ m logical sentences defined on $x_1, x_2, \ldots, x_n$ with the operators $\vee$ (or), $\wedge$ (and) and $\neg$ (not). Let S_0 be a tautology. Assume a vector $\pi = (\pi_0, \pi_1, \ldots, \pi_m)$ of probability values to be given with $\pi_0 = 1$; π_i is the probability that S_i is true for $i = 0, 1, \ldots, m$. Then consider the vectors X^k for $k = 1, 2, \ldots, 2^n$, called configurations, obtained by assigning the values true or false to the x_j in all possible ways. To each configuration X^k associate an $(m+1)$ column vector A^k with $a_{0k} = 1$, $a_{ik} = 1$ if S_i is implied by X^k and $a_{ik} = 0$ otherwise, for $i = 1, 2, \ldots, m$. Setting $A = (A^k)$, the decision version of PSAT may be written : Is there a solution to the linear system

$$Ap = \pi, p \geq 0 \ ? \tag{1}$$

If the answer is yes, the values of the 2^n components p_k of p define a probability distribution on the set of configurations X^k such that for each sentence S_i the sum of probabilities of the configurations for which it is true is equal to its probability of being true. Note that the vectors A^k do not correspond to all possible truth assignments to the sentences S_i, but only to the logically compatible ones; those vectors are not necessarily all distinct. In view of the fact, already noted by Boole [3], that the probability of an event is equal to the probability of the truth of the proposition stating that this event occurs, the x_j can be viewed as associated with simple, not necessarily independent events and the S_i as associated with compound events. In the optimization version of PSAT an additional sentence S_{m+1} is considered and best lower and upper bounds on its probability of being true are looked for.

Let a_{m+1} denote the 2^n-row vector with $a_{m+1,k} = 1$ if S_{m+1} is implied by configuration X^k and $a_{m+1,k} = 0$ otherwise, then the optimization version of PSAT may be written (Hailperin [10]):

$$\max(\min)\{a_{m+1}p : Ap = \pi, p \geq 0\} \tag{2}$$

Example: Consider the following seven logical sentences and their associated probabilities of being true:

$$\begin{array}{lcl} S_1: & x_1 & \pi_1 = 0.6 \\ S_2: & \neg x_1 \vee x_2 & \pi_2 = 0.4 \\ S_3: & x_2 \vee x_3 & \pi_3 = 0.8 \\ S_4: & x_3 \wedge x_4 & \pi_4 = 0.3 \\ S_5: & \neg x_4 \vee x_5 & \pi_5 = 0.5 \\ S_6: & x_2 \vee x_5 & \pi_6 = 0.6 \\ S_7: & x_5 & \pi_7 = ? \end{array}$$

The matrix A is then:

$$\begin{pmatrix} 1&1&1&1&1&1&1&1&1&1&1&1&1&1&1&1&1&1&1&1&1&1&1&1&1&1&1&1&1&1&1&1 \\ 1&1&1&1&1&1&1&1&1&1&1&1&1&1&1&1&0&0&0&0&0&0&0&0&0&0&0&0&0&0&0&0 \\ 1&1&1&1&1&1&1&1&0&0&0&0&0&0&0&0&1&1&1&1&1&1&1&1&1&1&1&1&1&1&1&1 \\ 1&1&1&1&1&1&1&1&1&1&1&1&0&0&0&0&1&1&1&1&1&1&1&1&1&1&1&1&0&0&0&0 \\ 1&1&0&0&0&0&0&0&1&1&0&0&0&0&0&0&1&1&0&0&0&0&0&0&1&1&0&0&0&0&0&0 \\ 1&0&1&1&1&0&1&1&1&0&1&1&1&0&1&1&1&0&1&1&1&0&1&1&1&0&1&1&1&0&1&1 \\ 1&1&1&1&1&1&1&1&1&0&1&0&1&0&1&0&1&1&1&1&1&1&1&1&1&0&1&0&1&0&1&0 \end{pmatrix} \tag{3}$$

and the objective function row:

$$(1\ 0\ 1\ 0\ 1\ 0\ 1\ 0\ 1\ 0\ 1\ 0\ 1\ 0\ 1\ 0\ 1\ 0\ 1\ 0\ 1\ 0\ 1\ 0\ 1\ 0\ 1\ 0\ 1\ 0\ 1\ 0) \tag{4}$$

Solving the corresponding linear program (2) gives when minimizing a lower bound of 0.2 on π_7, with $p_{13} = 0.2$, $p_{10} = 0.3$, $p_{12} = 0.1$, $p_{20} = 0.2$, $p_{22} = 0.2$, all other $p_k = 0$; and when maximizing an upper bound of 0.5 on π_7, with $p_{11} = 0.1$, $p_{13} = 0.1$, $p_{27} = 0.3$, $p_{10} = 0.3$, $p_{14} = 0.1$, $p_{22} = 0.1$, all other $p_k = 0$.

Both versions of PSAT are due to Boole [3] where they are called "*conditions of possible experience*" and "*general problem in the theory of probabilities*". Boole proposes algebraic techniques for their solution. Hailperin [10], [11] in an important paper and a book on "*Boole's logic and Probability*" shows that Boole's most efficient method is equivalent to Fourier elimination, and formulates PSAT as a linear program. Hailperin ([10], [11]) also proposes another way to obtain an analytical expression of best possible bounds for the optimization version of PSAT: maxima or minima of linear expressions in the variables π_i associated to all the vertices of the dual program of (1) are shown to yield such bounds. This result has recently been completed [13] by the proof that all conditions of possible experience are given by linear expressions in the variables π_i associated with the extreme rays of this polytope. So a complete analytical solution for a given system of sentences and probabilities can be obtained in an automated way [13]. Consistency conditions for a subclass of Horn clauses are also obtained in [1] by a polyhedral combinatorics approach.

PSAT has been often rediscovered, among others by Nilsson [19] in a well-known paper on "*Probabilistic Logic*". As the number of variables p_k in (1) and (2) increases exponentially with the number n of logical variables, doubts have been expressed [8], [19], [20], [24], [25] about the possibility to solve numerically large instances of PSAT in reasonable time. PSAT is NP-hard [9], and hence may require exponential time in worst case. However the column generation technique of linear programming may be used to solve it while keeping its expression implicit [2], [9], [15], [16], [26]. Note that writing the problem explicitly would already require exponentiel time. Moreover, polynomial cases have been identified [9], [16], [15]. Recall that when solving a linear program by column generation, a compact tableau is kept; at each iteration the entering column is found by solving an auxiliary combinatorial subproblem and the tableau is updated following the rules of the revised simplex method. For PSAT the subproblem of determining a column with maximum (or minimum) reduced cost can be expressed as the minimization of a nonlinear function in 0-1 variables. It is obtained as follows: the reduced cost for a generic column at the current iteration is

$$c_k - \sum_{i=1}^{m+1} a_{ik}u_i \tag{5}$$

where the u_i are the current dual variables. Associating the value true with 1 and false with 0, (5) may be rewritten

$$S_{m+1} - u_0 - \sum_{i=1}^{m} S_i u_i \tag{6}$$

which is an algebraic expression in the $0-1$ variables x_j, $j = 1, 2, \ldots, n$, with boolean operators $\vee$, $\wedge$, and $\neg$. These can be eliminated using $a \vee b = a + b - ab$, $a \wedge b = a \times b$ and $\neg a = 1 - a$, where a and b are logical variables.

Example (continued). The generic expression of the reduced cost is

$$\begin{aligned} & x_5 - u_0 - u_1x_1 - u_2(1 - x_1 + x_1x_2) - u_3(x_2 + x_3 - x_2x_3) \\ & -u_4x_3x_4 - u_5(1 - x_4 + x_4x_5) - u_6(x_2 + x_5 - x_2x_5) \\ = & -u_0 - u_2 - u_5 + (u_2 - u_1)x_1 - (u_3 + u_6)x_2 - u_3x_3 + u_5x_4 \\ & -(u_6 - 1)x_5 - u_2x_1x_2 + u_3x_2x_3 + u_6x_2x_5 - u_4x_2x_3 - u_5x_4x_5 \end{aligned}$$

where $x_1, x_2, \ldots, x_5 \in \{0, 1\}$.

As generating a column with a positive (negative) reduced cost which is not necessarily maximum (minimum) is sufficient at any current iteration, a *tabu search* heuristic may be used to find a corresponding column as long as possible. When this is no more the case an exact nonlinear $0-1$ programming algorithm must be used, as, e.g., that of [6]. Experiments on a SUN 3 workstation, with the XMP code for linear programming [15] have shown instances of PSAT with up to 140 variables and 300 clauses may be solved in reasonable time. The simplex iterations take about 90% of the computing time. This seems to be mostly due to density of the matrix A, which precludes using an interior-point method to reduce the computing time. So, except for better linear programming codes and computers, further progress lies in obtaining a form of PSAT with sparse matrix of coefficients. We will see in the next section that such a form exists.

Several extensions of PSAT have been studied: intervals of probabilities for the truth of the sentences can be used instead of single values [10], [15], [16]. Conditional probabilities can also be accomodated. If they appear in the constraints the models remains linear; if the objective is a conditional probability an hyperbolic program arises, which may be reduced to a linear program with one more variable by a standard technique [11]. Assuming the given probabilities to be inconsistent, consistency may be restored by a minimum increase in the width of the probabilities intervals, still by linear programming [15], or by deletion of a minimum number of sentences. This last case corresponds to the *probabilistic maximum satisfiability problem* [12], which may be solved by combining column generation with branch-and-bound techniques.

3 A decomposition-oriented version of PSAT

PSAT has been criticized on the grounds that the probability intervals obtained may be too large and hence of little pratical use [24], [25] and that independence relations are not taken into account [2], [24], [25]. As the bounds are, in fact, best possible, they reflect the knowledge the expert has been willing to provide. Getting more precise bounds requires further information. This is illustrated in [14] for an application of PSAT to two-terminal network reliability, where probabilities of simultaneous failure of pairs of edges significantly improve bounds obtained using only data on single edge failures. Efficient treatment of independence in belief networks suggests to combine the graphical tools they use for that purpose with PSAT. Van der Gaag [24], [25] proposes to extend the linear programming approach in that way. Another recent proposal, called "*Bayesian Logic*" [2], leads to nonlinear nonconvex programs, which are difficult to solve. Independence relations between variables are assumed to be represented by an *I-map*, i.e., an undirected graph $G = (V, E)$ with vertices $v_j \in V$ associated with the variables x_j and such that the absence of an edge $\{v_r, v_s\}$ indicates conditional independence between variables x_r and x_s (see Pearl [21], Van der Gaag [24] for details). It is also assumed that edges have been added with the minimum fill-in algorithm of [23] until all cycles of length greater than three have a cord, i.e, an edge joining non successive vertices. Then G is a *decomposable I-map*. It is further assumed that all initially given probabilities are local to the maximal cliques [1] of G, and the same holds for the probability to be bounded. Under these conditions the joint probability distribution P can be expressed as a product of marginal probability distributions on the cliques of G, adequately scaled. So the problem will be solved on each of the cliques $Cl_1, Cl_2, \ldots, Cl_t$ of G; however it is necessary that the marginal distributions so obtained agree on the intersections of the cliques. (In fact, not all pairwise intersections need be considered but only those of a join-tree, see again Pearl [21], Van der Gaag [24] for details). The corresponding problem (PSAT_d) may be written

$$\max(\min) \quad a_{m+1}p$$

[1] We will use the term clique for maximal clique below.

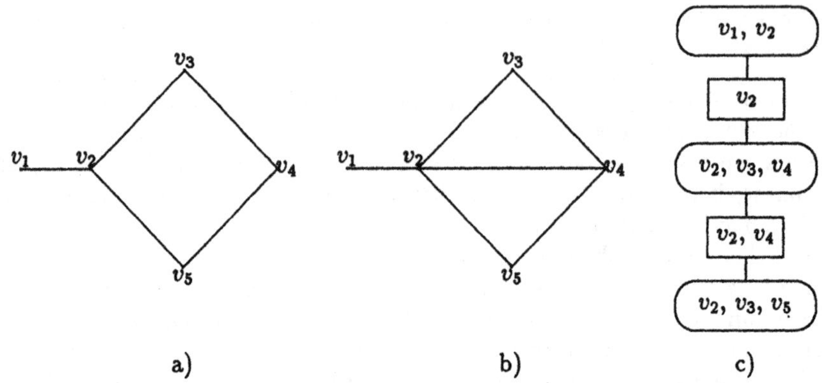

Figure 1: I-map, decomposable I-map and join tree

subject to:

$$\begin{aligned} A^i p^i &= \pi^i \quad i = 1, 2, \ldots, t \\ T_{ij} p^i - T_{ji} p^j &= 0 \quad i = 1, 2, \ldots, t \\ & \qquad j \text{ such the cliques } Cl_i \text{ and } Cl_j \\ & \qquad \text{are adjacent in the join tree} \end{aligned} \tag{7}$$

$$p^i \geq 0 \text{ for } i = 1, 2, \ldots, t$$

where t is the number of cliques. The first set of constraints correspond to the PSAT problems on each clique and the second set of constraints to compatibility conditions between the marginal distributions on the clique intersections of the join-tree.

Example (continued). An I-map for the example defined above is given in Figure 1a, a decomposable I-map in Figure 1b and a corresponding join-tree in Figure 1c.

The problem matrix and right-hand side in the decomposition form (7) of PSAT are:

S_i	p^1_1	p^1_2	p^1_3	p^1_4	p^2_1	p^2_2	p^2_3	p^2_4	p^2_5	p^2_6	p^2_7	p^2_8	p^3_1	p^3_2	p^3_3	p^3_4	p^3_5	p^3_6	p^3_7	p^3_8	
S^1_0	1	1	1	1																	= 1
x_1	1	1	0	0																	= 0.6
$\neg x_1 \vee x_2$	1	0	1	1																	= 0.4
$(x_2 = 1)$	1	0	1	0	−1	−1	−1	−1	0	0	0	0									= 0
S^2_0					1	1	1	1	1	1	1	1									= 1
$x_2 \vee x_3$					1	1	1	1	1	1	0	0									= 0.8
$x_3 \wedge x_4$					1	0	0	0	1	0	0	0									= 0.3
$(x_2 = 1, x_4 = 1)$					1	0	1	0	0	0	0	0	−1	−1	0	0	0	0	0	0	= 0
$(x_2 = 1, x_4 = 0)$					0	1	0	1	0	0	0	0	0	0	−1	−1	0	0	0	0	= 0
$(x_2 = 0, x_4 = 1)$					0	0	0	0	1	0	1	0	0	0	0	0	−1	−1	0	0	= 0
S^3_0													1	1	1	1	1	1	1	1	= 1
$\neg x_4 \vee x_5$													1	0	1	1	1	0	1	1	= 0.5
$x_2 \vee x_5$													1	1	1	1	1	0	1	0	= 0.6

and the objective function row:

(0 0 0 0 0 0 0 0 0 0 0 0 1 0 1 0 1 0 1 0).

Solving the corresponding linear program (7) gives when minimizing a lower bound of 0.2 on π_7, with $p_2^1 = 0.6$, $p_3^1 = 0.4$, $p_2^2 = 0.3$, $p_3^2 = 0.1$, $p_5^2 = 0.3$, $p_6^2 = 0.1$, $p_7^2 = 0.1$, $p_8^2 = 0.1$, $p_2^3 = 0.1$, $p_4^3 = 0.3$, $p_6^3 = 0.4$, $p_7^3 = 0.2$, all other $p_k^i = 0$; and when maximizing an upper bound of 0.5 on π_7, with $p_2^1 = 0.6$, $p_3^1 = 0.4$, $p_2^2 = 0.3$, $p_3^2 = 0.1$, $p_5^2 = 0.3$, $p_6^2 = 0.1$, $p_7^2 = 0.1$, $p_8^2 = 0.1$, $p_2^3 = 0.1$, $p_3^3 = 0.3$, $p_6^3 = 0.4$, $p_7^3 = 0.2$, all other $p_k^i = 0$.

That both forms of PSAT give the same bounds is not a coincidence.

Proposition 1 *The lower and upper bounds on the probabilility of truth of S_{m+1} given by* PSAT *and* PSAT$_d$ *are the same.*

Sketch of Proof.

(i) To any feasible solution of PSAT corresponds a feasible solution of PSAT$_d$ of same value. Indeed, it suffices to build by grouping terms the marginal probability distributions on each of the cliques.

(ii) To any feasible solution of PSAT$_d$ corresponds a feasible solution of PSAT of same value. Indeed, as G is a decomposable I-map then (Pearl [21], chapter 3, Theorem 8) there is a corresponding joint probability distribution given by

$$p_k = \text{Prob}(X^k) = \prod_{i=1,\ldots,t} \frac{\text{Prob}(Cl_i(X^k))}{\text{Prob}(S_i(X^k))} \tag{8}$$

where $\text{Prob}(Cl_i(X^k))$ denotes the probability of the restriction of X^k to clique Cl_i and $\text{Prob}(S_i(X^k))$ the probability of the restriction of X^k to the intersection of cliques S_i. □

Note that the probability distribution obtained by the procedure described above will usually not be that one given by the simplex algorithm. In particular it may not be a basic solution.

Example (continued). For the configuration $X^{10} = (1\,0\,1\,1\,0)^T$ one has in the minimization case

$$\begin{aligned} p_{10} &= \text{Prob}(Cl_1(1\,0)^T \times \frac{\text{Prob}(Cl_2(0\,1\,1)^T)}{\text{Prob}(S_2(0))} \times \frac{\text{Prob}(Cl_3(0\,1\,0)^T)}{\text{Prob}(S_3(0\,1)^T)} \\ &= 0.6 \times \frac{0.3}{0.3 + 0.1 + 0.1 + 0.1} \times \frac{0.4}{0.4} = 0.3 \end{aligned}$$

and similarly $p_{11} = 0.1$, $p_{14} = 0.1$, $p_{15} = 0.1$, $p_{20} = 0.3$, $p_{22} = 0.1$, all other $p_k = 0$.

The joint distribution of (8) does satisfy all properties of conditional independence expressed in the decomposable I-map G. Proposition 1 thus shows that the usual version of PSAT implicitly satisfies these constraints in the sense that adding them would not change the optimal value.

4 Algorithms

PSAT$_d$ compared to PSAT has:

(i) usually many less columns: $\sum_{i=1}^{t} 2^{|Cl_i|}$ instead of $2^{|V|}$;

(ii) more rows, i.e. $m + \sum_{i=1}^{t} 2^{|S_i|}$ instead of m;

(iii) a sparse coefficient matrix.

The reduction in columns is an advantage, but only a limited one if column generation techniques are used: indeed when this is the case few columns are explicitly considered (e.g., about 600 for a problem with 2^{70} columns [15]). The increase of the number of rows is detrimental as it increases the size of the bases. This increase is exponential in the size of clique intersections, so the form (7) is only useful if $|S_i|$ is small for all i. When this is not the case, one may chose to consider larger subproblems, with only S_i of small cardinality. Finally, sparsity is a clear advantage when program (7) is solved with or without decomposition. Linear programming codes such as CPLEX indeed exploit sparsity quite thoroughly. Van der Gaag [24], [25] proposes a method to exploit to its fullest the structure of (7). The essence of her algorithm (see [24], [25] for a complete description using an object-oriented style of discussion) is to eliminate subproblems one at a time beginning from the leaves of the join-tree by:

(i) finding their feasible set F_i from the local system of constraints $A^i p^i = \pi^i$;

(ii) projecting this feasible set on clique intersection S_i , i.e., finding the set $\{T_{ij}p^i, p^i \in F_i\}$;

(iii) transmitting these restrictions to the neighboring subproblem by the equations $T_{ij}p^i - T_{ji}p^j = 0$;

(iv) iterating until only the problem corresponding to the root of the join-tree and containing the objective function remains;

(v) solving this last problem, with all additional constraints by linear programming (and then the other subproblems if a solution is desired in addition to the bounds).

Van der Gaag provides no details on how to perform these operations. The usual way would be to use vertex and face enumeration techniques for polytopes. This may be time-consuming. Indeed, the number of vertices of polytopes with fixed number of dimensions often augments exponentially with the number of constraints (Dyer [7], Chen *et al.* [4], [5]). The number of non redundant constraints in the projection of such polytopes may itself grow exponentially. Moreover, as feasible set determination and projection are iterated the number of additional constraints is likely to build up. Therefore, contrary to statements in [24], [25] the proposed decomposition algorithm is not guaranteed to be polynomial in the case where the maximum clique size is bounded. Note that using the usual form of PSAT, the column generation technique, Kachian's algorithm (at least in principle) and the *basic algorithm revisited* of non-linear $0-1$ programming to solve the subproblem, gives a polynomial algorithm for that case [6], [9], [15].

An alternative to the algorithm just discussed would be to use again column generation. The auxiliary subproblem of finding the minimum reduced cost is more complex than in the case of the form (2). Separate computation must be made for each clique. The reduced cost expresssion will be similar to (6) but with the sentences corresponding to the clique only and with additional terms for all configurations of the clique intersections (except the configurations with all variables corresponding to the intersection negated, as a configuration per intersection is redundant).

Example (continued) For the first clique the reduced cost expression becomes

$$-u_1 - u_2x_1 - u_3(1 - x_1 + x_1x_2) - u_4x_2 = -u_1 - (u_2 + u_3)x_1 - u_4x_2 - u_3x_1x_2;$$

for the second clique

$$\begin{aligned} & u_4x_2 - u_5 - u_6(x_2 + x_3 - x_2x_3) - u_7x_3x_4 - u_8x_2x_4 - u_9(x_2 - x_2x_4) - u_{10}(x_4 - x_2x_4) \\ = \; & -u_5 + (u_4 - u_6 - u_9)x_2 - u_6x_3 - u_{10}x_4 + u_6x_2x_3 + (u_9 + u_{10} - u_8)x_2x_4 - u_7x_3x_4; \end{aligned}$$

and for the third clique

$$\begin{aligned} & x_5 - u_8x_2x_4 + u_9(x_2 - x_2x_4) + u_{10}(x_4 - x_2x_4) - u_{11} \\ & - u_{12}(1 - x_4 + x_4x_5) - u_{13}(x_2 + x_5 - x_2x_5) \\ = \; & - u_{11} - u_{12} + (u_9 - u_{13})x_2 - u_{12}x_4 - (u_{13} - 1)x_5 \\ & - (u_9 + u_{10})x_2x_4 + u_{13}x_2x_5 - u_{12}x_4x_5, \end{aligned}$$

where $x_1, x_2, \ldots, x_5 \in \{0, 1\}$.

So more subproblems must be solved, but with simpler objective functions. This may prove an asset, particularly when at the last iteration an exact solution must be obtained. The main advantage lies in the sparsity of the matrix which should be reflected by a sharp decrease in computing time per simplex iteration. However, only experimentation will show to what extent using form (7) instead of form (2) allows solution of larger instances of PSAT. Work in that direction is under way and will be reported in a future paper.

References

[1] Andersen, K.A., *Characterizing Consistency for a Subclass of Horn Clauses*, Mathematical Programming, 66, 257-271, 1994.

[2] Andersen, K.A., and J.N. Hooker, *Bayesian Logic*, Decision Support Systems 11, 191-210, 1994.

[3] Boole, G., *An Investigation of the Laws of Thought, on which are Founded the Mathematical Theories of Logic and Probabilities*, London: Walton and Maberley, 1854 (reprint New York: Dover 1958).

[4] Chen, P.C., P. Hansen and B. Jaumard, On-Line and Off-Line Vertex Enumeration by Adjacency Lists, *Operations Research Letters* 10(7) (1991) 403-409.

[5] Chen, P.C., P. Hansen and B. Jaumard, Partial Pivoting in Vertex Enumeration, *GERAD Research Report 92-15*, Montréal, 1992.

[6] Crama, Y. P., P. Hansen and B. Jaumard, The Basic Algorithm for Pseudo-Boolean Programming Revisited, *Discrete Applied Mathematics* 29 (1990) 171-186.

[7] Dyer, M.E., On the Complexity of Vertex Enumeration Methods, *Mathematics of Operations Research* 8(3) (1983) 381-402.

[8] Frisch, A. M., and P. Haddawy, Anytime Deduction for Probabilistic Logic, *Artificial Intelligence* 69 (1994) 93-122.

[9] Georgakopoulos, G., D. Kavvadias and C.H.Papadimitriou, Probabilistic Satisfiability, *Journal of Complexity* 4 (1988) 1-11.

[10] Hailperin, T., Best Possible Inequalities for the Probability of a Logical Function of Events, *American Mathematical Monthly* 72 (1965) 343-359.

[11] Hailperin, T., *Boole's Logic and Probability*, Studies in Logic and Foundations of Mathematics 85, New York: North Holand, 1986, 2nd edition (first edition, 1976).

[12] Hansen, P., B. Jaumard and M. Poggi de Aragão, Mixed-Integer Column Generation Algorithms and the Probabilistic Maximum Satisfiability Problem, *Integer Programming and Combinatorial Optimization II*, (Balas, E., G. Cornuejols and R. Kannan, Editors), Pittsburgh: Carnegie Mellon University, 165-180, 1992.

[13] Hansen, P., B. Jaumard and M. Poggi de Aragão, Boole's Conditions of Possible Experience and Reasoning Under Uncertainty, to appear in *Discrete Applied Mathematics*, 1995.

[14] Hansen, P., B. Jaumard and G.B. Douanya Nguetsé, Best Second Order Bounds for Two-terminal Network Reliability with Dependent Edge Failures, *GERAD Research Report* G-94-01, February 1994.

[15] Jaumard, B., P. Hansen and M. Poggi de Aragão, Column Generation Methods for Probabilistic Logic, *ORSA Journal on Computing* 3 (1991) 135-148.

[16] Kavvadias, D., and C.H. Papadimitriou, Linear Programming Approach to Reasoning about Probabilities, *Annals of Mathematics and Artificial Intelligence* 1 (1990) 189-205.

[17] Kachian, L.G., A Polynomial Algorithm in Linear Programming (in Russian), *Doklady Akademii Nauk* SSSR 224 (1979) 1093-1096 (English translation: Soviet Mathematics Doklady 20 (1979) 191-194).

[18] Lauritzen, S.L., and D.J. Spiegelhalter, Local Computations with Probabilities on Graphical Structures and their Applications to Expert Systems, *Journal of the Royal Statistical Society* B50 (1988) 157-224.

[19] Nilsson, N.J., Probabilistic Logic, *Artificial Intelligence* 28 (1986) 71-87.

[20] Nilsson, N.J., Probabilistic Logic Revisited, *Artificial Intelligence* 59 (1993) 39-42.

[21] Pearl, J., *Probabilistic Reasoning in Intelligent Systems: Networks of Plausible Inference*, Morgan Kaufmann, San Mateo, California, 1988.

[22] Shachter, R., Evaluating Influence Diagrams, *Operations Research* 34 (1986) 871-882.

[23] Tarjan, R.E., and M. Yannakakis, Simple Linear-time Algorithms to Test Chordality of Graphs, Test Acyclicity of Hypergraphs and Selectively Reduce Acyclic Hypergraphs, *SIAM Journal of Computing* 13 (1984) 566-579.

[24] Van der Gaag, L.C., *Probability-Based Models for Plausible Reasoning*, Ph.D. Thesis, University of Amsterdam, 1990.

[25] Van der Gaag, L.C., Computing Probability Intervals Under Independency Constraints, in P.P. Bonissone, M. Henrion, L.N. Kanal and J.F. Lemmer (Editors) *Uncertainty in Artificial Intelligence* 6 (1991) 457-466.

[26] Zemel, E., Polynomial Algorithms for Estimating Networks Reliability, *Networks* 12, 439-452, 1982.

Update postulates without inertia

D. Dubois, F. Dupin de Saint-Cyr and H. Prade

I.R.I.T., 118 route de Narbonne, 31062 Toulouse Cedex, France.
e-mail: {dubois,dupin,prade}@irit.fr

Abstract. Starting from Katsuno and Mendelzon postulates, a new set of postulates which is minimal and complete has been defined, these postulates characterize an update operator. The update operator class which is obtained is larger than Katsuno and Mendelzon's one, since it includes updating operators which are not inert, and which allow for the existence of unreachable states. The main property is that every update operator satisfying this new set of postulates admits an underlying ranked transition graph. The rank-ordering of its transitions has not to be faithful as in Katsuno and Mendelzon system.

1 Introduction

This paper deals with reasoning about change and especially with updating. The problem is to take into account the arrival of a new piece of information concerning a system which is represented by a knowledge base. Winslett [7] and later on Katsuno and Mendelzon [6] have shown that this piece of information can be of two kinds: either the piece of information describes the system itself, then the knowledge about the system is evolving, and the knowledge base should be *revised*; or it describes the evolution of the system, and then the knowledge base should be *updated*.

Katsuno and Mendelzon introduce 9 postulates in order to characterize an update operator. They point out that having an update operator verifying those postulates is equivalent to having, for each possible world ω, a pre-ordering relation which rank-orders every states of the world with respect to ω. They also demonstrate that, semantically, in order to update a knowledge base, you can make each of its models evolve independently towards the closest (with respect to the pre-ordering mentioned above) model in agreement with the new information, and then perform the union of all the resulting models.

These postulates are essentially criticized on one point: an update operator satisfying them must always prefer inertia (staying in the same state) to strict evolution (evolving towards a different state). So, in such an approach, update operators cannot describe transient states. Another point is that an update operator of that kind is such that every state of the world is accessible from every other state. It should be interesting to have a less restrictive formalization, so the aim of this work is to propose a minimal set of update postulates characterizing more update operators.

In the first part, Katsuno and Mendelzon postulates are described, and critics are more precisely exposed, then in order to answer to those critics a new set of postulates is defined which leads to a representation of updating in terms of ternary rank-ordering relations similarly to Katsuno and Mendelzon theory.

2 Katsuno and Mendelzon update postulates

A very important result in the field of reasoning about change in artificial intelligence is Alchourrón, Gärdenfors and Makinson [1] theory based on *rationality postulates* which any revision operator should satisfy. These postulates are constraining the way in which it is possible to revise a knowledge base in order to take into account a new piece of belief. These authors have shown that the existence of a *rational* revision operator is equivalent to the existence of a rank-ordering over the set of all possible states of the world (and conversely).

Winslett [7] has clearly shown the difference between revising a knowledge base and updating it, and that AGM theory is not appropriate to deal with updating. In revision: we learn something new about the world (our knowledge increases), while in updating: we learn that the world has changed. Then, Katsuno and Mendelzon [6] have defined a set of postulates characterizing update as it has been done for revision. And similarly, they established that the existence of a rational update operator is equivalent to the existence of a ternary rank-ordering over possible worlds (this time, each state of the world ω is associated with a relation which rank-orders all the states of the world with respect to ω). Semantically an operator satisfying these postulates is equivalent to a transition graph between states of the world.

2.1 Formalization

Let Ω be the non-empty set of possible states of the world, and z be an hypothetical state of the world not belonging to Ω. An updating operator is a function which computes a final state given an initial state and an information about the final state. Here the most general case is considered, i.e., every piece of knowledge can be imprecise: for example, the initial state can be ill-known. So every information is represented by the set of possible states in which this information is true (if the knowledge is complete then the set contains only one possible state). Consequently, an update operator will be defined over subsets of possible states of the world Ω.

2.2 Katsuno and Mendelzon postulates in a set formalism

A set formalism is used instead of a logical one, because updating is syntax independent, and using sets is simpler. Let g be an update operator, $g : 2^{\Omega} \times 2^{\Omega} \rightarrow 2^{\Omega}$, X is the representation of the state of the system before the evolution and A is the new information characterizing the result of this evolution, here are Katsuno and Mendelzon postulates expressed in the set formalism:

U1: $\forall X \subseteq \Omega, \forall A \subseteq \Omega, \quad g(X, A) \subseteq A$

When the system is learned to have evolved in a way such that the resulting state can be partially described by the information A, then the representation of the system state must be updated in accordance with A.

U2: $\forall X \subseteq \Omega, \forall A \subseteq \Omega, \quad X \subseteq A \Rightarrow g(X, A) = X$

If the representation X of the system state is in accordance with the information A, which describes the system state after a change, then the representation of the system state, after updating it, will still be X. This postulate is the one that leads to always prefer inertia to spontaneous evolutions.

U3: $\forall X \subseteq \Omega, \forall A \subseteq \Omega, \quad X \neq \emptyset$ and $A \neq \emptyset \Rightarrow g(X, A) \neq \emptyset$

If the representation X of the system state is consistent, and if a plausible information A characterizes its evolution, then the update of this representation by this information is always possible. It implies that every state is reachable from any other state.

U4: $\forall X \subseteq \Omega, \forall A, B \subseteq \Omega, \quad X = Y$ and $A = B \Rightarrow g(X, A) = g(Y, B)$

This axiom is useless in a set formalism.

U5: $\forall X \subseteq \Omega, \forall A, B \subseteq \Omega, \quad g(X, A) \cap B \subseteq g(X, A \cap B)$

U6: $\forall X \subseteq \Omega, \forall A, B \subseteq \Omega, \quad g(X, A) \subseteq B, g(X, B) \subseteq A \Rightarrow g(X, A) = g(X, B)$

U7: $\forall X \subseteq \Omega, \forall A, B \subseteq \Omega, \quad g(\{\omega\}, A) \cap g(\{\omega\}, B) \subseteq g(\{\omega\}, A \cup B)$

U8: $\forall X \subseteq \Omega, \forall A, B \subseteq \Omega, \quad g(X \cup Y, A) = g(X, A) \cup g(Y, A)$

U9: $\forall \omega \in \Omega, \forall A, B \subseteq \Omega, \quad g(\{\omega\}, A) \cap B \neq \emptyset \Rightarrow g(\{\omega\}, A \cap B) \subseteq g(\{\omega\}, A) \cap B$

Katsuno and Mendelzon postulates have been criticized and they can be challenged (e.g. [2]) on two points particularly. First, U2 always favors inertia: if the new information about the system change follows the representation of the current system state, then the representation must not change, so in this case the system must be considered to have remained in the same state. Thus, this postulate does not allow for the existence of transient states, i.e., states which are left immediately after being reached. But, for instance, consider the case of an object falling down from a table, the state expressing that the object is falling is transient and evolves towards a state in which the object is on the floor. This kind of situation cannot be modelled by a KM-update operator. Secondly, U3 forces every evolution from any state to any state to be possible. Meanwhile, one might need to express that a state in which an object is on the floor cannot evolve directly towards a state in which the object is on the table again, and that intermediary states are needed between those two states.

Here is the fundamental theorem which is linking those postulates with the existence of a ternary rank-ordering family (i.e. the existence of a transition graph between states):

Theorem 1 (Katsuno, Mendelzon). *g satisfies U1, U2, U3, U4, U5, U8, U9* $\Leftrightarrow \forall \omega \in \Omega$, *it exists a complete pre-ordering* $\geq_\omega$ *s.t.* $\forall \omega' \in \Omega, \omega >_\omega \omega'$ *and* $g(X, A) = \bigcup_{\omega \in X} \{\omega' \in A \text{ s.t. } \forall \omega'' \in A, \omega' \geq_\omega \omega''\}$.

The main limitation of this theorem is that the complete pre-ordering $\geq_\omega$ built on each state of the world ω must be *faithful* ($\forall \omega' \in \Omega, \omega >_\omega \omega'$), i.e., the state of the world ω on which is founded the rank-ordering is always strictly preferred to any other world. This inertia condition seems too strong and it is only due to postulate U2.

3 A new set of postulates

Considering the criticisms made above, a new set of postulates is introduced: after having removed postulate U2 which was there only to generate inertia and having modified postulate U3 in order to have a less restrict postulate, a normalization postulate U10 has been added. Here, the update operator g is a mapping from $2^{\Omega} \times 2^{\Omega \cup \{z\}}$ to 2^{Ω}, where z is an unreachable state not belonging to Ω.

U1, U5, U8 and U9 are left untouched.

U3bis: $\forall X \subseteq \Omega, \forall A, B \subseteq \Omega, \quad g(X, A) \neq \emptyset \Rightarrow g(X, A \cup B) \neq \emptyset$

To update every consistent representation of a system by any information is no longer necessarily possible, but, if an update of an initial representation X, with an information A is possible, then an update is necessarily still possible learning a piece of information more general than A.

U10: $\forall \omega \in \Omega, \quad g(\{\omega\}, \{z\}) = \emptyset$

Here, an unattainable state z is introduced, it constitutes the minimal bound of every rank-ordering $\geq_\omega$ build on Ω and relative to a given state ω (cf. Proposition 8).

Remark 1 *U1 can be deduced from U3bis, U5 and U10*

Proof. $\forall A \subseteq \Omega \cup \{z\}$, let us suppose that $\exists b \in \Omega \cup \{z\}$ such that $b \in g(X, A)$ and $b \notin A$. Using U5, $g(X, A) \cap \{b\} \subseteq g(X, \emptyset)$, i.e., $b \in g(X, \emptyset)$. Using U3bis, $g(X, \emptyset) \neq \emptyset \Rightarrow g(X, \{z\}) \neq \emptyset$, but, by U10, $g(X, \{z\}) = \emptyset$, so, the first assumption was impossible. So $\forall b \in \Omega \cup \{z\}$ such that $b \in g(X, A)$, $b \in A$. □

3.1 Completeness of the set U3bis, U5, U8, U9 and U10

This new set is more general than Katsuno and Mendelzon's one, now, a similar fundamental theorem must be established in order to show its well-foundedness. This theorem will guarantee that the existence of a transition graph between states is equivalent to the existence of an update operator satisfying our postulates (and conversely).

Lemma 2. *If g verifies U1, U5 then g also verifies:*
1. $\forall A, B \subseteq \Omega, \quad B \subseteq g(X, A) \Rightarrow g(X, B) = B$
2. $\forall A, B \subseteq \Omega, \quad A \not\subseteq g(X, A) \Rightarrow A \not\subseteq g(X, A \cup B)$
3. $\forall A, B \subseteq \Omega, \quad g(X, A \cup B) \subseteq g(X, A) \cup g(X, B)$

Proof. 1. If $B \subseteq g(X, A)$, then $g(X, A) \cap B = B$. From U1, $g(X, A) \subseteq A$, hence $B \subseteq A$, therefore $A \cap B = B$. From U5, $g(X, A) \cap B \subseteq g(X, A \cap B)$, so $B \subseteq g(X, B)$. U1 gives the converse inclusion.
2. From U5, $g(X, A \cup B) \cap A \subseteq g(X, A)$. So if $A \not\subseteq g(X, A)$ then $A \not\subseteq g(X, A \cup B) \cap A$.
3. From U5, $g(X, A \cup B) \cap A \subseteq g(X, A)$ and $g(X, A \cup B) \cap B \subseteq g(X, B)$, so $g(X, A \cup B) \cap (A \cup B) \subseteq g(X, A) \cup g(X, B)$. From U1, $g(X, A \cup B) \subseteq A \cup B$, thus $g(X, A \cup B) \cap (A \cup B) = g(X, A \cup B)$, and the result. □

Note that Lemma 2.1 entails $\forall X, A \subseteq \Omega$, $g(X, g(X, A)) = g(X, A)$, a property expected for an update operator.

Lemma 3. *If g verifies U5 and U9 then g also verifies:*
U6bis: $\emptyset \subset g(\{\omega\}, A) \subseteq B, \emptyset \subset g(\{\omega\}, B) \subseteq A \Rightarrow g(\{\omega\}, A) = g(\{\omega\}, B)$

Proof. Let A, B and ω be s.t. $\emptyset \subset g(\{\omega\}, A) \subseteq B$, and $\emptyset \subset g(\{\omega\}, B) \subseteq A$. Since $\emptyset \subset g(\{\omega\}, A) \subseteq B$, then $g(\{\omega\}, A) \cap B \neq \emptyset$, so we can use U9 and U5: $g(\{\omega\}, A \cap B) = g(\{\omega\}, A) \cap B$. Conversely, we also have $g(\{\omega\}, B \cap A) = g(\{\omega\}, B) \cap A$. Thus $g(\{\omega\}, A) \cap B = g(\{\omega\}, B) \cap A$. Since by assumption $g(\{\omega\}, A) \subseteq B$ and $g(\{\omega\}, B) \subseteq A$, we get $g(\{\omega\}, A) = g(\{\omega\}, B)$. □

Lemma 4. *If g verifies U1, U3bis and U9 then g also verifies:*

$$U7 : g(\{\omega\}, A) \cap g(\{\omega\}, B) \subseteq g(\{\omega\}, A \cup B)$$

Proof. Let $A, B \subseteq \Omega$ and $\omega \in \Omega$
- If $g(\{\omega\}, A \cup B) \cap A \neq \emptyset$ and $g(\{\omega\}, A \cup B) \cap B \neq \emptyset$ then using U9, $g(\{\omega\}, A) = g(\{\omega\}, (A \cup B) \cap A) \subseteq g(\{\omega\}, A \cup B) \cap A \subseteq g(\{\omega\}, A \cup B)$. Similarly $g(\{\omega\}, B) \subseteq g(\{\omega\}, A \cup B)$. Thus U7 is verified.
- If $g(\{\omega\}, A \cup B) \cap A \neq \emptyset$ and $g(\{\omega\}, A \cup B) \cap B = \emptyset$ then from U9, $g(\{\omega\}, A) \subseteq g(\{\omega\}, A \cup B)$. By U1, $g(\{\omega\}, B) \subseteq B$ therefore $g(\{\omega\}, A) \cap g(\{\omega\}, B) \subseteq g(\{\omega\}, A \cup B) \cap B = \emptyset$, so $g(\{\omega\}, A) \cap g(\{\omega\}, B) = \emptyset$ and U7 is easily verified. The proof is identical in the case where $g(\{\omega\}, A \cup B) \cap A = \emptyset$ and $g(\{\omega\}, A \cup B) \cap B \neq \emptyset$.
- If $g(\{\omega\}, A \cup B) \cap A = g(\{\omega\}, A \cup B) \cap B = \emptyset$ then $\forall x \in A \cup B, x \notin g(\{\omega\}, A \cup B)$. Using U1, $g(\{\omega\}, A \cup B) \subseteq A \cup B$. Thus $g(\{\omega\}, A \cup B) = \emptyset$. Using the converse of U3bis, $g(\{\omega\}, A) = g(\{\omega\}, B) = \emptyset$. U7 is again verified. □

Proposition 5. *Let g be an update operator verifying U1 U3bis, U5, and U9. For a given $\omega \in \Omega$, the relation on $\Omega \cup \{z\} \times \Omega \cup \{z\}$ such that $\omega' >_\omega \omega'' \Leftrightarrow \omega' \neq \omega''$ and $g(\{\omega\}, \{\omega', \omega''\}) = \{\omega'\}$ is a strict ordering.*

In the following proofs, $g(\{\omega\}, \{a, b, c\})$ will be written $g(abc)$, and so on.

Proof. Transitivity: If $a >_\omega b$ and $b >_\omega c$, we have: $g(ab) = \{a\}, g(bc) = \{b\}$ and a, b, c are distincts. Using Lemma 2.2, $b \notin g(ab)$ thus $b \notin g(abc)$, in the same way $c \notin g(bc)$ so $c \notin g(abc)$. From U1: $g(abc) \subseteq \{a, b, c\}$. By U3bis $g(abc) \neq \emptyset$ since $g(ab) \neq \emptyset$. Consequently $g(abc) = \{a\} \subseteq \{a, c\}$. From U1: $g(ac) \subseteq \{a, c\} \subseteq \{a, b, c\}$. From Lemma 2.1, $a \in g(ab)$ so $g(a) = \{a\} \neq \emptyset$. So from U3bis $g(ac) \neq \emptyset$. Thus we can use U6bis, $g(abc) = g(ac)$ and thus $g(ac) = \{a\}$ i.e., $a >_\omega c$.
Asymmetry and *Anti-reflexivity* are trivial by definition of $>_\omega$. □

Intuitively, $\omega' >_\omega \omega''$ means that starting from ω, ω' is a strictly more plausible next state than ω''. Therefore updating a knowledge base, whose extension is reduced to only one initial state ω, with a piece of information saying that the world has evolved either in ω' or in ω'' will give a resulting knowledge base which extension is the state ω'.

Proposition 6. *Let g be an update operator verifying U1, U3bis, U5, and U9. For a given $\omega \in \Omega$, the relation on $\Omega \cup \{z\} \times \Omega \cup \{z\}$ such that $\omega' \geq_\omega \omega'' \Leftrightarrow \omega' \in g(\{\omega\}, \{\omega', \omega''\})$ or $g(\{\omega\}, \{\omega', \omega''\}) = \emptyset$ is a complete pre-ordering.*

Remark 2 *g satisfies U1 $\Rightarrow \geq_\omega$ and $>_\omega$ defined from g are such that $a \geq_\omega b \Leftrightarrow b \not>_\omega a$.*

Proof. NOT ($b \neq a$ and $g(ba) = \{b\}$) $\equiv b = a$ or $g(ba) \neq \{b\}$. So, by U1, $b \not>_\omega a \equiv a \in g(ab)$ or $g(ab) = \emptyset$. □

Proof of Proposition 6. Transitivity: If $a \geq_\omega b$ and $b \geq_\omega c$, there are four cases:
- $a \in g(ab)$ and $b \in g(bc)$. Note that then $g(abc) = \emptyset$ is impossible (because of U3bis), as well as $g(abc) = \{b\}$ or $g(abc) = \{c\}$ or $g(abc) = \{b, c\}$. Indeed using U9 it is easy to see that any of these hypotheses leads to a contradiction, since $g(ab) \subseteq g(abc) \cap \{a, b\}$ leads to $g(ab) = \{b\}$, for $g(abc) = \{b\}$ or $\{b, c\}$ and thus to $a \notin g(ab)$; similarly U9

leads to $g(bc) = \{c\}$ if $g(abc) = \{c\}$. Due to U1, the only remaining possible case is $a \in g(abc)$. Now using U5, $a \in g(abc) \cap \{a,c\} \subseteq g(ac)$.
- $a \in g(ab)$ and $g(bc) = \emptyset$ then using the converse of U3bis, $g(b) = g(c) = \emptyset$. Now, using Lemma 2.2: $b \notin g(abc)$ and $c \notin g(abc)$. By U3bis, $g(abc) \neq \emptyset$. Using U1, we have $g(abc) = \{a\}$, and, as above, we get $a \in g(ac)$.
- The case $g(ab) = \emptyset$ and $b \in g(bc)$ is impossible (by the converse of U3bis, $g(b) = \emptyset$ and by Lemma 2.2 $b \notin g(b) \Rightarrow b \notin g(bc)$).
- $g(ab) = \emptyset$ and $g(bc) = \emptyset$, we get $g(ac) = \emptyset$ (using Lemma 2.3 and $g(a) = g(c) = \emptyset$)
In all cases, $a \geq_\omega c$.

Reflexivity: Since $>_\omega$ is anti-reflexive then $\geq_\omega$ is reflexive.

Completeness: If $a \not\geq_\omega b$, then from U1, $b \in g(ab)$ i.e., $b \geq_\omega a$. □

Intuitively, $\omega' \geq_\omega \omega''$ means that ω' is at least as accessible than ω'' from ω. So, for sure, if it is possible, updating a knowledge base whose extension is reduced to one initial state ω with the information that, now, the state of the system is ω' or ω'' gives a resulting knowledge base whose extension must contain the state ω'.

Proposition 7. *Let g be an update operator verifying U1, U3bis, U5 and U6bis, for a given $\omega \in \Omega$, the relation on $\Omega \cup \{z\} \times \Omega \cup \{z\}$ such that $\omega' =_\omega \omega'' \Leftrightarrow g(\{\omega\}, \{\omega', \omega''\}) = \{\omega', \omega''\}$ or $g(\{\omega\}, \{\omega', \omega''\}) = \emptyset$ is an equivalence relation.*

Remark 3 *If g satisfies U1 then $\geq_\omega$ and $=_\omega$ defined from g are such that $a =_\omega b \Leftrightarrow (a \geq_\omega b)$ and $(b \geq_\omega a)$*

Proof. $(a \geq_\omega b)$ and $(b \geq_\omega a) \equiv (a \in g(ab)$ or $g(ab) = \emptyset)$ and $(b \in g(ab)$ or $g(ab) = \emptyset) \equiv \{a,b\} \subseteq g(ab)$ or $g(ab) = \emptyset$. By U1, $\{a,b\} \subseteq g(ab) \equiv \{a,b\} = g(ab)$. Hence the result. □

Proof of Proposition 7. Since the relation $\geq_\omega$ is a pre-ordering, the relation $=_\omega$ defined by $x =_\omega y$ iff ($x \geq_\omega y$ and $y \geq_\omega x$) is trivially transitive, reflexive and symmetric . □

Intuitively, $\omega' =_\omega \omega''$ means that from the initial state ω, it is as plausible to evolve towards ω' than towards ω''. Therefore, if it is possible, updating a knowledge base whose extension is the initial state ω with an information that the next state now is either ω' or ω'', gives the result that the world has evolved either in ω' or in ω'', (no more precision about this evolution is available).

Proposition 8. *If g verifies U1, U5 and U10 then $\geq_\omega$, defined from g, is such that $\forall a, \omega \in \Omega, a \geq_\omega z$*

Proof. Let us assume that $\exists a \in \Omega, z >_\omega a$, then since $a \neq z$, $g(\{\omega\}, \{a,z\}) = \{z\}$. But by U10, $g(\{\omega\}, \{z\}) = \emptyset$, so using Lemma 2.2, $z \notin g(\{\omega\}, \{a,z\})$. □

This proposition points out that given an update function g, z, the unattainable state from any initial state ω, is the lowest bound of all pre-ordering $\geq_\omega$ associated to g.

Theorem 9. $\exists g : 2^\Omega \times 2^{\Omega \cup \{z\}} \rightarrow 2^\Omega$ *satisfying U3bis, U5, U8, U9 and U10* $\Rightarrow \forall \omega \in \Omega$, *there exists a complete pre-ordering $\geq_\omega$ s. t. $\forall S, X \subseteq \Omega, g(X,S) = \bigcup_{\omega \in X}\{\omega' \in S^\star$ s.t. $\forall \omega'' \in S, \omega' \geq_\omega \omega''\}$ with $S^\star = \{\omega' \in S, \omega' >_\omega z\}$.*

Proof. If $\exists g : 2^{\Omega} \times 2^{\Omega \cup \{z\}} \to 2^{\Omega}$ satisfying U1, U3bis, U5, U8, U9 and U10.
- by Proposition 6, for a given $\omega \in \Omega$, the relation on $\Omega \cup \{z\} \times \Omega \cup \{z\}$ s.t.

$$\omega' \geq_\omega \omega'' \Leftrightarrow \begin{cases} \omega' \in g(\{\omega\}, \{\omega', \omega''\}) \\ or \\ g(\{\omega\}, \{\omega', \omega''\}) = \emptyset \end{cases} \quad \text{is a complete pre-ordering.}$$

- *let us show that* $g(\{\omega\}, S) \subseteq \{\omega' \in S^\star, \forall \omega'' \in S, \omega' \geq_\omega \omega''\}$. If $g(\{\omega\}, S) = \emptyset$, it's trivial. Let $a \in g(\{\omega\}, S)$. From U1,$a \in S$. From Lemma 2.1, $g(\{\omega\}, \{a\}) = \{a\}$. Using Lemma 2.3 $g(\omega, az) \subseteq g(\omega, a) \cup g(\omega, z)$. Using U10, $g(\omega, az) \subseteq \{a\}$. By U3bis, $g(\omega, az) \neq \emptyset$, so $g(\omega, az) = \{a\}$, i.e., $a >_\omega z$, therefore $a \in S^\star$. Let us assume that it exists $b \in S$ such that $b >_\omega a$, in this case $a \notin g(\omega, ab)$. From U5, $g(\{\omega\}, S) \cap \{a, b\} \subseteq g(\{\omega\}, ab)$, but $a \in g(\{\omega\}, S) \cap \{a, b\}$, so it's impossible. Therefore $a \in \{\omega' \in S^\star, \forall b \in S, \omega' \geq_\omega b\}$.
- *let us show that* $\{\omega' \in S^\star, \forall \omega'' \in S, \omega' \geq_\omega \omega''\} \subseteq g(\{\omega\}, S)$. Let $a \in \{\omega' \in S^\star$ s.t. $\forall \omega'' \in S, \omega' \geq_\omega \omega''\}$ then $a \in S^\star$. Let us note $\omega_1, \ldots \omega_n$ the elements of S. Since $a \in S, S = \{a, \omega_1\} \cup \cdots \cup \{a, \omega_n\}$. Since $a \in S^\star$, $g(az) = \{a\}$. By Lemma 2.1, $g(a) = \{a\}$. Using U3bis, $\forall \omega_i, g(a\omega_i) \neq \emptyset$. Moreover, $\forall \omega_i \in S, a \geq_\omega \omega_i$, so $a \in g(\{\omega\}, \{a, \omega_i\})$. Using U7, we get $\forall \omega_{1 \ldots n} \in S, a \in g(\{\omega\}, \{a, \omega_1\} \cup \cdots \cup \{a, \omega_n\})$.
- by U8, $g(X, S) = \bigcup_{\omega \in X} g(\{\omega\}, S)$. □

Here is the converse of the previous theorem:

Theorem 10. *There exists a function mapping each* $\omega \in \Omega$ *to a complete pre-order* $\geq_\omega$ *on* $\Omega \cup \{z\} \times \Omega \cup \{z\}$ *s.t.* $\forall \omega, \omega' \in \Omega, \omega' \geq_\omega z \Rightarrow \exists g : 2^{\Omega} \times 2^{\Omega \cup \{z\}} \to 2^{\Omega}$ *s. t.* $\forall S, X \subseteq \Omega, g(X, S) = \bigcup_{\omega \in X} \{\omega' \in S^\star$ *s.t.* $\forall \omega'' \in S, \omega' \geq_\omega \omega''\}$ *with* $S^\star = \{\omega' \in S, \omega' >_\omega z\}$, *which satisfies U3bis, U5, U8, U9 and U10*

Proof. g satisfies *U8* and *U10* by construction.
- *U3bis:* If $g(\{\omega\}, A) \neq \emptyset$, let $a \in g(\{\omega\}, A)$, i.e, $\forall \omega'' \in A, a \geq_\omega \omega''$, and $a \in A^\star$. Since $\geq_\omega$ is complete, $\forall B \neq \emptyset, \exists b \in B$ s.t. $\forall \omega'' \in B, b \geq_\omega \omega''$. If $b \geq_\omega a$ then, since $\geq_\omega$ is transitive, $\forall \omega'' \in A, b \geq_\omega \omega''$, so, $\forall \omega'' \in A \cup B, b \geq_\omega \omega''$. Moreover $b >_\omega z$ (else $z \geq_\omega a$ which is impossible), so $b \in (A \cup B)^\star$, thus, $b \in g(\{\omega\}, A \cup B)$. Otherwise $a \geq_\omega b$ then, similarly, $\forall \omega'' \in A \cup B, a \geq_\omega \omega''$, moreover, $a \in A^\star$, so, $a \in (A \cup B)^\star$ and $a \in g(\{\omega\}, A \cup B)$.

Now, if $g(X, A) \neq \emptyset$, i.e, $\bigcup_{\omega \in X} \{\omega' \in A^\star$ s.t. $\forall \omega'' \in A, \omega' \geq_\omega \omega''\} \neq \emptyset$ then $\exists \omega \in \Omega$ s.t. $\{\omega' \in A^\star$ s.t. $\forall \omega'' \in A, \omega' \geq_\omega \omega''\} \neq \emptyset$. For this ω, we have just seen that $g(\{\omega\}, A \cup B) \neq \emptyset$, so $g(X, A \cup B) \neq \emptyset$.
- *U5:* If $g(\{\omega\}, A) \cap B = \emptyset$, U5 is trivial. Let $a \in g(\{\omega\}, A) \cap B$, thus, $\forall \omega' \in A \cap B, a \geq_\omega \omega'$. Moreover, $a \in A^\star$ hence $a \in (A \cap B)^\star$. So $a \in g(\{\omega\}, A \cap B)$. Thus, $g(\{\omega\}, A) \cap B \subseteq g(\{\omega\}, A \cap B)$ and therefore $\bigcup_{\omega \in X} g(\{\omega\}, A) \cap B \subseteq \bigcup_{\omega \in X} g(\{\omega\}, A \cap B)$, then, by U8, $g(X, A) \cap B \subseteq g(X, A \cap B)$.
- *U9:* If $g(\{\omega\}, A) \cap B \neq \emptyset$, let $a \in g(\{\omega\}, A)$ and $a \in B$ therefore $a \in A^\star \cap B \subseteq A \cap B$ and $\forall \omega' \in A, a \geq_\omega \omega'$. Let $b \in g(\{\omega\}, A \cap B)$, so $b \in (A \cap B)^\star \subseteq B$ and $\forall \omega' \in A \cap B, b \geq_\omega \omega'$. Since $a \in A \cap B$, then $b \geq_\omega a$. By transitivity: $\forall \omega' \in A, b \geq_\omega \omega'$. Since $b \in (A \cap B)^\star, b \in A^\star$ and $b \in B$. Consequently $b \in g(\{\omega\}, A) \cap B$. □

These two theorems show that the existence of an update operator satisfying U3bis, U5, U8, U9 and U10 is equivalent to the existence of rank-orderings on each set of transitions starting from a given state of the system. Let us notice that, here, the update operation must always lead to *reachable* states, this condition is added because U3 has been modified, this allows us to deal with unattainable states. Moreover, the inertia condition is suppressed by removing postulate U2 and therefore the complete pre-ordering mapped to each state of the world, this time, has not to be *faithful* [6] i.e. it is not necessarily inert. These theorems point also out that the update of a knowledge base whose extension is a set of state, can be computed by updating independently the knowledge bases corresponding to each state of the set, and then by doing the union of the results. $\{\geq_\omega, \omega \in \Omega\}$ describe a transition graph between states. *Every update operator satisfying U3bis, U5, U8, U9, U10 always admit an underlying ranked transition graph.*

Proposition 11. *If there exists a mapping associating to each interpretation* $\omega \in \Omega$ *a complete pre-ordering* $\geq_\omega$ *on* $\Omega \cup \{z\} \times \Omega \cup \{z\}$, *s.t.* $\forall \omega, \omega' \in \Omega$, $\omega' \geq_\omega z$ *then* $\forall \omega, \omega' \in \Omega$, $z \geq_\omega \omega' \Leftrightarrow g(\{\omega\}, \{\omega'\}) = \emptyset$ *(*ω' *is not reachable from* ω*) where* g *from* $2^\Omega \times 2^{\Omega \cup \{z\}}$ *to* 2^Ω *is defined by:* $g(X, S) = \bigcup_{\omega \in X} \{\omega' \in S^\star, s.t. \forall \omega'' \in S, \omega' \geq_\omega \omega''\}$ *with* $S^\star = \{\omega' \in S, \omega' >_\omega z\}$.

Proof. If $\omega' \in \Omega$ is such that $z \geq_\omega \omega'$ then $\{\omega'\}^\star = \emptyset$ thus $g(\{\omega\}, \{\omega'\}) = \emptyset$. □

The above property shows the possible existence of unattainable states from a given state. From a family of pre-orderings $\geq_\omega$ on $\Omega \cup \{z\} \times \Omega \cup \{z\}$, where z is the lowest bound of every $\geq_\omega$, the unattainable states from ω for g (the update function g associated to this family) are the states under z with respect to $\geq_\omega$.

3.2 Minimality of postulates U3bis, U5, U8, U9 and U10

Proposition 12. *U3bis, U5, U8, U9 and U10 are constituting a minimal set.*

Proof. It must be shown that no postulate is deducible from the others, i.e, for each postulate, one must find a function g violating it and satisfying the five remaining ones. For instance, the independence of U9 can be proven using the function g such that $\forall X \subseteq \Omega, \exists a \in \Omega, g(X, \Omega) = \{a\}$ and $\forall A \subseteq \Omega \cup \{z\}, A \neq \Omega, g(X, A) = A^\star$. U3bis, U5, U8 and U10 are true, U9 is not verified because $g(X, \Omega) \cap \{a, b\} \neq \emptyset$ and $g(X, \Omega \cap \{a, b\}) = \{a, b\} \not\subset g(X, \Omega) \cap \{a, b\} = \{a\}$. □

4 Conclusion

In relation with Katsuno and Mendelzon postulates, Boutilier [2] has discussed the update of a knowledge base by an observation. He introduces events which are functions that maps each world to a set of worlds (result of the event). To compute the update of a world ω by an observation O, one has to find the most plausible event e which transforms ω into a set of worlds where O is true. Boutilier's analysis agrees with our view in the sense that his class of update operators is also more general than Katsuno and Mendelzon's one (it doesn't verify neither U2 nor U3). He shows, however, that his framework can be restrained in order to satisfy every KM-postulate from U1 to U9.

Let us notice that a set of update postulates is not enough to update a knowledge base practically, because it does not define the update operator precisely but only its properties. In [3] it is pointed out that these postulates can be verified by some operators that are not intuitively satisfying as update operators, and thus concludes that they are not constraining enough.

The ternary relation of the form $\omega' >_\omega \omega''$ which expresses "closeness" between states and whose existence is guaranteed by the new set of updating postulates we propose, can be seen as a justification of the use of possibilistic Markov chains introduced in [4]. Indeed the ternary relation $\omega' >_\omega \omega''$ reads in possibilistic terms $\pi(\omega'|\omega) > \pi(\omega''|\omega)$ where $\pi(.|\omega)$ is a conditional possibility distribution. It expresses that ω' is strictly more possible than ω'' as being the next state after ω. It should be clear that the use of the possibilistic view leads to commensurate $>_{\omega_1}$ and $>_{\omega_2}$, an hypothesis which is not required by Katsuno and Mendelzon. The construction of the function g from the ternary relation agrees with the extension principle in possibility theory which enables us to extend a function to (fuzzy) subsets of its domain; here, the function under consideration is the one which associates to ω its closest neighbours in A, and which is then extended to X. The coherence of Katsuno and Mendelzon postulates with possibility theory has been pointed out and established in [5].

5 Acknowledgement

This work is partially supported by the French national project "Inter PRC" entitled "Gestion de l'évolutif et de l'incertain" (Handling of Uncertainty in a Dynamical World), and by the European project ESPRIT-BRA n^o6156 DRUMS-II (Defeasible Reasoning and Uncertainty Management Systems).

References

1. C. Alchourrón, P. Gärdenfors, and D. Makinson. On the logic of theory change : partial meet contraction and revision functions. *Journal of Symbolic Logic*, 50:510–530, 1985.
2. C. Boutilier. An event-based abductive model of update. In *Proc. of the Tenth Canadian Conf. on Artficial Intelligence*, 1994.
3. Collectif. Inter-prc: Gestion de l'evolutif et de l'incertain. In *5^{ièmes} journées nationales du PRC GDR*, pages 77–119, Nancy, France, February 1995.
4. D. Dubois, F. Dupin de Saint-Cyr, and H. Prade. Updating, transition constraints and possibilistic Markov chains. In *Proc. of the 4th Conf. on Information Processing and Management of Uncertainty in Knowledge-Based Systems*, pages 826–831, Paris, France, July 1994.
5. D. Dubois and H. Prade. A survey of belief revision and updating rules in various uncertainty models. *International journal of Intelligent Systems*, 9:61–100, 1994.
6. H. Katsuno and A.O. Mendelzon. On the difference between updating a knowledge base and revising it. In J. Allen and al., editors, *Proc. of the 2nd Inter. Conf. on Principles of Knowledge Representation and Reasoning*, pages 387–394, Cambridge, MA, 1991.
7. M. Winslett. Reasoning about action using a possible models approach. In *Proc. of the 7th National Conference on Artificial Intelligence*, pages 89–93, St. Paul, 1988.

Similarity-based Consequence Relations

D. Dubois*, F. Esteva**, P. Garcia**, L. Godo** and H. Prade*

* Institut de Recherche en Informatique de Toulouse IRIT - CNRS, Université Paul Sabatier 31062 Toulouse Cedex, France

**Institut d'Investigació en Intel.ligència Artificial IIIA - CSIC, Campus Univ. Autònoma Barcelona 08193 Bellaterra, Spain

Abstract. This paper offers a preliminary investigation of consequence relations which make sense in a logic of graded similarity, and their application to interpolative reasoning.

1 Introduction

One of the possible semantics of fuzzy sets is in terms of similarity, namely a grade of membership $\mu_F(\omega)$ can be viewed as the degree of resemblance between ω and prototypes of the fuzzy set F. One way of proceeding is to equip the referential Ω with a similarity relation S, that is a reflexive ($S(\omega,\omega) = 1$), symmetric ($S(\omega,\omega') = S(\omega',\omega)$) and t-norm-transitive fuzzy relation ($S(\omega,\omega')\otimes S(\omega',\omega'') \leq S(\omega,\omega'')$) (a t-norm $\otimes$ is a nondecreasing semigroup of the unit interval with identity 1 and absorbing element 0). For any classical subset A of Ω, we define a fuzzy set A* by

$$\mu_{A^*}(\omega) = \mathrm{Sup}_{\omega' \in A}\, S(\omega,\omega') \qquad (1)$$

where $S(\omega,\omega')$ is the degree of similarity between ω and ω'. A* is the fuzzy set of elements close to A. In the following, logical formulas of a finite lenguage L will be denoted by p, q, r..., the set of interpretations over L, by Ω, and [p] will denote the set of models of p. In such a framework, an interesting question is how to devise a logic of similarity, where inference rules can account for the proximity between interpretations. This kind of investigation has been started by Ruspini (1991) with a view to cast fuzzy patterns of inference such as the generalized modus ponens of Zadeh (1979) into a logical setting. Indeed in the scope of similarity modeling, the generalized modus ponens can be expressed informally as follows,

$$\frac{\text{p is close to being true;} \qquad \text{p approximately implies q}}{\text{q is not far from being true}}$$

where "close", "approximately" and "not far" refer to the similarity relation S, while p and q are classical propositions. Eventually one may capture the notion of interpolation inside a logical setting. In this paper, we further investigate how a logic of similarity can be defined, namely, what are the different consequence relations that make sense in similarity-based reasoning. More concretely, after this introduction we present in section 2 how similarity naturally leads to a notion of approximate and graded entailment and we characterize its associated consequence relation. In section 3, we study three different extensions of the previous entailment to deal with background knowledge and we apply and discuss them in an example of interpolative reasoning in section 4. Finally, some comments are provided in section 5.

2 Similarity and Approximate Entailment

In the rest of the paper S will denote a ⊗-similarity relation on Ω, for a given t-norm ⊗ (e.g. Trillas and Valverde 1984) satisfying the discriminating property $S(\omega, \omega') = 1$ iff $\omega = \omega'$. If q is a classical proposition, it can be fuzzified into another proposition q* which means "approximately q" and whose fuzzy set of models is $[q^*] = [q]^*$ as defined via (1). Clearly, a logic dealing with propositions of the form q* is a fuzzy logic in the sense of a many-valued logic, whose truth-value set is [0,1]. The satisfaction relation is graded and denoted $\models_S^\alpha$, namely,

$\omega \models_S^\alpha q$ iff there exists a model ω' of q which is α–similar to ω, in the sense that $\mu_{[q^*]}(\omega) \geq \alpha$, i.e., ω belongs to the α-cut of $[q^*]$ (denoted by $[q^*]_\alpha$).

Note that one may have $\omega \models_S^\alpha \omega'$ for $\omega' \neq \omega$. Indeed it means $S(\omega,\omega') \geq \alpha$. For the sake of simplicity, the subscript S will be omitted from the symbol $\models_S^\alpha$ whenever no confusion is possible. One might be tempted by defining a multiple-valued logic of similarity. Unfortunately it cannot be truth-functional. Namely given S, the truth-value evaluation $\mu_{[q^*]}(\omega)$ associated to the interpretation ω is truth-functional neither for the negation nor for the conjunction. This fact stresses the difference between similarity logic and other logics underlying fuzzy sets such as Lukasiewicz logic or the more recent family of monoidal logics (Höhle, 1994). The reason is that here all fuzzy propositions are interpreted in the light of a single similarity relation, so that there are in some sense less fuzzy propositions here than in more standard many-valued calculi. Similarity logic is more constrained, since the set of fuzzy subsets of Ω corresponding to classical propositions $\{[q^*] \mid q \in L\}$ is only a proper subset of the set $[0, 1]^\Omega$ of all fuzzy subsets of Ω.

A more natural setting is the one of modal logics which is tailored to account for relations on the set of interpretations. The similarity relation S defines a family of nested accessibility relations R_α on the set of possible worlds Ω defined as $R_\alpha(\omega, \omega')$ iff $S(\omega, \omega') \geq \alpha$. Therefore, enlarging the logical language, we can define, for each α, a usual pair of dual modal operators $\Box_\alpha$ and $\Diamond_\alpha$ with the following standard semantics:

$\omega \models \Diamond_\alpha p$	iff	there exists ω' such that $R_\alpha(\omega, \omega')$ and $\omega' \models p$
$\omega \models \Box_\alpha p$	iff	for every ω' such that $R_\alpha(\omega, \omega')$ then it holds $\omega' \models p$

If the similarity relation is min-transitive, i.e., $S(\omega, \omega') \geq \min(S(\omega, \omega''), S(\omega'', \omega'))$, then R_α are equivalence relations, and therefore, for each α, $\Box_\alpha$ and $\Diamond_\alpha$ are a pair of dual S5 modal operators. It is easy to check that the above defined graded satisfaction $\models^\alpha$ is directly related to the possibility operator $\Diamond_\alpha$ in the sense that if q is a non-modal proposition, then the following equivalence holds: $\omega \models^\alpha q$ iff $\omega \models \Diamond_\alpha q$.

The graded satisfaction relation can be extended to a graded semantic entailment relation: A proposition p entails a proposition q at degree α, written $p \models^\alpha q$, if and only if, each p-world makes q* at least α-true:

$$p \models^\alpha q \text{ iff } [p] \subset [q^*]_\alpha.$$

The condition of this entailment relation can be also expressed using Ruspini's *implication measure* (Ruspini, 1991) as $p \models^\alpha q$ iff $I_S(q \mid p) = \mathrm{Inf}_{\omega \models p} \mathrm{Sup}_{\omega' \models q} S(\omega, \omega') \geq \alpha$. Note that $I_S(q \mid \omega) = \mu_{[q^*]}(\omega)$. A companion of this measure is the so-called *consistency measure* defined as $C_S(q \mid p) = \mathrm{Sup}_{\omega \models p} \mathrm{Sup}_{\omega' \models q} S(\omega, \omega')$ which will play a minor role in this paper. Remarkable properties of the entailment relation $\models^\alpha$ are:

Transitivity: if $p \models^\alpha r$ and $r \models^\beta q$ then $p \models^{\alpha \otimes \beta} q$ where $\otimes$ is a t-norm,
Reflexivity: $\forall \alpha$, $p \models^\alpha p$,
Right weakening: if $q \models r$ and $p \models^\alpha q$ then $p \models^\alpha r$,
Left strengthening: if $p \models r$ and $r \models^\alpha q$ then $p \models^\alpha q$ (monotonicity),
Left OR : $p \vee q \models^\alpha r$ iff $p \models^\alpha r$ and $q \models^\alpha r$,
Right OR: If r has a single model, $r \models^\alpha p \vee q$ iff $r \models^\alpha p$ or $r \models^\alpha q$.

The third and fourth properties are consequence of the transitivity property. The left OR is necessary to handle disjunctive information, and the right OR is a consequence of the decomposability for the OR connective in similarity logic. It must be noticed that $\models^\alpha$ does not satisfy the Right And property, i.e. from $p \models^\alpha q$ and $p \models^\alpha r$ it does not follow in general that $p \models^\alpha q \wedge r$. Hence the set of approximate consequences of p, in the sense of $\models^\alpha$, is not deductively closed. Moreover, as indicated also in (Dubois and Prade, 1995), another property, the so-called CUT, which holds for classical semantical entailment, does not hold either for $\models^\alpha$, that is,

$$p \models^\alpha r \text{ and } p \wedge r \models^\beta q \text{ do not imply } p \models^{f(\alpha, \beta)} q$$

with $\alpha > 0$ and $\beta > 0$ implying $f(\alpha, \beta) > 0$. A first result towards a characterization of the similarity-based graded entailment is given in the next theorem, where a consequence relation $p \models^\alpha q$ means "p entails q, approximately", and α is a level of strength. Proofs can be found in (Dubois et al., 1995).

Theorem 1 (Characterization of the $\models^\alpha$ consequence relations). Let L be a finite Boolean algebra of propositions. Suppose we have a family of consequence operators $\{\vdash^\alpha\}_{\alpha \in [0, 1]}$ (i.e. $\vdash^\alpha \subset L \times L$) fulfilling the following properties:

1) $\{\vdash^\alpha\}_{\alpha \in [0, 1]}$ is a nested family: $p \vdash^\alpha q$ implies $p \vdash^\beta q$ for any $\beta \leq \alpha$,
2) $\vdash^1$ is just the classical logic consequence relation and $\vdash^0$ is the universal one,
3) *symmetry*: $\omega \vdash^\alpha \omega'$ iff $\omega' \vdash^\alpha \omega$, for any pair of interpretations,
4) *$\otimes$-transitivity*: $p \vdash^\alpha q$ and $q \vdash^\beta r$ implies $p \vdash^{\alpha \otimes \beta} r$,
5) *Left Or:* $p \vee r \vdash^\alpha q$ iff $p \vdash^\alpha q$ and $r \vdash^\alpha q$,
6) *Decomposition*: $\omega \vdash^\alpha p \vee r$ iff $\omega \vdash^\alpha p$ or $\omega \vdash^\alpha r$.

Then, there exists a $\otimes$-similarity relation S on Ω such that $p \vdash^\alpha q$ iff $I_S(q \mid p) \geq \alpha$, for each $\alpha \in [0, 1]$. And conversely, for any similarity S on Ω, the consequence relation defined as $p \models^\alpha q$ iff $I_S(q \mid p) \geq \alpha$ verifies the above set of properties.

Using again the modal logic setting, $p \models^\alpha q$ is also $p \models \Diamond_\alpha q$. An alternative entailment in similarity logic would be: $p \models \Box_\alpha q$. By definition, $p \models \Box_\alpha q$ iff $[p^*]_\alpha \subset [q]$. As usual in modal logics, this notion of entailment is stronger than the classical entailment (both are equivalent only if $\alpha = 1$), and thus it does not correspond to the idea of approximate inference. Notice that the implication and consistency measures can also be expressed in terms of the modal entailments (Esteva et al., 1994a):

$$I_S(q \mid p) = \mathrm{Sup}\{ \alpha \mid p \models \Diamond_\alpha q \}$$
$$C_S(q \mid p) = \mathrm{Inf}\{ \alpha \mid p \models \Box_\alpha \neg q \} = \mathrm{Inf}\{ \alpha \mid p \models \neg \Diamond_\alpha q \}.$$

3 Consequence Relations generated by a background knowledge

A natural question about the entailment is how to deal with some prior information which is available under the form of a set K of formulas or a subset of worlds E (the so-called *evidential set* in Ruspini's papers). Several extensions of $p \models^{\alpha} q$ can be envisaged. In particular, we shall consider two monotonic entailments in detail in this section, and we shall also point out a non-monotonic entailment relation, all of them being extensions of the classical consequence relation, $p \models_K q$ iff $K \wedge p \models q$ iff $K \models \neg p \vee q$ iff $E \cap [p] \subset [q]$, where $E = [K]$, which is recovered whenever the similarity relation S reduces to the classical equality relation.

3.1 A first option: using K as a pre-condition in $\models^{\alpha}$

The first and direct option is just to take the set K as a restriction on the set of p-worlds, and thus considering the entailment $\models^{\alpha}_{K}$ defined as follows:

$$p \models^{\alpha}_{K} q \text{ iff } \quad K \wedge p \models^{\alpha} q \quad \text{iff} \quad [p] \cap [K] \subset [q^*]_{\alpha}.$$

This amounts to expressing that [q] must be stretched to the degree α (at least) in order to encompass the models of K which are models of p. Although this entailment verifies properties like Reflexivity, Right Weakening or Left Strengthening as $\models^{\alpha}$ does, it does not satisfy any transitivity property. Even the restricted form

$$\text{if } \models^{\alpha}_{K} r \text{ and } r \models^{\beta}_{K} q \text{ then } \models^{\alpha \otimes \beta}_{K} q$$

does not hold, due to the failure of the inequality $I_S(q \mid p) \geq I_S(q \mid p \wedge r) \otimes I_S(r \mid p)$ which is also the responsible of the failure of the CUT property for the previous entailment relation $\models^{\alpha}$ (see Dubois and Prade, 1995). A characterization result, which is an extension of the previous one for $\models^{\alpha}$, is given in the next theorem.

Definition (consequence relations of type I). Let L be a finite Boolean algebra of propositions, let $\{\vdash^{\alpha}\}_{\alpha \in [0,1]}$ be a family of nested binary relations on L, that is, $\vdash^{\alpha} \subset L \times L$ and $p \vdash^{\alpha} q$ implies $p \vdash^{\beta} q$ for any $\beta \leq \alpha$, and let p_o be a proposition of L different from *False*. The set $\{\vdash^{\alpha}\}_{\alpha \in [0,1]}$ is said to be a family of *consequence relations of type I* if it satisfies the following properties:

1) $p \vdash^{1} q$ iff $p \wedge p_o \models q$; $\quad \vdash^{0}$ is the universal consequence relation,
2) *restricted symmetry*: $\omega \vdash^{\alpha} \omega'$ iff $\omega' \vdash^{\alpha} \omega$, for $\omega \models p_o$ and $\omega' \models p_o$,
3) *restricted transitivity*:
   $\omega \vdash^{\alpha} \omega'$ and $\omega'' \vdash^{\beta} \omega'$ implies $\omega \vdash^{\alpha \otimes \beta} \omega''$, for $\omega \models p_o$ and $\omega'' \models p_o$,
   $\omega \vdash^{\alpha} \omega'$ and $\omega \vdash^{\beta} \omega''$ implies $\omega' \vdash^{\alpha \otimes \beta} \omega''$, for $\omega \models p_o$ and $\omega' \models p_o$,
4) *Left Or*: $p \vee r \vdash^{\alpha} q$ iff $p \vdash^{\alpha} q$ and $r \vdash^{\alpha} q$,
5) *Decomposition*: $\omega \vdash^{\alpha} p \vee r$ iff $\omega \vdash^{\alpha} p$ or $\omega \vdash^{\alpha} r$,
6) *Coherence:* $p \vdash^{\alpha} q$ iff $p \wedge p_o \vdash^{\alpha} q$.

Theorem 2 (characterization of consequence relations of type I). If $\{\vdash^{\alpha}\}_{\alpha \in [0,1]}$ is a family of consequence relations of type I, then the following equivalent statements hold:

- there exists a ⊗-similarity relation S on the set of worlds Ω such that for each $\alpha \in [0, 1]$, $p \vdash^{\alpha} q$ iff $p \models^{\alpha}_{S,K} q$, with $K = \{p_o\}$
- there exists a family of consequence relations $\{\vdash'^{\alpha}\}_{\alpha \in [0, 1]}$ verifying the conditions of Theorem 1, such that $p \vdash^{\alpha} q$ iff $p \wedge p_o \vdash'^{\alpha} q$.

And conversely, for any ⊗-similarity S on Ω and any subset of formulas K, the consequence relations $\models^{\alpha}_{S,K}$ are of type I. See (Dubois et al., 1995) for the proof.

3.2 A second option: an entailment based on fuzzy implication

An alternative to taking into account prior knowledge into the entailment relation, related to what Ruspini calls "conditional necessity functions" in his proposal, is to define the following entailment:

$$p \models^{\alpha}_{K} q \text{ iff } \quad [K] \subset [p^* \Rightarrow q^*]_{\alpha},$$

where $\Rightarrow$ stands for the implication connective relating fuzzy propositions and interpreted by a residuated implication of many-valued logic, i.e., $\mu_{[p^* \Rightarrow q^*]} = \mu_{[p^*]} \otimes\!\!\rightarrow \mu_{[q^*]}$ where $\otimes\!\!\rightarrow$ denotes the residuated implication function w.r.t. the t-norm $\otimes$ ($a \otimes\!\!\rightarrow b = \sup \{x \mid a \otimes x \le b\}$). In terms of set inclusion, this entailment relation is related to the conditional implication measure in the sense that

$$p \models^{\alpha}_{K} q \qquad \text{iff} \qquad I_{S,K}(q \mid p) \ge \alpha$$

with $I_{S,K}(q \mid p) = \inf_{\omega \models K} \mu_{[p^*]}(\omega) \otimes\!\!\rightarrow \mu_{[q^*]}(\omega)$[1]. Notice that when K is empty, i.e., $[K] = \Omega$, $p \models^{\alpha}_{K} q$ no longer coincides with $p \models^{\alpha} q$. Rather, the equivalence holds between $p \models^{\alpha} q$ and $\models^{\alpha}_{p} q$, that is, when taking $K = \{p\}$ as background knowledge. Moreover if $p = True$ then $[K] \subset [q^*]_{\alpha}$; this means that $K \subset \{q \mid True \models^{\alpha}_{K} q\}$.

The underlying reason in (Ruspini, 1991) for considering such a conditional measure was to model, in its simplest form, the so-called generalized modus ponens in fuzzy logic (Zadeh, 1979) that can be expressed using $\models^{\alpha}_{K}$ as follows: "From $\models^{\alpha}_{K} r$ and $r \models^{\beta}_{K} q$ infer $\models^{\alpha \otimes \beta}_{K} q$". Indeed, a stronger form of transitivity holds, namely:

⊗-Transitivity: If $p \models^{\alpha}_{K} r$ and $r \models^{\beta}_{K} q$ then $p \models^{\alpha \otimes \beta}_{K} q$

This property is a direct consequence of the transivity of the conditional implication measure, i.e., $I_{S,K}(q \mid p) \ge I_{S,K}(r \mid p) \otimes I_{S,K}(q \mid r)$. However, $\models^{\alpha}_{K}$ so defined does not verify the CUT property. Other properties of $\models^{\alpha}_{K}$ are listed in the proposition below and used to characterize this type of entailment in the next theorem.

Proposition. The consequence operators $\models^{\alpha}_{K}$ above defined satisfy:

(i) $p \models^{\alpha}_{K} q$ implies $p \models^{\beta}_{K} q$ for every $\beta \le \alpha$,
(ii) $\models^{1}_{K}$ contains the classical logical consequence and $\models^{0}_{K}$ is the universal one,
(iii) ⊗-transitivity: $p \models^{\alpha}_{K} q$ and $q \models^{\beta}_{K} r$ implies $p \models^{\alpha \otimes \beta}_{K} r$,
(iv) Left-OR: $p \vee r \models^{\alpha}_{K} q$ iff $p \models^{\alpha}_{K} q$ and $r \models^{\alpha}_{K} q$,
(v) If $p \wedge K \equiv q \wedge K$ then $p \models^{1}_{K} q$ and $q \models^{1}_{K} p$.

---

[1]In (Dubois and Prade, 1995) it is pointed out that $I_{S,K}(q \mid p) \ge \alpha$ if, and only if, for all β, $[K] \cap [p^*]_{\beta} \subset [q^*]_{\alpha \otimes \beta}$.

Definition (consequence relations of type II). Let L be a finite Boolean algebra of propositions and $\{\vdash^{\alpha}\}_{\alpha\in[0,1]}$ a nested family of consequence relations on L. Let $K = \{q \mid \mathit{True} \vdash^{1} q\}$ and define the following fuzzy binary relation on the set of propositions L,

$$\underline{S}(p, q) = \mathrm{Min}(\ \mathrm{Sup}\{\alpha \mid p \vdash^{\alpha} q\}, \mathrm{Sup}\{\beta \mid q \vdash^{\beta} p\})$$

Then the family $\{\vdash^{\alpha}\}_{\alpha\in[0,1]}$ of *consequence relations* is said to be *of type II* if it satisfies the properties (i-iv) of the above proposition and :

(vii) $[K] \neq \emptyset$

(viii) $\omega_0 \vdash^{\alpha} q$ iff for all $\omega \in [K]$, there exists $\omega'_0 \models q$ such that
$\underline{S}(\omega, \omega'_0) \geq \underline{S}(\omega, \omega_0) \otimes \alpha$

Theorem 3 (characterization of consequence relations of type II). Let L be the finite Boolean algebra of propositions under consideration, and let $\{\vdash^{\alpha} \mid \alpha \in [0,1]\}$ a family of consequence operators of type II on L. Then, $\underline{S}$ is a $\otimes$-similarity relation on L and $p \vdash^{\alpha} q$ if and only if, $p \models^{\alpha}_{\underline{S},K} q$. (See Dubois et al., 1995, for a proof).

It is surprising to realize that the entailment $\models^{\alpha}$ is always stronger than $\models^{\alpha}_{K}$ for any prior information K, i.e., $p \models^{\alpha} q$ implies $p \models^{\alpha}_{K} q$ for any propositions p and q. This is an easy consequence of the inequality $I_{S,K}(q \mid p) \geq I_S(q \mid p)$.

3.3 A third option: a non-monotonic entailment

In (Esteva et al., 1994b) a modified version of the conditional measure $I_{S,K}(p \mid q)$ is proposed by defining

$$I^2_{S,K}(q \mid p) = \inf_{\omega \models K} I_S(p \mid \omega) \otimes\!\!\rightarrow I_S(q \wedge p \mid \omega),$$

which is closer to what a conditional possibility definition is. Actually when $\otimes = \min$, $I^2_{S,K}(q \mid p)$ can be interpreted as the infimum of the family of conditional possibility measures $\{\Pi_\omega(q \mid p)\}_{\omega \models K}$, where $\Pi_\omega(r) = \mu_{[r^*]}(\omega)$. Notice that when p is a tautology T, we also have $I^2_{S,K}(q \mid T) = I_S(q \mid K)$. Moreover, $I^2_{S,K}$ verifies the *Reflexivity, Right weakening, Left strenghtening, Right Or* properties, and although it does not verify the transitivity property, the following *restricted* form holds:

$$I_{S,K}(q) \geq I_{S,K}(p) \otimes I^2_{S,K}(q \mid p) \qquad (2)$$

where for the sake of convenience we have written $I_{S,K}(p)$ for $I_S(p \mid K)$. This suggests us, for a given similarity relation S and a subset of formulas K, to consider a new entailment:

$$p \vdash^{\alpha}_{K} q \quad \text{iff} \quad [K] \subset [p^* \Rightarrow (p \wedge q)^*]_\alpha, \text{ or equivalently,}$$
$$\text{iff} \quad I^2_{S,K}(q \mid p) \geq \alpha$$

Unlike the previously introduced consequence relations $\models^{\alpha}$ and $\models^{\alpha}_{K}$, the entailment relation $\vdash^{\alpha}_{K}$ is clearly non-monotonic, since it can be the case that $I^2_{S,K}(q \mid p) \geq \alpha$ but $I^2_{S,K}(q \mid p \wedge r) < \alpha$, for instance when $[p] \cap [q] \neq \emptyset$ and $[p] \cap [q] \cap [r] = \emptyset$. Moreover, $\vdash^{\alpha}_{K}$ verifies the Cut rule, that is:

Cut rule: $p \vdash^{\alpha}_{K} r,\ p \wedge r \vdash^{\beta}_{K} q \Rightarrow p \vdash^{\alpha\otimes\beta}_{K} q$

since $I^2_{S,K}$ verifies the following remarkable property: $I^2_{S,K}(r \mid p) \geq \alpha$ and $I^2_{S,K}(q \mid p \wedge r) \geq \beta$ imply that $I^2_{S,K}(q \mid p) \geq \alpha \otimes \beta$. Notice that when p is a tautology T, due to (2) we also have for $\vdash^{\alpha}_{K}$ a restricted form of transitivity, i.e.,

$$T \vdash^{\alpha}_{K} p,\ p \vdash^{\beta}_{K} q \Rightarrow T \vdash^{\alpha\otimes\beta}_{K} q.$$

On the other hand, $\vdash^{\alpha}_{K}$ does not verify the Cautious Monotonicity property, and thus not the Rational Monotony (see Makinson, 1994). The full characterization of this entailment relation, denoted as type III, in a similar way as we have done for the previous ones, is a topic for further research.

4. Example of application to interpolative reasoning

Let us consider a simple interpolation problem, which is paradigmatically related to the techniques of fuzzy control. Suppose a two-dimensional domain U×V, with two variables X (input) and Y(output) over U and V respectively. Assume that all it is known about the relationship between the two variables is the two following pieces of knowledge:

If X is in A_1 then Y is in B_1 ; If X is in A_2 then Y is in B_2

where A_1 and A_2 are classical subsets of U and B_1 and B_2 classical subsets of V. This is obviously an incomplete description of a mapping. The problem is how to guess a value for variable Y if we know for instance that variable X has got a value $X = x_0$, where x_0 does not belong neither to A_1 nor to A_2. The intuition says that if x_0 is close to A_1, then the value of Y will be close to B_1, and if it is close to A_2, the value of Y will be close to B_2. To model this scenario, we equip UxV with a similarity relation. One can consider, for instance, a similarity S_U on U and a similarity S_V on V, and then combine them into the product similarity $S = S_U \times S_V$ on the product space U×V, defined as $S_U \times S_V((x, y), (x', y')) = \min(S_U(x, x'), S_V(y, y'))$. Then one can compute the highest degree in which the proposition "X is x_0" entails both the proposition "X is in A_1" and the proposition "X is in A_2". So, we will have in the domain U:

"X is x_0" $\models^{\alpha}$ "X is in A_1", with $\alpha = I_{S_U}(A_1 \mid x_0)$;
"X is x_0" $\models^{\beta}$ "X is in A_2", with $\beta = I_{S_U}(A_1 \mid x_0)$.

What we are looking for is the most specific proposition of type "Y is S" derivable from the above information. The key point in the interpolation procedure is how to encode the above information, and more precisely how to encode the two conditional expressions that relate values of X with values of Y. The idea is, for some suitable background knowledge K, to express for instance the first conditional as

"X is in A_1" $\models^{1}_{K}$ "Y is in B_1"

that together with $\models^{\alpha}_{K}$ "X is in A_1" would enable us to infer $\models^{\alpha}_{K}$ "Y is in B_1". The most natural choice for K seems to be K = {¬"X is in A_1" ∨ "Y is in B_1", "X is x_0"} but it turns out that:

- for the entailment of type I, "X is in A_1" $\models^{1}_{K}$ "Y is in B_1" does hold, but that the entailment relation is not transitive

- on the other hand, entailments of type II and III are transitive, but "X is in A_1" $\models^1_K$ "Y is in B_1" holds with none of them.

However, the problem can be solved for the latter case by enlarging K in such a way that the models of the new K' is actually included in the set $\{\omega \mid \mu_{[A_1{}^*]}(\omega) \leq \mu_{[B_1{}^*]}(\omega)\}$ with $\omega = (x, y)$. That is, the background information necessary to perform interpolation is no longer the set of models of the crisp proposition "X is in A_1" $\rightarrow$ "Y is in B_1" but the set of interpretations where the *fuzzy* proposition "X is in A^*_1" $\otimes\!\!\rightarrow$ "Y is in B^*_1" is fully true. It comes down to interpreting the rule as a "gradual rule" expressing that "the closer X is to A_1, the closer Y is to B_1" (Dubois and Prade, 1992). If we do so, and define K = { "X is in A^*_1" $\otimes\!\!\rightarrow$ "Y is in B^*_1", "X is in A^*_2" $\otimes\!\!\rightarrow$ "Y is in B^*_2", "X is x_0" } together with the input data encoded as

1) $\models^\alpha_K$ "X is in A_1" (since $[K]_{|U} = x_0$) 2) "X is in A_1" $\models^1_K$ "Y is in B_1",

then, by the transitivity property, we have: 3) $\models^\alpha_K$ "Y is in B_1".

This is equivalent to $K \models^\alpha$ "Y is in B_1", and this is equivalalent to $[K] \subset [B_1{}^*]_\alpha$.

Similarly: 3') $\models^\beta_K$ "Y is in B_2"

and hence we come up with $[K] \subset [B_2{}^*]_\beta$, and therefore $[K] \subset [B_1{}^*]_\alpha \cap [B_2{}^*]_\beta$. Therefore the resulting set for Y of the interpolation would be the least specific S satisfying the above constraint, that is, $S = [B_1{}^*]_\alpha \cap [B_2{}^*]_\beta$. This is the result obtained using gradual rule-based interpolation (Dubois and Prade, 1992). Notice that in the product similarity space $I^2_{S,K}$("Y is B" | "X is A") = $I_{S,K}$("Y is B" | "X is A"), since $a \otimes\!\!\rightarrow b = a \otimes\!\!\rightarrow \min(a,b)$, and thus the solution adopted also works for entailment of type III. This example is a first step towards a logical characterization of interpolative reasoning and contrasts with Klawonn and Kruse (1993)'s similarity-based justification of another fuzzy reasoning method.

5. Discussion

The approximate entailments based on similarity are quite different from the preferential entailment $\models_\pi$ of possibilistic logic (Dubois et al. 1994). In the latter case, Ω is equipped with a complete partial ordering that expresses how plausible interpretations are, and is encoded as a possibility distribution π. In this case $p \models_\pi q$ means that q is true in all the best models of p, which correspond to shrinking p (instead of stretching q). The inference relation $\models_\pi$ satisfies properties different from those of $\models^\alpha$ (see Dubois and Prade, 1995). However as indicated by Esteva et al.(1994a), π can always be constructed from a given subset A, taken as background information, and the similarity relation S, such that $\pi = \mu_{A^*}$ in the sense of (1). Then $p \models_\pi q$ can be interpreted as: all models of p that are "as close as possible" to A are models of q. Moreover, in the setting of sphere semantics (Lewis,1973) it is clear what possibilistic and similarity logics have both in common and what differentiates them. From the model construction point of view, possibilistic logic is built upon a unique complete partial ordering on the worlds which determines an absolute system of spheres (see Farinas and Herzig, 1991), whereas a similarity relation corresponds to a complete partial ordering attached to each world (Dubois et al., 95), and thus it leads to a centered system of spheres. From the inferential point of view, possibilistic inference is related to the counterfactual necessity, whereas the similarity-based entailment of type III is related to the counterfactual possibility. The long term perspective of this work could be to provide logical foundations to "fuzzy logic", and also case-based reasoning where similarity plays a basic role.

Acknowledgements

This work has been partially supported by the ESPRIT III Basic Research Action n° 6156 DRUMS II, and by the Spanish DGICYT project n°PB91-03334.

References

Dubois D., Lang J. and Prade H. (1994) Possibilistic logic. In : *Handbook of Logic in Artificial Intelligence and Logic Programing* Vol. 3 (Gabbay D. et al., eds.), Oxford Univ. Press, 439-513

Dubois D. Prade H. (1992) Gradual inference rules in approximate reasoning. *Information Sciences*, 61, 103-122.

Dubois D. Prade H. (1995) Comparison of two fuzzy set-based logics: Similary logic and possibilistic logic. *Proc. of the 4th IEEE Inter. Conf. on Fuzzy Systems* (FUZZ-IEEE'95), 1219-1226. Long version in Tech. Report IRIT/94-10-R, IRIT, Univ. P. Sabatier, Toulouse, France.

Dubois D., Esteva F., Garcia P., Godo L. and Prade H. (1995). Similarity -based Consequences Relations. IIIA Research Report 95/1, Barcelona, Spain.

Esteva F, Garcia P, Godo L. (1994a) Relating and extending semantical approaches to possibilistic reasoning. *Int. J. Approximate Reasoning* 10, 311-344

Esteva F, Garcia P, Godo L. (1994b). On conditioning in Similarity Logic. *Proc. IPMU'94 Conf.*, Paris, pp. 999-1005. Extended version to appear in *Fuzzy Logic and Soft Computing*, 1995, (B. Bouchon, R. Yager and L.A. Zadeh eds.).

L. Fariñas del Cerro, A. Herzig (1991), A modal analysis of possibility theory. *Lecture Notes in Computer Sciences*, Vol. 535, Springer Verlag, Berlin, 11-18

Höhle, U.(1994), Monoidal logic, In *Fuzzy Systems in Computer Science* (R. Kruse et al., eds.), Vieweg, FRG, 233-243

Klawonn F. Kruse R. (1993) Equality relations as a basis for fuzzy control. *Fuzzy Sets & Syst.*, 54, 147-156

Lewis D.(1973) *Counterfactuals*. Basil Blackwell. London.

Makinson D. (1994) General patterns in nonmonotonic reasoning. In *Handbook of Logic in Artificial Intelligence and Logic Programming*. Vol. 3 (Gabbay D. et al., eds.), Oxford Univ. Press, 35-110

Trillas E., Valverde Ll. (1984) On Implication and Indistinguishability in the setting of Fuzzy Logic. In *Management Decission Support Systems using Fuzzy Set and Possibility Theory* (R.R.Yager and J. Kacprzyk eds).Verlag TÜV, 198-212.

Ruspini E. (1991). On the semantics of fuzzy logic. *Int. J. Approximate Reasoning* , 5, 45-88

Zadeh L.A. (1979) A theory of approximate reasoning. In *Machine Intelligence*, 9, Elsevier, New-York, 149-194

Epistemic Approach to Actions with Typical Effects*

Barbara Dunin-Kęplicz
Institute of Informatics
Warsaw University
Banacha 2
02-097 Warsaw, Poland
keplicz@mimuw.edu.pl

Anna Radzikowska
Institute of Mathematics
Warsaw University of Technology
Plac Politechniki 1
00-661 Warsaw, Poland
annrad@im.pw.edu.pl

Abstract. We study a problem of actions with *typical*, but not certain effects. We show how this kind of actions can be incorporated in a dynamic/epistemic multi-agents system in which the knowledge, abilities and opportunities of agents are formalized as well as the results of actions they perform. To cope with complexity of a rational agent behaviour, we consider scenarios composed of traditionally viewed basic actions and atomic actions with typical effects. We focus on a specific type of scenarios reflecting a "typical" pattern of an agent's behaviour. Adopting a model-theoretic approach we formalize a nonmonotonic preferential strategy for these scenarios in order to reason about the final results of their realizations.

1 Introduction

In everyday life people usually undertake actions with typical, but not necessarily certain, results. To adequately model the behavioural patterns of a rational agent in a multi-agent system (see [1]) one has also to cope with the complexity of actions with typical results. Recently this kind of actions has not attracted much interest in AI literature (see [2], [7]). In fact problems arise firstly in formalizing a concept of this kind of actions, and secondly when combining them into scenarios.

Although there are many types of scenarios, rational agents usually deal with scenarios reflecting a "typical" pattern of behaviour. When realizing such a scenario s/he prefers as many as possible of typical performances of actions. To address the problem of a scenario realization, one must be aware which kind of scenario is applicable under given circumstances. This intuition can be formalized in terms of a *preferential strategy*.

*This work is supported by the ESPRIT III BRA No. 6156-DRUMS II. and the Programme MEDICIS.

To investigate the nature of reasoning and acting of rational agents in a multi-agent system, regarding correctness and typical character of their scenarios, we provide an extension of the framework presented in [3], [4], [5]. This formal system is designed to deal with both the knowledge and abilities of agents as well as the effects of actions they perform. It seems natural to extend this system by formalizing a concept of action with typical results. Adopting a model-theoretic approach different strategies of scenario realizations can be defined.

As in this paper we focus on scenarios reflecting a "typical" pattern of behaviour, we model a *nonmonotonic* preferential strategy that can be viewed as a minimization of atypical performances of actions. Within our epistemic framework we apply this strategy to reason about scenarios, i.e. to determine a set of *desirable conclusions* which can be derived from a given scenario.

The paper is organized as follows. In section 2 and 3 we discuss notions of actions with typical effects and scenarios build over the actions traditionally viewed as well as these of the new type. After having defined basic notions underlying our approach in section 4, we are able to formalize reasoning about scenarios in section 5. In section 6 we discuss options for further research.

2 Characterization of actions with typical effects

To formalize results of actions performed by an agent we consider an event $\mathrm{do}_i(\alpha)$ referring to the performance of the action α by the agent i. We assume that the action α is deterministic, therefore the results of an event are represented by the following formula from (propositional) dynamic logic $<\mathrm{do}_i(\alpha)>\varphi$, denoting the fact that the agent i has the *opportunity* to perform action α and that doing α leads to φ. This kind of actions with certain effects will be referred to as *basic* actions.

The novelty of the presented approach is an extention of the considered set of actions by actions with typical (default) effects which will be referred to as Δ-actions. The generic characteristics of Δ-actions is that they have different effects in typical and atypical performances. When executing some Δ-action an agent i may proceed in a typical or an atypical way, but s/he always prefers a typical execution of the action.

Analogously, the result of performing Δ-action is represented by the formula $<\mathrm{do}_i(\alpha)>\varphi,\psi$, denoting that the agent i has the opportunity to perform the action α and as a result of this event φ (always) holds and *typically* ψ holds. The Δ-actions under consideration are deterministic in the sense that after choosing the way of performing the action (typical or atypical), the event consisting of an agent realizing some action has a unique outcome.

Following [3] apart from opportunities we introduce a general notion of agent's *abilities*, covering physical, mental and moral capacities. Treating abilities as a separate concept allows us to remove them as a prerequisite of events like performing actions. To formalize agents abilities we use an operator **A**: an expression $\mathbf{A}_i\alpha$ states the fact that agent i is capable to perform the action α. Combinations $<\mathrm{do}_i(\alpha)>\varphi$ and $\mathbf{A}_i\alpha$ express the idea that α is a *correct* ($<\mathrm{do}_i(\alpha)>\varphi$) and a *feasible* ($\mathbf{A}_i\alpha$) plan for agent i to achieve φ. Analogous characterization of correctness is applied to Δ-actions.

3 Characterization of scenarios

Intuitively a notion of a *scenario* for an agent reflects a sequence of actions to be performed by this agent together with initial and final observations. In AI literature various types of scenarios have been studied (see [8]). Considering a *typical character* of action performance, different kinds of scenarios may be distinguished. For example, in order to increase the probability of achieving a goal, an agent may repeat a given action (e.g. shooting) several times, although the first performance of this action could have been successful (e.g. mortal shoot). On the other hand, when considering an action like parking a car we expect that in a typical case a car will not be stolen. If we leave it for a couple of nights, we intuitively plan to find it on a parking place.

These essentially different examples require different methods to model their realization and expected consequences. In the former case, we assume by default that in a sequence of several performances of the same action at least one realization is typical (see [7]), while in the latter case we expect all performances to be typical. Being aware that various types of scenarios are applicable in common-sence reasoning we focus on a scenario reflecting an agent's "agenda", i.e. the planned in advance sequence of actions intentionally leading to achieve some goals. These goals become a part of final observations. It is justified to assume that effectiveness of agent's behaviour depends on how typical performing of each element of the plan is. Possible disturbances – atypical performances of some actions – may either preclude achieving final goals, in the worst case, or may change a way to achieve them (e.g. by resigning from performing those actions which prerequisites are not satisfied any longer).

Following rationale underlying our understanding of a scenario, its realization by an agent may be viewed as a *nonmonotonic* notion. An agent intends possibly typical performances of actions but, depending on circumstances, some atypical executions may take place.

While modelling agent's behaviour his preferences will be reflected in some *preferential strategy*. In view of the typical character of scenarios considered in this paper, the adopted strategy amounts to minimization of atypical performances of actions. However, other types of scenarios may require different preferential strategies.

Adopting a common-sense point of view we assume the basic modelling assumption: when an agent cannot perform some action in the scenario (i.e. s/he has not the opportunity to perform this action or s/he is unable to execute it), the scenario will be resumed from the first executable one (i.e. which prerequisite is satisfied and the agent is able to perform it).

Although from the epistemic perspective this solution seems natural, it may be counterintuitive from other perspectives, for example in the area of programming languages. Let us stress, however, that the scenario revision is allowed only in a way that assures achieving agent's goals. This revision reduces exclusively to the resignation from performing certain actions or to the atypical execution of some of them (however always within a frame of a given scenario).

As usual, our approach to reasoning about scenarios leads to determining a set of *desirable conclusions*. Clearly, the realization of a given scenario, including an adequate preferential strategy, leads to certain situations (*states*). To complete scenario realization we will determine a set of desirable conclusions, i.e. all statements holding in these states.

4 The basic formalism

In this section we extend the framework defined in [3], [4] and [5] to formalize the behaviour of rational agents. This approach considers agent's knowledge, opportunities and abilities to perform particular actions and results of these actions.

Definition 4.1 (Language $\mathcal{L}$)
The language $\mathcal{L}$ is based on the following three sets:

- a denumerable set $\mathcal{P}$ of *propositional symbols (fluents* in AI terminology);
- a finite set $\mathcal{A}$ of *agents*, denoted by numerals $1, 2, \ldots, n$;
- a finite set $\mathcal{A}t$ of *atomic actions*, denoted by a or b; this set includes a non-empty subset $\mathcal{A}t_\Delta$ of atomic Δ-actions.

The language $\mathcal{L}$ is the smallest set satisfying the following conditions:

- $p \in \mathcal{L}$, for each $p \in P$;
- if $\varphi, \phi \in \mathcal{L}$, then $\neg\varphi \in \mathcal{L}$ and $\varphi \vee \phi \in \mathcal{L}$;
- if $i \in \mathcal{A}$ and $\varphi \in \mathcal{L}$, then $\mathbf{K}_i\varphi \in \mathcal{L}$;
- if $i \in \mathcal{A}$ and $\alpha \in \mathcal{A}c$, then $\mathbf{A}_i\alpha \in \mathcal{L}$;
- if $i \in \mathcal{A}$, $\alpha \in \mathcal{A}c$ and $\varphi, \psi \in \mathcal{L}$, then $<\mathrm{do}_i(\alpha)>\varphi \in \mathcal{L}, <\mathrm{do}_i(\alpha)>\varphi, \psi \in \mathcal{L}$

The class $\mathcal{A}c_B$ of basic actions is the smallest set such that

- $\mathcal{A}t \backslash \mathcal{A}_\Delta \subseteq \mathcal{A}c_B$;
- if $\varphi \in \mathcal{L}$, then $\mathbf{confirm}\,\varphi \in \mathcal{A}c_B$; (confirmation)
- if $\alpha_1, \alpha_2 \in \mathcal{A}c_B$, then $\alpha_1; \alpha_2 \in \mathcal{A}c_B$; (sequential composition)
- if $\varphi \in \mathcal{L}$ and $\alpha_1, \alpha_2 \in \mathcal{A}c_B$, then **if** φ **then** α_1 **else** α_2 **fi** $\in \mathcal{A}c_B$; (conditional action)
- if $\varphi \in \mathcal{L}$ and $\alpha \in \mathcal{A}c_B$, then **while** φ **do** α **od** $\in \mathcal{A}c_B$ (repetitive action)

The class $\mathcal{A}c$ of actions is the smallest set given by:

$$\mathcal{A}c_B \subseteq \mathcal{A}c; \quad \mathcal{A}t_\Delta \subseteq \mathcal{A}c; \quad \text{if } \alpha_1, \alpha_2 \in \mathcal{A}c \text{ then } \alpha_1; \alpha_2 \in \mathcal{A}c. \quad \blacksquare$$

The constructs $True$, $False$, $\wedge$, $\rightarrow$ and $\equiv$ are defined in the usual way. Moreover, the following abbreviations are introduced:
skip = **confirm** $True$; **fail** = **confirm** $False$; $\alpha^0 =$ **skip**; $\alpha^{k+1} = \alpha^k; \alpha$.

Remark 4.1 The formula $\mathbf{K}_i\varphi$ states that the agent i knows the fact represented by φ; $\mathbf{A}_i\alpha$ states that the agent i is able to perform the action α. ∎

The semantics of a language $\mathcal{L}$ is based on the notion of Kripke model.

Definition 4.2 (Kripke model)
A Kripke model is a tuple $\mathcal{M} = (S, val, R, r, t, c)$ such that

(1) S is a set of possible worlds, or states;

(2) $val : P \times S \rightarrow \{0,1\}$ is the function that assigns the truth values to fluents in states;

(3) $R : \mathcal{A} \rightarrow \wp(S \times S)$ is the function that yields the accessibility relation for a given agent i, i.e. $(s_1, s_2) \in R(i)$ states that s_2 is an epistemic alternative for the agent i in a state s. Since we assume the modal system KT, $R(i)$ is reflexive for all $i \in \mathcal{A}$;

(4) $r : \mathcal{A} \times \mathcal{A}t \rightarrow S \rightarrow \wp(S)$ is such that $r(i,a)(s)$ yields the result of performing the action a by the agent i in the state s; this function is such that

- $\forall a \notin \mathcal{A}t_\Delta \; \forall i \in \mathcal{A} \; \forall s \in S \;\; |r(i,a)(s)| \leq 1$
- $\forall a \in \mathcal{A}t_\Delta \; \forall i \in \mathcal{A} \; \forall s \in S \;\; |r(i,a)(s)| \in \{0,2\}$

where $|V|$ denotes the number of elements in the set V;

(5) $t : \mathcal{A} \times \mathcal{A}t_\Delta \rightarrow S \rightarrow \wp(S)$ is such that $t(i,a)(s)$ yields the result of typical performing of the action a by the agent i in the state s; this function is such that

$$\forall i \in \mathcal{A} \; \forall a \in \mathcal{A}t_\Delta \; \forall s \in S \;\; t(i,a)(s) \subset r(i,a)(s) \text{ and } |t(i,a)(s)| \leq 1;$$

(6) $c : \mathcal{A} \times \mathcal{A}t \rightarrow S \rightarrow \{0,1\}$ is the capability function such that $c(i,a)(s)$ indicates that the agent i is able to perform the action a in the state s. ∎

Remark 4.2 The function r specifies that each basic action is *deterministic*. The performance of atomic Δ-action may have two outcomes. Typical state transitions are specified by the function t. ∎

By $\mathbf{\mathcal{M}}$ we denote the class of all Kripke models.

Definition 4.3 (Defining $\models$)
Let $\mathcal{M} = (S, val, R, r, t, c)$ be a Kripke model from $\mathbf{\mathcal{M}}$. For any propositional or epistemic formula φ, $\mathcal{M}, s \models \varphi$ is defined in the usual way. For other formulas it is defined as follows:

$\mathcal{M}, s \models <\mathrm{do}_i(\alpha)> \varphi$	iff $\exists s' \in r^*(i,\alpha)(s)$ and $\mathcal{M}, s' \models \varphi$
$\mathcal{M}, s \models <\mathrm{do}_i(\alpha)> \varphi, \psi$	iff $\forall s' \in r^*(i,\alpha)(s) \; \mathcal{M}, s' \models \varphi$ and $\exists s'' \in r^*(i,\alpha)(s) \; \mathcal{M}, s'' \not\models \neg\psi$
$\mathcal{M}, s \models \mathbf{A}_i\alpha$	iff $c^*(i,\alpha)(s) = 1$

where r^*, c^* are the extensions of r and c, respectively, defined by [1]

$$
\begin{array}{ll}
r^* : & \mathcal{A}\times\mathcal{A}c \to S \to \wp(S) \\
r^*(i,a)(s) & = r(i,a)(s) \quad \text{for } a \in \mathcal{A}t \\
r^*(i,\mathbf{confirm}\ \varphi)(s) & = \begin{cases} \{s\} & \text{iff } \mathcal{M},s \models \varphi \\ \emptyset & \text{otherwise} \end{cases} \\
r^*(i,\alpha_1;\alpha_2)(s) & = r^*(i,\alpha_2)(r^*(i,\alpha_1)(s)) \\
r^*(i,\mathbf{if}\ \varphi\ \mathbf{then}\ \alpha_1\ \mathbf{else}\ \alpha_2)(s) & = \begin{cases} r^*(i,\alpha_1) & \text{iff } \mathcal{M},s \models \varphi \\ r^*(i,\alpha_2) & \text{otherwise} \end{cases} \\
r^*(i,\mathbf{while}\ \varphi\ \mathbf{do}\ \alpha\ \mathbf{od})(s) & = \{s' \in S : \exists k \in \mathbb{N}\ \exists s_0,\ldots,s_k.\ s_0 = s,\ s_k = s' \\
& \quad \text{and } \forall j < k.\ s_{j+1} \in r^*(i,\mathbf{confirm}\ \varphi;\alpha)(s_j) \\
& \quad \text{and } \mathcal{M},s' \models \neg\varphi\} \\
\text{and } r^*(i,\alpha)(\emptyset) & = \emptyset \\
 & \\
c^* : & \mathcal{A}\times\mathcal{A}c \to S \to \{0,1\} \\
c^*(i,a)(s) & = c(i,a)(s) \text{ for } a \in \mathcal{A}t \\
c^*(i,\mathbf{confirm}\ \varphi)(s) & = \begin{cases} 1 & \text{iff } \mathcal{M},s \models \varphi \\ 0 & \text{otherwise} \end{cases} \\
c^*(i,\alpha_1;\alpha_2)(s) & = \begin{cases} 1 & \text{iff } c^*(i,\alpha_1)(s) = 1 \text{ and} \\ & \quad c^*(i,\alpha_2)(s) = 1 \\ 0 & \text{otherwise} \end{cases} \\
c^*(i,\mathbf{if}\ \varphi\ \mathbf{then}\ \alpha_1\ \mathbf{else}\ \alpha_2\ \mathbf{fi})(s) & = \begin{cases} 1 & \text{iff } c^*(i,\mathbf{confirm}\ \varphi;\alpha_1)(s) = 1 \\ & \text{or } c^*(i,\mathbf{confirm}\ \neg\varphi;\alpha_2)(s) = 1 \\ 0 & \text{otherwise} \end{cases} \\
c^*(i,\mathbf{while}\ \varphi\ \mathbf{do}\ \alpha\ \mathbf{od})(s) & = \begin{cases} 1 & \text{iff } \exists k \in \mathbb{N}.\ c^*(i,\beta)(s) = 1, \text{ where} \\ & \beta = (\mathbf{confirm}\ \varphi;\alpha)^k; \mathbf{confirm}\ \neg\varphi \\ 0 & \text{otherwise} \end{cases} \\
\text{and } c^*(i,\alpha)(\emptyset) & = 1.
\end{array}
$$

■

A formula φ is said to be *satisfiable in $\mathcal{M}$ in a state s* iff $\mathcal{M}, s \models \varphi$.

Remark 4.3 A formula $< do_i(\alpha) > \varphi$ is satisfiable in $\mathcal{M}$ in a state $s \in S$ if there exists a state s' accessible from s (by performing the action α by the agent i) such that φ holds. On the other hand, a formula $< do_i(\alpha) > \varphi, \psi$ is satisfiable in $\mathcal{M}$ in a state $s \in S$ if in *all* states s' accessible from s φ holds and there exists an accessible state s'' such that $\neg\psi$ does not hold. ■

5 Reasoning about scenarios

In this section we provide a formalization of reasoning about scenarios for a given agent. We aim to determine a set of desirable conclusions resulting from the scenario realization. Let us recall postulates imposed on scenarios.

[1] Here the state $s \in S$ is identified with the singleton set $\{s\}$.

S1. The scenario contains sequences of basic actions of various types and atomic Δ-actions;
S2. Each Δ-action results in different effects in typical and atypical performance;
S3. The applied preferential strategy is based on the minimization of atypical performances of actions;
S4. Scenario realization admits agent's disability to perform some action(s). The sequence of actions is then resumed from the next executable one.
S5. The final goal of a scenario realization is to determine a set of statements characterizing the preferred concluding states.

Definition 5.1 (Scenario)
Let $\gamma_{pre}, \gamma_{post}$ be any formulas from $\mathcal{L}$. The sequence $<\alpha_1, \ldots, \alpha_n>$ of actions to be performed by the agent i, $\alpha_k \in \mathcal{A}c$, $k=1,\ldots,n$, with the precondition γ_{pre} and the postcondition γ_{post}, is said to be a *scenario for an agent* i and denoted by SCD$(i, \{\gamma_{pre}\}\alpha_1; \ldots; \alpha_n\{\gamma_{post}\})$ (or simply SCD). ■

Intuitively the precondition γ_{pre} and the postcondition γ_{post} indicate the initial and the final observations, respectively, i.e. statements which represent knowledge, abilities and/or opportunities of both the agent i or some other agents.

Definition 5.2 (Epistemic path)
Let SCD$(i, \{\gamma_{pre}\}\alpha_1; \ldots; \alpha_n\{\gamma_{post}\})$ be a scenario for an agent i and let $\mathcal{M}$ be a Kripke model. An *epistemic path* in $\mathcal{M}$ for SCD, denoted by $\pi_{\mathcal{M}}^{SCD}$, is a sequence $<s_0, \ldots, s_n>$, $s_k \in S$, $k=1,\ldots,n$, of states such that

P1. $\mathcal{M}, s_0 \models \gamma_{pre}$
P2. $\mathcal{M}, s_n \models \gamma_{post}$
P3. if $r^*(i, \alpha_{k+1})(s_k) = \emptyset$ or $c^*(i, \alpha_{k+1})(s_k) = 0$, $k = 0, \ldots, n-1$, then $s_{k+1} = s_k$; otherwise $s_{k+1} \in r^*(i, \alpha_{k+1})(s_k)$, where r^* and c^* are defined in Definition 4.3. ■

Remark 5.1 Note that in some Kripke models $\mathcal{M}$ there may be no states s satisfying the condition **P1** or **P2** for a given scenario SCD. In such a case an epistemic path $\pi_{\mathcal{M}}^{SCD}$ in $\mathcal{M}$ for SCD reduces to the empty sequence $<>$. the condition **P3** corresponds to the postulate **S4**. ■

By $\Pi(\text{SCD}, \mathcal{M})$ we denote the set of all non-empty epistemic paths in $\mathcal{M}$ for the scenario SCD.

Let SCD be a scenario for an agent i and let $\mathcal{M}$ be a Kripke model. We say that $\mathcal{M}$ is a *(Kripke) model for SCD* iff $\Pi(\text{SCD}, \mathcal{M}) \neq \emptyset$. By MOD(SCD) we denote the subset of $\boldsymbol{\mathcal{M}}$ containing all Kripke models for SCD.
Given a Kripke model $\mathcal{M}$ we define a function $\tau : \mathcal{A} \times (\mathcal{A}c_B \cup \mathcal{A}t_\Delta) \times S \times S \rightarrow \mathbb{N}$ such that for all $i \in \mathcal{A}$

$$\tau(i, \alpha, s_1, s_2) = \begin{cases} 1 & \text{iff } \alpha \in \mathcal{A}t_\Delta,\ s_2 \in r(i,\alpha)(s_1),\ s_2 \notin t(i,\alpha)(s_1) \text{ and } c(i,\alpha)(s_1) = 1 \\ 0 & \text{otherwise} \end{cases}$$ ■

This function may be viewed as a penalty imposed on a transition performed by the agent i resulting from an *atypical* execution of Δ-action α.

Definition 5.3 (Atypical state transition function)
Let SCD=SCD(i, $\{\gamma_{pre}\}\alpha_1;\ldots;\alpha_n\{\gamma_{post}\}$), $<\gamma_{pre},\gamma_{post}>$) be a scenario for an agent i and let $\mathcal{M}\in$ MOD(SCD) be a Kripke model for SCD. An *atypical state transition function* is a function $AST : \Pi(\text{SCD},\mathcal{M}) \rightarrow \mathbb{N}$ defined by

$$AST(\pi_{\mathcal{M}}^{SCD}) = \sum_{i=1}^{n} \tau(i,\alpha_i,s_{i-1},s_i), \qquad \text{where } \pi_{\mathcal{M}}^{SCD} = <s_0,\ldots,s_n>. \blacksquare$$

Given an epistemic path $\pi_{\mathcal{M}}^{SCD}$ in $\mathcal{M}$ for the scenario SCD, the value $AST(\pi_{\mathcal{M}}^{SCD})$ determines the number of state transitions on $\pi_{\mathcal{M}}^{SCD}$ corresponding to atypical performances of Δ-actions occurring in SCD (global penalty function).

Definition 5.4 (Preferred path)
Let $\pi_1,\pi_2\in\Pi(\text{SCD},\mathcal{M})$. We say that π_1 *is preferred to* π_2, written $\pi_1 \preceq \pi_2$, iff $AST(\pi_1) \leq AST(\pi_2)$. ■

Given a scenario SCD for an agent i and a Kripke model $\mathcal{M}$ we write $\Pi_{\preceq}(\text{SCD},\mathcal{M})$ to denote the set $\Pi_{\preceq}(\text{SCD},\mathcal{M}) = \{\pi \in \Pi(\text{SCD},\mathcal{M}) : \pi \preceq \pi' \text{ for all } \pi' \in \Pi(\text{SCD},\mathcal{M})\}$, i.e. the set of all preferred epistemic paths in $\Pi(\text{SCD},\mathcal{M})$.

Let SCD be a scenario for an agent i and $\mathcal{M} \in$ MOD(SCD) be a Kripke model for SCD. A *penalty value for SCD in* $\mathcal{M}$, written $Pen(\text{SCD},\mathcal{M})$, is given by $Pen(\text{SCD},\mathcal{M}) = AST(\pi)$, for all $\pi\in\Pi_{\preceq}(\text{SCD},\mathcal{M})$.

Definition 5.5 (Preferred model)
Let SCD be a scenario and $\mathcal{M}_1,\mathcal{M}_2\in \boldsymbol{\mathcal{M}}$ be Kripke models. We say that $\mathcal{M}_1$ *is preferred to* $\mathcal{M}_2$ *with respect to the scenario SCD*, written $\mathcal{M}_1 \preceq_{SCD} \mathcal{M}_2$, iff $\mathcal{M}_1,\mathcal{M}_2\in$ MOD(SCD) and $Pen(\text{SCD},\mathcal{M}_1) \leq Pen(\text{SCD},\mathcal{M}_2)$. ■

Given a scenario SCD for an agent i we write PMOD(SCD) to denote the class of all preferred models for SCD. Obviously, what we are actually interested in is the set of conclusions entailed by the given scenario SCD. As usual, this set is to be defined in terms of preferred models. Let $\pi_{\mathcal{M}}^{SCD} = <s_0,\ldots,s_n>$ be an epistemic path in a Kripke model $\mathcal{M}$ for a scenario SCD. We write Last($\pi_{\mathcal{M}}^{SCD}$) to denote the last state of the path $\pi_{\mathcal{M}}^{SCD}$, i.e. the state s_n.

Definition 5.6 (Conclusion states)
Let SCD be a scenario for an agent i and $\mathcal{M} \in$ PMOD(SCD) be a preferred model for SCD. *Conclusion states* for SCD in $\mathcal{M}$, written Conc(SCD, $\mathcal{M}$), is the set of last states of all preferred epistemic paths in $\mathcal{M}$, i.e. Conc(SCD, $\mathcal{M}$) = $\{s\in S : s = \text{Last}(\pi) \text{ for } \pi\in\Pi_{\preceq}(\text{SCD},\mathcal{M})\}$. ■

Definition 5.7 (Preferential Entailment $\approx\!\!\!\!|$)
Let SCD be a scenario for an agent i and let $\beta\in\mathcal{L}$ be a formula. We say that SCD *preferentially entails* β, written SCD $|\!\!\approx \beta$, iff for each $\mathcal{M} \in$ PMOD(SCD) and for each state $s\in$ Conc(SCD, $\mathcal{M}$), $\mathcal{M}, s \models \beta$. ■

The following definition specifies the set of desirable conclusions resulting from realization of a given scenario. (See postulate **S5**).

Definition 5.8 (Scenario completion)
Let SCD be a scenario for an agent i. A set $\Gamma(\text{SCD}) = \{\beta : \text{SCD} \mid\!\approx \beta\}$ is called a *scenario completion* for SCD. ■

6 Conclusions and future work

In this paper we semantically investigated a new type of actions – actions with typical, but not necessarily certain, effects.

There still remain several topics that need to be studied yet. First, the formal properties of our (extended) formalism should be investigated. Next, we are going to extend the class of actions by including compound actions with typical effects. Finally, other types of scenarios together with preferential strategies corresponding to them are to be characterized.

References

[1] B. Dunin-Kęplicz, J. Treur: Compositional formal specification of multi-agents systems, in M. Wooldridge, N. Jennings (eds.), *Intelligent Agents – Proc. of the 1994 Workshop on Agent Theories, Architectures and Languages*, Springer-Verlag, 1995, pp. 102-117.

[2] D. W. Etherington, J. M. Crawford: Formalizing reasoning about change: A qualitative reasoning approach, in *Proc. 10th AAAI*, San Jose, CA, 1994.

[3] W. van der Hoek, B. van Linder, J. -J. Ch. Meyer: A logic of capabilities, Technical Report IR-330, Vrije Universiteit Amsterdam, 1993.

[4] W. van der Hoek, B. van Linder, J. -J. Ch. Meyer: Tests as epistemic updates, in *Proc. 11th ECAI*, Amsterdam, 1994.

[5] W. van der Hoek, B. van Linder, J. -J. Ch. Meyer: Communicating rational agents, in *Proc. 18th German Annual Conference on Artificial Intelligence*, Saarbrücken, 1994.

[6] R. Moore: A formal theory of knowledge and action, Technical Report 320, SRI International, 1984.

[7] A. Radzikowska: Circumscribing features and fluents: Reasoning about action with default effects, *Proc. ECSQARU'95*. (In this volume)

[8] E. Sandewall: Features and fluents: A systematic approach to the representation of knowledge about dynamical systems, Technical report LITH-IDA, Linköping University, Sweden, 1994.

[9] B. Thomas: A logic for representing actions, beliefs, capabilities and plans, in Working Notes of the AAAI Spring Symposium on *Reasoning about Mental States: Formal Theories and Applications*, 1993.

Nonmonotonic Belief State Frames and Reasoning Frames (extended abstract)*

Joeri Engelfriet[a], Heinrich Herre[b] and Jan Treur[a]

[a] Free University Amsterdam, Department of Mathematics and Computer Science
De Boelelaan 1081a, 1081 HV Amsterdam, The Netherlands
Emails: {joeri,treur}@cs.vu.nl

[b] University of Leipzig, Department of Computer Science
Augustusplatz 10/11, 04109 Leipzig, Germany
Email: herre@isun01.informatik.uni-leipzig.de

Abstract In this paper five levels of specification of nonmonotonic reasoning are distinguished. The notions of semantical frame, belief state frame and reasoning frame are introduced and used as a semantical basis for the first three levels. Moreover, the semantical connections between the levels are formalized. It is shown that this general semantical framework is applicable for some well-known approaches such as preferential semantics and default logic.

1 Introduction

Nonmonotonic reasoning systems address applications where an agent reasoning about the world wants to draw conclusions that are not logically entailed by its (incomplete) knowledge about the world. Under such circumstances it is only possible to build a set of (additional) beliefs of hypothetical nature. Such a set of beliefs represents a hypothetical view on the world. In general it is not unique: multiple views are possible; an agent may (temporarily) commit itself to one view and switch its commitment to another one later. Each view leaves open a number of possible complete world descriptions. The additional knowledge defining the view an agent is committing to, may be sufficient for the agent to draw the required (defeasible) conclusions (within the context of that view).

One may focus on the intersection of the different possible sets of beliefs for the agent; this could be described by a nonmonotonic inference operator, e.g. as in [KLM90]. A disadvantage of this (sceptical) approach may be that hypothetical conclusions that are possible within one of the belief sets may be lost due to the restriction to the common beliefs. The semantics of a set X of beliefs can be defined by the set M(X) of models (worlds, interpretations) satisfying X; M(X) is said to be a belief state. In the present paper we study nonmonotonic reasoning in terms of (multiple) belief states.

Thus, to specify nonmonotonic reasoning the following five levels of abstraction can be distinguished:

1. *Specification of a set of intended models*
Specification of the global set of possible (intended) worlds and the beliefs that hold in them, abstracting from the specific underlying (multiple) belief states, the specific reasoning patterns that lead to them and the specific reasoning system generating these reasoning patterns.

---

* Part of this work has been supported by SKBS and the ESPRIT III Basic Research project 6156 DRUMS II.

2. *Specification of a set of intended multiple belief states*
Specification of the possible belief states for the agent abstracting from the specific reasoning patterns that lead to them and the specific reasoning system generating these reasoning patterns.
3. *Specification of a set of intended reasoning patterns*
Specification of the reasoning patterns that lead to the intended possible belief states, abstracting from the specific reasoning system generating these reasoning patterns.
4. *Specification of a reasoning system*
Specification of an architecture for a reasoning system that when executed (by use of heuristic control knowledge) can generate the intended reasoning patterns.
5. *Implementation*
At this level an implemented reasoning system is described in any implementation environment (implementation code).

Of course there exist connections between the levels in the sense that from a specification of a lower level of abstraction in an unambiguous manner a specification of each of the higher levels can be determined. One could say the specification at a lower level gives in some sense a refinement or specialisation of the specification at the higher level (as in the case of conventional software specifications at different levels of abstraction). Given specifications of two different levels, *relative verification* is possible: to establish whether the lower level one indeed refines the higher level one. At a lower level different specifications can refine the same higher level specification. As a parallel one may think of development of programs using the method of (top down) stepwise refinement, e.g., according to Dijkstra's approach. Note however that other methods (other than top down stepwise refinement) are possible as well.

In this paper we introduce a general semantical framework to cover the levels 1, 2 and 3. In Section 2 we present a semantical formalization of level 1 by the notion of model operator. In Section 3 we do the same for level 2 by the notion of belief state frame. Also here the connections between the levels 1 and 2 are described. In Section 4 we introduce a semantical formalization of level 3 by the notion of reasoning frame; here the connections between the levels 2 and 3 are described as well. In Section 5 conclusions and further perspectives are pointed out, including the relations to levels 4 and 5. During the paper it will be shown how our general semantical framework can be used to define formal semantics for some well known approaches to nonmonotonicity such as preferential semantics and default logic.

2 Semantical Frames

In this section we will give a semantical definition of level 1. Let $\mathbf{L}$ be a nonempty language whose elements are denoted by φ, ψ, χ. In the following $\mathbf{L}$ is the language of classical propositional calculus and $\mathbf{Cn} : \mathcal{P}(\mathbf{L}) \rightarrow \mathcal{P}(\mathbf{L})$ is the inference operation based on it. The semantics of $(\mathbf{L}, \mathbf{Cn})$ is defined by a logical system $\mathcal{G}_0 = (\mathbf{L}, \mathbf{Mod}, \models)$, where $\mathbf{Mod}$ is the set of all propositional interpretations, and $\models \subseteq \mathbf{Mod} \times \mathbf{L}$ is the satisfaction relation.

We introduce the following notions. Let $X \subseteq \mathbf{L}$, $\mathbf{Mod}(X) = \{m : m \in \mathbf{Mod}$ and $m \models X\}$, where $m \models X$ iff for every $\varphi \in X : m \models \varphi$. Let $M \subseteq \mathbf{Mod}$, then $\mathbf{Th}(M) = \{\varphi : \varphi \in \mathbf{L}$ and $M \models \varphi\}$, where $M \models \varphi$ iff for all $m \in M : m \models \varphi$. We use the notation $\mathbf{Cn}(X) = \{\phi : \mathbf{Mod}(X) \subseteq \mathbf{Mod}(\varphi)\}$, $X \models \varphi$ iff $\varphi \in \mathbf{Cn}(X)$. For $M \subseteq \mathbf{Mod}$ let $\overline{M} = \mathbf{Mod}(\mathbf{Th}(M))$. A subset $M \subseteq \mathbf{Mod}$ is *closed* if $\overline{M} = M$.

Nonmonotonic inference operations can be introduced semantically by adding an operator $\Phi : \mathcal{P}(\mathbf{L}) \rightarrow \mathcal{P}(\mathbf{Mod})$ to $\mathcal{G}_0$ satisfying the condition $\Phi(X) \subseteq \mathbf{Mod}(X)$ (see [He94]).

Definition 2.1 (Semantical Frame and Model Operator)
The tuple $(L, Mod, \models, \Phi)$ where $\Phi : \mathcal{P}(L) \to \mathcal{P}(Mod)$ satisfies $\Phi(X) \subseteq Mod(X)$ for all $X \subseteq L$ is called a *semantical frame* and Φ is called a *model operator*.
The model operator Φ is said to be *invariant* if $(\forall X \subseteq L)\ (\Phi(X) = \Phi(Cn(X)))$.
It is said to be *closed* if $\Phi(X) = \overline{\Phi(X)}$ for every set $X \subseteq L$.

For a given $X \subseteq L$ the set $\Phi(X)$ can be viewed the set of possible worlds that the agent considers in relation to its beliefs.

The framework of model operators presents a general method to attach semantics to every nonmonotonic inference operation C satisfying supraclassicality, left absorption, and congruence. Such standard semantics can be introduced for most of the known nonmonotonic systems (see [He94] and [Di94]): default logic (based on the intersections of the extensions), Poole systems, and nonmonotonic systems derived from belief revision operators.

3 Belief State Frames

Next we give a semantical description of level 2. The semantics of a set of beliefs of an agent can be defined by a set of models making them true. Usually, there can be many alternative sets of beliefs that can be justified on the base of a set X of given knowledge (multiple interpretations).

3.1 Belief State Operators and Belief State Frames

Multiple belief states of an agent can be modelled semantically by functors associating to sets of formulae sets of sets of models. Such functors are called belief state operators.

Definition 3.1 (Belief State Operator and Belief State Frame)
a) A *belief state operator* Γ is a function $\Gamma : \mathcal{P}(L) \to \mathcal{P}(\mathcal{P}(Mod))$ satisfying the following conditions for every $X \subseteq L$:
(i) Every $K \in \Gamma(X)$ is closed and $K \subseteq Mod(X)$ for every $K \in \Gamma(X)$
(ii) $\forall K, J \in \Gamma(X)\quad J \subseteq K \Rightarrow K = J$ (*noninclusiveness)*.
The tuple $\mathcal{SB} = (L, Mod, \models, \Gamma)$ is said to be a *belief state frame.*
b) A belief state operator Γ is called *invariant* if $\Gamma(X) = \Gamma(Cn(X))$ for all $X \subseteq L$.

The condition of non-inclusiveness can be motivated as follows: if an agent has two possible belief states, then it will choose the state with the most conclusions, this is the smallest state (with respect to set inclusion).

3.2 Connections Between Semantical Frames and Belief State Frames

In the following we consider connections between the levels 1 and 2, i.e., between model operators and belief state operators. The way up from level 2 to 1 is called abstraction; the way down specialisation.

3.2.1 Abstraction

A simple upward connection is provided as follows:

Definition 3.2 (Semantical Frame Associated to a Belief State Frame)
a) For a belief state operator Γ the *associated model operator* Φ_Γ is defined by

$$\Phi_\Gamma(X) = \bigcup \Gamma(X).$$

b) For a given model operator Φ we define

$$\Gamma(\Phi) = \{\Gamma \mid \Gamma \text{ is a belief state operator with } \Phi_\Gamma = \Phi\};$$

3.2.2 Specialisation

We analyse in more detail the set $\Gamma(\Phi)$ of possible belief state operators connected with a model operator Φ, by defining a parametrization of all these possibilities. A *non-inclusive covering* of a set $N \subseteq$ **Mod** is a family M of closed pairwise non-inclusive subsets of **Mod** whose union equals N. Non-inclusive coverings of $\Phi(X)$ can be used to represent Φ by belief state operators:

Definition 3.4 (Belief State Parameter)

a) A *belief state frame parameter* is a family $p = (C_X)_{X \subseteq L}$ where each C_X is a family of closed pairwise non-inclusive subsets of **Mod**.

b) If $p = (C_X)_{X \subseteq L}$ is a belief state frame parameter, then its *related belief state operator* Γ_p is defined by: $\Gamma_p(X) = C_X$

c) We say a belief state frame parameter $p = (C_X)_{X \subseteq L}$ is *suited for* Φ or a *covering family* for Φ if $\Phi(X) = \bigcup C_X$ for all $X \subseteq L$.

Such families parametrize all the possibilities of representing a given model operator by a belief state operator:

Theorem 3.5

Let a model operator Φ and a belief state operator Γ be given. The following conditions are equivalent:

(i) $\Phi_\Gamma = \Phi$

(ii) There exists a belief state frame parameter p suited for Φ such that $\Gamma_p = \Gamma$.

This theorem gives a description of the connection between the levels 1 and 2. We now collect some examples of belief state operators.

Example 1 (Preferential Semantics)

Let a preference relation $<$ on **Mod** be given. A model operator $\Phi_<$ can be defined in the following manner: for each $X \subseteq L$

$$\Phi_<(X) = \{\, m \in \text{Mod} \mid m \text{ is } <\text{-minimal in Mod}(X) \,\}$$

Preferential semantics essentially provides a level 1 description, abstracting from the lower levels. Approaches using a preference relation are sometimes also used at level 2 (see [Vo93]).

Example 2 (Default Logic)

Let D be a set of defaults. For $X \subseteq L$ let $\mathbb{E}(\langle X, D\rangle)$ denote the set of (Reiter) extensions of the default theory $\langle X, D\rangle$. The following belief state operator and model operator can be defined for $X \subseteq L$:

$$\Gamma_D(X) = \{\, \text{Mod}(E) \mid E \in \mathbb{E}(\langle X, D\rangle) \,\}$$

$$\Phi_D(X) = \bigcup \{\, \text{Mod}(E) \mid E \in \mathbb{E}(\langle X, D\rangle) \,\}$$

Compared to [Et87] (see also [Vo93]) we have the following relation:

$$\Gamma_D(X) = \{\, \text{Mod}(\text{Th}(M)) \mid M \ <_D\text{-minimal and } D\text{-stable} \}$$

Default logic essentially gives a description at level 2 (and 3 as we shall see later). It does not abstract from these lower levels.

4 Reasoning Frames

In the previous chapter we have seen how (nonmonotonic) reasoning can be described by assigning to each set X of initial formulae a set $\Gamma(X)$ of belief states, abstracting from the way in which the conclusions of these states have been reached. On a less abstract level, one would also like to be able to describe types of reasoning by specifying not only the final conclusions of the reasoning process, but also the reasoning path leading from the initial formulae to the final conclusions. To do this we will first formalize the notion of such a path, which we call a reasoning trace. After giving a formal semantical description of these traces, we will look at the links between the previous level and the current one.

4.1 Reasoning Traces and Reasoning Frames

Intuitively, the path from initial set of formulae to final conclusions can be seen as the behaviour of a reasoning process which starts with the initial formulae, then makes some inferences to arrive at a new state, again make some inferences, et cetera, possibly ad infinitum. The final conclusions of such a process can be seen as the union of all conclusions drawn at all stages. A formalization of such reasoning behaviour would have to describe which formulae have been derived at each stage. This can be done syntactically or semantically; we have chosen to follow the latter approach. First we will formalize the notion of an information state:

Definition 4.1 (Information State)

a) An *information state* $\mathbf{M}$ is a non-empty closed class of propositional models, that is, there is a theory of which it is the model class.

b) The *refinement ordering* $\leq$ on information states is defined by:

$$\mathbf{M}_1 \leq \mathbf{M}_2 \quad \Leftrightarrow \quad \mathbf{M}_2 \subseteq \mathbf{M}_1$$

c) The *set of all information states* is denoted by **IS**.

Using these notions we can now define a reasoning trace as a specific type of sequence of such information states. In general a reasoning process does not stop, so the traces will have infinite length; if a process cannot draw any more conclusions at any step, its knowledge will remain constant.

Definition 4.2 (Reasoning Trace and Limit Model)

a) A *reasoning trace* $\mathcal{M}$ is a function from the set of natural numbers to **IS** such that for all $s \in \mathbb{N}$:

(i) $\mathcal{M}_s \leq \mathcal{M}_{s+1}$

(ii) $\mathcal{M}_s = \mathcal{M}_{s+1} \quad \Rightarrow \quad \mathcal{M}_s = \mathcal{M}_t$ for all $t \geq s$.

b) The *refinement ordering* $\leq$ on reasoning traces is defined by:

$$\mathcal{M} \leq \mathcal{N} \quad \Leftrightarrow \quad \mathcal{M}_s \leq \mathcal{N}_s \text{ for all } s \in \mathbb{N}$$

c) The *limit model*, $\lim \mathcal{M}$ of a reasoning trace $\mathcal{M}$ is the information state defined by

$$\lim \mathcal{M} = \bigcap_{s=0}^{\infty} \mathcal{M}_s$$

d) A reasoning trace $\mathcal{M}$ is sometimes denoted by $(\mathcal{M}_s)_{s \in \mathbb{N}}$.

A (nonmonotonic) type of reasoning can now be described by giving its intended reasoning traces. Given a set of initial formulae, there may of course be several traces leading to different conclusion sets. We do, however, assume that the reasoning is deterministic in the sense that given the set of initial formulae and the final conclusion set, the trace between them is uniquely determined. Moreover, we do not allow two distinct traces leading to limit models of which one is a refinement of the other (non-inclusiveness of traces).

Definition 4.4 (Reasoning Frame)

a) A *reasoning frame* is a tuple $(\mathbf{L}, \mathbf{Mod}, \models, \mathcal{T})$ with $\mathcal{T}$ a set of traces such that for all $\mathcal{M}$ and $\mathcal{M}'$ in $\mathcal{T}$: if $\mathcal{M}_0 = \mathcal{M}'_0$ and $\lim \mathcal{M} \leq \lim \mathcal{M}'$ then $\mathcal{M} = \mathcal{M}'$.

For shortness, sometimes we also call $\mathfrak{F}$ by itself a reasoning frame.
b) If for all sets of formulae X there exists a trace $\mathcal{M}$ in $\mathfrak{F}$ such that $Th(\mathcal{M}_0) = Cn(X)$ then $\mathfrak{F}$ is called a *complete* reasoning frame. Otherwise it is called *partial*.

A reasoning frame formally defines a set of intended alternative behaviours for the reasoning process. Following the approach introduced in [ET93], [ET94], this set of behaviours can be considered a set of temporal models in a (linear time) temporal logic. We will not give details about this connection in the current paper.

4.2 Connections Between Belief State Frames and Reasoning Frames

The levels 2 and 3 both provide a means of describing (nonmonotonic) types of reasoning. Descriptions on level 2 are more abstract whereas those on level 3 provide more details of the reasoning process. But can they describe the same types of reasoning?

4.2.1 Abstraction

Level 2 descriptions give the final conclusion sets of a type of reasoning given the initial formulae, abstracting from the reasoning process. So if we want to abstract from a level 3 specification, given a trace we should look at the initial formulae and the final outcome, that is the limit model. If we have a reasoning frame of level 3, we can define an invariant belief state operator in a straightforward way.

Definition 4.5 (Belief State Operator of a Reasoning Frame)
a) Given a complete reasoning frame $\mathfrak{F}$ the *associated belief state operator* $\Gamma_{\mathfrak{F}}$ is defined as follows: for any set $X \subseteq L$,

$$\Gamma_{\mathfrak{F}}(X) = \{ \lim \mathcal{M} \mid \mathcal{M} \in \mathfrak{F},\ Th(\mathcal{M}_0) = Cn(X) \}$$

b) For a given invariant belief state operator Γ we define

$$\mathfrak{F}(\Gamma) = \{ \mathfrak{F} \mid \mathfrak{F} \text{ reasoning frame with } \Gamma_{\mathfrak{F}} = \Gamma \}$$

It is easy to see that for a given reasoning frame $\mathfrak{F}$ the defined $\Gamma_{\mathfrak{F}}$ is an invariant belief state operator.

4.2.2 Specialisation

Many reasoning frames can yield the same associated belief state operator, so we want to analyze the set $\mathfrak{F}(\Gamma)$ of possible reasoning frames related to a belief state operator Γ.

If we want to specify, for an invariant belief state operator Γ, an associated reasoning frame, what we have to do is, for all X and $M \in \Gamma(X)$, specify a trace from the information state related to the set of initial formulae X to a belief state $M \in \Gamma(X)$. Therefore a parameter should specify when the formulae of $Th(M)/Cn(X)$ can and have to be added during the reasoning. We can do this by assuming that each formula may depend on some other formulae and can only be added if the formulae it depends on have already been added in earlier stages. So, for each X and $M \in \Gamma(X)$ such a dependency ordering $\prec$ between propositional formulae has to be specified, where $\psi \prec \varphi$ means that φ depends on ψ. Therefore we have chosen a parametrization of $\mathfrak{F}(\Gamma)$ by means of functions p which assign to each theory X and Y where X are initial facts and Y is the theory of a belief state $M \in \Gamma(X)$ an ordering on the propositional formulae. In the reasoning trace one has to make sure the formulae are added to X respecting this order. Doing this, for each X and $M \in \Gamma(X)$, the traces are specified unambiguously.

Definition 4.6 (Reasoning Trace Parameter)

a) A *reasoning trace parameter* is a partial order $(L, \prec)$ on propositional formulae such that for each $\varphi \in L$ there is an $n \in \mathbb{N}$ such that $\{\psi \mid \psi \prec \varphi\}$ does not contain a chain of length more than n. A reasoning trace parameter is called *finitary* if for each $\varphi \in L$ the set $\{\psi \mid \psi \prec \varphi\}$ is finite.

b) Let $\mathbb{TH} = \{X \subseteq L \mid Cn(X) = X\}$ be the set of theories, and let $\mathbb{BE} = \{ (X, Y) \mid X, Y \in \mathbb{TH}, X \subseteq Y\}$ be the set of pairs of possible beginpoints and endpoints. Given a trace parameter $\prec$ and $(X, Y) \in \mathbb{BE}$ define a chain of sets of formulae $(S_i)_{i \in \mathbb{N}}$ as follows:

$$S_0 = X$$
$$S_{i+1} = Cn(S_i \cup \{ \varphi \in Y \mid \{\psi \in Y \mid \psi \prec \varphi\} \subseteq S_i\})$$

Now define a reasoning trace $(\mathcal{M}_i)_{i \in \mathbb{N}}$ by $\mathcal{M}_i = Mod(S_i)$. This trace will be denoted by $\sigma(\prec, X, Y)$.

It is easy to see that this indeed defines a reasoning trace with $Th(\mathcal{M}_0) = X$ and $Th(\lim \sigma(\prec, X, Y)) = Y$.

Definition 4.7 (Parametrized Reasoning Frame of a Belief State Operator)

Let $\mathbb{TP}$ be the set of all reasoning trace parameters. A function $p : \mathbb{B} \rightarrow \mathbb{TP}$ with $\mathbb{B} \subseteq \mathbb{BE}$ is called a *reasoning frame parameter*. For a reasoning frame parameter p let $\mathfrak{T}_p$ be the following reasoning frame:

$$\mathfrak{T}_p = \{ \sigma(p(X,Y), X, Y)) \mid (X,Y) \in \mathbb{B}\}$$

A reasoning frame parameter p is *suited for* a belief state operator Γ if
$\mathbb{B} = \{(X, Y) \mid X \in \mathbb{TH}, Y = Th(M)$ for some $M \in \Gamma(X)\}$

It is easy to verify that in case all $X \in \mathbb{TH}$ occur in $\mathbb{B}$, this defines a complete reasoning frame and that all reasoning frames associated to a given belief state operator are parametrized by these parameters:

Theorem 4.8

Let an invariant belief state operator Γ and a complete reasoning frame $\mathfrak{T}$ be given. The following conditions are equivalent:

(i) $\Gamma_{\mathfrak{T}} = \Gamma$

(ii) There exists a reasoning frame parameter p suited for Γ such that $\mathfrak{T}_p = \mathfrak{T}$

The reasoning frame parameter can be taken finitary.

Continued Example (Default Logic)

This example continues Example 2 in Section 3. For a given X and $E \in \mathbb{E}(<X, D>)$ the following trace $\mathcal{M}$ can be associated in a canonical manner: $\mathcal{M}_i = Mod(E_i)$ with

$E_0 = Cn(X)$, and for all $i \geq 0$:

$E_{i+1} = Cn(E_i \cup \{ \omega \mid (\alpha : \beta_1, \ldots, \beta_n) / \omega \in D$ **is applicable at level i** $\})$

where a default $(\alpha : \beta_1, \ldots, \beta_n) / \omega \in D$ is applicable at level i if

$\alpha \in E_i$ and $\neg \beta_1 \notin E, \ldots, \neg \beta_n \notin E$

Note that this is a trace definition based on the given set of defaults D. A related finitary reasoning trace parameter $\prec$ can be defined by: $\psi \prec \varphi$ if and only if φ is the consequent of a default rule applicable at level i (and not earlier) and ψ is the consequent of a default rule applicable at an earlier level. Note that for the case of a prerequisite-free default theory this will be the empty ordering.

5 Conclusions and Further Perspectives

In this paper five levels of specification of nonmonotonic reasoning are distinguished. The notions of semantical frame, belief state frame and reasoning frame were introduced and used as a semantical basis for the first three levels. Moreover, the semantical connections between the levels were identified. It was shown that this general semantical framework is applicable for various well-known approaches such as preferential semantics and default logic; it also works for Poole systems and revision operators.

Different formalisms for nonmonotonic reasoning available in the literature cover different levels of specification. For example, nonmonotonic logics defined by a preferential entailment relation aim at specifications of level 1. On the other hand, the development of default logic with its stress on default rules and (multiple) extensions has concentrated more on specifications at the levels 2 and 3. The above analysis shows why it is hard to make a sincere competitive comparison between default logic and preference relation based approaches: they essentially address specification at different levels of abstraction.

Given the semantical framework introduced here, a number of questions arise: what kind of (standard) languages are most appropriate for specifying nonmonotonic reasoning at these levels? Are there "natural" choices for the parameters in general, or in specific nonmonotonic reasoning formalisms ? How should level 4 be specified ?

References

[Et87] Etherington, D.W. : A Semantics for Default Logic, Proc. IJCAI-87, pp. 495-498; see also in: D.W. Etherington, Reasoning with Incomplete Information, Morgan Kaufmann, 1988

[ET93] Engelfriet, J., Treur, J.: A Temporal Model Theory for Default Logic. In: M. Clarke, R. Kruse, S. Moral (eds.), Proc. 2nd European Conference on Symbolic and Quantitative Approaches to Reasoning and Uncertainty, ECSQARU '93, Springer Verlag, 1993, pp. 91-96.

[ET94] Engelfriet, J., Treur, J.: Temporal Theories of Reasoning. In: C. MacNish, D. Pearce, L.M. Pereira (eds.), *Logics in Artifical Intelligence*, Proceedings of the 4th European Workshop on Logics in AI, JELIA '94, Lecture Notes in AI, vol. 838, Springer Verlag, pp. 279-299.

[He94] Herre, H.: Compactness Properties of nonmonotonic Inference Operations. In: C. MacNish, D. Pearce, L.M. Pereira (eds.), *Logics in Artifical Intelligence*, Proceedings of the 4th European Workshop on Logics in AI, JELIA '94, Lecture Notes in AI, vol. 838, Springer Verlag, 1994, pp. 19-33.

[KLM90] Kraus, S., D. Lehmann, M. Magidor: Nonmonotonic Reasoning, Preferential models and cumulative logics; AI Journal 44 (1990), 167 - 207

[MT93] Marek, V., M. Truszczynski: Nonmonotonic Logic, Springer-Verlag, 1993

[Ta56] Tarski, A.: Logic, Semantics, Metamathematics. Papers from 1923 -1938. Clarendon Press, Oxford, 1956

[Vo93] Voorbraak, F.: Preference-based Semantics for Nonmonotonic Logics, in: Bajcsy, R. (ed.), Proc. 13th International Joint Conference on Artificial Intelligence, IJCAI-93, Morgan Kaufmann, 1983, pp. 584-589

A Bayesian Network Based Learning System:
- Architecture and Performance Comparison with Other Methods -

Kazuo J. Ezawa
Room 7E-523
kje@ulysses.att.com

Til Schuermann
Room 7E-530
til@ ulysses.att.com

AT&T Bell Laboratories
600 Mountain Avenue
Murray Hill, N. J. 07974

Abstract

In this paper, we discuss the construction of Bayesian network models from data using the Advanced Pattern Recognition & Identification (APRI) system. It is designed for classification of low probability events as well as mixed data types, discrete *and* continuous, with large amounts of available training data (a few million records for a typical application) where other methods such as discriminant analysis and classification trees have difficulty in doing the task. We show here that APRI does as well and in some cases better then these other methods with less demanding problems. We will discuss the architecture of the system as an example of Bayesian network learning system. We present a comparison of this system with the classification tree system C4.5 and statistical discriminant analysis using standard data sets, namely voting record and CRX credit card application. We show that despite the fact that APRI was not designed for small data set applications, it nevertheless performs well. We discuss functional advantages and disadvantages between classification tree (C4.5) and Bayesian network (APRI) methods.

Keywords: Bayesian Classification, Bayesian Learning, and Bayesian Networks.

I. Introduction

Currently, discriminant analysis from statistics and classification trees from machine learning are popular methods for analyzing information for classification. However, we believe we can improve classification accuracy by applying a non-parametric Bayesian classification where a vast amount of quantitative information is available in databases. This method allows explicit representation of dependencies among the attributes of classification without imposing any distributional assumptions. While discriminant analysis allows for such dependence between attributes, it does so within a pre-specified distributional framework such as multivariate normality [M1]. Classification trees, meanwhile, do not make such assumptions but allow for only a limited implicit modeling of dependencies. In theory, a "Bayesian classifier" [1] [F1] provides the optimal classification performance, but in practice so far, it has been considered impractical due to enormous data processing requirements. Recent advances in evidence (observation) propagation algorithms [S1, L1, J1, E1] as well as advances in computer hardware allow us to explore this Bayesian classifier in the Bayesian network form [C1, E2].

We discuss Advanced Pattern Recognition & Identification (APRI) which is a Bayesian network based learning system. For reasons of computational efficiency, APRI is based on propagation of evidence on the Bayesian network. It is designed as a standalone classification system and can also be used as a subsystem for a normative decision support system[2] or for a normative expert system. These systems are based on the influence diagram paradigm for seamless system integration of user interface and data exchange.

APRI has been in development for several years and has started to demonstrate its effectiveness in telecommunication related classification applications. The main application is the classification and detection of low probability events (1.0 to 10.0 %) where other methods such as discriminant analysis and classification trees have difficulty in doing the task. This requires the system to use large amounts of data (10^5 to 10^6 records) for training to obtain minimum sample size for the detection of such low probability events. It is designed to handle large amount of data efficiently and to perform classification task in real time [E2]. In this paper we seek to test this new approach against existing, albeit less demanding, data sets to provide for a kind of benchmark.

In the following section, we introduce a Bayesian network. In Section III, we discuss training using voting records and CRX credit card application examples, two commonly used data sets from the University of California Irvine repository. Section IV discusses a classification algorithm and other features of the system. In Section V, we conduct a comparison between APRI and C4.5 [Q1], as well as standard discriminant analysis.

II. Bayesian Network

A Bayesian network is a structure we use to represent the knowledge accumulated through a learning process [C1, G1, L2]. The attribute and model selection metric used in our method is the entropy-based concept of mutual information. In this section we provide a short description of the Bayesian network, creation of the Bayesian network from the training dataset, and classification of new data from the test dataset using evidence propagation on the Bayesian network.

The following are the definitions and notations we use to describe Bayesian network models:

Each *node i* is a chance (probabilistic) node with an associated variable X_i, and outcome space Ω_i where x_i represents a particular outcome of Ω_i. $P\{X_i\}$ represents the probability distribution of the conditionally independent variable X_i.

---

1 Bayes theorem provides a way to update beliefs given new evidence.

2 One such normative decision support system is CADET: Computer-Aided Decision Engineering Tool which is based on influence diagram paradigm[E1].

$P\{X_i|X_j\}$ represents the probability distribution of the conditionally dependent variable X_i given X_j. An *arc (i,j)* is a directed path between two nodes *i* and *j*. A successor (or descendant) of node *i* is a node on a directed path emanating from node *i*. A successor node that is adjacent to node *i* is called a *direct successor* of node *i* and denoted by S_i. A predecessor (or ancestor) of node *i* is a node on a directed path terminating at node *i*. A predecessor that is adjacent to node *i* is called a *direct predecessor* of node *i*. The set of all direct predecessors of node *i* is denoted as $C(X_i)$ (as *conditioning* nodes). A node *i* holds a probability distribution $P\{X_i|C(X_i)\}$or simply $P\{X_i\}$ if it has no predecessors.

Given that there is an arc *(i, j)* between chance nodes *i* node *j*, but no other path from node *i* to node *j*, arc *(i, j)* can be reversed to *(j, i)* using Bayes' Theorem. After the *arc reversal* between node *i* and node *j*, each node inherits the other's direct predecessors.

A *Bayesian network* is an acyclic network that describes the form of the joint probability distribution of a chance node called the *prime node* (PN) and its *k* attribute/field nodes (F_i). This product distribution represented by the Bayesian network is:

$$P\{X_1^F,\ldots,X_k^F,X^{PN}\} = \left[\sum_{i=1}^{k} P\{X_i^F|C(X_i^F)\}\right] \cdot P\{X^{PN}\}.$$

The superscripts F and PN denote field and prime node. The prime node contains the classification categories and associated (prior) probabilities. The attribute/field nodes contain their attribute outcomes and conditional (prior) probabilities (i.e., it has at least one predecessor, the prime node).

III. Training

The training data consists of preclassified data which provides the actual classification for each record (i.e., the outcomes for the prime node) and its attributes' outcomes. The first task of the training step is to encode the knowledge of the expert by identifying the prime node as well as naming each attribute node and its characteristics. For continuous variables, we have two options. One is to discretize the variable by setting the level of precision and rounding required for the training model. We also set a global minimum sample size for each outcome set of the continuous variables. If an outcome of the outcome set does not meet this requirement, it will be automatically merged to the neighboring outcome until it meets this minimum sample size in the training. The other option is to estimate the density function directly (such as via kernel density estimation). For automatic segmentation of outcomes, we employ either sequential application of binary discretization using the entropy method [Q1], or uniform probability discretization for the segmentation of outcome sets of an attribute.

APRI uses the entropy-based mutual information metric for both variable (or feature) as well as dependency selection. Mutual information is defined for a pair of discrete random variables X, Y as

$$MI(X;Y) = \sum_{x,y} Pr(x,y) \log \frac{Pr(x,y)}{Pr(x)\,Pr(y)},$$

where the sum is taken across all possible outcomes. In words, MI(X;Y) is the reduction in uncertainty in X due to knowledge about Y. Clearly, if X and Y are independent, mutual information is zero.

Mutual information is used to rank population characteristics (or field nodes, to use the language of APRI) by how well they can discriminate between two or more groups. It can also be used to find dependencies *between* these field nodes in order to create a conditionally dependent model. Note that the mutual information metric is used only to determine model size and structure: how many field nodes to keep and which field-to-field node dependencies to allow for in a conditionally dependent model. This is analogous to variable selection for model specification in statistical discriminant or regression analysis. To impose independence may be ignoring some information contained in the data; to allow full dependency will usually result in too complex a model.

One clear distinction between the classification tree approach and APRI in the training is that a classification tree does a greedy search one attribute and one segmentation of the outcomes of the variable at a time, whereas APRI first identifies a set of attributes to use (or keep) and then selects a set of dependencies among the attributes.

Algorithm 1: APRI Training

1) define schema file
    a) select cumulative entropy threshold (percentage)
        • prime to field T_{pf} ($0 \leq T_{pf} \leq 1$)
        • field to field T_{ff} ($0 \leq T_{ff} \leq 1$)
    b) select moving window size
        • single record
        • multiple record
2) compute outcome sets for each variable from training data
    a) discrete
        • full outcome set
        • merge outcomes to subsets
    b) continuous
        • discretize via entropy measure or equal probability
        • estimate conditional density directly: set kernel density estimation parameter
3) conduct variable selection: compute main effects
    a) compute all pairwise mutual information between prime and each field node
        $MI(X^{PN};X^{F}_{i})\ \ \forall\, i = 1,\ldots,k$ possible attribute variables
    b) select field variables in descending order until T_{pf} is reached
4) select field to field node dependencies: compute interaction effects
    a) compute all pairwise mutual information between field nodes conditional on the prime node
        $MI(X^{F}_{j};X^{F}_{i})\ \ \forall\, j \neq i.$
    b) select field to field dependencies in descending order until T_{ff} is reached

5) collect all conditional probabilities (prior) for selected nodes and dependencies
- compute $P\{X_i|C(X_i)\}$
- compute unconditional (prior) probability of prime node $P\{X^{PN}\}$ as well as conditional probabilities for selected nodes and dependencies $P\{X^F_i|C(X^F_i)\}$

We designed APRI to address two major bottlenecks found in telecommunication applications. One is the computational address limit. In the case of a 32 bit operating system, this is about 2GB. Since model complexity is partially determined by the entropy thresholds T_{pf} and T_{ff}, the higher those thresholds, the better the prediction accuracy, thanks in part to the pruning algorithm. However, APRI runs out of computational address space before we can estimate an "optimal" model as defined by considering all field to field dependencies (setting $T_{ff} = 100\%$). Moving to a 64 bit operating system would effectively eliminate this problem.

The second bottleneck is the time it takes to read the data set. APRI is designed to minimize the repeated read of a dataset. For other methods such as discriminant analysis and decision trees, the data set, especially when it is large, needs to be read every time a test is conducted. In the case of discrete outcome classification, APRI needs to read the data set only four times regardless of the number of attributes or associated outcomes.

IV. Classification

Once we have refined the trained model of the data set, we can classify a new data set. Standard operations for the propagation of evidence have been discussed previously [S1, E1]. The algorithm to perform evidence propagation on a Bayesian network is described in Algorithm 2 which is a modification of the standard operations by taking advantage of the two layer structure of the Bayesian network for updating the probability distribution of the prime node's outcomes. The advantages of this algorithm are 1) avoiding unnecessary arc reversals between S(PN) and PN, and 2) handling missing information efficiently using techniques such as barren node removal (which is the deletion of a node) or simply skipping to the next field node.

The instantiation of evidence, or outcome realization, on a chance node and propagation of evidence among chance nodes involve some of the following operations depending on the network structure:

Evidence absorption: instantiation of evidence x^F_j on node *i* is just the table lookup of the observed outcome,

$$\text{i.e., } P\{X^F_i = x^F_i | C(X^F_i)\}$$

Evidence propagation: propagation of evidence x^F_i to its successor node *j* is the identification of still valid potential outcomes,

$$\text{i.e., } P\{X^F_j | C(X^F_j) \setminus X^F_i \cap (X^F_i = x^F_i)\} \cdot P\{X^F_i = x^F_i | C(X^F_i)\}$$

Evidence reversal: evidence absorption of x^F_j on *j* and arc reversal between *j* and its predecessor *k* and the propagation of evidence x^F_j.

This method allows us to minimize the unnecessary computation and makes the operations more like table lookup operations.

Now we describe the algorithm that takes advantage of the above operations. N indicates the number of nodes involved for the particular evidence propagation operation.

Algorithm 2: APRI Classification (Evidence Propagation on a Bayesian Network)

1) If we have evidence (observations) for all nodes j except PN, then multiply the observed probability of all nodes with evidence x_j^F in descending order of prime/field entropy level,

$$P\{\sim x^{PN}\}^{new} = \left[\sum_{j=1}^{k} P\{X_j^F = x_j^F | C\{X_j^F)\}^{old} \right] \cdot P\{x^{PN}\}^{old}$$

go to 3)

2) Set $P\{\sim x^{PN}\}^{new} =: P\{x^{PN}\}^{old}$, where ~x indicates the value of x before normalization with respect to the sum of the probabilities (see 3)).

a) Instantiate and propagate evidence for node F_j for all nodes with evidence and predecessors with no missing information except for the prime node.

option 1) In descending order of prime/field entropy level, update the unconditional probability of the prime node:

$$P\{\sim x^{PN}\}^{new} =: P\{\sim x^{PN}\}^{old} \cdot P\{X_j^F = x_j^F | C(X_j^F)\}^{old}$$

Then remove barren node(s).

option 2)

a) j = argmin. N $(C(X_j^F))$. This is to minimize the number of arc reversals which is desirable because arc reversals are very computationally intensive.

b) j = argmax $N(S(X_j^F))$. This will eliminate downstream arc reversal because once evidence has been propagated, that arc is eliminated.

Now, update the unconditional probability of the prime node:

$$P\{\sim x^{PN}\}^{new} =: P\{\sim x^{PN}\}^{old} \cdot P\{X_j^F = x_j^F | C(X_j^F)\}^{old}$$

Then remove barren node(s).

b) Perform a) for all nodes with evidence and predecessors with missing information

3) Re-normalize

$$P\{x^{PN}\}^{new} =: \frac{P\{\sim x^{PN}\}^{old}}{\sum_{x^{PN} \in X^{PN}} P\{\sim x^{PN}\}^{old}}$$

Both options 1 and 2 of step 2 are heuristic rules. The former is more computationally intensive than the latter but considers the most important fields first, where importance is measured by the mutual information between the prime node and a field node. Which option to choose is very much application dependent.

If X_j^F is a continuous variable, the only difference is that $P\{X_j^F|C(X_j^F)\}$ becomes a continuous density function, i.e., $f(X_j^F|C(X_j^F))$. If x_j^F is the observed outcome, then we obtain the specific probability by $P\{X_j^F = x_j^F|C(X_j^F)\} = f(X_j^F = x_j^F|C(X_j^F))$.

Avoidance of Probability of 1 ("Pruning")

The avoidance of probability of 1 at the tail end of the evidence propagation operation in the classification process provides protection against "overfitting" to the training dataset. This feature allows us to separate the impact of model complexity from overfitting. The feature is simple. We skip a field node which causes $P\{\cdot\} = 1$ in the classification process as we would if we had missing infomation (or missing observation) for that field node. It is essentially the "pruning" of the tail-end attributes in the process of classification. Note that this effect of "pruning" is not explicitly observable on the network itself. It is implicitly hidden in the data structure under each field node.

V. Comparison

In this section, we discuss a comparison of two data sets, voting record and CRX credit card application. We used the data sets provided in C4.5 [Q1], a standard in the literature. The voting record data set contains only discrete variables while the CRX credit card application data set contains both continuous and discrete variables. All results are out-of-sample using the test data set.

Voting Record Data Set[3]

This data set represents votes for each of the House of Representatives Congressmen on the 16 key votes identified by the Congressional Quarterly Almanac. It contains a 300 record training data file and a 135 record test data file. Table 4 shows the summary of error rate comparison of these two systems.

APRI	error rate	Tree (C4.5)	error rate
Dependent (w/o pruning)	5.9 %	Before Pruning	5.2 %
Dependent (pruning)	1.5 %	After Pruning	3.0 %
Independent (8 vars)	7.4 %		

Table 1: Comparison of APRI and C4.5 using Voting Record Data Set

Using the same number of variables, explicitly modeling conditional dependencies reduces the error rate considerably for APRI. Moreover, we see that APRI with pruning out-performs the analogous C4.5 model. C4.5 before pruning uses 7 variables, i.e., "physician_fee", "budget", "education", "mx", "exports", "synfuels", and "water". APRI selected 8 variables, where only 4 variables are the same as C4.5,

3 Since the voting data set contains exclusively categorical variables, we did not not fit a statistical discriminant model to it.

i.e., "physician_fee", "budget", "education", and "mx". Furthermore, "water" was the least influencing variable for the classification as measured by the mutual information metric. Another interesting feature in Figure 1 is that only one field node is conditionally independent; all others have some dependencies. In a classification tree, you cannot explicitly observe these conditional dependency and independency explicitly.

CRX Data Set

This data set contains credit card application approval records with both continuous and categorical feature data, allowing us to also make a comparison with statistical discriminant analysis. We fit a linear and quadratic normal discriminant model, as well as a non-parametric one which makes no distributional assumptions. The conditional density is estimated with a normal kernel. The data set has a 490 record training data file and a 200 record test data file. The unconditional credit card approval rate is 44.3%.

APRI	error rate	Tree (C4.5)	error rate	Discr. Anal.	error rate
Dep. (no prune)	15.5%	Default	17.5%	linear	16.6%
Dep. (prune)	13.5%	- s[4]	17.4%	quadratic	16.9%
Indep.	16.5%	- m15[5]	14.5%	nonparametric	19.1%

Table 2: Comparison of APRI and C4.5 using CRX data set

APRI appears to have a slightly better overall performance, though all three methods produce rather similar results.

Current disadvantages:

Asymmetry: A tree is a more natural knowledge representation for asymmetric problems (unbalanced tree) than a Bayesian network. The current implementation of APRI does not exploit asymmetry as well as classification trees do. For example, in the voting record classification tree, the tree algorithm first looks at "physician_fee"; if the outcome is "no", check "budget"; if "yes", check "synfuels"; if "undecided", check "water." For now we do not exploit this outcome dependent asymmetry as cleanly and explicitly as the classification tree does. Note that in the Bayesian network, the asymmetric relations are implicitly represented in the network as conditional probabilities.

Model size and complexity: A Bayesian network model is larger in size (byte) and more complex (more dependencies) than a comparable tree model. It requires more memory and computational power for model creation and classification of new data.

Explanability: Decision rules created by the classification tree are easy to explain to users. In a Bayesian network, these rules are hidden within the network.

---

4 This option casuses the values of discrete attributes to be grouped for tests.

5 A minimum number of cases or observations threshold (here 15).

Current advantages:

Better accuracy: Although both C4.5 and APRI employ pruning, because of the "avoidance of probability of 1," APRI avoids overfitting and therefore provides better accuracy for classification.

Knowledge representation: The Bayesian network provides a parsimonious representation of the relationships among the variables.

Continuous outcome prediction: The prime node can be a continuous variable. When we discretize prime node outcomes, we can compute conditional expected values for the segments, and use them as outcomes[6] for the prime node. After the update of the class probability, we can compute the overall expected value for the prime node.

Moving windows: APRI can model record dependency which is often manifested as the passage of time. It can create a model based on a set of variables over a specific length of a sequence. For example, we can create a weather forecasting model based on the past three days' information on temperature, humidity, etc. (which includes dependency of temperature on day 1 , day 2 and day 3, etc.). C4.5 can do so only with extensive dataset reformatting.

Efficient handling of categorical and continuous data: Discretization of continuous information results invariably in information loss. One of the main advantages here of statistical discriminant analysis is its strength in modeling using continuous information, yet it falls short when the data is categorical. By contrast, machine learning algorithms such as C4.5 can handle categorical information more efficiently. APRI does *both* well.

Bayesian network based learning is still in its infancy. There are many missing pieces and questions, such as techniques to handle asymmetry, etc.. But it represents a logical way to approach the "ultimate" classifier -- the Bayesian classifier which provides optimal accuracy with no self-imposed restrictions. We have shown in this paper that the Bayesian network based learning can perform quite well.

Summary

In this paper, we discussed the construction of Bayesian network models from data. We discussed the architecture of the system as an example of such a Bayesian network learning system. We compared this system to the classification tree system C4.5 and statistical discriminant analysis and found it to be superior in performance based on two standard data sets. We discussed that APRI still has disadvantages in handling of asymmetry but advantages in efficient data handling, continuous variable classification, moving windows, handling of missing information and use of continuous probability functions. While classification trees can readily generate decision rules as output, a Bayesian network has a very intuitive representation of the relationship among the variables. Finally, in work currently under way we find that APRI's real power is seen when one of the classes occurs very

6 The ranges are hidden; e.g. the segment may have a range from 1.0 to 2.0 and be represented by 1.5 as the expected value.

rarely. The classification of such low probability events is virtually impossible with decision trees or discriminant analysis [E2].

References

C1. Cooper, G. F., and Herskovits, E., "A Bayesian Method for Constructing Bayesian Belief Networks from Databases," *Proceedings of the Seventh Conference on Uncertainty in Artificial Intelligence*, pp 86-94. Los Angeles: Morgan Kaufmann, 1991.

E1. Ezawa, K., "Value of Evidence on Influence Diagrams," *Proceedings of the Tenth Conference on Uncertainty in Artificial Intelligence*, pp 212-220, Morgan Kaufmann, 1994

E2. Ezawa, K. and T. Schuermann, "Fraud/Uncollectible Debt Detection Using a Bayesian Network Based Learning System: A Rare Binary Outcome with Mixed Data Structures", submitted to UAI'95

F1. Fukunaga K., *Introduction to Statistical Pattern Recognition*, Academic Press, 1990.

G1 Geiger, D., "An Entropy-Based Learning Algorithm of Bayesian conditional Trees", *Proceedings of the Eighth Conference on Uncertainty in Artificial Intelligence*, pp 92-97, Morgan Kaufmann, 1992.

J1. Jensen, V., Olesen K. G., and Andersen S. K., "An Algebra of Bayesian Universes for Knowledge-Based Systems", *Networks*, Vol. **20** pp. 637-659, John Wiley & Sons, Inc., 1990

L1. Lauritzen, S. L., and Spiegelhalter, D. J., "Local Computations with Probabilities on Graphical Structures and their Application to Expert Systems", *J. R. Statist. Soc* **B**, **50**, No.2 pp 157-224, 1988.

L2. Langley, Pat and Stephanie Sage, "Induction of Selective Bayesian Classifiers", in *Proceedings of the Tenth Conference on Uncertainty in Artificial Intelligence*, pp399-406, Morgan Kaufman, 1994.

M1. McLachlan, Geoffrey J., *Discriminant Analysis and Statistical Pattern Recognition*, John Wiley & Sons, 1992

Q1. Quinlan, J. R., *C4.5 Programs for Machine Learning*, Morgan Kaufmann, 1993.

S1. Shachter, R. D., "Evidence Absorption and Propagation through Evidence Reversals", *Uncertainty in Artificial Intelligence*, Vol. 5, pp. 173-190, North-Holland, 1990.

Specificity by Default

P. Geerts [1] and D. Vermeir [2]

[1] Dept. of Mathematics and Computer Science, University of Antwerp, UIA
[2] Dept. of Computer Science, Free University of Brussels, VUB

Abstract
The concept of prioritization, either implicitly or explicitly, has been generally recognized as a tool to eliminate spurious extensions. Implicit priority information can be used when specificity is the preference criterion by means of which extensions are selected. Sometimes, it is necessary to take other preference criteria into account, and explicit means of expressing priorities are required. Here we present an argument based approach to nonmonotonic reasoning, in which implicit and explicit priorities are combined. The idea is that arguments are ranked according to a preference relation based on implicit specificity information. Additional explicit priorities can be supplied by the user, so that specificity can be considered as the preference criterion by default.

1. Introduction

One of the basic ideas in nonmonotonic reasoning is that a defeasible statement can be believed only in the absence of any evidence to the contrary. This idea can be translated to reasoning with arguments: a statement, supported by some argument, can be concluded only in the absence of any counterargument. Recently, the concept of prioritization has been generally recognized as a tool to improve on the early non-monotonic formalisms, because they offer an attractive way to eliminate some undesirable extensions. The same tendency can be found in nonmonotonic formalisms based on arguments: arguments and counterarguments are compared based on specificity. Several formalisms rely on arguments, although their appearance can be quite different: sometimes, arguments need to have a certain structure[10, 13] , otherwise they are just sets of rules[14, 15] , possibly with some additional minimality requirement.

In this paper, we present a defeasible logic based on arguments, where we are interested in maximal consistent sets of rules in which each rule contributes to what can be concluded from this argument. The idea is that such an argument directly corresponds to an extension. Furthermore, we derive a method to compare maximal arguments based on the specificity information, implicitly present in the knowledge base. As there may be several preferred maximal arguments, and therefore also several extensions, this approach can be considered to be credulous. The ranking on all maximal arguments is based entirely on specificity. However, sometimes there are other preference criteria required, such as recency, authority, ... which can not be built into the proof theory. The fact that all maximal arguments are retained and ranked, makes it possible to integrate explicit priorities and select the most preferred arguments satisfying these additional priorities. Such an approach would be impossible if the formalism were skeptical or if it retained only the preferred arguments. Because a most preferred argument satisfying additional priorities doesn't need to be preferred with respect to the ranking in its entirety, it is clear that explicit priorities can override the implicit specificity priorities. From this point of view, specificity can be considered as the preference criterion by default: whenever no additional priorities are given, specificity is used as a selection tool, but explicit priorities may defeat the specificity criterion.

The paper is organized as follows. In section 2 we present a credulous argument based approach to nonmonotonic reasoning, and derive a preference relation on maximal arguments based on implicit specificity information. Section 3 shows how explicit priorities can be easily integrated in the framework presented in section 2. This extension makes it possible to rely on specificity when no other preference criteria are required or known, but also to refine or even defeat the specificity based priorities by adding explicit priorities. In section 4 we discuss related formalisms and consider other specificity based approaches which could be used for our purposes.

2. Prioritization of Arguments Based on Implicit Specificity Information

A literal is a propositional constant p or the negation $\tilde{}p$ of a propositional constant; p and $\tilde{}p$ are complements of each other. Where p is any literal, we denote the complement of p as $\neg p$. Where A is a finite set of literals and p is a literal, a rule is a pair $(A\ ,\ p)$, denoted $A \rightarrow p$. We usually omit the set brackets when the antecedent set has only one member, and we usually omit an empty antecedent set altogether. Thus $\{p\} \rightarrow q$ is usually written $p \rightarrow q$ and $\emptyset \rightarrow q$ is usually written $\rightarrow q$. With a set of rules R we associate an immediate consequence mapping R which transforms a set of literals: $R(X) = \{p \mid (C \rightarrow p) \in R \wedge C \subseteq X\} \cup X$. Since the mapping R is obviously monotone, it has a fixpoint for any set of literals. We use R^* to denote the fixpoint arising from the empty set, i.e. $R^* = \bigcup_i R^i$ where $R^1 = R(\emptyset)$, $R^2 = R(R^1), ..., R^n = R(R^{n-1})$.

Definition 1. Let R be a set of rules. An *argument* is any subset $A \subseteq R$ such that A^* is consistent and $\forall\ B \subset A : B^* \subset A^*$. An argument is maximal if it is not contained in any larger (w.r.t. the subset order) argument.

The above definition is based on the intuition that each rule in an argument should be responsible for a certain conclusion. All rules in our formalism are defeasible and are interpreted in a unidirectional way, i.e. contraposition is not allowed. As usual in this kind of formalisms, a rule $C \rightarrow p$ is said to be applicable in a set of literals S whenever $C \subseteq S$. Furthermore, $C \rightarrow p$ is said to be applicable in an argument A whenever it is applicable in A^*, i.e. when $C \subseteq A^*$. Therefore, the notion of applicability can be used both for a set of literals and for an argument.

Example 1. Consider $R = \{\rightarrow p, p \rightarrow b, b \rightarrow a, a \rightarrow \neg f, b \rightarrow f, p \rightarrow \neg f\}$, where p stands for penguin, b for bird, a for animal and f for the ability to fly. There are 3 maximal arguments, given by $A_1 = \{\rightarrow p,\ p \rightarrow b,\ b \rightarrow a,\ a \rightarrow \neg f\}$, $A_2 = \{\rightarrow p,\ p \rightarrow b,\ b \rightarrow a,\ b \rightarrow f\}$ and $A_3 = \{\rightarrow p,\ p \rightarrow b,\ b \rightarrow a,\ p \rightarrow \neg f\}$. The arguments A_2 and A_3 are in conflict since $A_2 \cup A_3$ is not an argument. However, our intuition tells us that A_3 is to be preferred because A_3 uses "more specific" information. For the same reason, A_2 should be preferred to A_1. What follows is an attempt to formalize this preference in a simple way. The idea is that for each argument, the set of rules which are "violated", is considered. Such a violated set can be used to define the "uncontroversial" part of an argument, the kernel. Arguments with a larger kernel are preferred. Several attempts to capture these ideas into our formalism ran into serious problems. First of all, when we compare two arguments, we should consider only the information in these arguments, instead of the entire knowledge base. Therefore, violated sets and kernels should always be defined with respect to another argument. A second problem originated from the observation that kernels should not be unique.

Definition 2. Let R be a set of rules and A_1 and A_2 arguments in R. The *violated set* of A_1 *with respect to* A_2, denoted $VS(A_1,A_2)$, is defined as the set of rules from A_2 which are applicable, but not present in A_1: $VS(A_1,A_2)= \{C \rightarrow p \in A_2 - A_1 \mid C \subseteq A_1^*\}$.

With this definition, every rule under consideration which is applicable in A_1^* but not present in A_1 is considered to be violated. This implies that whenever an applicable rule is not in a maximal argument because of the presence of another rule with the same conclusion, this rule is also regarded as violated.

Definition 3. Let R be a set of rules and A_1 and A_2 arguments in R. A *kernel* $\hat{A}_1(A_2)$ of A_1 *with respect to* A_2 is a maximal subargument of A_1 such that every violated rule of A_1 with respect to A_2 becomes inapplicable: $\hat{A}_1(A_2) = \max\{B \subseteq A_1 \mid B$ is an argument and $\nexists\ r \in VS(A_1,A_2)$ applicable in $B^*\}$. The set of kernels of A_1 with respect to A_2 is denoted $Ker(A_1,A_2)$.

The following theorem gives an alternative way to characterize kernels.

Theorem 1. Let R be a set of rules and A_1 and A_2 arguments in R. $Ker(A_1,A_2) = \{B \mid B$ is a maximal subargument of A_1 such that $VS(B,A_2) \subseteq A_1\}$.

Sometimes, $Ker(A_1,A_2)$ can be empty. This is the case when there is a rule $\rightarrow p$ in A_2 which is violated in A_1, since there is no way to make this rule inapplicable. Because we consider a rule $\rightarrow p$ to be less specific than a rule $C \rightarrow p$ or $D \rightarrow \neg p$, we would like to obtain that A_1 is preferred to A_2, whenever A_1 contains such a rule $C \rightarrow p$ or $D \rightarrow \neg p$ which is applicable in A_2. However, A_2 can be more specific concerning another rule. Therefore, we also need to define kernels in which violated rules with empty antecedent are thrown overboard.

Definition 4. For two arguments A_1 and A_2, $Ker(A_1,A_2)_\emptyset$ is the set of kernels of A_1 with respect to $A_2 - \{ \rightarrow p \mid \rightarrow p \in VS(A_1,A_2)\}$.

It is obvious that when no rule with empty antecedent is violated in A_1 with respect to A_2, we get that $Ker(A_1,A_2)_\emptyset = Ker(A_1,A_2)$.

Arguments can be compared with respect to their kernels, based on the idea that a larger kernel implies that more specific information is used.

Definition 5. Let R be a set of rules and let A_1 and A_2 be two maximal arguments in R. $A_1 \leq A_2$ iff

(a) $\exists \rightarrow p \in VS(A_1,A_2)$ such that $\exists\ C \rightarrow p$ or $D \rightarrow \neg p$ in $VS(A_2,A_1)$; or

(b) $Ker(A_1,A_2) \neq \varnothing$ and $\forall A \in Ker(A_1,A_2)$, $\exists B \in Ker(A_2,A_1)_\varnothing$ such that $B \subseteq A$.

We say that A_1 is preferred to A_2, denoted $A_1 < A_2$ iff $A_1 \leq A_2$ and $A_2 \not\leq A_1$. We say that a maximal argument A is preferred if there is no maximal argument B such that $B < A$.

Example 1 (Ctd'). For example 1, we have that

$$\begin{array}{ll} VS(A_1,A_2) = \{b \rightarrow f\} & Ker(A_1,A_2) = \{\{\rightarrow p\}\} \\ VS(A_2,A_1) = \{a \rightarrow \neg f\} & Ker(A_2,A_1) = \{\{\rightarrow p, p \rightarrow b, b \rightarrow f\}\} \\ VS(A_1,A_3) = \{p \rightarrow \neg f\} & Ker(A_1,A_3) = \{\varnothing\} \\ VS(A_3,A_1) = \{a \rightarrow \neg f\} & Ker(A_3,A_1) = \{\{\rightarrow p, p \rightarrow b, p \rightarrow \neg f\}\} \\ VS(A_2,A_3) = \{p \rightarrow \neg f\} & Ker(A_2,A_3) = \{\varnothing\} \\ VS(A_3,A_2) = \{b \rightarrow f\} & Ker(A_3,A_2) = \{\{\rightarrow p, p \rightarrow \neg f\}\} \end{array}$$

As a result, $A_3 < A_2 < A_1$, which corresponds to our intuition.

The following example shows that kernels don't have to be unique and illustrates the impact of violated rules with empty antecedents.

Example 2. Consider $R = \{\rightarrow a, \rightarrow b, \rightarrow \neg c, a \rightarrow c, \{a,b\} \rightarrow \neg c\}$. There are three maximal argument, given by $A_1 = \{\rightarrow a, \rightarrow b, \rightarrow \neg c\}$, $A_2 = \{\rightarrow a, \rightarrow b, a \rightarrow c\}$ and $A_3 = \{\rightarrow a, \rightarrow b, \{a,b\} \rightarrow \neg c\}$. The kernels are:

$$\begin{array}{ll} Ker(A_1,A_2)=\{\{\rightarrow b, \rightarrow \neg c\}\} & \\ Ker(A_2,A_1)=\varnothing & Ker(A_2,A_1)_\varnothing = \{A_2\} \\ Ker(A_1,A_3)=\{\{\rightarrow a, \rightarrow \neg c\},\{\rightarrow b, \rightarrow \neg c\}\} & \\ Ker(A_3,A_1)=\varnothing & Ker(A_3,A_1)_\varnothing = \{A_3\} \\ Ker(A_2,A_3)=\{\{\rightarrow a, a \rightarrow c\},\{\rightarrow b\}\} & \\ Ker(A_3,A_2)=\{\{\rightarrow b\}\} & \end{array}$$

Therefore, $A_3 < A_2 < A_1$, which corresponds to our intuition.

Definition 6. Let R be a set of rules. A *specificity extension* for R is given by A^*, where A is a preferred argument in R.

Intuitively, a specificity extension is supported by an argument which is preferred with respect to a preference relation based on specificity.

Until now, we assumed that knowledge bases contained rules only. In such a knowledge base, an observation can be simulated by adding the corresponding rule (with empty antecedent) to the information. Whenever there are no other rules contradicting this translated observation, this approach will do fine. However, when a translated observation can be defeated, and we don't want this to happen (i.e. the rule with empty antecedent is really an observation, and not some kind of a presumption), observations should be dealt with differently. With some minor adaptions, the same ideas can be used when a set of observations is added to the knowledge base as a separate component. Such an observation corresponds to a literal which should hold in each argument, unless the set of observations is inconsistent.

Definition 7. A theory is a pair (R,O), where R is a set of rules and O is a set of observations. Let $R_O = \{ \rightarrow o \mid o \in O\}$ be the set of rules corresponding to the observations. An argument is any subset $A \subseteq R \cup R_O$ such that $R_O \subseteq A$, A^* is consistent and $\forall B \subset A : B^* \subset A^*$.

After this, the same definitions as before can be used. The following example shows that the two different treatments of observations also give two different results.

Example 3. Consider the default knowledge that birds fly $(b \rightarrow f)$ and suppose we observe a non-flying bird. If every piece of information is interpreted as a default, we get the set of rules $R = \{ \rightarrow b, b \rightarrow f, \rightarrow \neg f\}$. In this case, there are 2 maximal arguments, namely $\{ \rightarrow b, b \rightarrow f\}$ and $\{ \rightarrow b, \rightarrow \neg f\}$, of which the first one is preferred. However, if we divide the information into two components, we get the theory $T = (\{b \rightarrow f\}, \{b, \neg f\})$, for which only one maximal argument, namely $\{ \rightarrow b, \rightarrow \neg f\}$, exists.

The nice thing about maximal arguments is that they contain the information by which the corresponding extension can be explained. However, when redundant information is involved, the preference relation on arguments can yield unintuitive results. Intuitively, a rule is redundant if nothing new can be learnt from it.

Example 4. If we add the rule $p \rightarrow a$ to the knowledge base of example 1, this rule can be considered as redundant information, because we already know that penguins are birds and birds are animals. However, as a result of adding this new rule, we get 3 additional maximal arguments: $A_4 = \{ \rightarrow p, p \rightarrow b, p \rightarrow a, a \rightarrow \neg f\}$, $A_5 = \{ \rightarrow p, p \rightarrow b, p \rightarrow a, b \rightarrow f\}$ and $A_6 = \{ \rightarrow p, p \rightarrow b, p \rightarrow a, p \rightarrow \neg f\}$. The presence of the redundant rule $p \rightarrow a$ in the arguments A_4, A_5 and A_6 hides the specificity information that birds are a special kind of animals. Therefore, it is not surprising that the preference relation on arguments gives unintuitive results: we get that $A_6 < A_3 < A_2 < A_1$, $A_6 < A_5 < A_2 < A_1$ and $A_6 < A_4 < A_2 < A_1$. The preferred argument is A_6, which we could agree upon, but there is no intuitive reason why A_4 should be preferred to A_2. On the other hand, we would expect preferences which are not reflected in the obtained result.

The obvious solution for this kind of problems is to eliminate redundant rules, as they cause problems by disturbing the specificity information. For this purpose, we should make clear what we understand by a redundant rule. It is obvious that for each argument A_1 containing a redundant rule r_1, there will be another argument A_2 without rule r_1, from which the same conclusions can be derived. This argument A_2 will contain a rule r_2 with the same consequent as r_1, where r_2 is less specific than r_1. The reason for this is that the redundant rule r_1 can be considered to short-circuit a chain of rules having r_2 as final rule. As a result, argument A_1, containing the redundant rule, will always be preferred to the (similar) argument A_2 (the "twin" argument).

Definition 8. A rule $C \rightarrow p$, with $C \neq \emptyset$, is a *redundant* rule if $\forall A_i$ containing $C \rightarrow p$ such that $\exists A_j$ containing $C \rightarrow p$ and $A_j < A_i$:

(1) $\exists A_k$ such that $A_i < A_k$ and $C \rightarrow p \notin A_k$; and

(2) $\forall A_k$ such that $A_i < A_k$, $C \to p \notin A_k$ and $C \to p \in A_l$ for each A_l with $A_i < A_l < A_k$, we have that $A_i^* = A_k^*$ and $D \to p \in A_k$ where $D \not\trianglelefteq C$.

Intuitively, we consider the preferred arguments containing a rule r which we investigate with respect to its redundancy. If it is the case that for each such most preferred argument, all the immediate succesors lacking r yield the same set of conclusions, then r is indeed redundant.

Example 4 (Ctd'). In trying to show that rule $p \to a$ is redundant, we should consider the preferred argument containing $p \to a$, which is argument A_6. There is only one immediate successor of A_6, if we disregard the ones containing $p \to a$, and that is argument A_3. Because A_6 and A_3 give the same extension, we can conclude that rule $p \to a$ is redundant. Therefore, if we leave out the redundant arguments (arguments containing a redundant rule), we get $A_3 < A_2 < A_1$.

Example 5. Consider the set of rules $R = \{ \to a, a \to b, a \to c, a \to d, b \to d, c \to \neg d\}$. There are 3 maximal arguments, given by $A_1 = \{ \to a, a \to b, a \to c, b \to d\}$, $A_2 = \{ \to a, a \to b, a \to c, c \to \neg d\}$ and $A_3 = \{ \to a, a \to b, a \to c, a \to d\}$. The preference relation on the arguments is given by $A_3 < A_1$ and $A_3 < A_2$. The rule $a \to d$ is not redundant, because A_3 has an immediate successor yielding a different extension, namely A_2.

The following theorem shows that, although redundant information has an impact on the ordering of arguments, it has no influence on the specificity extensions.

Theorem 2. Let R be a set of rules. Then, if A_1 is a preferred argument containing a redundant rule, there will be an argument A_2 which is preferred if we leave out the redundant arguments, for which $A_1^* = A_2^*$.

3. Combining Implicit Specificity Information and Explicit Priorities

A major criticism against nonmonotonic formalisms based on specificity is that sometimes, other preference criteria (such as recency, authority, reliability of sources, ...)[3, 5, 9] are required. However, this does not mean that we should forget about specificity completely, as is done in formalisms relying entirely on some kind of explicit priority ordering. Whereas the specificity criterion can be built into the proof theory, other criteria may need to be explicitly stated. In other words, what we need is a combination of the use of specificity information implicitly present inside the knowledge base and explicit priorities between rules. In the previous section, we presented a method to rank arguments based on specificity. When additional priorities among defaults are explicitly stated, we can use this ranking method to select the most specific arguments satisfying these explicit priorities. The integration of additional priorities makes it therefore possible to override specificity as a selection tool, so that specificity can be considered as the default preference criterion. The fact that the presented method to deal with implicit specificity information results in an ordering of arguments, makes it easier to extend it with an additional tool for explicitly stated priorities, in contrast to other specificity based approaches which are skeptical. Even for a credulous specificity based approach, this extension is not so obvious when only the preferred extensions are obtained, instead of an ordering on all arguments.

One way of dealing with explicit priorities is to provide some kind of extra-logical ordered structure, e.g. an ordered set of nodes, perspectives[6, 16] or subtheories containing defaults[1] , or an ordering of defaults[2, 11] . When these explicit priorities are strict, a similar mechanism can be used to extend our argument based approach: the implicit specificity information determines the most specific arguments, which can then be examined with respect to the explicit priorities. However, when the additional priorities are not static, but defeasible, we have to be able to reason about priorities. Therefore, we have to represent priorities within the logical language, so that statements concerning priorities can be derived, but also defeated. To make this possible, we will allow named defaults, in a similar way as Brewka[3] . Brewka gives a unique name to each default, and uses a predicate symbol (denoted <) to represent default priority. However, in contrast to his work, we don't need a name for each default, but only for defaults which are involved in a priority relation different from specificity.

First of all, we need an extension of our logical language. A rule can be an ordinary rule $C \rightarrow p$ or a named rule $r_i : C \rightarrow p$. The consequent of a rule can now also be a formula $r_i < r_j$, expressing that r_i has priority over r_j. $<$ is a strict partial order. No two named rules can have the same name. A named rule is considered to be applicable whenever its corresponding unnamed rule is. For a set of rules R, R_u denotes the set of corresponding unnamed rules. The consequence mapping associated with a set of unnamed rules A will be extended by assuring the transitivity of the explicit priority ordering: $A(X) = \{p \mid (C \rightarrow p) \in A \wedge C \subseteq X\} \cup \{r_i < r_j \mid (r_i < r_k) \in X \wedge (r_k < r_j) \in X\} \cup X$. Once again, we are interested in the fixpoint arising from the empty set, denoted A^*. The definition of consistency of a set of unnamed rules is extended by the requirement that the explicit priority ordering needs to be irreflexive.

Definition 9. Let A be a set of unnamed rules. We say that A^* is consistent if it doesn't contain two complementary literals and if it doesn't contain $r_i < r_i$ for some default name r_i.

The definition of an argument is slightly adapted: it is sufficient to consider unnamed rules instead of rules.

Definition 10. Let R be a set of rules. An *argument* is any subset $A \subseteq R_u$ such that A^* is consistent and $\forall B \subset A$: $B^* \subset A^*$.

The definitions for violated sets, kernels and the preference relation on maximal arguments, are the same as in section 2. As a next step, we have to explore which of these maximal arguments respect their own priority information.

Definition 11. Let R be a set of rules and let A be a maximal argument in R. We say that A *respects its own priority information* iff $\forall\, r_i < r_j \in A^*$: if $r_i : C \rightarrow p$ is applicable in A^*, but $C \rightarrow p$ is not in A, then the rule corresponding to r_j should not be in A.

In the following definition we distinguish between specificity extensions and priority extensions, where specificity extensions rely on specificity solely, and priority extensions † are obtained by the combination of specificity and explicit priorities.

† In[3] , the name priority extension is used to indicate those extensions which respect their own explicit priority information. Specificity is not considered.

Definition 12. Let R be a set of rules. A *specificity extension* for R is given by A^*, where A is a preferred argument in R when all maximal arguments are considered. Such an argument is also called a *specificity argument.* A *priority extension* for R is given by A^*, where A is a preferred argument in R when those maximal arguments respecting their own priority information are considered. The argument is called a *priority argument.*

It is obvious that whenever a set of defaults doesn't contain named rules, the priority extensions coincide with the specificity extensions.

The next example shows that not every priority extension is also a specificity extension. This is only the case when the default specificity criterion is overridden.

Example 6. Consider $R = \{ \rightarrow p, p \rightarrow b, r_1 : b \rightarrow f, r_2 : p \rightarrow \neg f, \rightarrow r_1 < r_2 \}$. In this case, the explicitly stated priority information contradicts the specificity information, and should therefore override the specificity criterion. There are 2 maximal arguments given by $A_1 = \{ \rightarrow p,\ p \rightarrow b,\ b \rightarrow f, \rightarrow r_1 < r_2 \}$ and $A_2 = \{ \rightarrow p,\ p \rightarrow b,\ p \rightarrow \neg f, \rightarrow r_1 < r_2 \}$. There is a unique specificity argument, A_2. However, A_2 doesn't satisfy its own explicit priority information: $r_1 < r_2$ is in A_2^*, $r_1 : b \rightarrow f$ is applicable in A_2^*, but not present in A_2 (while r_2 is).

It is possible to have a set of rules for which specificity arguments exist, but no priority arguments. In this case, we can argue that the user supplying the additional priorities has made an error. For an example, see[3] .

In the following example we try to give a more realistic application showing the need for defeasible rule priorities.

Example 7. Assume we want to drive from Antwerp to Charleroi. The shortest way is via the ring-road round Brussels. However, when there is a traffic jam on the ring-road round Brussels, we want to avoid this ring-road, unless we don't know any alternative route. This information is contained in $R = \{$ $\rightarrow$ from (Antwerp), $\rightarrow$ to (Charleroi), r_1 : {from(Antwerp),to(Charleroi)} $\rightarrow$ ring-road, r_2: traffic-jam $\rightarrow \neg$ ring-road, r_3 : $\rightarrow r_2 < r_1$, r_4: no_alternative_route $\rightarrow r_1 < r_2 \}$. With this information, there is a unique maximal argument, which is both a specificity and a priority argument: $A = \{ \rightarrow f(A), \rightarrow t(C), \{f(A), t(C)\} \rightarrow rr, \rightarrow r_2 < r_1 \}$. The additional information that there is a traffic jam results in two maximal arguments: $A_1 = \{ \rightarrow f(A), \rightarrow t(C), \rightarrow tj, \{f(A), t(C)\} \rightarrow rr, \rightarrow r_2 < r_1 \}$ and $A_2 = \{ \rightarrow f(A), \rightarrow t(C), \rightarrow tj, tj \rightarrow \neg rr, \rightarrow r_2 < r_1 \}$. Both arguments are specificity arguments, but only A_2 is also a priority argument. Here the additional explicit priorities made it possible to select one of two equally specific extensions. However, if we don't know an alternative route, we get the following maximal arguments: $A_3 = \{ \rightarrow f(A), \rightarrow t(C), \rightarrow tj, \rightarrow nar, \{f(A), t(C)\} \rightarrow rr, \rightarrow r_2 < r_1 \}$, $A_4 = \{ \rightarrow f(A), \rightarrow t(C), \rightarrow tj, \rightarrow nar, \{f(A), t(C)\} \rightarrow rr, nar \rightarrow r_1 < r_2 \}$, $A_5 = \{ \rightarrow f(A), \rightarrow t(C), \rightarrow tj, \rightarrow nar, tj \rightarrow \neg rr, \rightarrow r_2 < r_1 \}$ and $A_6 = \{ \rightarrow f(A), \rightarrow t(C), \rightarrow tj, \rightarrow nar, tj \rightarrow \neg rr, nar \rightarrow r_1 < r_2 \}$. In this case, A_4 is the unique priority argument. Rule r_3 is defeated, just like the corresponding rule priority.

4. Future and Related Work

An extensive comparison with related formalisms goes behind the scope of this paper, but will be the subject of further research. For now, we will just give some directives following which this work can be extended.

The proposed mechanism for using implicit specificity information ressembles the approach of conditional entailment (CE)[7] . Both formalisms use implicit specificity information and can be considered to be credulous. The most significant difference between them is that CE allows contraposition, while our formalism doesn't. In other words, we interpret rules to be unidirectional, while rules in CE are considered to be classical logic formulae. Even if we restrict CE to a unidirectional interpretation, some differences can be found between both formalisms. In CE, a preference relation on models is derived, instead of on arguments. This means that CE loses the information explaining how such a model is obtained. However, if we concentrate on extensions, there seems to be a correspondence between models preferred in CE and our extensions, resulting from preferred arguments. The fact that implicit specificity information is used to extract an ordering on defaults before the ordering on models is derived, makes CE a less interesting framework to be extended with explicit priorities.

Other formalisms dealing with implicit specificity information can be considered as frameworks to be extended with additional priorities. A general approach to specificity has been suggested in[4] . This approach appeals to techniques used in System Z[12] . Although System Z has its weaknesses, it turns out that it can be satisfactorily used to isolate conflicting subsets of defaults and determine specificity relations among conflicting defaults. The idea is to consider so-called *minimal conflicting sets* : minimal sets of defaults for which a non-trivial Z-ordering exists, i.e. a partition consisting of more than a single set of rules. A partition of a minimal conflicting set C will always be binary, i.e. $C = C_0 \cup C_1$, where C_0 contains the more normal, or less specific, information. Those rules in C_0 and C_1 which can be responsible for a conflict are called *minimal* ($\subseteq C_0$) and *maximal* ($\subseteq C_1$) *conflicting rules.* Based on this technique, a preference relation among maximal arguments can be defined by saying that $A_1 \leq A_2$ iff argument A_1 contains the maximal conflicting rules and argument A_2 the minimal conflicting rules of the same minimal conflicting set. By this definition, the redundancy problem will be avoided. However, different results are obtained, e.g. in the presence of rules with empty antecedents. Furthermore, the technique presented in[4] doesn't work when the set of defaults is not Z-consistent, i.e. when no Z-ordering exists. Our approach can also be used for Z-inconsistent sets of defaults, e.g. the set of defaults $\{ \rightarrow \neg p, \ \rightarrow \neg q, \neg p \rightarrow q, \neg q \rightarrow p\}$.

The most important feature of our approach is that it makes it possible to combine implicit and explicit priorities. System Z^+[8] is another formalism where the authors have recognized the difference between specificity preferences and priorities which are not specificity based and should be encoded on a rule-by-rule basis. However, in system Z^+, specificity can not be overriden. Furthermore, priorities are static: it is not possible to reason about priorities.

Acknowledgements

This research was supported by the ESPRIT III Basic Research Action No 6156 DRUMS II.

References

1. G. Brewka, "Preferred Subtheories: An extended logical framework for default reasoning," in *Proceedings IJCAI-89*, 1989.
2. G. Brewka, "Adding priorities and specificity to default logic.," Technical report, GMD, 1993.
3. G. Brewka, "Reasoning about priorities in default logic," in *Proceedings AAAI '94*, pp. 940-945, Seattle, 1994.
4. J.P. Delgrande and T.H. Schaub, "A general approach to specificity in default reasoning," in *Proceedings of the Fourth International Conference on Knowledge Representation and Reasoning, KR'94*, pp. 146-157, Morgan Kaufmann, 1994.
5. P. Geerts and D. Vermeir, "Prioritization in nonmonotonic reasoning and ordered logic: a comparative study," Technical Report 94-15, 1994.
6. P. Geerts, D. Nute, and D. Vermeir, "Ordered logic: defeasible reasoning for multiple agents," in *Decision Support Systems*, vol. 11, pp. 157-190, 1994.
7. H. Geffner, in *Default Reasoning: Causal and Conditional Theories*, The MIT Press, 1992.
8. M. Goldszmidt and J. Pearl, "System Z^+: a formalism for reasoning with variable-strength defaults," in *Proceedings AAAI-91*, pp. 399-404, 1991.
9. B.N. Grosof, "Generalizing Prioritization," in *Proceedings of the Second International Conference on Knowledge Representation and Reasoning, KR'91*, pp. 289-300, 1991.
10. R. Loui, "Defeat among arguments: A system of defeasible inference," *Computational Intelligence*, vol. 3, no. 2, pp. 100-106, 1987.
11. D. Nute, "Basic defeasible logic," in *Intensional Logics for Logic Programming*, ed. L. Farinas del Cerro, M. Pentonnen, pp. 125-154, Oxford University Press, 1992.
12. J. Pearl, "System Z: A natural ordering of defaults with tractable applications to nonmonotonic reasoning," in *Theoretical Aspects of Reasoning about Knowledge (TARK-III)*, pp. 121-135, Morgan Kaufmann, 1990.
13. J.L. Pollock, "Defeasible reasoning," *Cognitive Science*, vol. 11, pp. 481-518, 1987.
14. D. Poole, "On the comparison of theories: Preferring the most specific explanation," in *Proceedings IJCAI-85*, pp. 144-147, 1985.
15. G. Simari and R. Loui, "A mathematical treatment of defeasible reasoning and its implementation," *Artificial Intelligence*, vol. 53, pp. 125-157, 1992.
16. D. Vermeir, P. Geerts, and D. Nute, "A logic for Defeasible Perspectives," in *Proceedings of the Tubingen workshop on semantic nets, inheritance and nonmonotonic reasoning*, Tubingen, 1989.

Constructing Flexible Dynamic Belief Networks from First-Order Probabilistic Knowledge Bases

Sabine Glesner and Daphne Koller

Computer Science Division, University of California, Berkeley, CA 94720,
{glesner,daphne}@cs.Berkeley.EDU

Abstract. This paper investigates the power of first-order probabilistic logic (FOPL) as a representation language for complex dynamic situations. We introduce a sublanguage of FOPL and use it to provide a first-order version of *dynamic belief networks*. We show that this language is expressive enough to enable reasoning over time and to allow procedural representations of conditional probability tables. In particular, we define decision tree representations of conditional probability tables that can be used to decrease the size of the created belief networks. We provide an inference algorithm for our sublanguage using the paradigm of *knowledge-based model construction*. Given a FOPL knowledge base and a particular situation, our algorithm constructs a propositional dynamic belief network, which can be solved using standard belief network inference algorithms. In contrast to common dynamic belief networks, the structure of our networks is more flexible and better adapted to the given situation. We demonstrate the expressive power of our language and the flexibility of the resulting belief networks using a simple knowledge base modeling the propagation of infectious diseases.

1 Introduction

In recent years, *belief networks* (or *Bayesian networks*) [10] have emerged as the method of choice for reasoning under uncertainty. Belief networks utilize the underlying causal structure of the domain to make probabilistic reasoning practical, both in terms of knowledge representation and in terms of inference. The causal structure is represented graphically, as a directed acyclic graph. Each random variable of the modeled domain is represented by a node while edges represent direct causal influences between nodes. The topology of the network encodes a set of independence assumptions: that each node is independent of all its nondescendants given its parents. These independence assumptions allow us to concisely specify a joint probability distribution over the random variables in the network. It suffices to specify, for each node in the network, a *conditional probability table (CPT)*, which lists the probability that the node takes on each value given each possible combination of values for its parents. The structure of the network can also be used to make the probabilistic inference process more efficient. For example, the *join tree* algorithm, which is also used in our implementation, is a clustering method that has been implemented in the HUGIN system [1].

In spite of their success, belief networks have a significant limitation as a general framework for knowledge representation, since they lack the ability to generalize over (a potentially infinite set of) individuals. In fact, belief networks are essentially a probabilistic extension of propositional logic, and therefore do not even have the fundamental concepts of individuals, their properties, and the connections between them. In this paper, we use the theory of first-order probabilistic logic (FOPL) to overcome these difficulties. We show how FOPL can be used as a representation language for concisely describing *first-order belief networks*. We describe a sublanguage of FOPL, built over Prolog, and demonstrate its expressive power. In particular, we present a knowledge base modelling the propagation of infectious diseases. An example of another knowledge base, modeling the behavior of traffic, can be found in [4].

We present an inference algorithm for this language using the paradigm of *knowledge-based model construction*. This algorithm takes a knowledge base in our language and a particular situation and generates a standard belief network appropriate for this situation. More specifically, the algorithm takes a particular finite domain as input, and propositionalizes the knowledge base for that domain. It also takes a query Q and evidence E, and constructs a belief network with an appropriate structure. Standard belief network inference algorithms can then be used to derive probabilities for Q given E in the resulting network.

The paradigm of knowledge-based model construction from first-order schemata has been used before [2, 3, 5, 8, 6] (see also Sect. 2). There are a number of ways in which our approach extends some or all of these previous works.

First, our work focuses on dynamic domains, where we wish to represent a situation that changes over time. The standard approach for modeling such domains is using *dynamic belief networks*. The fundamental idea is to divide time into *time slices*, each representing the state of the world at a specific point in time. This state is described using some set of random variables; in general, each time slice in the network contains a copy of all these variables. Such a network is typically represented by describing the probabilistic relations between random variables in one time slice and the probabilistic relations between the random variables of two consecutive time slices. These are taken to be the same for all time slices. We use our first-order representation language to model these dynamic situations. Therefore, the networks resulting from our knowledge-based model construction process are *flexible dynamic belief networks* whose structure differs from one time slice to the other according to the given situation.

Our algorithm is based on the one given in [6]. There, the representation language does not allow a modular specification of the different influences on an event. For example, when modeling the propagation of infectious diseases, we want to specify the probability of infection from different sources separately, and then combine them as appropriate. As in [8, 5], our representation language allows a modular specification of the influences on each event in our system. These are then automatically combined by our system, using a combination function specified by the user. Typical combination functions are noisy-or, noisy-and, min, or max.

We also use the power of a first-order language to allow a compact functional representation of probabilities. Among other things, this allows us to represent continuous-valued variables in our framework. For example, we could have the location of a car be a Gaussian random variable whose mean depends on the location and velocity of the car at the previous time slice. Our first-order language is also rich enough to allow an easy specification of parameterized probabilities. For example, we could have the variance of this Gaussian depend on the width of the time slice, thereby allowing us to model the fact that the accuracy of our predictions decreases over time. The first-order character of the representation language can also be used to specify that certain variables should only appear in certain time slices. For example, we might have a variable denoting the weather appear less often (say once an hour). This can easily be specified in our language, and our algorithm will automatically generate networks with the appropriate structure.

The first-order character of our language can be used to formulate conditional probability tables very concisely. In particular, we can describe the CPT as a decision tree, thereby modeling situations where one variable affects another only in certain circumstances. For example, in certain circumstances the event "Person x has AIDS" might directly affect the event "Person y has AIDS", whereas in others it does not. Such a representation can be used by a knowledge-based model construction algorithm to produce much smaller networks tailored to specific circumstances.

2 FOPL and KBMC

The approach of first-order probabilistic logic puts a probability distribution on the set of possible worlds where a possible world is a model in the sense of classical first-order logic. In this framework it is possible to assign *probabilities* or *degrees of belief* to formulas which are true in some but not necessarily in all of the possible worlds. The degree assigned to a formula φ is the sum of the probabilities of those worlds in which φ is true. For the formal definitions we refer to [7]. FOPL is highly undecidable [7] but, as in first-order logic, it is possible to isolate interesting tractable cases. In the paradigm of *knowledge-based model construction*, systems rely on a representation language based on FOPL; they take a knowledge base written in this language and reduce it, given a particular example (or instance), to a propositional model, mostly specified in form of a belief or decision network. This approach has been successfully used in various systems [2, 3, 5, 8, 6, 11]. The essential idea behind most of these approaches is the same, although the details differ. We describe the work of Haddawy and Krieger [6] both as a prototypical knowledge-based model construction approach and as the starting point for our own work.

Haddawy and Krieger present an algorithm for dynamically constructing belief networks from first-order probabilistic knowledge bases. The overall aim is to represent a class of propositional belief networks using a first-order knowledge base. They choose a subset of the FOPL language defined by Halpern in [7] thereby giving their approach a well-defined semantics. Their knowledge base represents the topology and conditional probability tables of a first-order belief network in the FOPL language. For example, such a network for part of the burglar alarm domain might have three nodes, *Alarm(x)*, *Neighbor(n,x)*, and *Call(n,x)*, and two edges, from *Alarm(x)* and from *Neighbor(n,x)* to *Call(n,x)*. This models that for each x and any neighbor n of x, n is likely to call x whenever x's alarm goes off. The CPT for such a network can easily be represented in FOPL. The CPT for the node *Call(n,x)* would be represented as a collection of formulas such as $\forall x, n \, \Pr(\mathit{Call}(n,x) \mid \mathit{Alarm}(x) \wedge \mathit{Neighbor}(n,x)) = p$, one for each possible combinations of parents' and child's values. We call $\mathit{Call}(n,x)$ the head and $\mathit{Alarm}(x), \mathit{Neighbor}(n,x)$ the body of this rule.

Haddawy and Krieger make the following four assumptions in order to maintain the correspondence between the knowledge base and the belief networks it encodes: (1) Each rule body must also appear as the head of some rule; (2) all variables in the body must appear in the head; (3) the knowledge base does not contain two distinct rules that have ground instances (ground instances contain no variables) with identical heads; (4) the knowledge base is acyclic, i.e., there does not exist a set of ground instances $R_1, \ldots, R_n$ of the rules in the knowledge base such that $\textit{head}(R_1) \in \textit{body}(R_2)$, $\textit{head}(R_2) \in \textit{body}(R_3), \ldots, \textit{head}(R_n) \in \textit{body}(R_1)$. While the first and last restrictions seem to be inherently necessary for the specification of first-order belief networks, the second and third jeopardize the applicability of the representation language in many domains. We will show in the following sections how to weaken them.

Haddawy and Krieger present an algorithm that takes a probabilistic first-order knowledge base together with a query and a set of evidence as input and outputs the minimal belief network that contains all information relevant to the query. The algorithm performs three major steps: First, backward chaining from the query is done to find all predecessors of the query. In the second step, backward chaining from all the evidence nodes is performed. In the third step, by forward and backward chaining from the query, all nodes that do not influence the query node (there is no active path between them) are pruned away. The result of the third step is the minimal network containing all information relevant to the query. The constraints on the language guarantee that the knowledge base defines a unique distribution over any finite domain. The above described procedure is sound and complete with respect to this distribution.

3 Representation Language

As in the previous works on knowledge-based model construction, our fundamental structure is essentially a first-order belief network. We have a network whose nodes are the atomic formulas $R(x_1, \ldots, x_n)$ in our language. Each node is described using a rule, which defines the influences on the event $R(x_1, \ldots, x_n)$, and the associated probabilities. For example, the topology of the above mentioned network would be represented in our language, which is a subset of the Prolog programming language, as

```
rule(calling,call(N,X),[neighbor(N,X),alarm(X)]).
```

We want to weaken the restrictions that Haddawy and Krieger posed on their language. Although we still require that every formula in the body of some rule matches with the head of some other rule, we provide the user a more expressive language to describe the CPTs (see below). The acyclicity requirement seems to be necessary to keep a well-defined joint probability function in the belief networks. We enforce acyclicity using time parameters. Every predicate has a time argument such that the time argument in the rule head is at least one time step later than the time arguments of the predicates in the rule body. This allows us to model situations where there are cyclic dependencies that manifest themselves over time. For example, in one of our knowledge bases, where we model the behavior of traffic, we formulate a rule

```
rule(hlocation,hloc(X,T),[hloc(X,Q),hvelo(X,Q)]) :- Q is T-1.
```

stating that the horizontal location of car X at time step T depends on the horizontal velocity and location of X one time step earlier.

The assumption that only one rule can match with an atomic formula seems too restrictive in many domains. In the AIDS knowledge base, the random variable `aids(X,T)` has the intended meaning that person X was infected with the HIV virus at time point T. There are two influences which we model in our knowledge base: whether X was already infected one time step earlier or whether X had contact with another person Y who was infected.

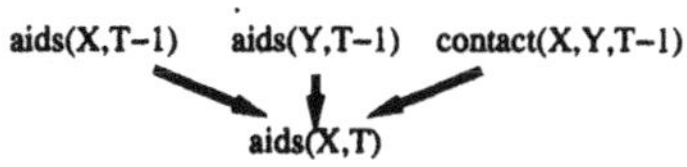

Fig. 1. Schema of the knowledge base for the AIDS domain

We represent these two influences using the construct of a *many-rule* which summarizes different influences on a random variable.

```
many_rule(aids,aids(X,T),[already_infected,sexual_contact]).
```

The third argument in this predicate is a statement containing the names of all rules that influence the head `aids(X,T)`.

In this example, we also want contact with different individuals Y to influence `aids(X,T)`. We therefore allow the head of a rule to contain variables that are not instantiated given a complete instantiation of the body. For example, in the rule above, it is not specified who the partner Y of X was, given only the instantiation of `aids(X,T)`. In principle, this free variable Y can be instantiated with every domain element. (This is the approach taken in our implementation.)

In both of these cases, we allow several rules or rule instantiations to influence a single random variable. In such cases, it is necessary to specify how the influences coming from different rules or rule instantiations should be combined. The combination functions are specified in combination statements. We allow noisy-or, noisy-and, min, and max. Noise-or is typically used to combine independent causes for an event. This is a good model for the AIDS domain, so that our knowledge base for that domain contains the assertion:

```
comb(aids,noisy_or).
```

Of course, we also need to specify CPTs for each individual rule. Haddawy and Krieger describe CPTs by stating a probability for each combination of parents' and child's values. We can do the same by using probability statements of the form

```
prob(calling,call,[neighbor,alarm],0.98).
```

Here, the name `calling` has to match with the name in a rule statement. The second argument is an instantiation of the head of the rule and the third argument is an instantiation of the body of the rule. The last argument states the probability for that specific instantiation. Our representation language also provides a far more expressive mechanism for specifying CPTs. It utilizes the first-order power of the language to describe the CPTs functionally. For example, in the case of the above mentioned many_rule in the AIDS knowledge base, if it is known that X was already infected in the previous time step, we do not need to take the values of the other parents into consideration. Our language allows such a functional representation by stating the probability statement as a Prolog routine:

```
prob(aids,Aids_X_T,[Aids_X_Q,Aids_Y_Q,Contact_X_Y_Q]) :
    % <Here comes the computation>.
```

In particular, we could use such a statement to represent CPTs as decision trees, as in Fig. 2. This allows us to model situations where, depending on the values which some of the random variables in the rule body take on, the head becomes independent of parts of the rule body. If we know, for example, that a person X was already infected with the HIV virus at time T-1, he will continue to be infected at time T. The HIV-infection status of other persons and their possible contacts with X are not relevant to the value of this variable. Similarly, the HIV-infection status of another person Y is not relevant if there was no contact between X and Y. The decision-tree representation allows us to model such situations concisely, and can also be used to prune the networks resulting from the knowledge-based model construction process (see below).

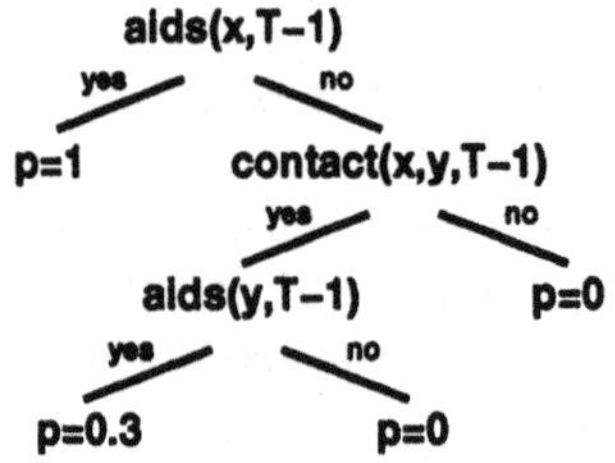

Fig. 2. CPT as a decision tree

We can also use the ability to specify CPTs functionally in other situations. In the traffic domain, for example, we model the random variables describing the location and the speed of a car as normally distributed random variables over the real numbers. The formalism of probability statements is able to capture this:

```
prob(hlocation,Head,Body,P) :- P is gaussian(U,V),
    % <computation for U and V>.
```

When constructing the propositional belief network, our implementation could express these variables as continuous-valued nodes. The inference on the resulting networks could be executed by stochastic simulation algorithms, since these are capable of doing inference in networks containing both discrete and continuous variables. In certain cases, the approach of [9] could also be used. Alternatively (although this is not yet implemented in our system), we could automatically discretize these nodes according to the user's specification.

4 Constructing the Models

Our network construction algorithm extends that of Haddawy and Krieger [6] to deal with procedural descriptions of CPTs and with modular specification of multiple influences on a node. In particular, our implementation allows more than one rule with the same head, and can also handle rules that have free variables in the body given the instantiated head. These variables are instantiated at run-time with all domain elements.

Roughly speaking, the algorithm works as follows. As in the algorithm of [6], it backward chains from the query and from the evidence. Each ground fact generated in this process forms a node A in the network. The parents of A are generated from the bodies of all the rules whose head match this ground fact. When the body of such a rule has free variables not instantiated in the head, these are instantiated with all possible domain elements. For each relevant rule, and for each instantiation of the variables, the algorithm computes the probabilities defined by each rule separately. Since these might be described procedurally (e.g., using a decision tree), this might require some computation. The influences from the different rules or rule instantiations are then combined using the combination function specified by the user. Our current implementation allows noisy-or, noisy-and, min, and max but this list is easily extendable. This completes the construction of the neighborhood of the node A (A, its parents, and the associated CPT). The backward chaining process then continues on the set of ground facts corresponding to A's parents. Finally, after the network is constructed, the d-separation criterion is used to prune the irrelevant parts of the network.

In Haddawy and Krieger's algorithm, the restrictions placed on the language guaranteed that the prior probability distribution is uniquely determined. Because of the use of combination rules and because of the use of time parameters to enforce acyclicity, this unique prior probability distribution property still holds for our extensions. Therefore the extended algorithm is sound and complete with respect to the distributions defined by our knowledge bases. (This is an easy extension of Haddawy and Krieger's theorem.)

In our implementation, we used two application domains as our main examples. The first domain models the propagation of infectious diseases; we used AIDS as our example. The second domain is a simple partial model of traffic behavior on highways; it emphasizes the random variable that a lane change is safe. For details of this second knowledge base, we refer to [4].

The first-order belief network structure for the AIDS knowledge base was given above in Fig. 1. As described in the previous section, our variables in this domain are `aids(X,T)` and `contact(X,Y,T)`. The probabilities for the `aids` rule are as specified in Fig. 2. The probability of `contact(X,Y,T)` is taken to be 0.1.

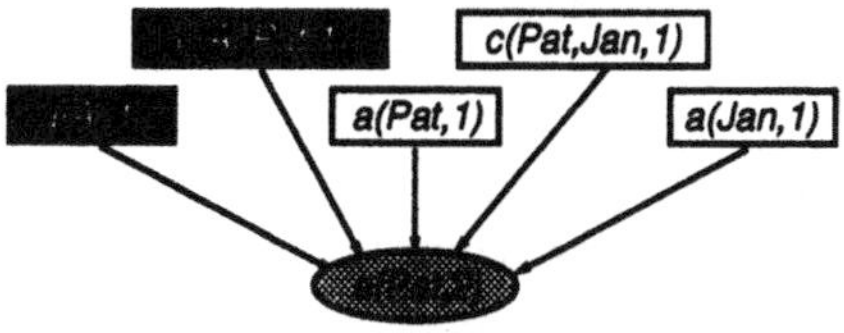

Fig. 3. Simple query for the AIDS knowledge base

Fig. 3 shows a flexible dynamic belief network produced by our algorithm from this knowledge base for a particular situation of interest. We mark evidence nodes by rectangles: black rectangles denote nodes that are set to true, and white rectangles nodes that are set to false. The query is denoted by a gray oval. In this example, we assume that the domain consists of three people: Al, Pat, and Jan. At time 1, Al is infected but Pat and Jan are not. Moreover we know that at this time point Al and Pat had contact with each other, but besides that there was no other contact. If we ask for the probability that Pat is infected at time 2, we get Fig. 3.[1] If we run this network on the HUGIN system, we obtain that the probability of `aids(Pat,2)` is 0.3.

The network changes considerably if we get the additional evidence that at time 3, Pat was diagnosed with the AIDS virus. We now have a significantly larger network for the same query, because other aspects of the problem become relevant. For example, Pat might have been infected via contact with Jan at time 2, so that Jan's HIV status (and its causes) becomes relevant. The network generated by our system is shown in Fig. 4. The resulting probability is 0.935.

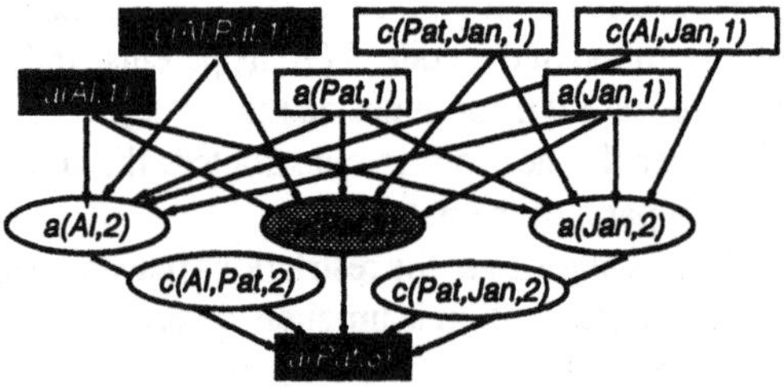

Fig. 4. Network for the same query with one additional piece of evidence

We mentioned in Sect. 3 that our language allows us to represent CPTs as decision trees. Although this is not yet implemented, the decision-tree representation can be used to prune the constructed belief network considerably. For example, we know that if an individual is infected at time `T-1`, he is also infected at time `T` independently of any other event. This would allow us to prune all the edges leading to the node `aids(Al,2)` except for the one from `aids(Al,1)`. Similarly, the fact that Jan had no contact with anyone at time 1 would allow us to prune some of the edges leading into `aids(Jan,2)`. Fig. 5 shows the network that would result from such a process. Since our system provides the infrastructure for the decision-tree representation, the implementation of the pruning routine should be straightforward.

[1] Currently, the knowledge base does not encode the fact the the `contact` relation is irreflexive and symmetric. Therefore, the network constructed by the algorithm would also contain the node `contact(Pat,Pat)`, which we have eliminated for clarity. A similar phenomenon occurs in Fig.s 4 and 5, where we have also eliminated the duplicate nodes resulting from symmetry (e.g., `contact(Pat,Al)`).

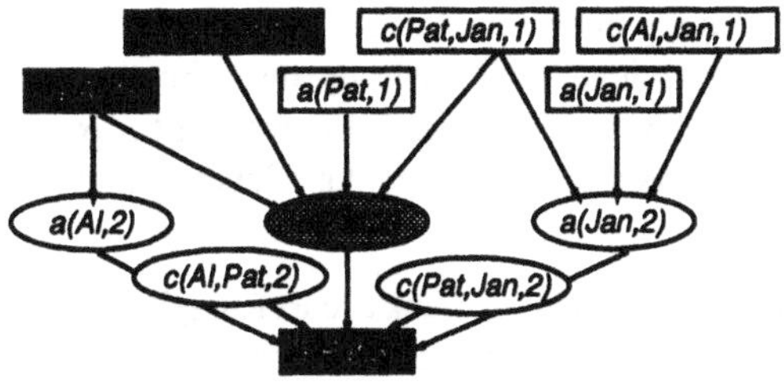

Fig. 5. The network obtained after pruning using the decision-tree representation

5 Conclusions and Further Work

In this paper we introduced a Prolog-based language for representing first-order dynamic belief networks. As our examples illustrate, this language is powerful enough to capture complex dynamic domains. In particular, it allows us to modularize the influences on an event and to combine them in different ways. It also allows us to use the first-order power of the language in representing the probabilities associated with an event. For example, we can easily provide a functional representation of the probabilities in the CPTs, which, in particular, allows us to easily include continuous random variables. We also described the implementation of an algorithm that takes knowledge bases in this format as input together with a query, evidence, and fixed domain and generates propositional dynamic belief networks. In contrast to standard dynamic belief networks, those resulting from our algorithm have a flexible structure that is adapted to the specific situation.

This ability to create flexible dynamic belief networks should have many other applications. In dynamic situations, we would often like to extend our current model further into the future, while "forgetting" things about the past. In the context of standard dynamic belief networks, new time slices are simply added to the existing network, while earlier time slices are marginalized into the newer ones. This process is called *roll-up*. It would be interesting to define a similar procedure for flexible dynamic belief networks, which would use our approach to generate new time slices with a structure that depends on the current situation. Such a flexible roll-up procedure would allow us to use our system in dynamic environments over time and not only for a given single situation.

We may also wish to model some variables more often than others. For example, it is probably not useful to update our weather variable five times a second, whereas such granularity is required when modeling vehicle behavior. The power of our representation language makes this very easy to accomplish. We can simply modify the rule corresponding to the weather variable so that the variable only exists in certain time slices (e.g., once every ten minutes), and update the rules for those variables that depend on the weather to refer to the latest copy of that variable. We could use the expressive power of the language to specify the required CPTs functionally, e.g., based on the time elapsed since the variable was last updated. This would allow us to treat frequency with which a particular variable is modeled as a parameter, and to change it without modifying the knowledge base. This may allow us to dynamically change this frequency, as required by the situation. For example, it is more important to provide accurate predictions for a nearby car that is changing lanes than for a distant car that is going at a steady rate. This idea can be combined with a flexible roll-up algorithm that creates new time slices as needed, thereby producing a very powerful paradigm for producing very compact flexible dynamic belief networks, where only the relevant variables are represented.

Acknowledgements We would like to thank Stuart Russell for many useful comments, and Timothy Huang and Keiji Kanazawa for helping us with information about the traffic domain. This research was supported by the German Fulbright Commission, the Studienstiftung des deutschen Volkes, a University of California President's Postdoctoral Fellowship, and an NSF Experimental Science Postdoctoral Fellowship.

References

1. S. K. Andersen, K. G. Olesen, F. V. Jensen, and F. Jensen. HUGIN—a shell for building Bayesian belief universes for expert systems. In *Proceedings of the Eleventh International Joint Conference on Artificial Intelligence (IJCAI-89)*, volume 2, pages 1080–1085, 1989.
2. Fahiem Bacchus. Using first order probability logic for the construction of bayesian networks. *Proceedings of the Sixth Conference on Uncertainty in Artificial Intelligence*, 1993.
3. John S. Breese. Construction of belief and decision networks. *Computational Intelligence*, 1992.
4. S. Glesner. Constructing flexible dynamic belief networks from first-order probabilistic knowledge bases. Master's thesis, Department of Electrical Engineering and Computer Science, University of California, Berkeley, 1994.
5. R. P. Goldman and E. Charniak. Dynamic construction of belief networks. *Proceedings of the Sixth Conference on Uncertainty in Artificial Intelligence*, pages 90–97, July 1990.
6. P. Haddawy and R. A. Krieger. Principled construction of minimal bayesian networks from probability logic knowledge bases. Submitted to Journal of AI Research.
7. J. Y. Halpern. An analysis of first order logics of probability. *Artificial Intelligence*, 46:311–350, May 1991.
8. M. C. Horsch and D. Poole. A dynamic approach to probabilistic inference using bayesian networks. *Proceedings of the Sixth Conference on Uncertainty in Artificial Intelligence*, pages 155–161, July 1990.
9. S. L. Lauritzen. Propagation of probabilities, means, and variances in mixed graphical association models. *Journal of the American Statistical Association*, 87(420):1098–1108, December 1992.
10. J. Pearl. *Probabilistic Reasoning in Intelligent Systems*. Morgan Kaufmann, 1988.
11. M. P. Wellman, J. S. Breese, and R. P. Goldman. From knowledge bases to decision models. *The Knowledge Engineering Review*, 7(1):35–53, November 1992.

On the Formalism of Stochastic Logic

Silviu Guiasu
Department of Mathematics and Statistics, York University
North York, Ontario, M3J 1P3, Canada

Abstract. Stochastic logic is a nonstandard logic that essentially takes interdependence and global connection into account. The present paper gives the basic operations and properties of this kind of nonstandard logic using the model provided by the stochastic sets defined by joint probability (or credibility) distributions. The Cantor sets are obtained when the joint distributions are degenerate.

1. Introduction

The stochastic logic proposed in this paper is a nonstandard logic. Its main aim is to take interdependence and connection into account and to deal with them in a global and flexible way. Such an attempt is motivated by the necessity of coping with uncertainty in dealing with real life problems. Uncertainty could have objective or subjective causes. Sometimes, the qualifications for being something are imprecise. Sometimes, the qualifications for being something else are precise, but there is real difficulty in determining whether or not certain subjects satisfy them. Stochastic logic, however, should not be identified to the standard probabilistic logic where the logical concept of probability replaces the two truth values (true, false) from the classical logic. Interdependence is universal and essentially influences the values of truth. When there is interdependence among entities, the degree of truth with which one of these entities satisfies a certain property depends in general on the degrees of truth with which the other entities satisfy that property or some other properties. Sometimes this interdependence is relatively weak and may be ignored, but when it is strong, such a simplification would distort reality.

The aim of this paper is to present basic properties of stochastic logic and the relationship between its concepts and the standard ones. The different probability distributions involved may be either objective, i.e. based on stable relative frequencies determined by repeating probabilistic experiments, or subjective, based on the principle of maximum uncertainty, for instance, in which case they are rather called credibility distributions. The formalism described has not been given a proof theory or a formal semantics. To the same extent to which Cantor's set theory offers a model for classical logic, the present paper gives the basic operations and properties of this kind of nonstandard logic using the model provided by the stochastic sets defined by joint probability (or credibility) distributions.

As mentioned above, the basic concept here is the joint distribution. If $X = \{x_1, x_2, \ldots, x_m\}$ is a set of interdependent entities and A, B are some properties, we start from an objective (or subjective) probability (or credibility) distribution on the joint statements of the form "entity x_1 has (or has not) properties A and B, *and* entity x_2 has (or has not) properties A and B, *and*,...,*and* entity x_m has (or has not) properties A and B". Such a joint distribution defines the stochastic set $A/X \otimes B/X$. From it, we can successively obtain the marginal stochastic sets A/X and B/X, their restrictions to subsets of entities, the complementary sets $\bar{A}/X, \bar{B}/X$, the intersection (logical operation 'and') $A \cap B/X$, the union (logical operation 'or') $A \cup B/X$, the inclusion, compatibility, similarity, De Morgan's realations, the law of double negation, the conditional stochastic sets, and the syllogisms. A stochastic set may induce belief, plausibility and fuzziness. Standard measures of uncertainty and global interdependence may be used in a natural way. The Cantor sets are obtained when the joint probability (credibility) distributions are degenerate.

A simple numerical example and the stochastic sets of murder suspects having motives and opportunity to murder from an Agatha Christie's detective story are also presented.

2. The Formalism

Basic joint stochastic set. Let $X = \{x_1, \ldots, x_m\}, Y = \{y_1, \ldots, y_n\}, \ldots$ be finite, not necessarily different, crisp sets of distinct entities. These sets are called universes. Let $A, B, \ldots$ be some properties or predicates, not necessarily different. The basic joint stochastic set $A/X \otimes B/Y \otimes \cdots$ is completely characterized by a joint membership probability (credibility) distribution $\chi_{A/X,B/Y,\ldots}$ on the binary crisp product set $\{0,1\}^m \times \{0,1\}^n \times \cdots$, showing the probability (credibility) that the entities of the given universes jointly satisfy or not the respective properties. If $m = 3$ and $Y = X$, for instance, then $\chi_{A/X,B/X}(1,0,0;1,0,1)$ is the probability (credibility) that entity x_1 satisfies both A and B, *and* x_2 does not satisfy A and B, *and* x_3 satisfies B but not A.

Restricted stochastic set. The restriction A/X of the basic joint stochastic set $A/X \otimes B/Y \otimes \cdots$ to property A and universe X is defined by the marginal membership probability (credibility) distribution $\chi_{A/X}$ obtained by saturating all the binary arguments of the joint membership probability (credibility) distribution $\chi_{A/X,B/Y,\ldots}$ except the first m ones, i.e.

$$\chi_{A/X}(i_1, \ldots, i_m) = \sum_{j_1,\ldots,j_n,\ldots \in \{0,1\}} \chi_{A/X,B/Y,\ldots}(i_1, \ldots, i_m; j_1, \ldots, j_n; \ldots).$$

The restriction of the stochastic set A/X to the crisp subset X^* of the universe X has as membership probability (credibility) distribution the marginal probability (credibility) distribution of $\chi_{A/X}$ relative to the elements of X^*. Thus, for instance,

$$\chi_{A/\{x_i\}}(k_i) = \sum_{k_1,\ldots,k_{i-1},k_{i+1},\ldots,k_m \in \{0,1\}} \chi_{A/\{x_1,\ldots,x_m\}}(k_1, \ldots, k_m)$$

represents the probability (credibility) that x_i has (if $k_i = 1$) or has not (if $k_i = 0$) property A regardless of what happens with the other entities of X. It defines the membership probability (credibility) distribution of $\chi_{A/X}$ to the subset $X^* = \{x_i\} \subset X$. The complement with respect to X of the stochastic set A/X^*, where $X^* \subset X$, is the stochastic set $A/(X - X^*)$. Thus, for instance, the complement of $A/\{x_i\}$ with respect to X is $A/\{x_1, \ldots, x_{i-1}, x_{i+1}, \ldots, x_m\}$ whose membership probability (credibility) distribution is

$$\chi_{A/\{x_1,\ldots,x_{i-1},x_{i+1},\ldots,x_m\}}(k_1, \ldots, k_{i-1}, k_{i+1}, \ldots, k_m) \\ = \sum_{k_i \in \{0,1\}} \chi_{A/\{x_1,\ldots,x_m\}}(k_1, \ldots, k_m).$$

Inclusion. The stochastic set A/X is included in the stochastic set B/X, i.e. $A/X \subset B/X$, relative to the basic stochastic set $A/X \otimes B/X$ if

$$\chi_{A/X,B/X}(i_1, \ldots, i_m; j_1, \ldots, j_m) = 0$$

whenever there is at least a pair (i_k, j_k), $(1 \leq k \leq m)$, such that $j_k = 0$ and $i_k = 1$.

Compatibility. Two stochastic sets A/X and B/X are compatible relative to the basic stochastic set $A/X \otimes B/X$ if $A/X \subset B/X$ and $B/X \subset A/X$.

Similarity. Two stochastic sets are similar, i.e. $A/X = B/X$, relative to the basic stochastic set $A/X \otimes B/X$, if $\chi_{A/X} = \chi_{B/X}$, which means $\chi_{A/X}(i_1, \ldots, i_m) = \chi_{B/X}(i_1, \ldots, i_m)$, for all values of $i_1, \ldots, i_m \in \{0, 1\}$. Obviously, $A/\{x_1, \ldots, x_m\} = A/\{x_1\} \otimes \ldots \otimes A/\{x_m\}$.

Induced fuzzy set. Let A/X be a stochastic set and let $A/\{x_1\}, \ldots, A/\{x_m\}$ its restrictions. The stochastic set A/X induces the fuzzy set whose membership function is $f_A : X \longrightarrow [0,1]$ defined by $f_A(x_i) = \chi_{A/\{x_i\}}(1)$.

Independent entities. The elements of universe X are independent with respect to property A if

$$\chi_{A/\{x_1,\ldots,x_m\}}(i_1, \ldots, i_m) = \chi_{A/\{x_1\}}(i_1) \cdots \chi_{A/\{x_m\}}(i_m). \tag{1}$$

Given a fuzzy set relative to property A defined by the membership function $f_A : X \longrightarrow [0,1]$, it generates the stochastic set A/X with independent entities whose membership probability (credibility) distribution is given by (1) where

$$\chi_{A/\{x_k\}}(1) = f_A(x_k), \; \chi_{A/\{x_k\}}(0) = 1 - f_A(x_k).$$

A crisp (Cantor) set A, i.e. the subset of X satisfying with certainty property A, is a particular stochastic set whose membership probability (credibility) distribution $\chi_{A/X}$ is degenerate, i.e. there is only one binary 0-1 vector $(k_1, \ldots, k_m)$ such that $\chi_{A/X}(k_1, \ldots, k_m) = 1$. The corresponding crisp subset of X is $A = \{x_i; k_i = 1\}$. Conversely, to any crisp subset $A = \{x_{i(1)}, \ldots, x_{i(r)}\} \subseteq X$ it corresponds the stochastic set $\chi_{A/X}$ for which $\chi_{A/X}(k_1, \ldots, k_m)$ is equal to 1 if $k_{i(1)} = \ldots = k_{i(r)} = 1, k_i = 0, (i \neq i(1), \ldots, i(r))$, and to 0 for all the other vectors $(k_1, \ldots, k_m)$.

Independent propositions. Two propositions A, B are independent with respect to the universe X if $\chi_{A/X,B/X} = \chi_{A/X}\, \chi_{B/X}$.

Intersection. If A/X and B/X are two stochastic sets then their intersection $A \cap B/X$ relative to the basic stochastic set $A/X \otimes B/X$ is the stochastic set having the membership probability (credibility) distribution defined by

$$\chi_{A\cap B/X}(i_1,\ldots,i_m) = \sum{}^{*} \chi_{A/X,B/X}(j_1,\ldots,j_m;k_1,\ldots,k_m) \tag{2}$$

where $\sum^{*}$ is taken in the following way: if $i_s = 1, (1 \le s \le m)$, then the sum contains all the terms for which $j_s = 1$ and $k_s = 1$; if $i_s = 0$, then the sum contains all the terms for which *either* $j_s = 1$ and $k_s = 0$ *or* $j_s = 0$ and $k_s = 1$, *or* $j_s = 0$ and $k_s = 0$. Obviously, if the two properties A and B are independent with respect to X then, in the above sum, $\chi_{A/X,B/X}$ should be replaced by the product$\chi_{A/X}\,\chi_{B/X}$.

Remark: If A and B are independent properties (predicates) with respect to X and the elements of universe X are independent with respect to these two properties (predicates) then, according to (2), the intersection of the fuzzy sets f_A and f_B induced by the stochastic sets $\chi_{A/X}$ and $\chi_{B/X}$, respectively, is

$$\begin{aligned} f_{A\cap B}(x_i) &= \chi_{A\cap B/\{x_i\}}(1) = \chi_{A/\{x_i\},B/\{x_i\}}(1;1) \\ &= \chi_{A/\{x_i\}}(1)\,\chi_{B/\{x_i\}}(1) = f_A(x_i)\,f_B(x_i), \end{aligned}$$

which, is a generalization for fuzzy sets of the usual intersection between crisp (Cantor) sets.

Union. If A/X and B/X are two stochastic sets then their union $A \cup B/X$ relative to the basic stochastic set $A/X \otimes B/X$ is the stochastic set having the membership probability (credibility) distribution defined by

$$\chi_{A\cup B/X}(i_1,\ldots,i_m) = \sum{}^{**} \chi_{A/X,B/X}(j_1,\ldots,j_m;k_1,\ldots,k_m) \tag{3}$$

where $\sum^{**}$ is taken in the following way: if $i_s = 0, (1 \le s \le m)$, then the sum contains all the terms for which $j_s = 0$ and $k_s = 0$; if $i_s = 1$, then the sum contains all the terms for which *either* $j_s = 1$ and $k_s = 0$ *or* $j_s = 0$ and $k_s = 1$, *or* $j_s = 1$ and $k_s = 1$. Obviously, if the two properties A and B are independent with respect to X then, in the above sum, $\chi_{A/X,B/X}$ should be replaced by the product $\chi_{A/X}\,\chi_{B/X}$.

Remark: If A and B are independent properties (predicates) with respect to X and the elements of universe X are independent with respect to these two properties (predicates) then, according to (3), the intersection of the fuzzy sets f_A and f_B induced by the stochastic sets $\chi_{A/X}$ and $\chi_{B/X}$, respectively, is

$$\begin{aligned} f_{A\cup B}(x_i) &= \chi_{A\cup B/\{x_i\}}(1) = \chi_{A/\{x_i\}}(1)\,\chi_{B/\{x_i\}}(0) \\ &\quad + \chi_{A/\{x_i\}}(0)\,\chi_{B/\{x_i\}}(1) + \chi_{A/\{x_i\}}(1)\,\chi_{B/\{x_i\}}(1) \\ &= f_A(x_j)\,[1 - f_B(x_j)] + [1 - f_A(x_j)]\,f_B(x_j) + f_A(x_j)\,f_B(x_j) \\ &= f_A(x_j) + f_B(x_j) - f_A(x_j)\,f_B(x_j), \end{aligned}$$

which, is a generalization for fuzzy sets of the usual union between crisp (Cantor) sets.

Distributivity. From the above definitions, if A, B, C are properties, then

$$A \cup (B \cap C)/X = (A \cup B) \cap (A \cup C)/X; A \cap (B \cup C)/X = (A \cap B) \cup (A \cap C)/X.$$

Complement. If A/X is a stochastic set and $\chi_{A/X}$ its membership probability (credibility) distribution, then its complement (or negation) with respect to property A is the stochastic set $\bar{A}/X$ whose membership probability (credibility) distribution is

$$\chi_{\bar{A}/X}(i_1, \ldots, i_m) = \chi_{A/X}(\bar{i}_1, \ldots, \bar{i}_m), \tag{1}$$

where $\bar{0} = 1$ and $\bar{1} = 0$. Also, if the joint membership probability (credibility) distribution $\chi_{A/X,B/X}$ is given, then

$$\chi_{\bar{A}/X,\bar{B}/X}(j_1, \ldots, j_m; k_1, \ldots, k_m) = \chi_{A/X,B/X}(\bar{j}_1, \ldots, \bar{j}_m; \bar{k}_1, \ldots, \bar{k}_m).$$

Remark: If $f_A : X \longrightarrow [0,1]$ is a fuzzy set on X, then the membership function of the complementary fuzzy set is $f_{\bar{A}} = 1 - f_A$. If the elements of X are independent then, according to (1), f_A and $f_{\bar{A}}$ completely determine the membership probability (credibility) distributions $\chi_{A/X}$ and $\chi_{\bar{A}/X}$ of the stochastic sets A/X and $\bar{A}/X$, respectively. As $\chi_{A/\{x_i\}}(k)$ is equal to $f_A(x_i)$ if $k = 1$ and to $1 - f_A(x_i)$ if $k = 0$, and $\chi_{\bar{A}/\{x_i\}}(k)$ is equal to $f_{\bar{A}}(x_i) = 1 - f_A(x_i)$ if $k = 1$ and to $1 - f_{\bar{A}}(x_i) = f_A(x_i)$ if $k = 0$, we have $\chi_{\bar{A}/\{x_i\}}(k) = \chi_{A/\{x_i\}}(\bar{k})$ and (1) implies (4).

De Morgan's relations. (a) $\overline{A \cup B}/X = \bar{A} \cap \bar{B}/X$;
(b) $\overline{A \cap B}/X = \bar{A} \cup \bar{B}/X$.

The law of double negation. $\bar{\bar{A}}/X = A/X$.

Conditional stochastic sets. If the joint stochastic set $A/X \otimes B/Y$ is given and A/X and B/Y are its restrictions to universes X and Y, respectively, then denote by $A/X \mid B/Y$ the family of conditional stochastic sets relative to property A in universe X given property B in universe Y, defined by the conditional membership probability (credibility) distributions

$$\chi_{A/X|B/Y}(i_1, \ldots, i_m \mid j_1, \ldots, j_n)$$
$$= \chi_{A/X,B/Y}(i_1, \ldots, i_m; j_1, \ldots, j_n)/\chi_{B/Y}(j_1, \ldots, j_n),$$

for those binary values of $j_1, \ldots, j_n$ for which the denominators are different from zero. In an abbreviated form, we can write the above equalities as $\chi_{A/X,B/Y} = \chi_{A/X|B/Y}\, \chi_{B/Y}$. A similar definition for $B/Y \mid A/X$, in which case $\chi_{A/X,B/Y} = \chi_{B/Y|A/X}\, \chi_{A/X}$. Thus, if $m = n = 2$, for instance, $\chi_{A/X|B/Y}(1, 0 \mid 0, 1)$ is the probability (or credibility) that x_1 has *and* x_2 has not property A *if* y_1 has not *and* y_2 has property B.

Syllogisms. (a) *Modus ponens:* Given $B/Y \mid A/X$, if A/X then B/Y, where

$$\chi_{B/Y}(j_1, \ldots, j_n) = \sum_{i_1, \ldots, i_m \in \{0,1\}} \chi_{B/Y|A/X}(j_1, \ldots, j_n \mid i_1, \ldots, i_m)\, \chi_{A/X}(i_1, \ldots, i_m).$$

The above equality may be abbreviated as $\chi_{B/Y} = \chi_{B/Y|A/X} \odot \chi_{A/X}$. Let us notice also that if $\chi_{A/X} \geq \alpha$ and $\chi_{B/Y|A/X} \geq \beta$, then $\chi_{B/Y} \geq \alpha\beta$.

(b) *Modus tollens:* Given $B/Y \mid A/X$, if B/Y then A/X,provided that the system of linear equations $\chi_{B/Y|A/X} \odot \chi_{A/X} = \chi_{B/Y}$ may be solved with respect to the unknown probability (credibility) distribution $\chi_{A/X}$.

Belief and plausibility induced by a stochastic set. Let A/X be a stochastic set with the membership probability (credibility) distribution $\chi_{A/X} : \{0,1\}^X \longrightarrow [0,1]$. The correspondence between the binary 0-1 vector $(i_1, \ldots, i_m)$ and the subset $\{x_j; i_j = 1\} \subseteq X$ induces the equivalence between $\{0,1\}^X$ and the class of all subsets of X, namely $\mathcal{P}(X)$. $\chi_{A/X}$ induces a probability (credibility) distribution on $\mathcal{P}(X)$, denoted by χ_A, i.e. $\chi_A(E) \geq 0, E \subseteq X$, $\sum_{E \subseteq X} \chi_A(E) = 1$. Let $\mathcal{F}_A$ be the class of focal subsets of X with respect to χ_A,

$$\mathcal{F}_A = \{E; E \subseteq X, \chi_A(E) > 0\} \subset \mathcal{P}(X).$$

The belief and plausibility induced by the stochastic set χ_A on $\mathcal{P}(X)$ are

$$Bel_A(E) = \sum_{F \subseteq E, F \neq \emptyset} \chi_A(F), \quad Pl_A(E) = \sum_{F \cap E \neq \emptyset} \chi_A(F),$$

for every nonempty $E \in \mathcal{P}(X)$. The standard definitions of the belief and plausibility functions assume that the basic probability assignment on $\mathcal{P}(X)$ has to be equal to zero for the empty subset of X. This is not the case here, as $\chi_A(\emptyset)$, which is $\chi_{A/X}(0, \ldots, 0)$, is not necessarily equal to zero. In our case, for each nonempty $E \subset X$ we have $\chi_A(\emptyset) + Bel_A(E) + Pl_A(X - E) = 1$.

Remark: As in the standard case, if the elements of $\mathcal{F}_A$ are nested, i.e. $E_1 \supseteq E_2 \supseteq \ldots$, then the belief and plausibility induced by χ_A on $\mathcal{P}(X)$ are called necessity and possibility, respectively.

Measures of uncertainty and interdependence. As the stochastic logic deals with membership probability (credibility) distributions, the classical measures of uncertainty may be used. Thus, denoting by $H(A/X)$ the Shannon entropy of the probability (credibility) distribution $\chi_{A/X}$, it gives the amount of uncertainty contained by this distribution.

Watanabe's measure of connection or interdependence between the restrictions A/X and B/Y of the joint stochastic set $A/X \otimes B/Y$ is

$$W(A/X \otimes B/Y; A/X, B/Y) = H(A/X) + H(B/Y) - H(A/X \otimes B/Y).$$

In particular, the amount of interdependence among the entities of the universe $X = \{x_1, \ldots, x_m\}$ with respect to property A is

$$W(A/\{x_1, \ldots, x_m\}; A/\{x_1\}, \ldots, A/\{x_m\}) = \sum_{i=1}^{m} H(A/\{x_i\}) - H(A/\{x_1, \ldots, x_m\}),$$

where $H(A/\{x_i\}) = -\chi_{A/\{x_i\}}(0) \ln \chi_{A/\{x_i\}}(0) - \chi_{A/\{x_i\}}(1) \ln \chi_{A/\{x_i\}}(1)$.

The entropic distance between the stochastic sets A/X and B/Y is

$$d(A/X, B/Y) = H(A/X \otimes B/Y) - W(A/X \otimes B/Y; A/X, B/Y).$$

Paradoxes. It is well-known that self-referential paradoxes appear in classical logic when there is a set for which a proposition A is both true and false, simultaneously. There is no such paradox in stochastic logic because each stochastic set is itself self-contradictory. In particular, the extreme events 'all the entities of the universe $X = \{x_1, \ldots, x_m\}$ have the property A' and 'no element of X has the property A' may be simultaneously possible when

$$\chi_{A/\{x_1,\ldots,x_m\}}(1, \ldots, 1) > 0, \text{ and } \chi_{A/\{x_1,\ldots,x_m\}}(0, \ldots, 0) > 0.$$

3. Examples

Numerical example. Using the notations from the previous section, let us take two entities, $X = \{x_1, x_2\}$, and two properties A, B. Given the stochastic set

$\chi_{A/X,B/X}$	.05	.06	.2	.1	.02	.0	.09	.1	.2	.05	.0	.06	.04	.01	.02	.0
$B : x_2$	0	1	0	1	0	1	0	1	0	1	0	1	0	1	0	1
$B : x_1$	0	0	1	1	0	0	1	1	0	0	1	1	0	0	1	1
$A : x_2$	0	0	0	0	1	1	1	1	0	0	0	0	1	1	1	1
$A : x_1$	0	0	0	0	0	0	0	0	1	1	1	1	1	1	1	1

we obtain from it

$\chi_{A/X}$	.41	.21	.31	.07
$A : x_2$	0	1	0	1
$A : x_1$	0	0	1	1

$\chi_{\bar{A}/X}$	.07	.31	.21	.41
$\bar{A} : x_2$	0	1	0	1
$\bar{A} : x_1$	0	0	1	1

$\chi_{A \cap B/X}$	.81	.11	.08	.00
$A \cap B : x_2$	0	1	0	1
$A \cap B : x_1$	0	0	1	1

$\chi_{A \cup B/X}$	.05	.08	.40	.47
$A \cup B : x_2$	0	1	0	1
$A \cup B : x_1$	0	0	1	1

Stochastic sets induced by evidence. In an Agatha Christie's detective story, Lord Edgware is murdered. The main characters are: j = Jane Wilkinson, an actress, the wife of Lord Edgware; c = Carlotta Adams, an actress who can perfectly impersonate j; b = Bryan Martin, an actor who loves j and is a friend of c; r = Captain Ronald Marsh, the nephew of Lord Edgware, in great need of money; s = Miss Carroll, Lord Edgware's secretary; d = Jenny Driver, the friend of c; g = Geraldine Marsh, Lord Edgware's daughter, who hated her father and is very fond of r; a = Duchess of Merton, an aristicrat old lady who wants to do anything possible in order to prevent the marriage of her religious son with j; h = Lord Edgware's handsome butler. The case is investigated by the detective Hercule Poirot. Let X_i be the universe of suspects at the i-th step of the investigation. Let M_i be the property 'having a motive to kill Lord Edgware at the i-th step of the investigation' and O_i the property 'having an opportunity to kill Lord Edgware at the i-th step of the investigation.' In his analysis, at each step of his investigation, Hercule Poirot applies Laplace's cautious Principle of Insufficient Reason, according to which if there is no reason to discriminate between the possible outcomes then the best strategy is to take them as being equally likely. The entities belonging to the intersection $M_i \cap O_i/X_i$, abbreviated as P_i/X_i, are the potential murderers of Lord Edgware at the i-th step of the investigation. Let us follow Hercule Poirot's steps in investigating the case:

Step 1: Evidence #1 {Jane wants her husband dead. Lord Edgware dies and Jane is seen at the place of the murder.} $\Longrightarrow X_1 = \{j\}$;
$\chi_{M_1/X_1,O_1/X_1}(1;1) = 1, \chi_{P_1/X_1}(1) = 1.$

Step 2: Evidence #1 and evidence #2 {Jane attended the dinner party at Sir Montagu Corner at the time when Lord Edgware was murdered.} $\Longrightarrow$
$X_2 = \{c\}$; $\chi_{M_2/X_2,O_2/X_2}(1;1) = 1$, $\chi_{P_2/X_2}(1) = 1.$

Step 3: Evidence #1, evidence #2, and evidence #3 {Carlotta dies and the letter sent to her sister incriminates Ronald.} $\Longrightarrow X_3 = \{c, r\}$;
$\chi_{M_3/X_3,O_3/X_3}(1,1;1,0) = 1/2$, $\chi_{M_3/X_3,O_3/X_3}(1,1;1,1) = 1/2$;
$\chi_{P_3/X_3}(1,0) = 1/2$, $\chi_{P_3/X_3}(1,1) = 1/2$.

Step 4: Evidence #1, evidence #2, and evidence #4 {Poirot discovers that a page was ingeniously removed from Carlotta's letter which now may incriminate any men not only Ronald.} $\Longrightarrow X_4 = \{c, r, b, h\}$;
$\chi_{M_4/X_4,O_4/X_4}(1,1,1,0;1,0,0,0) = 1/4, \chi_{M_4/X_4,O_4/X_4}(1,1,1,0;1,1,0,0) = 1/4,$
$\chi_{M_4/X_4,O_4/X_4}(1,1,1,0;1,0,1,0) = 1/4, \chi_{M_4/X_4,O_4/X_4}(1,1,1,0;1,0,0,1) = 1/4;$
$\chi_{P_4/X_4}(1,0,0,0) = 1/2$, $\chi_{P_4/X_4}(1,1,0,0) = 1/4$, $\chi_{P_4/X_4}(1,0,1,0) = 1/4$.

Step 5: Evidence #1, evidence #2, and evidence #5 {Poirot discovers that in Carlotta's letter the word ***he*** should be read ***she*** in which case the letter incriminates women not men.} $\Longrightarrow X_5 = \{c, a, d, g, s\}$;
$\chi_{M_5/X_5,O_5/X_5}(1,1,0,1,0;1,0,0,0,0) = \chi_{M_5/X_5,O_5/X_5}(1,1,0,1,0;1,1,0,0,0) = 1/5,$
$\chi_{M_5/X_5,O_5/X_5}(1,1,0,1,0;1,0,1,0,0) = \chi_{M_5/X_5,O_5/X_5}(1,1,0,1,0;1,0,0,1,0) = 1/5,$
$\chi_{M_5/X_5,O_5/X_5}(1,1,0,1,0;1,0,0,0,1) = 1/5$; $\chi_{P_5/X_5}(1,0,0,0,0) = 3/5,$
$\chi_{P_5/X_5}(1,1,0,0,0) = 1/5$, $\chi_{P_5/X_5}(1,0,0,1,0) = 1/5$.

Step 6: Evidence #1, evidence #5, and evidence #6 {Jane's humiliating gaffe about the judgment of Paris ('Paris?' she said. 'Why, Paris doesn't cut any ice nowadays. It's London and New York that count.') at Widburns' luncheon party at Claridge's distroys evidence #2, revealing that the sophisticated "Jane", who delighted the guests at the dinner- party at Sir Montagu Corner with her deep knowledge about the Greek mythology, was not the real Jane but Carlotta, the impersonator.} $\Longrightarrow X_6 = \{j\}$; $\chi_{M_6/X_6,O_6/X_6}(1;1) = 1$; $\chi_{P_6/X_6}(1) = 1$.

And Jane Wilkinson is arrested. She confesses murdering Lord Edgware.

References

1. B. Bouchon-Meunier: La logique floue. Paris: Presses Universitaires de France 1993
2. A. Christie: Lord Edgware dies. New York: Berkley Books 1984 (first published by Grosset & Dunlap in 1933)
3. D. Dubois, H. Prade: Fuzzy sets and systems. New York: Academic Press 1980
4. S. Guiasu: A unitary treatment of several known measures of uncertainty induced by probability, possibility, fuzziness, plausibility, and belief. In B. Bouchon-Meunier, L. Valverde, R.R. Yager (eds.): Uncertainty in intelligent systems. Amsterdam: North-Holland 1993, pp. 355-366
5. S. Guiasu: Fuzzy sets with inner interdependence. Information Sciences 79, 315-338 (1994)
6. S. Guiasu: Reaching a verdict by weighting evidence. In P.P. Wang (ed.): Advances in Fuzzy Theory and Technology, vol.2, Raleigh, North Carolina: Bookwrights 1994, pp. 167-180

Using Default Logic in Information Retrieval

Anthony Hunter

Department of Computing, Imperial College, London, UK

Abstract. Information retrieval involves uncertainty. In an information system, the user is not certain about the contents of the information system, and the system is not certain about the users needs. Information retrieval is about bridging this gap. In this paper, we show how this uncertainty problem can be addressed by using default logic.

1 Introduction

The aim of information retrieval is to provide a user with the "best possible" information from a database. The problem of information retrieval is determining what constitutes the best possible information for a given user. A common form of interaction for information retrieval is for the user to offer a set of keywords. These are then used by the information retrieval system to identify information that meets the users needs. For example, in a bibliographic database, a user might be interested in finding papers on some topic. The keywords would be an attempt to delineate that topic. This then raises key issues of precision (ensuring that a significant proportion of the items retrieved are relevant to the user) and recall (ensuring that a significant proportion of the relevant items are retrieved).

1.1 Statistical analysis versus semantic analysis

In order to determine how well matched an item in a database is for a query, most formal approaches to modelling the uncertainty in information retrieval use statistical information about keywords in the database. For example, a keyword in common between an item and a query, that occurs more in the item than in any other item, is a distinguishing feature of that item, and hence can increase the posterior probability that the item is of relevance to the user. A variety of such discriminating factors based on statistics have been proposed to quantify the similarity between items and queries (see for example Salton 1989, van Rijsbergen 1979).

Using probability theory has proven to be of significant value, and a variety of interesting proposals have been made including the probability ranking principle (Robertson 1977), and the binary independence model (van Rijsbergen 1989). Whilst there are a variety of problems with probabilisitc approaches (see for example Turtle 1995), we focus on the problem of the under-use of semantic information. In statistical analysis, the relationship between keyphrases is established by frequency ratios, whereas in semantic analysis, the relationship is established by "meaning". Not using semantic information is wasting valuable information that could be critical in matching a users needs to the information in the database. For example, suppose a search is undertaken using the keyword *car*, it would miss all items that only have the keywords *automobile* and *motor-car*. Similarly, suppose a search is undertaken using the request *computer-network or academic-communications*, an excessive number of items might be retrieved, whereas what might have been actually of interest to the user was the more specialized subject *internet*. Therefore, what is required is some formal representation of the semantic interrelationships between concepts, together with some ability to interpret users intended meanings when presenting requests.

1.2 The need for more than a thesaurus

Thesauri are widely-used tools in information retrieval. Essentially, a thesaurus is a database where for each keyword, there is a listing of synonyms, more specialized keywords, more general keywords, and related keywords. Usually they are not automated tools. Rather they are used directly by the user for consultation, with the onus being on the user to interpret and utilize the information in the course of composing a request.

In order to capture semantic information more fully in information retrieval, we need to automate the information in the thesaurus. In addition, we need more sophisticated information. In particular, we need context sensitivity. For example, suppose we have the keyword *car*. Then usually we would usually be interested in the synonym *automobile*. An exception would be if we also had the keyword *railway*. In which case we would usually be interested in the synonym *wagon*.

The lack of context dependency is one example of how there is no formal machinery for using thesauri. For automating the use of semantic information, we need to be able to specify when any particular specialization, generalization, synonym, or related term for a keyword can be used. Furthermore, we need to be able to extend this to resolving ambiguity such as arising from polysemes.

Previous approaches to semantic analysis in information retrieval do not provide a sufficiently expressive formal framework for exploiting semantic information. Yet, it is possible to use (non-monotonic) logics to handle semantic information about keywords, and so to identify logical relationships between items and queries. A logic-based approach can provide a richer alternative to probabilistic approaches.

In the following sections, we consider default logic as a formalism for semantic information in information retrieval. Default logic was proposed by Reiter (1980), and good reviews are available (Besnard 1989), and (Brewka 1991). Default logic, and variants, have well-understood properties including complexity and expressivity analyses. Whilst default logic is computationally problematical in the worst case, there are useful tractable subsystems. There is also promising work in approximations that is likely to provide, in the next few years, good quality reasoning with more appealing computational properties. In addition, viable theorem proving technology is now being developed, that should lead to robust inference engines in the next couple of years.

2 Using default rules for semantic information

In this section, we provide a framework, based on default logic, for capturing semantic information about keywords.

2.1 Keyphrase level

Let $\mathcal{K}$ be the usual set of formulae formed from a set of propositional letters and the connectives $\{\neg, \vee, \wedge\}$. We call $\mathcal{K}$ the set of keyphrases, and call any literal in $\mathcal{K}$ a keyword. The item keyphrase is a conjunction of literals. Intuitively this means the item contains information relating to each positive literal, and does not contain information relating to each negative literal. The request keyphrase is a specification by the user of what is of interest, and can be any formula in $\mathcal{K}$.

A factor in deciding whether an item is of interest to user, is whether the item keyphrase classically implies some or all of the request keyphrase. For example, take the item keyphrase α, and the request keyphrase $\alpha \vee \beta$, then the item would be of interest by this factor.

The choice of keyphrase can affect the recall and precision of the retrieval. A keyphrase might be based on concepts too general, or too specialized, or may fail to incorporate important synonyms. For each keyphrase, it is important to consider whether a more general, or specialized keyphrase should be used, or whether it should be used with some synonym, or even replaced by some synonym. We call this reasoning activity positioning.

2.2 Positioning for keyphrases

In order to formalize positioning for an item keyphrase, we assume semantic information is represented as a set of default rules. For this, let $\mathcal{L}$ be the set of predicates formed as follows: If α is a propositional letter in $\mathcal{K}$, then $in(\alpha)$ is in $\mathcal{L}$ and $out(\alpha)$ is in $\mathcal{L}$. Intuitively, $in(\alpha)$ is an argument for α being in the positioned keyphrase, and $out(\alpha)$ is an argument for α not being in the positioned keyphrase. We form the usual set of formulae from $\mathcal{L}$ and the connectives $\{\neg, \wedge, \vee\}$. We then form the default rules from $\mathcal{L}$ as usual.

For a default theory (D,W), D is some set of default rules and W is the smallest subset of $\mathcal{L}$ such that if α is a positive literal in the item keyphrase, then $in(\alpha)$ is in W.

For positioning, two important types of default rules are expansion and contraction. Expansion, of which the following is an example, intuitively states that if there is an argument for α being in the positioned keyphrase, then there is an argument for γ being in the positioned keyphrase.

$$\frac{in(\alpha) : in(\beta)}{in(\gamma)}$$

Contraction, of which the following is an example, intuitively states that if there is an argument for α being in the positioned keyphrase, then there is an argument for γ not being in the positioned keyphrase.

$$\frac{in(\alpha) : out(\beta)}{out(\gamma)}$$

The positioned keyphrase is generated as follows, where E is an extension generated as usual from (D,W).

$$keywords(E) = \{\alpha \mid in(\alpha) \in E \wedge out(\alpha) \notin E\}$$

If $keywords(E) = \{\alpha_1, .., \alpha_i\}$, then the positioned keyphrase is $\alpha_1 \wedge .. \wedge \alpha_i$. In this way the arguments 'for' and 'against' some α being in the positioned keyphrase are such that the arguments against α take precedence over arguments for α.

For example, suppose in a database of newspaper articles, we had an article with the item keyphrase, $mexico \wedge usa \wedge trade$. A reasonable generalization could be captured by the following expansion default rule:

$$\frac{in(trade) \wedge (in(mexico) \vee in(usa) \vee in(canada)) : in(nafta)}{in(nafta)}$$

Assume the default theory (D,W) where D is the above default, and W is $\{(in(mexico), in(usa), in(trade)\}$. Since $in(trade) \wedge (in(mexico) \vee in(usa) \vee in(canada))$ follows classically from W, and $in(nafta)$ is consistent with W, and the consequents of the defaults applied, then $in(nafta)$ holds. Hence the positioned keyphrase becomes $mexico \wedge usa \wedge trade \wedge nafta$.

In this example, we have positioned by using only one default rule. In practice, we would require many default rules.

2.3 Types of positioning

For a keyphrase β, we consider three types of positioning. These are defined, using the classical consequence relation $\vdash$, as follows, where β^* is the positioned keyphrase.

$$\text{(Strengthening) } \beta^* \vdash \beta \text{ and } \beta \not\vdash \beta^*$$

$$\text{(Weakening) } \beta^* \not\vdash \beta \text{ and } \beta \vdash \beta^*$$

$$\text{(Shifting) } \beta^* \not\vdash \beta \text{ and } \beta \not\vdash \beta^*$$

The intuitive nature of strengthening and weakening is clear. In shifting it is usually the case that there is some γ such that $\beta \vdash \gamma$ and $\beta^* \vdash \gamma$, and γ is only slightly weaker than both β and β^*. We show this by examples.

Suppose in our article database, we have an article with the item keyphrase, $in(olive) \wedge in(oil) \wedge in(cooking)$. A reasonable specialization could be captured by the following default rule.

$$\frac{in(oil) \wedge in(cooking) : in(\neg petroleum)}{in(\neg petroleum)}$$

Since $in(oil) \wedge in(cooking)$ follows classically from the item keyphrase, and $in(\neg petroleum)$ is consistent with the original item keyphrase, and consequents of the defaults applied, then $in(\neg petroleum)$ holds. So the positioned keyphrase becomes $olive \wedge oil \wedge cooking \wedge \neg petroleum$. This strengthening limits the ambiguity of the keyword *oil*, since the positioned keyphrase wouldn't be concerned with articles about *petroleum*.

Now suppose in our article database, we have an article with the keyphrase, $rail \wedge car$. Since *car* might not be regarded as an optimal keyword, the following could be useful.

$$\frac{in(rail) \wedge in(car) : in(wagon)}{in(wagon)} \quad \frac{in(rail) \wedge in(car) : out(car)}{out(car)}$$

From this, the positioned keyphrase becomes $rail \wedge wagon$. This is an example of shifting, and in this case it is intended to limit the ambiguity of using the keyword *car*.

Finally, we consider an example of weakening. Suppose we in our article database, we have an article with the item keyphrase $computer\text{-}networks \wedge internet$. Since there are now many articles on computer-networks, it is perhaps better to focus on this article being about internet. This can be achieved by the following default.

$$\frac{in(computer\text{-}networks) \wedge in(internet) : out(computer\text{-}networks)}{out(computer\text{-}networks)}$$

From this, the positioned keyphrase becomes *internet*.

3 Obtaining default rules

In order to obtain default rules, we need a strategy for training (or generating) default rules, and for testing (or validating) them. We consider these processes in outline below.

3.1 The training process

Let $\mathcal{I}$ be some set of identification numbers for items, and $\mathcal{K}$ is the set of keyphrases. Let $\mathcal{R}$ be the set of pairs $(n, \beta_1 \wedge .. \wedge \beta_i)$ where $n \in \mathcal{I}$ and $\beta_1, .., \beta_i$ are keywords in $\mathcal{K}$. Let $\Gamma \subseteq \mathcal{R}$. Each keyword denotes a class in which the item n is a member, and so n is in the intersection of $\beta_1, .., \beta_i$. Now let Γ be a training set for deriving default rules. We regard the set of items (identification numbers) as a space that is divided by the classes generated by the keywords. Then we ask a user, or appropriate substitute, to consider this space of items and use their own keywords to classify the items. The default rules are derived from the mapping between how the item keyphrases classify the items, and how the user classifies the items.

For example, let Γ contain $(23, ford \wedge car)$, $(25, volvo \wedge car)$, and $(26, fiat \wedge automobile)$, and suppose the user classifies 23, 25, and 26 as *motorcar*. For this a default rule could be as follows.

$$\frac{in(car) \vee in(automobile) : in(motorcar)}{in(motorcar)}$$

We would then repeat this process for a number of users. This would allows us to capture a number of the synonyms, polysemes, and related terms that the users would expect when identifying items such as those found in the training set.

This process assumes that the training set is a reasonable approximation of the whole possible space of items. If not the default rules derived might cover an inadequate subset of the items, and furthermore, errors could be introduced. If there are significant examples missing, then exceptions to default rules might not be identified. This means default rules could be generated that could be applied in incorrect circumstances. The only guard against these problems is taking a sufficiently large training set and sufficiently large number of users. What constitutes "sufficiently large" can only be estimated by repeated training and testing cycles. In this sense, there is a commonality with knowledge engineering and inductive learning issues.

3.2 The testing process

To test, we assume a form of retrieval defined as follows, where $\Delta \in \wp(\mathcal{R})$, and $(n, \alpha) \in \mathcal{R}$. Let α be a request keyphrase.

$$\Delta \mid\!\sim_x (n, \alpha) \text{ iff } (n, \beta) \in \Delta \text{ and } match_x(\alpha, \beta)$$

where $match_x$, and hence $\mid\!\sim_x$, could be defined in a number of ways. We consider the following definitions in more detail here, called $match_1$ and $match_2$, where β^* is the positioned version of β.

$$match_1(\alpha, \beta) \text{ if } \beta \vdash \alpha$$

$$match_2(\alpha, \beta) \text{ if } \beta^* \vdash \alpha$$

The first definition is classical, or Boolean, retrieval. For both definitions, an item is retrieved only if its keyphrase is totally exhaustive with respect to the request keyphrase.

For a test set Δ, we can ascertain the probabilities $p(retrieved_x)$, which is the proportion of items in Δ retrieved by $\mid\!\sim_x$, and $p(relevant)$, which is the proportion of items in Δ that are relevant. We assume that items are classified as *relevant* or $\neg$*relevant* by some oracle. We also assume that if the training process is successful, then we have the following inequalities,

$$[1]\ p(relevant \wedge retrieved_2) > p(relevant \wedge retrieved_1)$$

$$[2]\ p(relevant \mid retrieved_2) > p(relevant \mid retrieved_1)$$

In [1] and [2], we make explicit the assumption that after training positioning is better at retrieving relevant items than Boolean retrieval. Though of course, it is not necessarily the case that the following holds.

$$[3]\ p(retrieved_2) > p(retrieved_1)$$

Using these probabilistic terms, we can define recall and precision as follows.

$$precision_x = \frac{p(retrieved_x \wedge relevant)}{p(retrieved_x \wedge relevant) + p(retrieved_x \wedge \neg relevant)}$$

$$recall_x = \frac{p(retrieved_x \wedge relevant)}{p(retrieved_x \wedge relevant) + p(\neg retrieved_x \wedge relevant)}$$

From these definitions and assumptions, we can derive the following.

$$precision_2 > precision_1$$

$$recall_2 > recall_1$$

Note, if $p(retrieved_1 \wedge relevant)$ is already close to 1, then there seems to be little need to use positioning. The need for positioning increases as $p(retrieved_1 \wedge relevant)$ decreases.

4 Conclusions

The use of logic, and particularly default logic, offers a more lucid and more complete formalization of uncertainty between items and requests. In addition, statistical and syntactic information can also be presented as default rules. Clearly, qualitative abstractions of statistical information about relationships between keywords can be used. In addition, syntactical information is often of the form of heuristic rules, and hence can also be harnessed. To illustrate, consider that in English there are about 250 suffixes, and that heuristic rules can be identified for adding or removing these suffixes from words. Since a request keyword and item keyword might have the same stem, but different suffixes, they would not match without the hueristics to translate them into the same form.

Since the logic-based approach needs to be non-monotonic, and needs to formalize meta-level reasoning, terminological logics, such as MIRTL (Meghini 1993), that have been proposed for information retrieval, do not seem to be an adequate alternative to default logic. Elsewhere (van Rijsbergen 1986, Chiaramella 1992), a conditional logic with probabilistic semantics has been proposed to capture the uncertainty pertaining to pairs of items and requests. The work in this paper constitutes an improvement on that approach, since we are assuming some well-studies formalisms and analyses in non-monotonic logics. Another attempt to provide a logic-based framework for modelling information retrieval, dicusses in detail how strict co-ordinate retrieval and Boolean retrieval can be viewed logically (Bruza 1994). This complements the work presented here, since both pieces of work are contributions to an analysis of information retrieval at the level of the consequence relation, though the work here is more focussed on non-monotonic issues.

5 Acknowledgements

This work has been supported by the ESPRIT Defeasible Reasoning and Uncertainty Management Systems (DRUMS2) project. The author is grateful for discussions with Howard Turtle and Steve Robertson, and for feedback from Peter Bruza and Fabrizio Sebastiani.

6 References

Besnard Ph (1989) An Introduction to Default Logic, Springer

Brewka G (1991) Common-sense Reasoning, Cambridge University Press

Bruza P and Huibers T (1994) Investigating aboutness axioms using information fields, in Proceedings of the 18th ACM SIGIR Conference on Research and Development in Information Retrieval (SIGIR'94), ACM Press

Chiamaramella Y and Chevallet J (1992) About retrieval models and logic, The Computer Journal, 35, 233-242

Etherington D (1988) Reasoning with Incomplete Information, Pitman Press

Meghini C, Sebastiani F, Straccia U, and Thanos C (1993) A model of information retrieval based on a terminological logic, in Proceedings of the 16th ACM SIGIR Conference on Research and Development in Information Retrieval (SIGIR'93), 298-307, ACM Press

Reiter R (1980) A logic for default reasoning, Artificial Intelligence, 13, 81-132

van Rijsbergen C (1979) Information Retrieval, Cambridge University Press

van Rijsbergen C (1986) A non-classical logic for information retrieval, The Computer Journal, 29, 481-485

van Rijsbergen C (1989) Towards an information logic, in Proceedings of the 12th ACM SIGIR Conference on Research and Development in Information Retrieval, 77-86, ACM Press

Robertson S (1977) The probabiltiy ranking principle in information retrieval, Journal of Documentation, 33, 294-304

Salton G (1989) Automatic Text Processing, Addison-Wesley

Turtle H and Croft W (1995) Uncertainty in information retrieval, in Smets Ph and Motro A, Uncertainty Management in Information Systems: From Needs to Solutions, Kluwer

Sensitivity analysis in Bayesian networks

Finn V. Jensen[1], Søren H. Aldenryd[2], Klaus B. Jensen[2]

[1] Aalborg University, Dept. of Math. & Computer Science, DK-9000 Aalborg,
E-mail: fvj@iesd.auc.dk

[2] Systematic Software Engineering Inc., Søren Frichsvej 42 k, 8230 Aabyhøj,
E-mail: sha@systematic.dk & kbj@systematic.dk

Abstract. For systems based on Bayesian networks, evidence is used to compute posterior probabilities for some hypotheses. Sensitivity analysis is concerned with questions on how sensitive the conclusion is to the evidence provided. After the basic definitions and an example we conclude that the heart of sensitivity analysis is to compute probabilities for the hypotheses given various subsets of the evidence. We show how some of these probabilities come out as a side-effect of the HUGIN propagation method. Through a modification of the HUGIN method even more of the probabilities are achieved. Finally, we give methods for answering "what if"-questions, for determining the set of crucial findings, and determining minimal sufficient sets of findings.

1 Introduction

It is commonly agreed upon that any decision support system should have features for explaining how it has come up with its recommendations. Not only to help the user but also to establish confidence in the system.

For systems based on Bayesian networks, the explanation situation is that some evidence has been entered to the network, the probabilities of the variables have been updated, and now the user would like to have some kind of explanation of the connection between the evidence and the updated probabilities. There are roughly speaking three groups of explanatory questions:

Conflict analysis: Is the evidence coherent, and if not, can a conflict be traced?

Sensitivity analysis: How sensitive is the conclusion to the set of findings?

Path analysis: How is the chain of reasoning from evidence to conclusion?

Jensen, Chamberlain, Nordahl & Jensen (1991) define a measure of conflict which is easily calculated using the HUGIN propagation scheme. The INSITE explanation system by Suermondt (1992) extends this approach with a measure to be used when a particular hypothesis variable is in the focus of interest.

Spiegelhalter & Knill-Jones (1984) consider sensitivity analyses for simple Bayesian networks with a hypothesis variable on top and all findings being conditionally indpendent given the top variable. Due to this simple structure it is sufficient to measure the impact of each variable individually. Suermondt (1992) treats the general case of Bayesian networks, and he suggests to investigate the impact of all possible subsets of the given set og findings. This is exponential in the number of findings, and it is of course computationally unacceptable.

Path analysis for singly connected networks has been investigated by Henrion & Druzdel (1990). In Madigan & Mosurski (1993) it is described how path analysis can be performed on Berge networks. On these restricted classes of networks the methods are computationally efficient. Suermondt (1992) describes how path anlysis may be performed on Bayesian networks in general. However, the method described is computationally unacceptable on large networks.

So, for both sensitivity analysis and path analysis there is a need for computationally effective methods, and in this paper we shall present methods for sensitivity analysis.

2 Example and definitions

The following variant of a well-known example is used for illustration.

> In the morning when Mr Holmes leaves his house he realizes that his grass is wet. He wonders whether it has rained during the night or whether he has forgotten to turn off his sprinkler. He looks at the grass of his neighbours, Dr Watson and Mrs Gibbon. Both lawns are dry and he concludes that he must have forgotten to turn off his sprinkler.

The network for Holmes' reasoning is shown in Figure 1, and the initial probabilities are given in Table 1.

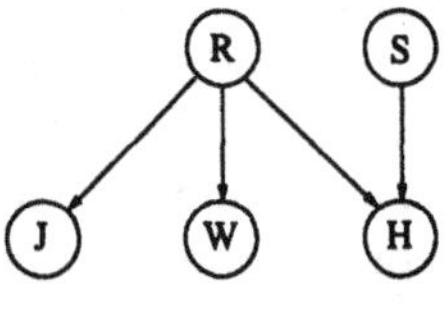

Fig. 1. Network for the wet grass example

The evidence e consists of the three findings e_H, e_W, e_J, and the hypothesis in focus is
h_s : "$S = y$". We have $P(h_s) = 0.1$, and $P(h_s \mid e) = 0.9999$.

We have $P(h_s \mid e_H) = 0.51, P(h_s \mid e_W) = 0.1 = P(h_s \mid e_J)$.[3] So neither e_W nor e_J alone have any impact on the hypothesis, but e_H is not sufficient for the

[3] A d-separation analysis (Geiger, Verma & Pearl 1990) could yield some of the results, however, this is not the point here.

Table 1. Tables for the wet grass example. $P(r) = (0.1, 0.9) = P(S)$.

	$R = y$	$R = n$
y	0.99	0.1
n	0.01	0.9

$P(J \mid R) = P(W \mid R)$

	$R = y$	$R = n$
$S = y$	(1, 0)	(0.9, 0.1)
$S = n$	(0.99, 0.01)	(0, 1)

$P(H \mid R, S)$

conclusion. Therefore the immediate conclusion that e_W and e_J are irrelevant for the hypothesis is not correct. We must conclude that evidence in combination may have a larger impact than the "sum" of the individual impacts.

To investigate further we must consider the impacts of subsets of the evidence. We have

$$P(h_s \mid e_W, e_J) = 0.1, P(h_s \mid e_H, e_J) = 0.988 = P(h_s \mid e_W, e_H)$$

To relate the probabilities above to their impact on the hypothesis we can divide them with the prior probability $P(h_s)$. This is the so-called *normalized likelihood.* It is called so because we by Bayes' rule have

$$\frac{P(h \mid e)}{P(h)} = \frac{P(e \mid h)}{P(e)}$$

We get the following normalized likelihoods:

(e_W, e_J, e_H) : 9.999; (e_W, e_H) : 9.88; (e_J, e_H) : 9.88; e_H : 5.1; the rest are 1.

We can conclude that though (e_W, e_J) alone has no impact on h_s these two findings cannot both be removed. Moreover, we see that the subsets (e_H, e_J) and (e_H, e_W) can account for almost all the change in the probability for h_s.

Definitions: Let e be evidence and h a hypothesis. Suppose that we want to investigate how sensitive the result $P(h \mid e)$ is to the particular set e.

We shall say that evidence $e' \subseteq e$ is *sufficient* if $P(h \mid e')$ is almost equal to $P(h \mid e')$. We then also say that $e \setminus e'$ is *redundant.* The term *almost equal* can be made precise by selecting a threshold θ_1 and require that $\left|\frac{P(h|e')}{P(h|e)} - 1\right| < \theta_1$. Note that $\frac{P(h|e')}{P(h|e)}$ is the fraction between the two likelihood ratios.

e' is *minimal sufficient* if it is sufficient, but no proper subset of e' is so.

e' is *crucial* if it is a subset of any sufficient set.

e' is *important* if the probability of h changes too much without it. To be more precise: if $\left|\frac{P(h|e\setminus e')}{P(h|e)} - 1\right| > \theta_2$, where θ_2 is some chosen threshold.

In the example above put $\theta_2 = 0.2, \theta_1 = 0.05$. Then (e_H, e_J) and (e_H, e_W) are minimal sufficient, (e_W, e_J) is important, and e_H is crucial.

3 Calculation of $P(h \mid e')$

As illustrated above, the heart of sensitivity analysis is the calculation of $P(h \mid e')$ for each $e' \subseteq e$. Since the number of subsets grows exponentially with the number of findings, the job may become very heavy, particularly when $P(h \mid e')$ has to be calculated through a propagation in a large network. Therefore we look for propagation methods which can yield easy access to $P(h \mid e')$. We shall call a subset e' *accessed* if $P(h \mid e')$ is achieved.

For single findings x we initially have $P(x)$. Now, enter h to the network and propagate. As a result we get $P(x \mid h)$. If the hypothesis h is a single finding we also have $P(h)$ initially, and if h is a compound set of findings $P(h)$ can be achieved as the normalizing constant for the propagation process (see e.g. (Jensen, Lauritzen & Olesen 1990)). By Bayes' rule we get $P(h \mid x)$.

To get $P(h \mid e')$ for sets of more than one finding it may seem that a full probability updating in the network is necessary for each subset e'. However, the propagation method may help us. We shall at first see what the HUGIN junction tree propagation method (Jensen et al. 1990) can give.

So, consider a junction tree over a triangulated graph where some evidence has been entered to it. In Figure 2 an example is given.

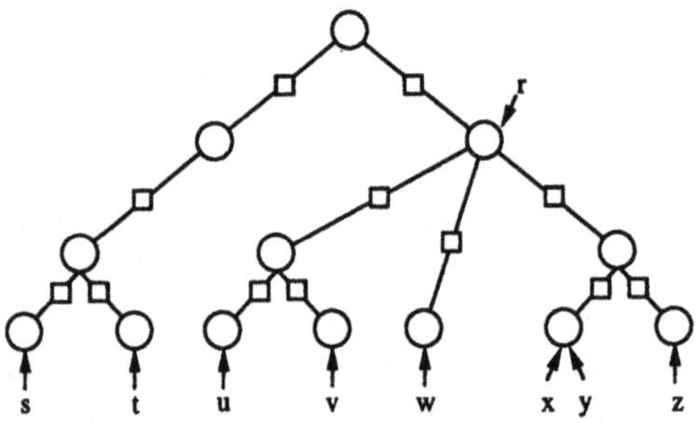

Fig. 2. A junction tree with evidence $e = \{r, s, t, u, v, w, x, y, z\}$ entered. The circles are nodes consisting of sets of variables, and the boxes are separators consisting of the intersection of the neighbouring nodes. The top node is the chosen root.

HUGIN propagation is performed in two phases, a *CollectEvidence* phase, where messages are sent from the leaves to a chosen root, and a *DistributeEvidence* phase, where messages are reversed. The content of the messages is explained below.

Consider the situation in Figure 3. Let the evidence e be divided by S into e_l and e_r.

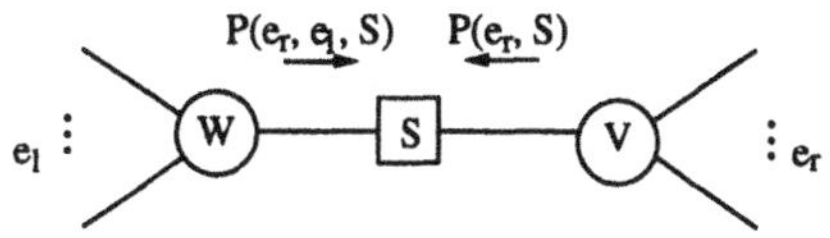

Fig. 3. The transmitted tables in a network where *CollectEvidence* is called at the left of W.

If *CollectEvidence* is called in a node at the left of W, the table to be transmitted from V to S is $P(e_r, S)$, and $\frac{P(e_r,S)}{P(S)}$ is transmitted further to W to be multiplied to $P(W)$. When later *DistributeEvidence* is activated, the table transmitted from W to S is $P(e_r, e_l, S)$ and $\frac{P(e_r,e_l,S)}{P(e_r,S)}$ is transmitted to V and multiplied to V's table ($\frac{0}{0}$ is set to 0).

Since $P(e_r, S)$ is calculated during propagation, we get

$$P(e_r) = \sum_S P(e_r, S).$$

Unfortunately, the situation is not symmetric. Due to 0's in $P(e_r, S)$ it is not in general possible to calculate $P(e_l, S)$ from $P(e_r, e_l, S)$, although e_r and e_l are independent given S.

Jensen (1995) presents a propagation method called *cautious propagation.* It is a modification of the HUGIN method to a architecture like (Shafer & Shenoy 1990), and it also incorporates *fast retraction* as proposed by Dawid (1992). The propagation method is called cautious because it does not change any table in the junction tree. Cautious propagation is slower than HUGIN propagation, normally by a factor 2 or 3 (varying with the topology of the junction tree), but it gives easy access to a large amount of $P(e')$s:

1. Each separator divides the evidence into two sets e_r and e_l. Cautious propagation gives access to both.
2. Each clique V with findings $f_1, \ldots, f_m$ entered and adjacent separators $S_1, \ldots, S_n$ divides the evidence into sets $\{f_1\}, \ldots, \{f_m\}, e_1, \ldots, e_n$. Cautious propagation gives access to any union of these sets. Note in particular that it gives access to $e \setminus \{f\}$ for any finding f.

In fact, for any clique V, cautious propagation places local to V the tables $P(e_i \mid S_i)$ and tables F_f for the findings f to multiply on $P(V)$. Then, for example

$$P(V, e_1, e_2, f) = P(V)P(e_1 \mid S_1)P(e_2 \mid S_2)F_f$$

In the example of Figure 2 cautious propagation gives access to

1. $\{s\}, e \setminus \{s\}, \{t\}, e \setminus \{t\}, \{u\}, e \setminus \{u\}, \{x\}, \{y\}, \{r\}, \{v\}, e \setminus \{v\}, \{w\}, e \setminus \{w\}$, $\{x, y\}, e \setminus \{s, y\}, \{z\}, e \setminus \{z\}, \{s, t\}, e \setminus \{s, t\}, \{u, v\}, e \setminus \{u, v\}, \{r, stuv, w\}$, $\{x, y, z\}$
2. $e \setminus \{x\}, e \setminus \{y\}, e \setminus \{r\}, \{s, t, r\}, \{u, v, w, x, y, z\}, \{s, t, u, v\}, \{r, w, x, y, z\}$, $\{s, t, w\}, \{r, u, v, x, y, z\}, \{s, t, x, y, z\}, \{r, u, v, w\}, \{r, s, t, u, v\}, \{w, x, y, z\}$, $\{r, s, t, w\}, \{u, v, x, y, z\}, \{r, s, t, x, y, z\}, \{u, v, w\}, \{s, t, u, v, w\}, \{r, x, y, z\}$, $\{s, t, u, v, x, y, z\}, \{r, w\}, \{s, t, w, x, y, z, \}, \{r, u, v\}$

To get $P(e' \mid h)$ for the same subsets we simply enter and propagate h before propagating e. Then all tables are conditioned by h, and Bayes' rule yields $P(h \mid e')$.

4 "What if"-questions, the set of crucial findings and minimal sufficient sets of findings

Consider the situation where evidence e has been entered and propagated cautiously. Assume that h is in the focus of interest, and that e also has been propagated in the junction tree conditioned on h.

Now, suppose we want to investigate the impact on h if a finding x is changed to y. This can be done for any finding without a new propagation. Let V be the clique to which the finding is entered. Due to cautious propagation, the situation is so that local to V we have $P(V), P(e_i \mid S_i)$ for all adjacent separators S_i, and tables F_f for the findings f to multiply on $P(V)$. It is then easy to substitute F_x with F_y and calculate $P(V, e \cup \{y\} \setminus \{x\})$ as the product of all tables local to V, and finally to marginalize V out to get $P(e \cup \{y\} \setminus \{x\})$. The same is done with the junction tree conditioned on h to get $P(e \cup \{y\} \setminus \{x\} \mid h)$.

Next, assume that the posterior probability of h is high and we want to determine the set of crucial findings. It may happen that some findings actually are evidence against h, but that they are overwritten by the entire set. We assume that the findings acting against h have been sorted out (can be done through $P(h \mid x)$ and $P(h \mid e \setminus \{x\})$ accessed through cautious propagation). For the remaining evidence we then can assume monotonicity: *No non-sufficient set contains a sufficient subset.*

If no proper subsets of e are sufficient then all findings are crucial. Else, the set of crucial findings is the intersection of all sufficient sets of the form $e \setminus \{x\}$. Suppose namely that x is not crucial, then due to monotonicity $e \setminus \{x\}$ is sufficient. On the other hand, if x is crucial then $e \setminus \{x\}$ cannot be sufficient.

When e is propagated cautiously, $P(h \mid e \setminus \{f\})$ can be calculated for all f, and thereby the set of crucial findings can be determined as the intersection of the sufficient subsets accessed.

A procedure for finding a minimal sufficient set of findings could be the following depth-first search.

1. Among the subsets e' accessed through cautious propagation, choose a sufficient set e_1^* with a minimal number of findings.
2. Enter e_1^* and perform a cautious propagation in an initialized junciton tree and in the one conditioned on h.
3. Perform steps 1 and 2 until no sufficient subset is accessed. The set entered last is a minimal sufficient set of findings.

The procedure terminates correctly due to the monotonicity assumption and the fact that all complements of single findings are accessed.

Take as an example the situation in Figure 2, and assume that $\{s, w, z\}$ is minimal sufficient. The search will then first identify $\{s, t, w, x, y, z\}$ as sufficient; next $\{s, w, z\}$ is identified, and finally it is concluded that $\{s, w, z\}$ is minimal sufficient. The search requires three pairs of cautious propagation.

The worst case for this search occurs when the evidence is entered as pairs of findings in leafs, and a minimal sufficient set consists of exactly one finding from each pair (see Figure 4).

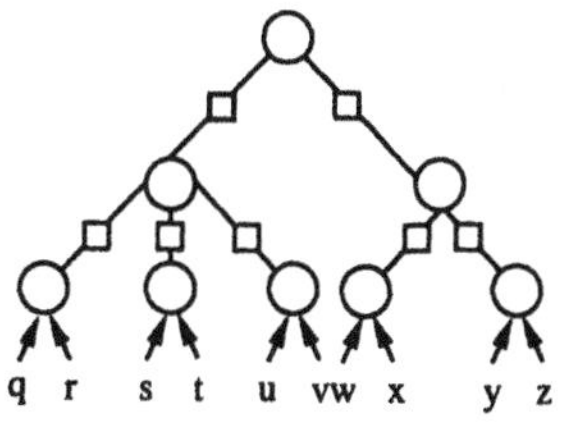

Fig. 4. A worst case for searching a minimal sufficient subset. $\{q, t, v, x, z\}$ is minimal sufficient. Six pairs of propagations are required.

In that case only one finding is removed in each round, and the search requires $n/2 + 1$ pairs of propagations.

If we want all minimal sufficient subsets, a breath-first search can be performed. If, in the example of Figure 2, $\{s, w, z\}, \{t, w, z\}, \{s, w, x, y\}$ and $\{t, w, x, y\}$ are minimal sufficient, then the sets to propagate are the following:

- initially e
- first round: $\{s, t, w, x, y, z\}, \{r, t, u, v, w, x, y, z\}, \{r, s, u, v, w, x, y, z\}, \{r, s, t, u, v, w, z\}, \{r, s, t, u, v, w, x, y, z\}$
- second round: $\{s, t, w, z\}, \{s, t, w, x, y\}, \{t, w, x, y, z\}, \{s, w, x, y, z\}, \{r, t, u, v, w, x, y\}, \{r, t, u, v, w, z\}, \{r, s, t, u, v, w, x, y\}, \{r, s, u, v, w, z\}$
- third round: $\{s, w, z\}, \{T, W, Z\}, \{s, w, x, y\}, \{t, w, x, y\}$

Altogether 18 pairs of propagation are required.

A worst case for searching all minimal sufficient subsets can be illustrated from Figure 4. Assume that all sets containing exactly one finding from the pairs $\{q,r\},\{s,t\},\{u,v\},\{w,x\}$ and $\{y,z\}$ are minimal sufficient. Then $3^5 = 243$ pairs of propagations are required. In the general case with n pairs of findings, 3^n pairs of propagations are required. This is seen in the following way: In the ith round we shall propagate sufficient subsets obtained by removing one finding from i pairs. So, in total we shall propagate all subsets, where we have removed 0 or 1 of two findings from each of the n pairs. This gives 3^n propagations.

Acknowledgements

Thanks to the ODIN group at Aalborg University (http:www.iesd.auc.dk/odin), in particular to Steffen L. Lauritzen, Stig K. Andersen and Søren Dittmer for valuable inputs and discussions. Also thanks to the anonymous referees for very constructive suggestions. This work is partially funded by the Danish Research Councils through the PIFT programme.

References

Dawid, A. (1992). Applications of a general propagation algorithm for probabilistic expert system, *Statistics and Computing* **2**: 25–36.

Geiger, D., Verma, T. & Pearl, J. (1990). d-separation: From theorems to algorithms, *in* M. Henrion, R. Shachter, L. Kanal & J. Lemmer (eds), *Uncertainty in Artificial Intelligence 5*, Elsevier Science Publishers.

Henrion, M. & Druzdel, M. (1990). Qualitative propagation and scenario-based approaches to explanation of probabilistic reasoning, *Proceedings of the 6th Conference on Uncertainty in Artificial Intelligence.*

Jensen, F. V. (1995). Cautious propagation in Bayesian networks, *Technical Report R-95-2004*, Aalborg University, Dept. of Mathematics and Computer Science.

Jensen, F. V., Chamberlain, B., Nordahl, T. & Jensen, F. (1991). Analysis in HUGIN of data conflict, *in* N.-H. Bonnisone et al. (ed.), *Uncertainty in Artificial Intelligence 6*, pp. 519–528.

Jensen, F. V., Lauritzen, S. L. & Olesen, K. G. (1990). Bayesian updating in causal probabilistic networks by local computations, *Computational Statistics Quarterly* **4**: 269–282.

Madigan, D. & Mosurski, K. (1993). Explanation in belief networks, *Technical report*, University of Washington, US and Trinity College, Dublin, Ireland.

Shafer, G. & Shenoy, P. (1990). Probability propagation, *Annals of Mathematics and Artificial Intelligence* **2**: 327–352.

Spiegelhalter, D. J. & Knill-Jones, R. P. (1984). Statistical and knowledge-based approaches to clinical decision-support systems, *Journal of the Royal Statistical Society, Series A* pp. 35–77.

Suermondt, H. J. (1992). *Explanation in Bayesian Belief Networks*, PhD thesis, Knowledge Systems Laboratory, Medical Computer Science, Stanford University, California, Stanford, California 94305. Report No. STAN-CS-92-1417.

Bayesian Approximation and Invariance of Bayesian Belief Functions

A. V. Joshi, S. C. Sahasrabudhe, K. Shankar

Electrical Engineering Department, Indian Institute of Technology,
Powai, Bombay, 400 076, India

Abstract. The Dempster-Shafer theory is being applied for handling uncertainty in various domains. Many methods have been suggested in the literature for faster computation of belief which is otherwise exponentially complex. Bayesian approximation is one such method. In this paper, we first present some results on invariance of Bayesian belief functions under Dempster's combination rule. Based on this, we interpret Bayesian approximation and further show that it inherits these properties from the combination operator of Dempster's combination rule. Finally, we bring into focus the limitation of Bayesian approximation.

1 Introduction

The Dempster-Shafer theory is quite popular in knowledge based applications. However, it's exponential computational complexity is a stumbling block. Several researchers worked on the problem of reducing the computational burden of the theory. The work in this direction was initiated by Barnett [1]. The approach of reducing the number of focal elements by certain approximation scheme was taken by Voorbraak [14], Dubois and Prade [2], and Tessem [13]. The work on propagation of belief in networks can be found in Gordon and Shortliffe [3], Shenoy and Shafer [10], Shafer and Logan [8], Shafer, Shenoy and Mellouli [9], Kohlas and Monney [6]. Kennes and Smets presented fast algorithms using möbius transforms [4, 5] and Wilson [15] gave a Monte-Carlo algorithm for belief computation. All these methods have given rise to efficient implementation of Dempster's combination rule.

Smets [11, 12] considered pignistic probability distribution based on belief function describing credal state for decision making. He arrived at this distribution based on axiomatic justification for generalized insufficient principle.

In this paper, we present results on invariance of Bayesian belief functions. These results help us to understand and interpret Bayesian approximation from a new perspective. In the light of this interpretation, we show that the properties of Bayesian approximation follow directly from the properties of the combination operator $\oplus$ of Dempster's combination rule. Further, given these set of properties, Bayesian approximation is unique in the class of approximations which can be obtained as a combination of Bayesian belief function and any other belief function. Finally, we show that Bayesian approximation has some limitations. Due to restrictions on number of pages, proofs of the theorem and corollaries are not included in this paper.

2 The Dempster-Shafer Theory

The Dempster-Shafer theory [7] assumes that the answer to a particular question lies in a finite set X, called *frame*. The elements of this set X are mutually exclusive and exhaustive. A mapping $m : 2^X \longrightarrow [0,1]$ satisfying

$$m(\emptyset) = 0; \tag{1}$$

$$\sum_{A \subseteq X} m(A) = 1 \ . \tag{2}$$

is called a ***basic probability assignment*** (BPA). A ***focal element*** is a subset of frame which has non-zero BPA. The union of all focal elements is termed as *core*. ***Total belief*** in a proposition $A \subseteq X$ is defined as:

$$Bel(A) \ = \ \sum_{B \subseteq A} m(B); \tag{3}$$

Thus, $Bel(A)$ is the sum of all BPA's which imply A. ***Plausibility*** of a proposition $A \subseteq X$ is defined as:

$$Pl(A) \ = \ 1 - Bel(\bar{A}); \tag{4}$$

Two belief functions Bel_1 and Bel_2 based on independent evidences bearing on a frame X can be combined using Dempster's rule combination. The combination rule is :

$$m(A) \ = \ \frac{\sum\limits_{B \cap C = A} m_1(B) \cdot m_2(C)}{1 - \sum\limits_{B \cap C = \emptyset} m_1(B) \cdot m_2(C)} \qquad \forall A \subseteq X \ . \tag{5}$$

provided, $\sum_{B \cap C = \emptyset} m_1(B) \cdot m_2(C) < 1$ where m_1 and m_2 are BPA's corresponding to Bel_1 and Bel_2 respectively.
A ***simple support function*** is a belief function with at most one focal element other than the frame itself. A ***separable support function*** is a simple support function or a combination of them. A belief function is said to be ***consonant*** if its focal element are nested. A ***vacuous*** belief function has frame as the only focal element.

3 Invariance of Bayesian Belief Functions

A Bayesian belief function, in simplest terms, is a belief function whose focal elements are singletons. It is mathematically defined in [7](p.44). One of the important property of Bayesian belief functions is that its combination with any other belief function (if they are combinable) is Bayesian. Shafer studied these belief function under the class of 'Quasi Support Functions' for they can always be obtained as the limit of a sequence of separable support functions. Here, we consider the problem of invariance of Bayesian belief functions under Dempster's rule of combination. In other words, if Bel_1 is a Bayesian belief function and Bel_2 is any other belief function, then, what should be the restrictions on Bel_2 such that the condition

$$Bel_1 \oplus Bel_2 = Bel_1 \tag{6}$$

holds? The following theorem gives the necessary and sufficient condition.

Theorem 1. *Let $X = \{x_1, x_2, \ldots, x_n\}$ be a frame and Bel_1 be a Bayesian belief function on this frame. If Bel_2 is any belief function on X, then*

$$Bel_1 \oplus Bel_2 = Bel_1$$

iff

$$\frac{\sum_{\substack{x_i \in A \\ A \subseteq X}} m_2(A)}{\sum_{B \subseteq X} m_2(B) \cdot |B|} = \frac{1}{n} \qquad i = 1, 2, \ldots n \ . \tag{7}$$

where $n = |X|$, m_1 and m_2 are BPA's corresponding to Bel_1 and Bel_2 respectively.

Alternatively, (7) can be written as

$$\frac{Pl_2(x_i)}{\sum_{x_i \in X} Pl_2(x_i)} = \frac{1}{n} \tag{8}$$

or

$$Pl_2(x_i) = \text{constant}, \qquad i = 1, 2, \ldots n \ .$$

What can we say about belief functions Bel_2 which satisfy (7) of Theorem 1? For the following corollaries, we assume that the frame consists of n elements.

Corollary 2. *Bel_2 is a vacuous belief function.*

Corollary 3. *if Bel_2 is Bayesian belief function, then*

$$Bel_2(x_i) = \frac{1}{n}, \qquad i = 1, 2, \ldots n \ .$$

Corollary 4. *Bel_2 is not a simple support function unless it is a vacuous belief function.*

Corollary 5. *Bel_2 is not a consonant belief function unless it is a vacuous belief function.*

Corollary 6. *Only the following kind of separable support function is possible: If Bel_2 is a separable support function induced by BPA m_2 such that A and B are its focal elements with $A \cap B = \emptyset$, $A \cup B = X$ then*

$$m_2(A) = m_2(B);$$

and

$$m_2(X) = 1 - m_2(A) - m_2(B)$$

Corollary 7. *If Bel_2 is a belief function with $\binom{n}{p}$ focal elements such that cardinality of each focal element is p, then,*

$$m_2(A) = \frac{1}{\binom{n}{p}} \qquad \forall A \subseteq X; \qquad 1 \leq p \leq n .$$

4 Bayesian Approximation

The Bayesian approximation gives a method of approximating any belief function by a Bayesian belief function. It was introduced by Voorbraak [14].

Definition 1. Let Bel be a belief function induced by the BPA m. The Bayesian approximation $[Bel]$ of Bel induced by the BPA $[m]$ is defined as:

$$[m](A) = \frac{\sum_{\substack{A \subseteq B \\ B \subseteq X}} m(B)}{\sum_{C \subseteq X} m(C) \cdot |C|}$$

if A is singleton; otherwise, $[m](A) = 0$.

Voorbraak showed that this approximation has following properties:

1. The maximum number of focal elements in the combination doesn't exceed $|X|$.
2. Combination of the approximation and approximation of combination give same results.
3. If Bel is Bayesian, then $[Bel] = Bel$.

$$[Bel] \oplus [Bel'] = Bel \oplus [Bel'] \tag{9}$$

$$= [Bel \oplus Bel'] \tag{10}$$

The definition of Bayesian approximation is similar to that of of 'relative plausibility' defined by Shafer [7] (p.205). While the definition of relative plausibility is defined for the class of support functions, Bayesian approximation is defined for any belief function. Nonetheless, if Bel is a support function then Shafer's [7] results, especially Theorem 9.7 and Theorem 9.8 (pp 205-206) are important.

5 An Interpretation of Bayesian Approximation

A closer look at the definition of Bayesian approximation and (7) reveals that they are precisely same. We can thus rephrase our Theorem 1 as:

Theorem 1. *Let X be a frame and Bel_1 be a Bayesian belief function on frame. If Bel_2 is any belief function on X and Bel_1 and Bel_2 are combinable, then*

$$Bel_1 \oplus Bel_2 = Bel_1$$

iff
Bayesian approximation of Bel_2

$$[m_2](x_i) = \frac{1}{n} \qquad \forall x_i \in X.$$

where m_1 and m_2 are the BPA's corresponding to Bel_1 and Bel_2 respectively.

We now show that Bayesian approximation can be viewed as a combination of belief function and a Bayesian belief function with equal basic probability mass on singletons.

Let $X = \{x_1, x_2, \ldots, x_n\}$ be a frame. If Bel_1 is a Bayesian belief function, Bel_2 is any other belief function and if they are combinable, then we can write

$$m_1 \oplus m_2(x_i) = \frac{\sum_{\substack{x_i \in B \\ B \subseteq X}} m_1(x_i) \cdot m_2(B)}{\sum_{\substack{i=1 \\ x_i \in B}}^{n} m_1(x_i) \cdot m_2(B)} \tag{11}$$

where m_1 and m_2 are the basic probability assignments corresponding to Bel_1 and Bel_2 respectively.

$$m_1 \oplus m_2(x_i) = \frac{m_1(x_i) \cdot \sum_{\substack{x_i \in B \\ B \subseteq X}} m_2(B)}{\sum_{\substack{i=1 \\ x_i \in B}}^{n} m_1(x_i) \cdot m_2(B)} \tag{12}$$

if we substitute, $m_1(x_i) = \frac{1}{n}; \quad n = |X|$
we obtain,

$$m_1 \oplus m_2(x_i) = \frac{\sum_{\substack{x_i \in B \\ B \subseteq X}} m_2(B)}{\sum_{\substack{i=1 \\ x_i \in B}}^{n} m_2(B)} \tag{13}$$

and we can easily prove the following identity

$$\sum_{\substack{i=1 \\ x_i \in B, B \subseteq X}}^{n} m_2(B) = \sum_{C \subseteq X} |C| \cdot m_2(C) \tag{14}$$

Thus we get,

$$m_1 \oplus m_2(x_i) = \frac{\sum_{\substack{x_i \in B \\ B \subseteq X}} m_2(B)}{\sum_{C \subseteq X} |C| \cdot m_2(C)} \tag{15}$$

It is important to note that the combination is a function of Bel_2 only. Expression (15), by definition, is Bayesian approximation of Bel_2. Hence, we arrive at an important conclusion:
Bayesian approximation of a belief function Bel_2 can be obtained by combining it with a Bayesian belief function Bel_1 such that
$Bel_1(x_i) = \frac{1}{n}, \ \forall\, x_i \in X; n = |X|$.

5.1 Properties

All the properties of Bayesian approximation can be obtained from the interpretation and results on invariance of Bayesian belief function dealt in the previous sections.

1. Let Bel_1 and Bel_2 be two combinable belief functions and bel is a Bayesian belief function with equal basic probability mass on each singleton. Then,

$$[Bel_1] \oplus [Bel_2] = (Bel_1 \oplus bel) \oplus (Bel_2 \oplus bel) \tag{16}$$
$$= (Bel_1 \oplus Bel_2) \oplus (bel \oplus bel) \tag{17}$$
$$= [Bel_1 \oplus Bel_2] \tag{18}$$

   since from Theorem 1 and Corollary 3, $bel \oplus bel = bel$.

2. If we rearrange Equation (17)

$$[Bel_1] \oplus [Bel_2] = Bel_1 \oplus (bel \oplus bel \oplus Bel_2) \tag{19}$$
$$= Bel_1 \oplus [Bel_2] \tag{20}$$
$$= Bel_2 \oplus [Bel_1] \tag{21}$$

   Equations (18), (20) and (21) are the properties which are true irrespective of the kind of belief function as long as they are combinable.

3. If Bel is Bayesian, then from Theorem 1,
   $[Bel] = Bel \oplus bel = Bel$

Notice that all the above properties were derived using commutativity and associativity property of the $\oplus$ operator. If we consider the set of approximations obtained by combining Bayesian belief function and a belief function, then such approximations, in general, do not satisfy the properties of Bayesian approximations. However, only Bayesian belief function with equal BPA for singletons combined with a belief function satisfy them. It is in this sense that Bayesian approximation is unique.

6 Limitations

Since a Bayesian approximation can be viewed as a combination of a Bayesian belief function with equal basic probability masses and a belief function to be approximated, it can only be used when the frame of discernment is rigid i.e. it doesn't undergo any refinement. Otherwise, as shown by Shafer [7] (example 9.2, p.208) one can obtain radically different degrees of belief. This severely restricts the applicability of Bayesian approximations.

7 Conclusion

In this paper we have given an interpretation to Bayesian approximation based on results of invariance of Bayesian belief functions. Also, we have shown that Bayesian approximation derives its properties from the combination operator of Dempster's combination rule. In the end, we have pointed out a limitation of Bayesian approximation.

Acknowledgements

This work was supported in part by Indian Space Research Organization. We are indebted to Prof. P.G.Poonacha, Electrical Engineering Department, I.I.T. Bombay for his valuable suggestions. We are also thankful to anonymous referees for their remarks and comments.

References

1. Barnett, J.: Computational methods for a mathematical theory of evidence, in Proceedings IJCAI-81, Vancouver, BC (1981) 868–875.
2. Dubois, D., Prade, H.: Consonant approximations of belief functions. Int. J. Approx. Reasoning. **4** (1990) 419–449.
3. Gordon, J., Shortliffe, E.: A method for managing evidential reasoning in a hierarchical hypothesis space. Artificial Intelligence. **26** (1985) 323–357.
4. Kennes, R., Smets, P.: Fast algorithms for Dempster-Shafer theory, in: Bouchon-Meunier B., Yager R.R., and Zadeh L. (eds.) Uncertainty in Knowledge Bases. Lecture Notes in Computer Science. **521** (Springer, Berlin, 1991) 14–23.

5. Kennes, R., Smets, P.: Computational aspects of the möbius transformation, in: Bonnisonne P.P., Henrion M., Kanal L.N. and Lemmer J.F. (eds.) Uncertainty in Artificial Intelligence. **6** (North-Holland, Amsterdam, 1991) 401–416.
6. Kohlas, J., Monney, P.: Propagating belief functions through constraints system, in: Bouchon-Meunier B., Yager R.R., and Zadeh L. (eds.) Uncertainty in Knowledge Bases. Lecture Notes in Computer Science. **521** (Springer, Berlin, 1991) 50–57.
7. Shafer, G.: A Mathematical Theory of Evidence (Princeton University Press, Princeton, NJ, 1976).
8. Shafer, G., Logan, R.: Implementing Dempster's rule for hierarchical evidence. Artificial Intelligence. **33** (1987) 271–298.
9. Shafer, G.,Shenoy, P., Mellouli, K.: Propagating belief functions in qualitative markov trees. Int. J. Approx. Reasoning. **1**, (1987) 349–400.
10. Shenoy, P., Shafer, G.: Propagating belief functions with local computations, IEEE Expert. **1:3** (1986) 43–52.
11. Smets, P.: Belief functions versus probability functions, in: Bouchon B., Saitta L. and Yager R. (eds.) Uncertainty and Intelligent Systems. Lecture Notes in Computer Science. **313** (Springer, Berlin, 1988) 17–24.
12. Smets, P.: Constructing the pignistic probability function in a context of uncertainty, in: Henrion M., Shachter R.D., Kanal L.N. and Lemmer J.F. (eds.) Uncertainty in Artificial Intelligence. **5** (North-Holland, Amsterdam, 1990) 29–39.
13. Tessem, B.: Approximations for efficient computation in the theory of evidence. Artificial Intelligence. **61** (1993) 315–329.
14. Voorbraak, F.: A computationally efficient approximation of Dempster-Shafer theory. Int. J. Man-Mach. Stud. **30** (1989) 525–536.
15. Wilson, N.: The combination of belief: when and how fast?, Int. J. Approx. Reasoning. **6** (May 1992) 377-388.

Model-Based Diagnostics Using Hints *

J. Kohlas, P.A. Monney, R. Haenni, N. Lehmann

Institute of Informatics
University of Fribourg
Regina Mundi
CH-1700 Fribourg
Switzerland

Phone: (+41 37) 298 322
Fax: (+41 37) 299 726
E-Mail: juerg.kohlas@unifr.ch

Abstract. It is often possible to describe the correct functioning of a system by a mathematical model. As long as observations or measurements correspond to the predictions made by the model, the system may be assumed to be functioning correctly. When, however, a discrepancy arises between the observations and the model-based predictions, then an explanation for this fact has to be found. The foundation of this approach to diagnostics has been laid by Reiter (1987). The explanations generated by his method, called diagnoses, are not unique in general. In addition, they are not weighed by a likelihood measure which would make it possible to compare them. We propose here the theory of hints – an interpretation of the Dempster-Shafer Theory of Evidence – as a very natural and general method for model-based diagnostics (for an introduction to the theory of hints, see (Kohlas & Monney, 1995)). Note that (Peng & Reggia, 1990) and (DeKleer & Williams, 1987) also discuss probabilistic approaches to diagnostic problems.

1 An Introductory Example

The problem is best introduced by an example. Figure 1 shows a logical circuit corresponding to a binary adder: in_1 and in_2 are the two bits to be added (in_3 is the carry bit from a previous addition) and out_1 is the sum of the three bits and out_2 is the carry bit of this sum. The components of this circuit are logical and-gates ($A1, A2$), exclusive or-gates ($X1, X2$) and an ordinary or-gate ($O1$). An and-gate is a device whose output is the logical conjunction of its two binary inputs, an exclusive or-gate puts 1 out if exactly one of its inputs equals 1 and an or-gate has as its output the logical disjunction of its two binary inputs. If the inputs $in_1 = 1, in_2 = 0$, $in_3 = 1$ and the outputs $out_1 = 1$ and $out_2 = 0$ are observed, then these observations are clearly in contradiction with the expected

* Research supported by grants No. 21-30186.90 and 21-32660.91 of the Swiss National Foundation for Research, Esprit Basic Research Activity Project DRUMS II (Defeasible Reasoning and Uncertainty Management).

behaviour of this system, namely $out_1 = 0$ and $out_2 = 1$. Therefore some gates are not working properly and the question is which ones.

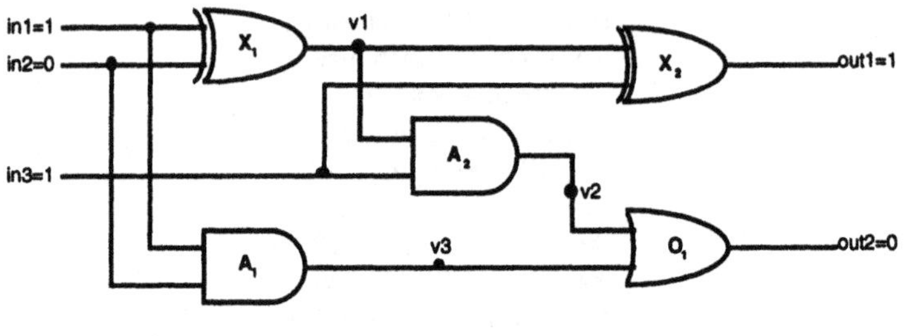

Fig. 1.

Reiter (1987) shows how certain selected subsets of components can be determined whose failure explains the discrepancy between observations and predictions. These are the possible diagnoses. More precisely, a diagnosis is a subset of components such that if they are assumed faulty and the other ones not faulty, then the consistency between the observations and the network is restored.

In contrast to this, the question we address here is how credible or plausible it is (in the sense of the Dempster-Shafer Theory of Evidence) that any given component is faulty or, more generally, how credible or plausible it is that at least one component is faulty in any particular subset of components. Thus both approaches are complementary: Reiter's method generates reasonable subsets of components to be investigated and the procedure presented below allows one to compute the credibility and plausibility that a subset actually contains a faulty component.

Suppose that there are known a priori probabilities for the failure of the components of the system. To be concrete, assume that all and-gates have the same probability of failure p_a, the exclusive or-gates the same probability of failure p_x and the or-gates the same probability of failure p_o, and that components fail independently from one another. Both input and output variables of a gate take values in the set $\Theta = \{0,1\}$ and the correct functioning of a gate is described by a relation between the input variables and the output variable, i.e. a relation $R \subseteq \Theta^3$. For an and-gate this relation is

$$R_a = \{(0,0,0),(1,0,0),(0,1,0),(1,1,1)\}, \tag{1}$$

for an exclusive or-gate

$$R_x = \{(0,0,0),(1,0,1),(0,1,1),(1,1,0)\} \tag{2}$$

and for an or-gate

$$R_o = \{(0,0,0),(1,0,1),(0,1,1),(1,1,1)\}. \tag{3}$$

But these relations hold only with probabilities $1 - p_a$ for an and-gate, $1 - p_x$ for an exclusive or-gate and $1 - p_o$ for an or-gate. In case of failure of a gate, one may assume for example that every combination of inputs and output is possible, which corresponds to the relation $R = \Theta^3$ in case of failure. Alternatively, one could also assume that in a failure mode the output is surely wrong, that is, for example, the relation

$$\{(0,0,1),(1,0,1),(0,1,1),(1,1,0)\} \tag{4}$$

for an and-gate, or that the output is always 0 for all inputs, etc. One could even allow for different failure modes corresponding to different input-output relations. Consider an and-gate with two possible operating modes $M_a = \{i, f\}$, where i stands for "the gate is intact" and f for "the gate is faulty". This determines the relation

$$\{(i,0,0,0),(i,1,0,0),(i,0,1,0),(i,1,1,1)\} \cup \{f\} \times \Theta^3 \tag{5}$$

in $M_a \times \Theta^3$. Such a relation can be considered as a constraint on $M_a \times \Theta^3$. So with each gate we associate a variable whose values are its possible operating modes. For example, the exclusive-or gate X1 in Figure 1 corresponds to the variable X1 taking values in $M_x = \{i, f\}$. A relation like the one given in (5) can be placed in the framework of hints (Kohlas & Monney, 1995) because a hint can be seen as an uncertain relation, i.e. with a known probability p_1 the relation R_1 holds, with a known probability p_2 the relation R_2 holds, etc... (the sum of all probabilities is 1). There are two interesting special cases. If there is only one relation (which must then hold with probability 1), then the hint is called deterministic. So the relation (5) defines a deterministic hint on $M_a \times \Theta^3$. The other special case is when every relation contains only one element. Then the hint is called precise. The a priori probabilities of the possible operating modes determine a precise hint (in the above example, probability $1 - p_a$ for i and probability p_a for f). Also, each observed value of a variable in the circuit defines a deterministic hint on $\Theta = \{0, 1\}$.

Now suppose that we want to know how credible it is that a particular gate of the circuit is faulty. Then all hints given above have to be combined by Dempster's rule and the resulting combined hint must be projected to the variable corresponding to that gate. This is a classical task in the Dempster-Shafer Theory of Evidence that can be carried out by doing local propagation in valuation networks (Shenoy, 1994). So the diagnostic problem considered in this paper can be solved by an application of Shenoy's valuation-based systems. The basic or fundamental structure of a valuation network is a Markov tree (or a hypertree) that is derived from a hypergraph. Let's see what this hypergraph is in the diagnostic problem considered here. Each uncertain relation is carried by a collection of variables in the circuit and these collections form the hyperedges of a hypergraph. The hypergraph corresponding to the system of Figure 1 is pictured in Figure 2. It has not an apparent hypertree structure and hence a covering hypertree has to be found first if we want to combine hints locally.

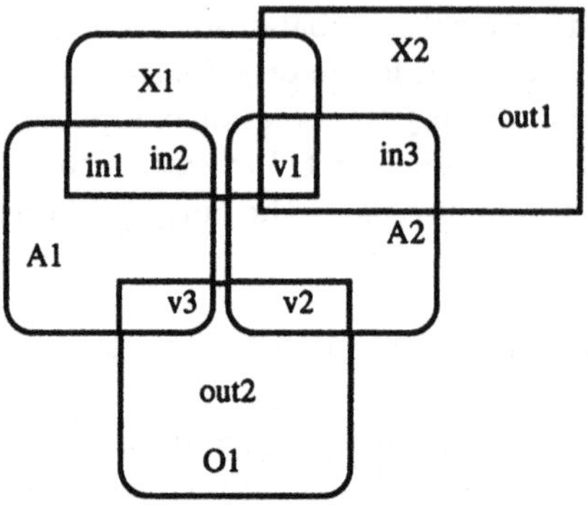

Fig. 2.

However, it will be shown below that in this type of problems a hypertree can always be obtained in a simple way.

Sets of components can also be studied in this framework. For example, consider the hypothesis that $X2$ and $A2$ are simultaneously faulty, or that $X2$ or $A2$ is faulty. To be able to judge these hypotheses, just add the new hyperedge $\{X2, A2\}$ to the hypergraph and let the vacuous hint be defined on it. Then, using a new covering Markov tree, propagate the hints locally to the hyperedge $\{X2, A2\}$. Hypotheses about $X2$, $A2$ can then be judged as usual with respect to the hint on $\{X2, A2\}$ obtained after completion of the propagation process. By the way, it can be shown that $\{X2, A2\}$ is a diagnosis in the sense of Reiter, and there are two other ones, namely $\{X1\}$ and $\{X2, O1\}$.

2 The General Model

The binary adder example already points out how a general system of model-based diagnostics, based on the theory of hints, can be designed. Let $C = \{c_1, c_2, \ldots, c_m\}$ be a set of components which are linked to each other in a network. The connections between components carry variables whose values must satisfy certain relations defined by the nature and the operating mode of the components of the system. Let $X = \{x_1, x_2, \ldots, x_n\}$ denote this set of variables. The possible values of a variable x_i form a set Θ_i called its frame. Each component c_j links a certain subset $X(c_j) \subseteq X$ of variables to which corresponds the product frame

$$\Theta(c_j) = \prod \{\Theta_k : x_k \in X(c_j)\}. \tag{6}$$

No distinction need be made for the purpose of the present analysis between input and output variables of a component.

Furthermore, with each component c_j is associated a set $M(c_j)$ of possible operating modes $\{m_0, m_1, \ldots, m_{rj}\}$ and we assume known a priori probabilities $p_j(m_h)$ on $M(c_j)$:

$$p_j(m_h) > 0; \sum \{p_j(m_h) : m_h \in M(c_j)\} = 1. \tag{7}$$

In general m_0 denotes the mode of correct functioning of the system, whereas $m_1, m_2, \ldots$ denote different failure modes. It is, however, also conceivable that a component has several different modes of correct functioning and several different failure modes. The probabilities (7) define a precise hint on the frame $M(c_j)$.

With each mode m_h of a component c_j is associated a relation $R_j(m_h) \subseteq \Theta(c_j)$ describing the possible values of the variables linked to the component, if the latter is in the operating mode m_h. This defines a relation

$$R_j = \{m_0\} \times R_j(m_0) \cup \{m_1\} \times R_j(m_1) \cup \cdots \subseteq M(c_j) \times \Theta(c_j) \tag{8}$$

between the frame of modes of c_j and the frame of the variables connected to c_j. This relation can be considered as a deterministic hint on $M(c_j) \times \Theta(c_j)$.

In addition to representing a component, let c_j also denote a variable whose possible values are in $M(c_j)$, i.e. the frame of the variable c_j is $M(c_j)$. Then the hints introduced so far define the hypergraph

$$\{\{c_1\} \cup X(c_1), \ldots, \{c_m\} \cup X(c_m)\} \tag{9}$$

over the variables $C \cup X$. In addition, a set of observed values o_j for the variables x_j in a subset $O \subseteq X$ is assumed to be available. If these observations are assumed to be precise and certain, then they correspond to deterministic and precise hints that have to be added to the model. However, more general models of observation may be adopted. Then the hyperedges $\{x_j\}$ for $x_j \in O$ have to be added to the hypergraph (this is not really essential as far as the search for a covering Markov tree is concerned because they are trivial hyperedges already contained in some $X(c_j)$).

Now suppose that we are interested in a particular subset D of components. Hypotheses about the operating modes of these components are represented by subsets of

$$\prod \{M(c_j) : c_j \in D\}. \tag{10}$$

So the new hyperedge D has to be included in the hypergraph and a covering Markov tree has to be found before the local propagation of the hints towards D (or its coverign hyperedge) can start. Then the resulting combined hint can be used to judge hypotheses represented by subsets of the frame 10. Note that since the combination of a precise hint with any other hint is again precise (Kohlas & Monney, 1995), the resulting hint on a subset of components is always precise. Of course we may not necessarily have a priori probabilities for the operating modes, but a more general hint. However, the solution principles presented above are still valid.

Besides the traditional heuristics to find a covering Markov tree, there is another trick that can be used when the observations are precise and deterministic. In the circuit of Figure 1, split the variable in_1 into two different varialbles in_{11} and in_{12} and link them to the gates $X1$ and $A1$ respectively. Also set the value of these variables to the value of in_1. If this splitting process is performed on in_2 and in_3 then one gets the network pictured in Figure 3.

Both networks are clearly equivalent as far as the diagnostic problem is concerned. The point is that the corresponding hypergraph, given in Figure 4, is now a hypertree that can be used to propagate hints locally.

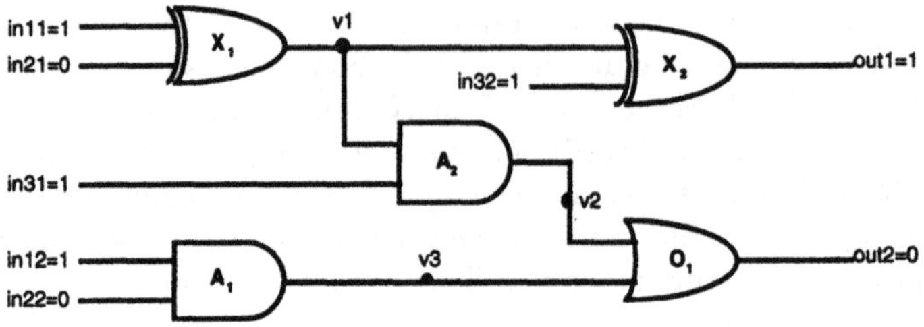

Fig. 3.

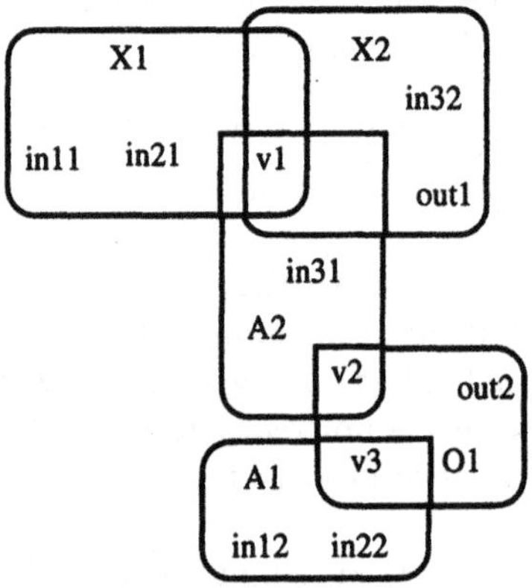

Fig. 4.

3 Numerical Examples

All examples in this section refer to the binary adder pictured in Figure 1. As already mentionned above, the resulting hints on the components are precise, i.e. the corresponding support and plausibility functions coincide and are probability measures. This means that for a single component it is sufficient to know the (a posteriori) probability that it is intact. We assume that the a priori probability that an and-gate is faulty is 0.01, for an exclusive-or it is 0.03 and for a regular or-gate it is 0.05. We will consider the five sets of observations given in Figure 5.

In addition, for every set of observation we consider two different behaviours of a faulty component. In case (A) we assume that the output of every component can be either 0 or 1, whereas in case (B) we assume that a faulty exclusive or-gate always produces 1 regardless of its input values, and a faulty or-gate or a faulty and-gate can again produce either 0 or 1. Figure 6 shows the a posteriori probability that a single component is intact in both cases (A) and (B) and for all five observation sets. Note that the last observation set is impossible in case (B) because $out1 = 0$ implies $X2$ is intact and hence $v1 = 0$ and hence $X1$ is

in1	in2	in3	out1	out2
1	0	1	1	0
1	1	0	1	0
1	0	1	0	0
1	1	0	0	0
0	1	0	0	1

Fig. 5. The five observation sets

intact. But since $in1 = 0$ and $in2 = 1$ and $X1$ is intact we should have $v1 = 1$, which is a contradiction.

Note that in case (A) with the first set of observations in Figure 5 (corresponding to those given in Figure 1), one should seriously consider checking the component $X1$ and in case (B) the components $X2$ and $O1$. Also note that the observation set number 2 gives the same results in both cases (A) and (B).

	X1	X2	A1	A2	O1
(A)	0.0546	0.9171	0.99	0.9814	0.9069
(B)	0.97	0	0.99	0.8319	0.1597
(A)	0.4924	0.4924	0.8319	0.99	0.1597
(B)	0.4924	0.4924	0.8319	0.99	0.1597
(A)	0.9564	0.9564	0.99	0.8343	0.1517
(B)	0.97	1	0.99	0.8319	0.1597
(A)	0.97	0.97	0.8319	0.99	0.1597
(B)	1	1	0.8319	0.99	0.1597
(A)	0.4924	0.4924	0.8549	0.8549	0.2744
(B)	-	-	-	-	-

Fig. 6. The a posteriori probability that a component is intact

4 Outlook

Even in a simple situation like the binary adder considered above (there are only five components) it is not at all easy to guess what components might be faulty. So the method discussed in this paper may prove very useful, especially if some decision procedures based on utility theory are introduced in order to actually decide what components to check and possibly replace. There are several interesting and important open questions to be addressed in this framework, like e.g. what is the next best measurement to make, or how should continuous input-ouput relations be treated. Finally, let's mention that the results presented here have been obtained by a computer program based on Shenoy's valuation networks developed by R. Haenni and N. Lehmann at the Institute of Informatics of the University of Fribourg.

References

DeKleer, J., & Williams, B.C. 1987. Diagnosing Multiple Faults. *Artificial Intelligence*, **32**, 97–130.

Kohlas, J., & Monney, P.A. 1995. *A Mathematical Theory of Hints. An Approach to the Dempster-Shafer Theory of Evidence.* Lecture Notes in Economics and Mathematical Systems, vol. 425. Springer.

Peng, Y., & Reggia, J. 1990. *Aductive Inference Model for Diagnostic Problem Solving.* Springer.

Reiter, R. 1987. A Theory of Diagnosis From First Principles. *Artificial Intelligence, Elsevier Science Publisher B.V. (Amsterdam)*, **32**, 57–95.

Shenoy, P. 1994. Using Dempster-Shafer's Belief Function Theory in Expert Systems. *Pages 395–414 of:* Yager, R.R., Kacprzyk, J., & Fedrizzi, M. (eds), *Advances The Dempster-Shafer Theory of Evidence.* Wiley.

An Axiomatic Approach to Extensional Probability Measures

Ivan Kramosil

Institute of Computer Science
Academy of Sciences of the Czech Republic
Pod vodárenskou věží 2, 182 07 Prague
Czech Republic
e-mail: kramosil@uivt.cas.cz

Abstract. Replacing the demand of countable additivity (σ-additivity), imposed on probability measures by the classical Kolmogorov axiomatic, by a stronger axiom, and considering only probability measures taking their values in the Cantor subset of the unit interval of real numbers, we obtain such an axiomatic system that each probability measure satisfying these axioms is extensional in the sense that probability values ascribed to measurable unions and intersections of measurable sets are functions of probability values ascribed to particular sets in question. Moreover, each such probability measure can be set into a one-to-one correspondence with a boolean-valued probability measure taking its values in the set of all subsets of an infinite countable space, e. g., the space of all natural numbers.

1 Introduction

Since the last two centuries probability calculus has continually played the role of the most powerful and most often used tool for uncertainty quantification and processing in various theoretical as well as practical domains of human activities. Kolmogorov probability theory conserved the main philosophical idea of all former probability calculi according to which probability values (or degrees) are related to the corresponding relative frequences of occurrences of certain random events in such a way that probabilities are the ideal and limit values of relative frequences, so that probabilities can be approximated, under certain conditions and in a certain sense, by appropriate relative frequences. Formalized mathematical expressions for this relation are the well-known laws of large numbers, known and proved also in the informal probability theory and respected also by the Kolmogorov axiomatic formulation.

However, due to the laws of large numbers the natural intensional (i. e., non-extensional) character of relative frequences has been transformed into the intensionality of probability measures. This is to say, in particular, that there do not exist binary functions F, G, taking pairs of real numbers from the unit interval $\langle 0,1\rangle$ into $\langle 0,1\rangle$ and such that for all random events A, B, for which their probabilities $P(A)$, $P(B)$ are defined, the equalities $P(A\cap B) = F(P(A), P(B))$, and $P(A\cup B) = G(P(A), P(B))$ would hold. Just as an example of an extensional calculus let us recall the classical propositional calculus, where the truthvalues of composed statements like "A and B" or "A or B" are defined by the well-known simple functions of truthvalues ascribed to A and B.

At least for two reasons the intensionality of probability measures leads to difficulties in practical applications of probability theory. First, the computations of probabilities of composed random events are of high computational complexity even if the set of marginal and conditional probabilities being at our disposal is rich enough to enable such a computation. Second, in the case when these probabilities are not known a priori and have to be estimated from a collection of statistical data or on the ground of subjective opinions of experts, it may be rather difficult to obtain good estimation of conditional probabilities with complicated and rarely occurring conditioning events. It is just because of these reasons that various extensional calculi for uncertainty quantification and processing like, e. g., fuzzy sets, have attracted the attention of specialists dealing with application of uncertainty processing methods, in spite of the lack of a bridge between uncertainty degrees and empirical results (like the laws of large numbers in probability theory), and in spite of difficulties involved by attempts to ontologize the uncertainty degrees, e. g., the membership degrees in the theory of fuzzy sets, and to find a natural and reasonable interpretation for them.

Consequently, it is perhaps not beyond any interest to ask, whether there exist probability measures which possess the property of extensionality, and, if the answer is affirmative, to characterize and investigate, in more detail, the class of such probability measures. In [5] we arrived at such probability measures by an appropriate numerical encoding of extensional boolean-valued probability measures taking their values in the set of all subsets of the set $\mathcal{N} = \{1, 2, \ldots\}$ of positive integers, and we stated and proved some simple results concerning the resulting extensional numerical probability measures. In what follows, we shall show that the class of such probability measures can be defined axiomatically, in a pattern strictly following that one applied in Kolmogorov axiomatic probability theory, just with the axiom of countable additivity (σ-additivity) replaced by a stronger one.

2 Strong Probability Measures

First of all, let us briefly recall and discuss the classical definition of probability measure.

Definition 1 Let Ω be a nonempty set. A nonempty system $\mathcal{A}$ of subsets of Ω is called *σ-field*, if it is closed with respect to the set-theoretic operations of complement and countable union, i. e., if for each sequence $A, A_1, A_2, \ldots$ of subsets of Ω which are in $\mathcal{A}$, also the sets $\Omega - A$ and $\bigcup_{i=1}^{\infty} A_i$ are in $\mathcal{A}$. The pair $\langle \Omega, \mathcal{A} \rangle$ is called *measurable space*.

Let $\mathcal{P}(\Omega) = \{S : S \subset \Omega\}$ denote the system of all subsets of Ω, i. e., the power-set over Ω (or: generated by Ω). As can be easily seen, $\{\emptyset, \Omega\}$ as well as $\mathcal{P}(\Omega)$ itself are σ-fields of subsets of Ω, here $\emptyset$ denotes the empty subset of Ω.

Moreover, the inclusions $\{\emptyset, \Omega\} \subset \mathcal{A} \subset \mathcal{P}(\Omega)$ obviously hold for each σ-field $\mathcal{A}$ of subsets of Ω.

Let $\langle 0,1 \rangle$ denote the closed unit interval of real numbers, let $\langle x_1, x_2, \ldots \rangle$ be an infinite sequence of non-negative real numbers (not necessarily from $\langle 0,1 \rangle$). Let $\sum_{i=1}^{\infty} x_i = \lim_{n\to\infty} \sum_{i=1}^{n} x_i$, if this limit value exists (i.e., if it is finite), let $\sum_{i=1}^{\infty} x_i = \infty$ otherwise, i.e., if $\sum_{i=1}^{n} x_i$ diverges. Obviously, $\sum_{i=1}^{\infty} x_i$ is defined for each sequence $\langle x_1, x_2, \ldots \rangle$ of non-negative real numbers.

$\langle A_1, A_2, \ldots \rangle$ is an infinite sequence of mutually disjoint sets, if $A_i \cap A_j = \emptyset$ holds for each $i, j \in \mathcal{N} = \{1, 2, \ldots\}$, $i \neq j$.

Definition 2 Let $\langle \Omega, \mathcal{A} \rangle$ be a measurable space. A real-valued function P defined on $\mathcal{A}$ is called *probability measure*, if it satisfies the following conditions:

(a) $P : \mathcal{A} \to \langle 0,1 \rangle$, hence, $0 \leq P(A) \leq 1$ for each $A \in \mathcal{A}$,
(b) $P(\Omega) = 1$,
(c) for each infinite sequence $\langle A_1, A_2, \ldots \rangle$ of mutually disjoint sets from $\mathcal{A}$ the equality $\sum_{i=1}^{\infty} P(A_i) = P\left(\bigcup_{i=1}^{\infty} A_i\right)$ holds.

Obviously, if the infinite sum $\sum_{i=1}^{\infty} x_i$ is taken as undefined in the case when $\lim_{n\to\infty} \sum_{i=1}^{n} x_i = \infty$, (c) should be replaced by

(c1) for each ...from $\mathcal{A}$, $\sum_{i=1}^{\infty} P(A_i)$ *is defined* and the equality ...holds.

Due to the condition that $\sum_{i=1}^{\infty} P(A_i) = P\left(\bigcup_{i=1}^{\infty} A_i\right)$, and due to the fact that $\bigcup_{i=1}^{\infty} A_i \in \mathcal{A}$, so that $P\left(\bigcup_{i=1}^{\infty} A_i\right) \leq 1$ follows from (a), both the definitions are equivalent. Let us present still another equivalent variant, perhaps less intuitive, but more close to the strong modification of (c), which will lead us to the notion of strong probability measure.

Let $\langle 0,1 \rangle^{\infty}$ denote the Cartesian product $\times_{i=1}^{\infty} H_i$, where $H_i = \langle 0,1 \rangle$ for each $i \in \mathcal{N}$, hence, $\langle 0,1 \rangle^{\infty}$ is the space of all infinite sequences of real numbers from the unit interval. Let $\sum^1$ be the partial mapping taking $\langle 0,1 \rangle^{\infty}$ into $\langle 0,1 \rangle$ and defined by $\sum^1 (\langle x_i \rangle_{i=1}^{\infty}) = \lim_{n\to\infty} \sum_{i=1}^{n} x_i = \lim_{n\to\infty}(x_1 + x_2 + \cdots + x_n)$ supposing that this limit value is in $\langle 0,1 \rangle$, $\sum^1 (\langle x_i \rangle_{i=1}^{\infty})$ being *undefined* otherwise, here $\langle x_i \rangle_{i=1}^{\infty}$ is a sequence from $\langle 0,1 \rangle^{\infty}$. To make the notation more close to the classical one introduced above, we shall write $\sum_{i=1}^{1\,\infty} x_i$ instead of $\sum^1 (\langle x_i \rangle_{i=1}^{\infty})$, leaving nevertheless the upper index 1 in $\sum^1$ to express explicitly the *partial* character in which this definition of countable addition on $\langle 0,1 \rangle$ differs from the two ones mentioned above. The items (c) or (c1) should then be replaced by

(c2) for each...from $\mathcal{A}$, $\sum_{i=1}^{1\,\infty} P(A_i)$ *is defined* and the equality $\sum_{i=1}^{1\,\infty} P(A_i) = P\left(\bigcup_{i=1}^{\infty} A_i\right)$ holds.

What makes this modification worth being formulated explicitly is that due to it, in order to define the classical probability measure, it is sufficient to define the countable addition just as a *partial* operation on $\langle 0,1 \rangle^{\infty}$ with the values in $\langle 0,1 \rangle$.

Let $\mathcal{C}$ be the well-known Cantor subset of $\langle 0, 1\rangle$. Formally defined, $\mathcal{C}$ is just the set of all real numbers from $\langle 0, 1\rangle$, for which there exist triadic decompositions (decompositions to the base 3) containing just the numerals 0 and 2. Moreover, for each $x \in \mathcal{C}$ there exists just one triadic decomposition containing only 0's and 2's (obviously, the alternative decomposition for $x_1, \ldots, x_n$, 0, 2, 2, 2, ..., i.e., $x_1, \ldots, x_n$, 1, 0, 0, 0, ... contains the numeral 1). Let $\langle y_1(x), y_2(x), \ldots\rangle \in \{0, 2\}^\infty$ denote the triadic decomposition of a number $x \in \mathcal{C}$ not containing 1, let $d(i, x) = y_i/2$ for each $i \in \mathcal{N}$, so that $D(x) = \langle d(1, x), d(2, x), \ldots\rangle$ is a binary sequence from $\{0, 1\}^\infty$. Set, for each $x \in \mathcal{C}$, $s(x) = \{i \in \mathcal{N} : d(i, x) = 1\}$ $\{i \in \mathcal{N} : y_i(x) = 2\}$, so that $D(x)$ can be taken as the characteristic function (identifier) of the subset $s(x)$ of $\mathcal{N}$. Obviously, D is a one-to-one mapping of $\mathcal{C}$ onto $\{0, 1\}^\infty$, so that, for each $\langle x_1, x_2, \ldots\rangle \in \{0, 1\}^\infty$, $D^{-1}(\langle x_1, x_2, \ldots\rangle)$ is defined, namely, $D^{-1}(\langle x_1, x_2 \ldots\rangle) = \sum_{i=1}^{\infty} 2x_i 3^{-i} \in \mathcal{C}$, where $\sum_{i=1}^{\infty}$ is the classical operation of countable addition.

Let $\mathcal{C}^\infty$ be the space of all infinite sequences of real numbers from the Cantor set, let $\sum^0$ be a partial operation defined on $\mathcal{C}^\infty$ in this way: if $\langle x_1, x_2 \ldots\rangle \in \mathcal{C}^\infty$, set $z_i = \text{card}\{j \in \mathcal{N} : d(i, x_j) = 1\}$, then $\sum^0 (\langle x_i\rangle_{i=1}^{\infty})$ (or $\sum_{i=1}^{0\,\infty} x_i$) is defined iff $\langle z_1, z_2, \ldots\rangle \in \{0, 1\}^\infty$ (i.e., iff for each $i \in \mathcal{N}$ there exists at most one j such that $d(i, x_j) = 1$) and, if this is the case, $\sum_{i=1}^{0\,\infty} x_i = D^{-1}(\langle z_1, z_2, \ldots\rangle) = \sum_{i=1}^{\infty} 2z_i 3^{-i}$, this value obviously is in $\mathcal{C}$.

Lemma 1 Let $\langle x_1, x_2, \ldots\rangle \in \mathcal{C}^\infty$. If $\sum_{i=1}^{0\,\infty} x_i$ is defined, then the sets $s(x_i)$, $i = 1, 2, \ldots$, are mutually disjoint, hence, $s(x_i) \cap s(x_j) = \emptyset$ for each $i, j \in \mathcal{N}$, $i \neq j$. (Because of the limited extent of this contribution all the proofs are omitted and will be published elsewhere).

So, we have arrived at the key definition of this paper.

Definition 3 Let $\langle \Omega, \mathcal{A}\rangle$ be a measurable space. A real-valued function π defined on $\mathcal{A}$ is called *strong probability measure*, if it satisfies the following conditions:

(a0) $\pi : \mathcal{A} \to \mathcal{C}$, hence, $0 \leq \pi(A) \leq 1$ for each $A \in \mathcal{A}$,

(b0) $\pi(\Omega) = 1$ ($1 = 0, 2222\ldots$ is obviously in $\mathcal{C}$),

(c0) for each infinite sequence $\langle A_1, A_2, \ldots\rangle$ of mutually disjoint sets from $\mathcal{A}$, $\sum_{i=1}^{0\,\infty} \pi(A_i)$ is defined and the equality $\sum_{i=1}^{0\,\infty} \pi(A_i) = \pi\left(\bigcup_{i=1}^{\infty} A_i\right)$ holds.

Theorem 1 Each strong probability measure defined on a measurable space $\langle \Omega, \mathcal{A}\rangle$ is also a classical probability measure on $\langle \Omega, \mathcal{A}\rangle$ in the sense of Definition 2.

Lemma 2 Let π be a strong probability measure defined on a measurable space $\langle \Omega, \mathcal{A}\rangle$, let $\emptyset$ be the empty subset of Ω, let $A \in \mathcal{A}$. Then the equalities $\pi(\emptyset) = 0$ and $\pi(\Omega - A) = 1 - \pi(A)$ hold.

3 Boolean-Valued Uncertainty Quantifications Induced by Strong Probability Measures

In the last chapter we stated, that for a sequence $\langle A_1, A_2, \ldots\rangle$ of mutually disjoint sets from $\mathcal{A}$ the corresponding support sets $s(\pi(A_1)), s(\pi(A_2)), \ldots$ are also mutually disjoint, in other words said, that for all pairs $i, j \in \mathcal{N}$, $i \neq j$, the equality $s(\pi(A_i)) \cap s(\pi(A_j)) = \emptyset = s(\pi(A_i \cap A_j)) = s(\pi(\emptyset)) = s(0)$. The following assertion proves, that this possibility to translate set-theoretic operations over sets from $\mathcal{A}$ into the same operations over the support sets of their strong probability values is more general and that it is not limited only to disjoint sets.

Theorem 2 Let π be a strict probability measure defined on a measurable space $\langle \Omega, \mathcal{A}\rangle$. Let $\langle A, A_1, A_2, \ldots\rangle$ be a sequence of sets from $\mathcal{A}$. Then the following set equalities hold in $\mathcal{P}(\mathcal{N})$:

(i) $s(\pi(\Omega - A)) = \mathcal{N} - s(\pi(A))$,
(ii) $s\left(\pi\left(\bigcup_{i=1}^{\infty} A_i\right)\right) = \bigcup_{i=1}^{\infty} s(\pi(A_i))$,
(iii) $s\left(\pi\left(\bigcap_{i=1}^{\infty} A_i\right)\right) = \bigcap_{i=1}^{\infty} s(\pi(A_i))$.

For a number of reasons explained in more detail, e. g., in [1] or [4], also non-numerical measures of degrees of uncertainty are worth being considered. Among these measures, attention is often concentrated to the set-valued or, more generally, boolean-valued measures of uncertainty because of the possibility to understand these degrees as sets of possible worlds satisfying some conditions or verifying some assertion, and because of the possibility to take profit from a relatively rich apparatus of notions and results concerning Boolean algebras. Namely, we shall define Boolean-valued probability measures as presented below.

Boolean algebra $\mathcal{B}$ is structure $\langle B, \vee, \wedge, \neg, \mathbf{0}, \mathbf{1}\rangle$, where B is a nonempty set, $\vee$ (supremum) and $\wedge$ (infimum) are two binary operations defined on $B \times B$ and taking their values in B, $\neg$ (complement) is a unary operation taking B into itself, $\mathbf{0} \in B$ is the zero element of $\mathcal{B}$ and $\mathbf{1} \in \mathcal{B}$ is the unit element of $\mathcal{B}$, in the case of necessity we can write $\mathbf{0}_{\mathcal{B}}$ and $\mathbf{1}_{\mathcal{B}}$. The operations $\vee$, $\wedge$, and $\neg$, as well as the elements $\mathbf{0}$ and $\mathbf{1}$ are supposed to satisfy the axioms of Boolean algebras which are known in various settings, e. g., that one presented in [7].

It is a well-known fact, cf., e. g., again [7], that the binary relation $\leq$, defined on B in such a way that, for each $x, y \in B$, $x \leq y$ holds iff $x \wedge y = x$ or, what turns to be the same, iff $x \vee y = y$, is a partial ordering relation on B and $x \vee y$ ($x \wedge y$, resp.) is just the supremum (the infimum, resp.) of x and y with respect to this partial ordering relation. Using the associativity and commutativity properties of both the operations $\vee$ and $\wedge$, we can immediately deduce by induction, that supremum and infimum of each finite set of elements of a Boolean algebra is defined. For an infinite set of elements, in general, this need not be the case. A Boolean algebra is called *complete*, if for *each* set of elements their supremum and infimum are defined, a Boolean algebra is called *σ-complete*, if for each *countable* set of elements their supremum and infimum are defined.

Definition 4 Let $\langle \Omega, \mathcal{A} \rangle$ be a measurable space, let $\mathcal{B} = \langle B, \vee, \wedge, \neg, \mathbf{0}, \mathbf{1} \rangle$ be a σ-complete Boolean algebra. A mapping ρ, defined on $\mathcal{A}$ and taking its values in B, is called *$\mathcal{B}$-valued Boolean probability measure* (or: Boolean-valued probability measure taking its values in the Boolean algebra $\mathcal{B}$), if

(i) $\rho(\Omega) = \mathbf{1}$
(ii) for each infinite sequence $\langle A_1, A_2, \ldots \rangle$ of mutually disjoint sets from $\mathcal{A}$, the subset $\{\rho(A_i) : i \in \mathcal{N}\}$ of $\mathcal{B}$ is a decomposition of the element $\rho\left(\bigcup_{i=1}^{\infty} A_i\right)$ of B. (In other words, for each $i, j \in \mathcal{N}$, $i \neq j$ implies that $\rho(A_i) \wedge \rho(A_j) = \mathbf{0}$ and $\bigvee_{i=1}^{\infty} \rho(A_i) = \rho\left(\bigcup_{i=1}^{\infty} A_i\right)$.)

The following assertion can be seen rather as a re-interpretation of the results of Theorem 2.

Theorem 3 Let π be a strict probability measure defined on a measurable space $\langle \Omega, \mathcal{A} \rangle$, let $\mathcal{B}_{\mathcal{N}} = \langle \mathcal{P}(\mathcal{N}), \cup, \cap, {}^c, \emptyset, \mathcal{N} \rangle$ be the complete Boolean algebra of all subsets of the set of all positive integers, where $\cap$, $\cup$ and ^{c} are the usual set-theoretic operations of union, intersection and complement. Then the mapping $\rho : \mathcal{A} \to \mathcal{P}(\mathcal{N})$, defined by $\rho(A) = s(\pi(A))$ for each $A \in \mathcal{A}$, is a $\mathcal{B}_{\mathcal{N}}$-valued Boolean probability.

4 Atomic and Extensional Properties of Strong Probability Measures

Definition 5 Let $\langle \Omega, \mathcal{A} \rangle$ be a measurable space, let P be a (classical) probability measure defined on $\langle \Omega, \mathcal{A} \rangle$. A set $A \in \mathcal{A}$ is called an *atom* of $\mathcal{A}$ with respect to P, if $P(A) > 0$ and for each $B \in \mathcal{A}$, $B \subset A$, either $P(B) = 0$ or $P(B) = P(A)$. Measure P is called *atomic* with respect to a set $At \subset \mathcal{A}$ of atoms of $\mathcal{A}$ with respect to P, if for each $B \in \mathcal{A}$ such that $P(B) > 0$ there exists an atom $A \in At$ such that $A \subset B$.

Given a strong probability measure π defined on a measurable space $\langle \Omega, \mathcal{A} \rangle$, we shall construct, in the sequel, the set of all atoms of $\mathcal{A}$ with respect to π. The following lemma will be useful for these sakes.

Lemma 3 Let π be a strong probability measure defined on a measurable space $\langle \Omega, \mathcal{A} \rangle$, let $\emptyset \neq \mathcal{S} \subset \mathcal{A}$ be a system of sets from $\mathcal{A}$. Then there exists a sequence $A_1^{\mathcal{S}}, A_2^{\mathcal{S}}, \ldots$ of sets from $\mathcal{S} \cup \{\emptyset\}$ such that

$$\bigcup_{A \in \mathcal{S}} s(\pi(A)) = \bigcup_{j=1}^{\infty} s(\pi(A_j^{\mathcal{S}})) = s\left(\pi\left(\bigcup_{j=1}^{\infty} A_j^{\mathcal{S}}\right)\right) \tag{1}$$

$$\bigcap_{A \in \mathcal{S}} s(\pi(A)) = \bigcap_{j=1}^{\infty} s(\pi(A_j^{\mathcal{S}})) = s\left(\pi\left(\bigcap_{j=1}^{\infty} A_j^{\mathcal{S}}\right)\right). \tag{2}$$

Set, for each $i \in \mathcal{N}$,

$$S_i = \bigcap_{A \in \mathcal{A},\, i \in s(\pi(A))} s(\pi(A)). \tag{3}$$

Obviously, $i \in S_i$ for each $i \in N$. Let $j \in S_i$ for some $j \in \mathcal{N}$, $j \neq i$, let $i \notin S_j$. Then there exists $A \in \mathcal{A}$ such that $j \in s(\pi(A))$, $i \notin s(\pi(A))$, hence, $j \notin s(\pi(\Omega - A)) = \mathcal{N} - s(\pi(A))$, but $i \in s(\pi(\Omega - A))$, so that $j \notin S_i$. We have arrived at a contradiction proving that $j \in S_i$ implies $i \in S_j$. But, $j \in S_i$ means by definition of S_i, that $(\forall A \in \mathcal{A})\ (i \in s(\pi(A))) \Rightarrow j \in s(\pi(A))$, in other terms, $\{A \in \mathcal{A} : i \in S(\pi(A))\} \subset \{A \in \mathcal{A} : j \in s(\pi(A))\}$, consequently, $S_j \subset S_i$. As $j \in S_i$ implies that $i \in S_j$, we obtain by the same way of reasoning that $S_i \in S_j$, hence, $j \in S_i$ implies that $S_j = S_i$. So, if $S_i \cap S_j \neq \emptyset$ for $i, j \in \mathcal{N}$, i. e., if there exists $k \in S_i \cap S_j$, then $S_i = S_k = S_j$. We can conclude that for each $i, j \in \mathcal{N}$ either $S_i \cap S_j = \emptyset$ or $S_i = S_j$, hence, the system $\mathcal{S}^* = \{S_1, S_2, \ldots\}$ of sets is a decomposition of the set $\mathcal{N}$ of all positive integers (let us recall that $\mathcal{S}^*$ is taken as a set of sets, so that repeated occurrences of some $S \subset \mathcal{N}$ in the *sequence* $\langle S_1, S_2 \rangle$ are not taken into consideration).

Let $\mathcal{S} \subset \mathcal{A}$ be a nonempty system of subsets of Ω. A sequence $A_1^{\mathcal{S}}, A_2^{\mathcal{S}}, \ldots$ of sets from $\mathcal{S}$ is called a *representation* of $\mathcal{S}$ (with respect to π), if $i \in s(\pi(A_i^{\mathcal{S}}))$ for each $i \in \bigcup_{A \in \mathcal{S}} s(\pi(A))$ (consequently, $\bigcup_{i=1}^{\infty} s(\pi(A_i^{\mathcal{S}})) = \bigcup_{A \in \mathcal{S}} s(\pi(A))$). A representation $\langle A_1^{\mathcal{S}}, A_2^{\mathcal{S}}, \ldots \rangle$ of $\mathcal{S}$ is called *minimal*, if $j \notin s(\pi(A_i^{\mathcal{S}}))$ holds for all $i, j \in \mathcal{N}$ such that $s(\pi(A_i^{\mathcal{S}})) \neq s(\pi(A_j^{\mathcal{S}}))$. When proving Lemma 3 we obtain that for each $\emptyset \neq \mathcal{S} \subset \mathcal{A}$ a representation of $\mathcal{S}$ exists. Let $\alpha(\mathcal{S})$ denote the set of all representations of $\mathcal{S}$ corresponding to different choices from the sets $\{A \in \mathcal{S} : i \in s(\pi(A))\}$ supposing that these sets are not singletons. In particular, let $\alpha^i = \alpha(\mathcal{S}_i)$, where $\mathcal{S}_i = \{A \in \mathcal{A} : i \in s(\pi(A))\}$.

Define, for each $i \in \mathcal{N}$,

$$At_i(\pi, \mathcal{A}) = \{A \in \mathcal{A} : s(\pi(A)) = S_i\}, \tag{4}$$

$$At(\pi, \mathcal{A}) = \bigcup_{i=1}^{\infty} At_i(\pi, \mathcal{A}). \tag{5}$$

Theorem 4 Let π be a strong probability measure defined on a measurable space $\langle \Omega, \mathcal{A} \rangle$. Then

(i) $At(\pi, \mathcal{A})$ is the set of all atoms of $\mathcal{A}$ with respect to π.

(ii) Each representation of $At(\pi, \mathcal{A})$ is minimal.

(iii) Measure π is atomic with respect to At.

(iv) Let $\langle B_1^{At}, B_2^{At}, \ldots \rangle$ be a representation of At. Then, for each $A \in \mathcal{A}$,

$$\pi(A) = \sum_{\substack{j \in \mathcal{N},\ s(\pi(B_j^{At})) \subset s(\pi(A)),\\ s(\pi(B_j^{At})) \neq s(\pi(B_k^{At}))\ \text{for all}\ k<j}} P(B_j^{At}). \tag{6}$$

Let us define the two following operations taking nonempty sets of real numbers from the Cantor set $\mathcal{C}$ into this set. Let $\emptyset \neq \mathcal{S} \subset \mathcal{C}$. Set

$$\bigvee_{x \in \mathcal{S}} x = \sum_{i \in \bigcup_{x \in \mathcal{S}} s(x)} 2 \cdot 3^{-i}, \tag{7}$$

$$\bigwedge_{x \in \mathcal{S}} x = \sum_{i \in \bigcap_{x \in \mathcal{S}} s(x)} 2 \cdot 3^{-i}. \tag{8}$$

We can write, abbreviatively, $\bigvee \mathcal{C}$ ($\bigwedge \mathcal{C}$, resp.) instead of $\bigvee_{x \in \mathcal{C}} x$ ($\bigwedge_{x \in \mathcal{C}} x$, resp.). Obviously,

$$s(\bigvee \mathcal{C}) = \bigcup_{x \in \mathcal{C}} s(x), \qquad s(\bigwedge \mathcal{C}) = \bigcap_{x \in \mathcal{C}} s(x), \tag{9}$$

and both the numbers $\bigvee \mathcal{C}$ and $\bigwedge \mathcal{C}$ are uniquely defined by these set equalities.

Theorem 5 Let π be a strong probability measure defined on a measurable space $\langle \Omega, \mathcal{A} \rangle$, let $\langle A_1, A_2, \ldots \rangle$ be a sequence of sets from $\mathcal{A}$. Then

$$\pi\left(\bigcup_{i=1}^{\infty} A_i\right) = \bigvee_{i=1}^{\infty} \pi(A_i), \tag{10}$$

$$\pi\left(\bigcap_{i=1}^{\infty} A_i\right) = \bigwedge_{i=1}^{\infty} \pi(A_i). \tag{11}$$

Theorem 5 can be re-formulated (or rather interpreted) in such a way that strong probability measures are *extensional* and *σ-extensional* in the sense that probability values ascribed to finite (in the case of extensionality) or countable (in the case of σ-extensionality) unions and intersections of measurable sets are *determined* by the probability values ascribed to the particular sets, in other words said, probabilities of at most countable unions and intersections are *functions* of probabilities of particular sets. Interesting enough, perhaps, in this paper we have arrived at a sub-class of probabilistic measures possessing the property of extensionality, and we have arrived at this sub-class of probability measures in a purely axiomatic way, just replacing the set $\langle 0, 1 \rangle$ of probability values by its Cantor subset $\mathcal{C}$ and the usual addition operation $\sum$ by its strengthened version $\sum^0$. And it is just the σ-extensionality property which motivates our choose of the Cantor set $\mathcal{C}$ as the space of possible probability values.

5 Definition of Classical Probability Measures Over Countable Spaces by Strong Probability Measures

Consider the following partial mapping w which takes the Cantor set $\mathcal{C}$ intó the unit interval of real numbers as follows. If $x \in \mathcal{C}$, set

$$w(x) = \lim_{n \to \infty} n^{-1} \sum_{i=1}^{n} d(i, x) \tag{12}$$

supposing that this limit values is defined, $w(x)$ being undefined otherwise. Hence, $w(x)$ is the limit value (if exists) of the relative frequences of the occurrences of the digit 2 in the initial segments of the uniques $0-2$ ternary decomposition of the number x.

Theorem 6 Let π be a strong probability measure defined on a measurable space $\langle \Omega, \mathcal{A}\rangle$. Then the system $\mathcal{A}_0 \subset \mathcal{A}$ of subsets of $\mathcal{A}$ for which the value $w(\pi(A))$ is defined is closed with respect to complements and to finite unions of mutually disjoint sets and $w(\pi(\cdot))$ is a non-negative, normalized and finitely additive real-valued measure defined on $\mathcal{A}_0$. □

As can be easily demonstrated, the measure $w(\pi(\cdot))$ is not, in general, σ-additive. Or, take $\langle \Omega, \mathcal{A}\rangle = \langle \mathcal{N}, \mathcal{P}(\mathcal{N})\rangle$, and take $\pi(A) = \sum_{i \in A} 2 \cdot 3^{-i}$. For each $i \in \mathcal{N}$ and for $A_i = \{i\}$ we obtain that $s(A_i) = \{i\}$, hence,

$$\begin{aligned} w(\pi(A_i)) &= \lim_{n\to\infty} n^{-1} \sum_{j=1}^{n} d(j(A_i)) = \\ &= \lim_{n\to\infty} n^{-1} \operatorname{card}\,(s(\pi(A_i)) \cap \{1,2,\ldots,n\}) = \\ &= \lim_{n\to\infty} n^{-1} \operatorname{card}\,(\{i\} \cap \{1,2,\ldots,n\}) = \lim_{n\to\infty} n^{-1} = 0, \end{aligned} \tag{13}$$

so that $\sum_{i=1}^{\infty} w(\pi(A_i)) = 0$, however,

$$w\left(\pi\left(\bigcup_{i=1}^{\infty} A_i\right)\right) = w(\pi(\mathcal{N})) = w(1) = 1, \tag{14}$$

hence, σ-additivity is violated.

The following question can perhaps arise: how large is the class of measures definable on $\langle \Omega, \mathcal{A}\rangle$, which can be defined by an appropriate strong probability measure π on $\langle \Omega, \mathcal{A}\rangle$ and by the mapping w in such a way that $P(A) = w(\pi(A))$ for each $A \in \mathcal{A}$? The following assertion proves that if the space Ω is at most countable, this class contains all the classical probability measures defined on $\langle \Omega, \mathcal{A}\rangle$.

Theorem 7 Let $\langle \Omega, A\rangle$ be a measurable space such that Ω is at most countable, let P be a classical probability measure defined on $\langle \Omega, A\rangle$. Then there exists a strong probability measure defined on $\langle \Omega, A\rangle$ such that, for all $A \in \mathcal{A}$, $P(A) = w(\pi(A))$.

The following remarks concerning the relation between classical probability measures and strong probability measures are perhaps worth being stated explicitly. If a strong probability measure π on $\langle \Omega, A\rangle$ is given, then $w(\pi(A))$ is defined uniquely for each $A \in \mathcal{A}$ for which the corresponding limit value exists. On the other side, given a classical probability measure P on $\langle \mathcal{N}, \mathcal{P}(\mathcal{N})\rangle$, the induced strong probability measure π on $\langle \mathcal{N}, \mathcal{P}(\mathcal{N})\rangle$ is defined uniquely only supposing that the sequences $x^i = \langle x_j^i\rangle_{j=1}^{\infty}$ are constructed according to the way described in the proof of Theorem 7. However, if $0 < r_i = p_i \left(\sum_{j=i}^{\infty} p_j\right)^{-1} < 1$, then there exists an infinite (uncountable, in fact) number of sequences $v^i = \langle v^i_j \rangle_{j=1}^{\infty} \in \{0,1\}^{\infty}$ such that $\lim_{n\to\infty} n^{-1} \sum_{j=1}^{n} v^i_j = r_i$, and each of them can be used instead of x^i when constructing the sequence y^i. Obviously, replacing x^i by v^i will result in different value of $\pi(\{i\})$, even if the equality $w(\pi(\{i\})) = p_i$ remains valid. When extending the proof of Theorem 7 to another countable set Ω (instead of $\mathcal{N}$) we must keep in mind, of course, that different enumeration of elements of Ω by positive integers will also lead to different strong probability measure π, as in this case already the measure P induced on $\langle \mathcal{N}, \mathcal{P}(\mathcal{N}) \rangle$ will depend on this enumeration.

As far as the items [2] and [6] in the list below are concerned, [2] can serve as a source dealing with discrete elementary combinatoric probabilities over finite or countable spaces, on the other side, [6] is a classical monography written or very high and abstract level and dealing with the axiomatic Kolmogorov probability theory in its most general setting.

References

1. A. Bundy: Incidence calculus – a mechanism for probabilistic reasoning. Journal of Automated Reasoning 1, 1985, no. 3, pp. 263–283.
2. W. Feller: An Introduction to Probability Theory and its Applications, vol. I, 2nd edition. J. Wiley and Sons, New York, 1957.
3. A. N. Kolmogorov: Grundbegriffe der Wahrscheinlichkeitsrechnung. Springer-Verlag, Berlin, 1933.
4. I. Kramosil: Expert systems with non-numerical belief functions. Problems of Control and Information Theory 17 (1988), no. 5, pp. 285–295.
5. I. Kramosil: Extensional processing of probability measures. International Journal of General Systems 22 (1994), no. 2, pp. 159–170.
6. M. Loève: Probability Theory. Van Nostrand, Princeton, 1955.
7. R. Sikorski: Boolean Algebras, second edition. Springer–Verlag, Berlin – Göttingen – Heidelberg – New York, 1964.

The Dynamics of Default Reasoning

(Extended Abstract)

B. van Linder, W. van der Hoek, J.-J. Ch. Meyer

Utrecht University, Department of Computer Science
P.O. Box 80.089, 3508 TB Utrecht, The Netherlands

Abstract. In this paper we look at default reasoning from a dynamic, agent-oriented, point of view. We introduce actions that model the (attempted) jumping to conclusions which is a fundamental part of reasoning by default. Application of such an action consists of three parts. First it is checked whether the formula that the agent tries to jump to is a default, thereafter it is checked whether the default formula can consistently be incorporated by the agent, and if this is the case the formula is included in the agent's beliefs. We define the ability and opportunity of agents to apply these actions, and the states of affairs following application. To formalize formulae being defaults, we introduce the modality of common possibility. To model the qualitative difference that exists between hard, factual knowledge and beliefs derived by default, we employ different modalities to represent these concepts, thus combining knowledge, beliefs, and defaults within one framework.

1 Introduction

The formalization of rational agents is a topic of continuing interest in Artificial Intelligence. Research on this subject has held the limelight ever since the pioneering work of Moore [13] in which knowledge and actions are considered. Over the years important contributions have been made on both *informational* [2] and *motivational* attitudes [1].

This paper is part of a research project [4, 5, 7, 8, 10, 11] in which we deal with a *theorist* logic for rational agents, i.e., a logic that is used to *specify*, and to *reason about*, (various aspects of) the behavior of rational agents. The main aim of this paper is to formalize a form of default reasoning by rational agents in our framework. The formalization that we present here has two remarkable features. The first is the attention we pay to the *dynamic* part of default reasoning: agents may execute certain actions that model the jumping to conclusions which forms the essential part of reasoning by default. The second remarkable feature is the use of the new modality of *common possibility* to define defaults. The idea underlying this definition is that a default is a formula which is considered epistemically possible by all agents.

Although we combine both features mentioned above in the framework presented in this paper, we would like to stress that the dynamic part depends in no way on the notion of common possibility to formalize defaults: any representation of defaults can be used in combination with the actions that constitute the dynamic part, and the notion of common possibility is also interesting in itself, without any reference to the dynamics of default reasoning.

The rest of the paper is organized as follows. In Sect. 2 we present some of our ideas on knowledge and action. Sect. 3 deals with our approach towards default reasoning: in 3.1 defaults are formalized, in 3.2 belief is introduced, in 3.3 an extended consistency check is defined, and in 3.4 the actual jump is formalized. In 3.5 the ability to jump is considered. In Sect. 4 we round off. This paper is an abstract; proofs and technical completions are to be found elsewhere [9].

2 Knowledge, abilities, opportunities, and results

Formalizing *knowledge* has been a subject of research both in analytical philosophy and in AI for quite some time [2, 3]. We follow, both from a syntactical and a semantic point of view, the approach common in epistemic logic: the formula $\mathbf{K}_i\varphi$ denotes that agent i knows φ, and is interpreted in a Kripke-style semantics.

At the action level we consider *results*, *abilities* and *opportunities*. In defining the result of an action, we follow ideas of Von Wright [15], in which the state of affairs brought about by execution of the action is defined to be its result. An important aspect of any investigation of action is the relation that exists between ability and opportunity. In order to successfully complete an action, both the opportunity and the ability to perform the action are necessary. Although these notions are interconnected, they are surely not identical: the abilities of agents comprise mental and physical powers, moral capacities, and human and physical possibility, whereas the opportunity to perform actions is best described by the notion of circumstantial possibility. We propose that in order to make a formalization of rational agents, like for instance robots, as accurate and realistic as possible, abilities and opportunities need also be distinguished in AI environments. The abilities of agents are formalized via the $\mathbf{A}_i$ operator; the formula $\mathbf{A}_i\alpha$ denotes the fact that agent i has the ability to do α. When using the definitions of opportunities and results as given above, the framework of (propositional) dynamic logic provides an excellent means to formalize these notions. Using events $\mathrm{do}_i(\alpha)$ to refer to the performance of the action α by the agent i, we consider the formulae $\langle \mathrm{do}_i(\alpha)\rangle\varphi$ and $[\mathrm{do}_i(\alpha)]\varphi$. In our deterministic framework, $\langle \mathrm{do}_i(\alpha)\rangle\varphi$ is the stronger of these formulae; it represents the fact that agent i has the opportunity to do α and that doing α leads to φ. The formula $[\mathrm{do}_i(\alpha)]\varphi$ is noncommittal about the opportunity of the agent to do α but states that should the opportunity arise, only states of affairs satisfying φ would result.

Definition 1. Let a finite set $\mathcal{A} = \{1, \ldots, n\}$ of agents, and some denumerable sets Π of propositional symbols and At of atomic actions be given. The language $\mathcal{L}$ is the smallest superset of Π such that:

- if $\varphi, \psi \in \mathcal{L}, i \in \mathcal{A}, \alpha \in Ac$ then $\neg\varphi, \varphi \vee \psi, \mathbf{K}_i\varphi, \langle \mathrm{do}_i(\alpha)\rangle\varphi, \mathbf{A}_i\alpha \in \mathcal{L}$

where Ac is the smallest superset of At such that if $\varphi \in \mathcal{L}$, $\alpha_1, \alpha_2 \in Ac$ then

- $\texttt{confirm}\ \varphi \in Ac$ — *confirmations*
- $\alpha_1; \alpha_2 \in Ac$ — *sequential composition*
- $\texttt{if}\ \varphi\ \texttt{then}\ \alpha_1\ \texttt{else}\ \alpha_2\ \texttt{fi} \in Ac$ — *conditional composition*
- $\texttt{while}\ \varphi\ \texttt{do}\ \alpha_1\ \texttt{od} \in Ac$ — *repetitive composition*

The purely propositional fragment of $\mathcal{L}$ is denoted by $\mathcal{L}_0$. Constructs $\wedge, \rightarrow, \leftrightarrow, \mathbf{tt}, \mathbf{M}_i\varphi$ and $[\mathrm{do}_i(\alpha)]\varphi$ are defined in the usual way. We adopt the convention that i and j, possibly marked, always refer to agents.

Definition 2. The class M contains Kripke models $\mathcal{M} = \langle \mathcal{S}, \pi, \mathrm{R}, \mathtt{r}, \mathtt{c} \rangle$ where

- $\mathcal{S}$ is a set of possible worlds, or states.
- $\pi : \Pi \times \mathcal{S} \rightarrow \{\mathbf{0}, \mathbf{1}\}$ assigns a truth value to propositional symbols in states.
- $\mathrm{R} : \mathcal{A} \rightarrow \wp(\mathcal{S} \times \mathcal{S})$ is a function that yields the epistemic accessibility relations for a given agent. It is demanded that $\mathrm{R}(i)$ is an equivalence relation for all i. We define $[s]_{\mathrm{R}(i)}$ to be $\{s' \in \mathcal{S} \mid (s, s') \in \mathrm{R}(i)\}$.
- $\mathtt{r} : \mathcal{A} \times At \rightarrow \mathcal{S} \rightarrow \wp(\mathcal{S})$ is such that $\mathtt{r}(i, a)(s)$ yields the (possibly empty) state transition in s caused by the event $\mathrm{do}_i(a)$. This function is such that for all atomic actions a it holds that $|\mathtt{r}(i, a)(s)| \leq 1$ for all i and s, i.e., these events are *deterministic*.
- $\mathtt{c} : \mathcal{A} \times At \rightarrow \mathcal{S} \rightarrow \{\mathbf{0}, \mathbf{1}\}$ is the capability function such that $\mathtt{c}(i, a)(s)$ indicates whether the agent i is capable of performing the action a in s.

Definition 3. Let $\mathcal{M} \in$ M, $s \in \mathcal{M}$. For φ in Π, a negation or a disjunction, $\mathcal{M}, s \models \varphi$ is defined as usual. For the other clauses it is thus defined:

$$\begin{array}{ll}
\mathcal{M}, s \models \mathbf{K}_i\varphi & \Leftrightarrow \forall s' \in \mathcal{S}[(s, s') \in \mathrm{R}(i) \Rightarrow \mathcal{M}, s' \models \varphi] \\
\mathcal{M}, s \models \langle \mathrm{do}_i(\alpha) \rangle \varphi & \Leftrightarrow \exists \mathcal{M}', s'[\mathcal{M}', s' \in \mathtt{r}(i, \alpha)(\mathcal{M}, s) \,\&\, \mathcal{M}', s' \models \varphi] \\
\mathcal{M}, s \models \mathbf{A}_i\alpha & \Leftrightarrow \mathtt{c}(i, \alpha)(\mathcal{M}, s) = \mathbf{1}
\end{array}$$

where r and c are defined by:

$$\begin{array}{ll}
\mathtt{r}(i, a)(\mathcal{M}, s) & = \mathcal{M}, \mathtt{r}(i, a)(s) \\
\mathtt{r}(i, \mathtt{confirm}\ \varphi)(\mathcal{M}, s) & = \mathcal{M}, s \text{ if } \mathcal{M}, s \models \varphi \text{ and } \emptyset \text{ otherwise} \\
\mathtt{r}(i, \alpha_1; \alpha_2)(\mathcal{M}, s) & = \mathtt{r}(i, \alpha_2)(\mathtt{r}(i, \alpha_1)(\mathcal{M}, s)) \\
\text{where } \mathtt{r}(i, \alpha)(\emptyset) & = \emptyset \\
\mathtt{c}(i, a)(\mathcal{M}, s) & = \mathtt{c}(i, a)(s) \\
\mathtt{c}(i, \mathtt{confirm}\ \varphi)(\mathcal{M}, s) & = \mathbf{1} \text{ if } \mathcal{M}, s \models \varphi \text{ and } \mathbf{0} \text{ otherwise} \\
\mathtt{c}(i, \alpha_1; \alpha_2)(\mathcal{M}, s) & = \mathtt{c}(i, \alpha_1)(\mathcal{M}, s) \,\&\, \mathtt{c}(i, \alpha_2)(\mathtt{r}(i, \alpha_1)(\mathcal{M}, s)) \\
\text{where } \mathtt{c}(i, \alpha)(\emptyset) & = \mathbf{1}
\end{array}$$

Validity and satisfiability are defined as usual.

The definition of $\mathtt{c}(i, \mathtt{confirm}\ \varphi)$ expresses that an agent is able to get confirmation for a formula φ iff φ holds. An agent is capable of performing a sequential composition $\alpha_1; \alpha_2$ iff it is capable of performing α_1 (now), and it is capable of executing α_2 after it has performed α_1. In [9] we incorporate the (abilities for) conditional and repetitive composition as well: for economical reasons, we do not consider them in this abstract.

3 Defaults and dynamics

The capacity to reason by default is very important when modelling rational agents. In default reasoning, reliable yet fallible conclusions are derived on the basis of the presence of certain information and the absence of other information. Usually an agent knows certain formulae to be true, other formulae to be false, and is uncertain with respect to still other formulae. The agent may try to fill in informational gaps by trying to jump to certain conclusions. These attempted jumps are modelled as explicit actions, `try_jump` φ for 'try to jump to φ', in our dynamic framework. The execution of such a `try_jump` φ action consists of three stages. In the first stage it is checked whether the formula φ is a suitable candidate to jump to. The formulae that are suitable candidates for a given agent in a given state are called its *defaults*. These formulae intuitively correspond to *supernormal* defaults in Reiter's default logic [14]. If the formula that the agent is trying to jump to is a default, the second stage of execution follows; if the formula is not a default, the jump fails. In the second stage of execution it is checked whether the default can consistently be adopted by the agent. If this is not the case, the jump reduces to the void action; otherwise the default is adopted, which constitutes the third stage of execution. In our opinion formulae *derived by default* are of a different nature than facts *known to be true*. To accommodate for this qualitative difference, we introduce a modality representing the *beliefs* of an agent. The implementation of the `try_jump` action is such that formulae derived by default are included in the agent's beliefs, and not in its knowledge.

3.1 Formalizing defaults: defaults as common possibilities

We want to formalize defaults by using concepts already present in our framework, thus allowing the entire process of reasoning by default to be formalized *within* the formal system. Therefore we need a modal translation of defaults. If one looks at some of the translations of defaults that have been proposed in the literature [12], it turns out that for supernormal defaults $\mathbf{tt} : \varphi/\varphi$ in an **S5** framework all of these translations amount to either the formula $\mathbf{M}_i\varphi \rightarrow \varphi$ or $\mathbf{M}_i\varphi \rightarrow \mathbf{K}_i\varphi$. These translations stem from the usual, *static*, account of default reasoning and are therefore not completely suitable for our *dynamic* framework. Intuitively, our notion of defaults corresponds to the antecedent of both the implications given above, whereas the consequents of these implications correspond to possible results of attempted jumps. Therefore it seems reasonable to consider the formula $\mathbf{M}_i\varphi$ as a candidate to represent our kind of defaults. However, this formalization would do no justice to the empirical character of defaults. More in particular, the idea of defaults being rooted in *common* sense is not visible when formalizing defaults as ordinary epistemic possibilities. In our multi-agent system, *common* sense is related to the knowledge and lack of knowledge of *all* agents. To capture this idea of defaults as determined by the (lack of) knowledge of all agents, we propose the modality of *common possibility*, intuitively corresponding to *being considered epistemically possible by all agents.* Although at first sight defaults as common possibilities have an *optimistic* flavor to them, agents that jump to these formulae are not that bold at all: no other agent could tell them that their jumps are made for incorrect reasons.

Definition 4. For all formulae φ, the formula $\mathbf{N}\varphi$, for nobody knows not φ, is defined by: $\mathbf{N}\varphi =^{\text{def}} \mathbf{M}_1\varphi \wedge \ldots \wedge \mathbf{M}_n\varphi$. The intuitive reading of $\mathbf{N}\varphi$ is that φ is a common possibility.

3.2 Formalizing belief

The formalization of belief as we present it, is a conceptual variant of the notion of belief as defined by Kraus & Lehmann [6]. Instead of an accessibility relation used to denote doxastic alternatives, we use for each world a set of designated worlds that together constitute the body of belief of the agent. Defining the semantics like this has two advantages as compared with the standard approach. The first is merely an intuitive one: by using a set, the worlds that define the beliefs of an agent have become more tangible. One can see at a single glance how the beliefs of the agent are determined, without having to examine a possibly complex accessibility relation. The second advantage is of a more technical nature: using sets instead of accessibility relations facilitates certain definitions.

Definition 5. The language $\mathcal{L}$ as given in Def. 1 is extended with formulae $\mathbf{B}_i\varphi$, representing the fact that agent i believes φ. Formulae without occurrences of any $\mathbf{B}_i$ operator are called *B-free* or *B-objective*. Kripke models are extended with a function $\mathrm{B} : \mathcal{A} \times \mathcal{S}/\mathrm{R} \to \wp(\mathcal{S})$, such that for all sets $[s]_{\mathrm{R}(i)}$ it holds that $\mathrm{B}(i, [s]_{\mathrm{R}(i)}) \subseteq [s]_{\mathrm{R}(i)}$ and $\mathrm{B}(i, [s]_{\mathrm{R}(i)}) \neq \emptyset$. Truth of belief formulae in states of a model is defined by: $\mathcal{M}, s \models \mathbf{B}_i\varphi \Leftrightarrow \forall s' \in \mathrm{B}(i, [s]_{\mathrm{R}(i)})[\mathcal{M}, s' \models \varphi]$.

Knowledge, belief, and defaults When defining the functions R and B as in Def. 2 and Def. 5 we end up with a notion of knowledge that obeys an S5 axiomatization, and a notion of belief validating a KD45 axiomatization; $\mathbf{K}_i$ and $\mathbf{B}_i$ are related as in the system of Kraus & Lehmann [6]. The common possibility operator $\mathbf{N}$ validates — as does the epistemic possibility operator — the dual KT4 axiomatization. However, whereas $\mathbf{M}_i$ validates the dual 5 axiom and the axiom of weak belief $\mathbf{M}_i(\varphi \vee \psi) \leftrightarrow (\mathbf{M}_i\varphi \vee \mathbf{M}_i\psi)$, $\mathbf{N}$ does not validate the first of these, and validates only the right-to-left implication of the latter.

Proposition 6. *Let $\varphi, \psi \in \mathcal{L}$. It holds that:*

1. $\mathbf{N}(\varphi \vee \psi) \to (\mathbf{N}\varphi \vee \mathbf{N}\psi)$ *is not for all φ, ψ valid*
2. $\models \varphi \to \psi \Rightarrow \models \mathbf{N}\varphi \to \mathbf{N}\psi$ *for all φ, ψ*
3. $\mathbf{N}\varphi \wedge \mathbf{N}(\varphi \to \psi) \to \mathbf{N}\psi$ *is not for all φ, ψ valid*
4. $\mathbf{N}\varphi \wedge \mathbf{N}\psi \to \mathbf{N}(\varphi \wedge \psi)$ *is not for all φ, ψ valid*
5. $\mathbf{N}\varphi \to \neg\mathbf{N}\neg\varphi$ *is not for all φ valid*

Item 1 of Prop. 6 indicates that disjunctive defaults are not necessarily trivialized, i.e., these disjunctions are not necessarily reduced to their disjuncts. This property is very important for the expressiveness of our framework: it allows the lottery paradox to be avoided, which is impossible using ordinary epistemic possibility. Items 4 and 5 show that the Nixon-diamond can be represented.

Proposition 7. *Let $\varphi \in \mathcal{L}$. It holds that:*

1. $\models \mathbf{K}_i\neg\varphi \to \neg\mathbf{N}\varphi$ *for all φ*
2. $\mathbf{B}_i\neg\varphi \wedge \mathbf{N}\varphi$ *is satisfiable for some φ*
3. $\models \mathbf{N}\mathbf{K}_i\varphi \leftrightarrow \mathbf{K}_i\varphi$ *for all φ*
4. $\models \mathbf{N}\mathbf{B}_i\varphi \leftrightarrow \mathbf{B}_i\varphi$ *for all φ*

5. $\models \mathbf{N}\neg\mathbf{K}_i\varphi \leftrightarrow \neg\mathbf{K}_i\varphi$ *for all* φ
6. $\models \mathbf{N}\neg\mathbf{B}_i\varphi \leftrightarrow \neg\mathbf{B}_i\varphi$ *for all* φ
7. $\models \mathbf{K}_i\neg\varphi \rightarrow \neg\mathbf{B}_i\mathbf{N}\varphi$ *for all* φ

Items 1 and 2 of Prop. 7 nicely emphasize the ontological difference between knowledge and belief: it is possible that an agent considers a formula to be a default although it *believes* the negation of the formula, whereas this is impossible if the agent *knows* the negation of the formula. Items 3 to 6 are related to the introspective properties that agents have for both knowledge and belief. The last item states that formulae known to be false are not believed to be defaults; this seems to be a desirable property for *rational* agents.

3.3 Checking consistency

Before adding a default to the beliefs of an agent, two different consistency checks need to be performed. The first of these is the obvious one, in which it is checked that the formula that is to be believed is consistent with the beliefs of the agent. The second consistency check is necessary due to the expressiveness of our framework in which defaults are not necessarily propositional formulae, but may contain all sorts of operators. Now when allowing non-propositional formulae, it is possible that an update with a formula that can consistently be assumed, does still not result in the agent actually believing the formula.

Example 1. Consider $\mathcal{M} = \langle \mathcal{S}, \pi, \mathrm{R}, \mathrm{B}, \mathbf{r}, \mathrm{c}\rangle$, with $\mathcal{S} = \{s_0, s_1\}$, $\pi(p, s_0) = \mathbf{1}$, $\pi(p, s_1) = \mathbf{0}$, $\mathrm{R}(i) = \mathcal{S}^2, \mathrm{B}(i, [s]_{\mathrm{R}(i)}) = [s]_{\mathrm{R}(i)}$, and $\mathbf{r}$ and c are arbitrary. Let φ be the formula $p \wedge \neg\mathbf{B}_i p$. In $\mathcal{M}$ it holds that $\mathbf{B}_i\neg\varphi$ is false at s_0, and hence φ is consistent with the beliefs of i in s_0. However, it is not possible to incorporate φ in the beliefs of the agent by performing a doxastic update as we propose it (see 3.4). For performing a doxastic update with φ results in a model $\mathcal{M}'$ such that $\mathrm{B}'(i, [s]_{\mathrm{R}(i)}) = \{s_0\}$. Then it holds that $\mathcal{M}', s_0 \not\models \mathbf{B}_i\varphi$.

The problem observed in Example 1 is solved by checking whether the update would be successful, which constitutes the second consistency check.

3.4 Jumping to conclusions

To formalize the actual *jumping* to conclusions, we introduce the `try_jump` action. In defining the semantics of this action, we use special 'low-level' actions that cause the beliefs of the agent to be updated appropriately. To emphasize the distinction between the high and the low-level informative actions, we introduce in addition to the set of rational agents a constant e, representing the *external environment* and in charge of performing low-level update actions.

Definition 8. The class Ac of actions is extended as follows: if φ is a formula then `try_jump` $\varphi \in Ac$. The set Ac_l of low-level actions is the union of the sets $\{$`dox_update` $(\varphi, j)\}$, representing the low-level action that performs *doxastic* updates, and $\{$`bel_update` $(\varphi, j)\}$ representing belief updates, where φ is a formula. The language $\mathcal{L}'$ is the set $\{\langle \mathrm{do}_e(\alpha)\rangle\varphi \mid \alpha \in Ac_l \text{ and } \varphi \in \mathcal{L}\}$.

Definition 9. For $\mathcal{M} \in \mathsf{M}$, $s \in \mathcal{M}$ and $\varphi \in \mathcal{L}$, the function $\mathtt{r}$ is extended by:

- $\mathtt{r}(i, \mathtt{try\_jump}\ \varphi)(\mathcal{M}, s) = \mathtt{r}(e, \mathtt{bel\_update}\ (\varphi, i))(\mathcal{M}, s)$ if $\mathcal{M}, s \models \mathbf{N}\varphi$
- $\mathtt{r}(i, \mathtt{try\_jump}\ \varphi)(\mathcal{M}, s) = \emptyset$ otherwise
- $\mathtt{r}(e, \mathtt{bel\_update}\ (\varphi, i))(\mathcal{M}, s) = \mathtt{r}(e, \mathtt{dox\_update}\ (\varphi, i))(\mathcal{M}, s)$ if $\mathcal{M}, s \models \neg\mathbf{B}_i\neg\varphi \wedge \langle \mathrm{do}_e(\mathtt{dox\_update}\ (\varphi, i))\rangle \mathbf{B}_i\varphi$
- $\mathtt{r}(e, \mathtt{bel\_update}\ (\varphi, i))(\mathcal{M}, s) = \mathcal{M}, s$ otherwise
- $\mathtt{r}(e, \mathtt{dox\_update}\ (\varphi, i))(\mathcal{M}, s) = \emptyset$ if $\mathcal{M}, s \models \mathbf{B}_i\neg\varphi$
- $\mathtt{r}(e, \mathtt{dox\_update}\ (\varphi, i))(\mathcal{M}, s) = \mathcal{M}', s$, where $\mathcal{M}' = \langle \mathcal{S}, \pi, \mathrm{R}, \mathrm{B}', \mathtt{r}, \mathtt{c}\rangle$ with $\mathrm{B}'(i, [s]_{\mathrm{R}(i)}) = \mathrm{B}(i, [s]_{\mathrm{R}(i)}) \cap [\![\varphi]\!]$ otherwise

Proposition 10. *Let φ, ψ be formula. It holds that:*

1. $\models \mathbf{N}\varphi \leftrightarrow \langle \mathrm{do}_i(\mathtt{try\_jump}\ \varphi)\rangle \mathtt{tt}$ *for all* $\varphi \in \mathcal{L}$
2. $\models \langle \mathrm{do}_i(\mathtt{try\_jump}\ \varphi)\rangle \mathtt{tt} \leftrightarrow \langle \mathrm{do}_j(\mathtt{try\_jump}\ \varphi)\rangle \mathtt{tt}$ *for all* $\varphi \in \mathcal{L}$
3. $\langle \mathrm{do}_i(\mathtt{try\_jump}\ \varphi)\rangle \mathbf{B}_i\varphi \to \langle \mathrm{do}_j(\mathtt{try\_jump}\ \varphi)\rangle \mathbf{B}_j\varphi$ *is not for all* φ *valid*
4. $\models \mathbf{N}\varphi \wedge \mathbf{B}_i\neg\varphi \to (\psi \leftrightarrow \langle \mathrm{do}_i(\mathtt{try\_jump}\ \varphi)\rangle \psi)$ *for all* $\varphi, \psi \in \mathcal{L}$
5. $\models \mathbf{N}\varphi \wedge \neg\mathbf{B}_i\neg\varphi \to \langle \mathrm{do}_i(\mathtt{try\_jump}\ \varphi)\rangle \mathbf{B}_i\varphi$ *for B-free formulae* φ
6. $\models \mathbf{B}_i\psi \to [\mathrm{do}_i(\mathtt{try\_jump}\ \varphi)]\mathbf{B}_i\psi$ *for* $\psi \in \mathcal{L}_0$ *and* $\varphi \in \mathcal{L}$

Item 1 of Prop. 10 states that being a default sets up the opportunity for jumps. By item 2, agents have equal opportunities with respect to attempted jumps to conclusions. Although agents have equal opportunities, item 3 states that an attempted jump may work out differently for different agents, dependent on the beliefs of the jumping agent. Item 4 states that attempting to jump to an unacceptable default does not cause any change at all, and item 5 states that a jump to an acceptable default results in the acquisition of belief in the default. By item 6, attempts to jump preserve purely propositional beliefs.

3.5 The ability to jump

For informative actions like observing and communicating, the agents' abilities are closely related to the information they posses. This seems to hold *a fortiori* for the action that consists of jumping to a default conclusion. For when observing or communicating, at least some interaction takes place, either with the real world in case of observing, or with other agents when communicating, whereas jumping to conclusions interacts with the agent's information only. The formalization that we present is such that an agent is able to jump to those formulae that it *knows* to be defaults, i.e., agents have to *know* their defaults in order to be *able* to use them.

Definition 11. Let $\mathcal{M} \in \mathsf{M}$, $s \in \mathcal{M}$ and $\varphi \in \mathcal{L}$. The capability function $\mathtt{c}$ is extended by: $\mathtt{c}(i, \mathtt{try\_jump}\ \varphi)(\mathcal{M}, s) = \mathbf{1} \Leftrightarrow \mathcal{M}, s \models \mathbf{K}_i\mathbf{N}\varphi$.

Proposition 12. *For all $\varphi \in \mathcal{L}$ it holds that:*

1. $\not\models \mathbf{A}_i\mathtt{try\_jump}\ \varphi \leftrightarrow \mathbf{A}_j\mathtt{try\_jump}\ \varphi$
2. $\models \mathbf{A}_i\mathtt{try\_jump}\ \varphi \leftrightarrow \mathbf{K}_i\mathbf{A}_i\mathtt{try\_jump}\ \varphi$
3. $\models \mathbf{A}_i\mathtt{try\_jump}\ \varphi \to \langle \mathrm{do}_i(\mathtt{try\_jump}\ \varphi)\rangle \mathtt{tt}$

Item 1 of Prop. 12 states that agents do not necessarily have equal abilities with regard to the application of defaults. Hence, even though the *opportunities* are identical for all agents, this is not the case for their *abilities*. By item 2, agents know of their abilities to apply defaults, and by item 3 the try_jump action is **A**-*realizable* [4], a property typical for actions without circumstantial prerequisites.

4 Discussion

In this paper we semantically investigated default reasoning from a dynamic, agent-oriented point of view by defining actions actions that model the jumping to conclusions typical of default reasoning. Execution of an action try_jump φ consists of three stages: first it is checked whether φ indeed is a *default*, thereafter it is checked whether φ can *consistently* be included in the beliefs of the agent and if this is the case the beliefs of the agent are *updated* accordingly. To model formulae being defaults we introduce the modality of common possibility. Due to the fact that we allow updates with arbitrary formulae, a strengthening of the usual consistency check of consistency-based default reasoning is necessary. The eventual belief update that follows application of the try_jump action is formalized using doxastic updates. The ability of an agent to jump to a default is defined in terms of its knowledge: the agent is able to attempt a jump to a formula only if it *knows* the formula to be a default.

Acknowledgements This research is partially supported by Esprit III BRA project No.6156 'Drums II', Esprit III BRWG project No.8319 'ModelAge', and the Vrije Universiteit Amsterdam; the third author is furthermore partially supported by the Katholieke Universiteit Nijmegen.

References

1. P. Cohen and H. Levesque. Intention is ... *AI*, 42:213–261, 1990.
2. J. Halpern and Y. Moses. A guide to completeness and complexity for modal logics of knowledge and belief. *AI*, 54:319–379, 1992.
3. J. Hintikka. *Knowledge and Belief*. Cornell University Press, 1962.
4. W. van der Hoek, B. van Linder, and J.-J. Meyer. A logic of capabilities. In Nerode and Matiyasevich, eds. , *Procs. of LFCS'94*, LNCS 813, pp. 366–378.
5. W. van der Hoek, B. van Linder, and J.-J. Ch. Meyer. Unravelling nondeterminism. In Jorrand and Sgurev, eds., *Proceedings of AIMSA'94*, pp. 163–172.
6. S. Kraus and D. Lehmann. Knowledge, belief and time. *TCS*, 58:155–174, 1988.
7. B. van Linder, W. van der Hoek, and J.-J. Meyer. Actions that Make you Change your Mind. TR UU-CS-1994-53.
8. B. van Linder, W. van der Hoek, and J.-J. Meyer. Communicating rational agents. In Nebel and Dreschler-Fischer, eds., *Proceedings of KI-94*, LNCS 861, pp. 202–213.
9. B. van Linder, W. van der Hoek, and J.-J. Meyer. The dynamics of default reasoning. TR UU-CS-1994-48.
10. B. van Linder, W. van der Hoek, and J.-J. Meyer. Tests as epistemic updates. In Cohn, ed., *Proceedings of ECAI'94*, pp. 331–335. John Wiley & Sons, 1994.
11. B. van Linder, W. van der Hoek, and J.-J. Meyer. Seeing is Believing. TR UU-CS-1995-08.
12. V.W. Marek and M. Truszczyński. *Nonmonotonic Logic*. Springer-Verlag, 1993.
13. R. Moore. Reasoning about knowledge and action. TR 191, SRI, 1980.
14. R. Reiter. A logic for default reasoning. *AI*, 13:81–132, 1980.
15. G.H. von Wright. *Norm and Action*. Routledge & Kegan Paul, 1963.

Lemma Handling in Default Logic Theorem Provers

Thomas Linke[1] and Torsten Schaub[2]*

[1] AG Knowledge-Based Systems, Faculty of Technology, University of Bielefeld, D-33501 Bielefeld, tlinke@techfak.uni-bielefeld.de
[2] Theoretische Informatik, TH Darmstadt, Alexanderstraße 10, D-64283 Darmstadt, schaub@iti.informatik.th-darmstadt.de

Abstract. We develop an approach for lemma handling in automated theorem provers for query-answering in default logics. This work builds on the concept of so-called *lemma default rules*. We show how different forms of such lemmas can be incorporated for reducing computational efforts.

1 Introduction

In automated theorem proving, one often caches *lemmas*, ie. auxiliary propositions used in the demonstration of several propositions, in order to reduce computational efforts. This renders the integration of lemma handling of great practical relevance in automated theorem proving. Unfortunately, such a technique is not applicable in *default logics* [8], since the addition of derived propositions to default theories may change the entire set of conclusions [7].

The central concepts in default logic are *default rules* along with their induced *extensions* of an initial set of facts. Default logic augments classical logic by default rules that differ from standard inference rules in sanctioning inferences that rely upon given as well as absent information. Hence, a default rule $\frac{\alpha:\beta}{\gamma}$ has two types of antecedents: A *prerequisite* α which is established if α is derivable and a *justification* β which is established if β is consistent in a certain way. If both conditions hold, the *consequent* γ is concluded by default. A set of such conclusions (sanctioned by a given set of default rules and by means of classical logic) is called an *extension* of an initial set of facts. At this point it should be clear that the need to incorporate lemmas is even greater in default theorem proving than in standard theorem proving, since computation in default logics not only involves deduction but also consistency checks.

We further develop an approach to lemma handling in default logics, introduced in [9]. The idea is to change the status of a default conclusion whenever it is added to a world-description by turning it into a new default rule. This default rule comprises information about the default proof of the original conclusion and so tells us when its proof is valid or not. In what follows, we elaborate the implementation of this method. This is accomplished by extending an existing algorithm for query-answering in default logics [10]. The whole approach is developed for a variant of default logic, known as *constrained default logic* [3].

2 Lemma Handling in Default Logics

Knowledge is represented in default logics by *default theories* (D, W) consisting of a consistent[3] set of formulas W and a set of default rules D. A *normal default*

* On leave from IRISA, Campus de Beaulieu, 35042 Rennes Cedex, France

[3] The restriction to consistent set of facts is not really necessary, but it simplifies matters.

theory is restricted to ***normal default rules*** whose justification is equivalent to the consequent. In any default logic, default rules induce one or more extensions of an initial set of facts.

Since [8], it is well-known that query-answering in default logics is only feasible in the presence of the property of *semi-monotonicity*: If $D' \subseteq D$ for two sets of default rules, then if E' is an extension of (D', W) then there is an extension E of (D, W) such that $E' \subseteq E$. Given this property, it suffices to consider a relevant subset of default rules while answering a query, since applying other default rules would only enlarge or preserve the partial extension at hand. Also, semi-monotonicity implies that extensions are constructible in a truly iterative way by applying one applicable default rule after another. Due to the semi-monotonicity of constrained default logic, one thus obtains the following specification [10]:

Theorem 1. *For a default theory (D, W) and sets of formulas E and C, (E, C) is a constrained extension of (D, W) iff there is some maximal $D' \subseteq D$ that has an enumeration $\langle\delta_i\rangle_{i\in I}$ such that for $i \in I$ the following conditions hold.*

1. $E = Th(W \cup Cons(D'))$ *and* $C = Th(W \cup Just(D') \cup Cons(D'))$
2. $W \cup Cons(\{\delta_0, \ldots, \delta_{i-1}\}) \vdash Pre(\delta_i)$
3. $W \cup Cons(\{\delta_0, \ldots, \delta_{i-1}\}) \cup Just(\{\delta_0, \ldots, \delta_{i-1}\}) \not\vdash \neg Just(\delta_i) \vee \neg Cons(\delta_i)$

Condition *(2)* spells out that D' has to be grounded in W. In general, a set of default rules D is *grounded* in a set of facts W iff there exists an enumeration $\langle\delta_i\rangle_{i\in I}$ of D that satisfies Condition *(2)*. Condition *(3)* expresses the notion of *incremental consistency*. Here, the "consistent" application of a default rule is checked at each step, whereas this is done wrt to the final set of constraints in the usual definition of a constrained extension (cf. [3]). A *default proof* D_φ for a formula φ from a default theory (D, W) is a a sequence of default rules $\langle\delta_i\rangle_{i\in I}$ such that $W \cup \{Cons(\delta_i) \mid i \in I\} \vdash \varphi$ and Condition *(2)* and *(3)* in Theorem 1 are satisfied for all $i \in I$. Then, one can show that $\varphi \in E'$ for some constrained extension (E', C') of (D, W) iff φ has a finite default proof D_φ from (D, W).

[9] introduced an approach to lemma handling in Reiter's and constrained default logic. In what follows, we focus on the latter and introduce the notion of a *lemma default rule*: For lemmatizing[4] a default conclusion, we take this conclusion along with one of its default proofs and construct the corresponding lemma default rule in the following way [9].

Definition 2. *Let D_φ be a default proof of a formula φ from default theory (D, W). We define a lemma default rule δ_φ for φ wrt (D, W) as*

$$\delta_\varphi = \frac{: \bigwedge_{\delta\in D_\varphi} Just(\delta) \wedge \bigwedge_{\delta\in D_\varphi} Cons(\delta)}{\varphi}.$$

[9] shows that the addition of lemma default rules does not alter the constrained extensions of a given default theory: Let δ_φ be a lemma default rule for φ. Then, (E, C) is a constrained extension of (D, W) iff (E, C) is a constrained extension of $(D \cup \{\delta_\varphi\}, W)$. So, the approach provides a simple solution for generating and using lemma defaults. Whenever we lemmatize a conclusion, we change its representation into a default rule and add it to the default rules of a considered

[4] Ie. to introduce a derivable theorem as a lemma by adding it to the initial theory.

default theory. So lemma defaults are abbreviations for the default inferences needed for deriving a conclusion. This approach is discussed in detail in [9]. There, it is also contrasted with the one taken in [2].

In fact, we do not have to transform a default conclusion into a lemma default rule if we focus on constrained extensions that are "compatible" with the underlying constraints imposed by the conclusion's default proof:

Theorem 3. *Let δ_φ be a lemma default rule for φ wrt a default theory (D, W). Then, we have for all sets of formulas E and C where $C \cup Just(\delta_\varphi) \cup \{\varphi\}$ is consistent that (E, C) is a constrained extension of (D, W) iff (E, C) is a constrained extension of $(D, W \cup \{\varphi\})$.*

This result justifies the use of so-called *dynamic lemmas*, which are applicable in the course of a proof search without consistency checks due to the (previously established) consistency of $Just(\delta_\varphi) \cup \{\varphi\}$ with the default proof segment at hand. In contrast to dynamic lemmas, we call a lemma default rule δ_φ *static*, if it was generated in an independent default proof. In such a case, merely the consistency with the default proof segment at hand has to be checked in order to apply δ_φ. Algorithmically, let $\mathcal{A}(\varphi, D, W)$ be a boolean algorithm returning true iff φ is in some constrained extension (E, C) of (D, W). Then, a lemma default rule δ_φ of (D, W) is supplied as a *static* lemma to $\mathcal{A}$ if it is used as a default rule, as in $\mathcal{A}(\varphi, D \cup \{\delta_\varphi\}, W)$. If additionally for some $D' \subseteq D$, we have $W \cup Just(D') \cup Cons(D') \cup Just(\delta_\varphi) \cup \{\varphi\}$ is consistent, then δ_φ is *dynamically* usable, via a "call" $\mathcal{A}(\varphi, D, W \cup \{\varphi\})$. With Theorem 3 we have $\mathcal{A}(\varphi, D \cup \{\delta_\varphi\}, W)$ iff $\mathcal{A}(\varphi, D, W \cup \{\varphi\})$ for dynamic lemma default rules.

Consider for example the statements "profs are typically adults", "adults are typically employed", "employed people typically have money", and "employed people having money typically buy cars", which yields the following theory.

$$\left(\left\{\frac{P:A}{A}, \frac{A:E}{E}, \frac{E:M}{M}, \frac{E \wedge M:B}{B}\right\}, \{P\}\right) \tag{1}$$

Consider the query B, asking whether profs buy cars. Proving this, by definition of a default proof, is to form a sequence $\langle\delta_i\rangle_{i \in I}$ of default rules such that B follows from $\{P\} \cup \{Cons(\delta_i) \mid i \in I\}$. For proceeding in a query-oriented manner, we have to form this sequence by starting with the rightmost default rule in sequence $\langle\delta_i\rangle_{i \in I}$ and working our way "down" to the facts while satisfying Condition *(2)* and *(3)* of Theorem 1. So let us put the default rule $\frac{E \wedge M:B}{B}$ at the end of the sequence. This can be done, if we can derive $(E \wedge M)$ from the remaining default rules together with $\{P\}$. That is, we have to prove in turn E and, independently, M. This can be done by means of the default proofs $D_E = \left\langle\frac{P:A}{A}, \frac{A:E}{E}\right\rangle$ and $D_M = \left\langle\frac{P:A}{A}, \frac{A:E}{E}, \frac{E:M}{M}\right\rangle$ for E and M, respectively. For the query B, we then obtain the default proof $D_B = \left\langle\frac{P:A}{A}, \frac{A:E}{E}, \frac{E:M}{M}, \frac{E \wedge M:B}{B}\right\rangle$. Observe that this approach bears a certain redundancy due to $D_E \subseteq D_M$. That is, if we build the default proof D_B in the aforementioned way, we consider the subsequence $\left\langle\frac{P:A}{A}, \frac{A:E}{E}\right\rangle$ twice. Consequently, we also have to check conditions *(2)* and *(3)* of Theorem 1 twice for each default rule in this default proof segment. However, this redundancy can be avoided by means of lemma default rules. Suppose, we first build the default proof $D_E = \left\langle\frac{P:A}{A}, \frac{A:E}{E}\right\rangle$ and lemmatize the conclusion E afterwards. This yields the lemma default rule $\delta_E = \frac{:A \wedge E}{E}$. Notably, this lemma default rule can be used for simplifying the second default proof

$D_M = \langle \frac{P:A}{A}, \frac{A:E}{E}, \frac{E:M}{M} \rangle$ to $D'_M = \langle \frac{:A \wedge E}{E}, \frac{E:M}{M} \rangle$

without any consistency checks. That is, not even the justification of δ_E, $A \wedge E$, has to be checked for consistency, since the underlying default proof D_E constitutes a viable segment of the actual default proof. In fact, the treatment of $\frac{:A \wedge E}{E}$ in the course of the proof search for B gives an example for handling dynamic lemma default rules. That is, a dynamic lemma default rule is applicable without any consistency checks due to the contribution of the underlying default proof to the default proof of the original query. Clearly, this approach is of great practical relevance since it reduces computational efforts in a significant way.

In addition to using δ_E as a dynamic lemma, we can generate and keep lemma default rules, like δ_E and $\delta_M = \frac{:A \wedge E \wedge M}{M}$, for later usage. Then, during a later proof search, we can use δ_E and δ_M as static default rules with the usual consistency check. Notably, in any case, none of the default proofs underlying δ_E and δ_M, namely D_E and D_M, have then to be reconsidered. Note also that the use of static lemma default rules leads to even shorter proofs than in the case of dynamic lemmas, because we can directly jump to the desired conclusions.

3 Lemma Handling while Query-Answering

The general idea of our algorithmic approach is to proceed in a query-oriented manner. For this, we extend the approach taken in [10]. In fact, [10] gives an algorithm following the line of Theorem 1. Even though this algorithm relies on the connection method [1], it can as well be seen as an algorithm based on model elimination [6]. Both deduction methods allow for testing the unsatisfiability of formulas in conjunctive normal form (CNF) and can be outlined as follows.[5] The proof procedures are carried out by means of two distinct inference operations, called *extension* and *reduction* operation. An extension operation amounts to Prolog's use of input resolution. That is, a subgoal, say K, is resolved with an input clause, say $\{J, \neg K, L\}$, if the subgoal is complementary to one of the literals in the selected clause, here $\neg K$. This yields two new subgoals, J and L. The reduction operation renders the inference system complete: If the current subgoal is complementary to one of its ancestor subgoals, then the current subgoal is solved. In the connection method the ancestor goals are accumulated in a so-called *path*, which intuitively corresponds to a path through a CNF obtained by taking the ancestor subgoal from each previous input clause.

In what follows, we refine the approach taken in [10] in order to incorporate the generation and application of lemma default rules. For this purpose, we redefine the predicate $compl(p, C_W, C_D)$ used in [10] as a declarative description of a query-answering algorithm in default logics. But first let us introduce some notions we use later on. We say a default theory (D, W) is in *atomic format* if all formulas occuring in the defaults in D are atomic. A general method to transform default theories in their atomic format is described in [10]. In what follows, we consider only propositional default theories in atomic format.

[5] For a detailed description the reader is referred to [1, 6].

In order to find out whether a formula φ is in some extension of a default theory (D, W) we proceed as follows: First, we transform the default rules in D into their sentential counterparts. This yields a set of indexed implications: $W_D = \{\alpha_\delta \rightarrow \gamma_\delta \mid \frac{\alpha_\delta : \beta_\delta}{\gamma_\delta} \in D\}$. Second, we transform both W and W_D into their clausal forms, C_W and C_D. The clauses in C_D, like $\{\neg\alpha_\delta, \gamma_\delta\}$, are called *δ-clauses*; accordingly, *lemma δ-clauses* are simple unit-clauses, like $\{\gamma_\delta\}$; all other clauses like those in C_W are referred to as *ω-clauses.* For any set of formulas S, let C_S be the set of clauses corresponding to the CNF of S.

Now, let us turn to our extension of the algorithm proposed in [10]: We define a predicate *compl* such that $compl(\neg\varphi, C_W, C_D)$ is true iff there is a default proof of φ from (D, W). The first argument of the predicate is a set of literals describing a partial path containing all ancestor goals, the second argument represents a set of ω-clauses, and the last argument accounts for δ-clauses. For incorporating lemma generation, we define a lemma operator as follows. Let (D, W) be default theory and S some set of literals. For $C_{D'} \subseteq C_D$, we define

$$C_W^S(C_{D'}) = \{\{\varphi\} \mid \varphi \in S \text{ and } compl(\{\neg\varphi\}, C_W, C_{D'})\}.$$

For distinguishing the components of the default theory, say (D°, W°), from formal parameters, let C_W° and C_D° be fixed sets of ω- and δ-clauses corresponding to the original sets W° and D°, respectively. C_W and C_D function as parameters.

Definition 4. *Let $C_W \subseteq C_W^\circ$ be a set of ω-clauses, $C_D \subseteq C_D^\circ$ be a set of δ-clauses, $C_L \subseteq C_{W^\circ}^S(C_D^\circ)$ be a set of (static) lemma δ-clauses and S be a set of literals. Let $C_{DL} = C_D \cup C_L$ be the set of all δ-clauses. Then, we define $compl(p, C_W, C_{DL})$ relative to C_W° as follows.*

1. *If $C_W \cup C_{DL} = \emptyset$ then $compl(p, C_W, C_{DL})$ is false.*
2. *If $C_W \neq \emptyset$ and $c \in C_W$ then $compl(p, C_W, C_{DL})$ is true iff the following two conditions hold for $c = c_1 \cup c_2$.*
   (a) *for all $K \in c_1$, K is complementary to some literal of p.*
   (b) *for all $K \in c_2$, there is a set of δ-clauses $C_{D(K)} \subseteq C_{DL}$ and a set of (dynamic) lemma δ-clauses $C_L^\star \subseteq C_{W^\circ}^S(\bigcup_{K\in c_2} C_{D(K)})$ such that the following two conditions hold.*
      i. *$compl(p \cup \{K\}, (C_W \setminus \{c\}) \cup C_L^\star, C_{D(K)})$ is true.*
      ii. *$compl(Just(\bigcup_{K\in c_2} D(K)), C_W^\circ \cup \bigcup_{K\in c_2} C_{D(K)}, \emptyset)$ is false.*
3. *If $C_D \neq \emptyset$ and $c \in C_D$ then $compl(p, C_W, C_{DL})$ is true iff the following two conditions hold for $c = \{\neg\alpha_\delta, \gamma_\delta\}$.*
   (a) *γ_δ is complementary to some literal of p.*
   (b) *There is a set of δ-clauses $C_{D(\neg\alpha_\delta)} \subseteq C_{DL}$ and a set of (dynamic) lemma δ-clauses $C_L^\star \subseteq C_{W^\circ}^S(C_{D(\neg\alpha_\delta)})$ such that $\{\neg\alpha_\delta, \gamma_\delta\} \in C_{DL} \setminus C_{D(\neg\alpha_\delta)}$ and the following two conditions hold.*
      i. *$compl(\{\neg\alpha_\delta\}, C_W^\circ \cup C_L^\star, C_{D(\neg\alpha_\delta)})$ is true.*
      ii. *$compl(Just(D(\neg\alpha_\delta) \cup \{\delta\}), C_W^\circ \cup C_{D(\neg\alpha_\delta)} \cup \{\{\neg\alpha_\delta, \gamma_\delta\}\}, \emptyset)$ is false.*
4. *If $C_L \neq \emptyset$ and $c \in C_L$ then $compl(p, C_W, C_{DL})$ is true iff the following two conditions hold for $c = \{\gamma_\delta\}$.*
   (a) *γ_δ is complementary to some literal of p.*
   (b) *$compl(Just(\delta), C_W^\circ \cup \{\{\gamma_\delta\}\}, \emptyset)$ is false.*

The preceding algorithm is an extension of the standard algorithm for the connection method given in [4]. In fact, the first two conditions provide a sound and complete algorithmic characterization of the standard connection method (see [4] for details) when discarding all δ-clauses. While Condition *(1)* accounts for the limiting case, Condition *(2)* deals with ω-clauses. *(2a)* corresponds to the aforementioned reduction operation, while *(2bi)* is an extension operation. Condition *(2bii)* was added in [10] in order to guarantee the compatibility of multiple subproofs found in *(2bi)*. Condition *(3)* deals with δ-clauses:[6] *(3a)* corresponds to *(2a)* and says that the consequent of a default rule γ_δ can be used for query-answering as any other proposition—provided *(3bi)* and *(3bii)* are satisfied. In fact, *(3bi)* "implements" Statement (*2*) in Theorem 1 and ensures that the prerequisite α_δ of a default rule is derivable in a non-circular way. Correspondingly, *(3bii)* "implements" Statement (*3*) in Theorem 1. This treatment is discussed in detail in [10], so that we focus now on the treatment of lemma default rules.

While static lemma δ-clauses are globally supplied by C_L, dynamic lemma δ-clauses are generated "on the fly" from the default proofs at hand. Dynamic lemmas are represented by $C_L^\star$; they are formed by considering all δ-clauses used in proving the set of subgoals under consideration, namely those in c_2 and $\{\neg\alpha_\delta\}$ in *(2b)* and *(3b)*, respectively. In this way, the resulting lemma δ-clauses can be treated in the subproof as if they were standard ω-clauses. The consistency of the corresponding justifications is ensured by *(2bii)* and *(3bii)*. Accordingly, dynamic lemma δ-clauses are added to the current ω-clauses in *(2bi)* and *(3bi)* via $(C_W \setminus \{c\}) \cup C_L^\star$ and $C_W^\circ \cup C_L^\star$, respectively.

Condition *(4)* deals with the application of static lemma δ-clauses. The treatment is analogous to that of δ-clauses in *(3)* with the exception that no prerequisite has to be proven. Consequently, there are no subproofs to be accomplished, which renders further lemma generation obsolete. In contrast to the treatment of dynamic lemmas in *(3)*, the consistency of the justification of the corresponding lemma default rule has to be checked in *(4b)*.

Let us illustrate $compl(p, C_W, C_D)$ by reconsidering the derivation of B from default theory (1), given at the end of Section 2. Since algorithm 4 is defined for default theories in atomic format, we partially transform our initial default theory in atomic format: For a new atom EM, the default theory

$$\left(\left\{\frac{P:A}{A}, \frac{A:E}{E}, \frac{E:M}{M}, \frac{EM:B}{B},\right\}, \{P\} \cup \{E \wedge M \rightarrow EM\}\right) \tag{2}$$

is a conservative extension of default theory (1). This theory yields the set of original ω-clauses $C_W^\circ = \{\{P\}, \{\neg E, \neg M, EM\}\}$, so that we have to show that

$$compl(\{\neg B\}, C_W^\circ, \{\{\neg P_{\delta_1}, A_{\delta_1}\}, \{\neg A_{\delta_2}, E_{\delta_2}\}, \{\neg E_{\delta_3}, M_{\delta_3}\}, \{\neg EM_{\delta_4}, B_{\delta_4}\}\}). \tag{3}$$

We select clauses in a connection-driven way. Thus, we select the δ-clause $\{\neg EM_{\delta_4}, B_{\delta_4}\}$ since B_{δ_4} is complementary to the literal $\neg B$ on the active path. This establishes Condition *(3a)*. Next, we have to verify *(3b)*. For this, we have to find a subset $C_{D(\neg EM_{\delta_4})}$ of the remaining δ-clauses in

[6] Note that default (sub)proofs are given as existentially quantified sets of default rules, such as $C_{D(K)}$ or $C_{D(\neg\alpha_\delta)}$ in *(2b)* and *(3b)*, respectively, in order to retain maximum degrees of freedom.

$\{\{\neg P_{\delta_1}, A_{\delta_1}\}, \{\neg A_{\delta_2}, E_{\delta_2}\}, \{\neg E_{\delta_3}, M_{\delta_3}\}\}$ satisfying *(3bi)* and *(3bii)*. For illustration, we direct our subsequent choices along the line sketched by the derivation in Section 2: For $C_{D(\neg EM_{\delta_4})} = \{\{\neg P_{\delta_1}, A_{\delta_1}\}, \{\neg A_{\delta_2}, E_{\delta_2}\}, \{\neg E_{\delta_3}, M_{\delta_3}\}\}$, we then obtain for *(3bi)* and *(3bii)*: [7]

$$compl(\{\neg EM_{\delta_4}\}, C_W^{\circ}, \{\{\neg P_{\delta_1}, A_{\delta_1}\}, \{\neg A_{\delta_2}, E_{\delta_2}\}, \{\neg E_{\delta_3}, M_{\delta_3}\}\}) \text{ is true and} \quad (4)$$

$$compl(\emptyset, C_W^{\circ} \cup \{\{\neg P_{\delta_1}, A_{\delta_1}\}, \{\neg A_{\delta_2}, E_{\delta_2}\}, \{\neg E_{\delta_3}, M_{\delta_3}\}, \{\neg EM_{\delta_4}, B_{\delta_4}\}\}, \emptyset) \text{ is false} \quad (5)$$

As can be easily seen, (5) is reducible by successive applications of *(2)* to $compl(\{P, A_{\delta_1}, E_{\delta_2}, M_{\delta_3}, EM, B_{\delta_4}\}, \emptyset, \emptyset)$ is false.

For showing (4), namely *(3bi)*, we select the ω-clause $\{\neg E, \neg M, EM\}$ from C_W° because EM is complementary to $\neg EM_{\delta_4}$ on the active path in (4); this establishes *(2a)*. For showing *(2b)*, we have to determine $C_{D(\neg E)}$, $C_{D(\neg M)}$ and $C_L^{\star}$ such that *(2bi)* and *(2bii)* hold. Observe that *(2bi)* has to be separately satisfied by $C_{D(\neg E)}$ and $C_{D(\neg M)}$, while *(2bii)* has to be jointly satisfied by $C_{D(\neg E)}$ and $C_{D(\neg M)}$. Since the choice of $C_L^{\star}$ is an arbitrary one, let us illustrate how $C_L^{\star} \subseteq C_W^S \circ (C_{D(\neg E)} \cup C_{D(\neg M)})$ can be successively build along the lines sketched in Section 2.

Let $C_{D(\neg E)} = \{\{\neg P_{\delta_1}, A_{\delta_1}\}, \{\neg A_{\delta_2}, E_{\delta_2}\}\}$ and let $C_L^{\star}$ be an arbitrary set of lemma δ-clauses at this point. Then, we have to show *(2bi)*:

$$compl(\{\neg EM_{\delta_4}, \neg E\}, \{\{P\}\} \cup C_L^{\star}, \{\{\neg P_{\delta_1}, A_{\delta_1}\}, \{\neg A_{\delta_2}, E_{\delta_2}\}\}) \text{ is true.} \quad (6)$$

By continuing along the same argumentation leading from (3) to (4) and (5), we first select the δ-clause $\{\neg A_{\delta_2}, E_{\delta_2}\}$; second we select the δ-clause $\{\neg P_{\delta_1}, A_{\delta_1}\}$ while applying *(3)* twice. In this way, we confirmed (6), viz. *(2bi)*, for $C_{D(\neg E)}$ without any usage of lemma δ-clauses. This corresponds intuitively to proving E from $\{P\}$ by means of the default proof D_E in Section 2.

For choosing $C_{D(\neg M)}$ (and $C_L^{\star}$), we have two extreme possibilities. First let

$$C_{D(\neg M)} = \{\{\neg P_{\delta_1}, A_{\delta_1}\}, \{\neg A_{\delta_2}, E_{\delta_2}\}, \{\neg E_{\delta_3}, M_{\delta_3}\}\} \quad \text{and} \quad C_L^{\star} = \emptyset . \quad (7)$$

In this case, no dynamic lemmas are used. On the other hand, we have established (6) without any use of dynamic lemmas. This allows us to draw dynamic lemma δ-clauses according to the definition of C_W^S. In this way, we can take advantage of the fact that we have proven E in (6) and obtain the following alternative choice for $C_{D(\neg M)}$ (and $C_L^{\star}$):

$$C_{D(\neg M)} = \{\{\neg E_{\delta_3}, M_{\delta_3}\}\} \quad \text{and} \quad C_L^{\star} = \{\{E\}\}. \quad (8)$$

Depending on our choice of $C_{D(\neg M)}$ and $C_L^{\star}$, we are faced with the following conditions establishing *(2bi)*:

$$compl(\{\neg EM_{\delta_4}, \neg M\}, \{\{P\}\}, \{\{\neg P_{\delta_1}, A_{\delta_1}\}, \{\neg A_{\delta_2}, E_{\delta_2}\}, \{\neg E_{\delta_3}, M_{\delta_3}\}\}) \text{ is true} \quad (9)$$

$$compl(\{\neg EM_{\delta_4}, \neg M\}, \{\{P\} \cup \{E\}\}, \{\{\neg E_{\delta_3}, M_{\delta_3}\}\}) \text{ is true} \quad (10)$$

The latter can be reduced to $compl(\{\neg EM_{\delta_4}, \neg M, P, E\}, \emptyset, \{\{\neg E_{\delta_3}, M_{\delta_3}\}\})$ by successive applications of *(2)*, while the former yields $compl(\{\neg EM_{\delta_4}, \neg M, P\}, \emptyset, \{\{\neg P_{\delta_1}, A_{\delta_1}\}, \{\neg A_{\delta_2}, E_{\delta_2}\}, \{\neg E_{\delta_3}, M_{\delta_3}\}\})$. In this way, we can solve (10) by means of *one* default inference, namely Condition *(3)*, due to the usage of dynamic lemmas, while we are faced with *three* default inferences in (9) if we fail to notice dynamic lemmas.

[7] Since we deal with normal default rules no justifications have to be added in (5) to the path.

Finally, we have to check *(2bii)* for $C_{D(\neg E)}$ and $C_{D(\neg M)}$: [8]

$compl(\emptyset, C^{\circ}_{W} \cup \{\{\neg P_{\delta_1}, A_{\delta_1}\}, \{\neg A_{\delta_2}, E_{\delta_2}\}, \{\neg E_{\delta_3}, M_{\delta_3}\}\}, \emptyset)$ is false.

As above, this can be confirmed by successive applications of *(2)* (no matter which choice, (7) or (8)). That is, $compl(\{P, A_{\delta_1}, E_{\delta_2}, M_{\delta_3}, EM\}, \emptyset, \emptyset)$ is false. Now, we have shown items (4) and (5) confirming Condition *(3bi)* and *(3bii)* so that our proof of B is completed.

Finally, we obtain the following result showing that our incremental algorithm with lemma handling is correct and complete for query-answering in constrained default logic:

Theorem 5. *Let (D, W) be a default theory in atomic format, φ an atomic formula and L a set of lemma default rules. Then, $\varphi \in E$ for some constrained extension (E, C) of (D, W) iff $compl(\{\neg\varphi\}, C_W, C_D \cup C_L)$ is true, where C_W is the matrix of W, C_D is the matrix of W_D and C_L is the matrix of L.*

4 Conclusion

We have implemented our approach and tested it on numerous examples. Due to space restrictions however we had to remove this part of the paper. The experimental results are given in [5]. What has been achieved? One of the original postulates of default formalisms was to "jump to conclusions" in the absence of information. But since the computation of default conclusions involves not only deduction but also expensive consistency checks, the need to incorporate lemmas is even greater in default theorem proving than in standard theorem proving. Hence, default lemmas can be seen as a step in this direction.

References

1. W. Bibel. *Automated Theorem Proving.* Vieweg, 1987.
2. G. Brewka. Cumulative default logic: In defense of nonmonotonic inference rules. *Artificial Intelligence*, 50(2):183–205, 1991.
3. J. Delgrande, T. Schaub, W. Jackson. Alternative approaches to default logic. *Artificial Intelligence*, 70(1–2):167–237, 1994.
4. E. Eder. *Relative Complexities of First Order Calculi.* Vieweg, 1992.
5. Th. Linke and T. Schaub. Lemma handling in default logic theorem provers. Technical report, Faculty of Technology, University of Bielefeld, 1995. (in preparation).
6. D. Loveland. *Automated Theorem Proving: A Logical Basis.* North-Holland, 1978.
7. D. Makinson. General theory of cumulative inference. In M. Reinfrank et al, eds, *Proc. 2nd Int. Workshop on Non-Monotonic Reasoning*, 1–18. Springer, 1989.
8. R. Reiter. A logic for default reasoning. *Artificial Intelligence*, 13(1–2):81–132, 1980.
9. T. Schaub. On constrained default theories. In B. Neumann, ed, *Proc. of the European Conf. on Artificial Intelligence*, p. 304–308. Wiley, 1992.
10. T. Schaub. A new methodology for query-answering in default logics via structure-oriented theorem proving. *Journal of Automated Reasoning*, 1995. Forthcoming.

[8] Since we deal with normal default rules no justification have to be added in *(2bii)* to the path.

Uncertain Reasoning in Concept Lattices

Thomas Lukasiewicz

Lehrstuhl für Informatik II, Universität Augsburg, Universitätsstr. 2,
86135 Augsburg, Germany, lukasiewicz@uni-augsburg.de

Abstract. This paper presents concept lattices as a natural representation of class hierarchies in object-oriented databases and frame based knowledge representations. We show how to extend concept lattices by uncertainty in the form of conditional probabilities. We illustrate that uncertain reasoning within the hierarchical structure of concept lattices can be performed efficiently and makes uncertain conclusions more precise.

1 Introduction

The aim of this paper is to integrate uncertainty into class hierarchies of object-oriented databases and frame based knowledge representations.

Extensional subclass relationships and disjointness statements are characteristic of class hierarchies. They can naturally be represented by *concept lattices* (see e.g. [15]). A concept is a pair consisting of a set of objects and a set of properties that all these objects share. The concept order is based on a coupled extensional and intensional order. For our purpose it is sufficient to concentrate just on the intensional part.

Uncertainty is integrated into concept lattices by a model based on conditional probabilities with intervals (see e.g. [11], [12], [13]). Surprisingly, uncertain reasoning in concept lattices has a lot of advantages. We show that the availability of conceptual knowledge yields an enormous search space reduction and that conceptual knowledge can be exploited for precise conclusions.

The technical details can be found in [8]. More details about the integration of uncertainty into object-oriented databases in the form of *uncertain constraints* are provided by [7] and [9].

2 Syntax and Semantics of Conceptual Knowledge

We start with the definition of a language for conceptual knowledge. We introduce *c-terms* as a means to refer to concepts. Classification among concepts can then be formulated by conceptual formulas.

Definition 2.1 (Syntax of c-terms) We consider an alphabet $\mathcal{A} := \{\emptyset, \mathcal{U}, B_1, \ldots, B_k\}$ of constants. The set $\mathcal{C}$ of all *c-terms* is the minimal set with $\mathcal{A} \subseteq \mathcal{C}$ and $C, D \in \mathcal{C} \Longrightarrow CD \in \mathcal{C}$.

Definition 2.2 (Semantics of c-terms) An *interpretation* $\mathcal{J} := (\mathcal{U}, J)$ of the set of c-terms $\mathcal{C}$ consists of a finite set of objects $\mathcal{U}$ and a mapping $J: \{B_1, \ldots, B_k\} \longrightarrow 2^{\mathcal{U}}$. J is extended to $\mathcal{C}$ by: $J(\boldsymbol{\mathcal{U}}) := \mathcal{U}$, $J(\boldsymbol{\emptyset}) := \emptyset$, $J(CD) := J(C) \cap J(D)$. In the sequel, we identify $\boldsymbol{\mathcal{U}}$ with $\mathcal{U}$ and $\boldsymbol{\emptyset}$ with $\emptyset$.

Definition 2.3 (Syntax of conceptual formulas) Let C, D, $D_1, \ldots, D_m \in \mathcal{C}$. The set of all conceptual formulas $\mathcal{CF}$ comprises *subclass formulas* $C \subseteq D$, *equality formulas* $C = D$ and *disjointness formulas* $D_1 \parallel \ldots \parallel D_m$.

Definition 2.4 (Semantics of conceptual formulas) An interpretation $\mathcal{J} = (\mathcal{U}, J)$ of $\mathcal{C}$ is extended to an interpretation of $\mathcal{CF}$ as follows:

1. $\mathcal{J} \models C \subseteq D$, iff $J(C) \subseteq J(D)$,
2. $\mathcal{J} \models C = D$, iff $\mathcal{J} \models C \subseteq D$ and $\mathcal{J} \models D \subseteq C$,
3. $\mathcal{J} \models D_1 \parallel \ldots \parallel D_m$, iff $\mathcal{J} \models D_i \cap D_j = \emptyset$ for all $i, j \in [1:m]$ with $i < j$.

The notions of models, satisfiability and logical consequence are defined as usual.

Definition 2.5 (Conceptual knowledge-base) A *conceptual knowledge-base* consists of a set of conceptual formulas.

Example 2.6 The conceptual knowledge that penguins are birds, that birds are winged animals, that penguins do not fly and that all flying objects are winged can be expressed by the following conceptual knowledge-base over the alphabet $\mathcal{A} = \{\emptyset, \mathcal{U}, \mathsf{penguins}, \mathsf{birds}, \mathsf{animals}, \mathsf{flying}, \mathsf{winged}\}$:

$$\mathcal{T}_1 = \{\mathsf{penguins} \subseteq \mathsf{birds},\ \mathsf{birds} \subseteq \mathsf{winged\,animals},\ \mathsf{penguins} \parallel \mathsf{flying},\ \mathsf{flying} \subseteq \mathsf{winged}\}\ .$$

3 Concept Lattices

A conceptual knowledge-base can completely be represented by a concept lattice.

Definition 3.1 (Concept lattice) Let $\mathcal{T}$ be conceptual knowledge-base. Let the equivalence relation $\sim_{\mathcal{T}}$ on $\mathcal{C}$ be defined by $C_1 \sim_{\mathcal{T}} C_2 :\Leftrightarrow \mathcal{T} \models C_1 = C_2$. Let $\mathcal{C}_{\mathcal{T}} := \mathcal{C}_{/\sim_{\mathcal{T}}}$ and $C_{\mathcal{T}} := [C]_{\sim_{\mathcal{T}}}$ for all $C \in \mathcal{C}$. The elements of $\mathcal{C}_{\mathcal{T}}$ are called *concepts*. $\emptyset_{\mathcal{T}}$ is called *empty concept*, $\mathcal{U}_{\mathcal{T}}$ is called *universal concept*. $(B_1)_{\mathcal{T}}, \ldots, (B_k)_{\mathcal{T}}$ are called *basic concepts*.

The partial order $\subseteq$ on $\mathcal{C}$ is canonically extended to a partial order $\subseteq_{\mathcal{T}}$ on $\mathcal{C}_{\mathcal{T}}$ by $A_{\mathcal{T}} \subseteq_{\mathcal{T}} B_{\mathcal{T}} :\Leftrightarrow (AB)_{\mathcal{T}} = A_{\mathcal{T}}$. The finite partially ordered set $(\mathcal{C}_{\mathcal{T}}, \subseteq_{\mathcal{T}})$ is a complete lattice. It is called the *concept lattice* for $\mathcal{T}$.

Example 3.2 Figure 1 shows the Hasse-diagram of $(\mathcal{C}_{\mathcal{T}_1}, \subseteq_{\mathcal{T}_1})$. We use the constants of the alphabet $\mathcal{A}$ as a label to the corresponding nodes in the Hasse-diagrams. This way we can get a representative for all non-labeled nodes: each node contains the conjunction of all constants attached to upper nodes.

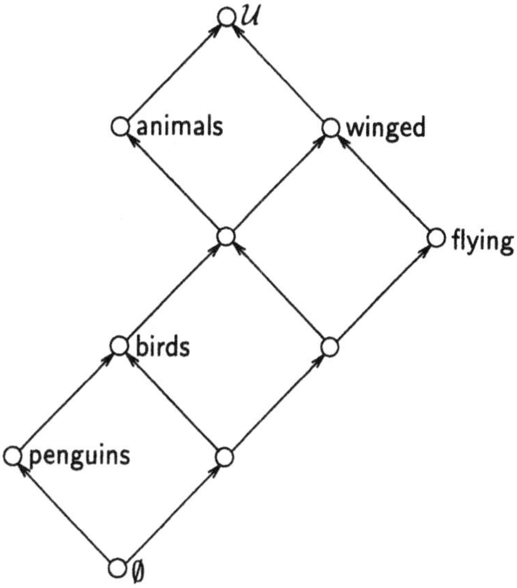

Fig. 1. The concept lattice for Ex. 2.6

4 Representation of Concept Lattices

Concepts can be internally represented by subsets of $\mathcal{A}$. The operation $\vee$ can be realized by intersection, the operation $\wedge$ can be performed by the use of a hull-operator on $2^{\mathcal{A}}$ based on a set of subclass formulas equivalent to the given conceptual knowledge-base. The time complexity of the hull-operator on $2^{\mathcal{A}}$ and hence of the operation $\wedge$ is linear in the number of subclass formulas ([1], [10]).

Definition 4.1 Let $\mathcal{A}(\cdot) : \mathcal{C} \to 2^{\mathcal{A}}$ be defined by $\mathcal{A}(C_1C_2\ldots C_l) := \{C_1, C_2, \ldots, C_l\}$ for all $C_1C_2\ldots C_l \in \mathcal{C}$ with $C_i \in \mathcal{A}$ for all $i \in [1:l]$, $l \geq 1$. Let $\mathcal{I} \subseteq \mathcal{CF}$ be a set of subclass formulas. Let the unary function $\mathcal{F}_{\mathcal{I}}$ on $2^{\mathcal{A}}$ be defined by:

$$\mathcal{F}_{\mathcal{I}}(A) := A \cup \bigcup\{\mathcal{A}(C) \mid P \subseteq C \in \mathcal{I},\ \mathcal{A}(P) \subseteq A\} \ .$$

Let the unary function $\mathcal{F}_{\mathcal{I}}^{\star}$ on $2^{\mathcal{A}}$ be defined by $\mathcal{F}_{\mathcal{I}}^{\star}(A) := \mathcal{F}_{\mathcal{I}}^{n}(A)$ with $n \in [0:k]$ such that $\mathcal{F}_{\mathcal{I}}^{n}(A) = \mathcal{F}_{\mathcal{I}}^{n+1}(A)$ and n minimal.

Theorem 4.2 *a) The partially ordered set* $(\mathcal{F}_{\mathcal{I}}^{\star}(2^{\mathcal{A}})\backslash\{\emptyset\}, \subseteq)$ *is a complete lattice with* $A \wedge B = \mathcal{F}_{\mathcal{I}}^{\star}(A \cup B)$ *and* $A \vee B = A \cap B$ *for all* $A, B \in \mathcal{F}_{\mathcal{I}}^{\star}(2^{\mathcal{A}})\backslash\{\emptyset\}$.
b) $(\mathcal{F}_{\mathcal{I}}^{\star}(2^{\mathcal{A}})\backslash\{\emptyset\}, \subseteq)$ *is anti-isomorphic to* $(\mathcal{C}_{\mathcal{I}}, \sqsubseteq_{\mathcal{I}})$.

Proof. For the proof of a) refer to [3] or [4], for the proof of b) refer to [9].

Example 4.3 An equivalent set of subclass formulas for the conceptual knowledge-base $\mathcal{T}_1$ is given by:

$\mathcal{I} = \{\text{penguins} \subseteq \text{birds, birds} \subseteq \text{winged animals, flying penguins} \subseteq \emptyset,$
$\text{flying} \subseteq \text{winged, winged} \subseteq \mathcal{U}, \text{animals} \subseteq \mathcal{U}, \emptyset \subseteq \text{flying penguins}\}$.

5 Syntax and Semantics of Uncertain Knowledge

The notations for the probabilistic model are adapted from [5] and [12].

Definition 5.1 (Syntax of probabilistic formulas) Let A, B, $C \in \mathcal{C}$ and $x_1, x_2, y_1, y_2 \in [0,1]$ with $x_1 \le x_2$ and $y_1 \le y_2$. The set of all probabilistic formulas $\mathcal{PF}$ comprises *positive probability statements* pos(A), *uncertain rules* $A \xrightarrow{x_1,x_2} B$ and *correlation rules* $A \underset{y_1,y_2}{\overset{x_1,x_2}{\longleftrightarrow}} B$.

Definition 5.2 (Semantics of probabilistic formulas) An interpretation $\mathcal{J} = (\mathcal{U}, J, P)$ of $\mathcal{PF}$ consists of an interpretation $(\mathcal{U}, J)$ of $\mathcal{C}$ and a probability measure $P : \mathcal{S} \longrightarrow [0,1]$ for the measure space $(\mathcal{U}, \mathcal{S})$.[1]

1. $\mathcal{J} \models pos(A)$, iff $P(J(A)) > 0$,
2. $\mathcal{J} \models A \xrightarrow{x_1,x_2} B$, iff $P(J(A)) = 0$ or $x_1 \le P(J(B)|J(A)) \le x_2$,[2]
3. $\mathcal{J} \models A \underset{y_1,y_2}{\overset{x_1,x_2}{\longleftrightarrow}} B$, iff $\mathcal{J} \models A \xrightarrow{x_1,x_2} B$ and $\mathcal{J} \models B \xrightarrow{y_1,y_2} A$.

The notions of models, satisfiability and logical consequence are defined as usual. The uncertain rule $A \xrightarrow{z_1,z_2} B$ is a *precise* logical consequence of $\mathcal{R} \subseteq \mathcal{CF} \cup \mathcal{PF}$ (denoted $\mathcal{R} \models_{precise} A \xrightarrow{z_1,z_2} B$), iff z_1 is the greatest lower bound and z_2 is the least upper bound for P$(B|A)$ that follows from $\mathcal{R}$ and the laws of probability.

Definition 5.3 (Probabilistic knowledge-base) A conceptual knowledge-base, extended by a non-empty set of probabilistic formulas, is called a *probabilistic knowledge-base*. Let V be an infinite set of variables. For $A, B \in \mathcal{C} \cup V$, $x_1, x_2 \in [0,1] \cup V$, the expression $?A \xrightarrow{x_1,x_2} B$ is called a *probabilistic rule query*.

Example 5.4 Gaining the uncertain knowledge that between 10 and 20 per cent of all animals are winged, that between 70 and 80 per cent of all winged animals fly, that between 40 and 50 per cent of all winged animals are flying birds, that between 50 and 60 per cent of all winged animals are birds, that between 10 and 20 per cent of all birds are penguins, that there are penguins and flying birds, we can add the set of uncertain rules

$$\mathcal{P} = \{\text{animals} \xrightarrow{0.1,0.2} \text{winged, winged animals} \xrightarrow{0.7,0.8} \text{flying,}$$
$$\text{winged animals} \xrightarrow{0.4,0.5} \text{flying birds, winged animals} \xrightarrow{0.5,0.6} \text{birds,}$$
$$\text{birds} \xrightarrow{0.1,0.2} \text{penguins, pos(penguins), pos(flying birds)}\}$$

to our conceptual knowledge-base $\mathcal{T}_1$.

---

[1] $\mathcal{S}$ denotes the smallest σ-algebra over $J(\mathcal{C})$.
[2] $P(J(B)|J(A))$ is the conditional probability of $J(B)$ under $J(A)$.

6 Uncertain Knowledge in Concept Lattices

Uncertain rules and correlation rules are extended from $\mathcal{C}$ to $\mathcal{C}_\mathcal{T}$ by:

$$A_\mathcal{T} \xrightarrow{x_1,x_2} (AB)_\mathcal{T} :\Leftrightarrow A \xrightarrow{x_1,x_2} B \ .$$

Positive probability statements are extended from $\mathcal{C}$ to $\mathcal{C}_\mathcal{T}$ by:

$$\mathrm{pos}(A_\mathcal{T}) :\Leftrightarrow \mathrm{pos}(A) \ .$$

Example 6.1 Figure 2 shows the Hasse-diagram of $(\mathcal{C}_{\mathcal{T}_1}, \subseteq_{\mathcal{T}_1})$ enriched by uncertain rules and positive probabilities. Uncertain rules are graphically represented by dashed, downward arcs and positive probabilities by black-filled nodes.

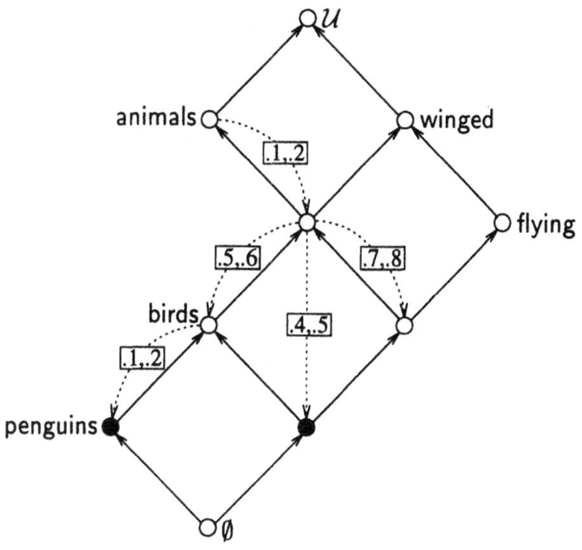

Fig. 2. Concept lattice with uncertain knowledge

7 Uncertain Deduction in Concept Lattices

Uncertain deduction is now performed on the complete lattice $(\mathcal{C}_\mathcal{T}, \subseteq_\mathcal{T})$, reducing the search space enormously.

Example 7.1 Table 7.1 gives a comparison of the number of elements in $\mathcal{C}_\mathcal{T}$, the number of uncertain and correlation rules over $\mathcal{C}_\mathcal{T}$ occuring w.r.t. $\mathcal{T} = \emptyset$ and $\mathcal{T} = \mathcal{T}_1$.

Table 1. Search space reduction by conceptual knowledge

	$\mathcal{T} = \emptyset$	$\mathcal{T} = \mathcal{T}_1$
number of elements in $\mathcal{C}_\mathcal{T}$	33	10
number of uncertain rules over $\mathcal{C}_\mathcal{T}$	276	47
number of correlation rules over $\mathcal{C}_\mathcal{T}$	1089	100

Conceptual knowledge can be exploited for increased precision of uncertain conclusions. This can be illustrated by referring to the chaining of correlations with the inference pattern $\{A \longleftrightarrow B, B \longleftrightarrow C\} \vdash A \longleftrightarrow C$. This syllogism is widely explored in the literature (see e.g. [2], [6], [12]), but all these considerations are based on the assumption that the involved events A, B and C are *elementary*. If A, B and C are implicitly or explicitly conceptually related, the inference rules presented in the literature for this pattern are not precise anymore. This is shown by the following theorem that provides the precise bounds under conceptual relationships between A, B and C. Note that conceptual relationships are directly encoded in the representation of concepts. Hence we get just one inference rule in which the conceptual relationships are evaluated on the representation of the concepts A, B and C.

Theorem 7.2 *Let* $\mathcal{T} \subseteq \mathcal{CF}$ *and* $\mathcal{P} = \{A \overset{u_1,u_2}{\underset{v_1,v_2}{\longleftrightarrow}} B, \mathrm{pos}(A), B \overset{x_1,x_2}{\underset{y_1,y_2}{\longleftrightarrow}} C\}$ *with* $u_1, v_1, x_1, y_1 > 0$, $u_1 = 1 \Leftrightarrow \mathcal{T} \models A \subseteq B$, $v_1 = 1 \Leftrightarrow \mathcal{T} \models B \subseteq A$, $x_1 = 1 \Leftrightarrow \mathcal{T} \models B \subseteq C$, $y_1 = 1 \Leftrightarrow \mathcal{T} \models C \subseteq B$, $\mathcal{T} \not\models A \subseteq C$, $\mathcal{T} \not\models AC = \emptyset$ *and* $\mathcal{T} \cup \mathcal{P}$ *satisfiable. It holds* $\mathcal{T} \cup \mathcal{P} \models_{precise} A \xrightarrow{z_1,z_2} C$ *with*

$$z_1 = \begin{cases} \frac{u_1}{y_2} & \text{if } \mathcal{T} \models C \subseteq A, \mathcal{T} \models AB \subseteq C \\ \frac{u_1 x_1}{v_2 y_2} & \text{if } \mathcal{T} \models C \subseteq A, \mathcal{T} \not\models AB \subseteq C \\ u_1 & \text{if } \mathcal{T} \not\models C \subseteq A, \mathcal{T} \models AB \subseteq C \\ \frac{u_1 x_1}{v_2} & \text{if } \mathcal{T} \not\models C \subseteq A, \mathcal{T} \not\models AB \subseteq C, \mathcal{T} \models BC \subseteq A \\ \max(0, u_1 - \frac{u_1}{v_1} + \frac{u_1 x_1}{v_1}) & \text{otherwise} \end{cases}$$

$$z_2 = \begin{cases} \min(1 - u_1, \frac{u_2(1-y_1)\min(x_2, 1-v_1)}{v_1 y_1}, \\ \quad \frac{(1-y_1)\min(x_2,1-v_1)}{y_1 v_1 + (1-y_1)\min(x_2,1-v_1)}) & \text{if } \mathcal{T} \models ABC = \emptyset \\ \min(u_2, \frac{u_2 x_2}{v_1}) & \text{if } \mathcal{T} \not\models ABC = \emptyset, \mathcal{T} \models AC \subseteq B \\ \min(1, \frac{u_2 x_2}{v_1 y_1}, 1 - u_1 + \frac{u_1 x_2}{v_1}, \frac{u_2}{y_1}, \\ \quad \frac{x_2}{v_1 y_1 + (1-y_1) x_2}) & \text{if } \mathcal{T} \not\models ABC = \emptyset, \mathcal{T} \not\models AC \subseteq B, \\ & \quad \mathcal{T} \models BC \subseteq A \\ \min(1, \frac{u_2 x_2}{v_1 y_1}, 1 - u_1 + \frac{u_1 x_2}{v_1}, \\ \quad u_2 - \frac{u_2 x_2}{v_1} + \frac{u_2 x_2}{v_1 y_1}, \frac{x_2}{y_1 v_1 + (1-y_1) x_2}) & \text{otherwise} \end{cases}$$

Proof. For the proof of Theorem 7.2 refer to [8].

Example 7.3 Let $\mathcal{A} = \{\emptyset, \mathcal{O}, \mathsf{A}, \mathsf{B}, \mathsf{C}\}$,

$$\mathcal{T}_1 = \emptyset,\ \mathcal{P}_1 = \{\mathsf{A} \overset{0.4,0.4}{\underset{0.1,0.3}{\longleftrightarrow}} \mathsf{B},\ \mathrm{pos}(\mathsf{A}),\ \mathsf{B} \overset{0.3,1}{\underset{0.8,0.8}{\longleftrightarrow}} \mathsf{AC}\}\ ,$$

$$\mathcal{T}_2 = \{\mathsf{BC} \subseteq \mathsf{A}\},\ \mathcal{P}_2 = \{\mathsf{A} \overset{0.4,0.4}{\underset{0.1,0.3}{\longleftrightarrow}} \mathsf{B},\ \mathrm{pos}(\mathsf{A}),\ \mathsf{B} \overset{0.3,1}{\underset{0.8,0.8}{\longleftrightarrow}} \mathsf{C}\}\ .$$

We get $\mathcal{T}_1 \cup \mathcal{P}_1 \models_{precise} \mathsf{A} \xrightarrow{0.5,0.5} \mathsf{C}$ and $\mathcal{T}_2 \cup \mathcal{P}_2 \models_{precise} \mathsf{A} \xrightarrow{0.4,0.5} \mathsf{C}$. These results can be computed with Theorem 7.2, since it holds $\mathcal{T}_1 \models \mathsf{AC} \subseteq \mathsf{A}$ and $\mathcal{T}_2 \models \mathsf{BC} \subseteq \mathsf{A}$. In contrast, all the inference rules for the chaining of correlation, which do not incorporate implicit or explicit conceptual knowledge between the correlated events, just enable us to compute the lower bound 0 and the upper bound 1.

8 Related Work

In [6] Heinsohn integrates uncertainty into terminological languages. Our approach is similar, but much more tractable for the use in object-oriented databases and frame-based knowledge representations, since we do not consider disjunction and negation. Furthermore we show how to reduce the search space by conceptual knowledge and how to integrate conceptual knowledge into the deduction of uncertain knowledge for an increased precision. The problem of uncertain deduction can also be solved by linear optimization. In [14] von Rimscha shows how to use certain knowledge to eliminate some variables of a linear optimization problem.

9 Summary and Outlook

We extended concept lattices by uncertainty in the form of conditional probabilities. We illustrated that uncertain reasoning within the hierarchical structure of concept lattices can be performed efficiently and makes uncertain conclusions more precise. Concept lattices seem to be a promising tractable subclass of the general problem of uncertain reasoning with conditional probabilities. There is more work to be done to find out in which special cases we can draw globally precise conclusions. Another topic for future work is the integration of objects in uncertain reasoning within concept lattices.

10 Acknowledgements

I'm grateful to Werner Kießling, Ulrich Güntzer, Gerhard Köstler and Helmut Thöne for fruitful discussions. I'm also grateful to the referees for useful comments.

References

1. C. Beeri and P. A. Bernstein. Computational problems related to the design of normal form relational schemas. *ACM Transactions on Database Systems*, 4:30–59, 1979.
2. D. Dubois, H. Prade, L. Godo, and R. L. de Màntaras. A symbolic approach to reasoning with linguistic quantifiers. In D. Dubois, M. P. Wellman, B. D. Ambrosio, and P. Smets, editors, *Proc. of the 8 th Conference on Uncertainty in Artificial Intelligence*, pages 74–82, Stanford, CA, Jul. 1992. Morgan Kaufmann Publishers.
3. V. Duquenne. Contextual implications between attributes and some representation properties for finite lattices. In B. Ganter, R. Wille, and K. E. Wolff, editors, *Beiträge zur Begriffsanalyse*, pages 241–254. B. I.-Wissenschaftsverlag, Mannheim, 1987.
4. B. Ganter and R. Wille. Implikationen und Abhängigkeiten zwischen Merkmalen. In P. O. Degens, H.-J. Hermes, and O. Opitz, editors, *Die Klassifikation und ihr Umfeld*, pages 171–185. INDEKS Verlag, Frankfurt, 1986.
5. U. Güntzer, W. Kießling, and H. Thöne. New directions for uncertainty reasoning in deductive databases. In *Proc. ACM SIGMOD Conference*, pages 178–187, Denver, CO, May 1991.
6. J. Heinsohn. *ALCP: Ein hybrider Ansatz zur Modellierung von Unsicherheit in terminologischen Logiken.* PhD thesis, Universität Saarbrücken, 1993.
7. W. Kießling, T. Lukasiewicz, G. Köstler, and U. Güntzer. The TOP database model – taxonomy, object-orientation and probability. In *Proc. Int'l Workshop on Uncertainty in Databases and Deductive Systems*, Ithaca, New York, Nov. 1994.
8. T. Lukasiewicz. Uncertain reasoning in concept lattices. Technical Report 323, Math. Institut, Universität Augsburg, March 1995.
9. T. Lukasiewicz, W. Kießling, G. Köstler, and U. Güntzer. Taxonomic and uncertain reasoning in object-oriented databases. Technical Report 303, Math. Institut, Universität Augsburg, Aug. 1994.
10. Y. Sagiv, C. Delobel, D. S. Parker, and R. Fagin. An equivalence between relational database dependencies and a fragment of propositional logic. *Journal of the Association for Computer Machinery*, 28(3):435–453, Jun. 1981.
11. L. Sombé. Reasoning under incomplete information in artificial intelligence: A comparison of formalisms using a single example. *International Journal of Intelligent Systems*, 5(4):323–472, 1990.
12. H. Thöne, U. Güntzer, and W. Kießling. Towards precision of probabilistic bounds propagation. In D. Dubois, M. P. Wellman, B. D. Ambrosio, and P. Smets, editors, *Proc. of the 8 th Conference on Uncertainty in Artificial Intelligence*, pages 315–322, Stanford, CA, Jul. 1992. Morgan Kaufmann Publishers.
13. H. Thöne, W. Kießling, and U. Güntzer. On cautious probabilistic inference and default detachment. *Special issue of the Annals of Operations Research*, 32, 1994. to appear.
14. M. von Rimscha. The determination of comparative and lower probability. In *Workshop Uncertainty in Knowledge-Based Systems, FAW-B-90025*, volume 2, pages 344–376, Ulm, Germany, 1990. FAW Ulm.
15. R. Wille. Restructuring lattice theory: an approach based on hierarchies of concepts. In I. Rival, editor, *Ordered sets*, pages 445–470. Reidel, Dordrecht, Boston, 1982.

A theorem prover for default logic based on prioritized conflict resolution and an extended resolution principle

Jérôme Mengin

Laboratoire de Recherche en Informatique
Bât. 490 - Université Paris Sud
91405 ORSAY CEDEX - FRANCE
Jerome.Mengin@lri.fr

Abstract. This paper presents a theorem prover for Reiter's default logic, one of the most studied nonmonotonic logics. Our theorem prover is based on a decomposition of default logic into two main elements: we describe an extension of the resolution principle, that handles the "monotonic" aspect of the defaults, and we provide a generalization of Reiter's and Levy's algorithms for the computation of hitting sets, that takes care of the nonmonotonic part of default logic. Lastly, we describe how these two components can be separately modified in order to obtain theorem provers for other variants of default logic, notably prioritized default logic.

1 Introduction

Default reasoning occurs whenever an agent must complete the certain information he has about a domain, with some knowledge which is plausible but not infallible. Pieces of such knowledge, also called pieces of default knowledge or *defaults* for short, enable the agent to draw reliable conclusions, which may have to be retracted in presence of new information.

In many logical approaches to default reasoning, the certain information is completed with defaults that are *coherent* with one another, to generate an *extension* of the certain information. As there are, usually, several possible combinations of defaults that are coherent with one another, several extensions can be built. This notion of coherence can be the consistency in the sense of classical logic [23, 10] or of some modal logics [30, 31]. Other notions of coherence have been shown [16, 9] to underly Reiter's default logic [24] and its variants.

In order to restrict the number of extensions, it is often necessary to use priorities among the defaults, like the so-called specificity principle, widely used in taxonomy. Other kinds of priorities, studied in the context of default reasoning, include ordering relations among the defaults, representing their relative reliabilities [4, 13, 11, 6], or some notions implicitly embedded in fixed-point constructs, as it is the case in Reiter's default logic [25, 5, 8].

A growing number of studies deal with algorithmic problems related to the computation of extensions. Some of these studies are based on TMS like algorithms [14, 13]. Other methods rely on more *ad hoc* approaches [22, 28, 29, 12, 26].

In this paper, following an approach by Levy [16], we present two methods that separately handle the notion of coherence between the defaults, and that of priorities among them.

More precisely, we propose a generalization of the resolution principle to defaults. That is, we define so-called "extended clauses", that are some kind of clausal representations of defaults, and we then define some new resolution rules for these extended clauses. We can then check the coherence of a set of defaults using these resolution rules, by trying to generate an empty clause.

We then propose a generalization of Levy's [17] algorithm for the computation of sets of defaults that generate extensions. This algorithm works by "eliminating", from an initial set of defaults, as many defaults as possible in order to restore some coherence of this set. The particularity of our algorithm is that it is not specially designed for default logic. It can handle a wide class of priorities among pieces of default knowledge.

In the next section, we present Reiter's original definition of default logic, and we recall the characterization that is used in our theorem prover. In Sect. 3, we describe our extended resolution principle, together with the new type of clauses that we introduce. Sect. 4 presents our elimination algorithm, and Sect. 5 describe some modifications that can be done to these two methods in order to obtain other variants of default logic.

2 Default logic

A *default theory* is a pair (W, D), where W is a set of closed formulas of first order predicate calculus, representing the certain information, and D is a set of *defaults*, of the.form $\frac{f:g}{h}$, where f, g, h are closed formulas of the language of first order predicate calculus. The default $\frac{f:g}{h}$ is intended to mean: "if f is true, and if nothing proves that g is false, then conclude h". We suppose, in the sequel, that W is consistent. Reiter [24] defines sets of theorems that are consequences of a default theory:

Definition 1 [24]. A set of formulas E is an *extension* of a default theory (W, D) iff $E = \Gamma(E)$, where $\Gamma(E)$ is the smallest set that is deductively closed, contains W, and such that for all $\frac{f:g}{h} \in D$, if $f \in \Gamma(E)$ and $\neg g \notin E$, then $h \in \Gamma(E)$.

In [19], we give another characterization of the extensions of a default theory, based on the following definitions:

Definition 2 [19]. Let (W, D) be a closed default theory. The set of formulas *generated* by a subset U of D, denoted by $\mathrm{Th}^{\mathrm{def}}(W \cup U)$, is the smallest set of formulas that contains W, is deductively closed (in the sense of predicate calculus), and such that for all $\frac{f:g}{h} \in U$, if $f \in \mathrm{Th}^{\mathrm{def}}(W \cup U)$ then $h \in \mathrm{Th}^{\mathrm{def}}(W \cup U)$. We will denote by Th the deduction operator of the predicate calculus.

Definition 3 [19]. A *conflict* of a default theory (W, D) is a subset C of D minimal that contains a default $\frac{f:g}{h}$ such that $f \wedge \neg g \in \mathrm{Th}^{\mathrm{def}}(W \cup U)$. In the sequel, Ξ denotes the set of conflicts of a theory.

Definition 4 [19]. An *elimination function* on a default theory (W, D) is a function ϕ that associates, to each conflict $C \in \Xi$, a set of pairs $(d, V) \in C \times 2^D$. A subset U of D is ϕ-preferred if it does not contain any conflict of the theory and verifies: $\forall d \in D \setminus U, \exists C \in \Xi, C \subseteq U \cup \{d\}$ and $(d, U) \in \phi(C)$

The intended meaning of $(d, V) \in \phi(C)$ is that, in order to resolve the conflict C, one can eliminate d, as soon as the elements of V are not themselves eliminated. See [19] for a more detailled presentation of these notions.

Theorem 5 [19]. *A set of formulas E is an extension of a default theory (W, D) iff E is generated by an ϕ^{DL}-preferred subset of D, where ϕ^{DL} is the elimination function defined by: $\phi^{\mathrm{DL}}(C) = \{(\frac{f:g}{h}, V) \in C \times 2^D \mid f \wedge \neg g \in \mathrm{Th}^{\mathrm{def}}(W \cup V)\}$.*

The next proposition shows that the extended deduction operator $\mathrm{Th}^{\mathrm{def}}$ is strongly related to the notion of conflict. It can be compared to a general result of classical logic: a formula f is classicaly entailed by a consistent set of formulas W if and only if $W \cup \{f \rightarrow \bot\}$ is inconsistent.

Proposition 6 [20]. *Given a default theory (W, D), whose set of conflicts is empty, then $f \in \mathrm{Th}^{\mathrm{def}}(W \cup U)$ iff $\frac{f:\bot}{\bot}$ is in a conflict of the theory $W, U \cup \{\frac{f:\bot}{\bot}\}$.*

Let us now outline the major steps taken by our theorem prover. Given a default theory (W, D) and a formula f, we want to decide whether f is in at least one extension of the theory:

1. Compute the conflicts of $(W, D \cup \{\frac{f:\bot}{\bot}\})$ (including those of (W, D)).
2. Compute ϕ^{DL} on the conflicts of (W, D).
3. Compute the ϕ^{DL}-preferred subsets of D.
4. f is in the extension generated by an ϕ^{DL}-preferred subset U of D iff there is a conflict $V \cup \{\frac{f:\bot}{\bot}\}$ of $(W, D \cup \{\frac{f:\bot}{\bot}\})$ such that $V \subseteq U$.

3 An extended resolution principle

In order to compute the conflicts of a default theory, we extend the classical resolution principle to defaults.

Definition 7. The *clausal form* of a default $d = \frac{\neg CN:CN'}{CN''}$, where CN, CN' and CN'' are conjunctions of clauses, is the set of defaults $\overline{d} = \{\frac{\neg c:c'}{c''}{}_d \mid c \in CN, c' \in CN', c'' \in CN''\}$. We will denote by $\overline{D}$ the union of the clausal forms of the set of defaults D, and call *extended clauses* the elements of $\overline{D}$.

Figure 1 presents the "extended resolution rules", that we will use together with the classical one.

Rules (1) and (2) are used to prove the prerequisite of a default d from the clauses of W and the consequents of other defaults obtained from rule (3) (see below): we make resolutions against the negation of the prerequisite of the default

$$\frac{c_1 \quad \frac{\neg c_2 : c'}{c''}_d}{\frac{\neg c : c'}{c''}_d}\,(1) \qquad \frac{\frac{\neg c_1 : c'}{c''}_d \quad \frac{\neg c_2 : c'}{c''}_d}{\frac{\neg c : c'}{c''}_d}\,(2) \qquad \frac{\frac{\neg \Box : c'}{c''}_d}{c''}\,(3) \qquad \frac{\frac{\neg \Box : c'}{c''}_d}{\frac{\neg \Box : c'}{\top}_d}\,(4) \qquad \frac{c_1 \quad \frac{\neg \Box : c_2}{\top}_d}{\frac{\neg \Box : c}{\top}_d}\,(5) \qquad \frac{\frac{\neg \Box : c_1}{\top}_d \quad \frac{\neg \Box : c_2}{\top}_d}{\frac{\neg \Box : c}{\top}_d}\,(6)$$

Fig. 1. Extended resolution rules (c_1 and $c2$ denote two clauses whose resolvent is c)

only. Therefore, when the extended clause "$\frac{\neg \Box : c'}{c''}_d$" is produced, the prerequisite of this default is proved.

Once the prerequisite of d has been proved, its consequent can be used like any formula of W (rule 3). However, the consistency of its justification is checked by making resolutions on it (rules 5-6). The production, using these rules, of an extended clause of the form $\frac{\neg \Box : \Box}{\top}_d$proves a conflict.

Rule (4) is there to avoid producing again the consequent of d using rule (3) everytime a resolution is made on its justification.

The production of an empty clause, using these extended resolution rules and the classical one, shows that the falsity is a consequence, in the sense of $\mathrm{Th}^{\mathrm{def}}$, of the set of defaults. In this case, the negation of the justification of any default can also be proved, therefore it also proves a conflict.

Notice how the indexes of the extended defaults have to be taken into account in rules (2) and (6): we can only make a resolution between the prerequisites (respectively the justifications) of two extended clauses if they have the same indexes, that is, if they have been produced from the same default. We will see the effect of relaxing these conditions in Sect 5.

Theorem 8 [20]. *Let (W, D) be a default theory, such that W is a finite set of clauses and D is finite and can be put under clausal form. A subset C of D is a conflict of the theory iff it is minimal such that the empty clause or an extended clause of the form $\frac{\neg \Box : \Box}{\top}_d$ can be produced from $W \cup \overline{C}$ using rules (1) to (6) and the classical resolution rule.*

Example 1. Let $W = \{p \vee q, \neg r \vee \neg s\}$ and $D = \{d, d'\}$, where $d = \frac{p \vee q : r}{s}$ and $d' = \frac{q : t}{t}$. Figure 2 shows the extended resolutions produced to prove that $\{d\}$ is a conflict of the theory.

In order to compute all the conflicts of a theory, we use [20] Besnard et al.'s *saturation by set* [2], which returns all conflicts of a set of (extended) clauses, and which is incremental: given two sets of clauses, it is possible to saturate $E \cup F$ using the result of the saturation of F. Thus, given a default theory (W, D), we will first saturate $W \cup D$ in order to compute the conflicts of the theory. Given some formula f, this result significantly simplify the saturation of $W \cup D \cup \{\frac{f : \perp}{\perp}\}$. Our implementation uses a particular resolution strategy, the *head-literal resolution*, which was proved in [3] to be complete and decidable for the class of so-called *groundable clauses*.

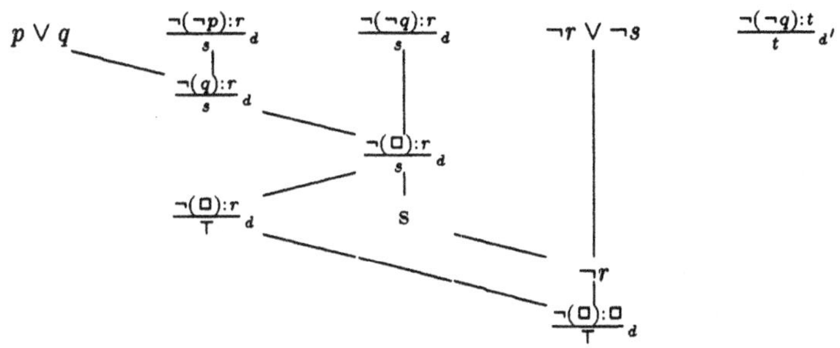

Fig. 2. Extended resolutions on Example 1

Lastly, let us briefly describe the computation of ϕ^{DL}: a default d can be eliminated in a context V iff its prerequisite and the negation of its justification can be proved from V. This corresponds to the production of extended clauses of the form $\frac{\neg(\Box):c}{c'}{}_d$ and $\frac{\neg(\Box):\Box}{\top}{}_d$ during the saturation process. Thus, the elimination function ϕ^{DL} can be computed from the result of the saturation.

4 Prioritized conflict resolution

The computation of the ϕ-preferred subsets of D, given a default theory (W, D), is done using an adaptation of Levy's algorithm for the computation "augmented HS-trees" [17]. Levy's has shown how his algorithm can be used for the computation of Reiter's default logic. We generalize below this result, by extending his notion of *exception* to a wider class of elimination functions. This result will be used in the next section, when we describe how to adapt our theorem prover to other variants of default logic.

Definition 9. An elimination function ϕ on the set of conflicts Ξ of a default theory (W, D) is *2-monotonic* if for all $C \in \Xi$ and $(d, V \cup V') \in D \times 2^D$, if $(d, V) \in \phi(C)$ then $(d, V \cup V') \in \phi(C)$. An *exceptions* is a pair $(d, V \cup (C \setminus \{d\}))$ where $C \in \Xi$ and $(d, V) \in \phi(C)\}$. (d, V) is *minimal* if for no exception of the form (d, V'), $V' \subset V$. We denote by Σ the set of minimal exceptions of a theory. Given a subset E of Σ, we denote $E_1 = \{d \mid \exists V \subseteq D, (d, V) \in E\}$ and $E_2 = \cup_{V \in \{V' \mid \exists d \in D, (d, V') \in E\}} V$.

Theorem 10. *Let (W, D) be a default theory, and ϕ a 2-monotonic elimination function on Ξ. A subset U of D is ϕ-preferred iff there exists $E \subseteq \Sigma$ such that $U = E_1$, $E_1 \cap E_2 = \emptyset$ and $\forall C \in \Xi, C \cap E_1 \neq \emptyset$.*

Proof (sketch). Suppose U is ϕ-preferred, then $\forall d \in D \setminus U, \exists C_d \in \Xi, C_d \setminus \{d\} \subseteq U$ and $(d, U) \in \phi(C_d)$. Let $V_d \subseteq U \cup (C_d \setminus \{d\})$ be minimal such that $(d, V_d) \in \Sigma$, and let $E = \{(d, V_d) \mid d \in D \setminus U\}$. Clearly $U = D \setminus E_1$. One can check that $E_1 \cap E_2 = \emptyset$ and $\forall C \in \Xi, C \cap E_1 \neq \emptyset$. For the converse, let $E \subseteq \Sigma$ s.t. $E_1 \cap E_2 = \emptyset$ and $\forall C \in \Xi, C \cap E_1 \neq \emptyset$, and let $U = D\backslash E_1$. For all $C \in \Xi$, since $E_1 \cap C \neq \emptyset$, $C \not\subseteq U$. Moreover let $d \in D\backslash U = E_1$, and let $V \subseteq D$ and $C \in \Xi$ s.t. $(d, V \cup (C \setminus \{d\})) \in E$: since $E_1 \cap E_2 = \emptyset$, $V \subseteq U$ and $C \setminus \{d\} \subseteq U$. By definition of Σ, $(d, V) \in \phi(C)$, hence $(d, U) \in \phi(C)$.

We compute the ϕ-preferred subsets of D by constructing a binary tree, whose nodes are labelled by pairs of the form (χ, Υ), where $\chi \subseteq 2^D$ and $\Upsilon \subseteq D$: χ is a set of conflicts that remain to be solved, and Υ is a set of defaults that cannot be eliminated any more, because they justify previous eliminations. The root is labelled by $(\Xi, \emptyset)$, and we consider an enumeration of Σ. Consider a new exception (d, V) in this enumeration. For each leaf of the tree labeled by (χ, Υ), if $d \notin \Upsilon$, and if $\emptyset \notin \{C \setminus V \mid C \in \chi, d \notin C\} = \chi'$, build two edges. The first one, labelled by d, leads to a new leaf labelled by $(\chi', \Upsilon \cup V)$. The second one is not labelled, and leads to a leaf labelled by (χ, Υ). Then U is an ϕ-preferred subsets of D iff U is the complementary in D of the set of labels of the edges on a path from the root to a leaf labelled by a pair of the form $(\emptyset, \Upsilon)$.

This tree can be pruned by a depth-first search. Let U be the ϕ-preferred subset of D corresponding to a leaf labelled by $(\emptyset, \Upsilon)$. Consider a node labelled by (χ', Υ'), such that the set L of labels of the edges from the root to this node, joined with $\cup_{C \in \chi'} C$, is included in $D \setminus U$: if this branch leads to a new solution U', it will be the complementary of a set included in $L \cup (\cup_{C \in \chi'} C)$. Since ϕ-preferred subsets of D are *maximal* such that they do not contain any conflict of the theory, we cannot obtain a new solution in the branches below this node.

5 Other variants of default logic

A major interest of this decomposition of the theorem prover into two completely independent tasks is that it enables us to adapt it to several other variants of default logic. In this section, we describe three such modifications.

Strong regularity Whereas Reiter's default logic requires that the justifications of the defaults used to generate an extension are separately consistent with the extension, several variants put a stronger condition: they require that the justifications of all the defaults together are consistent with the extensions [5, 27]. Froidevaux and Mengin [9] formalize it with a definition similar to the following one:

Definition 11 [9]. A set of defaults D is *strongly regular* w.r.t. a set of formulas W if $\mathrm{Th}^{\mathrm{def}}(W \cup D)$ is consistent with $\{g \mid \frac{f:g}{h} \in D\}$.

We can modify the definitions of conflict and of irregularity accordingly. In order for our extended resolution procedure to compute these irregularities, we simply have to replace rule (6) with rule (6') above,where c is the resolvent of c_1 and c_2. So we are now allowed to make resolutions between clauses that have been produced with the justifications of several defaults. If this leads to some extended clause $\frac{\neg\Box:\Box}{\top}$, then it means that the set of defaults is strongly irregular.

$$\frac{\frac{\neg\Box:c_1}{\top}d_1 \quad \frac{\neg\Box:c_2}{\top}d_2}{\frac{\neg\Box:c}{\top}d_1}\ (6') \qquad \frac{\frac{\neg c_1:c'_1}{c''_1}d_1 \quad \frac{\neg c_2:c'_2}{c''_2}d_2}{\frac{\neg c:c'_1}{c''_1 \vee c''_2}d_1}\ (2') \qquad \frac{\frac{\neg c_1:c'_1}{c''_1}d_1 \quad \frac{\neg c_2:c'_2}{c''_2}d_2}{\frac{\neg c:c'_2}{c''_1 \vee c''_2}d_2}\ (2'')$$

Fig. 3. Modified extended resolution rules

Reasoning by cases It is well-known that Reiter's default logic does not enable one to reason by cases using defaults: from the theory defined by $W = \{a \vee b\}$ and $D = \{\frac{a:c}{c}, \frac{b:d}{d}\}$ it is not possible to conclude $c \vee d$. Several authors have propose to modify Reiter's definition of the extension in order to allow such reasoning by cases. The idea is that one must be able to fire defaults "by sets", that is, to conclude the disjunction of the consequences of some defaults once the disjuction of their prerequisite has been proved. In order to adapt our theorem prover to reasoning by cases, we simply have to replace rule (2) with rules (2') and (2") abobe, where c is the resolvent of c_1 and c_2. As an example, it is possible to deduce the empty clause, using rules (1), (3) to (6), the above rule and the classical resolution rule, from $W \cup D \cup \{\frac{c:\Box}{\Box}, \frac{d:\Box}{\Box}\}$, where the latter set contains the extended clausal form of $\frac{c \vee d:\Box}{\Box}$.

Moinard [21] describes how this modification of default logic leads to some unwanted contrapositions of the defaults. He proposes to remedy to this problem by strenghtening the consistency condition on the justifications of the defaults, and the condition that allows one to eliminate a default. It would be interesting to specify the notion of irregularity as well as the elimination function that correspond to Moinard's definitions.

Prioritized default logic Several authors have proposed to add to default logic the possibility to define an ordering among the defaults, such that $d_1 \leq d_2$ means that the default d_1 is less reliable than the default d_2. The idea is that if d_1 and d_2 are conflicting, then one must use d_2 to generate an extension rather that d_1. In [19], we have proposed to associate, to such an ordering, the elimination function $\min_{\leq}$, such that $\min_{\leq}(C) = \{(d, V) \in C \times 2^D \mid \forall d' \in C, d' \not< d\}$. The meaning of this elimination function is that in order to resolve a conflict, one must eliminate one of its minimal (for $\leq$) elements. In order to adapt our theorem prover to the use of such a relation among the defaults, we simply have to apply the elimination algorithm to the set of conflicts of a theory, considering the elimination function $\min_{\leq} \circ \phi^{\mathrm{DL}}$: $\min_{\leq} \circ \phi^{\mathrm{DL}}(C) = \{(d, V) \in \phi^{\mathrm{DL}}(C) \mid \forall d' \in C, d' \not< d\}$.

6 Conclusion

We have described here the two main elements of a theorem prover for default logic. The first one generalizes the resolution principle to the (monotonic) deductions that can be made using defaults. The main interest of our presentation, by means of the introduction of special resolution rules, is that it is completely independent from any resolution strategy. We have implemented a theorem prover for default logic that uses theses rules combined to a resolution strategy by Bossu and Siegel [3], the resolution on head literals. But other resolution strategies could have been used. It is important to note that the resolution steps obtained using rules (1) to (6) correspond to resolution steps that would be obtained using the classical rule only on a clausal form of $W \cup \{\neg f, g, h \mid \frac{f:g}{h} \in D\}$. Consequently, any resolution strategy that is complete and that terminates on some particular class of clauses can be generalized to an extended resolution strategy that terminates and is complete on the corresponding class of extended clauses.

In comparison to many other theorem provers for default logic, we do not simply use some classical theorem prover to compute proofs for the prerequisites of the defaults or counter-arguments against their justifications. We provide, together with the extension of the resolution principle, a kind of "deduction theorem" that permits to make the link between the notion of conflicting defaults and that of monotonic deduction with defaults. Notice also that we do not need the introduction of any new propositional variable, as it is the case for the theorem provers that use some kind of traduction of the defaults into classical logic. This results in a greater clarity of the resolution steps, and simpler implementation. We have also described how simple modifications of some of the extended resolution rules can lead to other variants of default logic, that strengthen the consistency condition on the justification of the defaults or allow one to reason by cases.

Whereas the first part of our theorem prover is specific to default logic, the second one, that is, the elimination algorithm, is completely independent from any particular nonmonotonic logic. Levy [17] gives a detailed comparison between his algorithm and TMS-based algorithms used to compute extensions of default logic. As the algorithm that we have presented in this paper is not fundamentally different from Levy's one, this comparison still holds for our algorithm.

The main difference between Levy's algorithm and ours is that we do not need to check that the leaves of our tree correspond to valid sets of defaults generating extensions.

We have described in [20] how the notion of prioritized conflict resolution underlies some other famous nonmonotonic logic, like McDermott and Doyle's one [18]. In [19], we have also shown how elimination functions are interesting from the knowledge representation point of view.

The elements presented above are part of a system for prioritized default reasoning that we have implemented in Caml Light, a language of the ML family.

Acknowledgements

The author is greatly indebted to Christine Froidevaux, who helped a lot during this work, and to Philippe Chatalic and Viorica Ciorba for their sound criticisms on the algorithms. The author also acknwledges sound criticisms by two anonymous referees.

References

1. James Allen, Richard Fikes, and Erik Sandewall, editors. *Principles of Knowledge Representation and Reasoning: Proceedings of the Second International Conference (KR'91)*, The Morgan Kaufmann Series in Representation and Reasoning. Morgan Kaufmann, 1991.
2. Philippe Besnard, René Quiniou, and Patrice Quinton. A theorem prover for a decidable subset of default logic. In *Proceedings of the National Conference on Artifical Intelligence (AAAI'83)*, pages 27–30. American Association for Artificial Intelligence, 1983.
3. Geneviève Bossu and Pierre Siegel. Saturation, nonmonotonic reasoning and the closed world assumption. *Artificial Intelligence*, 25:13–63, 1985.
4. Gerhard Brewka. Preferred subtheories: An extended logical framework for default reasoning. In *Proceedings of 11th International Joint Conference on Artificial Intelligence (IJCAI 89)*, pages 1043–1048, 1989.
5. Gerhard Brewka. Cumulative default logic: In defense of nonmonotonic inference rules. *Artificial Intelligence*, 50:183–205, 1991.
6. Claudette Cayrol. Un modèle logique général pour le raisonnement révisable. *Revue d'Intelligence Artificielle*, 6(3):255–284, 1992.
7. A.G. Cohen, editor. *Proceedings of the 11th European Conference on Artificial Intelligence (ECAI'94)*. John Wiley & Sons Ltd., 1994.
8. James P. Delgrande and W. Ken Jackson. Default logic revisited. In Allen et al. [1], pages 118–127.
9. Christine Froidevaux and Jérôme Mengin. Default logics: a unified view. *Computational Intelligence*, 10(3):331–369, 1994.
10. Peter Gärdenfors and David Makinson. Nonmonotonic inference based on expectations. *Artificial Intelligence*, 1994.
11. Hector Geffner and Judea Pearl. Conditional entailment: bridging two approaches to default reasoning. *Artificial Intelligence*, 53:209–244, 1992.
12. M. Hopkins. Default logic: Orderings and extensions. In M.R.B. Clarke, Rudolph Kruse, and Serafin Moral, editors, *Symbolic and Quantitative Approaches to Reasoning and Uncertainty (European Conference ECSQARU'93)*, volume 747 of *Lecture Notes in Computer Science*, pages 174–179. Springer-Verlag, 1993.
13. Ulrich Junker and Gerhard Brewka. Handling partially ordered defaults in TMS. In Kruse and Siegel [15], pages 211–218.
14. Ulrich Junker and Kurt Konolige. Computing the extensions of autoepistemic and default logics with a truth maintenance system. In *Proceedings of the National Conference on Artifical Intelligence (AAAI'83)*, pages 278–283. American Association for Artificial Intelligence, 1990.
15. Rudolph Kruse and Pierre Siegel, editors. *Symbolic and Quantitative Approaches to Uncertainty (European Conference ECSQAU'91)*, volume 548 of *Lecture Notes in Computer ScienceLecture Notes in Computer Science*. Springer Verlag, 1991.
16. François Levy. Computing extensions of default theories. In Kruse and Siegel [15], pages 219–226.
17. François Levy. Reason maintenance systems and default theories. Pré-publication 92-2, LIPN, Université Paris Nord, Avenue J.B. Clément, 93430 Villetaneuse, July 1992.
18. D. MacDermott and John Doyle. Non-monotonic logic 1. *Artificial Intelligence*, 13:41–72, 1980.

19. Jérôme Mengin. Prioritized conflict resolution for default reasoning. In Cohen [7], pages 376–380.
20. Jérôme Mengin. *Raisonnement par défaut : résolutions de conflits et priorités.* Thèse de doctorat, Université Paris Sud, 1994.
21. Yves Moinard. Reasoning by cases without contraposition in default logic. In Cohen [7], pages 381–385.
22. Ilkka Niemelä. Decision procedures for autoepistemic logics. In *Proceedings of the 9th International Conference on Automated Deduction*, volume 310 of *Lecture Notes in Computer Science*, pages 676–684, 1991.
23. David L. Poole. A logical framework for default reasoning. *Artificial Intelligence*, 36:27–47, 1988.
24. Raymond Reiter. A logic for default reasoning. *Artificial Intelligence*, 13:81–132, 1980.
25. Raymond Reiter and G. Criscuolo. On interacting defaults. In *IJCAI-7*, pages 270–276, 1981.
26. Ken Satoh. A top down proof procedure for default logic by using abduction. In Cohen [7], pages 65–69.
27. Torsten Schaub. Assertional default theories: a semantical view. In Allen et al. [1], pages 496–506.
28. Camilla Schwind. A tableau-based theorem prover for a decidable subset of default logic. In *Proceedings of the 10th International Conference on Automated Deduction (CADE 10)*, pages 541–546. Springer Verlag, 1990.
29. Camilla Schwind and Vincent Risch. A tableau-based characterization for default logic. In Kruse and Siegel [15], pages 310–317.
30. Camilla Schwind and Pierre Siegel. Modal semantics for hypothesis theory. In *Proceedings of the 4th International Workshop on Nonmonotonic Reasoning*, pages 200–217, 1992.
31. Marek Truszczyński. Modal interpretation of default logic. In *Proceedings of 12th International Joint Conference on Artificial Intelligence (IJCAI 91)*, 1991.

A Theorem Prover for Lukaszewicz' Open Default Theory

Pascal NICOLAS
E Mail : pn@univ-angers.fr

Béatrice DUVAL
E Mail : bd@univ-angers.fr

Université d'Angers
Laboratoire d'Etudes et de Recherche en Informatique d'Angers
2, bd Lavoisier
49045 ANGERS cedex 01 FRANCE

Abstract : We present here a correct and complete theorem prover for a certain class of formulas in Lukaszewicz' default logic. Whereas many papers are concerned by calculus of extensions for some default logic, we have developed a theorem prover, that means a computation method to check whether a given formula belongs to some extension of a default theory. This theorem prover works in Lukaszewicz' default logic, which ensures that an extension always exists. More precisely, we define a class of formulas called range-restricted Horn default logic. The restriction to Horn logic enables to use SLD-resolution to build proofs. Moreover range restriction, the constraint on variables occurring in the formulas, enables to deal with open defaults by using the unification mechanism. This point is quite original since open defaults are usually replaced by a set of instanciated defaults. Another point is the fact that computing a proof (in a backward chaining way), instead of building an extension (in a forward chaining way or by eliminating conflicts between defaults), allows us to hope a better efficiency in presence of open defaults.

1. Introduction

Since original definition by Reiter [Reiter, 80], many works have been done to study the properties of default reasoning. Whereas many papers are concerned by calculus of extensions for some default logic, this paper presents a theorem prover, that means a computation method to check whether a given formula belongs to some extension of a default theory. This theorem prover works in Lukaszewicz' default logic. This framework and the notion of a formula proof are presented in section 2 which also describes the difficulties induced by management of open defaults. In section 3, we define a class of formulas called range-restricted Horn default logic. The restriction to Horn logic enables to use SLD-resolution to build proofs. Moreover range restriction, the constraint on variables occurring in the formulas, enables to deal with open defaults by using the unification mechanism. This point is quite original since open defaults are usually replaced by a set of instanciated defaults. The following of section 3 presents in detail our theorem prover, illustrates it by an example, and gives correctness and completeness results,. Section 4 concludes by explaining what can be the following of this work.

2. Lukaszewicz' Default Logic

2.1. Presentation

Default logic was proposed by Reiter [Reiter, 80] and has been the subject of many works (see [Besnard, 89], [Froidevaux, 93], [Froidevaux, Mengin, 92] for a formalization and a survey of different variants of default logic). First of all, we just present the most important features of this formalism.

A default is an expression like $\frac{\alpha:\beta_1,\ldots,\beta_n}{\omega}$ where α, β_i and ω are first order formulas which are respectively called *prerequisite, justifications* and *consequent* of the default. Such an expression can be read in the following way: "*if α is satisfied, and in absence of proof of $\neg\beta_i$ for all i in {1,...,n}, then conclude ω*".

A *default theory* is a pair T=(W,D) where W is a set of first order formulas and D a default set. We shall use the following notations. Let $d = \frac{\alpha:\beta_1,\ldots,\beta_n}{\omega}$ be a default, then Pre(d)={α}, Jus(d)={$\beta_1,\ldots,\beta_n$} and Cons(d)={ω}, and we note also $PRE(D)= \bigcup_{d\in D} Pre(d)$, $JUS(D)= \bigcup_{d\in D} Jus(d)$ $CONS(D)= \bigcup_{d\in D} Cons(d)$

A default is *closed* if it contains no free variable and a default theory is said to be closed if all its defaults are closed.

The most important point in default logic is the notion of *extension*. Briefly speaking, an extension is a maximal deduction set which can be obtained from W and consequents of defaults whose prerequisites are satisfied and justifications not contradicted in this extension. We shall not detail the definition of extension in Reiter's default logic. We just recall that an extension is based on a fixed point operator and a non normal default theory(1) may have no extension.

In order to avoid the problem of theory without extension, Lukaszewicz has proposed a variant of default logic [Lukaszewicz, 84] that we present here in detail.

In this framework, a default theory is also defined as a pair (W,D), and characterization of an *m-extension* (modified extension) of (W,D) is given below. As in Reiter's work, the study focuses on closed default theory.

Definition of Lukaszewicz' m-extension

Let (W,D) be a closed default theory and E and F two formula sets.
E is an *m-extension* of (W,D) with respect to F iff $E = \Gamma_1(E, F)$ and $F = \Gamma_2(E, F)$ where $\Gamma_1(E, F)$ and $\Gamma_2(E, F)$ are the smallest sets such that

i) $W \subseteq \Gamma_1(E,F)$

ii) $Th(\Gamma_1(E,F)) = \Gamma_1(E,F)$

iii) $\forall \frac{A:B_1,\ldots,B_n}{C} \in D$, if $\begin{cases} A \in \Gamma_1(E,F) \\ \forall x \in F \cup \{B_1,\ldots,B_n\}, E \cup \{x,C\} \text{ is consistent} \end{cases}$

then $\begin{cases} C \in \Gamma_1(E,F) \\ B_1,\ldots,B_n \in \Gamma_2(E,F) \end{cases}$

F is said to be the *set of justifications supporting* E.

If E is an m-extension of (W,D) with respect to F, a *generating default set* DG is such that DG={d $\in$ D / Pre(d) $\in$ E and $\forall$ j $\in$ F, E $\cup$ Cons(d) $\nvdash \neg$j}. This set contains all the defaults which are used to "build" the m-extension.

Example of m-extension

Let (W,D) be a default theory such that $W = \{A_1, A_2, \neg C_1 \vee B_2, \neg C_2 \vee B_1\}$ and $D=\{d_1,d_2\}$ where $d_1 = \frac{A_1:\neg B_1}{C_1}$ and $d_2 = \frac{A_2:\neg B_2}{C_2}$, then (W,D) has 2 m-extensions:

---

1 A default theory is normal if all its defaults are normal, a default is normal if it is of the form $\frac{\alpha:\beta}{\beta}$.

$E_1 = Th(W \cup \{C_1\})$ with $F_1 = \{\neg B_1\}$ and $DG_1=\{d_1\}$
$E_2 = Th(W \cup \{C_2\})$ with $F_2 = \{\neg B_2\}$ and $DG_2=\{d_2\}$

Some authors have treated the problem of extension computation, either with the original definition of Reiter or with the definition of some variants of default logic (see [Besnard et al, 83], [Gottlob , Mingyi, 94], [Junker, Konolige, 90], [Levy, 91], [Lukaszewicz, 84], [Mengin, 94], [Moinard, 93], [Papadimitriou, Sideri, 94], [Reiter, 80], [Risch, 93], [Schwind, Risch, 91]).

Instead of computing a whole extension, we may be interested by a query answering approach in default logic [Schaub, 95]. A query answering, or theorem proving approach, means that we are interested by checking whether a given formula belongs to some extensions. This approach is possible only if the considered default logic is semi-monotonic. This is the case of Lukaszewicz' default logic. Moreover Lukaszewicz proposed the following definition of default proof.

Definition of a default proof

Let (W,D) be a closed default theory and ϕ a formula.
A *default proof* of ϕ in (W,D) is a finite sequence $\{d_1,..., d_n\} \subseteq D$ such that

i) $\{d_1,..., d_n\}$ is *grounded in W*
i e : $\forall$ i, $1 \le i \le n$ $W \cup CONS(\{d_1,...,d_{i-1}\}) \vdash Pre(d_i)$

ii) $\{d_1,..., d_n\}$ is *regular* (or justified)
i e : $\forall$ i, $1 \le i \le n$ $\forall x \in JUS(d_i)$, $W \cup CONS(\{d_1,...,d_n\}) \nvdash \neg x$

iii) $W \cup Cons\{d_1,..., d_n\} \vdash \phi$

The important result, proved by Lukaszewicz [Lukaszewicz, 84], is that a formula ϕ belongs to an m-extension of a default theory (W,D) if and only if ϕ has a default proof in (W,D). This notion is the basis of our present work : we propose to determine whether ϕ is a theorem by searching a default proof of this formula. At this point, we must precise the notion of theorem. A formula ϕ is a *credulous theorem* of (W,D) if it belongs to at least one m-extension of (W,D), ϕ is a *skeptical theorem* of (W,D) if it belongs to every m-extension of (W,D). So, theorems obtained by a default proof are credulous theorems.

It is easy to see that a default proof is a subset of the generating default set of the m-extension containing ϕ. So we can hope very less expansive computations than those required to determine a whole m-extension. Another aspect of our work is to propose an explicit management of open default theories. The next section presents the difficulties involved by open defaults.

2.2. Open default theories

In almost every paper dealing with default logic, authors consider closed default theory (W,D). In fact, if the initial set D contains some open defaults, Reiter [Reiter, 80, p.117] has defined an equivalent closed default theory (W', D') such that :
W' = skolemization of W
D' = Closed-defaults(D) = $\{d(t) / d(x) \in D$ x is the nuple of free variables in d, and t is a nuple of ground terms of $H(F \cup \Sigma)\}$

where $H(F \cup \Sigma)$ is the set of all terms constructable over F (set of all function symbols, including constants) and Σ (set of Skolem functions issued from the skolemization of W).

This transformation is valid from a theoretical point of view but it may lead to some practical problems, high computational complexity for instance [Baader, Hollunder, 92].

If the language contains at least one n-ary function, n>0, and one open default as for $W=\{P(f(5))\}$, $D=\left\{\frac{:\neg Q(x)}{R(x)}\right\}$, then (W,D) is equivalent to (W',D') with $D'=\left\{\frac{:\neg Q(5)}{R(5)},\frac{:\neg Q(f(5))}{R(f(5))},\frac{:\neg Q(f(f(5)))}{R(f(f(5)))},\dots\right\}$. So, in this example, and in many practical cases the set of closed defaults and the set of generating defaults of an m-extension are infinite. Furthermore, the number of possible extensions may be infinite, as in the following example where $W=\{P(f(5))\}$ and $D=\left\{\frac{:Q(x)}{Q(x)},\frac{:\neg Q(x)}{\neg Q(x)}\right\}$ which gives $D'=\left\{\frac{:Q(5)}{Q(5)},\frac{:\neg Q(5)}{\neg Q(5)},\frac{:Q(f(5))}{Q(f(5))},\frac{:\neg Q(f(5))}{\neg Q(f(5))},\dots\right\}$. It is clear that a generating default set of an extension of (W',D') cannot contain both defaults $\frac{:Q(\alpha)}{Q(\alpha)}$ and $\frac{:\neg Q(\alpha)}{\neg Q(\alpha)}$ (α in {5, f(5),...}), then the number of extensions is the number of parts of D'.

Baader and Hollunder in [Baader, Hollunder, 92] have proposed a new interpretation of open defaults in order to solve some of these difficulties. They consider default theories (W,D) where W is a set of formulas in a terminological representation system, a sublanguage of first order logic. Furthermore, they interpret an open default as a set of closed defaults obtained by instanciation of free variables with only constants occurring in W. Their choices guarantee that the obtained closed default theory is finite (if W and D are finite). So, in this context they expose that some methods of computation of extension (those of Junker and Konolige and of Schwind and Risch) are efficient.

Our work, exposed in the following section, deals with open defaults via unification mechanism. This avoids to translate explicitly open defaults into their equivalent closed form, but we shall prove that with some language restrictions, our method leads to the same results.

3. A theorem prover for Lukaszewicz' default logic

3.1. Well formed formulas

We shall now present the language restrictions that we have considered. These limitations provide a subset of first order default logic to which an efficient proof mechanism can be applied.

Given a formula ϕ, we define *Var(ϕ)* the set of all variables occurring in ϕ.

A *positive Horn clause* is a formula Cl such that :

$Cl = B \vee \neg A_1 \vee \dots \vee \neg A_n$ where $n \geq 0$

$B, A_1 \dots A_n$ are positive literals

$\forall x \in Var(Cl)$, x is universally quantified

Such a Horn clause Cl is *range-restricted* if $Var(B) \subseteq Var(\neg A_1 \vee \dots \vee \neg A_n)$.

We extend now these well known definitions to defaults.

Definition of range-restricted Horn default

$d = \frac{A_1 \wedge \dots \wedge A_n : \neg B_1, \dots, \neg B_p}{C}$ is a *range-restricted Horn default* if

- $n \geq 0$ and $p \geq 0$

- all variables in d are free
- A_1 , ..., A_n and C are positive literals
- B_1,..., B_p are conjunctions of positive literals
- $Var(C) \subseteq Var(A_1 \wedge ... \wedge A_n)$
- $\forall$ i = 1,...,p, $Var(B_i) \subseteq Var(A_1 \wedge ... \wedge A_n)$

Ex : $\dfrac{bird(x) : \neg ostrich(x), \neg penguin(x)}{fly(x)}$, $\dfrac{P(x, y, z) : \neg(R(x) \wedge S(y))}{Q(y)}$, $\dfrac{: \neg P(5)}{Q(4)}$

are range-restricted Horn defaults.

A *range-restricted Horn default theory* is a pair (W,D) such that W is a set of range-restricted Horn clauses and D a set of range-restricted Horn defaults.

Restriction to Horn logic obviously limits the expressive power of the language, nevertheless it enables to deal with many practical problems as Prolog systems do and is required to use SLD-resolution [Lloyd, 87] which leads to efficient proof mechanism. Concerning the justifications of a default, we must point out that all justifications are negative. But this is not a new different restriction : this is a straightforward consequence of the Horn restriction. It is useless to consider positive justification B in a default d, because it is impossible to prove ¬B in a Horn theory. Thus, such a positive justification B would never block the use of default d. Constraints on variables of clauses and defaults will be justified during the description of the theorem prover.

3.2. Default proof procedure

The main idea of our proof procedure is inspired by Lukaszewicz' definition of a default proof. To achieve this goal we transform a default theory (W,D) into a set of labelled clauses CL(W,D).

Definition of CL(W,D)

Let (W,D) be a range-resricted Horn default theory.
For a default d in D, $Cl(d) = (Cons(d) \vee \neg Pre(d))_{\{d\}}$.
$CL(W,D) = \{(f)_{\emptyset}, f \in W\} \cup \{ Cl(d), d \in D\}$

So, from the default $\dfrac{A_1 \wedge ... \wedge A_n : \neg B_1, ..., \neg B_p}{C}$ a clause $(C \vee \neg A_1 \vee ... \vee \neg A_n)_{\{d\}}$ is built by forgetting the justifications.

Definition of labelled SLD-resolution

For two clauses from CL(W,D) a *labelled SLD-resolution* is a classical SLD-resolution based on the following rule

$$\frac{(A \vee \neg B_1 \vee ... \vee \neg B_n)_{\Delta_1} \qquad (\neg C \vee \neg D_1 \vee ... \vee \neg D_p)_{\Delta_2}}{(\sigma(\neg B_1 \vee ... \vee \neg B_n \vee \neg D_1 \vee ... \vee \neg D_p))_{\sigma(\Delta_1 \cup \Delta_2)}}$$

where σ is the most general unifier of A and C. The notation $\sigma(\Delta_1 \cup \Delta_2)$ represents the union of defaults sets Δ_1 and Δ_2 where unifier σ has been propagated.

We can now expose our proof method. Let ϕ be a conjunction of literals. In order to prove if ϕ has a default proof in a range-restricted Horn default theory (W,D) we proceed as follows. In a first time we build CL(W,D). Secondly, we try to find a labelled SLD-refutation of$\{\neg\phi\}\cup CL(W,D)$. As the only modification we do is to label every clause we keep all results of correctness and completeness of classical SLD-resolution. If we find a proof of ϕ which ends with the empty clause $()_\Delta$, Δ contains all defaults d such that the clause Cl(d) is used in the proof. Then we finally check whether Δ is regular or not. As we shall demonstrate below, Δ is a grounded default set such that $W\cup CONS(\Delta)\vdash\phi$. So if it is regular then we have found a default proof of ϕ (that is Δ), otherwise we try to find another proof using other defaults. Let us recall that Δ is regular if for all justification J in JUS(Δ), $W\cup CONS(\Delta)\nvdash\neg J$. This verification can easily be done by a classical SLD-proof of $\neg J$ from $W\cup CONS(\Delta)$. Finally, if no labelled SLD-proof of ϕ ends with the empty clause, or if all labelled SLD-proofs end with $()_\Delta$ where Δ is not regular, then ϕ is not a theorem of (W,D).

The next example shows how our algorithm finds a default proof of C(1) on (W,D), with $W=\{\neg C(x)\vee B(x), I(6,4), H(1,6,4), H(1,7,1), H(1,0,0)\}$ and $D=\{d_1,d_2\}$ where $d_1=\dfrac{A(z,t):\neg B(t),\neg D(t)}{C(z)}$ and $d_2=\dfrac{H(u,v,w):\neg I(v,w)}{A(u,w)}$

We show in figure 1 the three SLD-refutations of $\neg C(1)$ in CL(W,D) we need to prove that C(1) is a theorem of (W,D).

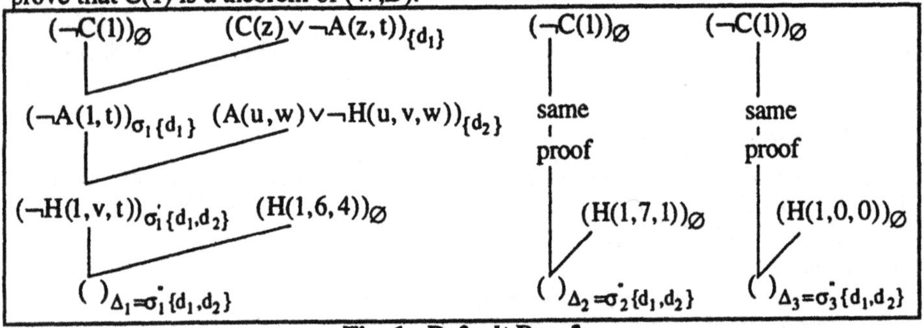

Fig. 1 : Default Proof

$W\cup\{C(1), A(1,4)\}\vdash I(6,4)$, so $\Delta_1=\left\{\dfrac{A(1,4):\neg B(4),\neg D(4)}{C(1)}, \dfrac{H(1,6,4):\neg I(6,4)}{A(1,4)}\right\}$ is not regular

$W\cup\{C(1), A(1,7)\}\vdash B(1)$, so $\Delta_2=\left\{\dfrac{A(1,1):\neg B(1),\neg D(1)}{C(1)}, \dfrac{H(1,7,1):\neg I(7,1)}{A(1,7)}\right\}$ is not regular

$\Delta_3=\left\{\dfrac{A(1,0):\neg B(0),\neg D(0)}{C(1)}, \dfrac{H(1,0,0):\neg I(0,0)}{A(1,0)}\right\}$ is regular since none of its justification is deducible from $W\cup\{C(1), A(1,0)\}$.

Property

> If a labelled SLD-proof of a formula ϕ in CL(W,D) ends with the labelled empty clause $()_\Delta$, then Δ is a set of closed defaults which terms belong to $H(F\cup\Sigma)$.

The SLD-refutation of a formula ϕ from a set of range-restricted Horn clauses (in particular unit clauses are ground) leads to a ground substitution of all variables of all clauses used in the proof. So, each default d in Δ is such that Pred(d) and Cons(d) do not contain free variable. Since $Var(Jus(d))\subseteq Var(Pre(d))$, all variables in d are substituted by a ground term of $H(F\cup\Sigma)$.

This property is important because it proves that, for an open default theory (W,D), unification gives the same results as those obtained by working explicitly on (W'D') the equivalent closed default theory .

We give now the following important result.

Theorem

> Let (W,D) be a range-restricted Horn default theory. Let ϕ be a conjunction of positive literals. There exists a default proof $\{d_1,\ldots, d_n\}$ of ϕ in (W,D) iff there exists a labelled SLD-proof of ϕ in CL(W,D) which ends with the empty clause $()_\Delta$, where Δ is regular and $\Delta \subseteq \{d_1,\ldots,d_n\}$.

Proof of the theorem.

<u>$\Leftarrow$:</u> If the labelled SLD-proof of ϕ in CL(W,D) ends with the empty clause $()_\Delta$, where $\Delta=\{d_1,\ldots,d_n\}$ is regular, then there exists the following ground proof of $\neg\phi'$ (an instanciation of ϕ) where, for all k in $\{1,\ldots,n\}$, the clause $Cl(d_k)=\left(Cons(d_k)\vee\neg Pre(d_k)\right)_{\{d_k\}}$ occurs.

$$(\neg\phi')_\varnothing$$
$$\vdots$$
$$(\neg Cons(d_k)\vee\varphi_k)_\delta \qquad (Cons(d_k)\vee\neg Pre(d_k))_{\{d_k\}}$$
$$(\varphi_k\vee\neg Pre(d_k))_{\delta\cup\{d_k\}}$$
$$\vdots$$
$$(\;)_\Delta$$

From this tree, and by considering that clauses $Cl(d_k)$ are numbered from the empty clause to $\neg\phi$ we can conclude :

$$W\cup\left(\bigcup_{i=1}^{k-1}\{Cons(d_i)\vee\neg Pre(d_i)\}\right)\vdash\neg\left(\varphi_k\vee\neg Pre(d_k)\right) \text{ for all } k=1,\ldots,n.$$

$$W\cup\left(\bigcup_{i=1}^{k-1}\{Cons(d_i)\vee\neg Pre(d_i)\}\right)\vdash Pre(d_k), \text{ for all } k=1,\ldots,n$$

$$W\cup\left(\bigcup_{i=1}^{k-1}\{Cons(d_i)\}\right)\vdash Pre(d_k)\ ^{(2)} \text{ for all } k=1,\ldots,n\,.$$

In the same way $W\cup\left(\bigcup_{i=1}^{n}\{Cons(d_i)\}\right)\vdash\phi$.

So conditions i), ii) and iii) of definition of a default proof are satisfied, so Δ is a default proof of ϕ.

<u>$\Rightarrow$:</u> Let $\{d_1,\ldots, d_n\}$ be a default proof of ϕ in (W,D). So $W\cup CONS(\{d_1,\ldots, d_n\})\vdash\phi$.

Then, by completeness of SLD-resolution, we obtain the following proof tree A.

$$\begin{array}{ccl} & \neg\phi & \\ A & \vdots & \text{on } W\cup CONS(\{d_1,\ldots,d_n\}) \\ & () & \end{array}$$

Now, we prove by induction on n that we can compute a labelled SLD-proof of ϕ in CL(W,D) which ends with $()_\Delta$ where Δ is a regular subset of $\{d_1,\ldots, d_n\}$.

<u>n=0 :</u> In this case A is a proof tree using only clauses of W. Each clause can be labelled with $\varnothing$, so A is a proof tree is on CL(W,D) that ends with the empty clause $()_\varnothing$ and $\varnothing$ is trivially regular.

<u>Suppose that property holds for $0\le i\le n$:</u> Let $\{d_1,\ldots, d_{n+1}\}$ be a default proof of ϕ in (W,D). Then A is as follows

---

2 This is obtained by successive applications of $W\cup\{B\vee\neg A\}\vdash C$ implies $W\cup\{B\}\vdash C$

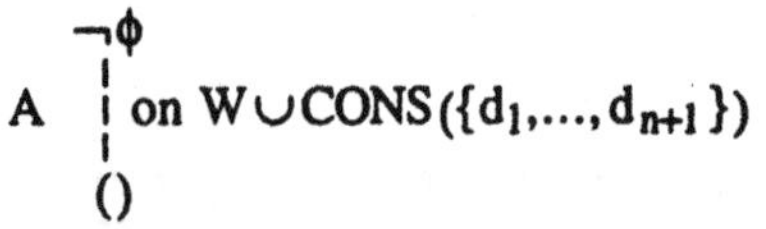

Let us consider that there exists k in $\{1,\dots,n+1\}$ such that $Cons(d_k)$ is used in this proof tree. Otherwise, that means that A only uses W and that is equivalent to the case n=0.

Then, considering such a k we can draw A as follows

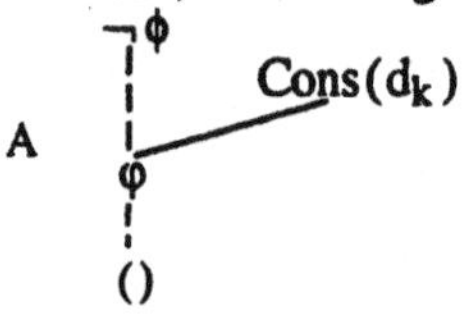

and we can complete this tree to obtain

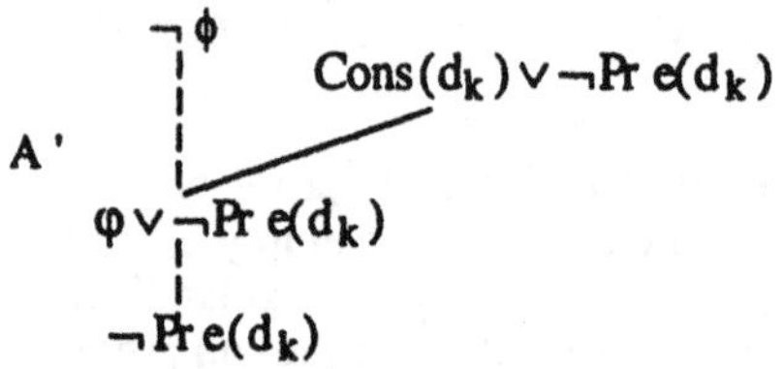

Furthermore, since $\{d_1,\dots, d_{n+1}\}$ is a default proof, we have

(α) $W \cup CONS(\{d_1,\dots, d_{k-1}\}) \vdash Pre(d_k)$

(β) $\forall\, i=1,\dots,k-1,\ W \cup CONS(\{d_1,\dots, d_{i-1}\}) \vdash Pre(d_i)$

(γ) $\{d_1,\dots, d_{k-1}\}$ is regular since $\{d_1,\dots, d_{n+1}\}$ is regular

Thus (α), (β) and (γ) $\Rightarrow$ $\{d_1,\dots, d_{k-1}\}$ is a default proof of $Pre(d_k)$ on (W,D), so by induction hypothesis, there exists a labelled SLD-proof of ϕ in CL(W,D) which ends with the empty clause $()_\Delta$, where Δ is regular and $\Delta \subseteq \{d_1 ,\dots,d_{k-1}\}$.

This can be represented by the tree B

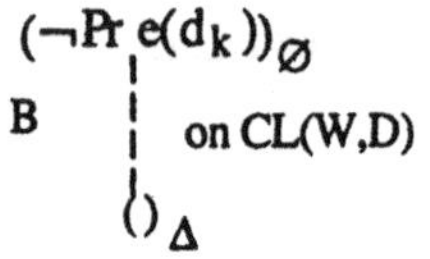

by labelling A' and adding B we obtain

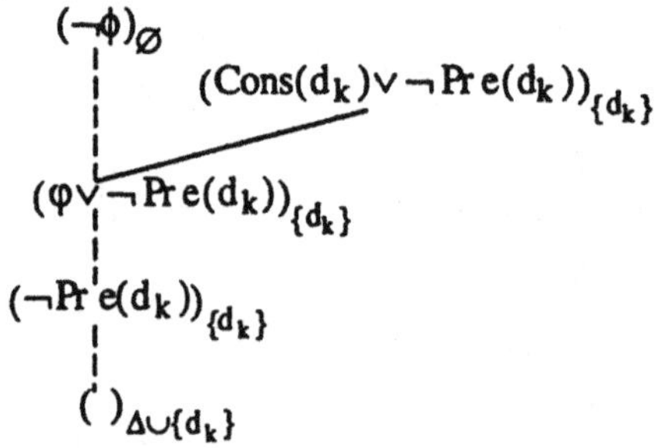

By applying this process for each occurrence of $Cons(d_k)$ that is used in the original tree A, we can replace all these $Cons(d_k)$ by $(Cons(d_k) \vee \neg Pre(d_k))_{\{d_k\}}$ and we obtain (in a finite number of iterations) the tree of a labelled SLD-proof of ϕ in CL(W,D) which ends with the empty clause $()_\Delta$ where $\Delta \subseteq \{d_1,\dots, d_{n+1}\}$. Let us notice that it is possible that Δ is not equal to $\{d_1,\dots, d_{n+1}\}$ because the original definition of a default proof does not require that all consequents of defaults are necessary to prove the given formula ϕ.

Finally, it is obvious that Δ is regular since it is a subset of $\{d_1,\dots, d_{n+1}\}$.

Thus the property holds for n+1, which ends the proof of the theorem.

In view of this result of correctness and completeness we have implemented this method in Common Lisp.

4. Conclusion

The major contribution of this paper is to demonstrate that a classical resolution method can be efficiently used to handle a class of open default theories in Lukaszewicz' default logic. Range restriction on variables of Horn defaults and clauses guarantees that the proof procedure ends with a default set where every default is closed as required by the definition of m-extension. This condition is probably too strong and a next work is to find a weaker constraint on formulas which would ensure the same results.

We can remark also that this theorem prover could be integrated in a method of m-extension calculus in the following way. Suppose that one is interested by computing one complete particular m-extension containing a given formula ϕ. Then, in a first time one can use our proof method to build a set Δ which is a default proof of ϕ. In a second time one can add defaults to Δ until to obtain the generating default set of one m-extension that necessarily contains ϕ. This approach has the advantage to focus only on m-extensions which contains the desired formula.

An other subject of research may be to extend this approach to others semi-monotonic variants of default logic.

Acknowledgment : We thank J. MENGIN for his personnal communication about some difficulties relative to the treatment of open defaults.

References

[Baader, Hollunder, 92] Baader F., Hollunder B., *Embedding defaults into terminological knowledge representation formalism*, In proceedings of KR 92, pp 306-317, 1992.

[Besnard et al., 83] Besnard P., Quiniou R., Quinton P., *A decidable subset of default logic*. Proc. of AAAI, Washington, 1983.

[Besnard, 89] Besnard P., *An introduction to default logic*. Springer Verlag, 1989.

[Froidevaux, Mengin, 92] Froidevaux C., Mengin J., *A framework for default logics*. In proceedings of JELIA 92, Lecture notes in AI, vol 633 Springer Verlag, pp154-173, Berlin, 1992.

[Froidevaux, 93] Froidevaux C., *Thèse d'habilitation à diriger des recherches*. (in french) In research report n° 835, LRI University of Paris Sud, 1993.

[Gottlob , Mingyi, 94] Gottlob G., Mingyi Z., *Cumulative default logic : finite characterization, algorithms, and complexity*. AI 69, vol 69 (1-2), pp 329-345, 1994.

[Junker, Konolige, 90] Junker U., Konolige K., *Computing the extensions of autoepistemic and default logics with a Truth Maintenance System*. Proc of AAAI, 1990.

[Levy, 91] Levy F., *Computing extensions of default theories*. In Symbolic and quantitative approachs to uncertainty. Lecture notes in Computer Science, vol 548 Springer Verlag, Berlin, 1991.

[Lloyd, 87] Lloyd J. W., Foundations of logic programming. Springer Verlag, 1987.

[Lukaszewicz, 84] Lukaszewicz W., *Considerations on default logic : an alternative approach*. Computer Intelligence, vol 4, pp 1-16, 1988.

[Mengin, 94] Mengin J., *Prioritized conflict resolution for default reasonning*. In Proceedings of ECAI 94, pp 376-380, 1994.

[Moinard, 93] Moinard Y., *Unifying various approaches to default logic*. Proc of IPMU 93, Lecture notes in Computer Science, vol 682, pp33-42, Springer Verlag, Berlin, 1993.

[Papadimitriou, Sideri, 94] Papadimitriou C. H., Sideri M., *Default theories that always have extensions*. AI 69, vol 69 (1-2), pp 347-357, 1994.

[Reiter, 80] Reiter R., *A logic for default reasoning*. AI 13, pp 81-132, 1980.

[Risch, 93] Risch V. *Caractérisations en termes de tableaux sémantiques pour la logique des défauts de Lukaszewicz*. (in french) Revue d'Intelligence Artificielle, vol 7, n° 1, pp 95-123, 1993.

[Schaub, 95] Schaub T., *A new methodology for query-answering in default logics via structure-oriented theorem proving*. Forthcoming in Journal of Automated Reasoning.

[Schwind, Risch, 91] Schwind C., Risch V., *A tableau-based characterization for default logic*. In Symbolic and quantitave approachs to uncertainty. Lecture notes in Computer Science, vol 548, pp310-317, Springer Verlag, Berlin, 1991.

Two Different Types of Discontinuity of Bayesian Learning in Causal Probabilistic Networks.

Ulrich G. Oppel

Mathematisches Institut der Ludwig - Maximilians - Universität München
Theresienstr. 39, D 80333 München, Germany
Email: ulrich@oppel2.mathematik.uni-muenchen.de

1. Introduction

A causal probabilistic network (CPN) is a directed graph and a family of Markov kernels. The nodes of the graph may be used to represent subsystems of a system, its directed edges are used to describe the dependency structure of the subsystems of the system qualitatively. The conditional probabilities of the Markov kernels are determining stochastic cause-effect relations quantitatively. This makes a CPN suitable to represent the knowledge base of an expert system which is subject to uncertainty and randomness. The total knowledge about such a system represented by a CPN is given by a (usually tremendously complex) multivariate probability distribution on the joint state space of the random variables describing the states of the subsystems. For theoretical purposes this multivariate probability distribution may be obtained from a process of iterative integrations; some properties of it will be cited in Section 2.

One of the great advantages of the representation of a knowledge by a CPN is its possibility to introduce and to propagate (deterministic or stochastic) evidence within the system. Powerful algorithms and tools are available for this purpose, exact ones (e.g. see Pearl [10], Lauritzen et al. [4], Neapolitan [6], Håjek et al. [2]) and approximate ones (e.g. see Henrion [3] and Shachter et al. [11]). Introduction and propagation of evidence in causal probabilistic networks is Bayesian learning which is nothing but conditioning (with respect to the total knowledge) and mixing (with respect to the given evidence). Hence, Bayesian learning is a process of desintegration and integration of probability measures. We shall make this precise for very general state spaces in Section 3.

In any kind of application we usually have available knowledge which is imprecise, incomplete, partial, or approximate in one sense or another. Hence, we are able to construct a CPN from our data or expert knowledge which represents the given system only approximately. Therefore it is necessary to think about concepts of approximation and convergence for CPNs and about the effects of this approximation or convergence on the operations to which we subject our CPNs.

We have shown earlier that the process of construction of the associated multivariate probability distribution to a CPN from the family of Markov kernels is fairly continuous with respect to many topologies; see Matthes et al. [5] and Section 2 below for a short review. This is important to know, since at present we have only available exact algorithms for propagation for finite discrete state spaces (e.g. the Lauritzen-Spiegelhalter algorithm) or aproximative algorithms for propagation for fairly general state spaces (e.g. based on variance reduced Monte Carlo simulations).

In contrary to the process of construction of the associated multivariate probability distribution, Bayesian learning is pretty discontinuous. We observe two different kinds of discontinuity of Bayesian learning, one with respect to the total knowledge and one with respect to the introduced evidence. In Section 4 we shall make this precise and give some examples of such discontinuities and prove some continuity results. In the concluding Section 5 we shall point out the importance of knowing conditions for the continuity of Bayesian learning for the construction and for the operation of expert systems based on CPNs.

2. Causal Probabilistic Networks and Their Associated Multivariate Distribution

A *causal probabilistic network (CPN)* is a directed graph $G:=(V,E)$ with $E\subset V\times V$ and $(u,v)\notin E$ for $(v,u)\in E$ and a family $\mathcal{P}:=(\mathcal{P}_v:\ v\in V)$ of Markov kernels

$$\mathcal{P}_v:\ S(Pa(v))\times\mathfrak{S}_v\to[0,1] \text{ with } ((x_u:\ u\in Pa(v)),B)\to\mathcal{P}_v((x_u:\ u\in Pa(v));B)$$

where $Pa(v):=\{u\in V:\ (u,v)\in E\}$ is the set of the parents of v in G. For $\emptyset\neq U\subset V$

$S(U):=\prod_{u\in U} S_u$ is the product set and $\mathfrak{S}(U):=\bigotimes_{u\in U}\mathfrak{S}_u$ is the product-σ-algebra of the family $((S_u,\mathfrak{S}_u):\ u\in U)$ of state spaces $(S_u,\mathfrak{S}_u)$.

(A Markov kernel P from a measurable space $(Y,\mathfrak{Y})$ to a measurable space $(Z,\mathfrak{Z})$ is a mapping $P:\ Y\times\mathfrak{Z}\to[0,1]$ with $(y,B)\to P(y;B)$ such that for fixed $y\in Y$ the mapping $P(y;.):\ \mathfrak{Z}\to[0,1]$ is a probability measure and for each fixed B the mapping $P(.\,;B)$: $(Y,\mathfrak{Y})\to[0,1]$ is measurable.)

For every CPN with an acyclic finite graph $G:=(V,E)$ exists a uniquely determined probability measure $\mathbb{P}:\ \mathfrak{S}(V)\to[0,1]$ which is the joint distribution of random variables X_v with state space $(S_v\mathfrak{S}_v)$, has the given Markov kernels $\mathcal{P}_v$ as conditional distributions of X_v given the values of the "parent" variables X_u, and is a directed Markov field. We call this probability measure $\mathbb{P}$ the *multivariate joint probability* or the *multivariate distribution associated to this CPN*. This can be shown by iterative integration:

Find an ancestral enumeration $V=\{v_i:\ i=0,\ \dots\ ,n\}$ of V (i.e. no node is enumerated before any of its ancestors) and define

$S^{(i)}:=S(\{v_j:\ j=0,\ \dots\ ,i\})$ the product set and

$\mathfrak{S}^{(i)}:=\bigotimes_{j=0}^{i}\mathfrak{S}_{v_j}$ the product σ-algebra for $0\le i\le n$.

Defining Markov kernels

$P_i:\ S^{(i-1)}\times\mathfrak{S}_v\to[0,1]$ for $i=0,\ \dots\ ,n$

$((x_{v_0},\ \dots\ ,x_{v_{i-1}}),B)\to P_i(x_{v_0},\ \dots\ ,x_{v_{i-1}};B):=\mathcal{P}_{v_i}((x_u:\ u\in Pa(v_i));B)$

The probability measure $\mathbb{P}:\ \mathfrak{S}(V)\to[0,1]$ is obtained by iterative integration:

(*) $\quad\mathbb{P}(A):=$

$$:=\int_{S_{v_0}}\int_{S_{v_1}}\dots\int_{S_{v_n}}1_A(x_{v_0},\ \dots\ ,x_{v_n})\ \ P_n(x_{v_0},\ \dots\ ,x_{v_{n-1}};dx_{v_n})\ \dots\ P_1(x_{v_0};dx_{v_1})\ P_0(dx_{v_0})$$

for $A\in\mathfrak{S}:=\mathfrak{S}^{(n)}=\mathfrak{S}(V)$.

The probability measure $\mathbb{P}:\ \mathfrak{S}(V)\to[0,1]$ determined by (*) does not depend on the chosen enumeration and is a directed Markov field (see Oppel [7] or [8]).

The iterative construction (*) is continuous for several norms and topologies; see Matthes et al. [5]:

Let us consider a sequence $(C_n:\ n\in\mathbb{N})$ of CPNs C_n with a finite acyclic directed graph

$G := (V,E)$ and a sequence $(\mathcal{P}_{(n)}: n \in \mathbb{N})$ of families $\mathcal{P}_{(n)} := (\mathcal{P}_{n,v}: v \in V)$ of Markov kernels

$\mathcal{P}_{n,v}: S(Pa(v)) \times \mathfrak{S}_v \to [0,1]$ with $((x_u: u \in Pa(v)), B) \to \mathcal{P}_{n,v}((x_u: u \in Pa(v)); B)$ and associated multivariate distributions $\mathbb{P}_n: \mathfrak{S} \to [0,1]$

and a CPN $\mathbb{C}$ with the same graph G and the family $\mathcal{P} := (\mathcal{P}_v: v \in V)$ of Markov kernels

$\mathcal{P}_v: S(Pa(v)) \times \mathfrak{S}_v \to [0,1]$ with $((x_u: u \in Pa(v)), B) \to \mathcal{P}_v((x_u: u \in Pa(v)); B)$ and the associated multivariate distribution $\mathbb{P}: \mathfrak{S} \to [0,1]$.

If the sequence $(\mathcal{P}_{(n)}: n \in \mathbb{N})$ converges uniformly to $\mathcal{P}$, i.e.

$\lim_{n\to\infty} \| \mathcal{P}_{n,v} - \mathcal{P}_v \| = 0$ for all $v \in V$ where $\| \mathcal{P}_{n,v} - \mathcal{P}_v \| :=$
$\sup\{ |\mathcal{P}_{n,v}((x_u: u \in Pa(v)); B) - \mathcal{P}_v((x_u: u \in Pa(v)); B)|: ((x_u: u \in Pa(v)); B) \in S(Pa(v)) \times \mathfrak{S}_v\}$,

then the sequence $(\mathbb{P}_n: n \in \mathbb{N})$ of associated multivariate distributions $\mathbb{P}_n$ converges uniformly to $\mathbb{P}$, i.e.

$\lim_{n\to\infty} \| \mathbb{P}_n - \mathbb{P} \| = 0$ where $\| \mathbb{P}_n - \mathbb{P} \| := \sup\{ |\mathbb{P}_n(A) - \mathbb{P}(A)|: A \in \mathfrak{S}\}$.

The topologies of uniform convergence of Markov kernels and of measures are very fine topologies. Subsequently we assume that all the state spaces are polish and the σ-algebras are the σ-algebras of Borel subsets. Now, we may consider instead of these very fine topologies the much coarser topologies of pointwise weak convergence of Markov kernels and measures.

(A topological space Y is polish if it is separabel and completely metrizable. For applications we may assume polish state spaces. The σ-algebra $\mathfrak{Y}$ of Borel subsets of Y is generated by the open subsets. A sequence $(\mu_n: n \in \mathbb{N})$ of probability measures $\mu_n: \mathfrak{Y} \to [0,1]$ on a polish space Y with the σ-algebra $\mathfrak{Y}$ of Borel subsets converges weakly to a probability measure $\mu: \mathfrak{Y} \to [0,1]$ if the sequence $(\int f \, d\mu_n: n \in \mathbb{N})$ of integrals of f over Y with respect to μ_n converges in $\mathbb{R}$ to $\int f \, d\mu$ for every bounded continuous function $f: Y \to \mathbb{R}$.)

If we reduce the assumption of uniform convergence of the sequences $(\mathcal{P}_{n,v}: n \in \mathbb{N})$ to the Markov kernel $\mathcal{P}_v$ to pointwise weak convergence of the sequences $(\mathcal{P}_{n,v}: n \in \mathbb{N})$ to the Markov kernel $\mathcal{P}_v$ (i.e. the weak convergence of the sequences $(\mathcal{P}_{n,v}((x_u: u \in Pa(v)); \,.\,): n \in \mathbb{N})$ of probability measures to the probability measure $\mathcal{P}_v((x_u: u \in Pa(v)); \,.\,)$ for all $(x_u: u \in Pa(v)) \in S(Pa(v))$, then the weak convergence of the sequence $(\mathbb{P}_n: n \in \mathbb{N})$ of the associated multivariate distributions needs not to be true:

Example 2.1:

Let be $G := (V,E)$ with $V := \{0,1\}$ and $E := \{(0,1)\}$, $S_0 := \{0\} \cup \{1/n: n \in \mathbb{N}\}$ with the topology induced by the usual topology on $\mathbb{R}$, $S_1 := \{0,1\}$ with the discrete topology, and

$\mathcal{P}_0: \mathfrak{S}_0 \to [0,1]$ with $A \to \mathcal{P}_0(A) := 1/2\, \mu(A) + 1/2\, \delta_0(A)$,
$\mathcal{P}_1: S_0 \times \mathfrak{S}_1 \to [0,1]$ with $(x_0, B) \to \mathcal{P}_1(x_0; B) := \delta_0(B)$ for $x_0 = 0$ and $:= \delta_1(B)$ for $x_0 \neq 0$,
$\mathcal{P}_{n,0}: \mathfrak{S}_0 \to [0,1]$ with $A \to \mathcal{P}_{n,0}(A) := 1/2\, \mu(A) + 1/2\, \delta_{1/n}(A)$
$\mathcal{P}_{n,1} := \mathcal{P}_1$ where $\mu(\{1/n\}) := 2^{-n}$ for $n \in \mathbb{N}$.

The associated multivariate distributions $\mathbb{P}: \mathfrak{S} \to [0,1]$ and $\mathbb{P}_n: \mathfrak{S} \to [0,1]$ are

$\mathbb{P}(C) := 1/2\, \nu(C) + 1/2\, \delta_{(0,0)}(C)$ and $\mathbb{P}_n(C) := 1/2\, \nu(C) + 1/2\, \delta_{(1/n,1)}(C)$
where $\nu(C) := \int_{S_0} 1_C(x_0, 1)\, \mu(dx_0)$ for $C \in \mathfrak{S}$.

Obviously, the sequences $(\mathcal{P}_{n,0}: n\in\mathbb{N})$ and $(\mathcal{P}_{n,1}: n\in\mathbb{N})$ converge pointwise weakly to $\mathcal{P}_0$ and $\mathcal{P}_1$, respectively, but the sequence $(\mathbb{P}_n: n\in\mathbb{N})$ does not converge weakly to $\mathbb{P}$. Furthermore, we observe that the kernels $\mathcal{P}_1$ and $\mathcal{P}_{n,1}$ are no Feller kernels. All the other kernels are Feller kernels.

(A Markov kernel $P: Y\times\mathfrak{Z} \to [0,1]$ from a polish space $(Y,\mathfrak{Y})$ into a polish space $(Z,\mathfrak{Z})$ is a Feller kernel if for every sequence $(y_n: n\in\mathbb{N})$ in Y converging to $y\in Y$ the sequence $(P(y_n;.): n\in\mathbb{N})$ of probability measures $P(y_n;.)$ converges weakly to $P(y;.)$.)

The continuity assertion is true only under additional conditions such as: all Markov kernels are Feller kernels, have the strong Feller convergence property, and have the compact uniform tightness property; again see Matthes et al. [5]. For $n\in\mathbb{N}_0$ let be $P_n: Y\times\mathfrak{Z} \to [0,1]$ a Markov kernel from a polish space $(Y,\mathfrak{Y})$ into a polish space $(Z,\mathfrak{Z})$. Then $(P_n: n\in\mathbb{N})$ is said to have the strong Feller convergence property with respect to P_0 and the compact uniform tightness property if the following condition (SFCP) and (CUTP) is fulfilled, respectively:

(SFCP):
For every uniformly bounded sequence $(g_n: n\in\mathbb{N})$ of bounded continuous functions $g_n: Y\times Z \to \mathbb{R}$ converging uniformly on compact sets to the bounded continuous function $g_0: Y\times Z \to \mathbb{R}$ the sequence $(f_n: n\in\mathbb{N})$ of functions $f_n: Y \to \mathbb{R}$ with $y \to f_n(y) := \int g_n(y,z)\, P_n(y;dz)$ is converging uniformly on compact sets to the analoguously to g_0 and P_0 defined function f_0.

(CUTP):
For every compact subset C_Y of Y and for every $\varepsilon>0$ there is a compact subset C_Z of Z such that $P_n(y; Z\setminus C_Z) \leq \varepsilon$ for every $y\in C_Y$ and every $n\in\mathbb{N}_0$.

For finite state spaces (each with the discrete topology) all these conditions are fulfilled and the pointwise weak convergence coincides with the uniform convergence.

3. Bayesian Learning: Introducing Evidence into a Causal Probabilistic Network

Introducing new evidence into a CPN usually is done by Bayesian updating. This is nothing but first desintegrating (i.e. conditioning) and then integrating by the probability measure representing the new evidence. The new evidence may be deterministic or stochastic. The process of introducing and propagating new evidence may be iterated:

We consider a CPN with a finite acyclic directed grah $G:=(V,E)$ and the family $(\mathcal{P}_v: v\in V)$ of Markov kernels $\mathcal{P}_v: S(Pa(v))\times \mathfrak{S}_v \to [0,1]$ for polish state spaces S_v with Borel σ-algebras $\mathfrak{S}_v$. Let $\mathbb{P}: \mathfrak{S} := \mathfrak{S}(V) \to [0,1]$ be the multivariate probability measure associated to this CPN via (*). Furthermore, for $\emptyset \neq E \subset F \subset V$ let $\pi_{FE}: S(F) \to S(E)$ and $\pi_E: S:=S(V) \to S(E)$ be the canonical projections and let $\mathbb{P}_E := \mathbb{P}\circ\pi_E^{-1}: \mathfrak{S}(E) \to [0,1]$ with $\mathbb{P}_E(B) := \mathbb{P}(\pi_E^{-1}(B))$ be the projection of $\mathbb{P}$ with respect to π_E. Finally, let

$$P_E: S(E)\times\mathfrak{S} \to [0,1] \quad \text{with} \quad ((x_v: v\in E),B) \to P_E((x_v: v\in E);B)$$

be the desintegration kernel of $\mathbb{P}$ with respect to the canonical projection $\pi_E: S \to S_E$. This kernel P_E has the following property:

$$\mathbb{P}(C) = \int_{S(E)} P_E(x_E;C)\, \mathbb{P}_E(dx_E) \quad \text{for every} \quad C\in\mathfrak{S},$$

It is well known that such a desintegration kernel exists and that two such kernels coincide $\mathbb{P}_E$ - almost everywhere; e.g. see Parthasarathy [9].

We call such a desintegration kernel P_E a (version of the) *revaluation of* $\mathbb{P}$ *for evidence from E*. For $x_E := (x_V: v \in E) \in S(E)$ we call $P_E(x_E; \,.\,)$ the *revaluation of* $\mathbb{P}$ *for evidence* x_E *from* E.

The process of revaluation is iterative and does not depend on the kind of iteration. For $\emptyset \neq E \subset F \subset V$ we obtain:

$$P_E(\pi_E(\omega); \,.\,) = \int_S P_F(\pi_F(\eta); \,.\,) \; P_E(\pi_E(\omega); d\eta) \quad \text{for } \mathbb{P}\text{-almost all } \omega \in S$$

or

$$P_E(x_E; \,.\,) = \int_{S(F)} P_F(y_F; \,.\,) \; \tilde{P}_E(x_E; dy_F)$$

for $\mathbb{P}_E$ - almost all $x_E \in S(E)$ where $P_E(x_E; \,.\,) := \tilde{P}_E(x_E; \,.\,) \circ \pi_E^{-1}$.

Especially, for $E, F, G, H \subset V$ with $E \subset F \subset H$ and $E \subset G \subset H$ with $E \neq \emptyset$ we obtain:

$$P_E(x_E; \,.\,) = \int_{S(F)} \int_{S(H)} P_H(y_H; \,.\,) \; \tilde{P}_F(y_F; dy_H) \; \tilde{P}_E(x_E; dy_F)$$

and

$$P_E(x_E; \,.\,) = \int_{S(G)} \int_{S(H)} P_H(y_H; \,.\,) \; \tilde{P}_G(y_G; dy_H) \; \tilde{P}_E(x_E; dy_F)$$

for $\mathbb{P}_E$ - almost all $x_E \in S(E)$.

Hence the process of revaluation of $\mathbb{P}$ from H is independent from the iteration $E \subset F \subset H$ and $E \subset G \subset H$. For details see Oppel [8].

Let P_E be a revaluation of $\mathbb{P}$ for evidence from E and $\nu_E: \mathfrak{S}(E) \to [0,1]$ be a probability measure on S(E). We call the probability measure

$$P_{E,\nu}: \mathfrak{S} := \mathfrak{S}(V) \to [0,1] \qquad \text{with } C \to P_{E,\nu}(C) := \int_{S(E)} P_E(x_E; C) \; \nu(dx_E)$$

the *revaluation of* $\mathbb{P}$ *for evidence* ν *from* E. Obviously, a revaluation of $\mathbb{P}$ for evidence x_E from E is a revaluation of $\mathbb{P}$ for evidence $\nu := \delta_{x_E}$ from E.

Finally, we call a revaluation of $\mathbb{P}$ for evidence ν from E *consistent with* $\mathbb{P}$ if ν is absolutely continuous with respect to $\mathbb{P}_E$. Such revaluations avoid problems with sets of $\mathbb{P}$ - measure 0 and to get into conflict with the "old knowledge" $\mathbb{P}$.

4. Discontinuities of Bayesian Learning in Causal Probabilistic Networks

Bayesian learning in CPNs is revaluation as defined in Section 3. The process of revaluation of a CPN is dependent on the total knowledge (represented by the multivariate distribution $\mathbb{P}$ associated to the CPN) and the evidential knowledge (represented by the probability measure ν on the marginal space S(E) of evidence). Here we want to study two different types of continuity and discontinuity of Bayesian learning. First, we keep the total knowledge fixed and vary the evidential knowledge. Second, we keep the evidential knowledge fixed and vary the total knowledge. Of course, this can be done and is interesting with respect to various topologies, but we restrict ourselves to the weak topology of probability measures. We make the same assumptions as in Section 3.

First, we consider a fixed CPN with its associated multivariate distribution $\mathbb{P}$ and a fixed subset E of the sets of nodes. A revaluation P_E of $\mathbb{P}$ for evidence from E is in general not uniquely determined. We obtain a first continuity result:

If there is a version P_E of the revaluation of $\mathbb{P}$ for evidence from E which is a Feller kernel, then the process of revaluation is weakly continuous with respect to evidential evidence; i.e. if the sequence $(\nu_n: n\in\mathbb{N})$ of probability measures $\nu_n: \mathfrak{S}(E) \to [0,1]$ is weakly converging to the probability measure $\nu: \mathfrak{S}(E) \to [0,1]$, then the sequence $(P_{E,\nu_n}: n\in\mathbb{N})$ of revaluations $P_{E,\nu_n}: \mathfrak{S}(V) \to [0,1]$ of $\mathbb{P}$ for evidence ν_n from E is weakly convergent to the revaluation $P_{E,\nu}: \mathfrak{S}(V) \to [0,1]$ of $\mathbb{P}$ for evidence ν from E.

To prove this, let $g: S(V) \to \mathbb{R}$ be a bounded continuous function. Since P_E is a Feller kernel, the function $f: S(E) \to \mathbb{R}$ wih $x_E \to f(x_E) := \int g(y)\, P_E(x_E; dy)$ is continuous and bounded. From this, the weak convergence of $(\nu_n: n\in\mathbb{N})$ to ν, and the definition of P_{E,ν_n} follows the assertion.

If the revaluation P_E of $\mathbb{P}$ for evidence from E is not a Feller kernel, then there is a sequence $(x_n: n\in\mathbb{N})$ in S(E) converging to an $x\in S(E)$ such that the sequence $(P_E(x_n;.): n\in\mathbb{N})$ does not converge weakly to $P_E(x;.)$. Since the convergence of $(x_n: n\in\mathbb{N})$ to x implies the weak convergence of $(\delta_{x_n}: n\in\mathbb{N})$ to δ_x, we proved the converse of the assertion above, at least for a sequence of Dirac measures (which might be not consistent for $\mathbb{P}$).

Now, we consider a sequence $(\mathcal{C}_n: n\in\mathbb{N}_0)$ of CPNs $\mathcal{C}_n$ for a fixed graph $G:=(V,E)$ with the family $(\mathcal{P}_{n,v}: v\in V)$ of Markov kernels $\mathcal{P}_{n,v}: S(Pa(v))\times\mathfrak{S}_v \to [0,1]$, the associated multivariate distribution $\mathbb{P}_n$, and revaluations $P_{n,E}$ of $\mathbb{P}_n$ for evidence from E for $\emptyset \neq E \subset V$.

The following Example 4.1 shows that from the weak convergence of the sequence $(\mathbb{P}_n: n\in\mathbb{N})$ of associated multivariate distributions to $\mathbb{P}_0$ does follow neither the weak convergence of the sequence $(P_{n,E}(x_E;.): n\in\mathbb{N})$ to $P_{0,E}(x_E;.)$ for every $x_E\in S(E)$ nor the weak convergence of the sequence $(P_{n,E;\nu}: n\in\mathbb{N})$ to $P_{0,E;\nu}$ for every evidential probability $\nu: \mathfrak{S}(E) \to [0,1]$ and every $E\subset V$.

Example 4.1 and 4.2 show that this is true even if we impose the additional condition that δ_{x_E} or ν is consistent with $\mathbb{P}_n$ for every $n\in\mathbb{N}_0$.

To impose further conditions like the strong Feller convergence property (SFCP) (which implies that every kernel is a Feller kernel) and the compact uniform tightness property (CUTP) does not help to guarantee this type of continuity of Bayesian learning. This is shown by Example 4.3 which carries these properties over to other topologies with the help of Scheffé's lemma; e.g. see Billingsley [1].

Example 4.1:

Let the graph G and the state spaces $(S_0,\mathfrak{S}_0)$ and $(S_1,\mathfrak{S}_1)$ be as in Example 2.1 and define

$\mathcal{P}_{0,0}: \mathfrak{S}_0 \to [0,1]$ with $A \to \mathcal{P}_{0,0}(A) := \delta_0(A)$,

$\mathcal{P}_{0,1}: S_0\times\mathfrak{S}_1 \to [0,1]$ with $(x_0,B) \to \mathcal{P}_{0,1}(x_0;B) := \delta_1(B)$,

and for $n\in\mathbb{N}$:

$\mathcal{P}_{n,0}: \mathfrak{S}_0 \to [0,1]$ with $A \to \mathcal{P}_{n,0}(A) := (1-1/n)\,\delta_{1/n}(A) + 1/n\,\delta_0(B)$, and

$\mathcal{P}_{n,1}: S_0\times\mathfrak{S}_1 \to [0,1]$ with $(x_0,B) \to \mathcal{P}_{n,1}(x_0;B) := \delta_1(B)$ for $x_0 \neq 0$
$:= \delta_0(B)$ for $x_0 := 0$.

Then the sequence $(\mathbb{P}_n: n\in\mathbb{N})$ of associated multivariate distributions

$\mathbb{P}_n = (1-1/n)\,\delta_{(1/n,1)} + 1/n\,\delta_{(0,0)}$ of G and $(\mathcal{P}_{n,0},\mathcal{P}_{n,1})$

converges weakly to the associated multivariate distribution

$\mathbb{P}_0 = \delta_{(0,1)}$ of G and $(\mathcal{P}_{0,0}, \mathcal{P}_{0,1})$,

but the sequence $(P_{n,\{0\}}(0;.): n \in \mathbb{N})$ of revaluations $P_{n,\{0\}}(0;.)$ of $\mathbb{P}_n$ for evidence $0 \in S_{\{0\}} = S_0$ from $\{0\}$ does not converge weakly to the revaluation $P_{0,\{0\}}(0;.)$ of $\mathbb{P}$ for evidence 0:

$$P_{n,\{0\}}(0;.) = \mathbb{P}_n(.\,|X_0 = 0) \circ X_1^{-1} = \delta_{(0,0)} \circ X_1^{-1} = \delta_0 \qquad = \mathcal{P}_{n,1}(0;.) \quad \text{and}$$

$$P_{0,\{0\}}(0;.) = \mathbb{P}(.\,|X_0 = 0) \circ X_1^{-1} = \delta_{(0,1)} \circ X_1^{-1} = \delta_1 \qquad = \mathcal{P}_{0,1}(0;.)\ .$$

We observe that for $n \in \mathbb{N}$ the Markov kernels $\mathcal{P}_{n,1}$ are no Feller kernels and that for $E := \{0\}$ and $x_E := 0$ the Dirac measure δ_{x_E} is consistent with $\mathbb{P}_n$ for every $n \in \mathbb{N}_0$.

Example 4.2:

Let the graph G, the state spaces $(S_0, \mathfrak{S}_0)$ and $(S_1, \mathfrak{S}_1)$, and μ be as in Example 2.1, $\nu := 1/2\ \mu + 1/2\ \delta_0$, and define

$$\mathcal{P}_{0,0}: \mathfrak{S}_0 \to [0,1] \quad \text{with} \quad A \to \mathcal{P}_{0,0}(A) := 1/2\ \delta_0(A) + 1/2\ \nu,$$

$$\mathcal{P}_{0,1}: S_0 \times \mathfrak{S}_1 \to [0,1]$$
$$\text{with} \quad (x_0, B) \to \mathcal{P}_{0,1}(x_0; B) := 1/2\ \delta_0(B) + 1/2\ \delta_1(B) \qquad \text{for } x_0 \neq 0$$
$$:= 1/6\ \delta_0(B) + 5/6\ \delta_1(B) \qquad \text{for } x_0 := 0,$$

and for $n \in \mathbb{N}$:

$$\mathcal{P}_{n,0}: \mathfrak{S}_0 \to [0,1] \quad \text{with} \quad A \to \mathcal{P}_{n,0}(A) := 1/2\ \delta_{1/n}(A) + 1/2\ \nu, \qquad \text{and}$$

$$\mathcal{P}_{n,1}: S_0 \times \mathfrak{S}_1 \to [0,1]$$
$$\text{with} \quad (x_0, B) \to \mathcal{P}_{n,1}(x_0; B) := 1/2\ \delta_0(B) + 1/2\ \delta_1(B) \quad \text{for } x_0 \neq 1/n \qquad \text{and}$$

$$\mathcal{P}_{n,1}(1/n; B) := (2^{n+1} + 1)^{-1}\ \delta_0(B) + 2^{n+1}\ (2^{n+1} + 1)^{-1}\ \delta_1(B).$$

Then the sequence $(\mathbb{P}_n: n \in \mathbb{N})$ of associated multivariate distributions

$$\mathbb{P}_n = 1/2\ \delta_{(1/n,1)} + 1/4\ \nu \times \delta_0 + 1/4\ \nu \times \delta_1 \qquad \text{of G and } (\mathcal{P}_{n,0}, \mathcal{P}_{n,1})$$

converges weakly to the associated multivariate distribution

$$\mathbb{P}_0 = 1/2\ \delta_{(0,1)} + 1/4\ \nu \times \delta_0 + 1/4\ \nu \times \delta_1 \qquad \text{of G and } (\mathcal{P}_{0,0}, \mathcal{P}_{0,1}),$$

but the sequence $(P_{n,\{0\}}(0;.): n \in \mathbb{N})$ of revaluations $P_{n,\{0\}}(0;.)$ of $\mathbb{P}_n$ for evidence $0 \in S_{\{0\}} = S_0$ from $\{0\}$ does not converge weakly to the revaluation $P_{0,\{0\}}(0;.)$ of $\mathbb{P}$ for evidence 0:

$$P_{n,\{0\}}(0;.) = \mathbb{P}_n(.\,|X_0 = 0) \circ X_1^{-1} = 1/2\ \delta_0 + 1/2\ \delta_1 \qquad = \mathcal{P}_{n,1}(0;.) \quad \text{and}$$

$$P_{0,\{0\}}(0;.) = \mathbb{P}_0(.\,|X_0 = 0) \circ X_1^{-1} = 1/6\ \delta_0 + 5/6\ \delta_1 \qquad = \mathcal{P}_{0,1}(0;.)\ .$$

We observe that for $n \in \mathbb{N}$ the Markov kernels $\mathcal{P}_{n,1}$ are no Feller kernels and that for $E := \{0\}$ and $x_E := 0$ the Dirac measure δ_{x_E} is consistent with $\mathbb{P}_n$ for every $n \in \mathbb{N}_0$. In addition to that here every singleton of the joint state space has positive measure, therefore every evidential probability measure is consistent with all the multivariate distributions.

Example 4.3:

Let the set of nodes $V := \{0,1\}$, the state spaces $(S_0, \mathfrak{S}_0)$ and $(S_1, \mathfrak{S}_1)$, and μ be as in Example 2.1 , $\nu := 1/2\ \mu + 1/2\ \delta_0$, but consider the graph $\mathfrak{G} := (V, \mathfrak{E})$ with $\mathfrak{E} := \{(1,0)\}$ instead of the graph $G := (V, E)$ with $E := \{(0,1)\}$. Take the sequence $(\mathbb{P}_n: n \in \mathbb{N}_0)$ of multivariate distributions $\mathbb{P}_n: \mathfrak{S}(V) \to [0,1]$ from Example 4.2. For $n \in \mathbb{N}_0$ define the Markov kernels

$\mathfrak{P}_{n,1} := \mathbb{P}_n \circ X_1^{-1}: \mathfrak{S}_1 \to [0,1]$,

$P_{n,0}: S_1 \times \mathfrak{S} \to [0,1]$ to be the desintegration kernel of $\mathbb{P}_n$ with respect to X_1, and

$\mathfrak{P}_{n,0}: S_1 \times \mathfrak{S}_0 \to [0,1]$ with $\mathfrak{P}_{n,0}(x_1;.) := P_{n,0}(x_1;.) \circ X_0^{-1}$.

Here these Markov kernels are uniquely determined. Since S_1 is discrete, every kernel is a Feller kernel. Furthermore, all spaces are compact. Therefore, the two sequences fulfil the (SFCP) and the (CUTP). From the construction it follows that $\mathfrak{G}$ with $(\mathfrak{P}_{n,0}, \mathfrak{P}_{n,1})$ is a CPN with the associated multivariate distribution $\mathbb{P}_n$. The sequence of these associated multivariate distributions is weakly convergent and the sequence of its revaluations (which coincide with the ones given in Example 4.2) does not converge weakly.

5. Conclusions

First, we saw that Bayesian learning in causal probabilistic networks (and not only here) is twofold discontinuous and therefore may be risky. In applications we have to be aware of that and have to take precautions. Second, we should look out for situations where Bayesian learning is continuous. This will help us also to develop better procedures for the estimation of the Markov kernels of a CPN from data and expert knowledge.

References:

[1] Billingsley, P.: Convergence of Probability Measures. J. Wiley and Sons: New York - London - Sidney - Toronto, 1968.

[2] Hájek, P.; Havránek, T. Jiroušek.R.: Uncertain Information Processing in Expert Systems. CRC Press: Boca Raton - Ann Arbor - London - Tokyo: 1992.

[3] Henrion, M.: Propagating uncertainty in Bayesian networks by probabilistic logic sampling. In: Lemmer, F.J.; Kanal, L.N. (eds.): Uncertainty in Artificial Intelligence 2. Elsevier Science Publishers B.V. (North - Holland): 1988.

[4] Lauritzen, S.L.; Spiegelhalter, D.: Local Computations with Probabilities on Graphical Structures and Their Application to Expert Systems. J. Roy. Stat. Soc. B, 50 (2) (1988), 157 - 224.

[5] Matthes, R.; Oppel, U.G.: Convergence of causal probabilistic networks. In: Bouchon - Meunier, B., Valverde, L.; Yager, R.R.(ed.): Intelligent Systems with Uncertainty. Elsevier: Amsterdam - London - New York - Tokio, 1993.

[6] Neapolitan, R.E.: Probabilistic Reasoning in Expert Systems. Theory and Algorithms. J. Wiley and Sons: New York - Chichester - Brisbane - Toronto - Singapore, 1990.

[7] Oppel, U.G.: Every Complex System Can be Determined by a Causal Probabilistic Network without Cycles and Every Such Network Determines a Markov Field. In: Kruse, R.; Siegel, P. (eds.): Symbolic and Quantitative Approaches to Uncertainty. Lecture Notes of Computer Science 548. Springer: Berlin - Heidelberg - New York, 1991.

[8] Oppel, U.G.: Causal probabilistic networks and their application to metabolic processes. In: Mammitzsch, V.; Schneeweiß, H.: Proceedings of the Second Gauss Symposium, München, August 2 - 7, 1993. De Gruyter: Berlin, 1995.

[9] Parthasarathy, K.: Probability Measures on Metric Spaces. Academic Press: New York - London, 1969.

[10] Pearl, J.: Probabilistic Reasoning in Intelligent Systems: Networks of Plausible Inference. Morgan Kaufmann: San Matteo, 1988.

[11] Shachter, R.D.; Peot, M.A.: Simulation approaches to to general probabilistic belief networks. In: Henrion, M.; Shachter, R.D.; Kanal, L.N.; Lemmer, J.F. (eds.): Uncertainty in Artificial Intelligence 5. Elsevier Science Publishers B.V. (North - Holland): 1990.

Revision in extended propositional calculus

Odile Papini[1]* and Antoine Rauzy[2]

[1] LIM, Faculté des sciences de Luminy,163 Avenue de Luminy 13288 Marseille Cedex 9, France, papini@gia.univ-mrs.fr
[2] LaBRI, Université Bordeaux I, cours de la Libération, 33405 Talence Cedex, France, rauzy@labri.u-bordeaux.fr, France

Abstract. In this paper we propose a new modality, denoted by $\flat$, which allow preferences in propositional knowledge bases. Formulae with $\flat$ are interpreted in a weighted propositional calculus. This new modality can be used in order to define a revision operator that satisfy Alchouron, Gärdenfors and Makinson postulates modified by Katsuno et Mendelzon.

1 Introduction

In [7] we propose a mixed approach of revision in propositional calculus, the adopted stategy consists of determining the best set of clauses to remove from the knowledge base in order to restore consistency. To do that, we construct interpretations that are extended models of the added formula, and we label each interpretation by the set of unsatisfied clauses by this interpretation. To order these interpretations, we provide syntactic criteria stemming from the syntax of the added formula.

In the present paper we place ourselves in the context of the semantic approaches of revision [2, 3, 6, 9]. The knowledge base K is represented by a propositional formula ψ such that $K = \{\phi, \psi \vdash \phi\}$. The knowledge base revision by a formula μ ,denoted $\psi \circ \mu$, consists of finding the model of μ which is the closest possible to a model of the knowledge base ψ. Katsuno and Mendelzon [6] establish a correspondence between $K * \mu$ and $\psi \circ \mu$ and reformulate the Gärdenfors postulates [6, 1]. The principle of minimal change for revision takes the form of finding a model of the added formula closest to a model of the initial knowledge base. This leads to the definition of orders between interpretations, for example, number of propositional variables on which two models differ for Dalal [3], or sets of propositional variables on which two models differ for Bordiga [2]. These orders are external to the language and seem to be relatively arbitrary. On the other hand these approaches stem from the principle of irrelevance of syntax, but firstly, some knowledge bases can describe situations where some formulas can't be removed, for example physical laws, so syntax has to be taken into account. Secondly, two equivalent knowledge bases can be revised in different ways, as shown in the example proposed by Hansson and cited by Gärdenfors.

Even if our approach is within the framework of the semantic approaches of revision, we want to define preferences from the syntax. To do that, we introduce in the propositional calculus, a new modality, denoted $\flat$, which allow us to define

* This work has been sponsored by the ESPRIT Working Group 7035 "LAC" and the inter-PRC project "gestion de l'évolutif et de l'incertain".

the revision operation as $(\psi \circ \mu = (\flat\psi) \wedge \mu)$, where the added formula μ is preferred trying to take into account, when it is possible, the formula ψ. When a new item of information is consistent with the knowledge base we want to meet again the propositional calculus, and in case of inconsistency the proposed semantics allow to prefer a model of the added formula. The general philosophy is to consider that an old assertion is less sure than a new one, like for example for civil state data or meteorogical data. One of the interests of this approach is that it allow to really perform multiple revision, and to represent the history of the knowledge base.

We thus extend the propositional calculus adding a new connective, this leads to an appropriate definition of syntax and semantics of the new language. As we represent the knowledge base as unic formula, we define the syntactic notion of polarity to express the contribution of a sub-formula to the satisfaction or the unsatisfaction of a formula. The semantics is defined by means of weighted interpretations, the weight of a formula is defined in an interpretation and is computed from the weight of its sub-formulae in this interpretation. The weight of a formula is an infinite word built on the integer alphabet. These words are provided with an order and two operations $+$ and $\downarrow$ which allow to compute the weight of a formula from the weight of its sub-formulae. The weight of a satisfied formula in an interpretation is the null word. The weight of an unsatisfied formula in an interpretation is a not null word, it depends on its sub-formulae and on the number of $\flat$ connectives that prefix the formula. The bigger is this number, the smaller is the weight. The weight of a formula in an interpretation provides an order between interpretations and in case of inconsistency, the models of smaller weight are preferred. This approach find to minimize inconsistency.

After the definition of the syntax and the semantics of the extended propositional language in (section 2), we then show in (section 3) how the $\flat$ operator can be used to perform revision, finally we present some related works in (section 4) before concluding.

2 Propositional calculus with flat

2.1 Syntax

The items of the knowledge are expressed in a propositional language $\mathcal{L}$ which is the classical propositional calculus with additional unary connective $\flat$.

Definition 1. The rules of formation for well-formed formulae of $\mathcal{L}$ are defined as follows : 0 and 1 are formulae, a variable is a formula. If F and G are formulae then $\neg F$, $\flat F$, $F \vee G$ and $F \wedge G$ are formulae. Usual notations like parenthesis, will be used, when it is more convenient.

We place ourselves in the context of semantic approaches to revision, so we represent a knowledge base as a unic formula called the reference formula. Therefore, dealing with a formula amounts to deal with its sub-formulae. We then define the syntactic notion of polarity which express the contribution of a sub-formula to the satisfaction or the unsatisfaction of the reference formula. The sub-formula polarity is determined by the number of negations which prefix this sub-formula relatively to the reference formula :

Definition 2. The *polarity* of a well-formed sub-formula G relatively to the reference formula F, denoted $pol_F(G)$, belongs to $\{0,1\}$ and is defined as follows :

- $pol_F(F) = 1$, where F is the reference formula.
- If G is of the form $A \vee B$ ou $A \wedge B$, then $pol_F(A) = pol_F(B) = pol_F(G)$.
- If G is of the form $\flat A$ then $pol_F(A) = pol_F(G)$.
- If G is of the form $\neg A$ then $pol_F(A) = 1 - pol_F(G)$.

Example 1. Let $F = a \vee \neg(b \wedge \neg c)$. The sub-formulae F, a, $\neg(b \wedge \neg c)$ and c have a polarity equal to 1, and the sub-formulae $(b \wedge \neg c)$ and b have a polarity equal to 0. This example illustrate the fact that the polarity of a sub-formula is equal to 1 iff it is prefixed by an even number of negations.

2.2 Semantics

Definition 3. The set $\mathbb{N}^\omega$ is the set of infinite words built on the integers alphabet ($\mathbb{N}$).

The semantics of $\mathcal{L}$ is defined by means of weighted interpretations, the weight of a formula in an interpretation is element of $\mathbb{N}^\omega$. Intuitivelly, in an infinite word $w_0w_1\ldots$ each component w_i represent the number of variables which are prefixed i times by the $\flat$ connective, and which interpretations unsatisfy the formula. As we deal with finite formulae, we only use a subset of $\mathbb{N}^\omega$, that is the set of the infinite words equal to zero everywhere excepted on a finite prefixe. The use of infinite words just simplifies the notations because it unifies the treatment of formulae with different length. We define a total order on $\mathbb{N}^\omega$ as follows :

Definition 4. We define a total order on $\mathbb{N}^\omega$ denoted $<$: $v_0v_1\ldots < w_0w_1\ldots$ iff there exists an integer k such that $v_i = w_i$ for each $i < k$ and $v_k < w_k$. $\leq$ denotes the reflexive closure of $<$.

We define two operations in order to compute the weight of a formula by means of weight of its sub-formulae :

Definition 5. Let $v, w \in \mathbb{N}^\omega \times \mathbb{N}^\omega$, $v = v_0v_1\ldots$ and $w = w_0w_1\ldots$ $\downarrow v = 0v_0v_1\ldots$ and $v + w = (v_0 + w_0)(v_1 + w_1)\ldots$.

We are now able to define interpretations :

Definition 6. Let F and G be two formulae, an interpretation σ is defined as follows :

$$\sigma(p) \in \{0,1\} \text{ if p is a propositional variable }, \sigma(0) = 0 \text{ and } \sigma(1) = 1,$$
$$\sigma(F \wedge G) = min(\sigma(F), \sigma(G)) , \sigma(F \vee G) = max(\sigma(F), \sigma(G)),$$
$$\sigma(\neg F) = 1 - \sigma(F) , \sigma(\flat F) = \sigma(F),$$

Definition 7. Let F be a reference formula, G a sub-formula of F and σ an interpretation. The weight of G induced by σ *relatively to* F, denoted $I_\sigma^F[G]$ is defined by :

$$I_\sigma^F[G] = I_\sigma[< G, pol_F(G) >].$$

In the following i denotes the polarity of a sub-formula relatively to the reference formula. The *weight* induced by σ *relatively to* the reference formula, denoted I_σ is an element of $\mathbb{N}^\omega$ defined by :

- If $\sigma(G) = i$ then $I_\sigma[< G, i >] = 0^\omega$.
- otherwise ($\sigma(G) \neq i$) :
  - $I_\sigma[< G, i >] = 1.0^\omega$ if G is a constant or a variable.
  - $I_\sigma[< \neg G, i >] = I_\sigma[< G, i >]$,
  - $I_\sigma[< G \vee H, i >] = I_\sigma[< G, i >] + I_\sigma[< H, i >]$,
  - $I_\sigma[< G \wedge H, i >] = I_\sigma[< G, i >] + I_\sigma[< H, i >]$.
  - $I_\sigma[< \flat G, i >] = \downarrow I_\sigma[< G, i >]$.

In the above definition, when the interpretation of a sub-formula is equal to its polarity relatively to the reference formula, then the weight is the null infinite word, otherwise the weight depends on its length and on the number of $\flat$ connectives that prefix it. We now define classical and non-classical models.

Definition 8. Let F be a formula and σ an interpretation. σ is a classical model of F iff $I_\sigma^F[F] = 0^\omega$.

Definition 9. Let F be a formula and σ an interpretation. σ is a non-classical model of F iff $I_\sigma^F[F] < 1.0^\omega$ and for any other interpretation γ, $I_\sigma^F[F] \leq I_\gamma^F[F]$.

Example 2. Let $F = (a \vee b) \wedge \flat(\flat\neg a \wedge \neg b)$.

$$I^F_{[a\leftarrow 0, b\leftarrow 0]}[F] = (1.0^\omega + 1.0^\omega) + 0^\omega = 2.0^\omega$$
$$I^F_{[a\leftarrow 0, b\leftarrow 1]}[F] = 0^\omega + \downarrow (0^\omega + 1.0^\omega) = 01.0^\omega$$
$$I^F_{[a\leftarrow 1, b\leftarrow 0]}[F] = 0^\omega + \downarrow (\downarrow 1.0^\omega + 0^\omega) = 001.0^\omega$$
$$I^F_{[a\leftarrow 1, b\leftarrow 1]}[F] = 0^\omega + \downarrow (\downarrow 1.0^\omega + 1.0^\omega) = 011.0^\omega$$

F does'nt admit any classical model and admits a non-classical one : $[a \leftarrow\ 1, b \leftarrow\ 0]$. The first interpretation is not a model because the weight of F in this interpretation is greater than 1.0^ω. The second and the fourth interpretations can't be models because the weight of F in these interpretations is not minimal.

Example 3. Let the following formula $F = \flat(a \wedge a \wedge \neg a)$.

$I^F_{[a\leftarrow 0]}[F] = \downarrow (1.0^\omega + 1.0^\omega + 0^\omega) = 02.0^\omega$ and $I^F_{[a\leftarrow 1]}[F] = \downarrow (0^\omega + 0^\omega + 1^\omega) = 01.0^\omega$

F does'nt admit any classical model and admits a non-classical one: $[a \leftarrow\ 1]$. This example show that within the framework of the logic with $\flat$, we distinguish a from $a \wedge a$. This recall the notion of ressource in the linear logic [5].

Remark : If we consider formulae without $\flat$ connective, we meet again the propositional calculus.

The semantics defined above leads to the definition of weak and strong equivalences between formulae.

Definition 10. Let F and G two formulae. F *weakly implies* G, denoted $F \models_w G$, if any interpretation σ which is a non-classical model of F is a non-classical model of G. F and G are *weakly equivalent*, denoted $F \equiv_w G$, if $F \models_w G$ and $G \models_w F$.

Definition 11. F and G are *strongly equivalent*, denoted $F \equiv_s G$, if for any interpretation σ, $I_\sigma^F[F] = I_\sigma^G[G]$.

Remark : The definition of the stong equivalence remove the interest of the strong implication, and of course the weak and strong equivalences are not equivalent. For example, for any formula that doesn't contain $\flat$ connective, $\flat F \equiv_w \flat^2 F$, but if F is unsatisfiable $\flat F \not\equiv_s \flat^2 F$.

2.3 Some properties

Property 12 *Let F be a formula, the formula $F\prime$, obtained from F deleting the $\flat$ connectives, is satisfiable if $I_\sigma^F[F] = 0^\omega$.*

Property 13 *A formula in the form $\flat F$ is always satisfiable.*

In an epistemic point of view, preference is not obligation.

Property 14 *Let F and G be two formulae, then,* $\flat\neg F \equiv_s \neg\flat F$ (1), $\flat\ (\ F \vee G) \equiv_s \flat F \vee \flat G$ *(2)*, $\flat(F \wedge G) \equiv_s \flat F \wedge \flat G$ *(3).*

Proof. These properties can be easily verified. For instance, let σ be an interpretation and assume that $\sigma(F \vee G) \neq pol(F \vee G))$:

$$I_\sigma[\flat(F \vee G)] = \downarrow (I_\sigma[F] + I_\sigma[G]) = \downarrow I_\sigma[F] + \downarrow I_\sigma[G] = I_\sigma[\flat F \vee \flat G].$$

These properties are very important since they allow to drive the $\flat$ connectives down to the variables in the same way that it is done for negations. It follows that the classical transformations , incuding the transformation of a a formula in a set of clauses, can be performed in $\mathcal{L}$ too. The literals are then in the form $\flat^n p$ ou $\flat^n \neg p$.

Example 4. The formula $F = \flat(\flat(a \vee b) \wedge a) \wedge \neg a$ can be rewritten into $F\ =\ (\flat^2 a \vee \flat^2 b) \wedge \flat a \wedge \neg a$.

Property 15 *Let F any formula then,* $\lim_{n \to \infty} \flat^n F = 1$.

This property means, in an informal way, that a condtion too weakened is not restrictive any more.

3 A new revision operation

3.1 Formal framework

As we follow the semantic approaches of revision [2, 3, 6, 9]. The knowledge base K is represented by a propositional formula ψ such that $K = \{\phi, \psi \vdash \phi\}$. The knowledge base revision by a formula μ ,denoted $\psi \circ \mu$, consists of finding the model of μ which is the closest possible to a model of the knowledge base ψ. Katsuno and Mendelzon [6] establish a correspondence between $K * \mu$ and $\psi \circ \mu$ and reformulate the Gärdenfors postulates [6, 1]. Several authors proposed metrics leading to the definition of orders between interpretations. Dalal [3] proposed the Hamming distance between interpretations, Bordiga [2] proposed an order stemming from the sets of propositional variables on which two interpretations differ.

3.2 Revision with flat

In the above papers, the history of the knowledge base is not taken into account, the revision process has no memory. Nethertheless, when dealing with dynamical knowledge, in a lot of cases, it seems reasonable to decrease with time the confidence that one has in a item of information, this is the reason why we define our revision operator as follows:

Definition 16. Let ψ and μ be two formulae. The revision ($\circ$) of ψ by μ is defined by :

$$\psi \circ \mu \stackrel{\text{def}}{=} (\flat\psi) \wedge \mu$$

In the following, we limit ourselves in the case were μ is without $\flat$ coonectives. On the contary, ψ may have been obtained by revision, i.e. may be itself in the form $\psi_0 \circ \mu_0$. The KM postulates can be reformulated as follows:

modified KM postulates Let ψ, ϕ and μ two formulae.

($R1\flat$) $\psi \circ \mu \models \mu$.
($R2\flat$) If $\psi \wedge \mu$ is satisfiable, then $\psi \circ \mu \equiv_w \psi \wedge \mu$.
($R3\flat$) If μ is satisfiable, thens so is $\psi \circ \mu$.
($R4\flat$) If $\psi_1 \equiv_s \psi_2$ et $\mu_1 \equiv_s \mu_2$, Then, $\psi_1 \circ \mu_1 \equiv_s \psi_2 \circ \mu_2$
($R5\flat$) $(\psi \circ \mu) \wedge \phi \equiv_s \psi \circ (\mu \wedge \phi)$

($R1\flat$), ($R3\flat$) and ($R4\flat$) are the straightforward translation of the corresponding postulates. On the contrary, in ($R2\flat$), the weak equivalence is used. It permits to take into account the syntactical structure of the knowledge base as well as its history. According to the definition of the revision operator, the KM postulates with $\flat$, les postulats ($R5$) et ($R6$) can merge in a unic one ($R5\flat$). We can establish the following result :

Theorem 17. *The operator $\circ$ verifies the 5 above postulates.*

Proof. The proof is rather simple, and permits to precise some points :

($R1\flat$) and ($R3\flat$) : Let σ an interpretation, since μ is assumed to be without $\flat$ connectives, $I_\sigma[\mu] \in \{0^\omega, 1.0^\omega\}$. Thus, any model of $\psi \circ \mu$ is a model of μ. Moreover, a formula in the form $\flat F$ is always satisfiable since $I_\sigma[\flat F] = 0w_0w_1\ldots < 1.0^\omega$. ($R1\flat$) and ($R3\flat$) follow from this result.

($R2\flat$) : The result comes directly from the above remark, and property (3)

Property 18 *Let F be a formule that does'nt contain $\flat$ and G be any formula, then $\flat G \wedge F \equiv_w G \wedge F$.*

The two above formulae are weakly but not strongly equivalent : if the base is revised in the future, these formulae could induce different behaviour. They are equivalent now, but not for the future.

($R4\flat$) comes from the model based definition of $\circ$. Note that if ($R4\flat$) is weakened by requiring only a weak equivalence between formulae, then the property is no longuer verified. For instance, if $\psi_1 = (\flat a \vee b)$, $\psi_2 = (\flat b \vee a)$ and $\mu = (\neg a \wedge \neg b)$, we have $\psi_1 \equiv_w \psi_2$ but $\psi_1 \circ \mu$ admits as unic model $\{\neg a, b\}$, on the other hand $\psi_2 \circ \mu$ admits a unic model $\{a, \neg b\}$.

($R5\flat$) comes from the associativity of $\wedge$, (ϕ is assumed to be $\flat$ free).

Integrity constraints : A knowledge base can be often divided in two parts: an evolutive one (ψ) and a static one (π), often called integrity constraints, that typically models physical laws. Such constraints cannot be revised and are thus treated appart : : $\psi \circ^{\pi} \mu \overset{\text{def}}{=} \pi \wedge (\flat\psi) \wedge \mu$. This technics has been proposed in [6].

3.3 The fast food restaurant example

We now apply our revision operation to the famous example proposed by Hansson and cited by Gärdenfors.

Suppose we are standing in the street where there are two fast food restaurants a and b. We meet somebody eating french fried potatoes, we conclude that at least one of the fast food restaurant is open, $\psi_0 = \{a \vee b\}$ (1). Moreover seeing from a distance that the restaurant a has its lights on, we suppose that a is open, $\psi_1 = \{\flat(a \vee b), a\}$ (2). Upon reaching the fast food restaurant a, we find that it is closed for remodeling, $\psi_2 = \{\flat^2(a \vee b), \flat a, \neg a\}$ (3).

(1) ψ_0 admits 3 models : $\{a, \neg b\}$, $\{\neg a, b\}$ et $\{a, b\}$: at least one of the fast food restaurant is open.
(2) ψ_1 admits 2 models : $\{a, \neg b\}$ and $\{a, b\}$: the fast food restaurant a is open.
(3) ψ_2 admits 1 model : $\{\neg a, b\}$ the fast food restaurant b is open.

In contrast, suppose that we had not met anyone eating french fried potatoes, seeing from a distance that the fast food restaurant a has its lights on, we suppose that a is open, $\psi'_1 = \{a\}$ (1'). Upon reaching the restaurant a, we find that it is closed for remodeling, $\psi'_2 = \{\flat a, \neg a\}$ (2').

(1') ψ'_1 admits 1 model : $\{a\}$, : the fast food restaurant a is open.
(2') ψ'_2 admits 1 models : $\{\neg a\}$: the fast food restaurant a is closed.

With the proposed extented propositional logic, the syntax is taken into account and in the previous example $(a \vee b) \wedge a \not\equiv_s a$.

4 Related works

4.1 Ordinal conditional function

W. Spohn [4] provides a function called *ordinal conditional function* which associate to each model of a knowledge base an ordinal number. This function allows the expression of degrees of plausibility. He defines such a function in the case of revision of a knowledge base by a formula. This function decreases the ordinal number corresponding to the models of the initial base that are models of the added formula, and increases the ordinal number corresponding to the models of the initial base that are not models of the added formula. Our approach is rather similar because we define weights corresponding to interpretations, the definition of our revision operation $\psi \circ \mu \overset{\text{def}}{=} (\flat\psi) \wedge \mu$ allows to increase the weight of models of $\neg\mu$ and to decrease the weight of models of μ. Nevertheless the ordered degrees of plausibility seem to be arbitrary and external to the language.

4.2 T-calculus

G. H. von Wright [8] proposes the T-calculus to represent changes with time. Working within the framework of propositional calculus, he provides an additional binary connective which express the change of truth value of a formula with time. "pTq" denotes "*p and after q*". This expression can be translated in our language as " $\flat p \wedge q$ ". The T-calculus allows the representation of the history of the models of the knowledge base. When a new formula is added to a knowledge base, the axioms of the T-calculus provide a disjunction of possible models of the knowledge base, but there is not possibility to choose between them.

5 Conclusion

In this paper we have proposed a new modality $\flat$ which allow the introduction of preferences in a knowledge base, as well as the definition of a revision operation. This work follows the model-based approach, nevertheless the semantics using $\flat$ connective takes the syntax into account to prefer models. The $\flat$ connective allows the representation of the history of the knowledge base and allows multiple revision. We now have to efficiently implement our revision method. When dealing with situations where the last item of information has to be preferred, the $\flat$ connective is adequate, nevertheless in some other situations like the overbooking problem or the taxis reservation problem, the last item of information has not necessarly to be preferred in the immediate following state of the knowledge base. For that kind of situations, we want to introduce a $\sharp$ connective the dual connective of $\flat$. We also have to study how the $\flat$ and $\sharp$ connectives can be used to define update operations.

References

1. C. Alchourron, P. Gärdenfors, and D. Makinson. On the Logic of Theory Change: Partial Meet Functions for Contraction and Revision. *Journal of Symbolic Logic*, 50:510–530, 1985.
2. A. Bordiga. Language Features for Flexible Handling of Exceptions in Information Systems. *ACM Transactions on DataBase System*, 10, 1985.
3. M. Dalal. Investigations into Theory of Knowledge Base Revision. In *Proceedings of the 7th National Conference on Artificial Intelligence*, pages 475–164, 1988.
4. Gärdenfors. *Knowledge in Flux: Modeling the Dynamics of Epistemic States.* Bradford Books. MIT Press, Cambridge, 1988.
5. J.Y. Girard. Linear Logic. *Theoretical Computer Science*, 50:1–102, 1987.
6. H. Katsuno and A. Mendelzon. Propositional Knowledge Base Revision and Minimal Change. *Journal of Artificial Intelligence*, 52:263–294, 1991.
7. O. Papini and A. Rauzy. A Mixed Approach of Revision in Propositional Calculus. In R. Kruse M. Clarke and S. Moral, editors, *Proceedings of ECSQARU'93*, volume 747, pages 296–303. LNCS, 1993.
8. G. H. von Wright. And Next. *Acta Philos. Fenn. Fasc.*, 18:297–304, 1965.
9. M. Winslett. Reasoning about action using a possible models approach. In *Proc. of the 7th National Conf. on Artificial intelligence*, pages 89–93, 1988.

Using qualitative uncertainty in protein topology prediction

Simon Parsons

[1] Advanced Computation Laboratory, Imperial Cancer Research Fund, P.O. Box 123, Lincoln's Inn Fields, London WC2A 3PX, United Kingdom.
[2] Department of Electronic Engineering, Queen Mary and Westfield College, Mile End Road, London, E1 4NS, United Kingdom.

Abstract. The prediction of protein structure is an important problem in molecular biology. It is also a difficult problem since the available data are incomplete and uncertain. This paper describes models for the prediction of a particular level of protein structure, known as the topology, which handle uncertainty in a qualitative fashion.

1 Introduction

Proteins are large biological macromolecules that form the main components of living organisms and control most of the crucial processes in within them. The function of a particular protein is determined by the chemical interactions at its surface, and these are related to its three dimensional structure. Thus knowledge of protein structure is important. The structure of proteins can be described at various levels of detail from the primary structure, which consists of a list of the amino acids that make up the protein, through the secondary structure, which is a description of the way that the amino acids are grouped together into substructures such as β-strands and α-helices, to the tertiary structure, which is the set of three dimensional co-ordinates of every atom in the protein. Protein topology is an intermediate level somewhere between secondary and tertiary structure which specifies how the substructures are arranged.

Now, knowledge of three dimensional protein structure is sparse so that while the primary structures for many tens of thousands of proteins are known, only some hundreds of distinct proteins have had their three dimensional structure determined. This discrepancy motivates much research into determining protein structure including the use of computational techniques.

2 Protein Topology Prediction

The prediction of protein topology is interesting because the topology can be used to guide the choice of experiments to confirm protein structure. A major difficulty in this prediction is that a vast number of possible topologies can be hypothesized from a single secondary structure prediction, and one means to tackle this problem is to identify and apply constraints based upon analyses of known protein structures. For instance, for α/β sheets [1, 13] (which are topological structures combining α-helices and β-strands):

- C1. For parallel pairs of β-strands, β-α-β and β-coil[3]-β connections are right handed.
- C2. The initial β-strand is not an edge strand in the sheet.
- C3. Only one change in winding direction occurs.
- C5. All strands lie parallel in the β-sheet.
- F1. Strands are ordered in the sheet by hydrophobicity, with the most hydrophobic[4] strands central.
- F2. Parallel β-coil-β connections contain at least 10 amino acids.

Because these constraints are derived from aggregate properties of a collection of proteins, they do not apply to all proteins. When Shirazi et al. [12] assessed the validity of $C1$, $C2$, $C3$, $C5$ and $F2$ by checking them against 33 α/β sheet proteins, they found that only one protein satisfied all the constraints. Their results, reproduced in Table 1, show that while the folding rules are useful heuristics they are only true some of the time, leading us to suspect that explicitly modelling the uncertainty in the constraints might be advisable. One approach to doing this is to assess the validity of a structure based upon the constraints to which that structure conforms [7]. This paper explores an alternative method which fits in well with the constraint-satisfaction approach to protein topology prediction reported by Clark et al. [1].

In this constraint-based approach, the search proceeds by incrementally adding components (such as β-strands) to a set of possible structures. After each addition the set of structures is pruned by testing against every constraint. Thus following each step a structure can either conform to the same set of constraints as before, or to some subset or superset of it. So, after each step new evidence about whether or not a constraint holds may be available. If it is possible to relate the fact that a particular structure conforms to a particular constraint to that structure being correct, then the effect of the new knowledge may be

Protein ID	Constraints Violated	Protein ID	Constraints Violated	Protein ID	Constraints Violated
p1aat	C2 C5	p1tsl	C2 C5	p1ppd	C2 C5
p1bp2	C2 C5	p1ubq	C3 C5	p1rn3	C2 C5
p1cac	C2 C3 C5	p2b5c	C2 C3 C5	p1sbt	C1
p1cpb	C2 C3 C5	p2cab	C2 C3 C5	p1sn3	C2 C5
p1crn	C2 C5	p2cdv	C2 C5	p1srx	C2 C3 C5
p1cts	C2 C5	p2cts	C2 C5	p5cpa	C2 C3 C5
p1ctx	C5	p2lzm	C5	p3pgm	C5
p1hip	C2 C5	p2ssi	C5	p4cts	C2 C5
p1nxb	C3 C5	p3bp2	C2 C5	p4dfr	C3 C5 F2
p1ovo	C5	p3cts	C2 C5	p4fxn	
p1p2p	C2 C5	p3dfr	C3 C5	p4pti	C2 C5

Table 1. The results of checking constraints against 33 α/β sheet proteins.

[3] A protein has coil structure where it is neither a β-strand nor an α-helix.

[4] Lacking an affinity for water.

propagated to find out how it affects the likelihood that the structure is correct. Thus it is possible to tell whether the protein structure that is being assembled has become more or less likely to be correct, and whether it should be rejected or continued with accordingly.

Now, information about changes in the validity of a structure being correct with changes in evidence about which constraints it conforms to is exactly the kind of information that is handled by our qualitative approach to propagating uncertainty [8], and methods based upon this approach are what we consider here. In the tradition of experimental investigations of how to model uncertainty in a given problem [3, 4, 7, 10] we discuss a number of different ways in which the data from Table 1 may be represented. There are, of course, other possibilities which are not discussed here, and some of these are discussed in [6].

3 Single formalism approaches

The data in Table 1 may be interpreted as telling us how often constraints hold for real proteins, since every structure in the table occurs in nature. Thus the proportion of the proteins for which a given constraint holds is the conditional probability that the constraint holds given that the protein is real. Thus, for $C1$:

$$p(C1 \,|\, real) = \frac{\text{Number of proteins for which } C1 \text{ holds}}{\text{Total number of proteins}} = \frac{32}{33}$$

We have no information about the proportion of proteins for which $C1$ holds yet which are not real, so we cannot establish $p(C1 \,|\, \neg real)$ in the same way. Instead, we must employ the principle of maximum entropy to conclude that $p(C1 \,|\, \neg real) = 0.5$. From [8] we learn that these values are sufficient to establish the relationship between $p(C1)$ and $p(real)$ as being that $\frac{dp(C1)}{dp(real)} = [+]$, so that as $p(real)$ increases, so does $p(C1)$. This information, in turn [8], tells us that $\frac{dp(real)}{dp(C1)} = [+]$, allowing us to establish how $p(real)$ changes when we have information about $C1$ holding. Using the data about other constraints, we get Table 2. Note that $\frac{dp(real)}{dp(C2)} = [-]$ indicates that as $p(C2)$ increases, $p(real)$ decreases.

Constraint (x)	Cases of constraint failure	$\frac{dp(real)}{dp(x)}$	Change in $p(real)$ on adding the constraint
$C1$	1	[+]	[+]
$C2$	23	[−]	[−]
$C3$	10	[+]	[+]
$C5$	31	[−]	[−]
$F2$	1	[+]	[+]

Table 2. The probabilistic qualitative derivatives and their effects

It is possible to construct a valuation system model [11] which allows us to combine the effects of the various constraints. A suitable network is given in Fig 1—ovals denote variables, and boxes denote relations between variables. The propagation of qualitative values in this network may be carried out by the Mummu system [8], and using Mummu we can establish that the addition of $C1$, $C3$ and $F2$ causes $p(real)$ to rise, while the addition of $C2$ and $C5$ cause it to fall (Table 2).

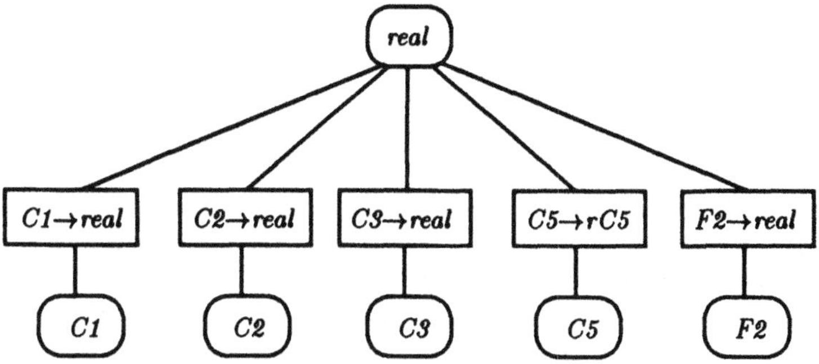

Fig. 1. A network for propagating qualitative changes

It is also possible to model the constraints using possibility theory. If a structure conforms to a constraint, then it is entirely possible that the structure is correct. However, if a structure fails to conform to a constraint then it becomes less possible that the structure is correct. Indeed, the possibility of the structure being a protein falls to a figure that reflects the proportion of naturally occurring proteins that do not conform to the constraint. So, considering the data in Table 1, we have:

$$\Pi(C1 \,|\, real) = \frac{\text{Number of proteins for which } C1 \text{ does not hold}}{\text{Total number of proteins}} = \frac{1}{33}$$

Since we have no information about proteins which are not real, we know nothing about $\Pi(C1 \,|\, \neg real)$ and $\Pi(\neg C1 \,|\, \neg real)$, and so set them both to 1 by the principle of minimum specificity [2]. These values, along with $\Pi(real) = \Pi(\neg real) = 1$ (again by the principle of minimum specificity) allow us to establish derivatives that define the relationship between $\Pi(real)$ and $\Pi(C1)$ [8] to be $\frac{d\Pi(C1)}{d\Pi(real)} = [0]$, $\frac{d\Pi(\neg C1)}{d\Pi(real)} = [\downarrow]$, $\frac{d\Pi(C1)}{d\Pi(\neg real)} = [0]$ and $\frac{d\Pi(\neg C1)}{d\Pi(\neg real)} = [0]$, meaning that $\Pi(\neg C1)$ may decrease when $\Pi(real)$ decreases, whilst it is independent of $\Pi(\neg real)$, and $\Pi(C1)$ is independent of $\Pi(real)$ and $\Pi(\neg real)$. From these values it is possible [8] to determine that $\frac{d\Pi(real)}{d\Pi(\neg C1)} = [\downarrow]$ with the other derivatives concerning $C1$ all being zero. Similar reasoning about the other constraints gives Table 3. When these derivatives are used with the network in Fig 1, and the effects of the application of individual constraints are propagated using Mummu, the results of the last column of Table 3 are generated. These results are rather different from

Constraint (x)	$\frac{d\Pi(real)}{d\Pi(x)}$	$\frac{d\Pi(real)}{d\Pi(\neg x)}$	$\frac{d\Pi(\neg real)}{d\Pi(x)}$	$\frac{d\Pi(\neg real)}{d\Pi(\neg x)}$	Change in $\Pi(real)$ on removing the constraint
$C1$	[↓]	[0]	[0]	[0]	[−]
$C2$	[↓]	[0]	[0]	[0]	[−]
$C3$	[↓]	[0]	[0]	[0]	[−]
$C5$	[↓]	[0]	[0]	[0]	[−]
$F2$	[↓]	[0]	[0]	[0]	[−]

Table 3. The possibilistic qualitative derivatives and their effects

those generated by the probabilistic modelling given above since they predict a change in possibility when a constraint is violated rather than a change in probability when a constraint is conformed to. At first sight it might appear that those constraints that, when added, cause a decrease in probability (that is $C2$ and $C5$), should, when removed, cause an increase in possibility. However, on reflection, this is seen not to be the case. Since, under our interpretation, violation of a constraint simply means that the possibility of a structure falls to reflect the proportion of structures that violate the constraint, when $C2$ and $C5$ are violated, the fall in possibility still occurs—it is just smaller than for other constraints.

4 Integrated approaches

It is also possible to integrate different representations of uncertainty using qualitative changes [8, 9], and this enables us to model the protein topology prediction problem in a slightly different way. There is another set of data about the applicability of the constraints [1, 7], which identifies some ambiguity in the data. This arises because there were a number of alternative structures for some of the proteins that were tested, and the constraints applied to some of these structures but not to others. In particular, $F1$ was found to hold for 1 of the 8 proteins tested, be violated for 5 of the proteins, and be ambiguous for 2, while $F2$ held for 6, was violated for 1, and was ambiguous for 1.

One way of modelling this ambiguity is to use Dempster-Shafer theory, and if the basic probability assignments that follow from the data given above are taken and interpreted as conditional beliefs, in the same way as the probabilistic data has previously been interpreted, then $bel(\{F1\} \mid \{real\}) = 0.125$, $bel(\{\neg F1\} \mid \{real\}) = 0.625$, $bel(\{F1, \neg F1\} \mid \{real\}) = 0.25$. Since there is no data about proteins that are not real we employ the Dempster-Shafer model of ignorance to get $bel(\{F1\} \mid \{\neg real\}) = 0$, $bel(\{\neg F1\} \mid \{\neg real\}) = 0$, $bel(\{F1, \neg F1\} \mid \{\neg real\}) = 1$, $bel(\{F1\} \mid \{real, \neg real\}) = 0$, $bel(\{\neg F1\} \mid \{real, \neg real\}) = 0$ and $bel(\{F1, \neg F1\} \mid \{real, \neg real\}) = 1$. These values tell us [8] that $\frac{dbel(\{F1\})}{dbel(\{real\})} = [+]$, $\frac{dbel(\{\neg F1\})}{dbel(\{real\})} = [+]$ and $\frac{dbel(\{F1, \neg F1\})}{dbel(\{real\})} = [-]$ and these may be transformed [8] to give $\frac{dbel(\{real\})}{dbel(\{F1\})} = [+]$, $\frac{dbel(\{real\})}{dbel(\{\neg F1\})} = [+]$ and $\frac{dbel(\{real\})}{dbel(\{F1, \neg F1\})} = [-]$. All other derivatives relating $F1$ and $real$ have value [0]. Repeating this procedure for $F2$ gives the derivatives of Table 4.

Constraint (x)	$\frac{dbel(\{real\})}{dbel(\{x\})}$	$\frac{dbel(\{real\})}{dbel(\{\neg x\})}$	$\frac{dbel(\{\neg real\})}{dbel(\{x\})}$	$\frac{dbel(\{\neg real\})}{dbel(\{\neg x\})}$	$\frac{dbel(\{real\})}{dbel(\{x,\neg x\})}$	$\frac{dbel(\{\neg real\})}{dbel(\{x,\neg x\})}$
$F1$	[+]	[+]	[0]	[0]	[−]	[0]
$F2$	[+]	[0]	[0]	[0]	[−]	[0]

Table 4. The Dempster-Shafer qualitative derivatives

These values may be used in conjunction with the probabilistic ones given above in the network of Fig 2. This network is simply that of Fig 1 extended to include the dependency of *real* on $F1$. The relationships between $C1$, $C2$, $C3$, $C5$ and *real* are determined using qualitative probabilities, while those between $F1$, $F2$ and *real* are determined using qualitative beliefs. The approach using qualitative changes that we are employing allows the combined use of different

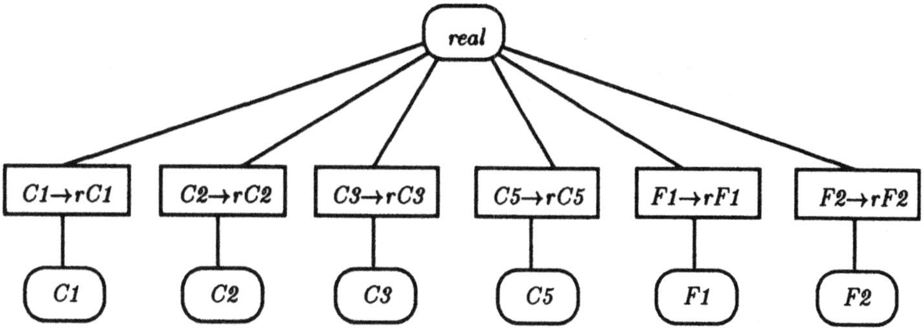

Fig. 2. A second network for propagating qualitative changes

formalisms together, simply translating a value of [+] (a definite increase) in belief functions to [0, +] (a possible increase) in probability, and [−] into [0, −], and giving the overall change at *real* as a qualitative probability. As before it is possible to consider changes in the value of *real* when new evidence is obtained

Constraint Added	Change in probability of *real*
$C1$	[+]
$C2$	[−]
$C3$	[+]
$C5$	[−]
$F1$	[+, 0]
$F2$	[+, 0]

Table 5. The results of using the probabilistic and Dempster-Shafer qualitative derivatives

Constraint Added	Change in possibility of *real*
$C1$	[0]
$C2$	[0]
$C3$	[0]
$C5$	[0]
$F1$	[+, 0]
$F2$	[+, 0]

Constraint Violated	Change in possibility of *real*
$C1$	[−]
$C2$	[−]
$C3$	[−]
$C5$	[−]
$F1$	[−, 0]
$F2$	[−, 0]

Table 6. The results of using the possibilistic and Dempster-Shafer qualitative derivatives

about a constraint holding, since Mummu implements the integration of changes in value discussed in [8, 9]. The results of applying Mummu are given in Table 5.

It is also possible to integrate possibility and belief values using the same network. Belief changes concerning $F1$ and $F2$ are propagated using the derivatives in Table 4, and changes in possibilities concerning $C1$, $C2$, $C3$ and $C5$ are propagated using the derivatives of Table 3. Translation from beliefs to possibilities are carried out in the same way as from beliefs to probabilities, and the overall change in *real* is given as a qualitative possibility. Since changes in possibility of the leaf nodes of the network in only occur when constraints are violated, both the addition and violation of constraints is considered. This set-up generates the results of Table 6.

Thus the use of both the single and combined formalism approaches make it possible to establish the change in validity of protein structure as components are added. The qualitative information that is provided is sufficient to assess how valid the addition is, and thus is sufficient to guide the addition of components during the constraint-based search.

5 Discussion

Unfortunately there is no obvious "gold standard" [3] against which to compare the results so that it is not possible to prove that they are helpful. However, it is possible to make several arguments for their being worth having and for the modelling experiment having been worthwhile. Firstly, it is a demonstration that purely qualitative methods for handling uncertainty can be useful. Thus it provides a useful counterpart to [5], which showed that qualitative probability could be usefully used in a diagnosis problem. Secondly it extends the comparative study of the use of differing uncertainty handling techniques [3, 4, 7, 10] to cover a new problem—that of modelling the impact of changing constraints in protein topology prediction. This problem contains a number of different types of uncertainty, and the fact that different models seem appropriate from different points of view provides empirical evidence for the validity of work on the different models. In addition, since no model seems to naturally model every aspect of the uncertainty, the protein topology problem provides motivation for working on using the different models in combination in the same problem. Further to this motivation, this paper, as is the case with the companion paper [7], has suggested some means of combining different methods within one problem, and, using results generated using the implementation of this work in the Mummu system, has illustrated the use of combinations of formalisms in solving a real problem. Thus the paper has provided some empirical demonstration that using combinations of formalisms is both feasible and useful.

References

1. Clark, D. A., Shirazi, J., and Rawlings, C. J. 1992. Protein topology prediction through constraint-based search and the evaluation of topological folding rules *Protein Engineering*, **4**:751–760.
2. D. Dubois and H. Prade 1991 Fuzzy sets in approximate reasoning, Part1: inference with possibility distributions, *Fuzzy sets and systems*, **40**:143–202.
3. Heckerman, D. E. 1990. An empirical comparison of three inference methods. In *Uncertainty in Artificial Intelligence 4*, (R. D. Shachter, T. S. Levitt, L. N. Kanal, and J. F. Lemmer, eds.), Elsevier, Amsterdam.
4. Heckerman, D. E., and Shwe, M. 1993. Diagnosis of multiple faults: a sensitivity analysis, *Proceedings of the Ninth Conference on Uncertainty in Artificial Intelligence*, Washington D. C.
5. Henrion, M., Provan, G., del Favero, B., and Sanders, G. 1994. An experimental comparison of diagnostic performance using infinitesimal and numerical bayesian belief networks, *Proceedings of the Tenth Conference on Uncertainty in Artificial Intelligence*, Seattle.
6. Parsons, S. 1995. Softening constraints in constraint-based protein topology prediction, *Proceedings of the 3rd International Conference on Intelligent Systems for Molecular Biology*, Cambridge, UK.
7. Parsons, S. 1995. Hybrid models of uncertainty in protein topology prediction, *Applied Artificial Intelligence*, **9**:335–351.
8. Parsons, S. 1993. Qualitative methods for reasoning under uncertainty, PhD Thesis, Queen Mary and Westfield College, London (to be published by MIT Press).
9. Parsons, S. and Saffiotti, A. 1993. Integrating uncertainty handling techniques in distributed artificial intelligence, in: *Symbolic and Quantitative Approaches to Reasoning and Uncertainty*, (M. Clarke, R, Kruse and S. Moral, eds.), Springer Verlag.
10. Saffiotti, A., Parsons, S. and Umkehrer, E. 1994. A case study in comparing uncertainty management techniques, *Microcomputers in Civil Engineering — Special Issue on Uncertainty in Expert Systems*, **9**:367–380.
11. Shenoy, P. P. 1991. A valuation-based language for expert systems, *International Journal of Approximate Reasoning*, **3**:383–411.
12. Shirazi, J., Clark, D. A. and Rawlings, C. J. 1990. Constraint-based reasoning in molecular biology: predicting protein topology from secondary structure and topological constraints, BCU/ICRF Technical Report.
13. Taylor, W. R. and Green, N. M. 1989. The predicted secondary structure of the nucleotide binding sites of six cation-transporting ATPases leads to a probable tertiary fold *European Journal of Biochemistry*, **179**:241–248.

Circumscribing Features and Fluents: Reasoning about Action with Default Effects*

Anna Radzikowska

Institute of Mathematics, Warsaw University of Technology
Plac Politechniki 1, 00-661 Warsaw, Poland
e-mail: annrad@im.pw.edu.pl

Abstract. In this paper we consider action scenarios where actions with default effects are permitted. We present one of the possible preferential strategies applicable for reasoning about such scenarios. This method, intuitively motivated, is provided in terms of circumscription. We adopt the occlusion concept introduced by Sandewall. The analysis is based on the standard two-sorted FOPC with temporal terms and discrete time.

1 Introduction

The formalization of reasoning about action and change is considered one of the central problems in the theory of knowledge representation. A number of various approaches have been presented in the framework of situation calculus [6]. As it turned out, it is surprisingly difficult to discuss the possibilities and limitations of the available methods in a precise and general way. For instance, until quite lately Baker's approach [1] has been found one of the most interesting and more robust than other proposals. Recently, however, Kartha [5] has pointed out some drawbacks of this approach in the case of nondeterministic actions.

Sandewall [7] has recently presented a number of entailment methods and assessed their range of applicability for particular classes of dynamical systems. The broadest class he considers, $\mathcal{K}$-IA (and its associated preferential relation PMON), covers scenarios with nondeterministic actions, actions with duration, partial specification at any state of the system and incomplete specification of the timing and order of actions. $\mathcal{K}$-IA is probably the widest class of scenarios for which the preferential method has been proven to give correct results.

Doherty [2] has provided a syntactic characterization of PMON in terms of the two-sorted FOPC and a circumscriptive axiom.

Strangely enough, no much interest has been attracted to study scenario problems involving actions with default effects ([3],[4]). In everyday life people usually undertake actions which have typical, but not necessarily certain effects (e.g. flipping the switch may fail to light the lamp). In many cases we are

*This work was supported by the ESPRIT Basic Research Action No. 6156-DRUMS II.

unable or unwilling to anticipate all circumstances under which some effects of the action may fail. Modelling a behaviour of intelligent agents, it seems natural to study such action scenarios.

In the paper we consider a class Υ_δ of action scenarios where some actions may have default effects. As we shall notice, various preferential strategies may be applied to solve such scenario problems. Our intend is to present one of these methods, MINP, reflecting minimal expectations one may have about the course of events. This method, intuitively motivated, is provided in terms of circumscription. We adopt the occlusion concept introduced by Sandewall [7]. The analysis is based on the standard two-sorted FOPC with temporal terms and discrete time.

The paper is structured as follows. The next section specifies the class Υ_δ of action scenarios. In Section 3 we briefly present the fluent logic FL1. The occlusion concept and the PMON policy are outlined in Section 4. Next, in Section 5, we present a preferential strategy, MINP, and provide its syntactic characterization. A simple example will show how this strategy works. Finally, in Section 6, we provide concluding remarks and briefly discuss future works.

2 The class Υ_δ of action scenarios

The $\mathcal{K}$-IA family of action scenarios can be naturally extended for the case where actions with default effects are permitted. Formalizing such actions we focus on modelling a typical course of the action performance. More specifically, we want to express that the action causes some (typical) effects, provided that any unexpected events take place during the action performance.

In principle, a typical performance of the action should be considered in the context of some particular effects of the action. Clearly, the action may be executed typically with respect to some results, yet atypically with respect to others. To simplify the discussion we restrict ourselves to distinguishing, in general sense, a typical from an atypical manner of the action performance.

In this paper we consider actions (henceforth referred to as δ-actions) which may be described by the following schema:[1]

> If a precondition π holds, then values of fluents $f_1, \ldots, f_n$ change and, additionally, values of fluents $g_1, \ldots, g_k$ are *typically* changed; in an atypical case, however, fluents $g_1, \ldots, g_k$ remain unchanged.

The class Υ_δ covers scenarios where δ-actions are permitted. In the framework of the taxonomy introduced by Sandewall, Υ_δ is a subclass of the $\mathcal{K}$-IAN family of scenarios characterized by the general treatment of normality of fluents.

[1] There are also other types of actions with default effects: actions which cause some additional changes only in atypical cases (e.g. parking a car usually leaves it untouched, yet atypically it may be stolen), and those which have different effects depending on their typical and atypical performances (e.g. unlocking the door usually makes it open, but atypically the lock is made out of order).

2.1 Action scenario descriptions

Most of the problems involving reasoning about action can be represented in terms of *scenario descriptions*. A scenario description Γ is a partial specification in a logical language of the states of the system, combined with descriptions of some actions that have occurred and their duration. Such specification may be formalized as *observation statements* and *action statements*. The former express states of the system at particular timepoints, whereas the latter are used to represent either action occurrences or action descriptions. In what follows, the symbols "obs" and "acs" will be used to denote an observation statement and an action statement, respectively.

3 Fluent Logic FL1

In this section we briefly present the fluent logic FL1 based on the logic FL introduced in [2]. FL1 is a two-sorted FOPC with equality including a sort for temporal entities and a sort for truth-valued fluents. We assume a linear discrete model of time containing all natural numbers.

An *alphabet* of FL1 consists of a denumerable set of *temporal variables*, denoted by the letters t and s; a denumerable set of *temporal constants*, denoted by the numerals 0,1,...; a denumerable set of *fluent variables*, denoted by the letter f; a denumerable set of *fluent constants*, denoted by italic lowercase letters; the equality predicate $=$; function symbols $+$, $-$ and binary predicate symbols $<$, $\leq$ (interpreted on natural numbers in the usual way); the binary predicate symbols *Holds* and *Occlude*, which take a temporal and a fluent term as arguments[2] and a denumerable set of binary predicate symbols: *action predicate symbols* (A-predicate symbols) and *action abnormality predicate symbols* (*Ab*-predicate symbols), which take two temporal terms as arguments. If A is an A-predicate symbol and t, s are temporal terms, then $\mathrm{A}(t,s)$ states that the action A occurs[3] during the period t to s. Similarly, $Ab(t,s)$ states that some action has an *abnormal* performance during the period t to s.

All variables and constants may be subscripted and/or primed.

The set of *temporal terms* is the smallest set satisfying the following conditions: (1) each temporal variable and each temporal constant is a temporal term; (2) if s and t are temporal terms, then so is $s+t$ and $s-t$. A *fluent term* is either a fluent constant or a fluent variable.

Atomic formulas are of the following types: (1) $t=s$, $t<s$, $t\leq s$, where t,s are temporal terms; (2) $Holds(t,f), Occlude(t,f), \mathrm{A}(t,s)$ and $Ab(t,s)$, where t,s are temporal terms, f is a fluent term and A, Ab are an A-predicate symbol and an Ab-predicate symbol, respectively.

---

[2] $Holds(t,f)$ states that the fluent f is true at time t; the meaning of the predicate *Occlude* will be explained in the next section.

[3] Note that $\mathrm{A}(t,s)$ does not state that the action A is performed. Since the precondition of A need not hold at time t, the execution of this action may fail (i.e. A has no effects).

The *set of formulas* is constructed in the straightforward way by using logical connectives and quantifiers over temporal and fluent variables.

To distinguish between different types of formulas in a scenario description the following notation will be useful. We write $\Gamma_{\Upsilon} = \Gamma_{ACS} \cup \Gamma_{OBS} \cup \Gamma_{UNA}$ to state that the scenario description Γ_{Υ}, representing the scenario Υ, consists of the set of observation axioms (Γ_{OBS}), the set of action axioms (Γ_{ACS}) and the set of appropriate unique name axioms (Γ_{UNA}).

4 The occlusion concept and PMON

Each action is assumed to change some fluents when it is performed. By virtue of the commonsense law of inertia, only fluents the action affects may change their values, while all others must remain unchanged. Also, no changes are allowed when no action takes place. In consequence, a fluent f may change its value only if the action which affects f is executed. On the other hand, if the action is performed longer than a single unit of time, then we assume that, unless otherwise is specified, one remains agnostic about the exact time of changes the action brings about. All one should know is that at the end of the action specific fluents obtain specific values. To capture these ideas Sandewall [7] introduced the occlusion predicate.

The predicate *Occlude* takes a fluent and a timepoint as arguments. $Occlude(t,f)$ states that a fluent f is *occluded* at time t with the intended meaning that there is no preference for f to retain its value in the transition from $t-1$ to t. In other words, $Occlude(t,f)$ says that at time t the fluent f is exempt from the global persistence assumption. Accordingly, all fluents affected by the action must be occluded during the time of the action performance. For example, the action of loading the gun can be represented in $\mathcal{L}$(FL1) by the following schema (here l is a fluent constant standing for *loaded*):

$$\forall t_1, t_2.\ \mathrm{Load}(t_1, t_2) \rightarrow Holds(t_2, l) \land (\forall t.\ t_1 < t \leq t_2 \rightarrow Occlude(t, l)).$$

Moreover, to specify that a fluent may change its value only when it is occluded, the *nochange axiom* is additionally introduced:

$$\Gamma_{NCH} = \forall t, f.\ \neg Occlude(t+1, f) \rightarrow [Holds(t, f) \equiv Holds(t+1, f)].$$

PMON stands for *Pointwise Minimization of Occlusion with Nochange Premises* and is an entailment relation covering the $\mathcal{K}$-IA family of action scenarios in the sense that it provides the intended models for this class. The idea of this method is to minimize occlusion globally relative only to action axioms Γ_{ACS} of a given scenario description Γ_{Υ} and then to intersect the obtained models with those of Γ_{Υ} and Γ_{NCH}. The syntactic characterization of this policy provides the circumscription axiom

$$\mathrm{CIRC}_{PMON}(\Gamma_{\Upsilon}) = \Gamma_{\Upsilon} \land \Gamma_{NCH} \land \mathrm{CIRC}_{SO}(\Gamma_{ACS}; Occlude; \mathbf{A}),$$

where $\mathbf{A} = (A_1, \ldots, A_n)$ is a tuple of all A-predicates occurring in Γ_Υ and $\mathrm{CIRC}_{SO}(\Gamma_{ACS}; \mathit{Occlude}; \mathbf{A})$ is the second-order circumscription formula.[4]

5 Minimal Expectation Policy

In this section we present one of the preferential strategies applicable for reasoning about δ-action and provide its syntactic characterization in terms of circumscription.

To begin with, consider a scenario $\Upsilon \in \Upsilon_\delta$, where some δ-action takes place once. The intuition dictates that this action, if it is performed, will be typically executed.

Suppose, however, that the scenario specifies several occurrences of the same δ-action. Since the scenario may be viewed as a plan (e.g. an agenda) constructed to achieve some goals, the question arises what the intention is to repeat the action several times. One may admit that the planner tends to increase the probability of achieving some goals. For instance, consider a shooter who wants to kill a turkey. Despite of the fact, that his shot is usually well-aimed, he will probably fire several times to ensure that the turkey will be finally dead. Similarly, if one has an important message to mail, s/he is likely to send it twice expecting that at least one of them will reach the receiver. From these examples it would follow that *at least one* performance of the δ-action is expected to succeed in the sense that the action will have desired effects. In fact, this policy seems to reflect minimal expectations one may have about the course of events. We call it the *Minimal Expectation Policy* (MINP policy, for short).

Suppose, however, that after the performance of some δ-action A, another action B takes place which (possibly) affects changes usually invoked by A. In such a case, it is inessential whether A is performed in a typical manner or not, since B is supposed to cancel normal effects of A. This suggests that the following assumption is required in order to limit the range of applicability for the MINP policy.

Assumption: In the course of events, between any two performances of some δ-action A, no action B is permitted, such that B influences results normally invoked by A.

Clearly, this strategy is not the only one which may be applied for reasoning about δ-actions. It is often desirable to conclude that, unless otherwise is known, each performance of a δ-action is typical. Sometimes one may prefer at least first (resp. last) typical execution of such action. Then, in general case, a scenario description should specify the appropriate policy for each type of δ-action. This specification will then guide the process of reasoning. In practice, this process may combine various preferential methods relevant to particular δ-actions.

---

[4] In [2], the PMON circumscription axiom is also based on second-order circumscription with *Holds* fixed, but no predicates are allowed to vary. Here, due to introducing A-predicates, we must take all of them as variables while minimizing occlusion.

Regardless of the adopted preferential strategy, the actual reasoning process proceeds in three stages which correspond to:

(1) for each combination of abnormalities, determining all potential histories constrained by the assumption of inertia;
(2) comparing the results with observations to rule out inappropriate histories;
(3) selecting histories with minimal[5] abnormalities from among the remaining.

Technically, this is realized via the following two-step process:

(1) global minimization of occlusion, where all A-predicates vary while *Holds* and all *Ab*-predicates are fixed;
(2) minimization of *Ab*-predicates.

The first step is realized by the PMON-Circumscription. The second step is the one which differs various preferential methods. In the sequel, we present its formalization for the Minimal Expectation Policy.

5.1 Syntactic characterization of the MINP policy

As we previously noted, the MINP preferential policy may be adopted for reasoning about some type of δ-actions, later referred to as δ_{MIN}*-actions*.

Before providing a syntactic characterization of this policy, some auxiliary notation should be introduced.

Let Φ and Ψ be binary predicates which take two temporal terms as arguments, A be an A-predicate corresponding to some δ_{MIN}-action and $\pi_{\mathrm{A}}(t)$ be a formula denoting the precondition of this action. Then $\mathrm{A}(t_1,t_2) \wedge \pi_{\mathrm{A}}(t_1)$, denoted later by $\mathrm{Ex}_{\mathrm{A}}(t_1,t_2)$, states that the action A is performed during the period t_1 to t_2. We write $\Phi \prec_{\mathrm{Ex}} \Psi$ to denote the formula

$$[\forall t_1, t_2.\, \mathrm{Ex}_{\mathrm{A}}(t_1,t_2) \rightarrow \Psi(t_1,t_2)] \wedge [\exists t_1, t_2.\, \mathrm{Ex}_{\mathrm{A}}(t_1,t_2) \wedge \neg\Phi(t_1,t_2)] \wedge \\ \wedge [\forall t_1, t_2.\, \neg\mathrm{Ex}_{\mathrm{A}}(t_1,t_2) \rightarrow \neg\Phi(t_1,t_2)].$$

Intuitively this formula states that whenever the action A is performed, the condition Ψ holds, there is an execution of A which does not satisfy Φ and Φ does not hold, provided that A is not executed.
Similarly, if $\mathbf{\Phi} = (\Phi_1,\ldots,\Phi_k)$, $\mathbf{\Psi} = (\Psi_1,\ldots,\Psi_k)$ are tuples of binary predicates with two temporal terms as arguments and $\mathbf{Ex} = (\mathrm{Ex}_1,\ldots,\mathrm{Ex}_k)$ is a tuple of predicate expressions such that $\mathrm{Ex}_i(t_1,t_2)$ stands for $\mathrm{A}_i(t_1,t_2) \wedge \pi_{\mathrm{A}_i}(t_1)$, where A_i, π_{A_i} are defined above, then $\mathbf{\Phi} \prec_{\mathbf{Ex}} \mathbf{\Psi}$ is an abbreviation for $\bigwedge_{i=1}^{k} [\Phi_i \prec_{\mathrm{Ex}_i} \Psi_i]$.

As we have already stated, the first step of the MINP policy is realized by the PMON-Circumscription. Let us denote the resulting theory by Γ_{PMON}. Since we aim to formalize that each δ_{MIN}-action, if it is performed, has at least one typical execution, *Ab*-predicates are to be minimized globally in Γ_{PMON} with respect to the preferential relation $\prec_{\mathbf{Ex}}$.

[5] The term "minimal" refers to the specific preferential relation.

Definition 1 (MINP-Circumscription) Let Γ_Υ be a scenario description representing a scenario $\Upsilon \in \Upsilon_\delta$ by the set of appropriate axioms in $\mathcal{L}$(FL1). Assume that $\mathbf{A} = (A_1, \ldots, A_n)$ is a tuple of all A-predicates occurring in Γ_Υ, $\mathbf{A}^* = (A_1, \ldots, A_k)$, $k \leq n$, is a tuple of all A-predicates representing δ_{MIN}-actions and $\boldsymbol{Ab} = (Ab_1, \ldots, Ab_k)$ is a tuple of Ab-predicates corresponding to δ_{MIN}-actions which occur in Γ_Υ. Let $\mathbf{Ex} = (\mathrm{Ex}_1, \ldots, \mathrm{Ex}_k)$ be a tuple of predicate expressions defined above. The *MINP-Circumscription* is the following formula

$$\mathrm{CIRC}_{\mathrm{MINP}}(\Gamma_\Upsilon) = \mathrm{CIRC}(\mathrm{CIRC}_{PMON}(\Gamma_\Upsilon);\ \boldsymbol{Ab}/\mathbf{Ex};\ \mathbf{A}, Holds, Occlude),$$

where $\mathrm{CIRC}(\mathcal{T};\ \boldsymbol{Ab}/\mathbf{Ex};\ \mathbf{A}, Holds, Occlude)$ denotes the formula
$\mathcal{T}(\boldsymbol{Ab}, \mathbf{A}, Holds, Occlude) \wedge \forall \boldsymbol{\Phi}, \boldsymbol{\Psi}, \Theta_1, \Theta_2. \neg[\mathcal{T}(\boldsymbol{\Phi}, \boldsymbol{\Psi}, \Theta_1, \Theta_2) \wedge \boldsymbol{\Phi} \prec_{\mathbf{Ex}} \boldsymbol{Ab}]$. ■

5.2 An example

The following default version of the Yale Shooting Problem will be useful to show how the MINP policy actually works.

Example 1 (YSP$_\delta$) Initially the gun is loaded and the turkey is alive. The gun is firing during the period 0 to 1, then it is loaded from 1 to 2 and firing again from 2 to 3. Loading the gun makes the gun loaded. If the gun is loaded at the begining of firing, then it becomes unloaded and the turkey is *typically* not alive at the end of firing; otherwise firing has no effect.

This scenario can be represented in $\mathcal{L}$(FL1) as follows (here l and a are fluent constants standing for *loaded* and *alive*, respectively, whereas Load and Fire are A-predicates):

obs1 $Holds(0, a) \wedge Holds(0, l)$
acs1 $\forall t_1, t_2. \mathrm{Load}(t_1, t_2) \rightarrow Holds(t_2, l) \wedge (\forall t. t_1 < t \leq t_2 \rightarrow Occlude(t, l))$
acs2 $\forall t_1, t_2. \mathrm{Fire}(t_1, t_2) \rightarrow [Holds(t_1, l) \rightarrow$
$\neg Holds(t_2, l) \wedge (\forall t. t_1 < t \leq t_2 \rightarrow Occlude(t, l)) \wedge$
$(\neg Ab(t_1, t_2) \rightarrow \neg Holds(t_2, a) \wedge (\forall t. t_1 < t \leq t_2 \rightarrow Occlude(t, a)))]$
acs3 $\mathrm{Fire}(0, 1) \wedge \mathrm{Load}(1, 2) \wedge \mathrm{Fire}(2, 3)$.

Applying the MINP policy, we first determine minimal occluded areas for each combination of firing abnormalities where observations are satisfied. This is realized by the PMON-Circumscription and results in three classes of models: first, where both firings are atypical, second, where both firings are typical and third, where exactly one performance of firing is normal. Next, by minimizing abnormalities (wrt $\prec_{\mathbf{Ex}}$) we prune all remaining models where both firings are performed abnormally. This process leads to three models shown in Tab.1.

Suppose that the turkey is alive at time 4. Then we add the following axiom

obs2 $Holds(4, a)$.

It is easily verified that the PMON-Circumscription leads to models of Γ where both firings are atypical (i.e. the turkey is not shot). Then we rule out models with abnormalities of hypothetical firings, i.e. those which are not provided by the scenario description. Consequently, we get a model shown in Tab.2. ■

The tables below show the preferred models obtained in the example. Here asterisks indicate occluded fluents at particular timepoints.

Tab.1: YSP_δ (prediction)

	$\mathcal{M}_1$	$\mathcal{M}_2$	$\mathcal{M}_3$
0	a, l	a, l	a, l
1	$\neg a^*, \neg l^*$	$a, \neg l^*$	$\neg a^*, \neg l^*$
2	$\neg a, l^*$	a, l^*	$\neg a, l^*$
3	$\neg a^*, \neg l^*$	$\neg a^*, \neg l^*$	$\neg a, \neg l^*$
4	$\neg a, \neg l$	$\neg a, \neg l$	$\neg a, \neg l$
$\vdots$	$\neg a, \neg l$	$\neg a, \neg l$	$\neg a, \neg l$
Ab	$\emptyset$	$\{(0,1)\}$	$\{(2,3)\}$
Load	$\{(1,2)\}$	$\{(1,2)\}$	$\{(1,2)\}$
Fire	$\{(0,1),(2,3)\}$	$\{(0,1),(2,3)\}$	$\{(0,1),(2,3)\}$

Tab.2: YSP_δ (postdiction)

	$\mathcal{M}$
0	a, l
1	$a, \neg l^*$
2	a, l^*
3	$a, \neg l^*$
4	$a, \neg l$
$\vdots$	$a, \neg l$
Ab	$\{(0,1),(2,3)\}$
Load	$\{(1,2)\}$
Fire	$\{(0,1),(2,3)\}$

6 Conclusions and future work

We have presented the preferential method, MINP, applicable for reasoning about actions with default effects. This strategy has been provided using nested circumscription. Although this policy has not been assessed correct, it appears to be intuitive and works correctly. As far as we know our approach is one of the first that formalizes reasoning about actions with default effects.

As future works, we would like to consider other preferential strategies adequate for reasoning about action with default effects. More general approach to normality of fluents should also be studied. Finally, it seems really worthwhile to expand our idea in the direction of dealing with the qualification problem.

References

[1] A. Baker: Nonmonotonic reasoning in the framework of situation calculus, *Artificial Intelligence*, **49**, pp. 5-23, 1991.

[2] P. Doherty: Reasoning about action and change using occlusion, in *Proc. 11th ECAI-94*, 1994, pp. 401-405.

[3] B. Dunin-Kęplicz, A. Radzikowska: Epistemic Approach to Reasoning about Action with Typical Effects, in *Proc. ECSQUARU-95*, 1995.

[4] D. W. Etherington, J. M. Crawford: Formalizing reasoning about change: A qualitative reasoning approach, in *Proc. 10th AAAI*, San Jose, CA, 1994.

[5] N. Kartha: Two counterexamples related to Baker's approach to the frame problem, *Artificial Intelligence*, **69**, pp. 379-391, 1994.

[6] J. McCarthy, P. J. Hayes: Some philosophical problems from the standpoint of artificial intelligence, in: B. Meltzer and D. Michie, eds., *Machine Intelligence* **4** (American Elsevier, New York, 1969), pp. 463-502.

[7] E. Sandewall: Features and fluents: A systematic approach to the representation of knowledge about dynamical systems, Technical report LITH-IDA, Linköping University, Sweden, 1994.

Using Maximum Entropy to Compute Marginal Probabilities in a Causal Binary Tree Need not Take Exponential Time

Paul C Rhodes & Gerald R Garside†

In a previous paper, the present authors have argued that Maximum Entropy is worth pursuing as a technique for reasoning under uncertainty when information is missing. The main drawback is that maximising Entropy has been shown to be an NP–Complete problem. However, a Maximum Entropy approach to probabilistic reasoning is not necessarily exponentially large to compute in at least one case. This paper shows that given a tree of incomplete causal information (eg. as used by Pearl but with some of the information missing), the probability of the marginals can be found in linear space and time using Maximum Entropy.

Keywords: Maximum Entropy, Probability, Reasoning under Uncertainty, Probabilistic Inference, Computational Complexity, Incomplete Information, Expert Systems.

Introduction

Reasoning with incomplete and unreliable information is part of everyday life but human reasoning is highly intuitive and prejudiced and this is not satisfactory for many decision and deductive processes, eg in industry and public services. What is required is an accurate assessment of that which can be safely deduced from the information available. With uncertain events this means finding a minimally prejudiced distribution for the probability of all the possible outcomes of the events.

Historically, work in this field has concentrated on situations where complete information in a very specific format is available or can be collected. The original approaches used purely ad–hoc techniques, eg.[1], or methods based only loosely on probability theory, eg.[2]. In an attempt to become more quantitative, modified logics[3,4], fuzzy logic[5,6,7,8] and probability theory[9,10,11] were tried. All these approaches have their merits but probabilistic approaches are particularly suited to this type of work, see Cheeseman[12]. Probabilistic approaches have been refined by, for example, Pearl[13,14,15] and Lauritzen and Spiegelhalter[16,17,18] and all of this work has been neatly summarised in a book by Neapolitan[19]. These approaches require knowledge to be available in a specific form, ie. as causal information, and information must be available for all edges in the network.

In some applications, eg. Decision Support Systems, one cannot expect the user to be able to provide complete information in the form required by the graph based methods. There may also be knowledge available which is not causal, eg. expected values or mean values, and this cannot be expressed in graph form. Consequently, it would be desirable to develop a more general technique.

Maximising Entropy is a technique which is more general. Maung[20] has shown that, given a set of information measures, solutions which use Maximum Entropy deduce as much information as possible without prejudicing the results. This is precisely what we want and strongly supports the use of Maximum Entropy but Maung and Paris[21] have shown that, in general, finding a Maximum Entropy based solution is an

†*Dept. of Computing, University of Bradford, Bradford BD7 1DP, U.K.*

NP–Complete problem. One way to overcome this problem is to use analytical techniques wherever possible and only resort to numerical methods when a solution cannot be progressed any further analytically. This is particularly true if the purpose of the exercise is only to find marginals.

The method devised by the authors[22] uses an analytical technique published by Tribus[23] but originally proposed by Jaynes[24]. However, whilst this approach is much less compute intensive than those based on more general methods, eg Griffeath[25], Cheeseman[26], it is still exponentially large in general. Lauritzen and Spiegelhalter[18] overcome this problem by mapping their graph into a tree of cliques and Pearl[15] has shown that propagation of causal information through a tree is only O(n) (but, see Cooper[27]). The same may be true of Maximum Entropy solutions. Consequently, it may be possible to devise a polynomially complex Maximum Entropy method which will work on a large subset of problems and provide a flexibility which is not available with the other methods. In particular, it would work if some of the causal information was missing. Such a method could be based on some system of organising the available information into a tree. The simplest tree of events is a binary tree of two valued events. Consequently, the question arises "is a Maximum Entropy solution, for knowledge which can be represented by a simple binary tree of two valued events, computable in polynomial time?". This paper develops a computational method for doing this but first it is necessary to describe briefly how the Maximum Entropy solution is derived for causal information.

Computing Joint Probabilities Using Maximum Entropy with Causal Information

Consider a knowledge domain which can be represented by a set of n events numbered 0 to n−1, each of which can only have two outcomes namely E_i or $\overline{E}_i$ (ie. true or false). The system, representing this domain, can then only be in one of a finite set of states,

$$S_0 = E_0\, E_1\, E_2 \ldots E_{n-2}\, E_{n-1} \qquad S_1 = E_0\, E_1\, E_2 \ldots E_{n-2}\, \overline{E}_{n-1} \tag{1}$$

etc until

$$S_{2^n-2} = \overline{E}_0\, \overline{E}_1\, \overline{E}_2 \ldots \overline{E}_{n-2}\, E_{n-1} \qquad S_{2^n-1} = \overline{E}_0\, \overline{E}_1\, \overline{E}_2 \ldots \overline{E}_{n-2}\, \overline{E}_{n-1}$$

Causal systems require knowledge to be provided in forms such as:–

$$P(E_i) = C_i,\quad P(E_j \mid E_k) = C_{jk},\quad P(E_q \mid E_r E_s) = C_{qrs} \tag{2}$$

where the C's are constants. Maximum Entropy requires one to maximise $-\sum_i p_i \log p_i$ where $\{p_i\}$ is a joint distribution of probabilities so, for the case being considered here, a solution can be found by maximising

$$H = -\sum_{i=0}^{2^n-1} P(S_i) \log P(S_i) \tag{3}$$

whilst conforming with $m+1$ constraints, ie. m pieces of causal knowledge and the fact that the sum of the probabilities in a probability distribution is unity. Tribus[23] has shown that, if the constraints are linear, ie. have the form:

$$\sum_{i=0}^{2^n-1} \sigma_{j,i} P(S_i) = C_j \qquad j = 0..m \tag{4}$$

where $\sigma_{j,i}$ $i = 0..2^n-1; j = 0..m$ is the coefficient of the ith state in the jth constraint, then the general solution for the probability of a state is:

$$P(S_i) = \prod_{j=0}^{m} e^{-\lambda_j \sigma_{j,i}} \qquad i = 0..2^n-1 \tag{5}$$

where the λ_j 's are the Lagrange multipliers which have to be found by solving the $m+1$ simultaneous equations obtained by substituting (5) into (4).

This can be done by forming three matrices, the constraint/state matrix, **S**, the matrix of constants, **C**, and the Lagrange multiplier matrix, **L**, where each matrix has the form:

$$\mathbf{S} = \begin{bmatrix} \sigma_{0,0} & \sigma_{1,0} & \sigma_{2,0} & \cdots & \sigma_{2^n-1,0} \\ \sigma_{0,1} & \sigma_{1,1} & \sigma_{2,1} & \cdots & \sigma_{2^n-1,1} \\ \sigma_{0,2} & \sigma_{1,2} & \sigma_{2,2} & \cdots & \sigma_{2^n-1,2} \\ \vdots & \vdots & \vdots & & \vdots \\ \sigma_{0,m} & \sigma_{1,m} & \sigma_{2,m} & \cdots & \sigma_{2^n-1,m} \end{bmatrix} \quad \mathbf{L} = \begin{bmatrix} e^{-\lambda_0} \\ e^{-\lambda_1} \\ e^{-\lambda_2} \\ \vdots \\ e^{-\lambda_m} \end{bmatrix} \quad \mathbf{C} = \begin{bmatrix} C_0 \\ C_1 \\ C_2 \\ \vdots \\ C_m \end{bmatrix}$$

The set of simultaneous equations which have to be solved to find the Lagrange multipliers can then be expressed in the form $\mathbf{S} \circ \mathbf{L} = \mathbf{C}$ where $\circ$ is a rather unusual matrix operation which consists of forming a product of each element in **L** raised to the power of the equivalent element in a column of **S**, multiplying each of these by the appropriate coefficient in a row of **S** and putting the sum of these equal to the appropriate element of **C**. The result is the following set of nonlinear, simultaneous equations:

$$\sum_{i=0}^{2^n-1} \sigma_{j,i} \prod_{k=0}^{m} e^{-\lambda_k \sigma_{k,i}} = C_j \qquad j = 0..m \tag{6}$$

This set of equations can be simplified when one is only interested in causal information because there are only three types of constraint which arise, these being:

$$\sum_{i=0}^{2^n-1} P(S_i) = 1, \quad P(E_p) = C_g, \text{ and } P(E_q|E_pE_rE_s \ldots) = C_j \tag{7}$$

The first constraint in (7) is always required by Probability theory and, hence, it is convenient to decree that this will be the 0th constraint. As a consequence $\sigma_{0,i} = 1$ for all $i = 0..2^n-1$, $C_0 = 1$ and $e^{-\lambda_0}$ occurs as part of the product for the probability of every state. The 0th constraint, ie. when j=0, in (6) can, therefore, always be used to find $e^{-\lambda_0}$, viz.

$$e^{-\lambda_0} = 1 \Big/ \sum_{i=1}^{2^n-1} \prod_{k=1}^{m} e^{-\lambda_k \sigma_{k,i}} \tag{8}$$

Constraints arising from both the second and third equations in (7) can be expressed in the same form since $P(E_p) = C_g$ can be written as $(1-C_g)P(E_p) - C_gP(\bar{E}_p) = 0$ and $P(E_q|E_pE_rE_s \ldots) = C_j$ as $(1-C_j)P(E_qE_pE_rE_s \ldots) - C_jP(\bar{E}_qE_pE_rE_s \ldots) = 0$.

Constraints of this type are then expressed in the form:

$$(1 - C_j) \sum_{x \varepsilon X} P(S_x) - C_j \sum_{y \varepsilon Y} P(S_y) = 0 \tag{9}$$

where X is the set of state subscripts pertaining to all those states with event outcomes $E_q, E_p, E_r, E_s \ldots$ fixed as required by equation (7) and Y is similarly defined on states with $\bar{E}_q, E_p, E_r, E_s \ldots$ fixed. When the general solution for the probability of the states, (5), is substituted into (9) it becomes:

$$(1 - C_j) \sum_{x \varepsilon X} \prod_{k=0}^{m} e^{-\lambda_k \sigma_{k,x}} - C_j \sum_{y \varepsilon Y} \prod_{k=0}^{m} e^{-\lambda_k \sigma_{k,y}} = 0 \qquad (10)$$

But, $\sigma_{j,x} = 1 - C_j$ and $\sigma_{j,y} = - C_j$ where $x \varepsilon X$ and $y \varepsilon Y$ so $e^{-\lambda_j}$ is raised to the power $1 - C_j$ in every product of the first sum and $e^{-\lambda_j}$ is raised to the power $- C_j$ in every product of the second sum. Consequently, if equation (10) is multiplied through by $e^{-\lambda_j c_j}$ and re–arranged then

$$e^{-\lambda_j} = \left(\frac{C_j}{1 - C_j}\right) \sum_{y \varepsilon Y} \prod_{\substack{k=0 \\ k \neq j}}^{m} e^{-\lambda_k \sigma_{k,y}} \Bigg/ \sum_{x \varepsilon X} \prod_{\substack{k=0 \\ k \neq j}}^{m} e^{-\lambda_k \sigma_{k,x}} \qquad j=1..m \qquad (11)$$

It should be noted that, because the constraints were expressed in the form given by equation (9), the $e^{-\lambda_0}$ term will cancel in all but the first constraint. Hence, the m equations (11), which are derived from the first to the mth constraint, form a simultaneous set which can be solved by fixed point iteration as long as the number of events is not excessive. The equation arising from the 'sum to unity' constraint is not part of this simultaneous set and is used to compute a value for $e^{-\lambda_0}$. However, unless this method can be extended to find the marginals directly, the computation will still be exponentially large. We need to show that if we restrict ourselves to a causal tree of two valued events, it is possible to derive algebraic expressions for the marginals. Before we do this we will give an example of the application of the above method to a five node causal binary tree.

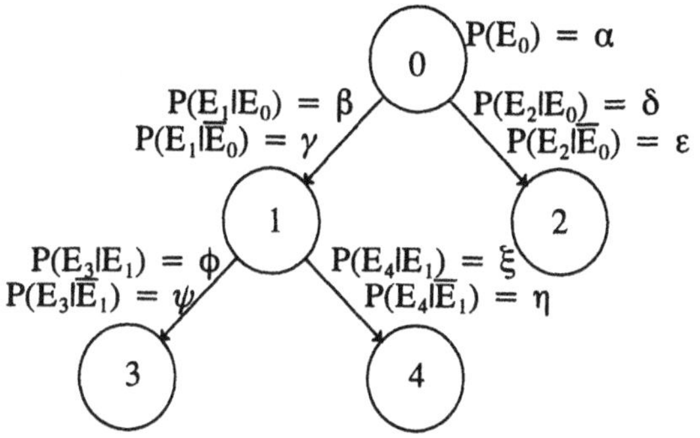

Fig. 1. A five node tree with complete causal information

The Maximum Entropy Solution for a Five Node, Causal Binary Tree

Consider the causal knowledge which can be represented by a five node binary tree as shown in Fig. 1. The nodes of the tree represent the events 0 to 4 which have associated variables e_i i=0..4 which can take the values E_i or $\overline{E}_i$. The causal knowledge given in Fig. 1 is not in the form required by Maximum Entropy, ie. that given in equation (9), so it has been converted into that form in equations (12) using the convention for numbering the states given in equation (1).

$$\sum_{i=0}^{31} P(S_i) = 1 \qquad (1-\alpha)\sum_{i=0}^{15} P(S_i) - \alpha \sum_{i=16}^{31} P(S_i) = 0 \qquad (1-\beta)\sum_{i=0}^{7} P(S_i) - \beta \sum_{i=8}^{15} P(S_i) = 0$$

$$(1-\gamma)\sum_{i=16}^{23} P(S_i) - \gamma \sum_{i=24}^{31} P(S_i) = 0 \quad (1-\delta)\sum_{i=0}^{3}\{P(S_i) + P(S_{i+8})\} - \delta \sum_{i=4}^{7}\{P(S_i) + P(S_{i+8})\} = 0$$

$$(1-\varepsilon)\sum_{i=16}^{19}\{P(S_i)+P(S_{i+8})\} - \varepsilon\sum_{i=20}^{23}\{P(S_i)+P(S_{i+8})\} = 0 \tag{12}$$
$$(1-\phi)\sum_{i=0,1,4,5}\{P(S_i)+P(S_{i+16})\} - \phi\sum_{i=2,3,6,7}\{P(S_i)+P(S_{i+16})\} = 0$$
$$(1-\psi)\sum_{i=8,9,12,13}\{P(S_i)+P(S_{i+16})\} - \psi\sum_{i=10,11,14,15}\{P(S_i)+P(S_{i+16})\} = 0$$
$$(1-\xi)\sum_{i=0}^{3}\{P(S_{2i})+P(S_{2i+16})\} - \xi\sum_{i=0}^{3}\{P(S_{2i+1})+P(S_{2i+17})\} = 0$$
$$(1-\eta)\sum_{i=4}^{7}\{P(S_{2i})+P(S_{2i+16})\} - \eta\sum_{i=4}^{7}\{P(S_{2i+1})+P(S_{2i+17})\} = 0$$

The constraints in equation (12) give rise to the constraints/state matrix shown in

$$\begin{bmatrix}
1&1&1&1&1&1&1&1&1&1&1&1&1&1&1&1&1&1&1&1&1&1&1&1&1&1&1&1&1&1&1&1\\
A&A&A&A&A&A&A&A&A&A&A&A&A&A&A&A&a&a&a&a&a&a&a&a&a&a&a&a&a&a&a&a\\
B&B&B&B&B&B&B&B&b&b&b&b&b&b&b&b&0&0&0&0&0&0&0&0&0&0&0&0&0&0&0&0\\
0&0&0&0&0&0&0&0&0&0&0&0&0&0&0&0&C&C&C&C&C&C&C&C&c&c&c&c&c&c&c&c\\
D&D&D&D&d&d&d&d&D&D&D&D&d&d&d&d&0&0&0&0&0&0&0&0&0&0&0&0&0&0&0&0\\
0&0&0&0&0&0&0&0&0&0&0&0&0&0&0&0&E&E&E&E&e&e&e&e&E&E&E&E&e&e&e&e\\
F&F&f&f&F&F&f&f&0&0&0&0&0&0&0&0&F&F&f&f&F&F&f&f&0&0&0&0&0&0&0&0\\
0&0&0&0&0&0&0&0&G&G&g&g&G&G&g&g&0&0&0&0&0&0&0&0&G&G&g&g&G&G&g&g\\
H&h&H&h&H&h&H&h&0&0&0&0&0&0&0&0&H&h&H&h&H&h&H&h&0&0&0&0&0&0&0&0\\
0&0&0&0&0&0&0&0&I&i&I&i&I&i&I&i&0&0&0&0&0&0&0&0&I&i&I&i&I&i&I&i
\end{bmatrix}$$

$a=\alpha$ $b=\beta$ $c=\gamma$ $d=\delta$ $e=\varepsilon$ $f=\phi$ $g=\psi$ $h=\xi$ $i=\eta$

$A=1-\alpha$ $B=1-\beta$ $C=1-\gamma$ $D=1-\delta$ $E=1-\varepsilon$ $F=1-\phi$ $G=1-\psi$ $H=1-\xi$ $I=1-\eta$

Fig. 2. The Constraint/State Matrix for a five node tree

Fig. 2. This in turn gives rise to the following general solution for the probability distribution of the states:

$$P(S_0) = e^{-\lambda_0}e^{-\lambda_1(1-\alpha)}e^{-\lambda_2(1-\beta)}e^{-\lambda_4(1-\delta)}e^{-\lambda_6(1-\phi)}e^{-\lambda_8(1-\xi)}$$
$$P(S_1) = e^{-\lambda_0}e^{-\lambda_1(1-\alpha)}e^{-\lambda_2(1-\beta)}e^{-\lambda_4(1-\delta)}e^{-\lambda_6(1-\phi)}e^{-\lambda_8(-\xi)}$$
$$P(S_2) = e^{-\lambda_0}e^{-\lambda_1(1-\alpha)}e^{-\lambda_2(1-\beta)}e^{-\lambda_4(1-\delta)}e^{-\lambda_6(-\phi)}e^{-\lambda_8(1-\xi)}$$
$$\cdots \qquad \cdots \qquad \cdots \tag{13}$$
$$P(S_{29}) = e^{-\lambda_0}e^{-\lambda_1(-\alpha)}e^{-\lambda_3(-\gamma)}e^{-\lambda_5(-\varepsilon)}e^{-\lambda_7(1-\psi)}e^{-\lambda_9(-\eta)}$$
$$P(S_{30}) = e^{-\lambda_0}e^{-\lambda_1(-\alpha)}e^{-\lambda_3(-\gamma)}e^{-\lambda_5(-\varepsilon)}e^{-\lambda_7(-\psi)}e^{-\lambda_9(1-\eta)}$$
$$P(S_{31}) = e^{-\lambda_0}e^{-\lambda_1(-\alpha)}e^{-\lambda_3(-\gamma)}e^{-\lambda_5(-\varepsilon)}e^{-\lambda_7(-\psi)}e^{-\lambda_9(-\eta)}$$

The Lagrangian expressions $e^{-\lambda_j}$ for $j = 4..9$ can be found by substituting (13) back into the constraints (12) and hence it can be shown that

$$e^{-\lambda_4} = \delta/(1-\delta) \qquad e^{-\lambda_5} = \varepsilon/(1-\varepsilon) \qquad e^{-\lambda_6} = \phi/(1-\phi)$$
$$e^{-\lambda_7} = \psi/(1-\psi) \qquad e^{-\lambda_8} = \xi/(1-\xi) \qquad e^{-\lambda_9} = \eta/(1-\eta) \tag{14}$$

It is convenient at this point to define

$$A = e^{-\lambda_1(-\alpha)}/(1-\alpha) \qquad B = e^{-\lambda_2(-\beta)}/(1-\beta) \qquad \Gamma = e^{-\lambda_3(-\gamma)}/(1-\gamma)$$
$$\Delta = \delta^{-\delta}/(1-\delta)^{1-\delta} \qquad E = \varepsilon^{-\varepsilon}/(1-\varepsilon)^{1-\varepsilon} \qquad \Phi = \phi^{-\phi}/(1-\phi)^{1-\phi} \tag{15}$$
$$\Psi = \psi^{-\psi}/(1-\psi)^{1-\psi} \qquad \Xi = \xi^{-\xi}/(1-\xi)^{1-\xi} \qquad H = \eta^{-\eta}/(1-\eta)^{1-\eta}$$

Then, by substituting (13), (14) and (15) into the third and fourth constraints in equations (12), it can be shown that

$$e^{-\lambda_2} = \frac{\Psi H}{\Phi \Xi}\left(\frac{\beta}{1-\beta}\right) \quad \text{and} \quad e^{-\lambda_3} = \frac{\Psi H}{\Phi \Xi}\left(\frac{\gamma}{1-\gamma}\right) \tag{16}$$

and by substituting equations (13), (14), (15) and (16) into the second equation in (12)

$$e^{-\lambda_1} = \frac{\Gamma E}{B\Delta}\left(\frac{\alpha}{1-\alpha}\right) \tag{17}$$

By substituting equations (13), (14), (15) and (16) into the first equation in (12)

$$e^{-\lambda_0} = 1/A\Gamma E\Psi H \tag{18}$$

The probability of the states can now be found by substituting equations (14) to (18) into equations (13), whence

$$\begin{aligned}
P(S_0) &= \alpha\beta\delta\phi\xi \\
P(S_1) &= \alpha\beta\delta\phi(1-\xi) \\
P(S_2) &= \alpha\beta\delta(1-\phi)\xi \\
&\text{etc.} \\
P(S_{15}) &= \alpha(1-\beta)(1-\delta)(1-\psi)(1-\eta) \\
P(S_{16}) &= (1-\alpha)\gamma\varepsilon\phi\xi \\
P(S_{17}) &= (1-\alpha)\gamma\varepsilon\phi(1-\xi) \\
&\text{etc.} \\
P(S_{29}) &= (1-\alpha)(1-\gamma)(1-\varepsilon)\psi(1-\eta) \\
P(S_{30}) &= (1-\alpha)(1-\gamma)(1-\varepsilon)(1-\psi)\eta \\
P(S_{31}) &= (1-\alpha)(1-\gamma)(1-\varepsilon)(1-\psi)(1-\eta)
\end{aligned} \tag{19}$$

We are now in a position to evaluate the a priori state of the tree, whence

$$P(E_1) = \sum_{i=0}^{7}\{P(S_i) + P(S_{i+16})\} = \alpha\beta + (1-\alpha)\gamma \tag{20}$$

$$P(E_2) = \sum_{i=0}^{3}\{P(S_i) + P(S_{i+8}) + P(S_{i+16}) + P(S_{i+24})\} = \alpha\delta + (1-\alpha)\varepsilon \tag{21}$$

$$\begin{aligned}
P(E_3) &= \sum_{i=0,2,4,6}\{P(S_i) + P(S_{i+8}) + P(S_{i+16}) + P(S_{i+24})\} \\
&= \{\alpha\beta + (1-\alpha)\gamma\}\phi + \{\alpha(1-\beta) + (1-\alpha)(1-\gamma)\}\psi
\end{aligned} \tag{22}$$

$$P(E_4) = \sum_{i=0}^{15} P(S_{2i}) = \{\alpha\beta + (1-\alpha)\gamma\}\zeta + \{\alpha(1-\beta) + (1-\alpha)(1-\gamma)\}\eta \tag{23}$$

The Maximum Entropy Solution for a Two Valued, Causal Binary Tree of any Depth

The previous example demonstrates that finding the marginal probabilities for a five node causal binary tree using Maximum Entropy is not a difficult problem but if we are to extend this to any binary tree, and in particular if we are to find a method which is O(n), we need to derive an appropriate computational scheme.

There is a hint in the previous example about how this might be done. We note that the Lagrange multipliers associated with the edges leading to leaf nodes can be derived from their own constraint and hence are independent of the rest of the simultaneous equations. However, we can also note that the Lagrange multipliers associated with the edges one layer further up in the tree can be derived from their own constraint and a knowledge of the Lagrange multipliers associated with the edges of their subtrees. This clearly indicates a possibility that the Lagrange multipliers can be evaluated sequentially from the bottom of the tree upwards.

Consider a causal binary tree whose nodes represent two valued events. Let events a and b be represented by two nodes which are adjacent and let the edge between them be depicted by <a,b>. Let the causal information associated with <a,b> be complete and be given by

$$P(E_b|E_a) = C_b \quad \text{and} \quad P(E_b|\overline{E}_a) = \overline{C}_b \tag{24}$$

and let the Lagrange multipliers associated with these be λ_b and $\overline{\lambda}_b$ respectively. Also, let the constraint at the root node be $P(E_0)=\alpha$ with associated Lagrange multiplier λ_1. In accordance with equation (9), the first equation in (24) can be written

$$(1 - C_b)\sum_{x\varepsilon X} P(S_x) - C_b \sum_{y\varepsilon Y} P(S_y) = 0 \tag{25}$$

where X and Y are sets of state subscripts similar to those introduced in equation (9) but which pertain to states with E_a, E_b fixed and E_a, $\overline{E}_b$ fixed respectively.

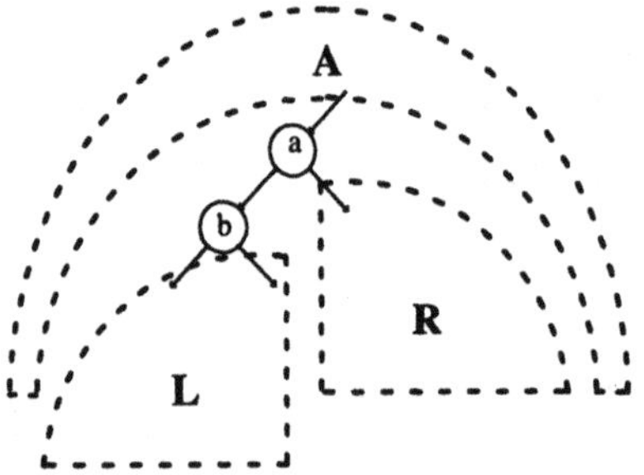

Fig. 3. Nodes a and b and the sub–trees which influence their probabilities

The situation is depicted in Fig. 3 where the set **A** depicts all the nodes which are not descendants of a, the set **L** depicts all the nodes which are descendants of b and the set **R** depicts all the nodes which are decendants of a but not b nor descendants of b. The sets of events represented by the nodes in **A, L** and **R** are capable of being in many different states and these states are denoted by A_i, L_j and R_k where the suffix indicates which state is being referenced. Now, because of independence, we can write

$$\sum_{x\varepsilon X} P(S_x) = P(E_aE_b)\sum_{i\varepsilon I_X} P(L_i|E_b)\sum_{j\varepsilon J} P(R_j|E_a)\sum_{k\varepsilon K} P(A_k|E_a) \tag{26}$$

where I_x is the set of all states of **L** which are compatible with E_b, and J and K are the sets of all states of **R** and **A** respectively which are compatible with E_a. Similarly

$$\sum_{y\varepsilon Y} P(S_y) = P(E_a\overline{E}_b)\sum_{i\varepsilon I_Y} P(L_i|\overline{E}_b)\sum_{j\varepsilon J} P(R_j|E_a)\sum_{k\varepsilon K} P(A_k|E_a) \tag{27}$$

where I_Y is is the set of all states of **L** which are compatible with $\overline{E}_b$. Now, if we consider the Maximum Entropy solution for the probability distribution given in equation (5) and note that $P(E_aE_b)$ is associated with $e^{\lambda_b(1-C_b)}$, $P(E_a\overline{E}_b)$ is associated with $e^{\lambda_b(-C_b)}$, all the Lagrange multipliers associated with **L** will appear in the sums over $\mathbf{I}_X$ and $\mathbf{I}_Y$, all the Lagrange multipliers associated with **R** will appear in the sum over J and all the Lagrange multipliers associated with **A** will appear in the sum over K then we can see that

$$\sum_{x\varepsilon X} P(S_x) = e^{-\lambda_0} e^{-\lambda_b(1-C_b)} \sum_{i\varepsilon I_X} \prod_{q\varepsilon Q_X} e^{-\lambda_q \sigma_{q,i}} \sum_{j\varepsilon J} \prod_{t\varepsilon T} e^{-\lambda_t \sigma_{t,j}} \sum_{k\varepsilon K} \prod_{u\varepsilon U} e^{-\lambda_u \sigma_{u,k}} \tag{28}$$

where Q_X is the set of Lagrange multipliers which are associated with the constraints on the edges of the subtree with root b and appear in $P(S_x)$ when $x\varepsilon X$. T and U are similarly defined for the regions **A** and **R** respectively. Similarly,

$$\sum_{y\varepsilon Y} P(S_y) = e^{-\lambda_0} e^{-\lambda_b(1-C_b)} \sum_{i\varepsilon I_Y} \prod_{q\varepsilon Q_Y} e^{-\lambda_q \sigma_{q,i}} \sum_{j\varepsilon J} \prod_{t\varepsilon T} e^{-\lambda_t \sigma_{t,j}} \sum_{k\varepsilon K} \prod_{u\varepsilon U} e^{-\lambda_u \sigma_{u,k}} \tag{29}$$

Q_Y is defined in a similar manner to Q_X but occurs when $y\varepsilon Y$ in $P(S_y)$. Substituting equations (28) and (29) into equation (25) gives

$$e^{-\lambda_b} = \left(\frac{C_b}{1 - C_b}\right) \sum_{i\varepsilon I_Y} \prod_{q\varepsilon Q_Y} e^{-\lambda_q \sigma_{q,i}} \Big/ \sum_{i\varepsilon I_X} \prod_{q\varepsilon Q_X} e^{-\lambda_q \sigma_{q,i}} \tag{30}$$

Now, if b is a leaf node I_X and I_Y are empty. Hence, when b is a leaf node

$$e^{-\lambda_b} = C_b/(1 - C_b) \quad \text{and} \quad e^{-\overline{\lambda}_b} = \overline{C}_b/(1 - \overline{C}_b) \tag{31}$$

So, every Lagrange multiplier associated with an edge terminating at a leaf node can be found directly from the causal information provided on that edge, ie. by a process of O(1). (The case when some information on the edge is missing is dealt with later in the paper). Note also that I_X, J and K are disjoint as are I_Y, J and K. Hence, even when b is not a leaf node, $e^{-\lambda_b}$ is a function of only those Lagrange multipliers which are associated with the subtree below it. Consequently, the Lagrange multipliers can be found by finding those at the leaves first and then progressing up the tree.

We now turn our attention to the case when the node representing b is not a leaf node, ie. I_X and I_Y are not empty. In order to do this we have to look more closely at $\sum_{i\varepsilon I_X} \prod_{q\varepsilon Q_X} e^{-\lambda_q \sigma_{q,i}}$ and $\sum_{i\varepsilon I_Y} \prod_{q\varepsilon Q_Y} e^{-\lambda_q \sigma_{q,i}}$. This requires us to refine Fig. 3 and this has been done in Fig. 4 where **L** has been broken down into the left and right offspring of node b, nodes v and w respectively, and the sets of nodes which are decendents of v and w namely **V** and **W** respectively. Now at this level of detail equation (26) becomes

$$\sum_{x\varepsilon X} P(S_x) = P(E_aE_b) \sum_{j\varepsilon J} P(R_j|E_a) \sum_{k\varepsilon K} P(A_k|E_a) P(e_v|E_b) \sum_{g\varepsilon G} P(V_g|e_v)\ P(e_w|E_b) \sum_{h\varepsilon H} P(W_h|e_w) \tag{32}$$

where $e_V = E_V$ or $\overline{E}_V$, $e_W = E_W$ or $\overline{E}_W$, G is the set of all states of **V** which are compatible with e_V and H is the set of all states of **W** which are compatible with e_W. There are four of these equations which are identical apart from the value of e_V and e_W. If we sum these four and gather terms, equation (32) becomes

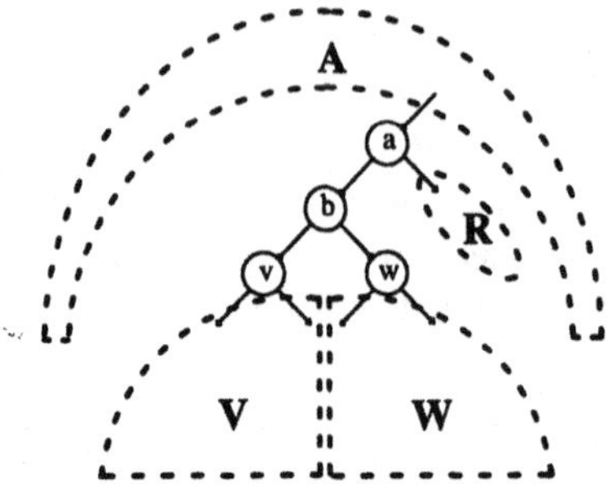

Fig. 4. A more detailed view of the tree below node b

$$\sum_{x\in X} P(S_x) = P(E_aE_b)\sum_{j\in J}P(R_j|E_a)\sum_{k\in K}P(A_k|E_a)\left\{P(E_v|E_b)\sum_{g\in G_{X'}}P(V_g|E_v) + P(\bar{E}_v|E_b)\sum_{g\in G_{Y'}}P(V_g|\bar{E}_v)\right\}$$

$$\left\{P(E_w|E_b)\sum_{h\in H_{X'}}P(W_g|E_w) + P(\bar{E}_w|E_b)\sum_{h\in H_{Y'}}P(W_g|\bar{E}_w)\right\} \qquad (33)$$

where $G_{X'}$, $G_{Y'}$, $H_{X'}$ and $H_{Y'}$ are defined like G_X, G_Y, H_X and H_Y but apply when e_v and e_w have been instantiated. Now, if we compare equation (33) with equations (26) and (27) and note that we are now interested in the edges <b,v> and <b,w>, it becomes clear that the terms in the first and second pairs of curly brackets in equation (33) are precisely those which feature in the constraints associated with the edges <b,v> and <b,w> respectively. In fact the first term in each curly bracket is analogous to the $\sum_{i\in I_X}$ term and the second is analogous to the $\sum_{i\in I_Y}$ term. Hence the constraints on <b,v> and <b,w> can be used to rewrite the first term in each pair of curly brackets in terms of the second term. Thus, equation (33) can be written

$$\sum_{x\in X} P(S_x) = P(E_aE_b)\sum_{j\in J}P(R_j|E_a)\sum_{k\in K}P(A_k|E_a)P(\bar{E}_v|E_b)\sum_{g\in G_{Y'}}P(V_g|\bar{E}_v)\left\{\frac{C_v}{1-C_v}+1\right\}$$

$$P(\bar{E}_w|E_b)\sum_{h\in H_{Y'}}P(W_h|\bar{E}_w)\left\{\frac{C_w}{1-C_w}+1\right\} \qquad (34)$$

Similarly,

$$\sum_{y\in Y} P(S_y) = P(E_a\bar{E}_b)\sum_{j\in J}P(R_j|E_a)\sum_{k\in K}P(A_k|E_a)P(\bar{E}_v|\bar{E}_b)\sum_{g\in G_{Y''}}P(V_g|\bar{E}_v)\left\{\frac{\bar{C}_v}{1-\bar{C}_v}+1\right\}$$

$$P(\bar{E}_w|\bar{E}_b)\sum_{h\in H_{Y''}}P(W_h|\bar{E}_w)\left\{\frac{\bar{C}_w}{1-\bar{C}_w}+1\right\} \qquad (35)$$

If we now examine the Maximum Entropy solution given by equation (5) in conjunction with equation (34) noting that $P(E_aE_b)$ is associated with $e^{\lambda_b(1-C_b)}$, $P(\bar{E}_v|E_b)$ is associated with $e^{\lambda_v(-C_v)}$, $P(\bar{E}_w|E_b)$ is associated with $e^{\lambda_w(-C_w)}$ and all the other Lagrange multipliers fall into four disjoint sets each of which is the subject of one of the sums in each of equation (34) or (35) and hence appear in both the X′ and Y′ pair or the X'' and Y'' pair. So, when the general Maximum Entropy solution for the probability distribution expressed in equation (5) is substituted into equation (25) the $P(\overline{E}_v|E_b)\sum_{g\varepsilon G_{Y'}} P(V_g|\overline{E}_v)\left\{\frac{C_v}{1-C_v}+1\right\}$ term results in a $\frac{e^{-\lambda_v(-C_v)}}{(1-C_v)}$ term and so

$$e^{-\lambda_b} = \left(\frac{C_b}{1-C_b}\right)\frac{\overline{K}_v\overline{K}_w}{K_vK_w} \tag{36}$$

where $K_v = \frac{e^{-\lambda_v(-C_v)}}{(1-C_v)}$, $\overline{K}_v = \frac{e^{-\overline{\lambda}_v(-\overline{C}_v)}}{(1-\overline{C}_v)}$, $K_w = \frac{e^{-\lambda_w(-C_w)}}{(1-C_w)}$ and $\overline{K}_w = \frac{e^{-\overline{\lambda}_w(-\overline{C}_w)}}{(1-\overline{C}_w)}$

Using an analogous argument, it can be shown that equation (35) gives

$$e^{-\overline{\lambda}_b} = \left(\frac{\overline{C}_b}{1-\overline{C}_b}\right)\frac{\overline{K}_v\overline{K}_w}{K_vK_w} \tag{37}$$

Note that the modifying term $\overline{K}_v\overline{K}_w/K_vK_w$ is the same in both cases and, if $e^{-\lambda_v}$, $e^{-\overline{\lambda}_v}$, $e^{-\lambda_w}$ and $e^{-\overline{\lambda}_w}$ have been previously computed, $e^{-\lambda_b}$ and $e^{-\overline{\lambda}_b}$ can be computed by a process of O(1).

Using the above techniques on the constraint $P(E_0) = \alpha$, it can be shown that

$$e^{-\lambda_1} = \left(\frac{\alpha}{1-\alpha}\right)\frac{\overline{K}_1\overline{K}_2}{K_1K_2} \tag{38}$$

where $\mathbf{K}_1$ and $\overline{\mathbf{K}}_1$ are associated with the constraints on the edge to the first offspring of the root node whilst $\mathbf{K}_2$ and $\overline{\mathbf{K}}_2$ are associated with the constraints on the edge to the second offspring of the root node. Similarly, it can be shown using the above techniques on the zeroth constraint, ie. the sum of the probability of the states is unity, that

$$e^{-\lambda_0} = 1\Big/A\prod_{i=1}^{n-1}K_i \tag{39}$$

where n is the number of nodes and $A = \frac{e^{-\lambda_1}}{(1-\alpha)}\frac{\overline{K}_1\overline{K}_2}{K_1K_2}$. If the values of $e^{-\lambda_i}$ and $e^{-\overline{\lambda}_i}$ are computed using a post order traversal of the tree, every such term can be computed by a process of O(1) and thus the whole process is O(n).

It is worth noting that the modifying term associated with the root of any subtree is $\overline{K}_l\overline{K}_r/K_lK_r$ where the suffices l and r have been used to indicate the left and right offspring respectively. This modifier is exactly the same as the one which would modify the expression for the Lagragrian multipliers which arise from the constraints on the edge entering the root node of the subtree from the tree higher up. Hence, in the parlance of Pearl, it can be viewed as a message passing up the tree which will be used to modify the Lagrange multiplier in the next layer up.

An O(n) Method for Finding Marginal Probabilities when Information is Missing

At this point we note that if the information is complete the marginal probabilities can be found with an O(n) process by propagating the probability associated with the root down the tree using the causal information, eg. $P(E_b) = P(E_b|E_a)P(E_a) + P(E_b|\overline{E}_a)P(\overline{E}_a)$. Consequently, there is little point in using Maximum Entropy if the information is complete. However, when the information is not complete, propagation is no longer possible and we need to find an alternative method.

If information is missing we can use the Maximum Entropy method described above but the constraint equations will have to be modified to remove those equations for which there is no information given, ie, the constant is unknown. An alternative approach is to put the Lagrangian expression equal to unity, ie. $e^{-\lambda_j} = 1$, if the C_j constant is missing. The Maximum Entropy solution for $P(S_i)$ $i=0..2^n-1$ given in equation (5) is identical whether we put $e^{-\lambda_j} = 1$ or remove the jth constraint. Consequently, equations (31), (36), (37) and (38) can either be used to find the Lagrange multiplier if the causal information is present or they can be used to find a value for the causal information which is consistent with the Maximum Entropy solution, ie. the minimally prejudiced value. If we rearrange the above equations, the formulas for finding the missing causal information are:

$$C_b = 0.5 \tag{40}$$

when C_b is associated with an edge which terminates in a leaf.

$$C_b = K_l K_r / (\overline{K}_l \overline{K}_r + K_l K_r) \tag{41}$$

when C_b is not associated with an edge which terminates in a leaf and K_l, $\overline{K}_l$ and K_r, $\overline{K}_r$ are the modifiers associated with the left and right offspring respectively.

$$\alpha = K_1 K_2 / (\overline{K}_1 \overline{K}_2 + K_1 K_2) \tag{42}$$

where α is the minimally prejudiced value which should be used if $P(E_0)$ is missing at the root of the tree.The zeroth constraint, the sum to unity, cannot be missing so equations (40), (41) and (42) are all that are needed to find the missing information.

Clearly, a post–order traversal of the tree could be used to find minimally prejudiced values for all missing information and a pre–order traversal could be used to propagate the information down the tree calculating values for the marginals as it proceeds. Both of these are O(n) operations so the marginals can be found with an O(n) process even if Maximum Entropy has been used to estimate the missing information.

Conclusion

Maximum Entropy is a very attractive paradigm because the information available does not have to be complete for reasoning about a system to be possible. But, since the time of the Maung and Paris paper[26], there has been a tacit assumption that finding the Maximum Entropy solution was an *NP*–Complete problem and hence intractable in real situations. This paper has shown this assumption to be wrong when the information available can be represented by a causal, two valued binary tree.

References

1. **Shortcliffe, E. H. and Buchanan, B. G.** A model of Inexact Reasoning in Medicine. *Mathematical Biosciences,* Vol. 23 (1975) pp 351–379.
2. **Duda, R.O., Hart, P.E. and Nilsson, N.J.** Subjective Bayesian Methods for Rule–based Inference Systems. National Computer Conference, AFIPS Conf. Proc. Vol.45 (1976) pp.1075–1082.
3. **McDermott, D. and Doyle, J.** Non–monotonic Logic I *Artificial Intelligence,* Vol 13 (1980) pp 41–72
4. **Reiter, R. A.** A logic for Inexact Reasoning. *Artificial Intelligence,* Vol 13 (1980) pp 81–132
5 **Zadeh, L A** A theory of approximate reasoning *Machine Intelligence* Vol 9 (1979) pp 149–193
6 **Zadeh, L A** The concept of a linguistic variable and its application to approximate reasoning *Learning Systems and Intelligent Robots* (Fu, K S and Tow, J T, **Eds.**) Plenum Press, New York, (1974) pp 1–10
7 **Zadeh, L A** The role of fuzzy logic in the management of uncertainty in expert systems *Fuzzy Sets and Systems* Vol 11 (1983) pp 199–227

8 **Baldwin, J F and Zhou, S Q** A fuzzy rational inference language *Fuzzy Sets and Systems* Vol 14 (1984) pp 155–174

9 **Dempster A.P.** A generalisation of Bayesian inference. *Journal of the Royal Statistical Society* Ser. B, Vol 30 (1968) pp 205–247

10 **Schafer G.** A mathematical Theory of Evidence Princeton University Press, Princeton (1976)

11 **Lemmer, J.F. and Barth, S.W.** Efficient Minimum Information Updating for Bayesian Inferencing in Expert Systems. *Proc. National Conf. on Artifical Intelligence,* Pittsburgh (1982) pp.424–427

12 **Cheeseman P.** In Defense of Probability In *Proceedings 8th International Joint Conference on AI (IJCAI–85)* Los Angeles (1985) pp 1002–1009

13 **Pearl J.** Reverend Bayes on Inference Engines:a distributed hierachical approach *Proceedings of the National Conference on AI* Pittsburgh (1982) pp 133–136

14. **Pearl, J.** Fusion, Propagation, and Structuring in Belief Networks. *Artificial Intelligence*, Vol.29, No.3 (1986) pp.241–288.

15. **Pearl, J.** *Probabilistic Reasoning in Intelligent Systems: Networks of Plausible Inference.* (1988) Morgan Kaufmann, San Mateo, California.

16. **Spiegelhalter, D.J.** Probabilistic Reasoning in Predictive Expert Systems. In *Uncertainty in Artificial Intelligence,* Kanal, L.N. and Lemmer, F.J. (Eds.) (1986) Elsevier Science Publishers B.V. (North Holland) pp 47–68

17. **Lauritzen, S.L. and Spiegelhalter, D.J.** Local Computations with Probabilities on Graphical Structures and Their Applications to Expert Systems. *J. Royal Statistical Society B.,* Vol.50, No.2 (1988) pp.157–224.

18. **Lauritzen, S.L. and Spiegelhalter, D.J.** Local Computations with Probabilities on Graphical Structures and Their Applications to Expert Systems. In *Readings in Uncertain Reasoning,* G. Shafer and J.Pearl (Eds), Morgan Kaufman, San Mateo, (1990) pp 415–433.

19. **Neapolitan, R.E.** *Probabilistic Reasoning in Expert Systems: theory and algoritms.* Wiley, New York (1990).

20. **Maung, I.** Measures of Information and Inference Processes. PhD Thesis, (1992) Department of Mathematics, University of Manchester.

21. **Maung, I. and Paris, J.B.** A Note on the Infeasibility of Some Inference Processes. *International Journal of Intelligent Systems*, Vol.5, No.5 (1990) pp.595–603.

22. **Rhodes, P.C. and Garside G.R.** The use of Maximum Entropy as a Methodology for Probabilistic Reasoning to be published in *Knowledge Based Systems*

23. **Tribus, M.** *Rational Descriptions, Decision and Designs.* Pergamon, New York (1969).

24. **Jaynes, E.T.** *Notes on Probability Theory in Science and Engineering.* Physics Dept., Washington University, St Louis (1969).

25. **Griffeath, D.S.** Computer Solution of the Discrete Maximum Entropy Problem. *Technometrics,* Vol.14 No.4 (1972) pp.891–897.

26. **Cheeseman, P.** A Method of Computing Generalised Bayesian Probability Values for Expert Systems *Proceeding of the 8th International Conference in Artificial Intelligence* (1983) pp198–202.

27. **Cooper, G. F.** Probabilistic Inference Using Belief Networks is *NP*–Hard, Technical Report KSL–87–27, Stanford University, Stanford, California. (1988).

Yet Some More Considerations On Cumulativity In Default Logics

Vincent Risch*

The University of Western Ontario
Department of Computer Science
Middlesex College
London, Ontario, Canada N6A 5B7
e-mail : risch@csd.uwo.ca

Abstract. From the time that [Makinson, 89] noticed the non-cumulativity of Reiter's and Łukaszewicz's default logics, many attempts have been made to introduce this property in full default logic. Following [Brewka, 91], many of these attempts are associated with the consistency of the set of justifications used for deriving an extension. But this modification of the original formalism of Reiter is not always suitable. Another point is that most of these attempts rely on a modification of the underlying langage and/or a weakening of cumulativity such as initially interpreted by [Makinson, 89]. In the present paper, a different approach to cumulativity in default logics is investigated. A (trivial) cumulative variant of default logic that does not require commitment to justifications is first introduced for skeptical reasoning in the sense of [Makinson, 89]. It can be noted that both Reiter's and Łukaszewicz's approaches are embedded in it, and that no extension of the underlying language is required. Then, using this framework and following a proposition of [Voorbraak, 93], a criterion is proposed to distinguish cumulative default theories in the sense of Łukaszewicz from non-cumulative ones.

1 Introduction

Cumulativity was introduced by [Gabbay, 85] as an interesting formal option for nonmonotonicity. Roughly, a cumulative agent is supposed to be complete in the sense that, although some part of his beliefs become verified as theorems, the previous state of his beliefs and the new one remain identical. Cumulativity is associated with attractive semantics and should improve nonmonotonic theorem provers by allowing the use of lemmas. From the time that [Makinson, 89] noticed the non-cumulativity of Reiter's and Łukaszewicz's default logics, different attempts have been made in order to introduce this property in full default logic. Following [Brewka, 91], most of these attempts ([Schaub, 91], [Dix, 92], [You, Li, 94]) have been associated with a reinterpretation of default rules due to [Poole, 88]. The basic idea is to require *commitment* to justifications, so that,

* Supported by a grant from the *Natural Science and Engineering Research Council of Canada*.

instead of simply reasoning with lack of given information, explicit assumptions must be done for deriving extensions. Hence, the initial meaning of a default rule is deeply modified. This modification has the advantage of both restoring cumulativity (in various forms) and providing a solution to the "broken arms" paradox (see [Brewka, 91]). However, it appears not to be suitable in *every* case. Now, it was also pointed out by [Brewka, 91] and [Schaub, 92] that cumulativity actually does not rely on commitment. However, cumulative default logics without commitment to justifications have received little attention, with the noteworthy exception of some very recent work (cf. [Wilson, 93] and [Giordano, Martelli, 94]).

Another, possibly more relevant point, is that different possible "cumulativities" can be considered in default logic. There are not only different ways of defining a nonmonotonic consequence operation (e.g. skeptical, credulous), but also there are different ways of understanding what "adding a formula" means. Since default theories are not homogeneous, some authors prefer to interpret it as naturally adding a classical formula (cf. [Makinson, 89], [Dix, 92]), whereas other authors reinterpret it as adding a default (cf. [Schaub, 91], [Schaub, 92]). However, in the latter case a slightly more complicated apparatus has to be considered. Anyway, both approaches suggest changing the nature of a formula. It can be pointed out that this aspect is lacking in the current abstract studies about cumulativity (cf. [Makinson, 89], [Kraus et Al., 90]). In these studies, there is no consideration of the possible repercussions due to the change of status of formulas moved from the right to the left of the inference relation sign (which in some sense may be interpreted as turning *belief* into *knowledge*). This aspect is also lacking in the studies of cumulative default logics based on the extension of the underlying language to assertions (cf. [Brewka, 91], [Makinson, 91], [Giordano, Martelli, 94]).

In this paper, a different approach to cumulativity in default logic is investigated. Following [Dix, 92], it focuses on a skeptical approach, but it also should be easily extendible to a credulous approach à la [Schaub, 92]. No extension of the first order language is required. Since no commitment between justifications is required, both Reiter's and Lukaszewicz's approaches are embedded in it, and can be easily characterized. Indeed, it distinguishes those default theories in the sense of Lukaszewicz which are cumulative from those which are not. Following [Voorbraak, 93], this provides a "filter" on "well formed" theories regarding cumulativity.

Our paper is organized in the following way: in the second section, basic abstract properties about cumulativity are briefly recalled. In the third section, the characterizations of three main default logics are given. The fourth section gives special attention to two different approaches of cumulativity in default logics. In the fifth section, commitment to justifications is discussed. In section six, guess default logic is introduced and its basic properties are given.

2 Cumulativity

Definition 1. [Makinson, 89], [Kraus et Al., 90] Let $\mid\!\sim$ be a nonmonotonic consequence relation, A a set of formulas, f and g any formulas; *Cut* and *Cautious Monotony* are defined by:

$$\textit{(Cut)} \qquad \frac{A \cup \{f\} \mid\!\sim g, \; A \mid\!\sim f}{A \mid\!\sim g}$$

$$\textit{(Cautious Monotony)} \qquad \frac{A \mid\!\sim f, \; A \mid\!\sim g}{A \cup \{f\} \mid\!\sim g}$$

Property 2 [Makinson, 89], [Kraus et Al., 90]. *Cut and Cautious Monotony together can be expressed jointly by* Cumulativity*:*

$$\textit{If } A \mid\!\sim f \textit{ then } (A \mid\!\sim g \textit{ iff } A \cup \{f\} \mid\!\sim g).$$

Definition 3. A set of nonmonotonic consequences derived from a set A of formulas is defined by

$$C(A) = \{f \mid A \mid\!\sim f\}.$$

Remark. Following [Makinson, 89], Cut and Cautious Monotony can be expressed infinitistically by:

$$\textit{(Cut)} \qquad A \subseteq B \subseteq C(A) \Rightarrow C(B) \subseteq C(A)$$

$$\textit{(Cautious Monotony)} \qquad A \subseteq B \subseteq C(A) \Rightarrow C(A) \subseteq C(B)$$

So, for Cumulativity we get:

$$\textit{(Cumulativity)} \; A \subseteq B \subseteq C(A) \Rightarrow C(A) = C(B)$$

That is, a cumulative agent keeps his beliefs when one of them becomes true.

3 Default theories

As defined by [Reiter, 1980], a closed default theory is a pair (W, D) where W is a set of closed first order sentences and D a set of default rules. A default rule has the form $\frac{\alpha : \beta}{\gamma}$ where α, β and γ are closed first order sentences. α is called the prerequisite, β the justification and γ the consequent of the default. $PREREQ(D)$, $JUST(D)$ and $CONS(D)$ are respectively the sets of all prerequisites, justifications and consequents that come from defaults in a set D. Whenever one of these sets is a singleton, we may identify it with the single element it contains. For instance, we prefer to consider $PREREQ(\{\frac{\alpha : \beta}{\gamma}\})$ as an element rather than a set. The following definition shows us how the use of a default is related to its prerequisite (cf. [Schwind, 90]):

Definition 4. [Schwind, 90] A set D of defaults is *grounded* in W iff for all $d \in D$ there is a finite sequence $d_0, \ldots, d_k$ of elements of D such that (1) $PREREQ(\{d_0\}) \in Th(W)$, (2) for $1 \leq i \leq k-1$, $PREREQ(\{d_{i+1}\}) \in Th(W \cup CONS(\{d_0, \ldots, d_i\}))$, and $d_k = d$.

An *extension* of a default theory is usually defined as a smallest fixed point of a set of formulas. It contains W, is deductively closed, and the defaults whose consequents belong to the extension verify a property which actually allows them to be used. The manner in which this property is considered is related to the variant of Default Logic under consideration. In what follows, we move directly to the characterizations previously obtained by Camilla Schwind and the author for the extensions in the sense of [Reiter, 1980], [Lukaszewicz, 88], [Schaub, 91] respectively. The first are called *R-extensions* (for Reiter's extensions), the second *j-extensions* (for justified extensions), and the third *c-extensions* (for constrained extensions).

Theorem 5. *Let $\Delta = (W, D)$ be a default theory. Let D' be any subset of D.*

- *[Schwind, Risch, 91], [Risch, 93] $E = Th(W \cup CONS(D'))$ is a R-extension of Δ iff D' is a maximal grounded subset of D such that $(\forall \beta \in JUST(D'))$ $(\neg\beta \notin E)$, and for each default $d \in D \setminus D'$, of the form $\dfrac{\alpha : \beta}{\gamma}$, either $\alpha \notin E$ or $\neg\beta \in E$.*
- *[Risch, 91] $E = Th(W \cup CONS(D'))$ is a j-extension of Δ with respect to $F = JUST(D')$ iff D' is a maximal grounded subset of D such that $(\forall \beta \in JUST(D'))(\neg\beta \notin E)$.*
- *[Risch, 93] $E = Th(W \cup CONS(D'))$ is a c-extension of Δ with respect to $C = Th(W \cup JUST(D') \cup CONS(D'))$ iff D' is a maximal grounded subset of D, such that $E \cup JUST(D')$ is consistent.*

Remark.
- Clearly, the only difference between Reiter's and Lukaszewicz's approach is in the behavior of the defaults that do not participate in the construction of an extension. In Reiter's default logic, the withdrawal of these defaults from the set of generating defaults has to be motivated by checking an additional condition. The present characterization sheds light on the intuition which stands behind Lukaszewicz's variant. In the latter, we are never allowed to revise a justification used for deriving the consequent of a default. According to Lukaszewicz, it is only in this precise way that we may speak of "justification" in a correct sense. Indeed, note that the only difference between Lukaszewicz's and Schaub's approaches concerns the consistency of the set of justifications related to an extension. Note that default reasoning is decidable on condition that Th is defined on a decidable language.
- Whatever is the variant under consideration (either R-, j-, or c-), given an extension E, the set D' is called *the set of generating defaults* of E, and is also denoted by $GD(E, \Delta)$.

- There are different ways for defining a nonmonotonic consequence relation from default theories. The most usual are the following:

  (Credulous reasoning) $W \mid\!\sim_{D,\cup} f$ iff $(\exists E$, extension of $(W,D))(f \in E)$
  (Skeptical reasoning) $W \mid\!\sim_{D,\cap} f$ iff $(\forall E$, extension of $(W,D))(f \in E)$.

  The operator C_D, associated with the corresponding form of reasoning, is defined on the basis of the previous general pattern:

$$C_D(W) = \{f \mid W \mid\!\sim_{D,s} f\} \text{ with } s \in \{\cup, \cap\}.$$

4 A brief account of some approaches of cumulativity in default logics

Let $\Delta = (W, D)$ be a default theory. Cumulativity in default logic is interpreted by [Makinson, 89] as the adding of a classical formula to W i.e.:

$$W \subseteq W \cup \{f\} \subseteq C_D(W) \Rightarrow C_D(W) = C_D(W \cup \{f\})$$

that is:

$$f \in C_D(W) \Rightarrow C_D(W) = C_D(W \cup \{f\}).$$

In this sense, neither Reiter's default logic nor Lukaszewicz's is cumulative as shown by [Makinson, 89]: let $\Delta = (W, D)$ with $W = \emptyset, D = \{\frac{:a}{a}, \frac{a \vee b : \neg a}{\neg a}\}$. Since there are only normal defaults (i.e. defaults with justification equal to the consequent), R- and j-extensions coincide. Δ has only one extension: $E^1 = Th(\{a\})$. Since $C_D(W) = Th(\{a\})$ (no matter whether it is defined skeptically or credulously), $(a \vee b) \in C_D(W)$. But adding $\{a \vee b\}$ to W modifies $C_D(W)$ since we have to consider now $\Delta_{\{a \vee b\}} = (W \cup \{a \vee b\}, D)$ which has two extensions: $E^1_{\{a \vee b\}} = Th(\{a\})$, $E^2_{\{a \vee b\}} = Th(\{\neg a\})$.

In order to introduce cumulativity in default logic, [Brewka, 91] followed by [Makinson, 91] and [Giordano, Martelli, 94] resorts to the notion of assertional default theories. On one hand this approach is an improvement since an assertion, being a quasi-default formula, seems to correspond to a homogenization of the initial formalism. However since the justification-part of an assertion is not logicaly closed, this can lead to an unatural behaviour when considering its abduction to a default theory. On the other hand with the extension of First Order formulas to assertions, a modification of how to interpret cumulativity in assertional default logic (called CDL) is achieved. Consider first this last point. The definition of cumulativity in CDL, such as proposed by Brewka is[2]: If there is a CDL extension F of a default theory (W, D) containing an assertion f, then E is a CDL extension of (W, D) containing f iff E is a CDL extension of $(W \cup \{f\}, D)$. Let us leave undefined what an assertion is for the time being.

[2] See Proposition 2.13, p. 191 of [Brewka, 91]

It is easy to check that the previous definition amounts to considering a set of nonmonotonic consequence relations $\mid\sim_{D,E}$ such that:

$$\textit{(Choice reasoning)}\ W \mid\sim_{D,E} f \text{ iff } (E, \text{extension of } (W, D))(f \in E).$$

Cumulativity is then considered as usual, but with the exception that it is defined regarding one nonmonotonic consequence relation for each extension[3]. Unlike [Makinson, 89], default reasoning is here considered as a process for generating a *family* of nonmonotonic consequence relations, rather than *one* nonmonotonic logic. This is quite reasonable. But it also has to be noticed that if formulas instead of assertions are used in the definition of $\mid\sim_{D,E}$, both Reiter's and Lukaszewic's approaches are cumulative as well. Hence, regarding cumulativity, the only difference between [Brewka, 91] and both Reiter's and Lukaszewicz's default logics concerns skeptical reasoning.

Now let us come back to the first point, that is the extension of First Order formulas to assertions. An assertion is any expression of the form $\langle p : J\rangle$ where, roughly speaking, J is a set of formulas supporting the belief in p. Note that whereas $\langle p : J\rangle$ expresses the belief in p supported by J, at least it is not the same as the belief in p expressed by $\langle p : K\rangle$ (although this does not mean that one assertion should be stronger than the other). Consider now the question of abducting an assertion to a default theory regarding cumulativity. What is usually shown is that given any extension of a default theory (W, D) containing the assertion $\langle p : J\rangle$, E is an extension of (W, D) containing $\langle p : J\rangle$ iff E is an extension of $(W \cup \{\langle p : J\rangle\}, D)$. But nothing is said in the case where instead of introducing in W the assertion $\langle p : J\rangle$ contained in a given extension of the default theory, we introduce $\langle p : K\rangle$. In other words, what happens if an expression previously considered as a certain kind of belief turns to be another kind of belief? Indeed, should the case $K = \emptyset$ be considered as a special case? Besides, this problem also concerns the syntax dependency of the sets of supports: e.g. the assertions $\langle p : \{a, a \vee b\}\rangle$ and $\langle p : \{a\}\rangle$ so far are not considered as equivalent. On the other hand there is some ambiguity concerning *what* is added regarding cumulativity in the framework of [Makinson, 89]. It remains unanswered whether this ambiguity is an advantage or not. However, [Schaub, 92] noticed that since adding the assertion $\langle p : J\rangle$ eliminates all the extensions that are inconsistent with this assertion (e.g. the default theory $(\emptyset, \{\frac{: a}{a}, \frac{: \neg a}{\neg a}\})$) it appears stronger than the abduction of a simple belief.

In order to avoid a modification of the language, [Schaub, 91] introduces *lemmata default rules* which, on the other hand, involve an adaptation of cumulativity. Actually, cumulativity in default logic was interpreted *a priori* from the adding of a classical formula to W by [Makinson, 89] (see above). But it is

[3] Actualy, the attentive reader may note that what is considered in the approach of Brewka is a generalization of *Choice Reasoning* regarding the side side effect of the adding of an assertion to W on *other* extensions containing the *same* assertion. We do not enter in the details because this difference has not effect on the comparisons with Reiter's and Lukaszewicz's approaches realized here

worthy noting that a default is a *contextual* inference rule since its application depends on the formulas which belong to it. In other words, a default is an intermediate form between a single formula and a whole inference rule. [Schaub, 91] makes the most of this remark by reinterpreting cumulativity as the adding of a default to D, although this turns out to require a slightly more complicated apparatus. Given a default theory $\Delta = (W, D)$, (1) let us define a new operator $\cup_D$ by:

$$(W, D) \cup_D \{f\} =_{\text{def}} (W, D \cup \{d_f\})$$

where d_f is a default corresponding to the formula f; (2) C_D is now extended to a new operator C on whole default theories:

$$C((W, D)) = \{f \mid (W, D) \mid\!\sim_D f\}$$

Now, we are able to redefine the usual cumulativity by the following ***D*-cumulativity**:

$$f \in C(\Delta) \Rightarrow C(\Delta) = C(\Delta \cup_D \{d_f\})$$

In what follows the term "cumulativity" is used to refer to the usual cumulativity[4], as opposed to "D-cumulativity". Note that whereas D-cumulativity corresponds to the abduction of a belief, usual cumulativity should now be interpreted as the abduction of a fact. It has been shown in [Schaub, 91] and [Schaub, 92] that both Reiter's and Schaub's default logics are D-cumulative regarding how d_f is defined.

In what follows let $\Delta = (W, D)$ be a default theory, and E be either a R-extension or a c-extension of Δ.

Definition 6. A default proof D_f of f in E is a minimal grounded subset of $GD(E, \Delta)$ such that $W \cup \{CONS(D_f)\} \vdash f$.

Definition 7 [Schaub, 91], [Schaub, 92]. Let $f \in E$, and D_f be a default proof of f. A *constrained lemmata default rule* for f is the following default:

$$d_f^c = \frac{: \bigwedge_{d \in D_f} JUST(\{d\}) \wedge \bigwedge_{d \in D_f} CONS(\{d\})}{f}.$$

A *Reiter's lemmata default rule* for f is the non-singular following default:

$$d_f^R = \frac{: JUST(\{d_1\}), \ldots, JUST(\{d_n\})}{f},$$

with $D_f = \{d_1, \ldots, d_n\}$.

Definition 8. Let $\mid\!\sim_D^\chi$ be the *credulous* nonmonotonic relations defined from $\Delta = (W, D)$ by: $(W, D) \mid\!\sim_D^\chi f$ iff $(\exists E, \chi\text{-extension of } (W, D))(f \in E)$ with $\chi \in \{R, c\}$.

---

[4] or, in other words, "W-cumulativity"...

Property 9 [Schaub, 91], [Schaub, 92]. *D-cumulativity holds for* $\mid\!\sim^c_D$ *and* $\mid\!\sim^R_D$ *regarding constrained and Reiter's lemmata default rules respectively.*

Example 1. [Makinson, 89] Let $\Delta = (W, D)$ with $W = \emptyset, D = \{\frac{:a}{a}, \frac{a \vee b : \neg a}{\neg a}\}$. Δ has only one c-extension: $E = Th(\{a\})$. Since $a \vdash a \vee b$, we may add the lemmata default rule $\frac{:a}{a \vee b}$ to D. $\Delta_{\{\frac{:a}{a \vee b}\}} = (W, D \cup \{\frac{:a}{a \vee b}\})$ has the same c-extension as $\Delta = (W, D)$: $E_{\{\frac{:a}{a \vee b}\}} = Th(\{a\})$.

Remark. Note that there are other ways of defining D-cumulativity. For instance, it seems easy to prove that D-cumulativity holds for the above variants of default logic when using the following lemmata default rule:

$$d_f = \frac{\bigwedge_{d \in D_f} CONS(\{d\}) : \top}{f},$$

where f and D_f are defined as in definition 7.

Commitment to justifications is not suitable in all cases. Also whatever assertions or lemmata default rules are considered, their abduction is weaker than the abduction of a first order formula in W, such as considered by [Makinson, 89]. Let us illustrate these points with the following two examples. The first one directly concerns a simple problem of knowledge representation regarding commitment to justifications. In the second example, it is stressed that commitment to justifications may involve an undesirable result with respect to cumulativity. Besides, it illustrates the fact that adding a formula to W has a different meaning than adding either a default or an assertion.

Example 2. Let us consider the following default theory: $\Delta = (W, D)$ with

$$W = \{\text{HIKE}\},$$
$$D = \{\frac{\text{HIKE} : \text{GOOD-WEATHER-FORECAST}}{\text{TAKE-SUNGLASSES}}, \frac{\text{HIKE} : \neg\text{GOOD-WEATHER-FORECAST}}{\text{TAKE-JACKET}}\}.$$

Since constraint default logic requires commitment to justifications, Δ has the two following extensions $E^1 = Th(\{\text{HIKE}, \text{TAKE-SUNGLASSES}\})$, $E^2 = Th(\{\text{HIKE}, \text{TAKE-JACKET}\})$. Now we are forced to choose one of the two extensions, and hence to gamble on the weather. But it should be stressed that (1) we *do not know* anything about the weather forecast and (in lack of any actual information) we probably prefer to leave this unknown, (2) two *contrary* but not necessarily *contradictory* actions are considered (taking sunglasses or taking a jacket). Here both Reiter's and Lukaszewicz's default logics have only one extension $E = Th(\{\text{HIKE}, \text{TAKE-SUNGLASSES}, \text{TAKE-JACKET}\})$ which seems more suitable.

Example 3. Couples are invited to a party. The corresponding default theory is $\Delta_W = (W, D)$ where

$$W = \{\text{COUPLE}(\text{Bogart}, \text{Bacall}), \text{COUPLE}(\text{Romeo}, \text{Juliet}), \text{COUPLE}(\text{Charles}, \text{Diana})\}$$

$$D = \{\frac{\text{COUPLE}(x,y) : \text{PRESENT}(x) \wedge \text{PRESENT}(y)}{\text{PRESENT}(x) \wedge \text{PRESENT}(y)},$$

$$\frac{\text{COUPLE}(x,y) \wedge (\text{PRESENT}(x) \vee \text{PRESENT}(y)) : \neg(\text{PRESENT}(x) \wedge \text{PRESENT}(y))}{\neg(\text{PRESENT}(x) \wedge \text{PRESENT}(y))}\}.$$

Let us stress the following points: (1) W denotes *actual* knowledge; (2) the first default expresses our *a priori* hope that couples should come; (2) the second default expresses the idea that we may have to consider the case where only one half of a given couple is present. Since the defaults are normal, R- and j-extensions coincide. So, let us simply speak of extensions, as opposed to c-extensions. In the present state the theory has only one extension:

$$E_W = Th(W \cup \{\text{PRESENT}(\text{Bogart}), \text{PRESENT}(\text{Bacall}), \text{PRESENT}(\text{Romeo}),$$
$$\text{PRESENT}(\text{Juliet}), \text{PRESENT}(\text{Charles}), \text{PRESENT}(\text{Diana})\}.$$

This theory is not cumulative: PRESENT(Diana) belongs to E_W as a belief, but if added to W as a fact, the new theory

$$\Delta_{W \cup \{\text{PRESENT}(\text{Diana})\}} = (W \cup \{\text{PRESENT}(\text{Diana})\}, D)$$

has two extensions:

$$E_{W \cup \{\text{PRESENT}(\text{Diana})\}} = E_W,$$
$$E'_{W \cup \{\text{PRESENT}(\text{Diana})\}} = Th(W \cup \{\text{PRESENT}(\text{Bogart}), \text{PRESENT}(\text{Bacall}),$$
$$\text{PRESENT}(\text{Romeo}), \text{PRESENT}(\text{Juliet}),$$
$$\neg\text{PRESENT}(\text{Charles}), \text{PRESENT}(\text{Diana})\}).$$

Note that in this example both constrained and Reiter's lemmata default rules corresponding to PRESENT(Diana) are the same, i.e.

$$d_{\text{PRESENT}(\text{Diana})} = \frac{: \text{PRESENT}(\text{Charles}) \wedge \text{PRESENT}(\text{Diana})}{\text{PRESENT}(\text{Diana})}.$$

The only c-extension of the theory $\Delta_{D \cup \{d_{\text{PRESENT}(\text{Diana})}\}}$ is E_W (with $d_{\text{PRESENT}(\text{Diana})}$ as lemmata default rule). But also $\Delta_{D \cup \{d_{\text{PRESENT}(\text{Diana})}\}}$ has E_W as the only non-contrained extension (either R- or j-). Clearly whatever is the variant considered, adding $d_{\text{PRESENT}(\text{Diana})}$ (or the corresponding assertion[5]) is weaker than adding PRESENT(Diana) to W. However, regarding the presence of new information (i.e. Diana *is* present, but we still know nothing about Charles) the last approach seems more realistic (for lack of being definitively optimistic about the presence of Charles). Let us note that the solutions given here to the non-cumulativity of default logics are such that they *restrict* the set of generated extensions.

[5] See [Giordano, Martelli, 94]

Remark. [Dix, 92] establishes *usual* cumulativity for a *skeptical* relation based on a twofold application of a fixed-point operator on default theories with commitment to justifications (that is, constrained default theories), whereas [You, Li, 94] establishes usual cumulativity for a *credulous* relation with respect to prerequisite-free constraint default theories.

5 Guess-default logic

We introduce now our variant, called *guess default logic*. Let us stress the following intuitive ideas:

- W denotes *actual* knowledge (corresponding to the "world" of [Reiter, 1980]);
- any prerequisite denotes a *local context* in which a corresponding default should be applied;
- any justification corresponds to a *plausible assumption* related both to a context and derived consequences of defaults;
- any consequence of a default is considered as a *guess* depending on both a context and the plausible assumptions.

Our idea is to obtain sets of guesses from maximal sets of plausible assumptions. We first try to put forward as many plausible assumptions as possible provided that they are consistent with the corresponding conclusions attached to them (i.e. the consequents of the corresponding default rules). In this way, pre-sets of guesses are obtained which are sound with respect to plausible assumptions. In order to get the actual guess, we keep only those which hold regarding the current contexts. More formally:

Definition 10. Let $\Delta = (W, D)$ be a default theory. Let D'' and D' be any subsets of defaults of D. $E = Th(W \cup CONS(D''))$ is a g-extension[6] of Δ with respect to $JUST(D')$ iff D' is a maximal subset of D such that $(\forall \beta \in JUST(D'))(\neg\beta \notin Th(W \cup CONS(D')))$ and D'' is a maximal grounded subset of D'.

Definition 11. Let $\Delta = (W, D)$ be a default theory. Let $E = Th(W \cup CONS(D''))$ be a g-extension of Δ with respect to $JUST(D')$.

- The set $JUST(D')$ is called *the set of plausible assumptions supporting* E, and D' itself is called the *support* of E.
- The set $PREREQ(D'')$ is called *the set of actual contexts of* E, and D'' itself is called the set of *generating defaults* of E.

Example 4. The default theory $(\emptyset, \{\frac{c : \neg a \wedge \neg b}{d}, \frac{: \neg a}{a \vee b}, \frac{: a}{a}\})$ has three g-extensions:

$$E^1 = Th(\emptyset) \text{ with } \{\neg a \wedge \neg b\} \text{ as support,}$$
$$E^2 = Th(\{a \vee b\}) \text{ with } \{\neg a\} \text{ as support,}$$
$$E^3 = Th(\{a\}) \text{ with } \{a\} \text{ as support.}$$

[6] for guess-extension...

Note that $E^1 \subseteq E^2 \subseteq E^3$.

Example 5. The default theory $(\{a\}, \{\frac{a:b}{b}, \frac{c:d}{e}, \frac{a:\neg e}{b}\})$ has two g-extensions:

$$E^1 = Th(\{a,b\}) \text{ with } \{b,d\} \text{ as support,}$$
$$E^2 = Th(\{a,b\}) \text{ with } \{b,\neg e\} \text{ as support.}$$

Since $E^1 = E^2$, it can also be considered that Δ has only one g-extension but with possibly two different sets of defaults as supports.

A g-extension is defined regarding a pre-extension for which the justification conditions hold. In this way, any g-extension is contained in a g-extension that could appear after the abduction of a previously derived formula. This is the key point of our approach: by giving up the idea of systematically getting maximal extensions we are able to recover cumulativity in default reasoning.

Definition 12. Let be $\mid\!\sim_D$ be the *skeptical* nonmonotonic relation defined from $\Delta = (W, D)$ by: $W \mid\!\sim_D f$ iff $(\forall E$, g-extension of $(W, D))(f \in E)$. The set of nonmonotonic consequences derived from W is: $C_D(W) = \{f \mid W \mid\!\sim_D f\}$.

Given a default theory Δ, and in order to establish that cumulativity holds for $\mid\!\sim_D$, it is necessary to consider how adding a formula f to W affects the behaviour of defaults. In the following lemma, we show that adding $\{f\}$ to W actually does not change the supports initially obtained from Δ.

Lemma 13. *Let $\Delta = (W, D)$ be a default theory, and f a formula. Let us call $\mathcal{D}_W$ and $\mathcal{D}_{W \cup \{f\}}$ the sets of supports of the g-extensions of (W, D) and $(W \cup \{f\}, D)$ respectively. We have:*

$$f \in C_D(W) \Rightarrow (\mathcal{D}_W = \mathcal{D}_{W \cup \{f\}}).$$

Theorem 14. *$\mid\!\sim_D$ is cumulative.*

Example 6. [Makinson, 89] Let $\Delta = (W, D)$ with $W = \emptyset, D = \{\frac{:a}{a}, \frac{a \vee b : \neg a}{\neg a}\}$. Δ has two g-extensions:

$$E^1 = Th(\{a\}) \text{ with } \{a\} \text{ as support,}$$
$$E^2 = Th(\emptyset) \text{ with } \{\neg a\} \text{ as support.}$$

The only guess generated under the assumption $\{\neg a\}$ are the tautologies (i.e. the content of W) since the corresponding context does not hold. Since $C_D(\emptyset) = \emptyset$, cumulativity trivially holds. Note that $\Delta_{\{a \vee b\}} = (W \cup \{a \vee b\}, D)$ still has two g-extensions:

$$E^1_{\{a \vee b\}} = Th(\{a\}) \text{ with } \{a\} \text{ as support,}$$
$$E^2_{\{a \vee b\}} = Th(\{\neg a\}) \text{ with } \{\neg a\} \text{ as support.}$$

$\Delta_{\{a\}} = (W \cup \{a\}, D)$ keeps $E^1_{\{a\}}$ as the only g-extension. Because there is more precise actual knowledge in W, fewer conjectures are possible. We have $E^i \subseteq E^i_{\{a \vee b\}}$, for $i \in \{1, 2\}$, and $E^1_{\{a \vee b\}} \subseteq E^1_{\{a\}}$. The lack of an extension $E^2_{\{a\}}$ can be considered as an extreme attempt to preserve consistency, when trying to apply the default $\frac{a \vee b : \neg a}{\neg a}$ facing the actual knowledge $W \cup \{a\}$.

The previous example concerning couples behaves in the same way. From the beginning two g-extensions are generated, associated with possible guesses regarding the actual knowledge of W. We get

$$E_1 = Th(W \cup \{\text{PRESENT(Bogart), PRESENT(Bacall), PRESENT(Romeo),}$$
$$\text{PRESENT(Juliet), PRESENT(Charles), PRESENT(Diana)}\},$$
$$E_2 = Th(W).$$

Since $C_D(\emptyset) = Th(W)$, cumulativity trivially holds.

Actually, the process involved by the generation of the g-extensions of a default theory corresponds to the opposite way for obtaining the c-extensions of this theory. Instead of removing the "too many" extensions, we try to initially generate the "missing" ones in order to establish cumulativity. Since we do not require commitment to the justification, we avoid any restriction on the reasoning of a cumulative agent. Indeed, we now have a cumulative approach of default logic in which two main non-cumulative approaches are embedded:

Theorem 15. *Let $\Delta = (W, D)$ be a default theory, and let us consider $E = Th(W \cup CONS(D''))$ with $D'' \subseteq D$. E is a j-extension of Δ iff E is a g-extension of Δ such that D'' is a maximal set of generating defaults.*

Example 7. Let be $D = \{\frac{c : \neg a \wedge \neg b}{d}\}$ and $D' = \{\frac{: \neg a}{a \vee b}, \frac{: a}{a}\}$. The default theory $(\emptyset, D)$ has only one g-extension which also is a j-extension: $E = Th(\emptyset)$. The default theory$(\emptyset, D \cup D')$ has three g-extensions: $E^1 = E = Th(\emptyset)$, $E^2 = Th(\{a \vee b\})$, $E^3 = Th(\{a\})$. Only E^2 and E^3 are j-extensions. Only E^3 is a R-extension. Note that $E^1 \subseteq E^2 \subseteq E^3$.

Hence:

- any j-extension is a g-extension;
- any R-extension is a g-extension (since following theorem 5 it is also a j-extension).

Guess default logic is cumulative whereas neither Łukaszewicz's nor Reiter's default logics are. However, it is clear that this kind of cumulativity may be considered of little interest (although coherent with the view of default reasoning developped so far) since in most cases the intersection of the g-extensions is nothing else than just $Th(W)$. Now, considering a given default theory $\Delta = (W, D)$, let us say that Δ itself is cumulative iff cumulativity holds regarding $C_D(W)$. In what follows, we are interested in the characterization of which default theories in the sense of Łukaszewicz are cumulatives and which are not. First, note that whatever is the variant under consideration, guess default logic allows us to get rid of those defaults which can never be used in the generation of new extensions.

Theorem 16. *Given a default theory $\Delta = (W, D)$ and any default $d = \frac{\alpha : \beta}{\gamma}$ of D, d is not in any support of any g-extension iff $\neg\beta \in Th(W \cup \{\gamma\})$.*

So, let us consider the defaults which are involved in the construction of g-extensions but do not generate j-extensions.

Definition 17. Let $\Delta = (W, D)$ be a default theory. Let $\mathcal{E}_j$ and $\mathcal{E}_g$ be, respectively, the set of the j-extensions and the set of the g-extensions of Δ. The *difference set of defaults* for Δ, $\mathcal{DS}(\Delta)$, is defined by the union of all the $D' \setminus D''$ such that, for any $E \in \mathcal{E}_g \setminus \mathcal{E}_j$, D' is the support of E and D'' is the set of generating defaults of E.

The following criteria holds for cumulative default theories in the sense of Łukaszewicz:

Property 18. *Let $\Delta = (W, D)$ be a default theory and let $C_D(W)$ be defined skeptically regarding the j-extensions of Δ. Let $\mathcal{DS}(\Delta)$ be the difference set of defaults for Δ. The default theory Δ understood in the sense of Łukaszewicz is cumulative iff for each default $d \in \mathcal{DS}(\Delta)$, of the form $\frac{\alpha : \beta}{\gamma}$, $(\alpha \in C_D(W) \Rightarrow \neg\beta \in C_D(W \cup \{\alpha\}))$.*

Example 8. Consider yet the default theory $\Delta = (W, D)$ with $W = \emptyset$, $D = \{\frac{: a}{a}, \frac{a \vee b : \neg a}{\neg a}\}$. Δ has two g-extensions: $E^1 = Th(\{a\})$, $E^2 = Th(\emptyset)$. Only E^1 is a j-extension. $C_D(W) = Th(\{a\})$, $\mathcal{DS}((W, D)) = \{\frac{a \vee b : \neg a}{\neg a}\}$. Δ is not cumulative regarding $C_D(W)$ since $(a \vee b) \in C_D(W)$ but $\neg\neg a \notin C_D(W \cup \{a \vee b\})$.

Example 9. Consider the default theory $\Delta = (W, D)$ with $W = \emptyset$, $D = \{\frac{c : \neg a \wedge \neg b}{d}, \frac{: \neg a}{a \vee b}, \frac{: a}{a}\}$. Δ has three g-extensions: $E^1 = Th(\emptyset)$, $E^2 = Th(\{a \vee b\})$, $E^3 = Th(\{a\})$. Only E^2 and E^3 are j-extensions. $C_D(W) = Th(\{a \vee b\})$, $\mathcal{DS}((W, D)) = \{\frac{c : \neg a \wedge \neg b}{d}\}$. Δ is cumulative regarding $C_D(W)$ since $c \notin C_D(W)$, and hence the implication trivialy holds.

6 Conclusion

A cumulative variant of default logic has been introduced. On one hand this variant matches the initial definition of cumulativity for default logic (see [Makinson, 89]), on the other hand Reiter's and Łukaszewicz's approaches are embedded in it. Indeed this variant can be used in order to select cumulative default theories in the sense of Lukaszewicz. This work is in progress and a lot of questions still require further study: it should be easy to show that guess default logic is D-cumulative. However, we would prefer to define a pure abstract link between usual W-cumulativity and D-cumulativity. Another remaining problem is the characterization of cumulative Reiter default theories inside our framework. A semantic characterization (for instance in the frameworks of [Besnard, Schaub, 92] or [Voorbraak, 93]) would certainly provide an essential tool for allowing a comparison with other approaches. Finally, whereas single extension nonmonotonic logics consider only one type of cumulativity (see [Kraus et Al., 90]), it seems essential to investigate in a deeper way the different types of cumulativities that are found in multiple extension nonmonotonic logics.

Acknowledgements. The author is gratefully indebted to Christine Froidevaux, Torsten Schaub, Camilla Schwind, and to anonymous referees for their helpful comments on earlier versions of the present paper. Thanks to Kevin Kennedy for his rereading. Special thanks to Robert E. Mercer for valuable arguments, discussions and feedback.

References

[Besnard, Schaub, 92] Besnard P., Schaub T., *Possible Worlds Semantics for Default Logics*. Proceedings of the 9th Canadian Conference on Artificial Intelligence, AI-92. Glasgow, Hadley (Ed), p. 148–155.

[Brewka, 91] Brewka G., *Cumulative Default Logic: in Defense of Nonmonotonic Inference Rule*. Artificial Intelligence, 50, p. 183–205.

[Dix, 92] Dix J., *Default Theories of Poole-Type and a Method for Constructing Cumulative Versions of Default Logic*. Proceedings of the 10th European Conference on Artificial Intelligence, ECAI-92. Neumann (Ed). John Wiley & Sons, p. 289–293.

[Gabbay, 85] Gabbay D., *Theoretical foundations for non-monotonic reasoning in expert systems*. in K.R. Apt (Ed), Logics and Models of Concurrent Systems, Springer Verlag.

[Giordano, Martelli, 94] Giordano L., Martelli A., *On Cumulative Default Logics*. Artificial Intelligence, 66, p. 161–179.

[Kraus et Al., 90] Kraus S., Lehman D., Magidor M., *Nonmonotonic Reasoning, Preferential Models and Cumulative Logics*. Artificial Intelligence, 44, p. 167–207.

[Lukaszewicz, 88] Lukaszewicz W., *Considerations on Default Logic - An Alternative Approach*. Computational Intelligence 4, p. 1–16.

[Makinson, 89] Makinson D., *A General Theory of Cumulative Inference*. Non-Monotonic Reasoning. Proceedings of the second international workshop. Siekmann (Ed). Lecture Notes in Artificial Intelligence 346, Springer Verlag, p. 1–18.

[Makinson, 91] Makinson D., *unpublished manuscript*. Quoted in [Brewka, 91].

[Poole, 88] Poole D., *A Logical Framework for Default Reasoning*. Artificial Intelligence, 36, p. 27–47.

[Reiter, 1980] Reiter R., *A Logic for Default Reasoning*. Artificial Intelligence, 13, 1, p. 81–132.

[Risch, 91] Risch V., 1991, *Démonstration à Base de Tableaux Sémantiques pour la Logique des Défauts au sens de Lukaszewicz*. Proceedings of the 8th conference AFCET "Reconnaissance des Formes et Intelligence Artificielle", Lyon, France, p. 355–361.

[Risch, 93] Risch V., *Les Tableaux Analytiques au Service des Logiques de Défauts*. PhD thesis, GIA, Faculté des Sciences de Luminy, Université Aix-Marseille II, France.

[Schaub, 91] Schaub T., *On Commitment and Cumulativity in Default Logics*. Proceedings of the European Conference on Symbolic and Quantitative Approaches for Uncertainty. Kruse, Siegel (Ed). Lecture Notes in Computer Science 548, Springer Verlag, p. 305–309.

[Schaub, 92] Schaub T., *On Constrained Default Theories*. Proceedings of the 10th European Conference on Artificial Intelligence, ECAI-92. Neumann (Ed). John Wiley & Sons, p. 304–308.

[Schwind, 90] Schwind C., *A Tableau-based Theorem Prover for a Decidable Subset of Default Logic*. Proceedings of the 10th International Conference on Automated Deduction, CADE 10, Springer Verlag, p. 541–546.

[Schwind, Risch, 91] Schwind C., Risch V., *A Tableau-Based Characterization for Default Logic*. Proceedings of the European Conference on Symbolic and Quantitative Approaches for Uncertainty. Kruse, Siegel (Ed). Lecture Notes in Computer Science 548, Springer Verlag, p. 310–317.

[Voorbraak, 93] Voorbraak F., *Preference-based Semantics for Nonmonotonic Logics*. Proceedings of 13th International Joint Conference on Artificial Intelligence, IJCAI-93. Bajcsy (Ed). Morgan Kaufmann Publishers, p. 584–589.

[Wilson, 93] Wilson N., *Default Logic and Dempster-Shafer Theory*. Proceedings of the European Conference on Symbolic and Quantitative Approaches to Reasoning and Uncertainty. Clarke, Kruse, Moral (Ed). Lecture Notes in Computer Science 747, Springer Verlag, p. 372–379.

[You, Li, 94] You J., Li L., *Two Cumulative Results On J- and PJ-Default Logics*. Proceedings of the 10th Canadian Conference on Artificial Intelligence, AI-94. Elio (Ed), p. 219–226.

A Two-Stage Approach to First Order Default Reasoning

Karl Schlechta
Laboratoire d'Informatique de Marseille, URA CNRS 1787
CMI, Technopôle de Château-Gombert
F-13453 Marseille Cedex 13, France
ks@gyptis.univ-mrs.fr

Abstract

We present a two stage approach to open normal defaults. The static or "descriptive" aspect of defaults is represented in an extension of classical first order logic by generalized quantifiers, the dynamic or "normative" aspect in a preference relation on the models of the default theory thus re-interpreted. The inference relation of this second stage is defined via a Limit Preferential Structure approach.

1 Introduction

The Reiter definition and generalized quantifiers Reiter's approach to open normal defaults, i.e. of the form $\frac{:\phi(x)}{\phi(x)}$ in the case without prerequisites, and of the form $\frac{\psi(x):\phi(x)}{\phi(x)}$ in the case with prerequisites (we follow Reiter's terminology, see [13]) via Skolem constants was criticized by F.Baader and B.Hollunder in [1] (see also [2]) for its sensibility to syntactic reformulations. In [2], we have suggested a Limit Preferential approach (as introduced by G.Bossu and P. Siegel in [6]), which, by its semantical basis, avoids above problems. It seems to capture well the "dynamic" or "inference-greedy" aspect of defaults, to make as many instances of the defaults true as possible.
In [14], we have taken a totally different approach to capture the "static" or "normality" aspect of defaults: That a default also expresses a fact about the world, and not only a strategy of the reasoner, i.e. roughly, that a default "normally, birds fly", expresses something like "most" birds fly, the "interesting" birds do, etc. E.g. Reiter's formalism [13] lacks this static, minimal requirement: If you say that normally birds fly, you have to produce at least one such flying bird, and even more, a substantial subset of the set of birds must be able to fly. If we accept that these are minimal conditions justifying a sentence like "normally $\phi(x)$", then we conclude that "normally $\phi(x)$" and "normally $\neg\phi(x)$" are impossible, on the premise that two such substantial subsets (of one base set) have non-empty intersection. In our opinion, this minimal

condition - $\phi(x)$ has to hold for a substantial subset to justify the sentence "normally $\phi(x)$" - leads naturally to a formalisation of "normally" via "important" or "large" subsets: "normally $\phi(x)$" holds iff there is an important subset A (of the universe, or of the set of birds etc.) such that for all $x \in A$ $\phi(x)$ holds.
We then have interpreted in [14] open normal defaults as generalized quantifiers, in strength between the classical existential and universal quantifier. More precisely, we have introduced a new quantifier "almost all" into first order logic (FOL), which was interpreted semantically by "large" subsets, characterized by a weak filter, added to a standard first order logic model, forming a more complex structure. A sound and complete axiomatization, extending classical FOL, for our semantics was given.
This approach had the advantage to give not only a notion of consistency of default theories - e.g. $\{\frac{:\phi(x)}{\phi(x)}, \frac{:\neg\phi(x)}{\neg\phi(x)}\}$ was ruled out as inconsistent - but also to allow the use of negated and nested defaults, and to give such formulas a clear meaning. Yet, it treated only the minimal, static aspect of defaults, not the dynamic, inference-greedy one: Apply the default as much as you can!
In the present approach, we marry both approaches in a two stage process, starting with the static aspect, and then, on the basis of this, make as many instances true as possible, by a preference relation on the extended FOL models of the default theory. Given a theory of classical and default information, we consider the set of extended FOL models of that theory - if it is consistent under our logic - and choose the "good" models among those by a preference relation, which reflects the "inference-greedy" aspect: as many instances as possible will be made to hold.
The fact that we choose only among the extended FOL models guarantees that the minimal, static requirements are met, i.e. that the default theory "means something objectively", that really the default properties hold for a "large" subset, and the preference relation makes the properties hold for as many elements as possible. E.g., for the theory $\{\frac{:\phi(x)}{\phi(x)}\}$ $\phi(x)$ will not only be true for a large subset - sufficient for the interpretation as generalized quantifiers - but for all elements of the universe, as there is nothing which contradicts this extension. $\{\frac{:\phi(x)}{\phi(x)}, \frac{:\neg\phi(x)}{\neg\phi(x)}\}$, however, will be ruled out immediately as inconsistent.
Examples and general considerations lead us to take the Limit Preferential Structure approach for the preference relation.
We conclude by presenting several examples, and show that this approach does not only abstractly capture some intuitions about defaults, but can solve some concrete and interesting cases as well.

Preferential Structures The basic idea is to interpret a primitive notion of "importance" or "value", by a function which chooses the subset of "best" models of a theory of that language.
In other words, we work on a set of "possible worlds", i.e. models of the underlying base logic, but do not accord the same importance or value to all such models. Given then a theory T of the base language and logic, we determine the semantical consequences of T in a structure $\mathcal{M}$ by considering only the subset of "best" models of T: $T \models_{\mathcal{M}} \phi$ iff ϕ holds in all best models of T in our structure. More formally, such a structure $\mathcal{M}$ will then consist of a set M of models or possible worlds for the base logic, and a choice function f on $\mathcal{P}(M)$ - the power set of M - which, for each base theory T, singles out the set $f(M(T)) \subseteq M(T)$ of best models of T in that structure

$\mathcal{M}$, where $M(T)$ is the set of all base models of T in $\mathcal{M}$. We thus define $T \models_{\mathcal{M}} \phi$ iff ϕ holds in all $m \in f(M(T))$. For historical reasons, we may call this approach the minimal case.

A refinement of the idea is to work not with one subset of "best" models, but with many subsets of "good" models, perhaps of increasing quality. This translates into the existence of several choice functions f_i in the structure $\mathcal{M}$, and we define $T \models_{\mathcal{M}} \phi$ iff there is some f_i such that ϕ holds in all $m \in f_i(M(T))$. This captures the intuition that we may not dispose of ideal models, but of ever better ones, which, in a sense, approximate the limit of the ideal case. Thus, each $f_i(M(T))$ may be non-empty, but $\bigcap\{f_i(M(T)) : i \in I\}$ may be empty. I shall call this the limit case.

A particular case for both approaches is to define the choice function(s) via a binary relation: smaller elements are preferred over bigger ones. This choice is a local one, context-free so to say, which results in strong logical properties (essentially one half of the deduction theorem). The minimal variant of these preferential structures were first considered, in a different context, in [8], and is quite well characterized by a number of soundness and completeness results (e.g. [9], [10], [15], [16]), the limit variant was introduced in [6], up to now, complete characterizations for this technically more difficult case seem to be missing, for partial results, see [3], [4], [5], [18].

A Two Stage Approach Thus, we start with the static aspect, and choose among the extended FOL models of the default theory T, defaults interpreted as generalized quantifiers, the "good" models by a preferential relation. The formal definition is given in the next section.

Basically, a model M is considered better than a model M' for the theory T, iff (1) for all defaults in T, M satisfies all positive instances of M' too (where c is a positive instance for the default $\frac{:\phi(x)}{\phi(x)}$, iff $\phi(c)$ holds in that model - the case for defaults with prerequisites is analogous), (2) for no default in T, there is a negative instance which holds in M, but not in M' (where c is a negative instance for the default $\frac{:\phi(x)}{\phi(x)}$, iff $\neg\phi(c)$ holds in that model - the case for defaults with prerequisites is again analogous), (3) there is at least one default in T, with one positive instance c in M, which is not positive in M'.

This definition is essentially taken from [2].

As our formalism with generalized quantifiers allows us to deduce defaults, e.g. by the axiom schema $\nabla x\phi(x) \wedge \forall x(\phi(x) \rightarrow \psi(x)) \rightarrow \nabla x\psi(x)$, it is not clear which defaults enter into the definition of the relation. But, consider a theory of two defaults (which we re-write immediately) $\nabla x\phi(x)$ and $\nabla x\psi(x)$, then we can deduce the defaults $\nabla x(\phi(x) \vee \neg\psi(x))$ and $\nabla x(\psi(x) \vee \neg\phi(x))$, which would block each other in an attempt to extend the positive instances. We therefore consider either only the defaults present in the original theory, or, alternatively, a set D of defaults mentioned explicitely - in all our examples, they will coincide.

The following example justifies a Limit Preferential Structure approach (beyond the abstract consideration, that the existence of ideal situations is perhaps not always guaranteed): Consider a language with one unary predicate $P(x)$, the default $\nabla xP(x)$, and the theory which says that we have infinitely many instances of $\neg P(x)$. All models will be infinite, we have no best models, as we can always make another element a positive instance, the theory is consistent, and we would like to deduce at least that we have infinitely many positive instances too. So not all models will have the same intuitive value, but none is the best, we have infinite descending chains, leading to an inconsistent set of conclusions in the Minimal Preferential Structure approach.

2 Definition and Examples

2.1 Repetitions of the Basic Definitions and Results on Defaults as Generalized Quantifiers

For proofs and further details, the reader is referred to [14].

Definition 2.1 Call $\mathcal{N}(M) \subseteq \mathcal{P}(M)$ (= the powerset of M) a $\mathcal{N}$-system over M iff (a) $M \in \mathcal{N}(M)$, (b) $A \in \mathcal{N}(M)$, $A \subseteq B \subseteq M \rightarrow B \in \mathcal{N}(M)$, (c) $A, B \in \mathcal{N}(M) \rightarrow A \cap B \neq \emptyset$ if $M \neq \emptyset$ (thus, $\emptyset \notin \mathcal{N}(M)$, if $M \neq \emptyset$). (Note that this is weaker than the corresponding axiom for filters.)

Definition 2.2 We augment the language of first order logic by the new quantifiers ∇ : If ϕ and ψ are formulas, then so is $\nabla x \phi(x)$ for any variable x.

Definition 2.3 Let $\mathcal{L}$ be a first order language, and M be a $\mathcal{L}$-structure. Let $\mathcal{N}(M)$ be a $\mathcal{N}$-system over M. Define $< M, \mathcal{N}(M) > \models \phi$ for any $\nabla - \mathcal{L}$-formula inductively as usual, with an additional induction step: $< M, \mathcal{N}(M) > \models \nabla x \phi(x)$ iff there is $A \in \mathcal{N}(M)$ s.t. $\forall a \in A$ $(< M, \mathcal{N}(M) > \models \phi[a])$.

Definition 2.4 Let any axiomatization of predicate calculus be given. Augment this with the axiom schemata (1) $\nabla x \phi(x) \wedge \forall x(\phi(x) \rightarrow \psi(x)) \rightarrow \nabla x \psi(x)$, (2) $\nabla x \phi(x) \rightarrow \neg \nabla x \neg \phi(x)$, (3) $\forall x \phi(x) \rightarrow \nabla x \phi(x) \rightarrow \exists x \phi(x)$, (4) $\nabla x \phi(x) \longleftrightarrow \nabla y \phi(y)$ if x does not occurr free in $\phi(y)$ and y does not occurr free in $\phi(x)$, (for all ϕ, ψ).

Theorem 2.1 The axioms given in Definition 2.4 are sound and complete for the semantics of Definition 2.1 and 2.3.

Extension to Normal Defaults with Prerequisites The extension to normal open defaults with prerequisites is straightforward: $\nabla x \phi(x) : \psi(x)$ ("if $\phi(x)$, then normally $\psi(x)$") is interpreted as a generalized quantifier relativized to $\{x : \phi(x)\}$, i.e. we consider an $\mathcal{N}$-system not over the whole universe, but only over the subset where $\phi(x)$ holds. See [14] for details.

Strengthening the Axioms of Normality The common use of defaults, as well as systems presented in the literature (see e.g. [9], [10]), motivate various extensions of our base system, i.e. of the semantics and axiomatization. On the semantic side, these extensions consist of adding properties to the $\mathcal{N}$-systems, e.g. making $\mathcal{N}$-systems filters, which corresponds to the "AND" rule on the syntactic side: $\nabla x \phi(x) \wedge \nabla x \psi(x) \rightarrow \nabla x(\phi \wedge \psi)(x)$. See again [14] for details.

2.2 Formal Definition of the Two Stage Approach

We start with the static aspect, and choose among the extended FOL models of the theory T, where defaults are interpreted as generalized quantifiers, the "good" models by a preferential relation.

Notation: We use the following abbreviations: $\phi_n[\psi] := \exists x_1 \ldots x_n(\psi(x_1) \wedge \ldots \wedge \psi(x_n) \wedge x_1 \neq x_2 \wedge \ldots \wedge x_{n-1} \neq x_n \wedge \forall y(y = x_1 \vee \ldots \vee y = x_n))$ says that the extension of $\psi(x)$ has exactly n elements, $\phi_{\leq n}[\psi] := \exists x_1 \ldots x_n(\psi(x_1) \wedge \ldots \wedge \psi(x_n) \wedge \forall y(y = x_1 \vee \ldots \vee y = x_n))$ says that the extension of $\psi(x)$ has at most n elements, $\phi_{\geq n}[\psi] := \exists x_1 \ldots x_n(\psi(x_1) \wedge \ldots \wedge \psi(x_n) \wedge x_1 \neq x_2 \wedge \ldots \wedge x_{n-1} \neq x_n)$ says that the extension of $\psi(x)$ has at least n elements, and we abbreviate $\phi_n[true]$ by ϕ_n.

The first stage: Let T be a consistent theory in the extended FOL language. (If so desired, the axioms of normality have been strengthened.) Let $M(T)$ be the set of its models.

Definition 2.5 (The second stage.) Given a set M and a binary relation $\prec$ on M, we call $X \subseteq M$ a minimizing segment of M, iff (a) for all $m \in M$ there is $x \in X$ s.th. $m = x$ or $x \prec m$, (b) for all $m \in M$ and $x \in X$, if $m \prec x$, then $m \in X$ - i.e. X is downward closed.
Given a language $\mathcal{L}$, a set of $\mathcal{L} - models$ M, a relation $\prec$ on M, a $\mathcal{L} - theory$ T, a $\mathcal{L} - formula$ ϕ, we define $T \models_{M,\prec} \phi$ iff there is a minimizing segment X of $M(T)$ s.t. $\forall m \in X.m \models \phi$.

Definition 2.6 Let m, m' be models (of classical or extended FOL).
(a) For any open normal default $d := \nabla x \phi(x) : \psi(x)$ (defaults without prerequisites may be rewritten equivalently as $\nabla x true(x) : \psi(x)$), and an element c in the universe of m, we call c a positive instance for d in m, iff $m \models \phi(c) \wedge \psi(c)$, and a negative instance for d in m iff $m \models \phi(c) \wedge \neg\psi(c)$. The set of positive (negative) instances for d in m will be denoted $P(d,m)$ ($N(d,m)$).
(b) Let D be a set of open normal defaults. Define $m \prec m'$ iff (1) $\forall d \in D\ P(d,m') \subseteq P(d,m)$ (2) $\forall d \in D\ N(d,m) \subseteq N(d,m')$ (3) $\exists d \in D\ P(d,m) \cap N(d,m') \neq \emptyset$. Note that $\prec$ is transitive, and by $P(d,m) \cap N(d,m) = \emptyset$, irreflexive.
(c) Let again D be a set of open normal defaults and $d \in D$ be fixed. Define $m \prec_d m'$ iff (1) $P(d,m') \subseteq P(d,m)$ (2) $N(d,m) \subseteq N(d,m')$ (3) $P(d,m) \cap N(d,m') \neq \emptyset$, and set $\prec'$ the transitive closure of the union of $\prec_d$ of all $d \in D$.

$\prec'$ was the order considered in [2] - in hindsight, $\prec$ may perhaps appear as the "cleaner" approach, it is chosen here. We now show that the two relations do not lead to the same consequence relations.

Example 2.1 Consider the language with the unary predicates P and Q, and the two constants a and b, and let $T := \{\phi_2, \neg\exists x(P(x) \wedge Q(x))\}$, and $D := \{d = \frac{:P(x)}{P(x)}, d' = \frac{:Q(x)}{Q(x)}\}$. T has 8 models, $M(T)$, which we may denote by $< P = Q = \emptyset >$, $< P = \emptyset, Q = \{a\} >$, $< P = \emptyset, Q = \{b\} >$, $< P = \emptyset, Q = \{a,b\} >$, $< P = \{a\}, Q = \emptyset >$, $< P = \{a\}, Q = \{b\} >$, $< P = \{b\}, Q = \emptyset >$, $< P = \{b\}, Q = \{a\} >$, $< P = \{a,b\}, Q = \emptyset >$.
In the relation $\prec$, the set of models $X := \{< P = \emptyset, Q = \{a,b\} >, < P = \{a\}, Q = \{b\} >, < P = \{b\}, Q = \{a\} >, < P = \{a,b\}, Q = \emptyset >\}$ forms an $\prec$ *-initial* segment, which is contained in all other initial segments of $M(T)$, its elements are $\prec$ *-minimal*. We thus have $T \models_{M(T),\prec} \phi \leftrightarrow X \models \phi$. Note that, by finiteness, X is definable, and there is a formula ϕ' s.th. $m \in X \leftrightarrow m \models \phi'$. Suppose $\prec'$ to be any other relation on $M(T)$ with $T \models_{M(T),\prec'} \phi \leftrightarrow T \models_{M(T),\prec} \phi$. Then there must be an

$\prec'$ *–initial* segment X' of $M(T)$ with $X' \models \phi'$, so $X' \subseteq X$. But if $X' \subsetneq X$, then X' defines, by finiteness, a strictly stronger theory, so $X' = X$. On the other hand, e.g. $< P = \{a\}, Q = \emptyset > \prec_d < P = \emptyset, Q = \{a,b\} >$, so X is not closed in $M(T)$ for $\prec'$. Consequently, the relations $\prec$ and $\prec'$ do not define the same inference relation. □

2.3 Some Logical Properties

The following axioms and rules are discussed and defined e.g. in [9], [10]): Right Weakening: $\vdash \alpha \rightarrow \beta, \gamma \mid\sim \alpha \Rightarrow \gamma \mid\sim \beta$, Reflexivity: $\alpha \mid\sim \alpha$, And: $\alpha \mid\sim \beta, \alpha \mid\sim \gamma \Rightarrow \alpha \mid\sim \beta \wedge \gamma$, Or: $\alpha \mid\sim \gamma, \beta \mid\sim \gamma \Rightarrow \alpha \vee \beta \mid\sim \gamma$, Left Logical Equivalence: $\vdash \alpha \leftrightarrow \beta, \beta \mid\sim \gamma \Rightarrow \alpha \mid\sim \gamma$, Cautious Monotony: $\alpha \mid\sim \beta, \alpha \mid\sim \gamma \Rightarrow \alpha \wedge \beta \mid\sim \gamma$, Rational Monotony: $\alpha \mid\sim \beta \Rightarrow \alpha \mid\sim \neg\gamma$ or $\alpha \wedge \gamma \mid\sim \beta$, One half of the Deduction Theorem: $\alpha \mid\sim \beta \Rightarrow \mid\sim \alpha \rightarrow \beta$.
We read these rules as follows: E.g. the rule "And" holds iff for all (fixed) sets of defaults D and classical formulas α, β, γ $D \cup \{\alpha\} \mid\sim \beta$, $D \cup \{\alpha\} \mid\sim \gamma \Rightarrow D \cup \{\alpha\} \mid\sim \beta \wedge \gamma$.
It is clear, that our approach is robust under logically equivalent reformulation, even for our stronger logic. In particular, the problem with Reiter's approach (classically equivalent reformulation of the classical information) does not arise. Care has to be taken, however, that also the set of defaults we want to treat in the second step stays equivalent.
So Right Weakening, Reflexivity, and Left Logical Equivalence will trivially hold, also for formulas of the extended FOL language, and the stronger logic of normality.

Lemma 2.2 Right And, Left Or, Cautious Monotony, and one half of the Deduction Theorem hold. (Transitivity of $\prec$ is crucial here.)

Example 2.2 Rational Monotony does not hold: Set $D := \{\nabla x P(x)\}, \alpha := \exists x \neg P(x)$, $\beta := \exists x(\neg P(x) \wedge \forall y(x \neq y \rightarrow P(y)))$, $\gamma := \exists x \forall y \neq x. \neg P(y)$. It is shown below, Example (4), that $\alpha \mid\sim \beta$ holds, by the arguments presented there, we also see that α does not entail $\neg\gamma$, as $< M, \mathcal{N} >$ with the universe $\{a,b\}$, $P(a)$, $\neg P(b)$, $\{a\} \in \mathcal{N}$ is minimal. But $\alpha \wedge \gamma$ does not entail β : Take $< M, \mathcal{N} >$ with the universe $\{a,b,c\}$, and $P(a)$, $\neg P(b)$, $\neg P(c)$, $\{a\} \in \mathcal{N}$. Changing one negative instance, e.g. b, into a positive one, while preserving the positive instance a leaves the models of $\alpha \wedge \gamma$, so this model is minimal, and β does not hold there. □

2.4 Examples

We conclude by discussing the examples presented in [2]. Note that, with exception of example (1), we consider theories with just one default, so $\prec$ and $\prec'$ coincide, and the results and arguments are often similar to those in [2]. In all cases, P and Q are unary predicates.
(1) $T := \{\nabla x P(x), \nabla x \neg P(x)\}$ is inconsistent.
(2) $T := \{\nabla P(x) : \neg P(x)\}$ is inconsistent too.
(3) $T := \{\nabla x P(x)\}$. Take $< M, \mathcal{N} > \models T$, so there is $A \in \mathcal{N}$ with $\forall x \in A.P(x)$. If $\exists x \neg P(x)$, then $< M', \mathcal{N} >$ with $P(x)$ for that x too, will be a better model. If $\forall x P(x)$, then $< M, \mathcal{N} >$ can't be improved, as we have no negative instances, so

Condition (3) in Definition 2.6 will not hold. So we can conclude $\forall x P(x)$, as this will hold in all $\prec$ – (or $\prec'$ –) best models.
(4) $T := \{\exists x \neg P(x), \nabla x P(x)\}$. Take $< M, \mathcal{N} > \models T$, so there is $A \in \mathcal{N}$ with $\forall x \in A.P(x)$. As we have one negative instance, and $\nabla x P(x) \rightarrow \exists x P(x)$, the universe of M has at least two elements. If we have two different x with $\neg P(x)$, we can improve, if not, we have just one negative instance. Turning that into a positive instance would force us to introduce a new negative instance so by Condition (2), the new model is not better than the old one. So the best models will all contain exactly one negative instance, we conclude that $\exists x(\neg P(x) \wedge \forall y(x \neq y \rightarrow P(y)))$ holds there.
(5) $T := \{\nabla x P(x)\} \cup \{\phi_{\geq n}[P] \rightarrow \phi_{n+1} : n \in \omega\}$. We can derive that all best models satisfy $\forall x P(x)$, and have an infinite universe.
(6) $T := \{\nabla x P(x)\} \cup \{\phi_n[\neg P] : n \in \omega\}$. There are no best models, but all sufficiently good models will contain an infinite set of positive instances.
(7) $T := \{\exists x P(x), \nabla P(x) : Q(x)\}$. $\exists x Q(x)$ will hold in all best models, which are those in which the extensions of P and Q coincide.
(8) $T := \{\neg P(b) \wedge \neg P(c), \nabla x P(x)\}$. In the best models $b = c$ will hold.

References

[1] F.Baader, B.Hollunder, "Embedding defaults into terminological knowledge representation formalisms", in Proceedings of the 3rd International Conference on Knowledge Representation and Reasoning, Cambridge, Mass., USA, 1992

[2] F.Baader, K.Schlechta, "A semantics for open normal defaults via a modified preferential approach", Research Report RR-93-13, Deutsches Forschungszentrum für Künstliche Intelligenz, Stuhlsatzenhausweg 3, D-66123 Saarbrücken, Germany, 1993

[3] C.Boutilier, "Conditional Logics of Normality as Modal Systems", AAAI 1990, Boston, p.594

[4] C.Boutilier, "Viewing Conditional Logics of Normality as Extensions of the Modal System S4", Toronto University, KRR-TR-90-4, June 1990

[5] C.Boutilier, "Conditional Logics for Default Reasoning and Belief Revision", Dept. of Comp. Sc., Univ. Brit. Columbia TR 92-1, Jan. 92, Vancouver, Canada

[6] G.Bossu, P.Siegel, "Saturation, Nonmonotonic Reasoning and the Closed-World Assumption", Artificial Intelligence 25 (1985) 13-63

[7] D.M.Gabbay, "Theoretical foundations for non-monotonic reasoning in expert systems". In: K.R.Apt (ed.), "Logics and Models of Concurrent Systems", Springer, Berlin, 1985, p.439-457

[8] B.Hansson: "An analysis of some deontic logics", Nous 3, 373-398. Reprinted in R.Hilpinen ed. "Deontic Logic: Introductory and Systematic Readings". Reidel, Dordrecht 1971, 121-147

[9] S.Kraus, D.Lehmann, M.Magidor, "Nonmonotonic reasoning, preferential models and cumulative logics", Artificial Intelligence, 44 (1-2), p.167-207, July 1990

[10] D.Lehmann, M.Magidor, "What does a conditional knowledge base entail?", Artificial Intelligence, 55(1), p. 1-60, May 1992

[11] D.Makinson, "Five Faces of Minimality", Studia Logica 52 (1993), p. 339-379

[12] D.Makinson, "General patterns in nonmonotonic reasoning", in D.Gabbay, C.Hogger, Robinson (eds.), "Handbook of Logic in Artificial Intelligence and Logic Programming", vol. III: "Nonmonotonic and Uncertain Reasoning", Oxford University Press, 1994, p. 35-110

[13] R.Reiter, "A logic for default reasoning", Artificial Intelligence 13 (1-2), p.81-132, 1980

[14] K.Schlechta, "Defaults as generalized quantifiers", to appear in Journal of Logic and Computation, Oxford (1994/95)

[15] K.Schlechta: "Some Results on Classical Preferential Models", Journal of Logic and Computation, Oxford, Vol.2, No.6 (1992), p. 675-686

[16] K.Schlechta: "Some Completeness Results for Stoppered and Ranked Classical Preferential Models", Research Report RR 15, 05/94, Laboratoire d'Informatique de Marseille, URA CNRS 1787, Université de Provence, 3 pl. Victor Hugo, F-13331 Marseille Cedex 3, France,

[17] K.Schlechta: "Preferential Choice Representation Theorems for Branching Time Structures" to appear in: Journal of Logic and Computation, Oxford (1994/95)

[18] K.Schlechta: "A Two-Stage Approach to First Order Default Reasoning" Research Report RR 36, 09/94, Laboratoire d'Informatique de Marseille, URA CNRS 1787, Université de Provence, 3 pl. Victor Hugo, F-13331 Marseille Cedex 3, France,

[19] Yoav Shoham: "A semantical approach to nonmonotonic logics". In Proc. Logics in Computer Science, p.275-279, Ithaca, N.Y., 1987

A Reduction of the Theory of Confirmation to the Notions of Distance and Measure

Karl Schlechta
Laboratoire d'Informatique de Marseille, URA CNRS 1787
CMI, Technopôle de Château-Gombert
F-13453 Marseille Cedex 13, France
ks@gyptis.univ-mrs.fr

Abstract

We present an analysis and formalization of confirmation of a theory through observation. The basic ideas are, first, to carry the results of single observations over to neighbouring cases by analogy, using an abstract distance relation as in the Stalnaker/Lewis semantics for counterfactual conditionals. A theory is then, in a second step, considered confirmed iff we have thus concluded positively for a "large" part of the universe - where "large" is interpreted by a weak filter. Formal semantics as well as sound and complete axiomatizations for the (trivial) first order and the propositional case are given.

1 Introduction

The basic idea The basic idea is to reason by analogy, taking the closest comparable cases as base. This can be expressed by the counterfactual conditional "observation carried out $\Rightarrow$ result corresponding to theory". (Philippe Besnard, Rennes, has pointed out to me that N.Goodman, see [1], had had this idea of expressing confirmation by counterfactuals too, before the advent of the Lewis/Stalnaker semantics (see e.g. [3], [11]). Our argument is, and was found, however, "one layer below" counterfactuals, and bases directly on the intuition of distance.) In a second step, we measure the quantity of cases thus directly or indirectly confirmed, and consider the theory itself to be confirmed, if a "large" number of cases have thus been confirmed, using our theory of "large" subsets, see [6]. Confirmation is thus tolerant to some exceptions.

Motivation and Context It was Popper's insight that usual scientific theories cannot be confirmed in the sense of classical logic: A (non-trivial) theory of the form $\forall x \phi$ can only be verified in the classical sense by examining an enormous amount of cases - many of which totally out of reach by distance and time. The domain of application of a theory of gravity, for instance, is the whole universe, at all moments of time. So, if there is a logic of confirmation, it cannot be classical logic. Yet scientific practice suggests that there is some such logic. We propose a combination of analogical and nonmonotonic reasoning, which seems to be an abstraction of some aspects of this successful scientific practice.

We start with a situation where some observations have been made: To take a classical example, some ravens have been observed and they turned out to be black. By analogical reasoning, we conclude that "nearby" ravens will (probably) be black too. "Nearby" can be read here geographically, in other cases, we will choose different relations of closeness. We thus base analogical reasoning on an underlying notion of distance, in parallel to the treatment of counterfacual conditionals in the Stalnaker/Lewis semantics. Finally, we consider a theory confirmed iff it is confirmed in a "large" number of cases, or in the "important" cases. A theory can thus be considered confirmed even in the presence of counterexamples, as scientific practice seems to permit (allowing for noisy data, future refinements of a theory etc.).

The standard abstraction in mathematics of a measure on a set X is a filter $\mathcal{F}(X)$ on X: $A \subseteq X$ is defined to be a large subset of X, iff $A \in \mathcal{F}(X)$. For various reasons, we have weakened this definition in [6] to that of an $\mathcal{N}$-system $\mathcal{N}(X)$ on X: If $A, B \in \mathcal{F}(X)$, then $A \cap B \in \mathcal{F}(X)$, we require only: If $A, B \in \mathcal{N}(X)$, then $A \cap B \neq \emptyset$. This seems to be the weakest reasonable abstraction of a system of "large" subsets of X.

We have introduced $\mathcal{N}$-systems as a semantics for nonmonotonic reasoning to cover a static aspect of "normality": If ϕ normally holds, it should really hold for a large number of cases. The corresponding syntactic operator is a generalized quantifier, in meaning between the classical two, introduced into the language of First Order Logic. The reader is referred to [6] for motivation and discussion.

From a methodological point of view, our argumentation is basically semantical. We do not pretend to formally reconstruct all aspects of the practice of confirmation of scientific theories. But we claim that our work is solid handcraft: We have constructed an intuitive semantics for confirmatory reasoning, created a formal semantics as abstraction thereof: a structure with distance relations and a weak filter, and developped a sound and complete formalism for reasoning about it.

Outline of the paper We first describe the type of theories we want to examine. Certain cases will be excluded, as they present unnecessary complications for a first approach, or are not really theories apt to confirmation by single cases.

We then prepare the logical framework by describing the kind of reasoning we want to be able to perform. In the formal part, we treat the first order case, and the - essentially - propositional case (with some quantifiers added). In the first case, there is nothing to show, as we can formulate conditionals in the first order framework through the underlying order. In the second case, we can use ideas and techniques from [6] and [7] to give a completeness proof, organized in several layers, in parallel to the definition of the language. En passant, we also give a new completeness result for preferential models with a (global) smallest element, as well as a new completeness proof for flat conditionals.

We conclude by discussing the Kraus/Lehmann/Magidor axioms, see [2], [4], in our framework and show that several crucial axioms cannot hold for very strong reasons.

Limitations of the approach It seems necessary to describe some restrictions and clear up some notions. This is done here in the first order framework, the treatment carries over to the propositional case without difficulties.
We work in a fixed universe U, for a language $\mathcal{L}$ which still needs some specifying, assume for the moment that it is the first order language, with a constant for each $a \in U$ - for simplicity to be denoted a too.
We are interested in theories which can be confirmed and disconfirmed locally. (1) A theory which is either always true or always false in our universe U shall not interest us. (2) A theory like $\exists x\phi(x)$ cannot be disconfirmed locally - unless the universe has only one element. (3) A theory like $\forall x\phi(x) \vee \forall x\neg\phi(x)$ cannot be falsified locally - we need to examine at least two elements.
Whereas theories described in (1) and (2) can be considered degenerate cases, (3) presents a more complicated situation, where the basic units of observation consist of more than one element. The formal development can also be carried out over such units (considering a relation of distance between pairs of elements etc.), but this is more complicated. Many "real life" theories will, however, express interdependencies between elements in the universe.
We turn these negative examples into positive - semantic - conditions: For simplicity, we consider "real" universal formulas of the type $\forall x\phi(x)$. (a) (Equivalence with $\forall\phi(x)$) For any interpretation I of $\mathcal{L}$ in to U, $\forall x\phi(x)$ holds in I iff all $\phi(a)$ hold in I. (b) (Independence of the $\phi(a)$) For an arbitrary truth assignment τ to the individual $\phi(a)'s$ there is an interpretation I_τ of $\mathcal{L}$ into U which respects it, i.e. I_τ makes $\phi(a)$ true iff τ assigned true to $\phi(a)$.
The above examples are excluded: (1) Choose I and I' making all $\phi(a)$ true or making at least one $\phi(a)$ false. (2) and (3) Choose for $a \in U$ I_a making all $\phi(b)$ true but for $b = a$.

The problem of observation We want to express: Wherever I have made a *relevant* observation, I found ravens to be black. We see an observation relevant to ϕ as a partition of truth (i.e. a set of mutually exclusive, consistent formulas ψ_i, whose disjunction is equivalent to truth), which permit to judge on ϕ, i.e. at least one of the $\psi_i's$ permits to deduce ϕ, and one $\neg\phi$.
It is like a scale from 0 to 10, one value has to hold, and I can say whether I have measured 5 or not. We further assume our observations to be correct. So I have really examined colour, and I found black, or red, or whatever. Some observations might be inconclusive, i.e. consistent with ϕ and $\neg\phi$, we just do as if we had not observed.

The intended type of reasoning We would like to conclude from evidence to hypotheses. Evidence shall be a formula describing a state of affairs at a point in the universe. A hypothesis shall essentially be a universally quantified formula. As we intend to pass via analogy, by a proximity relation, we express conditionals which permit to conclude from the state of affairs at $a_1 \ldots a_n$ to the state of affairs at a. It does not seem necessary here to treat nested conditionals, but boolean combinations of conditionals are desirable. We want to express that a property holds "almost everywhere", so we extend first order language by the generalized quantifier ∇ of [6]. We soften the conditions (i.e. ∇ instead of $\forall$) to tolerate exceptions, otherwise - as each element is closest to itself, in any reasonable notion of distance - a theory with one

counterexample could never be confirmed. We choose to apply ∇ after the conditional $\Rightarrow$, as a small set of counterexamples might have devastating effects on a theory: they might cover "strategic points" in the sense that there are many unobserved points close by.
So we want to say "had I made a ϕ-relevant observation at a, I would have found ϕ at a" in counterfactual terms, or, in more detail, and more intuitive too: "At the elements b closest to a, where I have made a ϕ-relevant observation, I have found $\phi(b)$". There is still a certain impreciseness there, because I am really speaking about $\phi(b)$-relevant observations. So, finally, we want to say: "At the elements b closest to a, where I have made a $\phi(b)$-relevant observation, I have found $\phi(b)$". We shall abbreviate this by $a \models (o_\phi \Rightarrow \phi)$ - the conditional evaluates to true at a.
Reasoning will then be e.g. of the form: If for all b $\phi(b) \rightarrow \psi(b)$, and, at the elements b closest to a, where I have made a $\phi(b)$-relevant observation, I have found $\phi(b)$, so I have $a \models (o_\phi \Rightarrow \phi)$, then I can conclude by analogy also to $\psi(a)$. (Note that in this argument, we use that any $\psi(b)$-negative observation will also be a $\phi(b)$-negative observation.)
To summarize: We have made a $\phi(a)$-relevant observation at some $a \in U$, we have found in some cases indeed $\phi(a)$, some were inconclusive, and some were counterexamples. We now use this evidence for reasoning by analogy, formally, we examine for which a $a \models (o_\phi \Rightarrow \phi)$ holds, and evidence supports ϕ iff $\nabla x.x \models (o_\phi \Rightarrow \phi)$ holds.

2 Definitions and Results

The First Order case is disappointing from the formal point of view: There is nothing to do! The propositional case is a little more interesting, but there is not much work to do either: We can largely use the ideas of [6] and [7] to construct a completeness result as wanted.

2.1 The first order case

Assume a first order language with a constant for each element of the universe, a generalized quantifier ∇ and a binary relation symbol $\prec_a$ for each element a to be given.
"$a \models \alpha \Rightarrow \beta$" can be expressed by the $\Rightarrow$-free formula $(\alpha(a) \wedge \beta(a)) \vee \neg\alpha(a) \wedge \forall x(\alpha(x) \wedge \neg\exists y(y \prec_a x \wedge \alpha(y)) \rightarrow \beta(x))$ - so no need to do any further work.
On the other hand, the fact that we can express finite cardinalities in First Order Logic (FOL) shows that we are not free to do all kinds of "bricolage" we might want to: In particular, we cannot multiply elements by making copies as is done abundantly e.g. in [7].
For the reader's convenience, we repeat the definitions and the main result of [6] - they will also be used (in slightly modified form) in the propositional case. On the semantic side, we formalize "large" subsets by a kind of weak filter, an $\mathcal{N}$-system. On the syntactic side, we introduce a new, generalized, quantifier, ∇, which should be read (approximatively) as "most". Soundness and completeness say that they correspond. For further motivation and discussion, the reader is referred to [6].

Definition 2.1 Call $\mathcal{N}(M) \subseteq \mathcal{P}(M)$ (= the powerset of M) a $\mathcal{N}$-system over M iff (a) $M \in \mathcal{N}(M)$, (b) $A \in \mathcal{N}(M)$, $A \subseteq B \subseteq M \rightarrow B \in \mathcal{N}(M)$, (c) $A, B \in \mathcal{N}(M) \rightarrow$

$A \cap B \neq \emptyset$ if $M \neq \emptyset$ (thus, $\emptyset \notin \mathcal{N}(M)$, if $M \neq \emptyset$). (Note that this is weaker than the corresponding axiom for filters.)

Definition 2.2 We augment the language of first order logic by the new quantifier ∇ : If ϕ and ψ are formulas, then so is $\nabla x\phi(x)$ for any variable x. (The results and definitions for the relativized version $\nabla x\phi(x) : \psi(x)$ are straightforward generalizations of the simple case, see [6] for details.)

Definition 2.3 Let $\mathcal{L}$ be a first order language, and M be a $\mathcal{L}-$*structure*. Let $\mathcal{N}(M)$ be a $\mathcal{N}$-system over M. Define $< M, \mathcal{N}(M) > \models \phi$ for any $\nabla - \mathcal{L}$-formula inductively as usual, with the additional induction step: $< M, \mathcal{N}(M) > \models \nabla x\phi(x)$ iff there is $A \in \mathcal{N}(M)$ s.th. $\forall a \in A$ ($< M, \mathcal{N}(M) > \models \phi[a]$).

Definition 2.4 Let any axiomatization of predicate calculus be given. Augment this with the axiom schemata (1) $\nabla x\phi(x) \wedge \forall x(\phi(x) \rightarrow \psi(x)) \rightarrow \nabla x\psi(x)$, (2) $\nabla x\phi(x) \rightarrow \neg\nabla x\neg\phi(x)$, (3) $\forall x\phi(x) \rightarrow \nabla x\phi(x) \rightarrow \exists x\phi(x)$, (4) $\nabla x\phi(x) \longleftrightarrow \nabla y\phi(y)$ if x does not occurr free in $\phi(y)$ and y does not occurr free in $\phi(x)$ (for all ϕ, ψ).

Theorem 2.1 The axioms given in Definition 2.4 are sound and complete for the semantics of Definition 2.3.

2.2 The (semi-) propositional case

We adapt our completeness results of [7] and [6] to counterfactuals.

(Very brief) outline of the proof: We first give a completeness result for theories without the generalized quantifier, and use for the full version the ∇-free consequences to construct a model by the first completeness result, on which we define a $\mathcal{N}$ -system, and show that in the full structure the full theory holds.
The first step uses largely ideas from [7], which need only a slight adaptation to account for the existence of a (global) smallest model. This is reflected by condition ($^{=}5$): Individial models correspond to consistent complete theories. So, en passant, we also find a new completeness result for another version of preferential reasoning. We use the result to treat flat counterfactual conditionals, the essential difference is that we work with single formulas, not with arbitrary theories. We thus have a new completeness proof for flat conditionals. The full proofs can be found in [9].
We work in a fragment of FOL with a generalized quantifier - in order to be able to do some reasoning. (What we really need is to differentiate e.g. between $\forall m(\phi \vee \psi)(m)$ and $(\forall m\phi(m)) \vee (\forall m\psi(m))$. Essentially, we can replace $\forall m\phi(m)$ by $R \vdash \phi$ and $\exists m\phi(m)$ by $Con(R, \phi)$ - where R is a classical background theory to be specified below.

Definition 2.5 Level 0: A classical propositional language. Level 1: Formulas of the type $m \models \alpha$ or $m \models \alpha \Rightarrow \beta$, where α and β are in Level 0, ($\Rightarrow$ expresses a conditional, and m, $\models$ have the usual meaning) and boolean combinations of such formulas. Level 2: Formulas of the type $\forall m\phi(m)$, $\exists m\phi(m)$, $\nabla m\phi(m)$, where $\phi(m)$ are of Level 1, and boolean combinations of such formulas.

For the definition of the ∇-semantics, we can take over almost all definitions and results of the first order case, with a slight modification of Definition 2.3.

Definition 2.6 Let $\mathcal{L}$ be a propositional language, M be a set of $\mathcal{L}-$*models*, and $< M, \{\prec_a : a \in M\} >$ be a structure for level 1 of the language, let $\mathcal{N}(M)$ be a $\mathcal{N}$ -system over M. Define $< M, \{\prec_a : a \in M\}, \mathcal{N}(M) > \models \nabla m\phi(m)$ with the additional induction step $< M, \{\prec_a : a \in M\}, \mathcal{N}(M) > \models \nabla x\phi(x)$ iff there is $A \in \mathcal{N}(M)$ s.t. $\forall a \in A\ (< M, \{\prec_a : a \in M\} > \models \phi[a])$

For the logic for ∇, we can take verbatim the above axioms, where FOL is suitably restricted.

Proposition 2.2 Let, for a language $\mathcal{L}, \mid\sim$ be a logic which is defined for some set $\mathcal{T}$ of $\mathcal{L}-$ theories, and $\vdash$ denote classical entailment. We abbreviate $\overline{\overline{T}} := \{\phi : T \mid\sim \phi\}$, and $\overline{T} := \{\phi : T \vdash \phi\}$. Let $R \subseteq S$ *be* $\mathcal{L}$-theories. Then there is a definability preserving classical preferential model $\mathcal{M}$ with smallest element $< m, i >$ with $m \models S$ and all points in M R-models, s.t. the logic $\mid\sim$ and the semantic entailment relation defined by the model coincide on $\mathcal{T}$, iff ($^=$1) $\overline{T \cup R} = \overline{T' \cup R} \rightarrow \overline{\overline{T}} = \overline{\overline{T'}}$, ($^=$2) $\overline{\overline{T}}$ is closed under the underlying logic, ($^=$3) $T \cup R \subseteq \overline{\overline{T}}$, ($^=$4) $\overline{T \cup R} \subseteq \overline{T' \cup R} \rightarrow \overline{\overline{T'}} \subseteq \overline{\overline{\overline{T}} \cup T' \cup R}$, ($^=$5) There is a consistent complete theory U with $S \subseteq \overline{U}$ s.th. $U \vdash T \rightarrow \overline{\overline{T}} = \overline{U}$ for all $T, T' \in \mathcal{T}$.

Corollary 2.3 The following axioms are sound and complete for flat conditionals (where $\Rightarrow$ expresses the counterfactual conditional):
(m1) $\forall m(m \models \phi \rightarrow ((\phi \Rightarrow \psi) \leftrightarrow \psi))$, (m2) $\forall m(m \models \psi \rightarrow \psi') \rightarrow \forall m(m \models (\phi \Rightarrow \psi) \rightarrow (\phi \Rightarrow \psi'))$, (m3) $\forall m(m \models (\phi \Rightarrow \psi) \wedge (\phi \Rightarrow \psi') \rightarrow (\phi \Rightarrow \psi \wedge \psi'))$, (m4) $\forall m(m \models \phi \leftrightarrow \phi') \rightarrow \forall m(m \models (\phi \Rightarrow \psi) \rightarrow (\phi' \Rightarrow \psi))$, (m5) $\forall m(m \models \phi \Rightarrow \phi)$, (m6) $\forall m(m \models (\phi' \wedge \phi \Rightarrow \psi) \rightarrow (\phi' \Rightarrow (\phi \rightarrow \psi)))$, where m ranges over all points in a fixed counterfactual conditional structure. (With, of course, the usual rules for $\models$: $m \models \phi \wedge \psi$ iff $m \models \phi$ and $m \models \psi$ etc.)

Theorem 2.4 The axioms given for ∇ and $\Rightarrow$, together with enough of FOL are sound and complete for our semantics.

3 Discussion

3.1 The Kraus/Lehmann/Magidor Axioms

Informal discussion: (For a discussion and motivation of these axioms, see [2], [4], and [5].) We read $\alpha \mid\sim \beta$ as follows: α is evidence and perhaps background theory, β is a hypothesis, $\alpha \mid\sim \beta$ says that evidence and background theory α confirm hypothesis β.
The KLM axioms Right Weakening, Reflexivity, and Left Logical Equivalence will always hold in an approach based on a semantics, whose base units consist of models of the underlying logic.
But already AND fails: Evidently, the same evidence can support many hypotheses. This is the reason why it is sometimes necessary to carry out an "experimentum crucis" deciding between hypotheses. But evidence will not support a contradiction, the conjunction of the two. This seems to be a deep reason. We should not hope that some logic generates for us from evidence - how feeble it might be - the ideal

hypothesis. Logic should have something to do with truths that hold in all possible situations, and a logic of confirmation should speak about hypotheses that can be reasonably upheld in the light of evidence; so it speaks about speculations about the nature of the universe at hand, which can be erroneous. The logic of confirmation should permit diverging hypotheses to be supported by the same evidence - but it should not support nonsense (a contradiction)!
Cautious Monotony fails for the same reason: Evidence might support two contradictory hypotheses, but adding one to the evidence as background theory should not permit to deduce the other!
OR fails in the presence of tolerated counterexamples. Let $e_i = e^+ \cup e_i^-$ be evidence supporting hypothesis h, with fixed positive evidence e^+, and varying negative evidence. Taking a (non-exclusive) or on the left hand side will add up all negative evidence - and in any finite reading one will arrive at the conclusion that there might be too many counterexamples.
Rational Monotony: As, in general, we can derive contradictory hypotheses, the axiom of rational monotony does not make much sense.

Formal discussion We work in the extended FOL. We fix a structure with its universe U, $\mathcal{N}$-system, and the orders $\prec_a$, $a \in U$, take some observations and look at the hypotheses which are confirmed by evidence and perhaps a background theory. Example 1: $U := \{a, b\}$ - the orders are trivial here - $\mathcal{N}(U) := \{U\}$, and consider an unary predicate p with $p(a)$ as evidence. Both $h := \forall x p(x)$ and $h' := \forall x(p(x) \leftrightarrow x = a)$ are confirmed by the evidence, but of course not their conjunction. Likewise, adding h to the evidence will disconfirm h'. Example 2: $U := \{a, b, c\}$, $\mathcal{N}(U) := \{X \subseteq U : card(X) \geq 2\}$ with a closest neighbour of both b and c. Assume a positive evidence for ϕ, b negative. Then $c \models o_\phi \Rightarrow \phi$, so ϕ is confirmed. If we take c instead of b as negative evidence, then $b \models o_\phi \Rightarrow \phi$, so ϕ is confirmed again. But taking a as positive, and both b and c as negative evidence will not confirm ϕ any more. So OR does not hold.

3.2 An extension:

One might have the feeling that some elements are too distant to count in any analogical reasoning. In trying to confirm that all ravens are black via the non-black non-ravens, we may feel that the tested non-black objects are too distant of some of the rest to conclude that they are non-ravens too. Thus, we may wish to add an unary predicate $d_a(x)$ for each element a, which expresses that x is too far away from a to count. Well-behaviour with $\prec_a$ will be needed: $d_a(x) \wedge (x \prec_a y) \rightarrow d_a(y)$. In the propositional case, d_a will of course just be a new propositional variable.

Acknowledgements Peter Flach, Tilburg, gave me through several articles and a talk given at a DRUMS meeting in fall 1994 at Malaga, Spain, the impression that some intuitive notions about induction should be clarified before trying a formatization. Both are attempted here.
An anonymous referee incited me to put in more explanation. I have tried to do so.

References

[1] N.Goodman, "Fact, Fiction, and Forecast", Harvard Univ. Press, 1955

[2] S.Kraus, D.Lehmann, M.Magidor, "Nonmonotonic reasoning, preferential models and cumulative logics", Artificial Intelligence, 44 (1-2), p.167-207, July 1990

[3] D.Lewis, "Counterfactuals", Harvard, Cambridge, Mass., USA, 1973

[4] D.Lehmann, M.Magidor, "What does a conditional knowledge base entail?", Artificial Intelligence, 55(1), p. 1-60, May 1992

[5] D.Makinson, "General patterns in nonmonotonic reasoning", in D.Gabbay, C.Hogger, Robinson (eds.), "Handbook of Logic in Artificial Intelligence and Logic Programming", vol. III: "Nonmonotonic and Uncertain Reasoning", Oxford University Press, 1994, p. 35-110

[6] K.Schlechta: "Defaults as Generalized Quantifiers", to appear in: Journal of Logic and Computation, Oxford (1994/95), also as Research Report RR 16, 05/94, Laboratoire d'Informatique de Marseille, URA CNRS 1787, Université de Provence, 3 pl. Victor Hugo, F-13331 Marseille Cedex 3, France

[7] K.Schlechta: "Some Results on Classical Preferential Models", Journal of Logic and Computation, Oxford, Vol.2, No.6 (1992), p. 675-686

[8] K.Schlechta: "Logic, Topology, and Integration", to appear in: Journal of Automated Reasoning, D.Reidel Publ. Company (1994/95)

[9] K.Schlechta: "A Reduction of the Theory of Confirmation to the Notions of Distance and Measure" Research Report RR 64, 12/94, Laboratoire d'Informatique de Marseille, URA CNRS 1787, Université de Provence, 3 pl. Victor Hugo, F-13331 Marseille Cedex 3, France

[10] K.Schlechta, D.Makinson: "Local and Global Metrics for the Semantics of Counterfactual Conditionals", Journal of Applied Non-Classical Logics, Hermes, Paris (1994)

[11] Stalnaker, "A theory of conditionals", in N.Rescher (ed.), "Studies in Logical Theory", Blackwell, Oxford, p. 98-112

Cluster-based Specification Techniques in Dempster-Shafer Theory*

Johan Schubert
Division of Information System Technology,
Department of Command and Control Warfare Technology,
National Defence Research Establishment,
S-172 90 Stockholm, SWEDEN
E-mail: schubert@sto.foa.se

Abstract. When reasoning with uncertainty there are many situations where evidences are not only uncertain but their propositions may also be weakly specified in the sense that it may not be certain to which event a proposition is referring. It is then crucial not to combine such evidences in the mistaken belief that they are referring to the same event. This situation would become manageable if the evidences could be clustered into subsets representing events that should be handled separately. In an earlier article we established within Dempster-Shafer theory a criterion function called the metaconflict function. With this criterion we can partition a set of evidences into subsets. Each subset representing a separate event. In this article we will not only find the most plausible subset for each piece of evidence, we will also find the plausibility for every subset that the evidence belongs to the subset. Also, when the number of subsets are uncertain we aim to find a posterior probability distribution regarding the number of subsets.

1 Introduction

In an earlier article [1] we derived a method, within the framework of Dempster-Shafer theory [2-3], to handle evidences that are weakly specified in the sense that it may not be certain to which of several possible events a proposition is referring. When reasoning with such evidences we must avoid combining evidences by mistake that refer to different events. The situation would become manageable if the evidences could be clustered into subsets representing events that should be handled separately. For this reason every proposition's action part must be supplemented with an event part describing to which event the proposition is referring. The event part may be more or less weakly specified dependent on the evidence.

An example from our earlier article illustrates the terminology:

Let us consider the burglaries of two bakers' shops at One and Two Baker Street, event 1 (E_1) and event 2 (E_2), i.e., the number of events is known to be two. One witness hands over an evidence, specific with respect to event, with the proposition: "The burglar at One Baker Street," event part: E_1, "was probably brown haired (B)," action part: B. A second anonymous witness hands over a nonspecific evidence with the proposition: "The burglar at Baker Street," event part: E_1, E_2, "might have been red haired (R)," action part: R. That is, for example:

---

*This paper is based on my Ph.D. thesis [6].

evidence 1:
proposition:
action part: B
event part: E_1
$m(B) = 0.8$
$m(\Theta) = 0.2$

evidence 2:
proposition:
action part: R
event part: E_1, E_2
$m(R) = 0.4$
$m(\Theta) = 0.6$

In this situation it is impossible to directly separate evidences based only on their proposition. Instead we will use the conflict between the propositions of two evidences as a probability that the two reports are referring to different events.

The general idea is this. If we receive evidences about several different and separate events and the evidences are mixed up, we want to sort the evidences according to which event they are referring to. Thus, we partition the set of all evidences χ into subsets where each subset refers to a particular event. In Figure 1 these subsets are denoted by χ_i and the conflict in χ_i is denoted by c_i. Here, thirteen evidences are partitioned into four subsets. When the number of subsets is uncertain there will also be a "domain conflict" c_0 which is a conflict between the current number

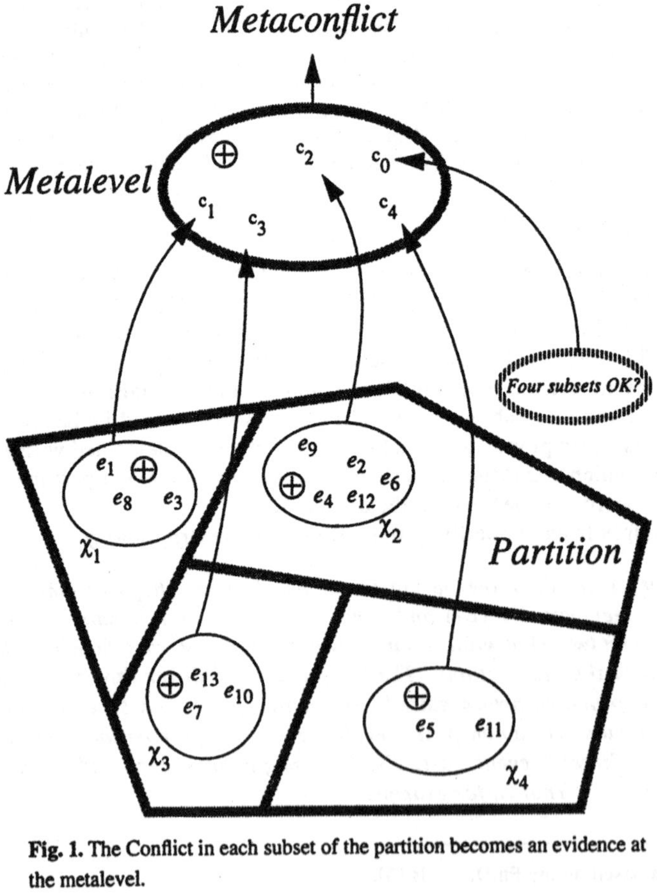

Fig. 1. The Conflict in each subset of the partition becomes an evidence at the metalevel.

of subsets and domain knowledge. The partition is then simply an allocation of all evidences to the different events. Since these events do not have anything to do with each other, we will analyze them separately.

Now, if it is uncertain to which event some evidence is referring we have a problem. It could then be impossible to know directly if two different evidences are referring to the same event. We do not know if we should put them into the same subset or not. This problem is then a problem of organization. Evidences from different problems that we want to analyze are unfortunately mixed up and we are having some problem separating them.

To solve this problem, we can use the conflict in Dempster's rule when all evidences within a subset are combined, as an indication of whether these evidences belong together. The higher this conflict is, the less credible that they belong together.

Let us create an additional piece of evidence for each subset where the proposition of this additional evidence states that this is not an "adequate partition". Let the proposition take a value equal to the conflict of the combination within the subset. These new evidences, one regarding each subset, reason about the partition of the original evidences. Just so we do not confuse them with the original evidences, let us call these evidences "metalevel evidences" and let us say that their combination and the analysis of that combination take place on the "metalevel", Figure 1.

In the combination of all metalevel evidences we only receive support stating that this is not an "adequate partition". We may call this support a "metaconflict". The smaller this support is, the more credible the partition. Thus, the most credible partition is the one that minimizes the metaconflict.

This methodology was intended for a multiple-target tracking algorithm in an anti-submarine intelligence analysis system [4]. In this application a sparse flow of intelligence reports arrives at the analysis system. These reports may originate from several different unconnected sensor systems. The reports carry a proposition about the occurrence of a submarine at a specified time and place, a probability of the truthfulness of the report and may contain additional information such as velocity, direction and type of submarine.

When there are several submarines we want to separate the intelligence reports into subsets according to which submarine they are referring to. We will then analyze the reports for each submarine separately. However, the intelligence reports are never labeled as to which submarine they are referring to. Thus, it is not possible to directly differentiate between two different submarines using two intelligence reports.

Instead we will use the conflict between the propositions of two intelligence reports as a probability that the two reports are referring to different submarines. This probability is the basis for separating intelligence reports into subsets.

The cause of the conflict can be non-firing sensors placed between the positions of the two reports, the required velocity to travel between the positions of the two reports at their respective times in relation to the assumed velocity of the submarines, etc.

2 Separating Nonspecific Evidence

In [1] we established a criterion function of overall conflict called the metaconflict function. With this criterion we can partition evidences with weakly specified propositions into subsets, each subset representing a separate event. We will use the minimizing of the metaconflict function as the method of partitioning the set of evidences into subsets. This method will also handle the situation when the number of events are uncertain.

An algorithm for minimizing the overall conflict was proposed. The proposed algorithm is based on the one hand on characteristics of the criterion function for varying number of subsets and on the other hand on an iterative optimization among partitionings of evidence for a fixed number of subsets.

The conflict in Dempster's rule measures the lack of compatibility between evidences. Since evidences referring to different events tend to be more incompatible than evidences referring to the same event, it is an obvious choice as a distance measure between evidences in a cluster algorithm.

We have a conflict between two pieces of evidence within the same subset in two different situations. First, we have a conflict if the proposition action parts are conflicting regardless of the proposition event parts since they are presumed to be referring to the same event. Secondly, if the proposition event parts are conflicting then, regardless of the proposition action parts, we have a conflict with the presumption that they are referring to the same event. The idea of using the conflict in Dempster's rule as distance measure between evidences was first suggested by Lowrance and Garvey [5].

The metaconflict used to partition the set of evidences is derived as the plausibility that the partitioning is correct when the conflict in each subset is viewed as a metalevel evidence against the partitioning of the set of evidences, χ, into the subsets, χ_i. We have a simple frame of discernment on the metalevel $\Theta = \{\mathrm{AdP}, \neg\mathrm{AdP}\}$, where AdP is short for "adequate partition", and a basic probability assignment (bpa) from each subset χ_i assigning support to a proposition against the partitioning:

$$m_{\chi_i}(\neg\mathrm{AdP}) \triangleq \mathrm{Conf}(\{e_j | e_j \in \chi_i\}),$$

$$m_{\chi_i}(\Theta) \triangleq 1 - \mathrm{Conf}(\{e_j | e_j \in \chi_i\})$$

where e_j is the jth evidence and $\{e_j | e_j \in \chi_i\}$ is the set of evidences belonging to subset χ_i and $\mathrm{Conf}(\cdot)$ is the conflict, k, in Dempster's rule. Also, we have a bpa concerning the domain resulting from a probability distribution about the number of subsets, E, conflicting with the actual current number of subsets, $\#\chi$. This bpa also assigns support to a proposition against the partitioning:

$$m_D(\neg\mathrm{AdP}) \triangleq \mathrm{Conf}(\{E, \#\chi\}),$$

$$m_D(\Theta) \triangleq 1 - \mathrm{Conf}(\{E, \#\chi\}).$$

The combination of these by Dempster's rule give us the following plausibility of the partitioning:

$$\mathrm{Pls}(\mathrm{AdP}) = (1 - m_D(\neg\mathrm{AdP})) \cdot \prod_{i=1} (1 - m_{\chi_i}(\neg\mathrm{AdP})).$$

Finding the most probable partitioning of evidences into disjoint subsets representing different events will then be the problem of maximizing the plausibility of possible partitionings, or the dual problem of minimizing one minus the plausibility. The difference, one minus the plausibility of a partitioning, will be called the metaconflict of the partitioning.

2.1 Metaconflict as a Criterion Function

Let E_i be a proposition that there are i subsets, $\Theta_E = \{E_0, ..., E_n\}$ a frame of domain propositions and $m(E_i)$ the support for proposition E_i.

The metaconflict function can then be defined as:

DEFINITION. *Let the* metaconflict function,

$$Mcf(r, e_1, e_2, ..., e_n) \triangleq 1 - (1 - c_0) \cdot \prod_{i=1}^{r} (1 - c_i),$$

be the conflict against a partitioning of n evidences of the set χ into r disjoint subsets χ_i. Here, c_i is the conflict in subset i and c_0,

$$c_0 = \sum_{i \neq r} m(E_i),$$

is the conflict between r subsets and propositions about possible different number of subsets.

Two theorems are derived to be used in the separation of the set of evidences into subsets by an iterative minimization of the metaconflict function. By using these theorems we are able to reason about the optimal estimate of the number of events, when the actual number of events may be uncertain, as well as the optimal partition of nonspecific evidence for any fixed number of events. These two theorems will also be useful in a process for specifying evidences by observing changes in the metaconflict when moving a single piece of evidences between different subsets.

THEOREM 1. *For all j with $j < r$, if $m(E_j) < m(E_r)$ then min $Mcf(r,e_1,e_2,...,e_n) <$ min $Mcf(j,e_1,e_2,...,e_n)$.*

This theorem states that an optimal partitioning for r subsets is always better than the other solutions with fewer than r subsets if the basic probability assignment for r subsets is greater than the basic probability assignment for the fewer subsets.

THEOREM 2. *For all j, if min $Mcf(r, e_1, e_2, ..., e_n) < \sum_{i \neq j} m(E_i)$ then min $Mcf(r,e_1,e_2,...,e_n) <$ min $Mcf(j,e_1,e_2,...,e_n)$.*

Theorem 2 states that an optimal partitioning for some number of subsets is always better than other solutions for any other number of subsets when the domain part of the metaconflict function is greater than the total metaconflict of the present partitioning.

For a fixed number of subsets a minimum of the metaconflict function can be found by an iterative optimization among partitionings of evidences into different subsets. This approach is proposed in order to avoid the combinatorial problem in minimizing the metaconflict function. In each step of the optimization the consequence of transferring an evidence from one subset to another is investigated.

The algorithm for finding the partitioning of evidences among subsets that minimizes the metaconflict is based on theorems 1 and 2 of the metaconflict function for finding the optimal number of subsets and an iterative optimization among partitionings of evidences for a fixed number of subsets. The iterative part of the algorithm guarantees, like all hill climbing algorithms, local but not global optimum.

3 Specifying Nonspecific Evidence

3.1 Evidences About Evidence

A conflict in a subset χ_i is interpreted as an evidence that there is at least one piece of evidence that does not belong to the subset;

$$m_{\chi_i}(\exists j.\, e_j \notin \chi_i) = c_i.$$

If an evidence e_q in χ_i is taken out from the subset the conflict c_i in χ_i decreases to c_i^*. This decrease $c_i - c_i^*$ is interpreted as an evidence indicating that e_q does not belong to χ_i, $m_{\Delta\chi_i}(e_q \notin \chi_i)$, and the remaining conflict c_i^* is an other evidence indicating that there is at least one other evidence e_j, $j \neq q$, that does not belong to χ_i - $\{e_q\}$,

$$m_{\chi_i - \{e_q\}}(\exists j \neq q.\, e_j \notin (\chi_i - \{e_q\})) = c_i^*.$$

The unknown bpa, $m_{\Delta\chi_i}(e_q \notin \chi_i)$, is derived by stating that the belief that there is at least one piece of evidence that does not belong to χ_i should be equal, no matter whether that belief is based on the original evidence $m_{\chi_i}(\exists j.\, e_j \notin \chi_i)$, before e_q is taken out from χ_i, or on a combination of the other two evidences $m_{\Delta\chi_i}(e_q \notin \chi_i)$ and $m_{\chi_i - \{e_q\}}(\exists j \neq q.\, e_j \notin (\chi_i - \{e_q\}))$, after e_q is taken out from χ_i, i.e.

$$\mathrm{Bel}_{\chi_i}(\exists j.\, e_j \notin \chi_i) = \mathrm{Bel}_{\Delta\chi_i \oplus (\chi_i - \{e_q\})}(\exists j.\, e_j \notin \chi_i).$$

where

$$\mathrm{Bel}_{\chi_i}(\exists j.\, e_j \notin \chi_i) = c_i$$

and

$$\mathrm{Bel}_{\Delta\chi_i \oplus (\chi_i - \{e_q\})}(\exists j.\, e_j \notin \chi_i) = c_i^* + m_{\Delta\chi_i}(e_q \notin \chi_i) \cdot [1 - c_i^*].$$

Thus, we have derived the evidence that e_q does not belong to χ_i from the variations in cluster conflict when e_q was taken out from χ_i:

$$m_{\Delta\chi_i}(e_q \notin \chi_i) = \frac{c_i - c_i^*}{1 - c_i^*}.$$

If e_q after it is taken out from χ_i is brought into another subset χ_k, its conflict will increase from c_k to c_k^*. The increase in conflict when e_q is brought into χ_k is interpreted as if there exists some evidence indicating that e_q does not belong to $\chi_k + \{e_q\}$, i.e.

$$\forall k \neq i . m_{\Delta\chi_k}(e_q \notin (\chi_k + \{e_q\})) = \frac{c_k^* - c_k}{1 - c_k}.$$

When we take out an evidence e_q from subset χ_i and move it to some other subset we might have a changes in domain conflict. The domain conflict is interpreted as an evidence that there exists at least one piece of evidence that does not belong to any of the n first subsets, $n = |\chi|$, or if that particular evidence was in a subset by itself, as an evidence that it belongs to one of the other n-1 subsets. This indicate that the number of subsets is incorrect.

When $|\chi_i| > 1$ we may not only put an evidence e_q that we have taken out from χ_i into another already existing subset, we may also put e_q into a new subset χ_{n+1} by itself. There is no change in the domain conflict when we take out e_q from χ_i since $|\chi_i| > 1$. However, we will get an increase in domain conflict from c_0 to c_0^* when we move e_q to χ_{n+1}. This increase is an evidence indicating that e_q does not belong to χ_{n+1}, i.e.

$$m_{\Delta\chi}(e_q \notin \chi_{n+1}) = \frac{c_0^* - c_0}{1 - c_0}.$$

We will also receive an evidence from domain conflict variations if e_q is in a subset χ_i by itself and moved from χ_i to another already existing subset. In this case we may get either an increase or decrease in domain conflict. First, if the domain conflict decreases $c_0^* < c_0$ when we move e_q out from χ_i this is interpreted as an evidence that e_q does not belongs to χ_i,

$$m_{\Delta\chi}(e_q \notin \chi_i) = \frac{c_0 - c_0^*}{1 - c_0^*}.$$

Secondly, if we observe an increase in domain conflict $c_0^* > c_0$ we will interpret this as a new type of evidence, supporting the case that e_q does belong to χ_i;

$$m_{\Delta\chi}(e_q \in \chi_i) = \frac{c_0}{c_0^*}.$$

3.2 Specifying Evidences

We may now make a partial specification of each piece of evidence. We combine all evidence from different subsets regarding a particular piece of evidence and calculate for each subset the belief and plausibility that this piece of evidence belongs to the subset. The belief in this will always be zero, with one exception, since every proposition states that our evidence does not belong to some subset. The exception is when our evidence is in a subset by itself and we receive an increase in domain conflict when it is moved to an other subset. That was interpreted as if there exists an evidence that our piece of evidence does belong to the subset where it is placed. We will then also have a nonzero belief in that our piece of evidence belongs to the subset.

For the case when e_q is in χ_i and $|\chi_i| > 1$ we receive, for example,

$$\forall k \neq n+1 . \mathrm{Pls}(e_q \in \chi_k) = \frac{1 - m(e_q \notin \chi_k)}{1 - \prod_{j=1}^{n+1} m(e_q \notin \chi_j)} .$$

In the combination of all evidences regarding our piece of evidence we may receive support for a proposition stating that it does not belong to any of the subsets and can not be put into a subset by itself. That proposition is false and its support is the conflict in Dempster's rule, and also an indication that the evidence might be false.

In a subsequent reasoning process we will discount evidences based on their degree of falsity. If we had no indication as to the possible falsity of the evidence we would take no action, but if there existed such an indication we would pay ever less regard to the evidence the higher the degree was that the evidence is false and pay no attention to the evidence when it is certainly false. This is done by discounting the evidence with one minus the support of the false proposition.

Also, it is apparent that some evidences, due to a partial specification of affiliation, might belong to one of several different subsets. Such a piece of evidence is not so useful and should not be allowed to strongly influence the subsequent reasoning process within a subset.

If we plan to use an evidence in the reasoning process of some subset, we must find a credibility that it belongs to the subset in question. An evidence that cannot possible belong to a subset has a credibility of zero and should be discounted entirely for that subset, while an evidence which cannot possibly belong to any other subset and is without any support whatsoever against this subset has a credibility of one and should not be discounted at all when used in the reasoning process for this subset. That is, the degree to which an evidence can belong to a subset and no other subset corresponds to the importance the evidence should be allowed to play in that subset.

Here we should note that each original piece of evidence regardless of in which subset it was placed can be used in the reasoning process of any subset that it belongs to with a plausibility above zero, given only that it is discounted to its credibility in belonging to the subset.

When we begin our subsequent reasoning process in each subset, it will naturally be of vital importance to know to which event the subset is referring. This information is obtainable when the evidences in the subset have been combined. After the combination, each focal element of the final bpa will in addition to supporting some proposition regarding an action also be referring to one or more events where the proposed action may have taken place. Instead of summing up support for each event and every subset separately, we bring the problem to the metalevel where we simultaneously reason about all subsets, i.e. which subsets are referring to which events. In this analysis we use our domain knowledge stating that no more than one subset may be referring to an event. From each subset we then have an evidence indicating which events it might be referring to. We combining all the evidence from all different subsets with the restriction that any intersection in the combination that assigns one event to two different subsets is false. This method has a much higher chance to give a clearly preferable answer regarding which events is represented by which subsets, than that of only viewing the evidences within a subset when trying to determine its event.

The extension in this article of the methodology to partition nonspecific evidence developed in the first article [1] imply that an evidence will now be handled similarly by the subsequent reasoning process in different subsets if these are of approximately equal plausibility for the evidence. Without this extension the most plausible subset would take the evidence as certainly belonging to the subset while the other subsets would never consider the evidence at all in their reasoning processes.

4 Deriving a Posterior Domain Probability Distribution

Here we aim to find a posterior probability distribution regarding the number of subsets by combining a given prior distribution with evidence regarding the number of subsets that we received from the evidence specifying process.

We use the idea that each single piece of evidence in a subset supports the existence of that subset to the degree that this evidence supports anything at all other than the entire frame. In the evidence specifying process of the previous article we discounted each single evidence m_q for its degree of falsity and its degree of credibility in belonging to the subset where it was placed, $m_q^{\%\%_i}$. For each subset separately, we now combine all evidence within a subset and the resulting evidence is the total support for that subset. Thus we have

$$m_{\chi_i}(\chi_i \in \chi) = 1 - \frac{1}{1-k} \cdot \prod_q m_q^{\%\%_i}(\Theta).$$

The degree to which the resulting evidence from this combination in its turn supports anything at all other than the entire frame, is then the degree to which all the evidence within the subset taken together supports the existence of this subset, i.e. that it is a nonempty subset that belongs to set of all subsets.

For every original piece of evidence we derived in the previous section an evidence with support for a proposition stating that this piece of evidence does not belong to the subset. If we have such support for every single piece of evidence in some subset, then this is also support that the subset is false. In that case none of the evidences that could belong to the subset actually did so and the subset was derived by mistake. Thus, we will discount the just derived evidence that support the existence of the subsets for this possibility.

Such discounted evidences $m_{\chi_i}^{\%}$ that support the existence of different subsets, one from each subset, are then combined. The resulting bpa $m_{\chi}^{\%}$ will have focal elements that are conjunctions of terms. Each term give support in that some particular subset belongs the set of all subsets, i.e. that it is a nonempty subset.

From this we can create a new bpa that is concerned with the question of how many subsets we have. This is done by exchanging each and every proposition in the previous bpa that is a conjunction of r terms for one proposition in the new bpa that is on the form $|\chi| \geq r$, where χ is the set of all subsets. The sum of support of all focal elements in the previous bpa that are conjunctions of length r is then awarded the focal element in the new bpa which supports the proposition that $|\chi| \geq r$;

$$m_\chi(|\chi| \geq r) = \sum_{\chi^* | |\chi^*| = r} m_\chi^{\%}((\ \wedge \chi^*) \in \chi),$$

where $\chi^* \in 2^\chi$ and $\chi = \{\chi_1, \chi_2, \ldots, \chi_n\}$.

A proposition in the new bpa is then a statement about the existence of a minimal number of subsets. Thus, where the previous bpa is concerned with the question of which subsets have support, the new bpa is concerned with the question of how many subsets are supported. This new bpa gives us some opinion that is based only on the evidence specifying process, about the probability of different numbers of subsets.

In order to obtain the sought-after posterior domain probability distribution we combine this newly created bpa that is concerned with the number of subsets with our prior domain probability distribution which was given to us in the problem specification.

Thus, by viewing each evidence in a subset as support for the existence of that subset we were able to derive a bpa, concerned with the question of how many subsets we have, which we could combine with our prior domain probability distribution in order to obtain the sought-after posterior domain probability distribution.

5 Conclusions

In this paper we have extended the methodology to partition nonspecific evidence developed in our previous article [1] to a methodology for specifying nonspecific evidence. This is in itself clearly an important extension in analysis, considering that an evidence will now in a subsequent reasoning process be handled similarly by different subsets if these are approximately equally plausible, whereas before the most plausible subset would take the evidence as certainly belonging to the subset while the other subsets would never consider the evidence in their reasoning processes.

We have also shown that it is possible to derive a posterior domain probability distribution from the reasoning process of specifying nonspecific evidence.

References

1. J. Schubert, On nonspecific evidence, *Int. J. Intell. Syst.* 8 (1993) 711-725.
2. A.P. Dempster, A generalization of Bayesian inference, *J. R. Stat. Soc. Ser. B* 30 (1968) 205-247.
3. G. Shafer, *A Mathematical Theory of Evidence*. Princeton University, Princeton, 1976.
4. U. Bergsten, and J. Schubert, Dempster's rule for evidence ordered in a complete directed acyclic graph, *Int. J. Approx. Reason.* 9 (1993) 37-73.
5. J.D. Lowrance and T.D. Garvey, Evidential Reasoning: An implementation for multisensor integration, Technical Note 307, SRI International, Menlo Park, CA, 1983.
6. J. Schubert, Cluster-based Specification Techniques in Dempster-Shafer Theory for an Evidential Intelligence Analysis of Multiple Target Tracks, Ph. D. Thesis, TRITA-NA-9410, Royal Institute of Technology, Stockholm, Sweden, 1994, ISBN 91-7170-801-4.

And/Or Trees for Knowledge Representation

Dr.Luminita State, Radu State, Graduate Student
Department of Mathematics and Computer Science
University of Bucharest,Romania

Abstract

Graph modelling is a modern branch of probability theory concerned with representations for the probability distributions as a product of functions of several variables as a base for possible ways to store high-dimensional distributions by means of a small number of parameters. During the last years, several attempts have been proposed as alternatives in solving this kind of problems [1]-[4]. In most of the practical applications of interest, dependency structures expressed in terms of probability distributions are too complex to allow convenable representations ; in such cases , a possible approach could be realised by approximating them keeping the computations at a certain level of complexity but at a convenable accuracy too.

The aim of the paper is to formulate an informational -based approach in decomposing probability distributions using tree-like structures . Our model will be stated in terms of features or actions meaning possible alternatives and their corresponding response effects.

Decision trees for knowledge representation

Throughout the paper we will accept the computation rules: 0/0=0 and 0log0=0. Also, all the probability distributions will be assumed to be finite.

Let $\Im = \{f_1, f_2, \ldots, f_m\}$ be a finite set of finite valued random elements defined on the probability space (Ω, Ξ, P). We will refer to the elements of $\Im$ as features. For any $f \in \Im$, we denote its range by $V(f)$, $V = \mathop{\times}\limits_{i=1}^{m} V(f)$

The meaning of the elements belonging to $\Im$ is that each $f \in \Im$ represents either a possible action in solving a certain problem or a measurement which can be taken or obtained through an observation process .

The concept of AND/OR DF-decision tree will be introduced as a basic structure for representing sequential processes where at each step , an unique feature has to be selected from the set of all available alternatives for the current state. The OR links represent the current available alternatives and each AND link corresponds to the connection between a selected feature and one of its possible values.

Definition 1. The structure $(T_0, \varphi, \Im)$ is an AND/OR DF-decision tree, if the following conditions hold:

1). T_0 is a AND/OR-directed rooted tree such that all even height nodes are of type OR and all nodes of odd height are AND type nodes. The root, denoted by r is considered as a OR-type node ; its height is by definition equal to 0.

2). The label function $\varphi : T_0 \setminus \{r\} \to \Im \cup \left(\bigcup_{i=1}^{m} V(f_i) \right)$ assigns to each node n $\in$ $T_0 \setminus \{r\}$ the label $\varphi(n)$, such that

a) if n is an AND-type , then $\varphi(n) \in \Im$

b) if n is an OR-type node, then $\varphi(n) \in V(\varphi(\overline{n}))$, where $\overline{n}$, is the parental node of n in T_0.

3). For any $n \in T_0$, all labels of the nodes belonging to the r-n path are pairwise different.

4). For any $n \in T_0$,

a) if n is an AND- type node, then od(n)= $|V(\varphi(n))|$

b) if n is an OR- type node, then od(n) $\in \{|\Gamma^+(n)|, 0\}$,

where od(n) stands for the outer degree of n and $\Gamma^+(n)$ is the set of features which do not appear as labels of the nodes belonging to the r-n path.

5). For any $n \in T_0$, the labels corresponding to its sons are pairwise different.

An AND/OR DF-decision tree allows us to represent different possible sequences of actions in solving a certain problem. According to Definition 1, it is possible that at the level of a certain node the process is stopped although some features are still available, but if a feature appears as a label of a node n, then all its values should be represented in T_0 as labels of the sons of n.

A particular trial is represented by a r-n path, where n is a terminal node of T_0; in each trial any feature can appear at most once.

We introduce the following notations:

For any $n \in T_0$,

- PP(n) is the r-n path in T_0. If n is an OR-type node, then PP(n)≡(n_0=r, n_1,...,n_{2k}=n), $\forall i, 1 \le i \le k,\ \ \varphi(n_{2i}) \in V(\varphi(n_{2i-1}))$, therefore, PP(n) can be represented as

PP(n)≡$\{f_1 = f_1', \dots, f_k = f_k'\}$, where $\forall i, 1 \le i \le k,\ \ f_i = \varphi(n_{2i-1}),\ f_i' = \varphi(n_{2i})$

- $\Gamma^-(n) = \{f \mid f \in \mathfrak{I}, \exists m \in PP(n), f = \varphi(m)\}$, $\Gamma^+(n) = \mathfrak{I} \setminus \Gamma^-(n)$. Hence $\Gamma^-(n)$, $\Gamma^+(n)$ are the sets of features which are "already considered" and respectively "still available" at the level of n
- δT_0 is the set on terminal nodes of T_0; obviously, all nodes of δT_0 are OR-type nodes.

Definition 2. An AND/OR DF-decision tree is complete, if for any $n \in \delta T_0$, $\Gamma^+(n) = \emptyset$.

Note that a complete AND/OR DF-decision tree could be seen as a map to represent all possible attempts solve a certain problem. In order to represent only a particular sequence of actions to solve the given problem we define the SF-decision tree structure .

Definition 3. Let $(T_0, \varphi, \mathfrak{I})$ be an AND/OR DF-decision tree.

The structure $(T, \overline{\varphi}, \mathfrak{I})$ is a SF-decision tree if the following conditions hold:

ι) T is a subtree of T_0 rooted in r,

ιι) $\overline{\varphi} = \varphi|_{T \setminus \{r\}}$

ιιι) For any n, non-terminal node of T,

a) if n is an OR -type node then , an unique son of n in T_0 belongs to T

b) if n is an AND-type node, then all its successors in T_0 belong to T

In order to simplify the notation, we will write φ instead of $\overline{\varphi}$.

Let Q be a probability distribution on V, and $(T_0, \varphi, \mathfrak{I})$ an AND/OR DF-decision tree. Then, each SF-decision tree corresponds to a possible decomposition of Q in the framework of $(T_0, \varphi, \mathfrak{I})$. For any OR-type node, such that $Q(PP(n)) \neq 0$, let $Q(\cdot \mid PP(n))$ be the conditional probability distribution on V:

$$\forall (f_1',\dots,f_m') \in V,\ Q((f_1',\dots,f_m') | PP(n)) = \begin{cases} 0, \exists p,k, 1 \le k \le j, 1 \le p \le m, h_k = f_p, h_k' \ne f_p' \\ \dfrac{Q((f_1',\dots,f_m'))}{Q(PP(n))}, \text{otherwise} \end{cases}$$

where $PP(n) = (h_1 = h_1',\dots,h_j = h_j')$ whe

To simplify the notation we assume $h_k = f_k, 1 \le k \le j$; also, we will write $Q(f_1 = f_1',\dots,f_m = f_m')$ instead of $Q((f_1',\dots,f_m'))$

Note that for any OR-type node n such that $Q(PP(n)) \ne 0, \Gamma^+(n) \ne \varnothing, Q(\cdot | PP(n))$ iisofa probability distribution on $\mathop{\times}\limits_{i=j+1}^{m} V(f_i)$. For any g $\in \Gamma^+(n)$, we denote by $Q(g | PP(n))$ the marginal of $Q(\cdot | PP(n))$ with respect to the feature g.

If $(T,\varphi,\mathfrak{I})$ is a SF-decision tree, and Q is a probability distribution on V, then we say that $(T,\varphi,\mathfrak{I})$ is a solution tree for Q. Let $(T,\varphi,\mathfrak{I})$ be a solution tree for Q. Then, for any n $\in \delta T$, $Q(PP(n))$ represents the Q-probabilistic mass along the path PP(n), that is at the end of the process consisting of the sequence of actions given by the features appearing as labels of the OR-nodes in PP(n), the corresponding values being given by the labels of the AND-sons. Therefore, $Q(\cdot | PP(n))$ represents the probabilistic mass still available in the process represented by PP(n). For soundness sake with respect to Q, we will assume in the following that the basic AND/OR DF-decision tree $(T_0,\varphi,\mathfrak{I})$ is such that for any n $\in \delta T_0$, $Q(PP(n)) \ne 0$.

Since $Q(\cdot | PP(n))$ is the "still not-explained" component of Q , according to the maximum entropy principle, along each PP(n), $Q(\cdot | PP(n))$ can be estimated by the product of its marginals. Therefore, for given a solution tree $(T,\varphi,\mathfrak{I})$,a global approximation for Q could be obtained by combining the local components of Q explained by $(T,\varphi,\mathfrak{I})$ to the local maximum entropy approximations of the not yet-explained components.

Definition 4. Let $(T,\varphi,\mathfrak{I})$ be a solution tree for the probability distribution Q. The function Q_T defined by:

$$Q_T = \sum_{n \in \delta T} Q(PP(n)) \prod_{g \in \Gamma^+(N)} Q(g | PP(n))$$

is called the ST-representation of Q .

The following results can be derived without difficulty:

Lemma 1. If $(T,\varphi,\mathfrak{I})$ is a solution tree for Q, then {Q(PP(n)),n $\in$ δT} is a probability distribution and Q_T is a probability distribution on V.

Lemma 2. If $(T,\varphi,\mathfrak{I})$ is a solution tree for Q , then for any n $\in$ δT, Q(PP(n)) = Q_T(PP(n)).

Corollary 1 If $(T,\varphi,\mathfrak{I})$ is a solution tree for Q, then Q and Q_T induce the same probability distribution on the set of all root-terminal node paths of T.

Corollary 2. Let $(T,\varphi,\Im)$ be a solution tree for Q ; then for any $(f_1',\ldots,f_m')\in V$,
$$Q(f_1=f_1',\ldots,f_m=f_m')=\sum_{n\in\delta T}Q(PP(n))Q(f_1=f_1',\ldots,f_m=f_m'\mid PP(n))$$

The quality or the potential of a certain SF-decision tree to approximate a given probability distribution Q will be expressed in terms of the Kullback-Leibler divergence of Q_T with respect to Q.

Definition 5. Let $\tau=(T,\varphi,\Im)$ be a SF-decision tree. The probability distribution Q on V is τ-representable, if $Q=Q_T$.

Let $(T_0,\varphi,\Im)$ be an AND/OR DF-decision tree and Q a probability distribution on V . We denote by τ^* its set of SF-decision trees. We would like to identify one of the best representations of Q in terms of Kullback-Leibler divergence, that is to find a solution tree $\tau=(T,\varphi,\Im)$ such that
$$K(Q,Q_T)=\min\{K(Q,Q_{T'})\mid\tau\in\tau^*,\tau=(T,\varphi,\Im)\}$$

Optimal Kullback-Leibler solution trees

Let $(T,\varphi,\Im)$ be a solution tree for the probability distribution Q such that for any $n\in\delta T$, $Q(PP(n))\neq 0$

The local disagreement between Q and Q_T at the level of $n\in\delta T$, denoted $K(Q,Q_T\mid PP(n))$ is defined by,
$$K(Q,Q_T\mid PP(n))=\begin{cases}0, & \Gamma^+(n)=\varnothing\\ \displaystyle\sum_{(g_1',\ldots,g_r')\in\times_{k=1}^{r}V(g_k)}Q(g_1=g_1',\ldots,g_r=g_r'\mid PP(n))\ln\frac{Q(g_1=g_1',\ldots,g_r=g_r'\mid PP(n))}{\prod_{j=1}^{r}Q(g_j=g_j'\mid PP(n))}, & \Gamma^+(n)=\{g_1,\ldots,g_r\}\end{cases}$$

Theorem 1. If $(T,\varphi,\Im)$ is a solution tree for the probability distribution Q, then the Kullback-Leibler divergence between Q_T and Q is the expectation of local Kullback-Leibler disagreements with respect to the probability distribution induced by Q on the set of root-terminal paths of T, that is,
$$K(Q,Q_T)=\sum_{n\in\delta T}Q(PP(n))K(Q,Q_T\mid PP(n))$$

For a given solution tree, the still available features at the level of each non-finished terminal node n can be considered as potential candidates to extend the given tree, in case a refinement in representing Q is intended. The following results supply possible ways to evaluate the amount of improvement if such extensions are performed.

Theorem 2. Let $\tau=(T,\varphi,\Im)$ be a solution tree for Q and n a non-terminal , OR-type node of T . If n' is the son of n in T, $\varphi(n')=g$, then for each $g'\in V(g)$ we denote by n(g') the son of n' labelled by g'. Then,
$$K(Q,Q_T\mid PP(n))\geq\sum_{g'\in V(g)}Q(g=g'\mid PP(n))K(Q,Q_T\mid PP(n(g')))$$

Suppose that $g=g_1$. Note that since the difference can be written as
$$\sum_{g'\in V(g)}Q(g=g'\mid PP(n))K(Q,Q_T\mid PP(n(g')))-K(Q,Q_T\mid PP(n))=$$

$$\sum_{i=2}^{r}\sum_{g_1'\in V(g_1)} Q(g_1=g_1'|PP(n)) \sum_{g_i'\in V(g_i)} Q(g_i=g_i'|PP(n)) \ln\frac{Q(g_i=g_i'|PP(n))}{Q(g_i=g_i'|PP(n(g_1')))}$$

therefore, in theorem 1 the equality holds if and only if the feature g_1 is such that

$$\forall g' \in V(g_1), \forall g_i \in \Gamma^+(n)\setminus\{g_1\},\quad Q(g_i=g_i'|PP(n)) = Q(g_i=g_i'|PP(n(g_1')))$$

We also get,

$$Q(PP(n))K(Q,Q_T|PP(n)) \geq \sum_{g_1'\in V(g_1)} Q(PP(n(g_1')))K(Q,Q_T|PP(n(g_1')))$$

hence, extending the already generated solution tree, the mean of the Kullback-Leibler distances is decreased.

Definition 6. Let $\tau=(T,\varphi,\Im)$ be a SF-decision tree, n∈ δT and g ∈ $\Gamma^+(n)$, k=| V(g) |. The SF-tree $\tau'=(T',\varphi',\Im)$ is the extension of ST at the level of n according to the decision g if the following conditions hold:

1. $T' = T\cup\{n',n_1,\dots,n_k\},\quad n',n_1,\dots,n_k \notin T$
2. $\varphi'|_T = \varphi$
3. **any pair of nodes belonging to T have the same connection in T' as in T,**
4. **n' is an AND- type node, its parental node in T' is n,$\varphi'(n')=g$**
5. **$n_1,\dots,n_k$ are the sons of n' in T'; all of them are OR-type nodes**
6. $\varphi'(n_i)=g^{(i)}, i=1,\dots,k,$ **where** $V(g)=\{g^{(1)},\dots,g^{(k)}\}$

To simplify the notation, we will write φ instead of φ'.

Obviously, the extension of any solution tree for the probability distribution Q is also a solution tree for Q.

Theorem 3. Let $\tau=(T,\varphi,\Im)$ a solution tree for the probability distribution Q and $\tau'=(T',\varphi',\Im)$ one of its extensions. Then, $K(Q,Q_T)\geq K(Q,Q_{T'})$

For a given probability distribution Q, we could determine an optimal Kullback-Leibler solution tree for Q, by simulating a search in the space represented by the full AND/OR DF-decision tree. Starting with a tree consisting of an unique node which is the root, at each step, the best terminal node n of the current solution tree and the best feature f still available for that node, will be selected, and the expansion of the current tree at the level of n according to f is obtained as the new current solution tree.

Let $\tau=(T,\varphi,\Im)$ be a solution tree for Q; and the function $\xi:\delta T\times\Im\to\Re$ defined by,

$$\xi(n,f)=\begin{cases} 0,\ f\in\Gamma^-(n), or\ n\in\delta T_0 \\ Q(PP(n))K(Q,Q_T|PP(n)) - \sum_{f'\in V(f)} Q(PP(n)\cup\{f=f'\}) \\ K(Q,Q_T|PP(n)\cup\{f=f'\}),\ otherwise \end{cases}$$

For any $n\in\delta T, f\in\Im$, $\xi(n,f)$ is a measure of the value of f in the solution tree $\tau=(T,\varphi,\Im)$ at the level of the terminal node n.

By direct computations, it can be proved that for any $n\in\delta T, f\in\Gamma^+(n)$,

$$\xi(n,f)=Q(PP(n))\left\{K(Q,Q_T|PP(n))-\sum_{f'\in V(f)}Q(f=f'|PP(n))K(Q,Q_T|PP(n)\cup\{f=f'\})\right\}$$

Therefore, in order to get the best expansion of a given solution tree $(T,\varphi,\Im)$, the terminal node to be expanded and the right alternative for it are selected according to the criterion : select n Î dT and $f\in\Gamma^+(n)$ such that $\xi(n,f)=\max\{\xi(\bar n,\bar f)|\bar n\in\delta T,\bar f\in\Gamma^+(\bar n)\}$

Depending on the particular problem we could desire to stop the decomposition process according to some prespecified conditions. Let C be the particular stopping condition; the decomposition process continues while C is false. Being given the probability distribution Q, the search for an optimal Kullback-Leibler solution tree can be described as follows:

1. Generate the tree $T=\{r,n_1,\dots,n_m\}$ where r is the root (OR-type node) and n_i, $1\le i\le m$ are its sons, all of them being AND-type nodes. For the AND-type nodes the labels are such that $\Im=\{\varphi(n_1),\dots,\varphi(n_m)\}$, where $|\Im|=m$;

2. For each n_i, $1\le i\le m$, $\varphi(n_i)=f_i$ if $k=|V(f_i)|$ then generate k new OR-type nodes $n_{i1},\dots,n_{ik}$ and to each n_{ij}, $1\le j\le k$, assign as label one of the values of f_i ; $V(f_i)=\{\varphi(n_{i1}),\dots,\varphi(n_{ik})\}$. Attach the new generated nodes as sons of n_i in T;

3. For each $n\in\delta T$, determine the best feature $f(n)\in\Gamma^+(n)$,i.e.

$$\sum_{f'\in V(f(n))}K(Q,Q_T|PP(n)\cup\{f(n)=f'\})Q(f(n)=f'|PP(n))=$$

$$\min_{f\in\Gamma^+(n)}\sum_{f'\in V(f)}K(Q,Q_T|PP(n)\cup\{f=f'\})Q(f=f'|PP(n))=$$

APPENDIX

Proof of Theorem 1:

Since $K(Q,Q_T)=\sum_{(f_1',\dots,f_m')\in\times_{j=1}^{m}V(f_j)}Q(f_1=f_1',\dots,f_m=f_m')\ln\frac{Q(f_1=f_1',\dots,f_m=f_m')}{Q_T(f_1=f_1',\dots,f_m=f_m')}$,

using the already established relations, we get,

$$K(Q,Q_T)=\sum_{n\in\delta T}Q(PP(n))\sum_{(f_1',\dots,f_m')\in\times_{j=1}^{m}V(f_j)}Q(f_1=f_1',\dots,f_m=f_m'|PP(n))$$

$$\ln\frac{Q(f_1=f_1',\dots,f_m=f_m'|PP(n))}{\prod_{g\in\Gamma^+(n)}Q(g=g'|PP(n))}=\sum_{n\in\delta T}Q(PP(n))K(Q,Q_T|PP(n))$$

Proof of Theorem 2:

If $PP(n)=\{f_1=f_1',\dots,f_j=f_j'\}$, $\Gamma^+(n)=\{g_1,\dots,g_r\}$, then

$$K(Q,Q_T|PP(n))=\sum_{(g_1',\dots,g_r')\in\times_{j=1}^{r}V(g_j)}Q(g_1=g_1',\dots,g_r=g_r'|f_1=f_1',\dots,f_j=f_j')$$

$$\ln\frac{Q(g_1=g_1',\dots,g_r=g_r'|f_1=f_1',\dots,f_j=f_j')}{\prod_{k=1}^{r}Q(g_k=g_k'|f_1=f_1',\dots,f_j=f_j')}=$$

$$\sum_{(g_1',\dots,g_r')\in \times_{j=1}^{r} V(g_j)} Q\left(g_2=g_2',\dots,g_r=g_r' \mid g_1=g_1', f_1=f_1',\dots,f_j=f_j'\right)$$

$$Q\left(g_1=g_{1r}' \mid f_1=f_1',\dots,f_j=f_j'\right)\ln\frac{Q\left(g_2=g_2',\dots,g_r=g_r' \mid g_1=g_1', f_1=f_1',\dots,f_j=f_j'\right)}{\prod_{k=1}^{r} Q\left(g_k=g_k' \mid f_1=f_1',\dots,f_j=f_j'\right)}=$$

$$\sum_{g_1'\in V(g_1)} Q\left(g_1=g_1' \mid f_1=f_1',\dots,f_j=f_j'\right)K\left(Q,Q_T \mid PP\left(n\left(g_1'\right)\right)\right)-$$

$$\sum_{g_1'\in V(g_1)} Q\left(g_1=g_1' \mid f_1=f_1',\dots,f_j=f_j'\right)$$

$$\sum_{i=2}^{r}\sum_{g_i'\in V(g_i)} Q\left(g_i=g_{ir}' \mid g_1=g_1', f_1=f_1',\dots,f_j=f_j'\right)\ln Q\left(g_i=g_{ir}' \mid g_1=g_1', f_1=f_1',\dots,f_j=f_j'\right)$$

Therefore, if g= g_1 then,

$$K\left(Q,Q_T \mid PP(n)\right)-\sum_{g_1'\in V(g_1)} Q\left(g_1=g_1' \mid f_1=f_1',\dots,f_j=f_j'\right)K\left(Q,Q_T \mid PP\left(n\left(g_1'\right)\right)\right)=$$

$$-\sum_{g_1'\in V(g_1)} Q\left(g_1=g_1' \mid PP(n)\right)\sum_{i=2}^{r}\sum_{g_i'\in V(g_i)} Q\left(g_i=g_i' \mid PP\left(n\left(g_1'\right)\right)\right)\ln Q\left(g_i=g_i' \mid PP(n)\right)\geq 0$$

Proof of Theorem 3

Let $n\in\delta T, g_1\in\Gamma^+(n)$ **such that the extension of** τ **is according to** (n,g_1). **Assume that** $|V(g_1)|=k,\ T'=\{n',n_1,\dots,n_k\},\ \varphi(n')=g_1,\ V(g_1)=\{\varphi(n_1),\dots,\varphi(n_k)\}$.

Obviously, for $\bar{n}\in\delta T\cap\delta T'$, $K\left(Q,Q_T \mid PP(\bar{n})\right)=K\left(Q,Q_{T'} \mid PP(\bar{n})\right)$

Therefore,

$$K\left(Q,Q_T\right)-K\left(Q,Q_{T'}\right)=Q\left(PP(n)\right)K\left(Q,Q_T \mid PP(n)\right)-$$

$$\sum_{g_1'\in V(g_1)} Q\left(PP(n)\cup\{g_1=g'\}\right)K\left(Q,Q_{T'} \mid PP(n)\cup\{g_1=g'\}\right)$$

from which, using the result given by theorem 2, we get $K\left(Q,Q_T\right)\geq K\left(Q,Q_{T'}\right)$

REFERENCES

[1] Jirousek R. "Decision Trees and their power to represent probability distributions" Workshop on Uncertainty Processing in Expert Systems, September 1991, Alsovice, Czechoslovakia

[2] Jirousek R. " Simple Approximations of Probability Distributions by Graph Models" IPMU'92, Palma de Mallorca, July 1992

[3] Jirousek R. " Solution of the Marginal Problem and Decomposable Distributions" Kybernetika, vol.20 (1991),no.5

[4] Pearl J. " Probabilistic Reasoning in Intelligent Systems: Networks of Plausible Inference" Morgan Kaufmann Publ.Inc. 1989

[5] Gallager R.G. " Information Theory and Reliable Communication" John Wiley& Sons, Inc. ,1968

Why Defeasible Deontic Logic needs a Multi Preference Semantics*

Yao-Hua Tan[1] and Leendert W.N. van der Torre[1,2]

[1] EURIDIS
Erasmus University Rotterdam
P.O. Box 1738, 3000 DR Rotterdam, The Netherlands
{ytan,ltorre}@euridis.fbk.eur.nl
[2] Tinbergen Institute and Department of Computer Science
Erasmus University Rotterdam
P.O. Box 1738, 3000 DR Rotterdam, The Netherlands

Abstract. There is a fundamental difference between a conditional obligation being violated by a fact, and a conditional obligation being overridden by another conditional obligation. In this paper we analyze this difference in the multi preference semantics of our defeasible deontic logic DEFDIODE. The semantics contains one preference relation for ideality, which can be used to formalize deontic paradoxes like the Chisholm and Forrester paradoxes, and another preference relation for normality, which can be used to formalize exceptions. The interference of the two preference orderings generates new questions about preferential semantics.

1 Introduction

In recent years deontic logics has become increasingly popular as a tool to model legal reasoning in expert systems [7, 10]. Deontic logic is a modal logic in which the modal operator O is used to express that something is obliged, see [2]. For example, if the proposition i stands for the fact that you insult someone, then $O(\neg i)$ means that you should not insult someone. The sentence $O(\neg i) \wedge i$ is consistent and expresses that the obligation not to insult someone is violated by the fact i that you insult someone. The most well-known deontic logic is so-called 'standard' deontic logic (SDL), a normal modal system of type KD according to the Chellas classification [2]. It satisfies, besides the propositional tautologies and the inference rules modus ponens $\frac{p, p \rightarrow q}{q}$ and necessitation $\frac{\vdash p}{\vdash O(p)}$, the axioms K: $O(p) \wedge O(p \rightarrow q) \rightarrow O(q)$ and D: $\neg(O(p) \wedge O(\neg p))$.

It is well-known that defeasible reasoning is a very important aspect of legal reasoning (see [6, 11]). In this paper we argue that in case of defeasible deontic logic, one needs two preference orderings in the semantics of such a logic. In a defeasible deontic logic, two kinds of defeasibility can be distinguished, so-called *factual defeasibility* and *overridden defeasibility*, see [16] for an analysis in terms of inference patterns. Factual defeasibility can be used to represent that an obligation is *overshadowed by a violating fact* and overridden defeasibility can be used to represent that an obligation is *cancelled*

* This research was partially supported by the ESPRIT III Basic Research Project No.6156 DRUMS II and the ESPRIT III Basic Research Working Group No.8319 MODELAGE.

by another obligation. The semantics contains a preferential ordering to model the deontic aspects and another ordering to model the normality aspects, which are used to model exceptional circumstances. Interestingly, it appears that these preference orderings interfere in a complicated way, thus generating new and interesting questions about preferential semantics.[3]

In this paper we use DEFDIODE to analyze the interference between the two preferential orderings. In DEFDIODE, the preferential orderings are very simple (they are subset orderings, defined on abnormality predicates). These orderings do not model all the subtleties of the individual orderings (see [8] for a detailed description of the subtle distinctions), but they are sufficient to analyze the interference problems. We will illustrate the interference of the two orderings by a simple example. In this example there is a situation which can be considered as a kind of overshadowing and as a kind of cancelling. The semantics clearly show that, in this example, overshadowing is preferred over cancelling.

2 DIODE

Three decades ago, Chisholm described in [3] a notorious paradox of deontic logic, the so-called Chisholm Paradox, which has led to the development of new deontic logics that were meant to solve the Chisholm paradox (see [2]). Two decades later, Forrester described in [4] his version of the paradox, the so-called Forrester paradox, which could not be solved by any of these new deontic logics. A set of sentences is called a paradox of a deontic logic when the (most obvious) formalization in the deontic logic is inconsistent. In [14] we introduced DIODE; a DIagnostic framework for DEontic reasoning. In these papers we showed how one can solve certain aspects of the Chisholm and Forrester paradoxes in DIODE. From a semantic point of view one could say that in DIODE the deontic modal operator is replaced by a preferential semantics as this was initially developed for conditional and non-monotonic logics. In this section, the details of this semantics will be explained.

The basic idea of DIODE is to translate a conditional obligation 'if α is the case, then it ought to be that β is the case' into the propositional formula $\alpha \wedge \neg V_i \rightarrow \beta$.[4] V_i is a propositional constant denoting whether the obligation is violated; the conditional obligation can be read as 'if α is the case and the obligation is not violated then β is the case'. For example, the obligation not to insult someone is formalized in DIODE by $\neg V_1 \rightarrow \neg i$ where i stands for insulting someone.

Let L be a propositional logic. L_V is L extended with (a finite number of) violation constants V_i. We write $\models$ for entailment in L_V. A deontic theory T of L_V consists of a set of factual sentences of L (denoted by the set F in Figure 1), a set of background knowledge sentences of L and a set of absolute and conditional obligations (deontic rules) of L_V, typically given by $\neg V_i \rightarrow \beta$ or $\alpha \wedge \neg V_i \rightarrow \beta$ with $\alpha, \beta \in L$. Every distinct

[3] Boutilier [1] also argues for a second normality preference ordering. This ordering is used in his logic to model factual defaults, not the defeasibility of conditional obligations. Therefore, his two orderings give rise to completely different problems than our two orderings.

[4] Usually such a conditional obligation is translated into either $\alpha \rightarrow O(\beta)$ or $O(\beta \mid \alpha)$, where O is a monadic or dyadic modal operator (see [2]).

deontic rule has a distinct violation constant V_i. For a detailed description of the syntax and proof theory of DIODE and related work, see [14].

DIODE contains a preferential semantics that defines a preference ordering on models (see e.g. [13]) using the V_i constants. This preference ordering orders all ideal and sub-ideal states. The motivation of the distinction between ideal and sub-ideal states is that not all obligations refer to an ideal situation, but also often to sub-ideal situations. These obligations are so-called *Contrary-To-Duty* (CTD) obligations. For example, if you are obliged not to insult someone $O(\neg i)$, then the conditional obligation that if you insult someone, you should apologize $i \rightarrow O(a)$ is a CTD obligation. A CTD obligation describes the *optimal* subideal state. They are well-known from the notorious Chisholm and Forrester paradoxes. In [12] several other examples of sub-ideal states and CTD obligations are given.

Definition 1. Let T be a theory of L_V and M_1 and M_2 two models of T. M_1 is preferred over M_2, written $M_1 \sqsubseteq M_2$, iff $M_1 \models V_i$ then $M_2 \models V_i$ for all i. We write $M_1 \sqsubset M_2$ (M_1 is strictly preferred over M_2) iff $M_1 \sqsubseteq M_2$ and not $M_2 \sqsubseteq M_1$.

Given this partial pre-ordering, we use the following basic definitions:

Definition 2. An interpretation M *preferentially satisfies* A (written $M \models_{\sqsubset} A$) iff $M \models A$ and there is no other interpretation M' such that $M' \sqsubset M$ and $M' \models A$. In this case we say that M is a *preferred model* of A. A preferentially entails B (written $A \models_{\sqsubset} B$) iff for any M, if $M \models_{\sqsubset} A$ then $M \models B$.

The notion of preferential entailment can be used to identify minimal (with respect to set inclusion) violation sets.

Definition 3. Let T be a theory of L_V and M a preferred model of T, i.e. $M \models_{\sqsubset} T$. The set $\{V_i \mid M \models V_i\}$ is a *preferred violation set* of T.

A deontic theory can have more than one preferred violation set. In the deontic context given by a DIODE theory T, the sentences of L which are true in all preferred models are called contextually obliged.

Definition 4. Let T be a theory of L_V. T provides a contextual obligation for α iff $T \models_{\sqsubset} \alpha$ and $\alpha \in L$.

Semantically, the deontic rules (together with the background knowledge sentences) define a preference ordering on the models which orders all ideal and sub-ideal states. The facts (a subset of T, represented by F) zoom in on this partial ordering by selecting the (sub)ideal states where the facts are true. This zooming in will be demonstrated by an instance of the Forrester paradox [4]: you should not kill, but if you kill you should do it gently.

Example 1. **(Forrester paradox)** Consider the following sentences of a theory T:

1. $\neg V_1 \rightarrow \neg i$: You should not insult someone;
2. $i \wedge \neg V_2 \rightarrow p$: If you insult someone you should do it in private;
3. $p \rightarrow i$: Insulting someone in private logically implies that you insult him;
4. i: You insult someone.

The preference ordering of the deontic rules (together with the background rule $p \to i$) of the Forrester 'Paradox' is given in Figure 1. This figure must be read as follows. The models are ordered by the subset relation on the violation constants V_i. The circles denote equivalence classes of this ordering (all models in a circle satisfy the same violation constants) and the arrows indicate which models are strictly preferred. The set of obligations which are violated in this equivalence class are written in the circle. Moreover, the circles also contain a set of propositions. These propositions are true in all the models of the equivalence class which are preferred for some set of factual sentences. Hence, only models which are relevant, i.e. which are minimal for the set of formulas of L they make true, are shown in the figure. For example, the models that satisfy $\neg i$ and V_1 are never preferred and are therefore not represented; all *relevant* models that satisfy V_1, also satisfy i. Equivalence classes without such relevant models, e.g. the equivalence class of V_2, are not shown. When the facts contain all the propositions that are written in some circle, then the preferred violation set is the set of obligations in this circle. Hence, the circles contain the minimal set of violated obligations that are consistent with the propositions in the circle. For example, in the i, p-circle, V_1 has to be true due to the obligation $\neg V_1 \to \neg i$.

In the ideal situation, given by the left circle, you do not insult someone. If you insult someone, i.e. for $F = \{i\}$, you only consider equivalence classes that contain i. Hence, the relevant models are restricted to the sub-ideal models containing V_1 and the sub-sub-ideal models containing V_1 and V_2. In Figure 1 this zooming in on the ordering is depicted by a dashed box. The optimal sub-ideal state, represented by the leftmost circle within the dashed box, represents the fact that you insult him in private. This means that $\{V_1\}$ is the only preferred violation set and T provides a contextual obligation for p. The worst state reflects, in a sense, two violations: the first one is the offense of insulting someone and the second one is doing it in public.

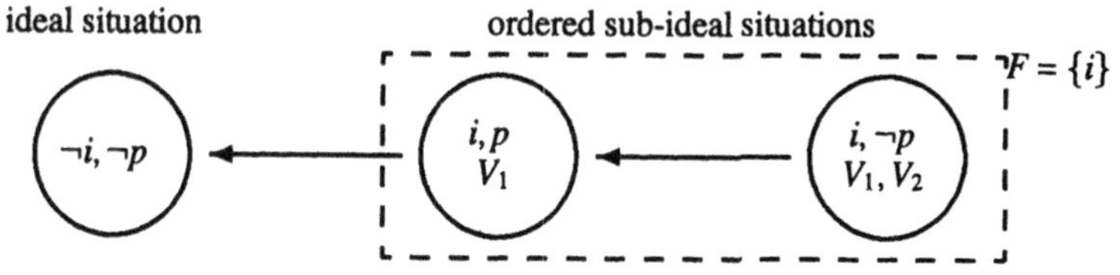

Fig. 1. Preference relation of the Forrester paradox

The previous example showed the two-phase mechanism of DIODE. The first phase consists of building a preference ordering on all models, given by the deontic rules and background knowledge (like $p \to i$ in the Forrester paradox). The second phase zooms in on this ordering by selecting the models where the facts are true. Two similar phases exist in the defeasible variant of DIODE which will be developed in the next section. However, in the first phase *two* preference orderings will be constructed; not only one for ideality but also one for normality.

3 DefDiode: Diode with exceptions

There is a fundamental difference between a conditional obligation being violated by a fact, and a conditional obligation being overridden by another conditional obligation. See [16] for a discussion of this difference in terms of inference patterns. For example, in a legal setting, when an obligation is violated you have to pay a fine for it, but when it is cancelled by another obligation, you cannot be fined for it. Horty [5] gives his well-known example of being served asparagus. You should not eat with your fingers. But if you are served asparagus, then you should eat with your fingers. In the special case where you are served asparagus, the first obligation is less specific and hence cancelled by the second one. Various authors, e.g. [5, 8, 9], have investigated the formalization of *defeasible* conditional obligations (traditionally called *prima facie* obligations), deontic rules which are subject to exceptions. Explicit exceptions can be introduced in Diode by formalizing a defeasible conditional obligation 'if α is the case then *usually* it ought to be that β is the case' by $\alpha \wedge \neg V_i \wedge \neg Ex_i \rightarrow \beta$, where Ex_i is a propositional constant denoting whether the defeasible conditional obligation is defeated (by some exceptional circumstances). For example, a defeasible conditional obligation that usually you should not insult someone can be formalized by $\neg V_1 \wedge \neg Ex_1 \rightarrow \neg i$. The Ex_i abnormalities are used to control the preferences between two conflicting defeasible conditional obligations. Hence, the rules that determine when an abnormality Ex_i holds are quite different from the rules that determine when a violation V_i holds. From a semantic point of view there are two independent preference relations on the models; one for minimizing the V_i constants and one for minimizing the Ex_i constants.

DefDiode is an extension of Diode in the sense that in DefDiode obligations might contain an exception constant Ex_i. Given a set of defeasible conditional obligations in DefDiode, the question remains how to determine when there are exceptional circumstances, i.e. when an exception constant is true. In this paper, we make the assumption that all exceptions are given explicitly and that in case of a conflict, violations are preferred over exceptions. Obviously, there is no a priori reason to prefer violations over exceptions; it follows from the assumption that *all* exceptions are given explicitly. For example, assume there is a second deontic rule that states that you should insult someone when he does harm the public interest, formalized by $h \wedge \neg V_2 \rightarrow i$ where h stands for someone harming public interest. An example of this obligation is that every journalist should expose Nixon in the Watergate affair. In that case, a so-called defeater rule must be added that states that a situation of public interest is an exception to the rule not to insult someone, $h \rightarrow Ex_1$. Semantically, the normality ordering is a subset ordering on exception constants Ex_i just like the ideality ordering on violation constants V_i (though the rules which determine when an abnormality Ex_i holds are quite different from the rules that determine when a violation V_i holds!).

The following definition of overridden is a formalization of the notion of specificity. This definition can be used in our framework to identify exceptional circumstances. The definition is borrowed from non-monotonic logics. However, as we will see later, this definition has to be adapted for defeasible *deontic* logic since it is too strong. In spirit it is similar to Horty's definition of overridden [5].

Definition 5. Let $F_b \subseteq T$ be the set of background knowledge sentences of T. A defeasible conditional obligation $\alpha_1 \wedge \neg V_1 \wedge \neg Ex_1 \rightarrow \beta_1 \in T$ is *overridden for* α_2 by $\alpha_2 \wedge \neg V_2 \wedge \neg Ex_2 \rightarrow \beta_2 \in T$ (or $\alpha_2 \wedge \neg V_2 \rightarrow \beta_2 \in T$) iff:

1. $F_b \wedge \beta_1 \wedge \beta_2$ is inconsistent, and
2. $F_b \wedge \alpha_2 \models \alpha_1$ and $F_b \wedge \alpha_1 \not\models \alpha_2$.

In all cases where a defeasible conditional obligation $\alpha_1 \wedge \neg V_1 \wedge \neg Ex_1 \rightarrow \beta_1$ is *overridden for* α_2 by $\alpha_2 \wedge \neg V_2 \wedge \neg Ex_2 \rightarrow \beta_2$ (or $\alpha_2 \wedge \neg V_2 \rightarrow \beta_2$), the explicit defeater rule $\alpha_2 \rightarrow Ex_1$ is added to T.[5] The next example is an instance of Horty's asparagus example: you should not eat with your fingers, but if you eat asparagus you should eat with your fingers [5].

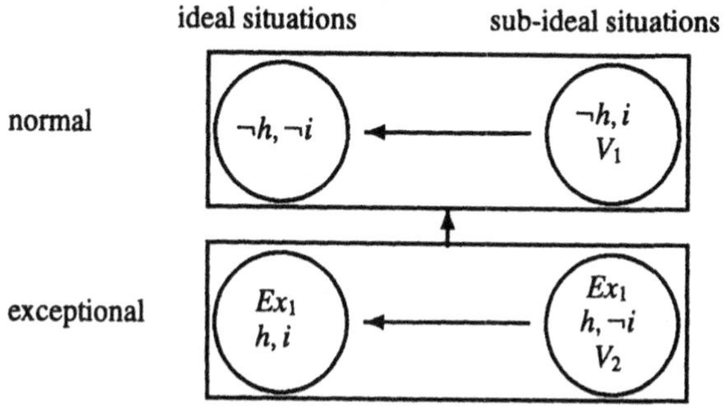

Fig. 2. Preference relation of Public Interest

Example 2. **(Public Interest)** Consider the following sentences of a theory T:

1. $\neg V_1 \wedge \neg Ex_1 \rightarrow \neg i$: Usually, you should not insult someone.
2. $h \wedge \neg V_2 \rightarrow i$: When someone does harm the public interest, you should insult him.

The second obligation overrides the first one for h so the clause $h \rightarrow Ex_1$ should be added. The idea of the preference ordering on normality is that the models with exceptional circumstances (public interest) are semantically separated from the normal situation. The intended preferential semantics are given in Figure 2. The boxes denote equivalence classes in the normality ordering and the 'vertical' arrow the normality preference ordering. The circles denote equivalence classes in the deontic ordering *within an equivalence class of the normality ordering*, and the 'horizontal' arrows the deontic preference ordering. The upper box represents the 'normal' models, which is determined by the fact that h is false, i.e. there is no situation of public interest. Deontically, the

[5] Notice that Definition 5 is syntax-dependent, since the logically equivalent $\alpha \wedge \neg V_i \rightarrow \beta$ and $\neg V_i \rightarrow (\alpha \rightarrow \beta)$ are treated differently. This is the consequence of the strong notion of implication used in DEFDIODE, which is the classical material implication. Notice that we can still use classical models, because the explicit defeater rules are added before the preferential orderings are built. There are several ways to solve this syntax dependence. Horty [5] solves this, for instance, by representing deontic rules as Reiter default rules.

$\neg h$-models are ordered according to the obligation that usually, you should not insult someone. The lower box contains the models where h is true and which are therefore exceptional, which is also denoted by Ex_1. These models are deontically ordered by the obligation that in this situation, you should insult him. Because of the exceptional circumstances, the models are not subject to the obligation that usually, you should not insult someone.

Without the explicit defeater $h \to Ex_1$, there is a conflict when h is true, because the first obligation implies that you should not insult, and the second obligation implies that you should. In the semantics, this conflict would be represented by the fact that h, i models are incomparable with $h, \neg i$ models. The introduction of the explicit defeater, and hence the exceptionality level in the multi preference semantics, results in two normality classes. Within these classes, all models are comparable. Hence, there is no conflict anymore: the explicit defeater has resolved the conflict.

Now we reconsider the Forrester paradox in a defeasible deontic setting. As we showed in [15], a strong definition of overridden like Horty's definition [5] or our Definition 5 above will give unintuitive results.

Example 3. **(Forrester paradox)** Reconsider the sentences of Example 1 in a defeasible setting:

1. $\neg V_1 \land \neg Ex_1 \to \neg i$: Usually, you should not insult someone;
2. $i \land \neg V_2 \to p$: If you insult someone, you should do it in private;
3. $p \to i$: Insulting someone in private implies that you insult him.

Given Definition 5 of overridden, the first sentence is overridden by the second one for i; i.e. we should add the formula $i \to Ex_1$. However, the addition of the formula is highly counterintuitive since it implies that the first obligation can never be violated. In our semantic analysis, we can see that the introduction of an explicit defeater is counterintuitive, because there is no conflict to be resolved. In the picture without explicit defeaters, i.e. Figure 1, there are no incomparable models! The intuitive reading of the example is that the second obligation is a CTD obligation of the first one, and hence the first and more general obligation should hold and not be overridden.

The problem here is that the CTD obligation is considered as an exception because the conclusions of the deontic rules are inconsistent and the condition of the second rule is more specific. For a defeasible deontic logic, this condition is too strong.

The previous example showed the interesting situation where a definition borrowed from non-monotonic logic is too strong for a defeasible deontic logic. In [15] we introduced therefore the following weaker notion of overridden which excludes this possibility by introducing a test (the third condition) whether the second sentence is a CTD obligation of the first sentence. The additional condition for the definition is very natural. A CTD obligation is an obligation where the reference situation is in contradiction with duty, namely $\alpha_1 \land \beta_1$. The condition is that $F_b \not\models \alpha_2 \to \alpha_1 \land \beta_1$. It can easily be seen that this reduces to condition 3.

Definition 6. Let F_b be the set of background knowledge sentences of T. A defeasible conditional obligation $\alpha_1 \land \neg V_1 \land \neg Ex_1 \to \beta_1 \in T$ is *overridden for* α_2 by $\alpha_2 \land \neg V_2 \land \neg Ex_2 \to \beta_2 \in T$ (or $\alpha_2 \land \neg V_2 \to \beta_2 \in T$) iff:

1. $F_b \wedge \beta_1 \wedge \beta_2$ is inconsistent, and
2. $F_b \wedge \alpha_2 \models \alpha_1$ and $F_b \wedge \alpha_1 \not\models \alpha_2$, and
3. $F_b \wedge \beta_1 \wedge \alpha_2$ is consistent.

For the Public Interest example the conditions are still satisfied. In the Forrester paradox, the defeasible deontic rule not to insult someone is no longer overridden for i according to Definition 6, because the last condition is not satisfied.

Acknowledgements. Thanks to Patrick van der Laag, Henry Prakken, Marek Sergot and Tina Smith for several discussions on the issues raised in this paper.

References

1. C. Boutilier. Toward a logic for qualitative decision theory. In *Proceedings of KR'94*, 1994.
2. B.F. Chellas. *Modal Logic: An Introduction.* Cambridge University Press, 1980.
3. R.M. Chisholm. Contrary-to-duty imperatives and deontic logic. *Analysis*, 24:33–36, 1963.
4. J.W. Forrester. Gentle murder, or the adverbial Samaritan. *Journal of Philosophy*, 81:193–197, 1984.
5. J.F. Horty. Deontic logic founded in nonmonotonic logic. *Annals of Mathematics and Artificial Intelligence*, 9:69–91, 1993.
6. A.J.I. Jones and M. Sergot. Deontic logic in the representation of law: Towards a methodology. *Artificial Intelligence and Law*, 1:45–64, 1992.
7. A.J.I. Jones and M. Sergot. *Proceedings of the Second Workshop on Deontic Logic in Computer Science (Deon'94).* Oslo, 1994.
8. D. Makinson. Five faces of minimality. *Studia Logica*, 52:339–379, 1993.
9. L.T. McCarty. Defeasible deontic reasoning. In *Fourth International Workshop on Nonmonotonic Reasoning*, Plymouth, 1992.
10. J.-J. Meyer and R. Wieringa. *Deontic Logic in Computer Science: Proceedings of the First Workshop on Deontic Logic in Computer Science (Deon'91).* John Wiley & Sons, 1993.
11. H. Prakken. *Logical Tools for Modelling Legal Argument, Ph-D thesis.* Amsterdam, 1993.
12. H. Prakken and M.J. Sergot. Contrary-to-duty imperatives, defeasibility and violability. In *Proceedings of the Second Workshop on Deontic Logic in Computer Science (Deon'94)*, Oslo, 1994.
13. Y. Shoham. *Reasoning About Change.* MIT Press, 1988.
14. Y.-H. Tan and L.W.N. van der Torre. Representing deontic reasoning in a diagnostic framework. In *Proceedings of the Workshop on Legal Applications of Logic Programming of the Eleventh International Conference on Logic Programming (ICLP'94)*, 1994.
15. L.W.N. van der Torre. Violated obligations in a defeasible deontic logic. In *Proceedings of the Eleventh European Conference on Artificial Intelligence (ECAI'94)*, pages 371–375. John Wiley & Sons, 1994.
16. L.W.N. van der Torre and Y.-H. Tan. Cancelling and overshadowing: two types of defeasibility in defeasible deontic logic. Technical Report WP 95.02.01, EURIDIS, 1995. To appear in: *Proceedings of the IJCAI-95.*

Numeric Defaults

About an expressive first-order framework for reasoning with infinitesimal probabilities

Emil Weydert
Max-Planck-Institute for Computer Science[1]
emil@mpi-sb.mpg.de

1. Introduction

Probability theory, refined through different modeling and inference techniques, certainly constitutes the most important and best-developed framework for representing and handling uncertain information. The corresponding mathematical tools are well-understood and their usefulness has been demonstrated on unnumerable occasions. Still, there are inferential tasks involving incomplete knowledge, partly well within the reach of human agents, where the usual numerical approaches are inappropriate, unintuitive or even meaningless. Default inference, a coarse-grained, common sense form of uncertainty management, is one of these areas. There have been lots of attempts to formalize its "jumping to conclusions", but most of them seriously conflict with our intuitions. Some progress has been made in recent years, but the research community has not yet reached an agreement about what would - depending on the intended application field - constitute, or just characterize a canonical formalism. It isn't really surprising that the most promising approaches - at least as far as foundational coherence and arguably correct behaviour are concerned - appear to be those derived from the probabilistic paradigm, e.g. ranking measures [Wey 91, 94] for interpreting default conditionals and the limiting-probability accounts for defeasible inference based on minimal information and indifference principles [GMP 90, BGHK 93]. Adopting a quasi-probabilistic perspective is interesting for several reasons. First of all, it guarantees a smooth transition between default conclusions and probabilistic judgments. Recall that the probabilistic viewpoint is strongly backed not only by practical considerations but also by the analysis of rational behaviour. Furthermore, it makes it easier to evaluate defeasible reasoning patterns by offering a reference point which allows us to identify and understand the relevant assumptions. A major advantage is of course the possibility to exploit powerful classical probabilistic tools. Last but not least, this approach facilitates decision-theoretic investigations, which are the main purpose of plausible reasoning in the real world.

In our paper, we are going to follow this line of research and present a simple but expressive integrated framework for extended probabilistic and default reasoning based on what we call an explicitly nonarchimedean probability logic. We begin with a critical look at the ranking measure paradigm for default knowledge and propose to replace it by a more powerful semantic perspective based on nonarchimedean probability measures, i.e. admitting infinitely small values. It allows us to interpret defaults by generalized probability constraints. Next, we introduce and investigate a flexible new two-sorted probability logic able to deal with infinitesimal values and more sophisticated algebraic notions like exponentiation. This is necessary to implement at the object-level interesting defeasible entailment strategies based on information theoretic concepts. Our task here is simplified by recent results from model-theoretic algebra. To conclude,

[1] Im Stadtwald, D-66123 Saarbrücken, Germany.

we discuss our numeric defeasible reasoning philosophy and exemplify it by an inference notion based on local entropy comparisons in a nonstandard context, made possible by the expressiveness of our framework.

2. Ranking measures

According to the descriptive philosophy, defaults express strong conditional expectations reflecting normal relationships in the real world or in our epistemic model of it. A reasonable translation of some default $\varphi \twoheadrightarrow \psi$ therefore might be "$\varphi\&\neg\psi$ *is negligible w.r.t.* φ" or "$\varphi\&\neg\psi$ *has lower qualitative magnitude than* $\varphi\&\psi$". These interpretations suggest a quasi-probabilistic semantics for default knowledge. It could be based, for instance, on what we call ranking measures[2], an approach first advocated in [Wey 91] and elaborated further in [Wey 94].

Definition 2.1 $\mathcal{R}$ is called a *ranking measure* iff $\mathcal{R} : \mathbf{B} \to \mathbf{V}$ is a function s.t.
1. $\mathcal{B} = (\mathbf{B}, \cap, \cup, -, \mathbf{0}, \mathbf{1})$ is a *boolean algebra,*
2. $\mathcal{V} = (\mathbf{V}, *, \ll)$ is a *ranking algebra* : $(\mathbf{V}\backslash\{\infty\}, *, \ll)$ is the negative half of a nontrivial ordered commutative group[3] with identity o and $-\infty$ is $\ll$-minimal and absorptive for $*$, i.e. for all $v \in \mathbf{V}$, $-\infty * v = v * -\infty = -\infty$,
3. $\mathcal{R}(\mathbf{0}) = -\infty$, $\mathcal{R}(\mathbf{1}) = o$ and $\mathcal{R}(A \cup A') = \max_{\ll}\{\mathcal{R}(A), \mathcal{R}(A')\}$ for $A, A' \in \mathbf{B}$,
4. $\mathcal{R}(A) = -\infty$ if $A = \bigcup_{\mathcal{B}}\{A_i \mid i \in I\}$ and for all $i \in I$, $\mathcal{R}(A_i) = -\infty$ (*coherence*).

The *conditional ranking measure* corresponding to $\mathcal{R}$ is defined by the equations $\mathcal{R}(A \cap B) = \mathcal{R}(B \mid A) * \mathcal{R}(A)$, for $\mathcal{R}(A) \neq -\infty$, and $\mathcal{R}(B \mid A) = -\infty$, for $\mathcal{R}(A) = -\infty$.

Ranking measure values can be seen - on the objective side - as coarse, simplified representations of extreme probabilities in the real world or - on the subjective side - as degrees of disbelief or potential surprise, i.e. the smaller $\mathcal{R}(\neg A)$, the stronger our belief in the proposition expressed by A. But first of all, they provide a transparent, descriptive semantics for default implication. Let L be a classical first-order language and $\mathcal{B}_L = (\mathbf{B}_L, \&, \vee, \neg, \mathbf{F}, \mathbf{T})$ be the corresponding compact boolean Lindenbaum-algebra[4] induced by first-order predicate logic. Then, we may stipulate

- $\mathcal{R}$ satisfies $\varphi \twoheadrightarrow \psi$ iff $\mathcal{R}(\neg\psi \mid \varphi) \ll o$ iff $\mathcal{R}(\varphi\&\neg\psi) \ll \mathcal{R}(\varphi\&\psi)$ or $\mathcal{R}(\varphi\&\neg\psi) = -\infty$.

This semantics guarantees that Lehmann's rationality postulates for default conditionals [KLM 90] are satisfied. In fact, in infinite contexts, it is more general than the standard possible worlds semantics, because it is immunized against the infinite version of the lottery paradox. But there are several problems with this approach. First of all, it is too coarse-grained for most decision-theoretic purposes. For instance, we cannot distinguish between a situation with 99 positive and 1 negative, but equally plausible outcomes and one where the odds are inversed. The reason is that equal ranking measure values don't add up, which is a major characteristic of this account. A second aspect is that ranking measure structures are too rudimentary to allow a direct exchange of information and powerful tools with classical probability theory.

---

[2] They turn out to generalize Spohn's natural conditional functions [Spo 90], i.e. Pearl's κ-rankings, and Dubois and Prade's [DP 88] possibility measures.

[3] $(G, *, \ll)$ is an ordered commutative group iff $*$ is associative, commutative, has a neutral element, admits inverses and satisfies $x \ll y \to x*v \ll y*v$.

[4] For the sake of notational economy, we sloppily denote the elements (the sets of classically equivalent L-formulas) resp. functions of $\mathcal{B}_L$ by their representatives from L resp. the corresponding propositional connectives.

Standard probablistic threshold interpretations, on the other hand, are even less suitable. Translating $\varphi \twoheadrightarrow \psi$ by $P(\neg\psi \mid \varphi) \leq \alpha$, for non-zero α, would be completely ad hoc and in flagrant conflict with our intuitions. But $P(\neg\psi \mid \varphi) \leq 0$ is inacceptable as well because it would induce the trivialization of defaults with an exceptional antecedent, e.g. automatically validating $\varphi\&\neg\psi \twoheadrightarrow \neg\phi$ and $\varphi\&\neg\psi \twoheadrightarrow \phi$. In addition, even if we don't require σ-additivity, there are some notorious theoretical defects. A very prominent one is the non-existence of uniform distributions on infinite sets if we want to reserve probability zero for the empty set. These difficulties illustrate the need for an extended framework.

3. Nonarchimedean measures

Because the traditional probabilistic strategy as well as its coarse-grained counterpart fail to satisfy our demands, we are now going to consider fine-grained generalizations of probability measures, with valuation algebras extending ([0, 1], +, x, <)[5]. The most interesting candidates are finitely additive measures taking values in the unit interval of suitable proper extensions[6] $\mathbb{R}' = (\mathbf{R}', 0, 1, +', x', <')$ of the standard ordered real number field $\mathbb{R} = (\mathbf{R}, 0, 1, +, x, <)$. First, note that if $\mathbb{R}'$ is a field, it is necessarily a nonarchimedean extension of $\mathbb{R}$. This means, it includes infinitesimally small non-zero numbers, i.e. $0 < \varepsilon$ with ε x' n < 1 for all positive integers n (written $\varepsilon << 1$). However, because we shall need an extended logarithm function for defining information measures aimed at nonarchimedean probability distributions, in fact, we have to look for adeqaute proper extensions $\mathbb{R}'$ of the real exponential field $\mathbb{R}_e = (\mathbf{R}, 0, 1, +, x, \exp, <)$, where exp(r) stands for 2^r. Their existence is guaranteed by the compactness theorem. Let L_{EF} be the language of exponential fields. There exists a tentative, correct axiomatization **RCE** of $\mathbb{R}_e$'s L_{EF}-theory Th($\mathbb{R}_e$), but completeness is still an open problem.

Definition 3.1 *Let* **RCF** *be the theory of real closed fields, i.e. ordered fields*[7] *where every polynomial of odd degree has a root (= theory of* $\mathbb{R}$*).* $\mathbb{F} = (\mathbf{F}, 0, 1, +, x, \exp, <)$[8] *is called a real closed exponential field iff* $\mathbb{F}$ *verifies* **RCE = RCF + E1 - E4**, *where*

E1 $\exp(1) = 1+1$, $\exp(v + w) = \exp(v)\exp(w)$,
E2 $v < w \rightarrow \exp(v) < \exp(w)$,
E3 $0 < v \rightarrow \exists w\, \exp(w) = v$,
E4 $\underline{n} \times \underline{n} < v \rightarrow v^n < \exp(v)$, for all $\underline{n} = 1 + \ldots + 1$ ($v^n = v \times \ldots \times v$, n times).

For practical and intuition-related reasons, we want $\mathbb{R}'$ to be as close to $\mathbb{R}_e$ as possible. Consequently, we consider only models of Th($\mathbb{R}_e$). But we know from Wilkie [Dri 94] that Th($\mathbb{R}_e$) is model-complete. That is, if $\mathbb{F}°$ is a substructure of $\mathbb{F}$ and both are models of Th($\mathbb{R}_e$), then $\mathbb{F}°$ is an elementary substructure of $\mathbb{F}$, i.e. every $L_{EF}(\mathbf{F}°)$-formula[9] satisfied by $\mathbb{F}°$ also holds in $\mathbb{F}$. In particular, this becomes true for $\mathbb{F}° = \mathbb{R}_e$ and $\mathbb{F} = \mathbb{R}'$. So, we may restrict ourselves to proper elementary extensions of $\mathbb{R}_e$. We are now ready to offer the formal definition of our extended probability measures.

Definition 3.2 *Let* $\mathbb{R}' = (\mathbf{R}', 0, 1, +, x, <)$ *be a proper elementary extension of* $\mathbb{R}_e$ *and* $\mathbb{B} = (\mathbf{B}, \cap, \cup, -, 0, 1)$ *be a boolean algebra. Then the function* $\mathbf{P} : \mathbf{B} \rightarrow \mathbf{R}'$ *is called a*

---

[5] Nonstandard probabilities in the context of default reasoning / belief revision were first considered in [LM 92] / [Spo 90].
[6] A structure N is called an extension of the structure M iff its restriction to the domain of M is just M.
[7] An axiom set can be found in [Bac 90] or in most standard books on algebra.
[8] To ease notation, we shall use from now on the same relation / function terminology for all structures.
[9] $L_{EF}(\mathbf{F}°)$ is the expansion of L_{EF} obtained by introducing a constant for each element of $\mathbf{F}°$.

$\mathbb{R}'$-valued, nonarchimedean probability measure iff for all A, B$\in$**𝔅**, **P(1)** = 1, **P**(A) $\geq$ 0 *and* **P**(A$\cup$B) = **P**(A) + **P**(B) *if* A$\cap$B = **0**. *We call it coherent iff* **P**(A) = 0 *implies* A = **0**.

Because $\mathbb{R}'$ is nonarchimedean, many bounded countable subsets from $\mathbb{R}_e$ have no supremum. In addition, we do not want to exclude uniform coherent distributions on infinite sets. Therefore, we cannot assume σ-additivity. Coherence, i.e. respecting impossibility, should only be a facultative requirement, given that important classical distributions - e.g. the Lebesgue measure on [0, 1] - violate this principle. Note that we may construct from every coherent $\mathbb{R}'$-valued probability measure **P** : **B** –> $[0, 1]_{\mathbf{R}'}$ a corresponding canonical ranking measure $\mathfrak{R}^{\mathbf{P}}$ by identifying those values in $[0, 1]_{\mathbf{R}'}$ diverging only by a finitely bounded factor. On the other hand, every nonarchimedean probability measure can be extended to one a full power set algebra.

Proposition 3.1 *Let* **𝔅** *be a boolean sub-algebra of the power-set-algebra* **𝔓𝔬𝔴**(S), $\mathbb{R}'$ *be as above and* **P** *be an* $\mathbb{R}'$*-valued probability measure on* **B**. *Then there is a* Th($\mathbb{R}_e$)*-model* $\mathbb{R}''$ *extending* $\mathbb{R}'$ *and an* $\mathbb{R}''$*-valued probability measure* **P'** *on* **Pow**(S) *extending* **P**.

What is the role of infinitesimal probabilities ? First of all, **P**(A | B) = ε, for $\varepsilon << 1$, simply means that within the context B - at least for finite boolean algebras - we may neglect the alternative A for utility considerations and decision-taking. The fine-grained distinctions offered by the extended probabilistic scale are only exploited to revise probabilities in a reasonable way when extreme conditioning on neglected evidence has to occur. In the following, we are going to use them for more sophisticated interpretations of default knowledge and default inference, which allows us to accommodate powerful probabilistic inference mechanisms.

How do we translate the descriptive content of defaults into this framework ? The obvious way would be to use the canonical ranking measure construction.

- φ –» ψ : $\mathbf{P}(\neg\psi \mid \varphi) << 1$ (*<<-classical*)

This interpretation supports the postulates of rational conditional logic. Another strategy would be to choose an infinitesimal ε for a nonarchimedean threshold reading.

- φ –» ψ : $\mathbf{P}(\neg\psi \mid \varphi) \leq \varepsilon << 1$ (*≤-bounded*)

It turns out that this type of linear inequality constraint is well suited for probabilistic defeasible inference strategies like entropy maximization. Technically speaking, almost all the rationality postulates are violated. Nevertheless, on an intuitive level, this condition is still quite similar to the previous one, because the infinitesimals in $\mathbb{R}'$ are highly indiscernible. In fact, Wilkie has also proved that $\mathbb{R}_e$ is o-minimal, which means that all its parameter-definable subsets are finite unions of open intervals and points. This gives us the following.

Proposition 3.2 *Let* $\mathbb{R}'$ *be an elementary extension of* $\mathbb{R}_e$ *and* ε, $\tau \neq 0$ *be two infinitesimals in* $\mathbb{R}'$. *Then, for all unary* $\varphi(x) \in L_{EF}(R)$, $\mathbb{R}' \models \varphi(\varepsilon)$ *iff there is* $0 < r \in \mathbf{R}'$ *s.t. for all* $s \in \mathbf{R}'$, $0 < s < r$ *implies* $\mathbb{R}' \models \varphi(s)$ *iff* $\mathbb{R}' \models \varphi(\tau)$.

That is, all the infinitesimals from $\mathbb{R}'$ satisfy the same unary $L_{EF}(\mathbf{R})$-formulas, which are already determined by the limit-behaviour of the reals. So, every infinitesimal in $\mathbb{R}'$ may be called generic. Our next task is now to present and investigate a logical framework which is sufficiently powerful for reasoning with such numeric default knowledge.

4. Nonarchimedean probability logic

Given a first-order language L, we want to construct an expansion $L^* \supseteq L$ suitable for talking about standard and nonstandard probabilities - and thereby about default knowledge - associated with L*-formulas resp. their semantic realizations.

Formally, we adopt the "objective" perspective for probabilistic statements. On the semantic level, this means that we are going to evaluate the probability of subsets of L-structures. On the syntactic level, we choose the single-variable conditional term-quantifier notation $\mathbf{P}x(\varphi(x) \mid \psi(x))$ to express the probability that $\varphi(x)$ holds given $\psi(x)$. Note that within this framework, we can also easily represent and handle subjective and multidimensional probability. This is quite important because infinitesimal probabilities might be interpreted epistemically and most probabilistic judgments rely heavily on plausible inference techniques and working assumptions about priors or random processes, which bring in a subjective element. To implement the subjective viewpoint, we need a unary predicate W to split up the domain into an epistemic (worlds) and an objective (individuals) part. Next, we have to replace each n-ary function or predicate symbol A from L by a fresh n+1-ary symbol A' for its world-indexed counterpart, i.e. we have to pass from $A(\underline{x})$ to $A'(w, \underline{x})$. In addition, we introduce for each object variable x_i a new unary function symbol X_i representing a random variable with domain W picking up elements from $\neg W$. To each L-formula φ now corresponds a world-indexed, $\neg W$-restricted formula φ' obtained by changing $A(\underline{x})$ into $A'(w, \underline{x})$ and restricting $\forall x$ and $\exists x$ to $\neg W(x)$.

Assuming independent and - at least for definable sets - equally distributed X_i, we can express the multidimensional objective or statistical probability of $\varphi(x_1, ..., x_n)$ w.r.t. a specific random process by $\mathbf{P}w(\varphi'(X_1(w), ..., X_n(w)) \mid W(w))$, and the subjective probability of $\varphi(a)$ - $\varphi(x)$ holds for the object denoted by the constant a - by $\mathbf{P}w(\varphi'(a'(w)) \mid W(w))$. This gives us a common representational framework for handling objective and epistemic probabilities. Note that the intended relationships between both types of probability, like direct inference, are to be handled at the level of nonmonotonic reasoning. This subjectivist strategy allows us to consider several distributions at once and to state their respective properties and relationships, e.g. independency. In particular, this might be useful to model multi-agent belief. So, our approach is quite flexible and, if the language is strong enough, we may choose the framework which best fits our needs.

In L*, of course, we want to state comparative, additive and multiplicative relationships, e.g. to express the laws of probability theory and dependencies. Furthermore, because some defeasible reasoning techniques make use of information measures, like entropy, we have to include a function symbol for logarithmization and/or exponentiation. To express our default constraints, we also need a possibility to talk about infinitesimality. Unfortunately, this concept cannot be entirely grasped by first-order means, it may only be approximated by a notion of extreme smallness or abstract infinitesimality. To achieve this, we introduce a new predicate R describing a non-cofinal, i.e. bounded model of $Th(\mathbb{R}_e)$, intended to represent the "standard" part of the full valuation structure. But note that we cannot exclude axiomatically that R holds for some proper infinitesimals. In this context, we say that a positive number is extremely small iff it is smaller than the strictly positive chunk of the structure delimited by R. If R is interpreted by the real exponential field, these are just the infinitesimal elements (and 0). In addition, we ask for a constant e denoting some "generic infinitesimal" serving as a reference point in the realm of smallness.

All this suggests a two-sorted language with variables for numbers and objects. Let L be a language of first-order predicate logic with individual variables x_i ($i \in \mathbb{N}$), m_i-ary function symbols f_i ($i \in I_f$) and n_i-ary predicate symbols P_i ($i \in I_p$). Formally, we construct L* from L by adding to our vocabulary numeric variables v_i ($i \in \mathbb{N}$), a numeric constant e, numeric functions +, x, exp, -, $^{-1}$, log, (of arities 2, 2, 1, 1, 1, 1), a unary numeric predicate R and a dyadic term-quantifier **P** binding a single object variable, together with the following rules. If φ, ψ are L*-formulas, s, s' numerical L*-terms, v a numerical and x an object variable, then

- $\neg\varphi$, $\varphi\&\psi$, $\varphi\vee\psi$, $\varphi\rightarrow\psi$, $\forall x\varphi$, $\exists x\varphi$, $\forall v\varphi$, $\exists v\varphi$, $s \leq s'$, $s < s'$, R(s) are L*-formulas,
- v_i, e, s + s', s x s' (= ss'), exp(s), -s, s^{-1}, log(s), **P**x(φ | ψ) are numerical L*-terms.

In addition, we abbreviate extreme smallness $\forall v'(R(v')\&0<v' \rightarrow v<v')\&\neg(v<0)$ by S(v). For practical purposes, we often restrict ourselves to fragments where the arguments of **P**x may only take specific forms or where we impose nesting constraints. But the full language, which is primarily meant to be a reference framework of high expressiveness, allows arbitrary nesting of connectives and quantifiers. It extends the language of Bacchus [Bac 90] insofar as it offers exponentiation and explicit reference to an abstract infinitesimal concept. We interpret L* by L-structures carrying suitable nonarchimedean probability measures.

Definition 4.1 ($\mathcal{A}$, $\mathcal{F}$, $\mathcal{P}$, $\mathfrak{h}$) is called an *extended probabilistic structure* iff

1. $\mathcal{A}$ is a first-oder L-structure with domain A,
2. $\mathcal{F}$ = (F, F°, 0, 1, ε, +, x, exp, <) is an *explicitly nonarchimedean canonical real closed exponential field* (**ENARCE**-field), that is

2.1 $\mathbb{F}$ = (F, 0, 1, +, x, exp, <) satisfies Th($\mathbb{R}_e$) (*valuation algebra*),

2.2 $\mathbb{F}$° = (F°, 0, 1, +, x, exp, <) satisfies Th($\mathbb{R}_e$) (*standard part*),

2.3 For all 0 < a ∈ **F**°, 0 < ε < a (*generic infinitesimal*).

3. $\mathcal{P}$: **Pow(A)** –> $[0, 1]_F$ is an $\mathbb{F}$-valued finitely additive measure.
4. $\mathfrak{h}$ interprets objective resp. numeric variables by elements of **A** resp. **R**.

The model completeness of Th($\mathbb{R}_e$) ensures that the "standard" core $\mathbb{F}$° is an elementary substructure of $\mathbb{F}$. From this and Prop. 3.2, it follows that all the infinitesimals w.r.t. $\mathbb{F}$° satisfy the same L_{EF}(**F**°)-formulas. By convenience $\mathcal{P}$ is defined for the full powerset of A. But in practice, we shall be mostly concerned with restrictions of $\mathbb{F}$-valued measures to the subalgebra of L-definable sets. Of course, we may choose for ($\mathbb{F}$, $\mathbb{F}$°) the pair ($\mathbb{R}$', $\mathbb{R}_e$) and for ε an arbitrary proper infinitesimal from $\mathbb{R}$'.

The satisfaction relation between extended probabilistic structures and L*-formulas is defined in the obvious way and denoted by ||=. R is interpreted by **F**°, e by ε and **P**x by $\mathcal{P}$. Let ||- be the corresponding monotonic, classical entailment relation. Given an axiomatization of Th($\mathbb{R}_e$), we could extract from the above semantic postulates a complete proof theory for our canonical nonarchimedean probability logic ||-.

5. Numerical default reasoning

Nonmonotonic reasoning with nonarchimedean probabilistic knowledge is a natural generalization of more traditional forms of probabilistic inference and defeasible reasoning with default conditionals. What these approaches have in common is that, given a collection of constraints on (probabilistic, ranking) valuations, they try to infer what we might reasonably expect or assume beyond certainty, for instance by looking at the most plausible ones. Let's have a glimpse at how this might be done within our framework. For reasons of space and transparency, we are going to restrict ourselves to very simple, flat numerical constraints of the form $\Phi(\mathbf{Px}(\varphi_1(x)), ..., \mathbf{Px}(\varphi_n(x)))$, where $\Phi(v_1, ..., v_n)$ is an L_{EF}-expression and the $\varphi_i(x)$ are L-formulas with at most one free variable bounded by **Px**. For instance, depending on the chosen interpretation paradigm, a finite knowledge base $\Delta = \{\varphi_i(x) \twoheadrightarrow \varphi'_i(x) \mid i \leq n\}$ of open defaults over L could be translated by the numerical assertions

- $\Phi_{\leq,s}(\Delta) = (\mathbf{Px}(\neg\varphi'_1(x) \mid \varphi_1(x)) \leq \varepsilon \ \& \ ... \ \& \ \mathbf{Px}(\neg\varphi'_n(x) \mid \varphi_n(x)) \leq \varepsilon)$ or
- $\Phi_{<<}(\Delta) = S(\mathbf{Px}(\neg\varphi'_1(x) \mid \varphi_1(x))) \ \& \ ... \ \& \ S(\mathbf{Px}(\neg\varphi'_n(x) \mid \varphi_n(x)))$.

How should we exploit these constraints to draw plausible conclusions $\psi(x)$ from some conjunction of L-facts (all we know) $\varphi(x)$ about an individual or world x ? The most natural strategy to define a plausible inference notion $\mid\approx$ seems to be the following one.

- $\varphi(x) \mid\approx_\Delta \psi(x)$ iff the most "reasonable" models of $\Phi(\Delta)$ validate $S(\mathbf{Px}(\neg\psi(x) \mid \varphi(x)))$.

That is, we base default inference for facts on reasonable inference for numeric conditions. Here, we accept only those defeasible relationships backed by an extremely small conditional probability for the negated conclusion. The properties of extreme smallness (S) then guarantee that $\mid\approx_\Delta$ is a preferential consequence relation. In general, to make nonmonotonic numerical inference invariant under logical equivalence w.r.t. $\Vdash$, we have to fix a finite boolean Lindenbaum-algebra **B** which takes into account the $\varphi_i(x)$ from a premise constraint $\Phi(\mathbf{Px}(\varphi_1(x)), ..., \mathbf{Px}(\varphi_n(x)))$. If **B** has p many atoms, we may then easily obtain a corresponding normalized form $\Phi°(\mathbf{Px}(\alpha_1(x)), ..., \mathbf{Px}(\alpha_p(x)))$ $\dashVv \Vdash$ $\Phi(\mathbf{Px}(\varphi_1(x)), ..., \mathbf{Px}(\varphi_n(x)))$ by splitting up the $\varphi_i(x)$ into their atomic components $\alpha_j(x)$ w.r.t. **B** and making use of finite additivity. Under these conditions, our *numerical default reasoning philosophy* then requires that what is a plausible conclusion Ψ of $\Phi(\mathbf{Px}(\varphi_1(x)), ..., \mathbf{Px}(\varphi_n(x)))$ should only depend on the building blocks $\alpha_j(x)$ of $\varphi_i(x)$, the L_{EF}-formula $\Phi°(v_1, ..., v_p)$, the identitifications $\mathbf{Px}(\alpha_j(x)) = v_j$ and the probabilistic consistency constraint $v_1 + ... + v_p = 1 \ \& \ 0 \leq v_1 \ \& \ ... \ \& \ 0 \leq v_p$. So, everything would come down to the choice of **B** and of a plausibility notion for finite valuations.

Canonical nonarchimedean probability logic is sufficiently powerful to describe different nonmonotonic inference strategies at the object-level. In particular, we may implement variants of the *minimum information principle.* The standard (lack of) information measure discussed in the literature is the entropy function. Among others, entropy and entropy maximization [Jay 78] can be justified by uniqueness results for different sets of postulates [PV 90]. Let $\mathcal{P}$ be a standard probability distribution on a finite boolean algebra **B** with atoms $A_1, ..., A_p$, represented by the tuple $(\mathcal{P}(A_1), ..., \mathcal{P}(A_p))$. Then the entropy of $\mathcal{P}$ is defined by

- $H(\mathcal{P}) = -\Sigma s_i$ with $s_i = \mathcal{P}(A_i)\log(\mathcal{P}(A_i))$ if $\mathcal{P}(A_i) \neq 0$ and $s_i = 0$ if $\mathcal{P}(A_i) = 0$.

It has been shown that for every closed convex set of valuation tuples, **H** admits a unique maximum. Obviously, we can state within L_{EF} that $(v_1, ..., v_p)$ is the maximum entropy solution of $\Phi \in L_{EF}$. Let $\mathbf{ME}(\Phi)(v_1, ..., v_p)$ be the corresponding formula. By our assumptions, all the L_{EF}-expressible results about finitary entropy-maximization are valid within our canonical nonarchimedean framework. This allows us, for instance, to define a numeric defeasible entailment relation $\mid\approx^*_B$ for constraints of the form $\mathbf{Px}(\psi(x)$

$\mid \varphi(x)) \leq s$ or $\geq s$, where s is an L_{EF}-term, $Px(\psi(x) \mid \varphi(x))$ has no free variables and the $\varphi_i(x), \psi_i(x) \in L$ are representatives of the finite Lindenbaum algebra **B** having p atoms.

- $\Phi(Px(\varphi_1(x)), ..) \mid\approx^*_B \Psi(Px(\psi_1(x)), ..)$ iff $\Vdash ME(\Phi^\circ)(v_1, ..., v_p) \rightarrow \Psi^\circ(v_1, ..., v_p)$.

It is not difficult to see that $\mid\approx^*_B$ is preferential on the relevant L*-fragment. The following examples may give an impression of its behaviour. We assume that Bird(x), Penguin(x), $\varphi(x)$, $\varphi'(x)$ and $\psi(x)$ are logically independent L-formulas. In each example, **B** should be just the Lindenbaum algebra spanned by the explicitly mentioned formulas.

- $Px(Bird(x) \mid Penguin(x)) = 1 \mid\approx^*_B Px(Bird(x)) = 2/3$.

This example shows that **ME** is hyperspeculative and should be used cautiously.

- $Px(\varphi(x) \mid \psi(x)) \leq \varepsilon \;\&\; Px(\varphi'(x) \mid \psi(x)) \leq \varepsilon^2 \mid\approx^*_B Px(\varphi(x)\&\varphi'(x) \mid \psi(x)) = \varepsilon^3$.

This pattern illustrates the independency and "probability-maximizing" features of **ME**.

- $\Phi_{\leq,s}(\Delta) \mid\approx^*_B Px(\neg\psi(x) \mid \varphi(x)) \leq \underline{n}^{-1}$, for all $n \in$ **Nat**, iff $\varphi(x), \Delta \mid\approx_{ME} \psi(x)$,

where $\Phi_{\leq,s}(\Delta)$ and Δ are as above and $\mid\approx_{ME}$ is the implementation of maximum entropy entailment which is based on convergent parametrized probability measures [GMP 90] and subsumed by the random worlds approach [BGHK 93]. Because we can explicitly refer to infinitesimal probabilities and information measures, our representational framework is more expressive and flexible than theirs. In particular, we can get rid of the cumbersome approximation methodology. Using more sophisticated versions of $\mid\approx^*_B$, suitable for the full flat language, we may also handle arbitrary premises lacking finite models, which is off limits for the random worlds account.

References

[Bac 90] F. Bacchus. *Representing and Reasoning with Probabilistic Knowledge*. MIT Press, Cambridge Mass., 1990.

[BGHK93] F. Bacchus, A.J. Grove, J. Y. Halpern. Statistical foundations for default reasoning. In *Proceedings of IJCAI 93*, Morgan Kaufmann, 1993.

[DP 88] D. Dubois, H. Prade. *Possibility Theory*. Plenum Press, New York 1988.

[Dri 94] L. van den Dries, A. Macintyre, D. Marker. The elementary theory of restricted analytic fields with exponentiation. In *Annals of Mathematics*, 140 (1994), 182-205.

[GMP 90] M. Goldsmidt, P. Morris, J. Pearl. A maximum entropy approach to nonmonotonic reasoning. In *Proceedings of AAAI 90*. Morgan Kaufmann 1990.

[Jay 78] E. T. Jaynes. Where do we stand on maximum entropy ? In R.D. Levine and M. Tribus (eds.), *The Maximum Entropy Formalism*. MIT-Press 1978.

[KLM 90] S. Kraus, D. Lehmann, M. Magidor. Nonmonotonic reasoning, preferential models and cumulative logics. *Artificial Intelligence*, 44: 167-207, 1990.

[LM 92] D. Lehmann, M. Magidor. What does a conditional knowledge base entail ? *Artificial Intelligence*, 55:1-60, 1992.

[PV 90] J.B. Paris and A. Vencovska. A note on the inevitability of maximum entropy. In *Internationl Journal of Approximate Reasoning*, 4:183-223, 1990.

[Spo 90] W. Spohn. A general non-probabilistic theory of inductive reasoning. In R.D. Shachter *et al.* (eds.), *Uncertainty in Artificial Intelligence 4*, North-Holland, Amsterdam 1990.

[Wey 91] E. Weydert. Qualitative magnitude reasoning. Towards a new semantics for default reasoning. In J. Dix *et al.* (eds.), *Nonmonotonic and Inductive Reasoning*. Springer-Verlag 1991.

[Wey 94] E. Weydert. General belief measures. In *Tenth Conference on Uncertainty in Artificial Intelligence*. Morgan Kaufmann, 1994.

Author Index

Springer-Verlag and the Environment

We at Springer-Verlag firmly believe that an international science publisher has a special obligation to the environment, and our corporate policies consistently reflect this conviction.

We also expect our business partners – paper mills, printers, packaging manufacturers, etc. – to commit themselves to using environmentally friendly materials and production processes.

The paper in this book is made from low- or no-chlorine pulp and is acid free, in conformance with international standards for paper permanency.

Lecture Notes in Artificial Intelligence (LNAI)

Vol. 766: P. R. Van Loocke, The Dynamics of Concepts. XI, 340 pages. 1994.

Vol. 770: P. Haddawy, Representing Plans Under Uncertainty. X, 129 pages. 1994.

Vol. 784: F. Bergadano, L. De Raedt (Eds.), Machine Learning: ECML-94. Proceedings, 1994. XI, 439 pages. 1994.

Vol. 795: W. A. Hunt, Jr., FM8501: A Verified Microprocessor. XIII, 333 pages. 1994.

Vol. 798: R. Dyckhoff (Ed.), Extensions of Logic Programming. Proceedings, 1993. VIII, 360 pages. 1994.

Vol. 799: M. P. Singh, Multiagent Systems: Intentions, Know-How, and Communications. XXIII, 168 pages. 1994.

Vol. 804: D. Hernández, Qualitative Representation of Spatial Knowledge. IX, 202 pages. 1994.

Vol. 808: M. Masuch, L. Pólos (Eds.), Knowledge Representation and Reasoning Under Uncertainty. VII, 237 pages. 1994.

Vol. 810: G. Lakemeyer, B. Nebel (Eds.), Foundations of Knowledge Representation and Reasoning. VIII, 355 pages. 1994.

Vol. 814: A. Bundy (Ed.), Automated Deduction — CADE-12. Proceedings, 1994. XVI, 848 pages. 1994.

Vol. 822: F. Pfenning (Ed.), Logic Programming and Automated Reasoning. Proceedings, 1994. X, 345 pages. 1994.

Vol. 827: D. M. Gabbay, H. J. Ohlbach (Eds.), Temporal Logic. Proceedings, 1994. XI, 546 pages. 1994.

Vol. 830: C. Castelfranchi, E. Werner (Eds.), Artificial Social Systems. Proceedings, 1992. XVIII, 337 pages. 1994.

Vol. 833: D. Driankov, P. W. Eklund, A. Ralescu (Eds.), Fuzzy Logic and Fuzzy Control. Proceedings, 1991. XII, 157 pages. 1994.

Vol. 835: W. M. Tepfenhart, J. P. Dick, J. F. Sowa (Eds.), Conceptual Structures: Current Practices. Proceedings, 1994. VIII, 331 pages. 1994.

Vol. 837: S. Wess, K.-D. Althoff, M. M. Richter (Eds.), Topics in Case-Based Reasoning. Proceedings, 1993. IX, 471 pages. 1994.

Vol. 838: C. MacNish, D. Pearce, L. M. Pereira (Eds.), Logics in Artificial Intelligence. Proceedings, 1994. IX, 413 pages. 1994.

Vol. 847: A. Ralescu (Ed.) Fuzzy Logic in Artificial Intelligence. Proceedings, 1993. VII, 128 pages. 1994.

Vol: 861: B. Nebel, L. Dreschler-Fischer (Eds.), KI-94: Advances in Artificial Intelligence. Proceedings, 1994. IX, 401 pages. 1994.

Vol. 862: R. C. Carrasco, J. Oncina (Eds.), Grammatical Inference and Applications. Proceedings, 1994. VIII, 290 pages. 1994.

Vol 867: L. Steels, G. Schreiber, W. Van de Velde (Eds.), A Future for Knowledge Acquisition. Proceedings, 1994. XII, 414 pages. 1994.

Vol. 869: Z. W. Raś, M. Zemankova (Eds.), Methodologies for Intelligent Systems. Proceedings, 1994. X, 613 pages. 1994.

Vol. 872: S Arikawa, K. P. Jantke (Eds.), Algorithmic Learning Theory. Proceedings, 1994. XIV, 575 pages. 1994.

Vol. 878: T. Ishida, Parallel, Distributed and Multiagent Production Systems. XVII, 166 pages. 1994.

Vol. 886: M. M. Veloso, Planning and Learning by Analogical Reasoning. XIII, 181 pages. 1994.

Vol. 890: M. J. Wooldridge, N. R. Jennings (Eds.), Intelligent Agents. Proceedings, 1994. VIII, 407 pages. 1995.

Vol. 897: M. Fisher, R. Owens (Eds.), Executable Modal and Temporal Logics. Proceedings, 1993. VII, 180 pages. 1995.

Vol. 898: P. Steffens (Ed.), Machine Translation and the Lexicon. Proceedings, 1993. X, 251 pages. 1995.

Vol. 904: P. Vitányi (Ed.), Computational Learning Theory. EuroCOLT'95. Proceedings, 1995. XVII, 415 pages. 1995.

Vol. 912: N. Lavrač, S. Wrobel (Eds.), Machine Learning: ECML – 95. Proceedings, 1995. XI, 370 pages. 1995.

Vol. 918: P. Baumgartner, R. Hähnle, J. Posegga (Eds.), Theorem Proving with Analytic Tableaux and Related Methods. Proceedings, 1995. X, 352 pages. 1995.

Vol. 927: J. Dix, L. Moniz Pereira, T.C. Przymusinski (Eds.), Non-Monotonic Extensions of Logic Programming. Proceedings, 1994. IX, 229 pages. 1995.

Vol. 928: V.W. Marek, A. Nerode, M. Truszczynski (Eds.), Logic Programming and Nonmonotonic Reasoning. Proceedings, 1995. VIII, 417 pages. 1995.

Vol. 929: F. Morán, A. Moreno, J.J. Merelo, P.Chacón (Eds.), Advances in Artificial Life. Proceedings, 1995. XIII, 960 pages. 1995.

Vol. 934: P. Barahona, M. Stefanelli, J. Wyatt (Eds.), Artificial Intelligence in Medicine. Proceedings, 1995. XI, 449 pages. 1995.

Vol. 941: M. Cadoli, Tractable Reasoning in Artificial Intelligence. XVII, 247 pages. 1995.

Vol. 946: C. Froidevaux, J. Kohlas (Eds.), Symbolic Quantitative and Approaches to Reasoning under Uncertainty. Proceedings, 1995. X, 430 pages. 1995.

Lecture Notes in Computer Science

Vol. 913: W. Schäfer (Ed.), Software Process Technology. Proceedings, 1995. IX, 261 pages. 1995.

Vol. 914: J. Hsiang (Ed.), Rewriting Techniques and Applications. Proceedings, 1995. XII, 473 pages. 1995.

Vol. 915: P. D. Mosses, M. Nielsen, M. I. Schwartzbach (Eds.), TAPSOFT '95: Theory and Practice of Software Development. Proceedings, 1995. XV, 810 pages. 1995.

Vol. 916: N. R. Adam, B. K. Bhargava, Y. Yesha (Eds.), Digital Libraries. Proceedings, 1994. XIII, 321 pages. 1995.

Vol. 917: J. Pieprzyk, R. Safavi-Naini (Eds.), Advances in Cryptology - ASIACRYPT '94. Proceedings, 1994. XII,

Vol. 918: P. Baumgartner, R. Hähnle, J. Posegga (Eds.), Theorem Proving with Analytic Tableaux and Related Methods. Proceedings, 1995. X, 352 pages. 1995. (Subseries LNAI).

Vol. 919: B. Hertzberger, G. Serazzi (Eds.), High-Performance Computing and Networking. Proceedings, 1995. XXIV, 957 pages. 1995.

Vol. 920: E. Balas, J. Clausen (Eds.), Integer Programming and Combinatorial Optimization. Proceedings, 1995. IX, 436 pages. 1995.

Vol. 921: L. C. Guillou, J.-J. Quisquater (Eds.), Advances in Cryptology – EUROCRYPT '95. Proceedings, 1995. XIV, 417 pages. 1995.

Vol. 922: H. Dörr, Efficient Graph Rewriting and Its Implementation. IX, 266 pages. 1995.

Vol. 923: M. Meyer (Ed.), Constraint Processing. IV, 289 pages. 1995.

Vol. 924: P. Ciancarini, O. Nierstrasz, A. Yonezawa (Eds.), Object-Based Models and Languages for Concurrent Systems. Proceedings, 1994. VII, 193 pages. 1995.

Vol. 925: J. Jeuring, E. Meijer (Eds.), Advanced Functional Programming. Proceedings, 1995. VII, 331 pages. 1995.

Vol. 926: P. Nesi (Ed.), Objective Software Quality. Proceedings, 1995. VIII, 249 pages. 1995.

Vol. 927: J. Dix, L. Moniz Pereira, T. C. Przymusinski (Eds.), Non-Monotonic Extensions of Logic Programming. Proceedings, 1994. IX, 229 pages. 1995. (Subseries LNAI).

Vol. 928:V.W. Marek, A. Nerode, M. Truszczynski (Eds.), Logic Programming and Nonmonotonic Reasoning. Proceedings, 1995. VIII, 417 pages. (Subseries LNAI).

Vol. 929: F. Morán, A. Moreno, J.J. Merelo, P. Chacón (Eds.), Advances in Artificial Life. Proceedings, 1995. XIII, 960 pages. 1995. (Subseries LNAI).

Vol. 930: J. Mira, F. Sandoval (Eds.), From Natural to Artificial Neural Computation. Proceedings, 1995. XVIII, 1150 pages. 1995.

Vol. 931: P.J. Braspenning, F. Thuijsman, A.J.M.M. Weijters (Eds.), Artificial Neural Networks. IX, 295 pages. 1995.

Vol. 932: J. Iivari, K. Lyytinen, M. Rossi (Eds.), Advanced Information Systems Engineering. Proceedings, 1995. XI, 388 pages. 1995.

Vol. 933: L. Pacholski, J. Tiuryn (Eds.), Computer Science Logic. Proceedings, 1994. IX, 543 pages. 1995.

Vol. 934: P. Barahona, M. Stefanelli, J. Wyatt (Eds.), Artificial Intelligence in Medicine. Proceedings, 1995. XI, 449 pages. 1995. (Subseries LNAI).

Vol. 935: G. De Michelis, M. Diaz (Eds.), Application and Theory of Petri Nets 1995. Proceedings, 1995. VIII, 511 pages. 1995.

Vol. 936: V.S. Alagar, M. Nivat (Eds.), Algebraic Methodology and Software Technology. Proceedings, 1995. XIV, 591 pages. 1995.

Vol. 937: Z. Galil, E. Ukkonen (Eds.), Combinatorial Pattern Matching. Proceedings, 1995. VIII, 409 pages. 1995.

Vol. 938: K.P. Birman, F. Mattern, A. Schiper (Eds.), Theory and Practice in Distributed Systems. Proceedings, 1994. X, 263 pages. 1995.

Vol. 939: P. Wolper (Ed.), Computer Aided Verification. Proceedings, 1995. X, 451 pages. 1995.

Vol. 940: C. Goble, J. Keane (Eds.), Advances in Databases. Proceedings, 1995. X, 277 pages. 1995.

Vol. 941: M. Cadoli, Tractable Reasoning in Artificial Intelligence. XVII, 247 pages. 1995. (Subseries LNAI).

Vol. 942: G. Böckle, Exploitation of Fine-Grain Parallelism. IX, 188 pages. 1995.

Vol. 943: W. Klas, M. Schrefl (Eds.), Metaclasses and Their Application. IX, 201 pages. 1995.

Vol. 944: Z. Fülöp, F. Gécseg (Eds.), Automata, Languages and Programming. Proceedings, 1995. XIII, 686 pages. 1995.

Vol. 945: B. Bouchon-Meunier, R.R. Yager, L.A. Zadeh (Eds.), Advances in Intelligent Computing - IPMU '94. Proceedings, 1994. XII, 628 pages.1995.

Vol. 946: C. Froidevaux, J. Kohlas (Eds.), Symbolic and Quantitative Approaches to Reasoning and Uncertainty. Proceedings, 1995. X, 420 pages. 1995. (Subseries LNAI).

Vol. 947: B. Möller (Ed.), Mathematics of Program Construction. Proceedings, 1995. VIII, 472 pages. 1995.

Vol. 948: G. Cohen, M. Giusti, T. Mora (Eds.), Applied Algebra, Algebraic Algorithms and Error-Correcting Codes. Proceedings, 1995. XI, 485 pages. 1995.